UNDERSTANDING
CORPORATE LAW

UNDERSTANDING CORPORATE LAW

THIRD EDITION

Arthur R. Pinto
Professor of Law & Co-Director of the
Center for the Study of International Business Law
Brooklyn Law School

Douglas M. Branson
W. Edward Sell Chair in Business Law
University of Pittsburgh School of Law

Library of Congress Cataloging-in-Publication Data

Pinto, Arthur R.
   Understanding corporate law / Arthur R. Pinto, Douglas M. Branson. -- 3rd ed.
      p. cm.
   Includes index.
   ISBN 978-1-4224-2959-4 (softbound)
   1. Corporation law -- United States. I. Branson, Douglas M. II. Title.
      KF1414.P56 2000
      346.73'066--dc22

                                                                2009028914

This publication is designed to provide accurate and authoritative information in regard to the subject matter covered. It is sold with the understanding that the publisher is not engaged in rendering legal, accounting, or other professional services. If legal advice or other expert assistance is required, the services of a competent professional should be sought.

NOTE TO USERS

To ensure that you are using the latest materials available in this area, please be sure to periodically check the LexisNexis Law School web site for downloadable updates and supplements at www.lexisnexis.com/lawschool.

Editorial Offices
121 Chanlon Rd., New Providence, NJ 07974 (908) 464-6800
201 Mission St., San Francisco, CA 94105-1831 (415) 908-3200
www.lexisnexis.com

MATTHEW BENDER

PREFACE

Understanding Corporate Law is intended to assist law students and lawyers with a basic understanding of the law of corporations as taught in most corporations courses. Significant business, economic and policy issues are highlighted in connection with a thorough analysis of the important cases and both state and federal statutory provisions used in the study of corporations. It includes the major theoretical approaches used in current corporate law literature. In each chapter, the authors identify important policies and discuss the relationship of the law as it has developed to those policies. Statutory issues are covered under both the General Corporation Law of the State of Delaware and the Business Corporation Act. In addition, significant sections from the Principles of Corporate Governance of the American Law Institute are covered. The corporate scandals of 2001 and 2002 and the enactment of the federal Sarbanes-Oxley Act of 2002 is also covered. This book is designed to be used with all of the major corporate law casebooks.

We also have written this volume so that non-lawyers who desire to progress beyond a rudimentary knowledge of corporate law may do so by reading this book.

Although the book was a collaborative effort, Professor Pinto wrote Chapters 1, 4, 5, 6, 8, 9, 10 and 12. Professor Branson wrote Chapters 2, 3, 7, 11, 13 and 14.

Professor Pinto would like to acknowledge the helpful suggestions on the chapters he wrote from his colleagues Professors Fanto and Neil Cohen. In addition, he would like to thank Todd Moore, Brooklyn Law School Class of 2009, for his editorial assistance. He would like to also acknowledge Stephen J. Bohlen for his constant support.

Professor Branson dedicates this book to Elizabeth, Clare and Annie.

The book is dedicated to our students past and present who have inspired this project.

Arthur R. Pinto
Douglas M. Branson

TABLE OF CONTENTS

TABLE OF CONTENTS

TABLE OF CONTENTS

TABLE OF CONTENTS

TABLE OF CONTENTS

TABLE OF CONTENTS

TABLE OF CONTENTS

TABLE OF CONTENTS

TABLE OF CONTENTS

TABLE OF CONTENTS

TABLE OF CONTENTS

TABLE OF CONTENTS

TABLE OF CONTENTS

Chapter 1

INTRODUCTION AND FORMATION

§ 1.01 INTRODUCTION

The corporation is one of several ways to structure a business. Partnerships, limited liability companies and sole proprietorships, as forms of business, far outnumber corporations. However, the economic impact of the corporate format is significant, since it is the form chosen by most large enterprises. Although there is no standard definition for the term "corporation," the United States Supreme Court in the *Dartmouth College* case described it as follows:

> A corporation is an artificial being, invisible, intangible, and existing only in contemplation of law. Being a mere creature of law, it possesses only those properties which the charter of its creation confers upon it, either expressly, or as incidental to its very existence.[1]

A corporation is a separate legal entity[2] which owes its existence to the state. Its owners, called shareholders (sometimes "stockholders" by some state statutes) because they own shares of stock, elect a distinct group, known as the board of directors, to oversee the management of the business and select officers to run it (the directors and officers are often called the "managers"). A significant aspect of the study of corporate law (which includes state corporate law and federal securities law) involves corporate governance and the means by which the relationships between shareholders and managers are governed.[3]

---

[1] *The Trustees of Dartmouth College v. Woodward*, 17 U.S. (4 Wheat.) 518, 636 (1819). In theory, one could establish most of the attributes of a corporation by contract among all participants. For a discussion of the corporation as a nexus of contracts, see § 5.03[C][3] *infra.*

[2] Issues have been raised to the extent that the corporation, as a separate legal entity, is protected under the Constitution. In *Santa Clara v. Southern Pacific Ry.*, 118 U.S. 394 (1886), the Supreme Court held that a corporation is entitled to equal protection under the Fourteenth Amendment. In *Minneapolis & St. Louis Ry. Co. v. Beckwith*, 129 U.S. 26 (1888), the Court held it was entitled to due process of law. But in *Hale v. Henkel*, 201 U.S. 43 (1906), a corporation was not entitled to the Fifth Amendment protection against self incrimination but was protected from unreasonable searches and seizures under the Fourth Amendment. The corporation's right to free speech under the First Amendment has also been raised. In *First Nat. Bank of Boston v. Bellotti*, 435 U.S. 765 (1978), the majority found that the state had not shown a compelling interest in regulating corporate expenditures in a referendum. There was no evidence of either a corrupting influence or need to protect the shareholders. But in *Austin v. Michigan St. Chamber of Commerce*, 494 U.S. 652 (1990), the Court upheld a Michigan law that prohibited corporate expenditures in state elections. The majority focused on the state providing the means by which corporations can amass large amounts of money that can be used unfairly in political contests. These cases are not only interesting from a constitutional point of view but the different opinions express a variety of views on the nature of a corporation and its relationship to the state.

[3] For a discussion of Corporate Governance, see § 5.02[A] *infra.*

While the number of experiences varies widely in business formation, we will describe one that may help the reader relate to the material in this book. A business often starts with an idea or invention but requires money or other people to get started or expand (contribution of goods or services is also possible). The initial business can be formed as a corporation, partnership, limited partnership or limited liability company. The capital can be invested in the business in two general ways.[4] If capital is lent, then the relationship between the lenders and the business creates a debtor-creditor relationship where the creditor is looking for eventual repayment plus some current return usually in the form of interest on the loan. If the capital is provided for an ownership stake, then the investors are willing to forgo a promise to be paid interest or a set return on the investment for the potential for sharing in the success of the business as owners. Their investment provides equity for the business. The source of debt or equity can be friends, family, banks or groups of private investors who are willing to invest to start up or expand a new business with the hope of making a profit when the business is successful. Usually these private investors invest in a later stage of the development of the business then the initial investors. Those private investors are often called venture capitalists which is a sub-category of investors called private equity.[5]

Many businesses continue to operate and expand with a small number of investors. These corporations are called closely-held corporations. But as businesses grow, they often require substantial capital. To attract capital, a business may have several options. It can attract capital by finding more private investors or having another established business invest in the business. Another alternative is for the business to sell its equity or debt more widely to the public in which case the corporate form is usually required.[6] This initial going public process for selling equity is called an "IPO," initial public offering, and is regulated by federal securities laws.[7] The money raised in going public can be used to fund expansion of the business or to pay back the initial investors or venture capitalists.[8] Once a corporation has a public offering, the shares are publicly traded in some stock market where investors can continually trade shares of the corporation.[9] Most of the well known large businesses in the United States are publicly held corporations, i.e., the shares are held by a large number of shareholders and the shares trade in a stock market.

---

[4] For a discussion of the financing of businesses in more detail, see Chapter 4.

[5] In 2007, venture capitalists invested $34.7 billion, the most since 2001. Rebecca Buckman, *In Silicon Valley, Start-Ups Begin Hitting the Brakes*, WALL ST. J., Feb. 15, 2008 at B1. The money supplied to venture capitalists can come from individuals or institutional investors. For a discussion of institutional investors and corporate governance, see § 5.02[E][2] *infra.*

[6] For a discussion of why the corporate form is used, see § 1.04[B] *infra.*

[7] For a discussion of federal securities laws and the process of going public, see § 7.03 *infra.*

[8] For example, in 2007, there were 231 public offerings, raising $53 billion. Associated Press, *The Strongest Year of U.S. IPOs Since 2000*, WASH. POST, December 23, 2007, at F02. A corporation may also decide to go public to provide a market for its shares so that those shares could be used to acquire other corporations or to support the use of employee stock options.

[9] The Securities and Exchange Act of 1934 deals with the stock markets and corporations that have publicly traded shares. *See* Chapters 7, 13.

As discussed in this book, there are different types of corporations which have different attributes, rules and legal issues depending upon the ownership structure. In closely held corporations, where there are few shareholders, the distinction between the shareholders and managers may be insignificant because they may substantially overlap. When there is a group of shareholders consti- tuting the majority who control the business and another group is in the minority, issues may arise as to their relationships and the control group taking advantage of the minority.[10] In some publicly held corporations, a group of shareholders (maybe the founders or their family) or another corporation may retain control and thus the public shareholders are minority shareholders.[11] Again, in that context, issues will arise as to the relationship between the majority and minority shareholders.[12] In many publicly traded corporations in the United States, the original or controlling shareholders may have sold off most of their shares and no longer control the corporation. In that case, there may not be any large group of shareholders controlling the business. Instead there are numerous and widely dispersed shareholders where no group of shareholders holds enough shares to control the election of the directors and hence, the management of the corporation. The dispersion of ownership allows the managers (the directors and officers) to control the corporation even though they might own relatively few shares. In this context, issues arise as how these dispersed publicly traded shareholders monitor those managers who run the corporation.[13]

A basic need for any business is capital and investors need some assurance that they will be protected. By buying shares they understand that there is risk that the business may not be successful. The fundamental problem shareholders face other than business risk when owning shares where they do not control the corporation is that those who manage or control the business will either mismanage the business or unfairly self deal, i.e., steal. In both cases the shareholders are harmed. Much of the discussion of corporate law in this book seeks ways to minimize those problems.[14]

§ 1.02 SOURCES OF CORPORATE LAW

Every state has a corporate law statute that provides the rules for corpora- tions incorporated in that state (hereinafter "the statute"). The statutes indicate how to incorporate, deal with financing and legal capital rules, establish the basic structure of the board of directors, deal with shareholder power and rights, and disposes of a variety of other issues. Every state also has judicially created law or common law applicable to corporations. The courts not only interpret the statutes but create important legal principles. For example, a shareholder's right

---

[10] For a discussion of closely held corporations, see Chapter 11.

[11] For example, Google is a large publicly held corporation but the original founders are significant shareholders and have effective control.

[12] For a discussion of controlling shareholders, see Chapter 10.

[13] For a discussion of corporate governance in these publicly traded corporations, see Chapter 5.

[14] Often these problems are viewed as an issue of agency costs. For a discussion of this view see § 5.03[C][1] *infra*.

to sue on behalf of the corporation in a derivative suit was developed by the courts.[15] Federal securities law is also a source of corporate law and much of its regulation is disclosure-oriented and intended to affect the relationships within the corporation.[16] The stock markets where the shares of publicly traded corporations are traded have rules with which corporations must comply.[17]

Independent legal organizations also influence the legislative and judicial development of corporate law. The American Law Institute (the "A.L.I.") which is known for its restatements of law has produced the *"Principles of Corporate Governance: Analysis and Recommendations."*[18] The Project attempts to look at corporate law and suggest an approach to corporate governance issues. The Project is not intended to be a restatement of the law but rather as a suggestion of good corporate practice and rules. The Model Business Corporation Act (the "MBCA") is a product of the American Bar Association and has also been influential in the development of various states corporate law statutes. The approach has not been to seek uniformity among the states, but to suggest an approach to issues allowing for local differences. A number of states have adopted the MBCA as their corporate statute.

§ 1.03 HISTORICAL BACKGROUND

Since the formation of a corporation is facilitated by the state, understanding the historical development of state regulation is significant to understanding modern corporate law. The historical development of American corporate law provides an interesting study of political and economic forces which influenced the development of that law.[19]

In the early 19th century, American law restricted the use of corporations. In order to form a corporation in the United States, one had to petition one's state legislature for a charter or articles of incorporation granting the right to operate as a corporation. Articles of incorporation were not freely given due to suspicion of the private power of corporations. However, the state understood that corporations could serve a useful public purpose. Thus, early American corporations were often established to allow private resources to accomplish public functions. For example, corporations were used to run the railroads, or build roads and bridges.

Over time, business practices changed and the economy grew, resulting in a greater demand for articles of incorporation. This led to the enactment of general corporate statutes under which legislative chartering was no longer required and articles of incorporation were standardized. It also turned the corporate form into a generally available right, as opposed to the privilege of a few.

---

[15] For a discussion of shareholder litigation, see Chapter 14.

[16] *See* MARC STEINBERG, UNDERSTANDING SECURITIES LAW (3d ed. 2001); *see also* Chapter 7.

[17] For an example of such rules, see § 5.02[C][2] *infra.*

[18] Sections of the A.L.I. project will be cited in the book as A.L.I. Corp. Gov. Proj.

[19] *See generally* LAWRENCE M. FRIEDMAN, A HISTORY OF AMERICAN LAW (3d ed. 2005).

Economic reality also dictated the need to use corporations for broader purposes. Throughout the 19th century, America expanded its frontiers and experienced the industrial revolution. The expansion of industry transformed America from an agrarian to an industrial society, in which large amounts of capital were required for business. In addition, the public began to invest in private corporations. With public investment in corporations, there was also a rise in financial scandals. As a result, corporate law also developed to try to protect investors. For example, shareholder suits developed to allow injured investors to recover for frauds or breaches of fiduciary duty by corporate managers.

In the late 19th century, a number of states lowered taxes on corporations and enacted corporate statutes removed many traditional limitations on the corporation and its managers. These statutes became more enabling and corporations were allowed broader powers. Some of the changes were viewed as more pro-management as opposed to pro-shareholders. It has been suggested that managers would chose a state in which to incorporate which had rules most favorable to management and least favorable to shareholders so states tried to attract incorporations by favoring the managers. New Jersey was the first state to liberalize its law. Delaware eventually took the lead and became the most attractive state for publicly held corporations.[20] Today, all state corporate statutes are generally enabling, although there are some differences among the states.

While state law became more "liberal," the federal government became more suspicious as the power of corporations grew. Thus, federal regulations were developed, including antitrust laws and regulation for certain industries, such as transportation. The stock market crash of 1929 and many of the frauds committed against public investors in the 1920s resulted in Congress enacting federal securities laws during the New Deal in the 1930s to protect these investors. However, Congress chose not to preempt most state law dealing with corporations.[21] In 2001 and 2002, there were corporate scandals associated with Enron, Worldcom and other publicly traded corporations what caused Congress to enact the Sarbanes-Oxley Act of 2002 to protect shareholders.[22]

§ 1.04 CHOICE OF FORM

In organizing and operating a business, the owners may choose a variety of forms. The major choices are corporations, partnerships, limited partnerships, sole proprietorships and limited liability companies. Factors that often influence the choice are the need for limited liability, free transferability of interests, continuity of existence, centralized management, costs, access to capital and taxation.

---

[20] For a discussion of Delaware's dominance among the states for incorporations, see § 1.08[A], *infra*. For an in-depth analysis of Delaware corporate law, see David A. Drexler, et al., *Delaware Corporation Law and Practice* (2003).

[21] *See generally* J. WILLARD HURST, THE LEGITAMACY OF THE BUSINESS CORPORATION IN THE LAW OF THE UNITED STATES 1780–1970 (1970).

[22] For a discussion of Sarbanes-Oxley, see § 5.08 *infra*.

[A]   Sole Proprietorship

The simplest form of business is the sole proprietorship, where an individual decides to go into business as the sole owner. There are no formal requirements for the formation or operation of a sole proprietorship and ownership and management can exist in the sole owner. The owner is the principal and can employ people as agents to represent and work for her business. As owner, she is personally liable for the obligations of the business. In addition, all profits and losses are personal and part of her individual tax return.

[B]   Partnership vs. Corporation

Once an individual decides to go into business with other people as owners, there are other choices she can make as to business form.[23]

Two choices for business format are partnership and corporation. To form and operate a corporation, one must comply with a list of requirements, one of which is the filing of articles of incorporation with the state.[24] The services of an attorney are often needed to help prepare the necessary documentation, which increases the costs of doing business.

Another format in which to conduct business is the partnership. The partnership is defined as "an association of two or more persons to carry on as co-owners a business for profit."[25] The formation of a partnership requires no formal action or written agreement. Individuals acting together to run a business may result in a partnership being formed.[26] However, it is advisable to have an agreement among partners or among shareholders of a closely held corporation to protect the interests of the parties. In the absence of an agreement, partnership law is generally more protective of all the owners than corporate law.[27]

---

[23] Although a sole owner can incorporate to take advantage of certain corporate benefits such as limited liability, a partnership requires at least two owners. U.P.A. § 6(1) (1914); R.U.P.A. § 101(6) (2008).

[24] For a discussion of formation, see § 1.07 *infra*.

[25] U.P.A. § 6(1) (1914); R.U.P.A. § 101(6) (2008).

[26] A partnership results from contract, either expressed or implied. If a court finds that the parties have in fact acted as partners, it will find the existence of a partnership with all the legal consequences that flow from it. Courts will usually look for two elements of co-ownership in determining the existence of a partnership: profit sharing and control. For example, under the definition of partnership, creditors who lend money and receive a share of profits and either contract for or act with extensive control, may be treated as partners with unlimited liability. In *Martin v. Peyton*, 246 N.Y. 213, 158 N.E. 77 (1927), a creditor was not found to be a partner and escaped liability even though a contract gave the creditor considerable control and profit sharing; the court found that the control existed primarily through the use of negative covenants designed to protect the creditor's loan. Generally, the receipt of profits is prima facie evidence of partnership status, except that certain situations are excluded, such as interest on a loan, wages or rents. *See* U.P.A. § 7(4) (1914); R.U.P.A. § 202(3) (2008).

[27] Partnership law originally developed under the common law, but in 1914 the Uniform Partnership Act was promulgated and now provides many of the rules governing partnerships. The Uniform Partnership Act allows partners to modify the rules by contract. In 1994, the Revised Uniform Partnership Act was adopted with the intent of superseding the Uniform Partnership Act.

The choice between the corporate form and partnership depends on comparing the different attributes of the two forms and then determining which attributes are significant to one's business. The key considerations are limited liability, free transferability of interests, continuity of existence, centralized management, costs, access to capital, and taxation. While these differences are significant, practical considerations may make them irrelevant.[28] It is also important to note that each of these attributes may be modified by contract among the interested parties.[29]

The major differences between the partnership and corporation flow primarily from the fact that partnerships are generally viewed as an aggregate that is composed of its owners, while the corporation is viewed as a separate legal entity distinct from its owners.[30] For example, since the partnership is generally legally viewed as the aggregate of its owners, it follows that each owner is personally liable for the debts of the partnership. Since the corporation is a separate legal entity, it is able to incur its own liabilities, shielding the shareholders as owners from personal liability.[31] Thus, the corporation's creditors cannot usually go after the personal assets of the shareholders and the creditors of the shareholders have no right to directly go after the assets of the corporation. This limited liability means that in most cases, the shareholders will only lose their investment in the corporation. In addition, the assets of the

---

Partnership law has been described as supplementary in the sense that if there is no contract, the Uniform Partnership Act provisions govern. The resulting rules tend to reflect what most parties in small businesses would have agreed to or expected in most cases. For example, most owners of a small business would assume that they would have a right to participate in management; this is provided under partnership law. See U.P.A. § 18(e) (1914); R.U.P.A. § 401(f) (2008). Corporate law provides that to be involved in management, a shareholder needs to be elected to the board by a majority vote. Most corporate statutes are traditionally more regulatory and designed to deal with both closely held corporations and large publicly held corporations. Thus the rules may not be as protective of minority shareholders in closely held corporations. In order to protect minority interest in a closely held corporation, there usually needs to be a contract to adapt the law, while most partnership law without a contract is protective. Thus, minority shareholders should provide by contract to have a voice or a return on their investment. For a discussion of contracts in closely held corporations, see § 11.03 *infra.*

[28] For example, there is free transferability in the corporate form which allows the shareholders to freely sell their shares. However, while shareholders may have the legal right to sell, there may be no real market for the shares, especially if the shares represent a minority interest in a closely held corporation. For a discussion of the problems of the minority shareholders of a closely held corporation, see § 11.01 *infra.*

[29] For example, although the corporate form provides limited liability, creditors may insist on personal guarantees from the shareholders to induce it to loan to the business. Conversely, in a partnership, if the partners are in a strong bargaining situation, they could contract for limited liability with the creditors of the partnership, agreeing to only go after the assets of the partnership. Contracting in the context of a small business is very important in both the partnership and closely held corporate context.

[30] The aggregate concept has been modified by the Uniform Partnership Act for particular situations. For example, under an aggregate approach, partnership property would have to be held in the name of each partner. However, the Uniform Partnership Act allows it to be held in the partnership name. See U.P.A. § 8 (1914). The Revised Uniform Partnership Act uses an entity approach in most cases, but does not change many of the basic differences between a partnership and a corporation. See R.U.P.A. § 201 (2008).

[31] Entity status need not have this or other attributes. For example, under early English law there were corporations with unlimited liability.

corporation are also shielded from the personal creditors of the shareholders who cannot go directly after those corporate assets. The shielding advantages are the primary reason why the corporate form is chosen for many businesses.

Partnership interests are not freely transferable, since any change in the identity of the partners will alter the aggregate. While new partners may be added, there must be a unanimous consent for changes in the makeup of the partnership[32] unless there has been a contractual modification of this rule. On the corporation side, since shareholders are separate from the corporation, they can freely transfer shares; different owners have no effect on the separate corporate entity.

If there is any change in the partnership, there is a dissolution of that partnership. This rule limits the continuity of the business.[33] Therefore, the death or bankruptcy of one partner causes a dissolution of the partnership because the aggregate changes when the original partner is replaced by another: death precipitates the appointment of an executor and bankruptcy heralds the designation of a trustee. Death or bankruptcy of a shareholder or desire of a shareholder to terminate ownership does not affect the corporation because it is a separate legal entity unaffected by changes in ownership. Thus, corporations provide for a perpetual existence.[34]

In addition, a partner may at any time cause the dissolution of the partnership by merely deciding to end the relationship.[35]

A dissolution of partnership does not necessarily mean an end to the business, particularly when there is a partnership agreement allowing for continuity. However, in the absence of such an agreement, there will be a winding up of the business.

Partners, as co-owners of the business, have the right to participate in the management of the partnership.[36] In addition, each partner has the power to bind the partnership as agent in the usual course of business.[37] In the corporate context, the corporation, as a separate legal entity from its owners, has a board of directors that manages the business. The board is elected by the

---

[32] See U.P.A. § 18(g) (1914); R.U.P.A. § 401(i) (2008). However, section 27 of the Uniform Partnership Act permits partners to transfer just their interest in profits of the partnership without dissolving the partnership or giving the assignee any other partnership rights. See U.P.A. § 27 (1914); R.U.P.A. § 502 (2008).

[33] U.P.A. § 29 (1914). A dissolution only means a change in the partnership makeup and does not always mean that there is a winding up or termination of the business if there was a contract to allow continuation.

[34] One can, however, provide in the articles for termination or a shorter duration for a corporation. See, e.g., Model Bus. Corp. Act Ann. § 3.02 (4th ed. 2008).

[35] U.P.A. § 31(1)(b) (1914). Under R.U.P.A. § 601, dissolution is defined differently, reducing the events which will actually dissolve the partnership. Instead, a "dissociation" may occur which will not always result in a winding up and termination. For example, unlike the U.P.A., the death of a partner is not a dissolution and does result in a winding up. R.U.P.A. §§ 601, 701 (2008).

[36] U.P.A. § 18(e) (1914); R.U.P.A. § 401(f) (2008). A majority vote will resolve differences on ordinary partnership matters. Unanimity is required for acts in contravention of any agreement between the partners. See U.P.A. § 18(h) (1914); R.U.P.A. § 401(j) (2008).

[37] U.P.A. § 9 (1914); R.U.P.A. § 301 (2008).

shareholders. The use of a board of directors allows for a group other than owners to manage and thus a centralization of management separate from the owners. Since a majority vote is usually required for election of the board, a minority shareholder must gain votes of other shareholders to participate in the management of the corporation. While in closely held corporations the shareholders may contract to place minority shareholders on the board, all shareholders (unlike partners) usually do not have the automatic right to manage or be on the board.

Businesses that need to raise large amounts of capital by attracting public investors as shareholders will choose the corporate form. Limited liability, free transferability, centralized management and continuity are all attributes that are necessary to attract public shareholders interested in passively investing and trading shares in the markets.[38] For example, it would be hard to imagine every shareholder of General Electric having a right to participate in management of the company. Limited liability is another important characteristic of the corporate format without which every investor would be personally liable for the obligations of the business. Without limited liability, each shareholder's joint liability would depend on the personal worth of the other owners. This would make it impossible to value and trade shares because share value would be dependent upon, among other things, the potential liability of different shareholders.[39]

§ 1.05 TAXATION

Another significant difference between the partnership and corporate formats is the respective tax treatment given each entity. One way in which the two are treated differently is that corporations, apart from its shareholders, pay taxes as a legal entity. By contrast, a partnership is considered an aggregate of individuals and usually not a legal entity; thus, the partnership is not subject to taxation. The partnership is required to file a tax return, known as an informational return. The purpose of an informational return is to determine how much tax the individual partners will pay on the income derived from the operation of the partnership business but not to tax the partnership.

[A] Double Taxation

Corporations pay tax on the profits they receive and when that profit is distributed to shareholders in the form of dividends, it is again taxed in the hands of the individual shareholders This practice has been called "double taxation" and often referred to as "flow-through" taxation.[40] Since the partnership pays no tax, the income from the business flows through to the

---

[38] For a discussion of shareholder passivity, see § 5.05[C][4] infra.

[39] For a discussion of limited liability and public ownership of shares, see § 3.01 infra.

[40] The top tax rate for corporations is 35% and dividends are paid out of after-taxed profits. Prior to 2003, dividends received by individual shareholders would be included in income and taxed again at as much as 38.6% and thus resulting in a high amount of double tax (total tax of 73.6% not including local taxes). The Tax Act enacted in 2003 lowered the tax rate paid by shareholders for dividends received to a maximum of 15% which lessens the impact of the double tax.

partners and is only taxed individually (even if the partnership income is never distributed). Thus, there is no double taxation.

In the corporate context, when there is a loss from the business operations, the corporation can use the loss to offset other corporate profits from the past or in the future. However, in the partnership, the partners report the losses on their individual tax returns. These losses may be used to offset other personal income and thus reduce personal taxes.

When there are expected to be business profits, tax advisors seek means of avoiding double taxation. Often, this means the formation of the business as a partnership or some other business form that allows a flow through of profits (or losses) to the investor without being taxed twice. In a large business, it is usually impossible to operate as a partnership because of other limitations of the partnership form, such as lack of free transferability of interests and the need for limited liability and centralized management. However, in a small business, the partnership form can be advantageous from a tax point of view.

Alternatively, the tax advisor may form the business as a corporation but seek to structure it to minimize the effect of double taxation. For instance, since income is only taxed a second time once it is distributed to the shareholder, a corporation may retain the earnings in the business and not pay a dividend. Another way to avoid double taxation is to distribute the funds to the shareholders in a form other than a dividend so that the corporation may deduct the payment as a business expense and not pay taxes on that amount. For example, if the shareholder is an employee, the amount which would otherwise be paid to him as a dividend could be paid to him as a salary. Similarly, if one's investment in a corporation is in the form of a bond or a note, the interest paid may substitute for dividends. If one owns the corporation's plant or equipment, rent paid is deductible by the corporation. The payments of salary, interest on debt and rent are usually tax deductible. There are important caveats to these comments since unreasonable attempts to avoid double taxation may result in tax penalties.[41]

[1]   Subchapter S Corporation

Another corporate format which plays a significant role in tax consequences is the S corporation. The S corporation is a corporation which has elected to be taxed under the provisions of Subchapter S of the Tax Code. This provision allows a corporation to pay no tax. Instead, all the corporate income is taxed to the shareholders, whether or not such income is actually distributed thereto. Subchapter S corporations are generally treated like partnerships for tax purposes. Certain restrictions may preclude election as a Subchapter S corporation, such as a the requirement that there be a maximum of 75 shareholders, or the preclusion of non-resident alien or corporate shareholders, or the use of only one class of shares.

---

[41] I.R.C. § 162(a). For example, the Internal Revenue Service may attack the retention of earnings or the payment of salaries as unreasonable and may consider the payments an illegal attempt to avoid double taxation. In the event of such a finding, the IRS would likely impose penalties in addition to the payment of taxes on those amounts.

[2]   Limited Liability Companies

All states have enacted legislation that authorizes the use of a new kind of business entity, called the "limited liability company." The limited liability company for tax purposes is an unincorporated organization.[42] The intent is to provide additional business organizations with limited liability, but without the double taxation consequence of corporations or the restrictions of the Subchapter S Corporation.

The limited liability company is not restricted as to the number of shareholders who may be called members (although too large a number may deem it publicly traded and subject it to double taxation), type of shareholders and capital structure. Although the legislation differs among the states, limited liability companies generally enjoy limited liability and can select centralized management by an entity such as a board of directors. Under the "check the box" regulations, limited liability companies now qualify for partnership tax treatment even if they have other corporate attributes such as free transferability and perpetual existence. States usually require a contract among members called an operating agreement. The operating agreement establishes or modifies the characteristics of the organization.

In order to provide some certainty on tax treatment, the IRS has provided for "check-the-box" regulations which simplify the issue of how a business organization will be treated for tax purposes. The regulations provide that every business organization that is not a corporation is a "pass-through entity," which means it will be treated like a partnership for tax purposes. The regulations list eight organizations which are corporations per se, including the statutory corporation.[43] More significantly the list does not include other business organizations such as limited partnerships and limited liability corporations. If not listed, then the organization is an eligible entity, allowing for a pass through tax treatment and no double taxation. Thus an eligible entity by default is treated like a partnership for tax purposes unless it elects to be treated like a corporation.

§ 1.06   LIMITED PARTNERSHIPS

A limited partnership is a business organization which provides partnership-style tax treatment and limited liability for some of the owners as limited partners.[44] A limited partnership must have at least one general partner with

---

[42] Limited liability partnerships and limited liability limited partnerships may also be formed in many states. These organizations require registration and partnership form but the partners are exempt from some of the partnership liabilities (*e.g.*, tortious conduct of a partner may not create liability to other partners). The limited liability partnership has been used by some accounting and law firms.

[43] I.R.C. § 7701 and regulations thereunder. Prior to 1997, the classification for tax purposes of different business entities depended on its characteristics which were: (1) associates, (2) an objective to carry on a business and divide the profits, (3) continuity of life, (4) centralized management, (5) limited liability, and (6) free transferability of interests.

[44] There are some publicly traded limited partnerships which attempted to avoid the double taxation of the corporate form. Currently under section 7704 of the Internal Revenue Code, a publicly

unlimited liability;[45] the other owners may be limited partners with limited liability (like shareholders). Unlike corporate shareholders who can serve as officers and directors and still have limited liability, if a limited partner gets involved in the control of the limited partnership, she may lose limited liability.[46] Unlike the partnership, it is created by compliance with state law which includes the paying of fees and the filing of a certificate.[47] Much of the structure of the limited partnership is usually established by the provisions of the certificate or contract among the participants.

§ 1.07 LIMITED LIABILTY COMPANY

This form of business entity seeks to combine the most sought-after features of corporation (limited liability) with those of partnership ("flow through" federal taxation), as does the limited partnership form. Unlike limited partnership law, LLC law permits unlimited participation in the business by some or all the owners, seen as another advantage to the LLC form of entity. A principal dividing line between groups of LLCs is "member managed" (similar to partnership) or "manager managed" (similar to corporation and board of directors). A practitioner forms an LLC by filing a brief document, known as the certificate, with a state official, often the secretary of state. The heart of an LLC

---

traded limited partnership is usually taxed as a corporation. I.R.C. § 7704.

[45] Under the Uniform Limited Partnership Act and the Uniform Partnership Act, corporations can serve as general partners of a limited partnership. States which permit a corporation to be the sole partner in a limited partnership have created limited liability for the general partner. A problem arises when a corporation is a general partner of a limited partnership and an individual limited partner also controls the corporation (the general partner). Does the limited partner become liable as a result of that control? If the limited partner acts on behalf of the corporation in controlling the corporation as general partner, there is usually no individual liability. While section 303(b) of the Revised Uniform Limited Partnership Act precludes liability when one acts for the corporation, the result is not as clear under the earlier Uniform Limited Partnership Act. *See* U.L.P.A. (1914); R.U.L.P.A. § 303(b) (2008); Frigidaire Sales Corp. v. Union Properties, Inc., 562 P.2d 244 (1977) (the limited partners acted solely as agents of the corporation and the third party did not rely on them as general partners).

[46] Section 7 of the original Uniform Limited Partnership Act created liability for a limited partner when she participates in the control of the business. The open ended concept of control resulted in litigation and uncertainty. U.L.P.A. § 7 (1914). The Revised Uniform Limited Partnership Act attempted to clarify the situation by enumerating certain conduct that a limited partner may carry on without being deemed to have taken part in control of the business. Under section 303 of the Revised Uniform Limited Partnership Act, a limited partner may, among other things, consult with and advise a general partner with respect to the business of the limited partnership; be a contractor agent, or employee of the limited partnership; act as surety or guarantor for the limited partnership; propose, approve or disapprove of a variety of actions involving the limited partnership. R.U.L.P.A. § 303 (2008).

[47] The Uniform Limited Partnership Act requires a certificate of limited partnership to be filed with the secretary of state (or some other state official). U.L.P.A. § 2 (1914). The certificate shall set forth the following information concerning the limited partnership: the name and address; the names and addresses of all agents for service of process; the names and business addresses of all general partners; the latest date upon which the limited partnership is to dissolve; and any matters the general partners determine to include. The limited partnership is formed at the time of the filing or any date specified in the certificate. In addition, section 201 of the Revised Uniform Limited Partnership Act allows for substantial compliance in filing, which is similar to the de facto incorporation doctrine. R.U.L.P.A. § 201 (2008). For a discussion of the doctrine, see § 2.03[B] *infra*.

is the operating agreement. The operating agreement contains governance provisions (*e.g.*, choice between member versus manager managed, limitations on managers' authority, procedures for election or removal of managers). It also contains financial provisions (*e.g.*, shares, fractional ownership, or, often, assignment to members of ownership percentages).

A hallmark of the LLC is nearly unlimited flexibility. For that reason, lengthy agreements may be necessary to select from a wide array of possible choices. Because agreements are lengthy and often hand-tailored, attorneys charge higher fees to form an LLC as opposed to a corporation. Because of the need for the operating agreement LLCs are often used by sophisticated investors such as private equity funds and investor vehicles as an alternative to limited partnerships.

As to legal issues, courts often employ many analogies to corporate law, for example, what fiduciary duty is and what it may require,[48] or adopting differing approaches to piercing the veil issues.[49]

§ 1.08 INCORPORATION AND ORGANIZATION

In forming a corporation, at least one person must act as the incorporator. She is responsible for filing the articles of incorporation (sometimes called a charter or certificate of incorporation). The articles of incorporation are usually filed with the secretary of state and in some states the filing can be done electronically. The process is simple and relatively inexpensive. The articles of incorporation contain some basic information about the company and must comply with statutory requirements.[50] The name of the corporation must be different from the name of any other corporation to avoid confusion or deception. Corporations must also use a denomination after the name, such as the words "Inc.," "Corp.," "Ltd." to make clear that the company is a corporation. The articles may also contain other significant discretionary provisions authorized by the statute.

Upon acceptance of the articles of incorporation by the state official, corporate existence commences. Once the corporation exists, all further actions on the corporation's behalf must be taken by the incorporator. In order to complete the formation of the corporation, the incorporator must adopt a set of bylaws, hold the initial shareholders' and directors' meetings, arrange for the election of directors and officers, open a bank account for the corporation, issue the shares and conduct other significant initial acts. The bylaws contain the internal rules dealing with the governance of the corporation.[51] Unlike the articles of incorpo-

---

[48] For a discussion of corporate fiduciary duty, see Chapters 8 and 9 *infra.*

[49] *See, e.g.*, the discussion in § 3.03[D] *infra.*

[50] For example under Model Bus. Corp. Act Ann. § 2.02(a) (4th ed. 2008), the articles of incorporation must include: a corporate name; the number of shares which the corporation is authorized to issue; the street address of the corporation's initial registered office, the name of its initial authorized agent; and the name and address of each incorporator.

[51] Bylaws often contain rules regarding important aspects of running the corporation such as shareholders' meetings (for example, the location, notice, waiver of notice, rules for special meetings, voting rights, rules for proxies, quorum requirements etc.); the operation of the board of directors, (such as their number, compensation, method of filling vacancies, and removal of directors and

ration, the bylaws are not publicly filed. Once established, the corporation must comply with the requirements of the state statutory scheme such as holding annual meetings of both directors and shareholders.[52]

Attorneys are often involved in this process. Counsel may advise the client on the advantages of the different business forms and draft the necessary legal papers. Often, the incorporation process is pro forma, using standard forms for the articles of incorporation and the bylaws. As discussed in Chapter 11, the articles and the bylaws may be modified, particularly to protect minority shareholders of a closely held corporation from potential oppression by majority shareholders. Thus, the preparation of the documents may involve potential or actual conflicts of interests among the shareholders. If retained, an attorney must identify these conflicts and disclose them. While it is advisable that all shareholders retain their own counsel to represent their interests, clients sometimes regard the need for individual counsel as an unnecessary expense, particularly when the parties prefer not to use corporate funds for legal fees.

The Code of Professional Responsibility allows an attorney to represent the corporation[53] and set up the business. However, it is important that all the parties understand the potential for conflicts of interest, particularly if a contract is written among the shareholders which addresses their relationship to the corporation and each other.

§ 1.09   CHOICE OF LAW

In organizing the corporation, the incorporator must choose the state in which to file the articles of incorporation.[54] State statutes indicate how to incorporate, deal with financing and legal capital rules, establish the basic structure of the board of directors, deal with shareholder power and rights, and a variety of other issues. Every state has a corporate statute that sets out the corporate rules. Although the state statutes are generally standard, a few statutory rules differ significantly from state to state. These differences may include treatment of shareholder voting rights, the ability to sue directors, and the extent of the directors' fiduciary duty.

Also, every state has a judicially created common law which governs various aspects of corporate life, such as the concept of fiduciary duty and its application

---

officers); the rules concerning officers, agents and employees (duties, salaries, titles, etc.); the rules for issuing share certificates and the transfer of shares; and the method for conducting special corporate acts, such as signing checks and amending the bylaws.

[52] Failure to comply with the formalities may be a factor in deciding whether to hold individual shareholders liable on a piercing of the corporate veil theory. See § 3.03[C] *infra.*

[53] Model Code of Prof'l Responsibility DR 5 (1980).

[54] Most corporations are creatures of state law, but some corporations actually are chartered under federal law. These federally-chartered corporations include such public and quasi-governmental entities as Fannie Mae and the FDIC and Congress has chartered railroads, construction companies, banks, savings associations, credit unions, and many other types of business entities. Paul Lund, *Federally-Chartered Corporations and Federal Jurisdiction*, 36 FLA. ST. U. L. REV. ___ (2008), *available at* http://papers.ssrn.com/sol3/papers.cfm?abstract_id=1274206#.

to the managers of the corporation.[55] While fiduciary duty is often defined by statute, the courts ultimately decide how to apply the statute to a particular set of facts. Court decisions have resulted in differences among states concerning the extent of protection of shareholders by corporate law.

The law of the state of incorporation should govern most intra-corporate relationships, such as between the corporation and its officers, directors and shareholders.[56] This is known as the internal affairs doctrine. With the use of a single law, the doctrine attempts to avoid a corporation being faced with conflicting demands, while it also encourages convenience and predictability of legal application. This does not mean that the law of the state of incorporation governs other corporate dealings, such as commercial transactions, contracts or tort law. In addition, a given state may have a sufficient interest in a corporation incorporated elsewhere but doing business in the state, to subject it to local taxation, jurisdiction for litigation and filing as a foreign corporation.

While Congress could have enacted a federal scheme of incorporation,[57] it has chosen, by not acting, to allow the states to provide the mechanism and law that govern the internal affairs of the corporation. As we will see in subsequent chapters, there is an extensive federal presence through federal securities laws that affects the internal affairs of a corporation. However, defining and regulating the relationship between the shareholders and the managers of the corporation remains primarily an issue of state law.

[A]   Delaware's Dominance

Local businesses usually incorporate in the state in which they maintain a principal place of business to avoid paying extra taxes or fees to a state in which the business has no real interest.[58] Larger corporations do not necessarily incorporate in the state in which they are headquartered. A large number of publicly held corporations have chosen to incorporate in Delaware. Of the corporations that make up the Fortune 500, more than one-half are incorporated in Delaware.[59] However, most of these companies have a small presence in Delaware. Why do corporations choose Delaware? Why do other states recognize Delaware law?

Most states have respected the internal affairs doctrine and do not attempt to impose their rules on corporations incorporated in other states. To some extent

---

[55] For an introduction to fiduciary duty, see Chapter 8.

[56] Restatement (Second) of the Conflict of Laws § 302 (1971).

[57] This theory would be premised on the Commerce Clause. Under the Commerce Clause, Congress has the power to regulate interstate activity, which would include most corporate activities.

[58] For example, if a local business operates primarily in New York but incorporates in Delware it may be considered a foreign corporation in New York, i.e., incorporated in another state but doing business in New York. As a result, it would pay Delaware fees and still have to file as a foreign corporation in New York and pay fees pursuant to N.Y.B.C.L. Article 13.

[59] It is no wonder that Delaware has become almost a brand name for the "business" of serving as the "official home for corporations." Lewis S. Black Jr, *Why Corporations Chose Delaware* 1 (2007), http://corp.delaware.gov/whydelaware/whycorporations_web.pdf (distributed by the State of Delaware).

the "full faith and credit clause"[60] and the Commerce Clause[61] of the United States Constitution support the idea that states should respect the laws of other states. However, the application of one state's corporate law is arguably more a principle of conflict of laws than constitutional law and some states have provisions of their corporate law that apply to foreign corporations (that is, corporations incorporated in another state, but with a presence in that state). Some states have attempted to apply some of their internal affairs laws to corporations incorporated in other states.[62] This practice is infrequent and its validity remains unclear.[63]

Delaware's prominence as a state of incorporation has been criticized as causing a "race to the bottom."[64] Some claim that Delaware has laws which favor corporate management over shareholders. Managers who decide where to incorporate will likely choose a state with favorable laws that protect their interests, such as Delaware.[65]

Why would Delaware provide this pro-management environment? In 2001 Delaware took in around $600 million in franchise taxes.[66] In addition, the corporate bar of Delaware is actively involved in representing corporations in litigation arising under Delaware law. Arguably, Delaware has a direct economic interest in encouraging incorporation within its borders.

Some commentators have argued contrary to the "race to the bottom" theory that incorporating in Delaware is beneficial to shareholders. They argue that corporate management would not choose to incorporate in a state with pro-management laws that hurt shareholders because to do so would depress the value of the shares, reflecting the potential opportunism of the managers. Lower priced shares would hurt the corporation and the managers. The lower priced shares could result in various market mechanisms being used to protect shareholders. For example, if shares are priced too low, the company could become a takeover target, where the purchasing company would likely replace the managers. Since managers fear replacement, they are more apt to try to keep the price of the shares high. According to this argument, managers can be

---

[60] U.S. Const. Art. 1, § 10.

[61] U.S. Const. Art. 1, § 8.

[62] *See, e.g.,* N.Y.B.C.L. §§ 1317–20.

[63] *See* Arthur R. Pinto, *The Constitution and the Market For Corporate Control: State Takeover Statutes After* CTS Corp., 29 WM. & MARY L. REV. 699, 754–774 (1988). The Delaware courts have indicated that the internal affairs doctrine requires application of the law of the state of incorporation based upon both the commerce clause and the need for uniformity that results from the application of a single law. Vantage Point Venture Partners 1996 v. Examen, Inc., 871 A.2d 1108 (Del. 2005). The holding, of course, furthers Delaware's dominance.

[64] "Lesser states, eager for the revenue derived from the traffic in articles of incorporation, had removed safeguards from their own incorporation laws. Companies were early formed to provide articles of incorporation in states where the cost was lowest and the laws least restrictive. The states joined in advertising their wares. The race was not one of diligence but of laxity . . . ." Liggett v. Lee, 288 U.S. 517, 557–58 (1933) (Brandeis, J., dissenting).

[65] *See generally* William Cary, *Federalism and Corporate Law: Reflections on Delaware,* 83 YALE L.J. 663 (1974).

[66] *See* U.S. Census Bureau, Delaware State Government Tax Collections: 2001 (2002), *available at* http://www.census.gov/govs/statetax/0108destax.html.

expected to seek state laws that will benefit shareholders and enhance the market value of the shares to avoid the takeover.[67] Thus, states can be expected to compete in the market for corporate charters to attract incorporations with optimal law.[68] However, empirical studies concerning manager influence in choice of state of incorporation fail to resolve the dispute and the debate continues.[69]

Ultimately, Delaware dominates state corporate law in the United States and influences the development of the law in other states.[70] One of the major advantages of incorporating in Delaware is that with so many corporations incorporated there, its bar and judiciary have an excellent understanding of the complexities of corporate law. Its extensive case law also facilitates planning and research on corporate law issues.

§ 1.10   ULTRA VIRES

Ultra vires results when a corporation has acted beyond its purpose (the object of the incorporation) or powers (the means by which the corporation carries out the object). For example, a corporation established for the purpose of washing windows would have the power to enter contracts to wash windows. However, a contract to replace windows might be ultra vires and beyond its purpose.

In the 19th century, incorporation was difficult because there were concerns about corporate influence and power. Legislatures would grant certificates of incorporation with limited purposes and powers. If a corporation was authorized only to build a road and decided to contract to build an inn so that travelers could stop on their travels, the contract could be ultra vires. The corporation or the party with which the corporation contracted could thus attempt to avoid the contract. Courts attempted to avoid the harsh results of ultra vires. For example, a court could find the corporation had an implied power to build an inn; or could use an estoppel argument based upon the reliance of the third party; or a quasi

---

[67] Professor Roberta Romano has described this federalism as "[t]he genius of American corporate law." *See* ROBERTA ROMANO, THE GENIUS OF AMERICAN CORPORATE LAW 1 (1993). While traditionally the competition is thought to be with other states, some have suggested that Delaware is not really competing with the other states but with the federal government. *See* Mark J. Roe, *Delaware's Competition*, 117 HARV. L. REV. 588 (2004).

For a discussion of other market mechanisms that protect shareholders, see § 5.02[C][2] *infra*.

[68] *See* Ralph K. Winter, *State Law, Shareholder Protection, and the Theory of the Corporation*, 6 J. LEG. ST. 251 (1977). Recently, North Dakota has enacted a shareholder friendly corporate law to hopefully attract incorporations. N.D. Cent. Code § 10-35-01 *et seq.*

[69] *See* Romano, *The State Competition Debate in Corporate Law*, 8 CARDOZO L. REV. 709, 710–12 (1987).

[70] *See generally* Brett H. McDonnell, *Two Cheers for Corporate Law Federalism*, 30 IOWA J. CORP. L. 99, 138–39 (2004) ("The presence of one dominant state allows companies to benefit from network effects in corporate law. A multiplicity of states offering corporate law provides for experimentation and some diversity in the law offered. Even with Delaware's dominance reducing the incentive of other states to innovate in order to attract new corporations, they still have incentive to innovate in order to better serve their own home corporations, or in Delaware's case, to maintain its reputation for responsiveness.").

contract theory. But even with judicial attempts to alleviate the unfairness of ultra vires, there was uncertainty.

Ultra vires is less significant now. Incorporation is much easier and there are no longer legislative restrictions so corporations can be formed with broad purposes and powers to act in any lawful means and purpose.[71] In addition, even if a corporate action is ultra vires, statutory provisions restrict the use of the ultra vires defense in order to protect third parties. For example, MBCA § 3.04 limits challenges based upon ultra vires only to shareholders seeking to enjoin executory contracts; shareholders suing the directors for the violation; or a proceeding by the attorney general to dissolve the corporation.[72] Even if the contract is executory and there is an attempt to enjoin it under the statute, that action must be equitable.[73]

Ultra vires may still be raised in some particular contexts.[74] Corporate guarantees of third party debts that do not benefit the corporation may be attacked.[75] In addition, nonprofit corporate activity such as excessive charitable contributions or unauthorized, unjustified payments to third parties may be wasteful and viewed as ultra vires.

[A]   Corporate Social Responsibility and Philanthropy

Issues of corporate social responsibility involve issues of corporate philanthropy and corporate governance. The issue involves determining whether a corporation should be managed solely to benefit its shareholders or should both societal concerns and stakeholders other than shareholders such as employees, consumers, creditors play a role.[76]

---

[71] "Every corporation incorporated under this Act has the purpose of engaging in any lawful business unless a more limited purpose is set forth in the articles of incorporation." Model Bus. Corp. Act Ann. § 3.01(a) (4th ed. 2008). Certain types such as banking and insurance may be subject to differing and more extensive formation requirements.

[72] In *Total Access, Inc. v. Caddo Electric Cooperative*, 9 P.3d 95 (Okla. App. 2000), the court applied its ultra vires statute to a claim of *quo warranto* which occurs when a corporation "abuses its power or intentionally exercises powers not conferred by law." The court found that since a disappointed competitor has no standing under the ultra vires statute it has no right to a claim of *quo warranto*.

[73] *See* Model Bus. Corp. Act Ann. § 3.04 (official comment) (4th ed. 2008). In *Goodman v. Ladd Estates Co.*, 427 P.2d 102 (Or. 1967), shareholders were unable to challenge a corporate guaranty having no business purpose even though it was ultra vires because Oregon had a similar statute. Plaintiff-shareholder claimed the guaranty was inequitable because it was ultra vires. The fact that the guaranty may have been ultra vires did not make it inequitable under the statute because the statute now validates ultra vires transactions. To be inequitable would require something more. In addition, it was not inequitable because the plaintiffs bought the shares of the corporation from the previous owner who was involved in the ultra vires guaranty and they had knowledge of the guaranty.

[74] When corporations act as partners in a partnership, issues of ultra vires are raised. The other partners can make decisions which adversely affect the corporation and impinge on the role of the directors in managing the business. But most statutes now explicitly permit a corporation to enter into partnerships *See, e.g.*, Model Bus. Corp. Act Ann. § 3.02(9) (4th ed. 2008).

[75] *See* Goodman, *supra*.

[76] For a discussion of the stakeholders and focus of corporate governance, see § 5.02[A] *infra*.

The advocates of shareholder-gain as the sole motive for corporations believe that corporations are formed to run a business for a profit and other activities should not be within their focus. Allowing managers to pick and choose philanthropic or socially beneficial activities permits use of corporate funds for management's personal charities and enables the managers to act as a sort of unelected civil servant. In addition, critics complain that profit is the yardstick used to measure the success of a business. Ultimately, profit maximization is the most socially responsible activity.[77]

Advocates for a broader view recognize that large publicly traded corporations have considerable power and resources that play a significant role in the economy. Corporations as part of the larger community gain from philanthropic activities by enhanced reputation and helping to preserve the advantages that the law provides for businesses. Thus philanthropy should be encouraged and the fiduciary duty of managers should be owed to the enterprise, not just to shareholders, and viewed in a larger context.[78]

Reasonable amounts of corporate philanthropy are not only specifically authorized by state statutes but are common and significant. Originally the issue of corporate philanthropy was raised in the context of the doctrine of ultra vires, that is, whether the contribution was beyond the power and purpose of a corporation. Most state statutes now authorize reasonable philanthropic activities.[79] Even prior to statutory enactments, courts have found philanthropy to be beneficial and within a corporation's implied powers. In *A.P. Smith Mfg. Co. v. Barlow*,[80] the corporation was incorporated prior to a statutory enactment allowing philanthropic corporate payments. It was argued that the change in the statute allowing philanthropy violated the Constitution's Contract Clause because it was a change in the contract (reflected in the law and the articles of incorporation) between the State and the corporation. However, the state had in its corporate statute a reserved power clause which allowed it to change the law subsequently to alter the articles of incorporation.[81] The court also recognized the importance of such contributions to society and to the corporation as a good citizen and thus within its power.[82]

---

[77] *See, e.g.*, MILTON FRIEDMAN, CAPITALISM AND FREEDOM (1962).

[78] A.L.I. Corp. Gov. Proj. § 2.01 takes a compromise position indicating that corporations should have as their objective business activities with a view to enhancing corporate profit and shareholder gain. Notwithstanding this objective, a corporation may take ethical considerations into account and devote reasonable amounts to public welfare, humanitarian, educational, and philanthropic purposes.

[79] *See, e.g.*, Model Bus. Corp. Act Ann. § 3.02(13) (4th ed. 2008).

[80] 98 A.2d 581 (N.J. 1953).

[81] *See, e.g.*, Model Bus. Corp. Act Ann. § 1.02 (4th ed. 2008).

[82] The court found a contribution to Princeton University within the power of a corporation even though not specifically authorized in its articles of incorporation. The court noted that the contribution was not made to a "pet" charity or motivated by personal considerations and would benefit a part of the community in which it operates. A.P. Smith Mfg. Co. v. Barlow, 98 A.2d 581 (N.J. 1953); *see* Theodora Holding v. Henderson, 257 A.2d 398 (Del. Ch. 1969) (the test is one of reasonableness and used the 5% of gross income federal tax deduction limitation as evidence of reasonableness). If the decision to contribute is made by independent directors in an informed manner and not wasteful, it would be protected by the business judgment rule. Kahn v. Sullivan, 594 A.2d 48 (Del. 1991). For a discussion of the business judgment rule, see § 8.03[B], *infra*.

Chapter 2

PROMOTERS' LIABILITY AND DEFECTIVE INCORPORATION

§ 2.01 INTRODUCTION

The issues in this chapter, and in the chapter that follows (piercing the corporate veil), are what English or Australians term issues of legal personality. These questions involve whether, or the extent to which, lenders, contractors, landlords, tort claimants, other creditors, courts, and even the IRS (Internal Revenue Service) will regard the business entity (corporation, LLC) as separate and distinct from its owners.

Before incorporating a business or forming an LLC, someone may take the responsibility of assuring that the business will, in fact, come into existence. She may bring the important parties together, raise capital and make arrangements for the business, such as necessary contacts. This person is known as the promoter.[1] If the corporation or LLC is not yet formed, two sets of issues arise. One is the liability of the promoter acting "on behalf of a corporation to be formed." The other is the liability of the newly formed corporation or LLC on contracts the promoter has made.

Defective incorporation occurs when there has been an improper or incomplete filing necessary to create the corporation or LLC or when, in midlife, the corporation is administratively dissolved by the secretary of state for failure to pay annual franchise taxes or file annual reports. The defective incorporation problems differ from promoters' liability because the parties assume that the corporation or LLC is in existence when contracting or performing other acts on the entity's behalf. Promoters, on the other hand, know that the entity does not yet exist. This chapter deals with both sets of problems: promoters' liability and defective incorporation.

---

[1] The SEC defines a promoter as a "person who acting alone or in conjunction with one or more persons, directly or indirectly, takes the initiative in founding and organizing the business or enterprise . . . ." Synonyms include "founder" and "organizer." *See* SEC Rule 405, 17 C.F.R. § 230.405 (2000).

§ 2.02 PROMOTERS' LIABILITY ON PREINCORPORATION CONTRACTS

[A] Overview

The issue of "corporate personality" involves those who act on behalf of a corporation "to be formed" or "in formation," namely, the promoter. The promoter may believe that once the corporation comes into existence, or even prior thereto based upon the intent of the parties, she will not be personally liable on the contract. More often than not, however, unless the promoter meticulously follows a detailed set of rules, she will find that she remains obligated to pay for goods or services supplied to the new corporation, even after the corporation is in existence.

[B] Liability of the Promoter

Assume, for instance, a retired police officer, Gyro Gearloose, who desires to open a doughnut shop near the police station. Gyro telephones Young Lawyer. Each element of Gyro's business plan has fallen into place. He has enlisted two fellow retired officers as investors. The strip mall storefront near the police station has become available for long term lease. Gyro's application for a Dunkin Donuts franchise has been approved by the Dunkin Donuts area representative, who has tendered a franchise agreement to Gyro. Gyro directs Young Lawyer to form a corporation, Altoona Dunkin Donuts, Inc. (ADD). What advice should Young Lawyer give to Gyro?

The best advice might be to wait. By quickly filing articles of incorporation, over the Internet in some states, with the secretary of state's office, an attorney may be able to form a corporation in a day or two. The corporation then, and the corporation alone, will enter into contracts. But Gyro may be an impatient fellow who does not want to wait even a few days.

Young Lawyer should tell Gyro to insure that in signing the lease and franchise agreement he clearly indicates his representative capacity. If Gyro signs "Altoona Dunkin Donuts, Inc., /S/ Gyro Gearloose," the inference may be that both are bound.[2] Instead, Gyro should sign "Altoona Dunkin Donuts, *by* Gyro Gearloose," or "Altoona Dunkin Donuts, /S/ Gyro Gearloose, *Promoter.*"

An agent, too, warrants the existence of his principal and this maxim represents a second trap for Gyro. Altoona Dunkin Donuts does not yet exist.[3] Gyro should sign "Altoona Dunkin Donuts, *in formation,*" or "Altoona Dunkin Donuts, *a corporation to be formed,* by /S/ Gyro Gearloose," clearly indicating the non-existence of the corporation.

These are not easy rules and an impatient Gyro might hang up on Young Lawyer before she has imparted her advice. But more advice there must be.

---

[2] *See, e.g., Colonial Baking Co. v. Dowie,* 330 N.W.2d 279 (Iowa 1983) (corporate promoter who signed check imprinted with the corporation's name also held liable because in signing he failed to indicate his representative capacity).

[3] *See, e.g., Weiss v. Baum,* 217 N.Y.S.2d 820 (App. Div. 1926).

Young Lawyer must also tell Gyro that in the body of the franchise agreement, and the lease, Gyro must provide that when the corporation comes into being, the other party will look to the corporation for performance. The documents must also expressly provide that Gyro will no longer be responsible (that he "drops out") when the corporation comes into being.

[C]   The Strict View of Promoters' Liability

In *RKO-Stanley Warner Theaters, Inc. v. Graziano*,[4] in their agreement to purchase a movie theater, promoters Graziano and Jenofsky provided: "Upon condition that such incorporation be completed by closing, all agreements, covenants, and warranties contained herein shall be construed to have been made between seller and the resultant corporation." The two promoters did form a corporation prior to closing. Nonetheless, the Pennsylvania Supreme Court held the promoters liable, observing that "[o]ne who acts on behalf of a non-existent principal is himself liable in the absence of an agreement to the contrary." In the court's view, no agreement to the contrary existed: "While paragraph 19 does make provision for recognition of the resultant corporation . . . it makes no mention of any release of personal liability."

A slightly more forgiving rule may be found in *Goodman v. Darden, Doman & Stafford Associates*.[5] Goodman, a real estate salesperson, sold an apartment building to the Darden partnership. He also represented that he was an experienced contractor who could do the extensive renovations needed. He signed a contract "Building Design and Development, Inc. (In Formation), John A. Goodman, President." The court quoted from *RKO-Stanley Warner Theaters v. Graziano*, but did "not believe the agreement to release a promoter from liability must say in so many words, 'I agree to release,'" as the Pennsylvania court had held. Yet the court found no evidence of intent to release the promoter, holding that the Darden partnership's execution of a contract with a corporation "in formation" was not enough to evidence an intent to release Goodman.

The substitution of a new party for a party to a contract is known as a novation. Novation requires three parties. In promoters' cases, however, only two parties are in existence at the time of contracting, the promoter and the other side. In reality, the promoter who gets it right is providing for a future novation, when and if the corporation comes into being. *Ex ante* (before the fact), then, the safest course for a promoter is expressly to provide for a novation *in futuro* and to do so in the body of the contract.[6]

---

[4] 355 A.2d 830 (Pa. 1976).

[5] 670 P.2d 648 (Wa. 1983).

[6] *Accord How & Associates, Inc. v. Boss*, 222 F. Supp. 936 (S.D. Iowa 1963). The defendant signed a contract for architectural services "By: Edwin Boss, Agent for a Minnesota Corporation to be formed, who will be the obligor." The court held "who will be the obligor" words insufficient also to release the promoter. "Adoption of the contract by the corporation is not sufficient to relieve the promoter of his liability. There must be a novation or agreement to that effect."

[D]   Reliance On the Intent of the Parties

Ex post (after the fact), other cases potentially offer more relief for promoters, although *ex ante* an attorney advising a promoter might not rely on them. These cases attempt to ascertain the intention of the parties from all the surrounding facts and circumstances. If those circumstances evince an attempt to look solely to the corporation when formed, then the promoter will not be held liable on the contract.

In *Sherwood & Roberts-Oregon, Inc. v. Alexander,*[7] plaintiff mortgage broker urged the defendant promoters to form a corporation to evade the Oregon usury law. Loans to an incorporated entity could be made at prevailing interest rates which were well above the then statutory usury rate. The promoters never did form the corporation. The mortgage broker then sought payment of the "good faith deposit" from the promoters themselves.

The Oregon court sought to:

> [d]etermine if there was any evidence that the plaintiff agreed to accept the obligation of a to-be-formed corporation solely from the defendants as individuals . . . .

> We find there was evidence that plaintiff looked solely to the to-be-formed corporation for payment of the note. Unlike the creditor in the usual case, the plaintiff in this case is the party that insisted that the contract show a corporation as the obligor and would not do business otherwise.[8]

This result would not be acceptable to courts taking the old-fashioned view. Those courts hold that parties to a contract do not intend their acts to be a nullity. Those parties intend the contract to bind someone. Therefore, until the corporation comes into being, or if the corporation is never formed, someone else must be bound. That someone is the promoter.[9]

Another "all the surrounding facts and circumstances" case is *Quaker Hill, Inc. v. Parr,*[10] in which plaintiff, a New York nursery, pushed for execution of a contract to purchase nursery stock before the growing season ended. Defendant promoter acceded to those wishes, signing "Denver Memorial Nursery, Inc., E.D. Parr, Pres."[11] Denver Memorial Nursery never was formed; another corporation was. Quaker Hill shipped the stock but it arrived too late. The stock died. Quaker Hill then sought to hold Parr personally liable.

The court gave lip service to the old-fashioned rule: "The general principle . . . is that promoters are personally liable on their contracts, though made on

---

[7] 525 P.2d 135 (Or. 1974).

[8] 525 P.2d 135, at 138–39.

[9] *See, e.g., White & Bollard, Inc. v. Goodenow,* 361 P.2d 571 (Wa. 1961).

[10] 364 P.2d 1056 (Co. 1961).

[11] Those acts alone, failure to indicate his representative capacity and failure to disclose the non-existence of his principal, would have rendered Parr personally liable at the outset, at least in some jurisdictions.

behalf of a corporation to be formed." The court then announced an exception capable of swallowing the rule: "[i]f the contract is made on behalf of a corporation and the other party agrees to look to the corporation and not to the promoters for payment, the promoters incur no personal liability."

The court looked to all the circumstances to divine the parties' intention. The court found "little evidence indicating intent on the part of the plaintiff to look to the defendants." It found much evidence the other way: "long distance dealing," "the great rush to complete" the transaction, and "the heavy emphasis on completion of the sale rather than on securing payment."[12]

In those jurisdictions in which courts attempt to determine the intention of the parties, not only from the contract but also from the surrounding circumstances, one key fact or circumstance stands out. That circumstance is the structure of the transaction: that is, using a to-be-formed corporation suited the convenience of the other party rather than the convenience of the promoter.

Before the fact, however, no cautious attorney would rely on *Sherwood & Roberts* or *Quaker Hill v. Parr.* Instead, she would advise the promoter client either (1) to wait until the corporation has been formed, or (2) to "make a contract at the time binding himself, with the stipulation or understanding that if a company is formed it will take his place and that then he shall be relieved of responsibility," as explained previously.

Other choices from a well known 1903 Pennsylvania decision, *O'Rorke v. Geary,*[13] are less desirable. For example, to "take on behalf [of the corporation to be formed] an offer from the other, which, being accepted after the formation of the company, becomes a contract" results in nothing more than an offer which may be revoked at any time prior to acceptance. Similarly, for a promoter "to bind himself personally without more and look to the proposed company, when formed, for indemnity" may amount to nothing more than a request by the promoter for charity.[14]

Even if a promoter such as Gyro does everything right, he runs risks. One risk is that the corporation will never be formed. Then, under the old-fashioned view, (but not perhaps under cases such as *Sherwood & Roberts*) promoter Gyro is liable nonetheless.

A last, and viable alternative, is to advise Gyro to take an assignable option on the storefront lease, or from the franchisor. When the corporation is formed, Gyro may then assign the options to the corporation which may then exercise

---

[12] The circumstances may indicate, or the creditor may admit to, knowledge that the corporation is not yet in existence. That alone is insufficient to release the promoter. To escape liability she must prove also that the creditor intended to look only to the corporation. *See, e.g., Coopers & Lybrand v. Fox,* 758 P.2d 683 (Col. App. 1988) (no agreement, express or implied, and no other evidence that creditor had agreed to look to the corporation; promoter held liable for accounting fees).

[13] 56 A. 541 (1903).

[14] In *O'Rorke v. Geary,* the promoter signed "D.J. Geary for a bridge company to be organized and incorporated." Geary was held personally liable because he failed to pursue any of the three courses of conduct the court outlined (take an offer; provide for novation *in futuro*; or bind himself and look for indemnity).

them.[15] To be irrevocable, this option will require that Gyro furnish consideration, which may prove to be expensive for the promoter.

The law governing liability of promoters for pre-incorporation contracts is thus a patchwork. *Ex ante*, the attorney-advisor must base her advice on the old fashioned, tough rules. Those rules are complex. *Ex post*, under the minority view, the promoter may be able to escape liability based upon the intent of the parties.

[E]   Liability of the Newly Formed Corporation or LLC

Once the corporation comes into existence, the initial board of directors should review and take action with respect to each contract made by the promoter on the corporation's behalf. Otherwise, through mere inaction, the corporation may find itself bound by contracts it later deems unsuitable or not in accord with its business plan.

Recall that in the Gyro Gearloose hypothetical, Gyro had recruited two fellow police department retirees as co-investors. After the Secretary of State returns the certificate of incorporation to the attorney, the next order of business is for the attorney to summon the participants to an organizational meeting of the corporation.[16] At the organizational meeting, one of the first agenda items will be the election by Gyro and his two confederates of themselves as the first directors of Altoona Dunkin Donuts.

Once the election of directors has taken place, the corporation should consider the promoter's contracts. The promoter should lay out all of the contracts he has made on the corporation's behalf. The new board of directors should then either accept them, or repudiate them. It is insufficient for the directors merely to review the contracts and accept no benefits from those the directors find not to their liking. Under the principle known as acquiescence, the corporation may be bound by the promoter's contracts given corporate knowledge and the passage of time.

In *McArthur v. Times Printing Co.*,[17] C. A. Nimocks, as promoter of a newspaper corporation to be formed, made a one year contract with plaintiff for his services as an advertising solicitor. Plaintiff solicited advertising for six months. He was then dismissed on grounds that his employment arrangement was week to week. Plaintiff sued the corporation on the contract. The trial court

---

[15] This alternative is suggested by *How & Associates, Inc. v. Boss, supra,* and by *Elggren v. Snyder,* 285 P. 640 (Utah 1930). One difficulty is that Gyro may end up out-of-pocket for the monies expended to procure the option. However, he may persuade the landlord to apply the option price to the first month's rent. Alternatively, Gyro's co-venturers probably will agree that when formed, the corporation will reimburse him. Another difficulty may arise if an option contract is unfamiliar to the other party. The landlord, for example, may say "Do you want the space or don't you?" All in all, though, despite those drawbacks, the option choice is an alternative the attorney-advisor should have in mind when she speaks with the promoter of a "corporation to-be-formed."

[16] The meeting may be a shareholders meeting if the shareholders are to manage the corporation's business and affairs. Alternatively, the meeting may be styled as a combined meeting of the shareholders and directors.

[17] 51 N.W. 216 (Minn. 1892).

found that "the defendant's board of directors never took any formal action with reference to the contract made on its behalf by Nimocks." Mr. Justice Mitchell propounded a broad rule for determining when a newly formed corporation will be bound:

> [W]hile a corporation is not bound by engagements made on its behalf by its promoters before its organization, it may, after its organization, make such engagements its own contracts . . . . [Yet] it is not requisite that such adoption or acceptance be expressed, but it may be inferred from acts or acquiescence on the part of the corporation, or its authorized agents . . . .[18]

Other courts have found adoption only in acceptance of benefits from promoters' contracts. However, given the possibility of an individual court finding the corporation bound through mere acquiescence, the safest advice to the directors of a new corporation is to review and affirmatively repudiate the contracts viewed negatively.

A more narrow question is whether, by its existence, a corporation becomes liable on a promoter's contract to pay for the legal services provided in forming the corporation. In responding in the negative, the Supreme Court of Iowa reasoned, in *Kridelbaugh v. Aldrehn Theaters Co.*:

> Does a corporation on coming into existence adopt by acquiescence the contract of its promoters to pay for legal services and expenses in its creation? Does its obligation to pay under the terms of the promoter's original contract come into being at the time the corporation has its birth without any act on its part . . . ? We answer again in the negative. This is not a case in which the corporation can accept or refuse the benefits of a contract. Under the instant record it had no choice. Like a child at its birth it must be born in the manner provided. There is no volition on its part.[19]

An Iowa court would require more than existence: adoption or ratification by the corporation of the contract to pay for legal services is necessary. Such an adoption "need not be shown by express acts, but it may be established by implication." A "formal act or resolution" is not necessary.[20]

The Iowa court, however, found express adoption. At the first meeting of the board of directors, one of the directors said to the attorney "we will pay you just as quick as we can sell some stock with which to pay you." The court therefore affirmed judgment for the attorney.

---

[18] 51 N.W. at 216.

[19] 191 N.W. 803, at 804 (1923).

[20] Several jurisdictions hold that, under either an acquiescence or acceptance of benefits test, by virtue of its existence, a corporation becomes liable for attorney services rendered in the corporation's creation. *See, e.g., Ong Hing v. Arizona Harness Raceway, Inc.*, 459 P.2d 107 (Ariz. Ct. App. 1969); *David v. Southern Import Wine Co.*, 171 So. 180 (La. Ct. App. 1936); *Ramsey v. Brooke County Bldg. & Loan Assn.*, 135 S.E. 429 (W. Va. 1926).

[F]   Promoters' Fiduciary Duties

Promoters owe duties of care and loyalty to their co-promoters, the corporation they form and to others with financial interests in the corporation.[21] A promoter may not self deal or secretly profit from her position. She must act in the best interests of the future corporation.[22]

Often, promoters convey property or an existing business to the corporation at an inflated value. Later, other shareholders, or even co-promoters, pay "full value" in money or money's worth for the shares that they receive. A question arises as to whether the corporation may recover the shortfall from the promoter.[23] Some courts take the position that the corporation may not recover the shortfall from the promoter, at least if all the promoters knew about and consented to the inflated transaction. In those cases, the corporation itself, being nothing more than the promoters themselves transformed into shareholders and directors, should be treated as having consented to the conveyance.[24] Other courts find liability if at the time of the inflated conveyance to the corporation, the promoters intended the future sale of shares to the public.[25]

§ 2.03 DEFECTIVE INCORPORATION

[A]   The Problem

Most often, defective incorporation involves shareholders acting as though a corporation has been formed when one has not. Sometimes, the reason for the defective incorporation is simple, such as the case of the paralegal or secretary who lost the articles of incorporation behind the filing cabinet and never filed them. Other times, defective incorporation may occur when the secretary of state or equivalent official returns the articles of incorporation for corrections or because of an error or defect in the check sent for filing and franchise fees.[26] In

---

[21] This may include a duty to creditors to protect them from fraud. *See Frick v. Howard*, 126 N.W.2d 619 (Wis. 1964). For a discussion of fiduciary duty generally, see Chapter 8 (Duty of Care) and Chapter 9 (Duty of Loyalty).

[22] In *Post v. United States*, 407 F.2d 319 (D.C. Cir. 1968), persons found to have been promoters of a country club in Washington, D.C., were held criminally liable for conspiracy to defraud and mail fraud. The court noted that the fiduciary duties of promoters "required that they exercise the utmost good faith in their relations with the corporation and the members, including fully advising the corporation and members and persons who it was anticipated would become members, of any interest the defendants had that would in any way affect the corporation, the members and anticipated members."

[23] In certain cases, subsequent shareholders may recover under the theory of common law fraud or under a statutory antifraud rule applicable to the purchase or sale of securities, such as SEC Rule 10b-5. See the discussion in Chapter 13.

[24] *See Old Dominion Copper Mining & Smelting Co. v. Lewisohn*, 210 U.S. 206 (1908).

[25] *Old Dominion Mining & Smelting Co. v. Bigelow*, 89 N.E. 193 (Mass. 1909).

[26] *Cantor v. Sunshine Greenery, Inc.*, 398 A.2d 571 (N.J. 1979) (delayed acceptance by Secretary of State); *Robertson v. Levy*, 197 F.2d 443 (D.C. Cir. 1964) (articles returned unfiled).

these cases, the parties usually believe that the corporation has been duly formed and venture out, doing business in the corporate name.[27]

Today, certain statutory developments have made defective incorporation easier to avoid. One of the most common causes of defective incorporation arose out of the dual filing requirement, which mandated that corporate documents be filed with both state and local offices. Many states have now eliminated the dual filing requirement. Most states have also eliminated minimum capitalization requirements ($500 or $1000) for all corporations. When a state does have a minimum capitalization requirement, the failure of the promoters to fund the required minimum before commencing business may necessitate the treatment of the business as defectively incorporated.[28]

Defects in corporate existence may arise at corporate death as well as at birth. Corporations that fail to file annual reports or to pay annual franchise fees may be administratively dissolved upon passage of a stated time after the failure to file or to pay.[29] Despite the dissolution, the participants in the enterprise may go about their business, contracting on behalf of a corporation they still believe to exist.

In *Bryant Construction Co. v. Cook Construction Co.*,[30] the court held that a corporation that had failed to pay annual franchise fees did not cease to exist but was only "suspended" pursuant to Mississippi law. Suspension meant that, "though it exists, [it] has been deprived of all power by the state."[31] Therefore, the contracts executed by the corporation during the period of suspension were held to be ultra vires.[32] Acts performed, including contracting, were not void but merely voidable in limited circumstances.[33]

---

[27] To be distinguished from the foregoing cases are instances in which parties pass themselves off as a corporation without any real factual basis for doing so, such as the con artist who merely has printed stationery and invoices with a corporate logo. Neither law nor equity offers protection to such practice.

[28] In *Sulphur Export Corp. v. Caribbean Clipper Lines*, 277 F. Supp. 632 (E.D. La. 1968), under the Louisiana statute requiring a minimum $1000 capitalization prior to transacting business, the directors and officers were found liable for the full amount of the defectively formed corporation's debts. By contrast, earlier versions of the Model Business Corporation Act expressly provided that the only effect of a minimum capital violation would be that the directors would be liable to pay in the amount ($1000 or $500) and not for all debts of the entity.

[29] *See, e.g.*, MBCA §§ 14.20–21.

[30] 518 So. 2d 625 (Miss. 1987).

[31] Compare *Richmond Wholesale Meat Co. v. Hughes*, 625 F. Supp. 584 (N.D. Ill. 1985) (under Illinois law failure to pay annual franchise tax results in dissolution of the corporation by the Secretary of State), discussed in § 2.03[C], *infra*.

[32] In similar fashion, the Model Business Corporation Act provides that "a corporation administratively dissolved continues its corporate existence but may not carry on any business except that necessary to wind up . . . ." MBCA § 14.21(c). Upon payment of back taxes, penalties and interest, however, a dissolved corporation may reinstate its existence as though nothing had occurred, with all contractual commitments intact. See the discussion in § 2.03[E], *infra*.

[33] See the discussion of ultra vires in § 1.09, *supra*.

[B]   The De Facto Corporation Doctrine and Corporation by Estoppel

Usually, in cases of defects at birth or resulting in death, the outcome is more extreme. Plaintiffs may sue the individual owners of the would-be corporation, contending that they should be held liable as if they were partners or treated as an unincorporated association of individuals. Defective incorporation cases thus involve loss of limited liability or limited liability that never existed.

The traditional defense to this claim has been the de facto corporation doctrine or a variant, corporation by estoppel. A duly formed corporation has de jure existence. Its existence is good as against all of the world, including the state. A corporation that made a good faith start toward existence may contend that although it is not de jure, it has de facto existence, that is, existence good against all the world except the state.

The de facto corporation defense has three elements. First, there must be a law pursuant to which the contemplated enterprise could have incorporated. In a world of general incorporation acts, usually such a law exists. Second, the defendants must prove a good faith or "colorable" attempt to incorporate under that law. Third, the defendants must demonstrate actual use or exercise of the corporate powers the participants believe themselves to have, which in the usual case will involve doing business under a corporate name.[34]

For example, in *Cantor v. Sunshine Greenery, Inc.*,[35] a shareholder-promoter, Brunetti, caused articles of incorporation to be filed on December 3. He negotiated a lease with Cantor on Dec. 16 but had no checks with which to make a deposit. Cantor urged Brunetti to sign a counter check. The following day, Brunetti's attorney repudiated the lease; Brunetti stopped payment on the check. Later it was found that "for some unexplained reason" the Secretary of State did not officially file the articles until Dec. 18. So Cantor sued Brunetti personally on the lease. The appellate court refused to hold Brunetti liable, finding "[a]mple evidence of the fact that it was a *de facto* corporation in that there was a *bona fide* attempt to organize the corporation some time before the consummation of the contract and there was an actual exercise of the corporate powers by the negotiations with plaintiffs and the execution of the contract."

If, however, an ersatz corporation is unable to establish the three elements of the de facto corporation doctrine, the defense could still inquire if the particular creditor dealt with the participants as if they were acting on behalf of or as a corporation. Persons who have dealt with a business as though it were a corporation may not later protest when attempting to hold shareholders individually liable on grounds that the corporation had been defectively formed. This fallback theory, "corporation by estoppel," was applied in *Cranson v. International Business Machines Corp.*[36] In *Cranson*, IBM supplied several electric typewriters to the Real Estate Service Bureau, Inc., which acted as though it were a corporation for seven months before discovering that the

---

[34] *See, e.g., Cranson v. International Business Machines Corp.*, 200 A.2d 33 (Md. 1964).

[35] 398 A.2d 571 (N.J. Super. 1979).

[36] *Cranson, supra*, 200 A.2d at 39.

articles of incorporation had not been filed. IBM had delivered the typewriters, invoicing the Bureau as though it were a corporation. The Maryland court held that IBM was not entitled to hold the individual defendant liable: "[w]e think that IBM having dealt with the Bureau as if it were a corporation and relied on its credit rather than that of Cranson, is estopped to assert that the Bureau was not incorporated at the time the typewriters were purchased."

[C]   Statutory Abolition of the De Facto Corporation Doctrine

The 1950 and 1969 versions of the Model Business Corporation Act provide that "[a]ll persons who assume to act as a corporation without authority so to do so shall be jointly and severally liable for all debts and liabilities incurred or arising thereof."[37]

The statutes also provide that "[u]pon issuance of the certificate of incorporation, the corporate existence shall begin, and such certificate of incorporation shall be conclusive evidence that all conditions precedent required . . . have been complied with and that the corporation has been incorporated under this Act . . . ."[38]

In *Timberline Equipment Co., Inc. v. Davenport,*[39] the Oregon Supreme Court held that the MBCA abolished the de facto corporation doctrine. Owing in part to the ease with which a corporation may be formed under modern statutes, an entity is either a corporation de jure or is nothing at all. The court found some wiggle room in the statutory wording "assume to act":

> We conclude that the category of "persons who assume to act as a corporation" does not include those whose only connection with the organization is as an investor. On the other hand, . . . [w]hen several persons carry on the activities of a defectively organized corporation, chance will frequently dictate which of the several active principals directly incurs a certain obligation . . . .

> We are of the opinion that the phrase "persons who assume to act as a corporation" should be interpreted to include those persons who have an investment in the organization and who actively participate in the policy and operational decisions of the organization. Liability should not necessarily be restricted to the person who personally incurred the obligation.[40]

The court held liable for equipment rentals not only the shareholder director who signed equipment leases on behalf of a defectively formed corporation but also two doctors who were shareholders and directors but who did not sign. The court found that "they endeavored to and did retain some control over [Davenport's] management." They co-signed checks and one of the doctors made

---

[37] MBCA § 139 (1950); MBCA § 146 (1969).

[38] MBCA § 50, today codified as MBCA § 2.03.

[39] 514 P.2d 1109 (Or. 1973).

[40] 514 P.2d at 1113–14.

frequent visits to the building site at which the leased equipment was in use. Thus, the wiggle room in the statute was of no help to the defendant doctors in *Timberline Equipment*.

Richmond Wholesale Meat Co. v. Hughes[41] involves a case of corporate death by administrative dissolution for failure to pay franchise taxes. The court agreed with *Timberline Equipment's* reasoning and prior Illinois precedent that "some element of knowledge, whether actual or constructive, is required by the statute." The court denied motions for summary judgment because an issue of fact existed as to whether the non-signing participant in a wholesale purchase of meat products by a dissolved corporation "knew or should have known of the corporation's dissolution."

[D]   Does Corporation by Estoppel Survive the Model Business Corporation Act?

In passing, the *Timberline Equipment* court seemed to think that the corporation by estoppel concept could survive the Model Business Corporation enactment. Other courts that have considered the question more closely have arrived at the opposite conclusion.

In *Robertson v. Levy*,[42] Levy was to purchase Robertson's business, taking an assignment of Robertson's lease. Levy agreed to do those things in the name of a corporation, "Penn. Ave. Record Shack, Inc." Meanwhile, the Superintendent of Corporations rejected the articles of incorporation. Levy refiled the articles and they were accepted on January 17, after Levy had taken a bill of sale from Robertson on January 8 and an assignment of the lease on January 2. Examining the Model Act, including the provision providing that "[u]pon issuance of the certificate of incorporation, the corporate existence shall begin, and such certificate of incorporation shall be conclusive evidence . . . ,"[43] the court held that under the Model Act there can be "no corporation de jure, de facto or by estoppel." Reviewing cases and commentary, the court found "[t]he authorities . . . unanimous in their belief that [the Model Act provisions] have put to rest de facto corporations and corporations by estoppel."[44]

A Tennessee appellate court applied *Robertson v. Levy* in *Thompson & Green Machinery Co. v. Music City Lumber Co.*[45] Examining the cases, the court found that "de facto corporations no longer exist" and that "[t]o allow an estoppel would be to nullify" the Tennessee version of the Model Act provisions.[46]

---

[41] 625 F. Supp. 584 (N.D. Ill. 1985).

[42] 197 F.2d 443 (D.C. Cir. 1964).

[43] MBCA § 50 (1950). Today's equivalent provision is MBCA § 2.03.

[44] Compare *Cantor v. Sunshine Greenery, Inc.*, 398 A.2d 571 (N.J. Super. 1979), finding a de facto corporation under a modern statute. New Jersey, however, is not a Model Act jurisdiction. It has no equivalent to MBCA § 2.04, formerly MBCA § 139.

[45] 683 S.W.2d 340 (Tenn. Ct. App. 1984).

[46] A similar case is *Don Swann Sales Corp. v. Echols*, 287 S.E.2d 577 (Ga. Ct. App. 1981), in which

[E]   Model Business Corporation Act Compromise

Robertson v. Levy, Thompson & Green Machinery, and similar cases abolishing all traces of the de facto and corporation by estoppel doctrines are harsh outcomes. The 1985 revision of the Model Act (MBCA) attempts to ameliorate their holdings. The MBCA codifies the interpretation of the statute made by the courts in *Timberline Equipment* and *Richmond Wholesale Meats.* The Model Act drafters thus add a knowledge requirement: "[a]ll persons purporting to act as or on behalf of a corporation, *knowing there was no incorporation under this Act,* are jointly and severally liable for all liabilities created while so acting."[47] In jurisdictions with newer versions of the Model Business Corporation Act, the purely or largely passive investor may escape liability for the obligations of an entity whose proper birth has not come about, if not for those of a corporation that has suffered a premature, unknown death.

[F]   Corporate Death

A defunct corporation may re-instate itself by paying back franchise taxes and penalties or by filing missing annual reports, at least if it does so within two years after administrative dissolution.[48] The MBCA makes clear that reinstatement within the time allotted solves all, or most, problems associated with corporate death: "When the reinstatement is effective, it relates back to and takes effect as of the effective date of the administrative dissolution and the corporation resumes carrying on its business as if the administrative dissolution had never occurred."[49]

Neither a shareholder or an attorney can bring a corporation back to life after the two year reinstatement window has closed. What happens thereafter? Are the shareholders sitting ducks for creditor claims based upon business done after the corporation had been administratively dissolved? At first, and even second, blush, it seems as through they would be, although *Equipto Division Aurora Equip. Inc. v. Yarmouth*[50] reaches a contrary result, using the MBCA's 1985 knowledge limitation to limit shareholder liability.

Yarmouth did business in the corporate name after the Secretary of State had administratively dissolved the corporation. The creditor (Equipto) brought

---

the defendant dealt in the name of Cupid's, Inc., even though the corporation was not registered until 10 months later. The court found that the Georgia version of the Model Act "has eliminated the doctrine of de facto corporations." The court also refused to find grounds for an estoppel, an equitable concept , when "[t]here is no equitable ground for application of the doctrine because persons who do business as a corporation without even a colorable organization must know that they are not a corporation and are not therefore misled or injured."

[47]   MBCA § 2.04 (emphasis added).

[48]   MBCA § 14.22.

[49]   *Id.* § 14.22(c). An Arkansas court applied the section in *Harris v. Looney,* 862 S.W.2d 282 (Ark. App. 1993), to hold liable only the incorporator of a defectively formed corporation (J & R Construction, Inc.) who had signed the purchase agreement. No proof existed, the court decided, that the two non-signing incorporators (1) had acted "on behalf of the corporation," and (2) had known that there had been "no incorporation under the Act."

[50]   950 P.2d 451 (Wash. 1998).

a collection action after the two year reinstatement window had closed. The court applied a provision in the Model Act's incorporation chapter, MBCA § 2.04, *supra*, to a situation following corporate death rather than one of corporate birth. The court held the knowledge limitation ("knowing there was no incorporation under this title") applied post-dissolution as well as to its formative years. Baring actual knowledge, Yarmouth would not be liable for business he did in the defunct corporation's name. The result was that no one would be bound by a valid contract. Whether courts in other states follow *Equipto*, with its counter-intuitive outcome, remains to be seen.

Chapter 3

PIERCING THE CORPORATE VEIL

§ 3.01 THE CONCEPT OF LIMITED LIABILITY

Limited liability does not mean an absence of liability. A corporation must satisfy judgments against it, at least to the extent of its assets. Shareholders who purchase shares in corporations take the risk that if the corporation is ultimately held liable, they will lose all or part of their investment. Since the median term of survival of American corporations is about seven years (more than half fail sooner), investments often sour.

The corporation is a separate juridical person and as such, is liable for its own debts. Creditors may not reach the assets (home, automobile, bank account, other investments) of the flesh-and-blood owners, the shareholders, or in the case of a subsidiary corporation, the incorporated owner, the parent corporation.

Limited liability encourages capital formation. Fewer persons would be willing to invest if, in doing so, they subjected all of their assets to the risks of the business enterprise. Under a joint and several liability corporate law scheme, potential investors would wish to know the level of other potential investors' wealth so as to able to undertake a assessment of their own risk exposure. If they had to do so in many cases, the development of impersonal trading over stock exchanges would never have developed. Limited liability encourages savings, investment, and the pooling of capital by numerous investors, often on a national or even global scale.[1]

Pooling of capital by different individuals and entities allows individuals better to make multiple investments, resulting in diversification. Among other things, pooling of capital and diversification makes it less imperative to monitor closely any one investment, aiding further in capital formation. Capital formation is necessary to finance enterprises that a single individual may not be willing to undertake due to unusual scope or risk.

Despite its role in achieving the goal of capital formation, the concept of limited liability has been under attack by some legal scholars who posit that limited liability forces suppliers, creditors, and especially tort claimants to subsidize promoters and other participants in incorporated enterprises.[2]

Limited liability induces managers of incorporated entities to take risks or to tolerate an overall level of risk they otherwise would avoid. With the present scheme, if an incorporated business fails with its liabilities far exceeding its

---

[1] *See* the discussion of stock exchanges in § 5.02[B], *infra.*

[2] See the discussion in § 3.02, *infra.*

assets, the owners need not bankrupt the business. Instead, the owners may simply toss the keys to the creditors and walk away.[3]

Even when the concept of limited liability is not under attack on a theoretical basis, in some individual cases, plaintiffs argue that due to abuse of the corporate form by persons in control of the corporation, limited liability should not be upheld. They plead an "add on" legal theory, contending that in the case at bar, the limited liability of the corporate entity should be disregarded. They contend that shareholders should be personally liable for corporate debts. The doctrine has many names, including "corporate disregard," "the alter ego theory," the "instrumentality" or "mere instrumentality" theory. Another doctrinal offshoot, "enterprise liability," may hold a group of corporations under common control, say, by a large multinational corporation (subsidiaries, parent and even grand-parent corporations), as one enterprise for liability and other purposes. Then Judge, later Justice, Cardozo found the entire body of doctrine as discussed or applied by courts and commentators to be "enveloped in the mists of metaphor."[4] Most lawyers today refer to the doctrine as "piercing the corporate veil."

A first thing to note about the doctrine, which is almost exclusively a creature of judge made law, is that before invoking the doctrine, a plaintiff must first establish an independent basis to hold the corporation liable. Having established corporate liability for a tort or a breach of contract, if the corporate defendant has insufficient assets to satisfy a prospective judgment, the plaintiff may then seek to pierce through the veil that protects the individual shareholders, or parent corporation, from liability for the defendant corporation's debts. Thus, with an "add on" to her complaint, a plaintiff hopes to establish a route to a deeper pocket.

Obviously, piercing the corporate veil is a favorite doctrine of litigators who attempt to invoke it whenever opposing small or mid-sized corporate defendants with assets insufficient to satisfy a potential judgment. The doctrine is invoked quite frequently.[5] Given the volume of cases, the law in the area tends to be complex and somewhat confusing.[6] Seemingly, every jurisdiction, every appellate court, every judge and every litigator seeks to add a wrinkle or two to the doctrine.[7] Nonetheless, common themes do emerge that enable one to make sense of it all.

---

[3] Under state laws, the euphemistic legal term for this act is an "assignment for the benefit of creditors."

[4] *Berkey v. Third Ave. Ry. Co.*, 244 N.Y. 84, 94, 155 N.E. 58, 61 (1926) (Cardozo, J., "Metaphors in law are to be narrowly watched, for starting as devices to liberate thought, they end often by enslaving it").

[5] In the late 1980s, Professor Robert Thompson conducted an empirical study of reported appellate decisions. He found 1400 appellate opinions in the Westlaw database through 1985. *See* Robert Thompson, *Piercing the Corporate Veil: An Empirical Study*, 76 Cornell L. Rev. 1036 (1991). Of course, reported appellate decisions represent only the tip of the iceberg. The theory is plead in countless trial court proceedings.

[6] Apropos of the conceptual murkiness, and the sheer number of cases, a treatise devoted entirely to piercing the corporate veil has been published. *See* Stephen Presser, PIERCING THE CORPORATE VEIL (1991).

[7] Because the doctrine is a creature of equity, the inquiry tends to be fact-specific in every case, reinforcing impressions that wide variation exists from case to case or from jurisdiction to

The doctrines of *ex ante* (before the fact) and *ex post* (after the fact) have tremendous implications for corporate planners.[8] In forming corporations, planners should seek to reduce the risk that a plaintiff may be able to pierce the corporate veil and must warn promoters and other corporate participants that certain conduct may result in loss of limited liability.

§ 3.02 THE LIMITED LIABILITY DEBATE

A lender such as a bank may take steps to protect itself when dealing with incorporated entities. A bank contemplating a loan to a corporation has enough at stake to warrant an investigation into whether the borrower is adequately capitalized (that is, has sufficient assets to meet the reasonably expected demands of creditors and insurance or assets to protect against risks of tort liability). The bank should also discern whether the corporation observes the formalities required of corporations and refrains from intermixture of the corporate and owners' affairs. As will be seen, the intermixture of affairs, inadequate capitalization and the like may be common grounds upon which courts rely in piercing the corporate veil.

After its investigation, or as a routine matter, the bank will then take steps to protect its interests. For example, the bank may insist upon taking a security interest in certain key assets which will allow the bank to liquidate the assets if it is not paid. The bank may require that some or all of the shareholders personally guarantee the corporate indebtedness. Since banks often conduct thorough investigations before lending money to corporations, these lenders may not necessarily need the assistance of a legal doctrine that lifts the veil when the corporate form has been abused.

Other contract claimants, however, do not have the ability to investigate first. A trade creditor may have hundreds of customers, each with a small account. The trade creditor would encounter significant, unbearable costs if she attempted the type of investigation undertaken by a bank. Similarly, putative employees may not have the bargaining power to obtain the information they may need in order to protect themselves.

One line of thought has been then that court should be more liberal in lifting the veil, especially in cases in which the incorporated entity has misrepresented its capitalization, how it conducts business, and so on:

---

jurisdiction. *See, e.g.,* Franklin A. Gevurtz, *Piercing Piercing: An Attempt to Lift the Veil of Confusion Surrounding the Doctrine of Piercing the Corporate Veil,* 76 Or. L. Rev. 853 (1997) ("piercing claims constitute the single most litigated area of corporate law" and "judicial opinions in this area have made it one of the most befuddled").

[8] *"Ex ante"* and *"ex post"* are helpful terms borrowed from the social sciences which describe the temporal perspective from which an event or transaction is viewed. Analysis *ex ante,* or before the fact, may differ greatly from an inquiry *ex post,* or after the fact. For example, *ex ante,* a tort lawyer might exhort bus drivers to "stop, look and listen" at every railroad crossing. In defending the driver or the bus company after an accident, the same lawyer will argue *ex post* that all that is required is reasonable care in the circumstances and that no hard and fast "stop, look and listen" rule of law exists.

Employees, consumers, trade creditors, and lenders are voluntary creditors. The compensation they demand will be a function of the risk they face. One risk is the possibility of nonpayment because of limited liability. Another is the prospect . . . that after the terms of the transaction are set the debtor will take increased risk, to the detriment of the lender.[9]

Firms which know or can assess the risks inherent in dealing with certain corporations can price their products or services accordingly. However, when incorporated entities misrepresent their assets or engage in fraud, the supplier firm or lender will likely make incorrect calculations and will bear the risk of insolvency without adequate compensation.

[C]reditors must be able to assess the risk of default accurately. If the creditor is mislead into believing that the risk of default is lower than it actually is, the creditor will not demand adequate compensation. This will lead to an excessive amount of risk taking by firms, because some of the costs are now shifted to creditors.[10]

For that reason, when an element of fraud or misrepresentation is present, courts should be much more inclined to pierce the veil.[11]

Recently, scholars have advanced arguments that limited liability should be abolished altogether, in small and publicly held corporate settings alike. They point to the opportunistic manipulation of limited liability by large corporations. An example of the latter would be a major oil company putting its oil tankers in a separate subsidiary corporation or, better yet, putting each individual tanker in a separate corporation. In that manner, the oil company could minimize its exposure in the case of an oil spill to one tanker and miscellaneous assets. Law professors advocate that a regime of pro rata shareholder liability (that is, each shareholder pays damages according to their respective ownership) should be implemented, at least for the torts of incorporated entities.[12]

Other scholars find that the regime of limited liability, even though it may create incentives for incorporated entities to engage in unduly risky activities, on balance seems justified, and merely needs some reform.[13]

Between the extremes are skeptics who argue that investors would develop devices to evade pro rata shareholder liability for the torts of incorporated

[9] Frank Easterbrook & Daniel Fischel, *Limited Liability and the Corporation*, 52 U. Chi. L. Rev. 89, 104 (1985).

[10] *Id.* at 105.

[11] Indeed, Professor Thompson's study, *supra* note 4, bears this out. If courts identified an element of misrepresentation in a case, they pierced the corporate veil in 98 of 107 contract cases examined, or 91.6% of the time. Conversely, if the court expressly noted the absence of misrepresentation, piercing occurred in only 7.7% of the cases.

[12] *See generally* Henry Hansman & Reinier Kraakman, *Toward Unlimited Liability for Corporate Torts*, 100 Yale L. J. 1879 (1991).

[13] *See* David Leebron, *Limited Liability, Tort Victims, and Creditors*, 91 Colum. L. Rev. 1565 (1991) (as a reform, suggesting that when individuals use multiple corporations to segment related but similar businesses, "all of the assets of such related businesses should be available to satisfy the claims of tort victims").

enterprises, were such a regime of pro rata liability to be implemented.[14] Another skeptic points out that in a torts case against a publicly held corporation, it is doubtful whether a state court could ever obtain territorial (personal) jurisdiction over a critical mass of shareholders made liable on a pro rata basis, given the widespread geographical dispersion of shareholders in publicly held corporations of any size.[15] Pro rata liability for shareholders of larger corporations might inhibit development of trading markets for their shares: prudent investors would investigate to ascertain their potential exposure, at least in cases in which they were uncertain as to whether the shares' market price reflected the risk. The cost of investigation would depress share prices and deter some investors altogether.

While informative, the proposal for unlimited liability is simply politically unfeasible. Throughout the United States, limited liability is central to the formation of small business endeavors that frequently utilize the corporate form.[16] Elimination of limited liability would entail legislative action. Nothing is less likely to pass a state legislature than a bill that legislators perceive to be "anti-small business."[17] Clearly, legislatures view the benefits of limited liability as outweighing the costs.

Recent legislative efforts have been going in precisely the opposite direction. Legislatures across the land have adopted limited liability company and limited liability partnership legislation that extends the protection of limited liability to investors in entities other than corporations.[18] The scholarly debate, then, may amount to the proverbial academic exercise of determining how many angels can dance on the head of a pin.

§ 3.03 GROUNDS FOR PIERCING THE CORPORATE VEIL

[A] Introduction

Piercing the corporate veil is an equitable theory in which the facts of each case are important. In almost every case in which the veil is pierced, the court has found the presence of two or more of the factors this section discusses. In

---

[14] *See, e.g.*, Joseph Grundfest, *The Limited Future of Unlimited Liability: A Capital Markets Perspective*, 102 Yale L. J. 387 (1992).

[15] Jane Cooper Alexander, *Unlimited Shareholder Liability Through a Procedural Lens*, 106 Harv. L. Rev. 387 (1992).

[16] *Accord* Leebron, *supra* note 12, at 1566 ("Despite the recent burst of scholarship, few topics are liable to strike the reader as less likely to produce changes in the law than analysis of limited liability. No principle seems more established in capitalist law, or more essential to the functioning of the modern corporate economy.") (footnotes omitted).

[17] Indeed, Professor Stephen Presser perceives a socio-economic justification for limited liability in that it encourages individual investment by those of modest means, as opposed to investment by the wealthy for whom the specter of pro rata liability would be less of a deterrent. *See* Stephen Presser, Piercing The Corporate Veil 1–12 (1991).

[18] See the discussion of limited liability companies and other new business forms in Chapter 1.

one case, *Sea-Land Services, Inc. v. Pepper Source*,[19] the court read Illinois law as directing a judge to "focus on four factors: (1) the failure to maintain adequate corporate records or to comply with corporate formalities, (2) the commingling of funds or assets, (3) undercapitalization, and (4) one corporation treating the assets of another corporation as its own." The court seemed to agree that all four bases were present in a case in which one individual owned the shares of six corporations which he operated as his "personal playthings."

Kinney Shoe Corp. v. Polan[20] found that the state law required the presence of two factors, "[g]rossly inadequate capitalization combined with disregard of corporate formalities, causing basic unfairness . . . sufficient to pierce the corporate veil." In the case of more sophisticated contract creditors, the court would impose a "third prong." "Where, under the circumstances, it would be reasonable for that type of party entering into the contract with the corporation, for example, a bank or other lending institution, to conduct an investigation of the credit of the corporation prior to entering into the contract, such party will be charged with the knowledge that a reasonable credit investigation would disclose."[21]

Courts may require multiple showings because the law permits citizens to incorporate precisely to limit their liability. Judges also know that by their findings they may be opening up to personal exposure ordinary citizens who may see their bank accounts, personal investments, automobiles, and so on, subjected to corporate creditors' claims.

[B]   Intermixture of Affairs

The term "intermixture of affairs," refers to the blurring of the distinction between the concerns of the corporation and those of the owners. When affairs are intermixed, it becomes difficult for a third party to determine where the affairs of the owner leave off and those of the incorporated business begin. This ground for piercing the corporate veil usually occurs in connection with, and is closely related to, the next ground, lack of observation of formalities.

In parent/subsidiary cases, intermixing of affairs often occurs to such a great extent that the subsidiary no longer has even a small portion of its agenda which it may call its own. In the case of individual shareholders, owners may take cash from the corporate treasury in the form of no interest, low interest, or undocumented loans. Corporate equipment may be utilized for personal gain. Corporate employees may be asked to complete personal tasks, or tasks associated with other business ventures.

Shareholders of small incorporated entities, or a parent corporation, may deal with their corporation, or with a subsidiary. The fact that the corporation is used to benefit the shareholders does not itself mean there will be a piercing. Were that so, piercing the veil would occur much more frequently.

---

[19] 941 F.2d 519 (1991), *after remand*, 993 F.2d 1309 (7th Cir. 1993).

[20] 939 F.2d 209 (4th Cir. 1991).

[21] Applying *Laya v. Erin Homes, Inc.*, 352 S.E.2d 93 (W. Va. 1986).

When affairs are intermixed, an inference is drawn that somehow, the individuals are more responsible for the corporate debts and obligations. Intermixture of affairs creates an express or implied representation that the individuals should be held accountable. To avoid the inference, shareholders must be above board and clearly document their dealings with their corporation.

When complete intermixture of affairs occurs, courts may apply the "instrumentality theory."[22] In the parent subsidiary context,

> [t]hree elements must be proved: [1] control by the parent to such a large degree that the subsidiary has become its mere instrumentality; [2] fraud or wrong by the parent through its subsidiary, *e.g.*, torts, violation of a statute or stripping the subsidiary of its assets; and [3] unjust loss or injury to the claimant, such as insolvency of the subsidiary.[23]

In *American Trading and Production Corp. v. Fischback & Moore*,[24] plaintiff exhibitor suffered losses in the destruction by fire of McCormick Place in Chicago, Illinois. Faulty wiring caused the fire. Plaintiff sued one of twenty subsidiaries which did actual wiring and the publicly held parent corporation (Fischback & Moore), invoking the instrumentality theory. The court did not accept the argument. Any intermixture of affairs was insufficient to lead to a finding of domination or control:

> [A]ll four of the Subsidiary's directors were also directors of the parent, and four of the Subsidiary's directors were also officers of the Parent. However, the corporations maintain separate offices and conduct separate directors' meetings. The financial books and records of the Subsidiary are maintained by its employees in Chicago . . . . The Subsidiary has its own bank accounts and negotiates its own loans from third parties . . . . On occasion, the Subsidiary has borrowed from the Parent; these loans are evidenced by notes and call for interest at the prime rate.

The district court continued for several more paragraphs, chronicling the course of dealing between the corporation and its owner, ultimately declining to pierce the veil on the basis of the instrumentality theory, which in the first instance is a theory based upon intermixture of affairs.

Moral indignation may creep into an appellate court's affirmation of a veil piercing. For example, in *Soerries v. Dancause*,[25] a young woman had been served while inebriated and then died in an automobile accident after leaving a nightclub owned by a corporation of which defendant was the sole owner. Employees testimony indicated that their employer paid some wages under the table. Comparison of corporate and individual tax returns indicated that the corporation deducted $43,000 for rent while defendant (also the landlord)

---

[22] See the discussion of instrumentality theories as a separate ground in § 3.03[F], *infra.*

[23] *Steven v. Roscoe Turner Aeronautical Corporation*, 324 F.2d 157, 160 (7th Cir. 1963).

[24] 311 F. Supp. 412 (N.D. Ill. 1970).

[25] 564 S.E.2d 356 (Ga. App. 2001).

reported $34,173 in rental income. The court took the evidence as a showing that the defndant "had disregarded the speparatness of legal entities by commingling and confusiion of properties [and] records." The case is one of many veil piercing cases in which courts "employ a character test." They conduct a "sort of genneral review of the defendant's businss ethics," affirming corporate disregard if they sense that defendant is a "sharp operator," even if the observation has little or nothing to do with the issues before the court.[26]

[C]   Lack of Corporate Formalities

Courts are more likely to pierce the veil of corporations which do not attend to corporate formalities. Such formalities include issuing stock certificates, holding meetings, electing officers, and documenting loans and other transactions. Failure to observe formalities may indicate an impermissible intermixture of affairs or may indicate the use of a corporation as a "mere instrumentality." Usually, when corporate formalities are found to have been ignored, courts require at least one other independent ground for piercing the corporate veil.

The Model Business Corporation Act Close Corporation Supplement negates the possibility that the corporate form will be disregarded on the basis of lack of corporate formalities alone. The relevant provision states:

> *Limited Liability.* The failure of a statutory close corporation to observe the usual corporate formalities or requirements relating to the exercise of its corporate powers or management of its business and affairs is not a ground for imposing personal liability on the shareholders for the liabilities of the corporation.[27]

The proposed statute may be an acknowledgment that in some non closely held corporation settings, lack of formalities alone may be a ground for piercing the corporate veil. However, the few courts confronting the question disagree. A New Mexico Court has stated that "disregard of corporate formalities" and "ignorance on the part of directors and officers as to its operation . . . are not enough to warrant disregarding the corporate entity."[28] A Texas court echoed those thoughts, finding that "plaintiff fails to point out how" failure to observe corporate formalities and keep financial affairs separate caused plaintiff to "fall victim to some basically unfair device by which the corporate form of business organization has been used to achieve an inequitable result."[29]

In conjunction with other findings, however, proof that defendant shareholders or parent corporation has failed to observe the formalities required of businesses operating in the corporate form frequently puts the plaintiff over the top in proof of his case. "[A] failure to observe corporate formalities coupled with inadequate capitalization has frequently been cited as a basis for disregarding

---

[26] *See* Franklin Gevurtz, *Piercing Piercing: An Attempt to Lift the Veil of Confusion Surrounding the Doctrine of Piercing the Corporate Veil*, 76 Ore. L. Rev. 853, 858 (1997).

[27] MBCA Close Corporation Supplement § 25.

[28] *Scott Graphics Inc. v. Mahaney*, 549 P.2d 623 (N.M. Ct. App. 1976).

[29] *Preston Farm & Ranch Supply v. Bio-Zyme Enterprises*, 615 S.W.2d 258 (Tex. Civ. App. 1981).

the corporate entity," observed the court in *Brunswick Corp. v. Waxman.*[30] By contrast, when formalities are lacking, third parties may be lead to believe that the individual owners or parent will be in some way be "good for" the debts of the corporation.

[D]   Veil Piercing in Limited Liability Companies (LLCs)

"We see no reason, in either law or equity, to treat LLCs differently than we treat corporations" but "the factors would be different." The principal difference is that "[o]rganizational formalities applicable to corporations do not apply to LLCs."[31] California's statute specifically provides that failure to observe formalities may not be a ground for veil piercing in an LLC.[32] "The analyses between corporate veil piercing and limited liability company veil piercing may not completely overlap," especially in the area of failure to observe formal requirements.[33]

[E]   Inadequate Capitalization

[1]   Overview

Professor Ballantine defined inadequate capitalization as a ground for piercing the corporate veil: "If the capital be trifling or illusory compared with the business to be done or the risks of loss, this is a ground for denying the separate entity privilege." Earlier in the same passage, Ballantine stated that "[i]t is coming to be recognized as the policy of the law that shareholders should in good faith put at risk of the business unencumbered capital reasonably adequate for its prospective liabilities."[34] The test requires incorporators and directors to peer into the future, at least for the intermediate term, funding the corporation in a manner adequate for the business plan (risk and size of the undertaking).

That said, a number of questions arise. When is the capital "trifling or illusory"? What is "capital" for these purposes? Is inadequacy of capital alone a sufficient grounds for piercing the corporate veil or, because the legislature allows persons to incorporate without capital or with minimum capital, must additional proofs be made? Must shareholders or a parent corporation "top off" capital as a business grows, or are they protected if the capital contributed at

---

[30] 459 F. Supp. 1222 (E.D.N.Y. 1978), *affirmed*, 599 F.2d 34 (2d Cir. 1979), citing, *inter alia*, *Anderson v. Abbott*, 321 U.S. 349 (1944); *DeWitt Truck Brokers v. W. Ray Fleming Fruit Co.*, 540 F.2d 681 (4th Cir. 1976). The court held that plaintiff Brunswick, as the supplier of bowling equipment, could not reach the individual shareholders of a no asset "dummy" corporation specifically formed for the purpose of taking title and assuming payment obligations on the bowling equipment. "Brunswick was under no illusion that the construction corporation was an agent for the Waxmans," concluded the court. "Brunswick was not mislead into doing business with a no asset corporation."

[31] *Kaysee Land and Livestock, Inc. v. Flahive*, 43 P.3d 333 (Wyo. 2002).

[32] Cal. Corp. Code § 1702(c).

[33] *Hollowell v. Orleans Regional Hospital*, 1998 U.S. Dist. LEXIS 8184 (E.D. La. May 29, 1998).

[34] H. Ballantine, BALLANTINE ON CORPORATIONS 303 (rev. ed. 1946).

formation was more than "trifling or illusory"? If the corporation is thinly capitalized, may a contract creditor pursue an alternative but related theory, subordination in contract, or the so-called Deep Rock doctrine?[35]

[2]   What is Capital for These Purposes?

To some individuals, capital consists of equity permanently contributed to the corporation, thereafter subject to control by the corporation's board of directors. To others, capital consists of all owner contributions (equity and loans) available to satisfy the corporation's liabilities. For certain purposes, liability insurance coverage may also be considered to be the capital of the business.

Legal authority exists to help define "capital." In *Baatz v. Arrow Bar*,[36] plaintiffs, injured in an automobile accident by a drunken patron of the Arrow Bar, pursued a dram shop theory against the tavern. They also sought to hold the shareholders personally liable on the grounds that in purchasing the bar, the owners had contributed only $5000 cash. But the shareholders had personally guaranteed a promissory note given to their sellers. Later, they substituted a $145,000 bank loan which they also personally guaranteed. The court held the capital adequate.

For purposes of torts claims, although thinly capitalized, many small corporations do carry liability insurance. For purposes of piercing the corporate veil, most attorneys consider insurance coverage to be capital or additional capital because insurance proceeds are available to meet some claims.

An argument to the contrary succeeded at trial in *Radaszewski v. Telecom Corp.*[37] There, the district judge reasoned that, "[u]ndercapitalization is undercapitalization, regardless of insurance." He was propelled no doubt by the equities. Plaintiffs, injured in an accident with a truck operated by a subsidiary of Telecom (Contrux, Inc.), had little capital available to satisfy a judgment but $11 million worth of liability insurance. "Unhappily," said the appellate court, "Contrux's insurance carrier became insolvent two years after the accident and is now in receivership." Nonetheless, the Eighth Circuit reversed the district judge:

> This distinction [between capital and insurance coverage] escapes us. The whole purpose of asking whether a subsidiary [or other corporation] is "properly capitalized" is precisely to determine its "financial respon- sibility." If the subsidiary is financially responsible, whether by means of insurance or otherwise, the policy behind [the case law] is met. Insur- ance meets this policy just as well, perhaps even better, than a healthy balance sheet . . . . Insurance is unquestionably relevant on the issue of "undercapitalization."

The case confirms most attorneys' understanding of the law in the area.

---

[35] This last issue is the subject of a separate subsection, see the discussion in § 3.04, *infra*.

[36] 452 N.W.2d 138 (S.D. 1990).

[37] 981 F.2d 305 (8th Cir. 1992) (Missouri law).

[3]   When is Capital Adequate?

There is surprisingly little instructive authority on what constitutes adequate capitalization, other than Professor's Ballentine's famous epigram about capital "trifling or illusory compared with the business to be done or the risks of loss." Courts employ a "know it when they see it," conclusionary approach, or leave the matter to a jury to determine. One court held $10,000 in equity adequate when the shareholders had also loaned the corporation $140,000.[38] However, in that case, the corporation engaged in the relatively unrisky business of installing commercial sound systems. The sum ($10,000) might have been "trifling or illusory" if the corporation operated snowmobiles and took tourists high into the mountains. There simply is not much analysis of when capitalization is inadequate.[39]

[4]   Is Inadequate Capitalization Alone a Sufficient Ground?

A much vexed question is whether inadequate capitalization alone can be grounds for veil piercing. Courts and commentators point out that corporate statutes no longer contain any form of minimum capital requirement. Older statutes did require that, prior to commencing business, corporations have $500 or $1000 actually paid in as capital.[40] Today, in most jurisdictions, acceptance of articles of incorporation by the Secretary of State or an equivalent official brings about limited liability. Courts should not be able to disregard limited liability by de facto re-requiring some form of minimum capital.

However, courts in some jurisdictions do so. In an *Erie* case, surveying state law decisions, the Ninth Circuit found that "[u]nder California law, inadequate capitalization of a subsidiary may alone be a basis for holding the parent corporation liable for the acts of the subsidiary."[41] California attorneys and jurists point to Justice Traynor's opinion in *Minton v. Cavaney.*[42]

In that case, the only acts to which Justice Traynor points are acts of undercapitalization.[43]

---

[38] *O'Hazza v. Executive Credit Corp.*, 431 S.E.2d 318 (Va. 1993).

[39] In addition to the dominance of conclusionary analysis in the area, another reason may be that a number of courts pierce the corporate veil based upon thin capitalization only when one or more of the other grounds for veil piercing is also present. See the discussion herein, § 3.03[D], *infra.*

[40] See the discussion of minimum capital requirements and defective incorporation in § 2.03[A], *supra.*

[41] *Slottow v. American Casualty Co.*, 1 F.3d 912, 917 (9th Cir. 1993).

[42] 56 Cal.2d 576, 15 Cal. Rptr. 641, 364 P.2d 473 (1961). *But see* 364 P.2d at 473, where Justice Traynor lists three alternative grounds for invocation of the doctrine:

> The equitable owners of a corporation . . . are personally liable when they treat the assets of the corporation as their own and add or withdraw capital from the corporation at will; when they hold themselves out as being personally liable for the debts of the corporation; or when they provide inadequate capitalization and actively participate in the conduct of corporate affairs.

(citations omitted).

[43] "[T]he evidence is undisputed that there was no attempt to provide adequate capitalization.

Yet even the California cases are contradictory on the point.[44] Still other authorities purport to be more authoritatively in the opposite direction. Judge Easterbrook has unequivocally stated that "we are unaware of any decision relying on undercapitalization alone as a grounds for disregarding the corporate entity in a contract case."[45] In *Consumer's Co-op v. Olsen*,[46] the Supreme Court of Wisconsin specifically rejected contentions that the veil may be pierced based upon thin capitalization alone.

In *Consumer's Co-op*, Chris Olsen capitalized his corporation with $7018. By the time the corporation closed its doors, principally through open account indebtedness to suppliers, the corporation had a minus net worth of $189,362. The court reversed a decision below which had pierced the veil:

> While significant, undercapitalization is not an independently suffi-
> cient ground to pierce the corporate veil. In order for the corporate veil
> to be pierced, in addition to undercapitalization, additional evidence of
> failure to follow corporate formalities or other evidence of pervasive
> control must be shown.
>
> [B]oth inadequate capitalization and disregard of corporate formali-
> ties are significant . . . .

Fletcher v. Atex, Inc.,[47] involved Eastman Kodak Company's centralized cash management system. In such a system, subsidiaries maintain zero balance bank accounts. "All funds transferred from the subsidiary accounts [to the parent] are recorded as credits to the subsidiary, and when a subsidiary is in need of funds, a transfer is made." The court indicated that "without considerably more," use of a centralized cash management system is insufficient to pierce the corporate veil, based upon inadequacy of capital.

The decision seems to do great violence to the veil piercing doctrine, permitting a subsidiary to be robbed of any financial independence, set up in disregard of Ballantine's maxim that capital, even of a subsidiary, must be adequate "compared with the business to be done or the risks of loss." Such systems also seem to consist of dishonest bookkeeping, allowing all of the excess cash flow and profits to be "upstreamed" to the parent corporation while the liabilities remain "bottled up" in a subsidiary.

While the cases may be inconclusive, most attorneys advise corporate owners that they must adequately capitalize the corporation or they may run a risk of personal liability. Corporate owners may also be advised that sufficient capitali-

---

Seminole never had any substantial assets. It leased the pool that it operated, and the lease was forfeited for failure to pay the rent. Its capital was 'trifling compared with the business to be done and the risks of loss . . . .' "

[44] *Compare Automotriz Del Golfo De California S. A. v. Resnick*, 47 Cal.2d 792, 306 P.2d 1, 4 (1957) ("it is inequitable that shareholders should set up such a flimsy organization to escape personal liability"), *with Arnold v. Brown*, 27 Cal. App. 3d 386, 103 Cal. Rptr. 775 (1972) (undercapitalization is merely a factor albeit an important one).

[45] *Seon Service Systems, Inc. v. St. Joseph Bank & Trust Co.*, 855 F.2d 406, 416 (7th Cir. 1988).

[46] 419 N.W.2d 211 (Wis. 1988).

[47] 68 F.3d 1451 (2d Cir. 1995).

zation may be comprised of a combination of some capital and a quantity of liability insurance sufficient to protect against most foreseeable claims.

[5]   Does a Duty Ever Arise to "Top Off" the Original Capital?

Consumer's Co-op raises an additional point concerning thin capitalization. Does a duty arise for shareholders to "top off" capital as the business grows, or risk a loss of limited liability? In *Consumer's Co-op*, the court ducked the issue, concluding that "we need not reach the question of whether the increase in the size of ECO's undertaking was of such a nature and magnitude that additional capital would be required," because "by continuing to extend credit . . . Consumer's Co-op waived the right to claim inadequacy of capital."

On a wider basis, however, the answer seems to be that once the capital of a corporation has proven to be sufficient for purposes of veil piercing, no such later duty to "top off" arises and no risk of corporate disregard reenters the picture. Courts confine their analysis to a "snapshot" taken of capitalization in the formative stages of corporate life.

For example, in *Arnold v. Phillips*,[48] the sole shareholder of a brewing business contributed $50,000 for shares and $75,000 as a loan. The corporation then had two years of success, followed by a downturn that required the owner to make additional loans to the corporation. The court found that the need later to advance additional funds did not prove the original capital inadequate, as "[t]he two series of advances differ materially as respects their nature and purpose." The corporation had had "two years of prosperity, with the original capital thus enlarged demonstrated to be sufficient." The instant case was not a case "where the corporate entity ought to be disregarded as being a sham, a mere obstacle to justice, or an instrument of fraud." On the other hand, if a corporation radically changed its focus, rather than having merely grown or expanded, with the new focus presenting an increase in risks for third parties, the adequacy of capital would have to be re-examined in that light.

Inadequacy of capital is present in many veil piercing cases. As has been seen, questions arise as to the definition of capital, the yardstick by which adequacy is measured, and the identity of other grounds which must accompany inadequacy of capital for the veil to be lifted. One last question may involve determining when, if ever, a need arises to supplement the capital originally supplied.

[F]   Evasion of a Contract or Statute or Use of a Corporation Solely to Work a Fraud

The emphasis here is on the word "solely." If a court finds that a corporation had no reason to exist other than evasion of a contract or a statute, the court may disregard the corporation. Assume, for example, that when the price of milk is $1 per gallon, Raskin and Bobbins, Inc., an ice cream manufacturer,

---

[48] 117 F.2d 497 (5th Cir.), *cert. denied*, 313 U.S. 583 (1941).

signs a requirements contract with Dairy Corp. to purchase all of its milk from
that supplier. In return, Dairy Corp. offers a discounted price, say, $0.90 per
gallon. Then the open market milk price falls to $0.75 per gallon. Rather than
re-negotiating with Dairy, Raskin and Bobbins forms a new corporation,
"Bypass, Inc." and causes that corporation to purchase milk on the open market
at the lower price. In suing, Dairy Corp. may well be able to reach beyond
Raskin and Bobbins to Bypass, Inc. because the sole reason for Bypass's
existence is evasion of the requirements contract.[49]

A Pennsylvania family that owned an automobile wrecking business formed a
corporation to hire family members as employees. In slow times, family
members would take turns being laid off, collecting unemployment insurance.
Previously, as self-employed persons in a partnership, under Pennsylvania law
they had not been employees and could not collect such benefits. The court
found that the sole purpose for the corporation was to evade the unemployment
security statute, concluding "that the corporate entity may be ignored in
determining whether the claimants were, in fact, unemployed under the act, or
were self-employed."[50]

In one case, the Ninth Circuit was asked to determine whether to ignore a
corporation formed solely to evade limitations on outside income under the
Social Security Act. Plaintiff owned a family farm and a duplex rental property.
Her income from the rental venture was so great that her social security
benefits were nil. In order to render herself eligible for Social Security benefits,
she formed a corporation to hold the assets of the family business and drew a
salary sufficiently meager so that she qualified for the benefits. The Ninth
Circuit held that although "Congress could have provided that the motivation to
obtain social security by organizing a corporation would defeat the end" — "It
did not." The court refused to disregard the corporation as having been formed
solely to evade a statute.[51]

The use of a corporation solely to work a fraud is illustrated by *Linn & Lane
Timber Co. v. United States.*[52] There, to put a parcel of real property beyond a
creditor's reach, the debtor formed a corporation, conveyed the property to it,
and re-conveyed the property after the statute of limitations had run. Courts
may disregard the corporation if the sole purpose of forming the corporation
was to perpetrate the fraud.[53]

---

[49] Based in part upon *Culinary Workers Local 596 v. Gateway Cafe, Inc.*, 588 P.2d 1334 (Wash.
1979) (second corporation named Bypass, Inc. utilized in attempt to evade collective bargaining
agreement and unfunded pension liabilities to culinary workers). *See also Dairy Co-operative Assn.
v. Brandes Creamery*, 30 P.2d 338 (Or. 1934); *Arctic Dairy Co. v. Winans*, 255 N.W. 290 (Mich. 1934).

[50] *Roccograndi v. Unemployment Comp. Bd. of Review*, 178 A.2d 786 (Pa. Super. Ct. 1962).

[51] *Stark v. Flemming*, 283 F.2d 410 (9th Cir. 1960).

[52] 236 U.S. 574 (1915).

[53] *Kinney Shoe Corp. v. Polan*, 939 F.2d 209 (4th Cir. 1991), discussed § 3.03[A], *supra*, may also
be viewed as such a case. In that case, defendant Polan formed a no asset corporation, in which no
meetings were held nor other formalities observed; the corporation was purportedly formed to act as
sublessee on an industrial lease. The inference was very strong that the sole purpose of the
corporation was to work a fraud on the plaintiff sublessor.

[G]   Instrumentality Theories

When a court finds that a corporation exists *solely* to carry out the owner's agenda, having no independent reason for its own existence, then the corporation is found to be the "mere instrumentality" of the owner. The corporation is disregarded and the owner held liable. To invoke the theory, "[t]here must be such domination of finances, policies and practices that the controlled corporation has, so to speak, no separate mind, will or existence of its own and is but a business conduit for its principal."[54]

As discussed,[55] extreme, or complete, intermixture of affairs may lead to invocation of the instrumentality theory. A well-known case reaching the "mere instrumentality" conclusion, and upholding liability on the part both of the individual shareholder and a related corporation, is *Zaist v. Olson.*[56] Martin Olson, a real estate developer, founded and controlled East Haven Homes, Inc., Martin Olson, Inc., New London Shopping Center, Inc., and Viking, Inc. Plaintiff, a contractor, had supplied $192,753 in services and materials to East Haven Homes, Inc. When East Haven became defunct, plaintiff sought to collect the $23,100 unpaid balance from Olson and Martin Olson, Inc. The Supreme Court of Connecticut invoked the instrumentality theory to uphold the lower court's liability rulings:

> Courts will disregard the fiction of separate legal entity when a corporation is "a mere instrumentality or agent of another corporation or individual owning all or most of its stock." . . . The circumstance that control is exercised merely through dominating stock ownership, of course, is not enough . . . . There must be 'such domination of finances, policies and practices that the controlled corporation has, so to speak, no separate mind, will or existence of its own . . . .'
>
> [When] . . . the corporation is so manipulated by an individual or another corporate entity as to become a mere puppet or tool for the manipulator, justice may require the courts to disregard the corporate fiction and impose liability on the real actor . . . . It is because of this that there have arisen what are called the 'instrumentality' or 'identity' rules.

Another instrumentality parent-subsidiary case is *OTR Associates v. IBC Services, Inc.,*[57] in which a franchisor (International Blimpy) negotiated leases in shopping malls for Blimpy franchisees. Blimpy used a subsidiary (IBC Services, Inc) with no assets of its own, no employees, and no business premises to hold the leases. IBC then sublet the leased premises to Blimpy franchisees who paid rent to IBC. OTR, a shopping mall owner, succeeded in having IBC Services characterized as the mere instrumentality of Blimpy International, which was held liable for $150,000 in rent arrearages. The court found "[d]omination and

---

[54] 1 FLETCHER'S ENCYCLOPEDIA OF CORPORATIONS 205.

[55] See the discussion in § 3.03[B], *supra.*

[56] 227 A.2d 552 (Conn. 1967).

[57] 401 A.2d 407 (N.J. App. 2002).

control by Blimpy of IBC [to be] patent" and that the "parent so dominated the subsidiary that is had no separate existence."

These "instrumentality" cases always contain one or more of the bases for veil piercing already discussed, namely, intermixture of affairs, lack of required formalities, inadequacy of capital, or use of the corporation solely to evade a contractual or statutory obligation. From an analytical standpoint, these bases are more helpful. For example, in evaluating whether she should add a veil piercing count to a complaint, a plaintiff's attorney will find it far more useful to ask whether capital was inadequate or affairs intermixed than to ask whether the corporation was the "mere instrumentality" of its owner. The latter may be a largely conclusionary finding not particularly helpful for purposes of analysis, used as a matter of emphasis or posturing by litigants and courts alike rather than as an independent ground or basis for piercing the veil. A court could buttress its findings, for example, by a statement that "not only was the capital trifling or illusory and the corporate interests intermixed with the interests of the principals, but the court finds further that the corporation in this case was but the mere instrumentality of the defendant X."

Nonetheless, courts also continue to use "mere instrumentality" analysis as an independent ground for piercing the corporate veil in cases of complete domination and control by the owner, including a parent corporation. A parent corporation could, for example, adequately capitalize and give functional independence to a subsidiary. Twenty or thirty years later, the parent could come so to dominate the subsidiary's affairs, bending it to serve the parent's needs and whims alone. Thus, even though in the subsidiary's early years the veil may not have been capable of being pierced, for inadequacy of capital and so on (traditional veil piercing), later on the subsidiary's corporateness might be disregarded because of complete domination and control. So viewed, instrumentality (alter ego) is a doctrine different from, but related to, traditional veil piercing, which tends more to focus on the corporation's formation and startup years.

[H] Torts Versus Contracts

Commentators have always posited that it should be easier to pierce the corporate veil in tort cases. In cases of smaller and mid size corporations, a first question to ask is if a shareholder, officer or director participated in the allegedly tortious conduct. If so, the person might be a tortfeasor, rendering it less necessary to pierce the corporate veil. An individual who commits a tort, or participates in the tortious conduct of others, is always liable, even though the corporate employer may be also liable on a vicarious basis.[58] In a contract situation, the plaintiff chooses to deal with the corporation and has an opportunity to investigate whether the corporation's capitalization is adequate and the owner's affairs segregated from those of the corporation. Conversely, in tort cases, the plaintiff often becomes involved with the defendant by chance.

---

[58] *Baatz v. Arrow Bar*, 452 N.W.2d 138 (S.D. 1990) (plaintiffs' attorney sought to discover whether the owners themselves served alcoholic beverages to the customer who had the automobile accident; if so, they would be liable themselves as tortfeasors).

> When, under the circumstances, it would be reasonable . . . for a bank or other lending institution to conduct an investigation of the credit of the corporation prior to entering the contract, such party will be charged with the knowledge that a reasonable credit investigation would disclose. If such an investigation would disclose that the corporation is grossly undercapitalized . . . such party will be deemed to have assumed the risk of gross under capitalization and will not be permitted to pierce the corporate veil.[59]

The court also wondered if the reasonable investigation requirement "should be extended beyond the context of the financial institution lender" to other creditors and types of contracts. It declined to do so in the case at bar, finding the reasonable investigation requirement to be "permissive and not mandatory" and the facts in the case before it to be egregious, justifying veil piercing.

The ability to investigate reflects reality as to major creditors. A trade creditor, however, with many customers purchasing goods and services on open account may be hard pressed to undertake much investigation at all. Professor Thompson, in his extensive study, found the results to be the opposite of what armchair empiricists had postulated. He found that courts upheld piercing the corporate veil in 41.98% of the contract cases while the corresponding number was only 30.97% in torts cases.[60]

Despite the difficulty in making the theory jibe with Professor Thompson's results, the theory does provide fodder for argument by the attorney defending a piercing claim brought by a major creditor. Counsel should point out the ability of the bank or other major creditor to investigate and that, unlike a tort victim, a contracting party willingly chooses to deal with the other party.

§ 3.04 EQUITABLE SUBORDINATION

The subordination of the claims of shareholders, including a parent corporation, in favor of those of outside creditors is also known as the "Deep Rock Doctrine."[61] In a bankruptcy or receivership, creditors invoke the theory, asking the court to order shareholders in their capacity as creditors to "go to the end of the line." At the end of the line, shareholders receive little or no payment for advances or other debts. The creditors thus benefit because they share with fewer persons, resulting in larger recovery.

Consider the following illustrative example. A corporation has $100,000 in assets but $500,000 in liabilities. Among those liabilities are debts to shareholders in the amount of $300,000, representing a major portion of the shareholders' investment when they formed the corporation. The corporation enters bankruptcy. If the shareholders participate with the general creditors, everybody

[59] *Kinney Shoe Corp. v. Polan*, 939 F.2d 209, 212 (4th Cir. 1991), quoting *Laya v. Erin Homes, Inc.*, 352 S.E.2d 93, 100 (W. Va. 1986).

[60] Robert Thompson, *Piercing the Corporate Veil: An Empirical Study*, 76 Cornell L. Rev. 1036 (1991).

[61] *Taylor v. Standard Gas & Elec. Co.*, 306 U.S. 307 (1939) (Deep Rock Oil Corp. was the name of the subsidiary involved in this case of first impression).

receives $0.20 on the dollar ($100,000 ÷ $500,000). By contrast, if the outside creditors persuade the court to subordinate ("deep rock") the shareholder debt, the general creditors will take $0.50 on the dollar ($100,000 ÷ $200,000), while the shareholders will receive nothing. Bolder still, if the general creditors can pierce the corporate veil, the shareholders would not recover the $300,000 and, in effect, would have to "pay in" an additional $100,000. The creditors would then recover $1 on the dollar.

Of course, in such a scenario, the shareholder-creditors would resist, maintaining that insofar as they are creditors, they should be permitted to stand "elbow-to-elbow" with the other creditors and receive the same $0.20 on the dollar that outside creditors receive.

Three observations may be made about the subordination theory: it arises frequently; the consequence is not so severe as complete disregard of the corporation; and the grounds for ordering subordination are very similar to those upon which piercing the corporate veil is decreed.

Subordination cases arise with frequency because participants in small corporations often structure a portion of their contribution as debt rather than equity. The owners contribute cash and or property to the corporation, taking back from it not just shares of stock but promissory notes as well. For example, in *Costello v. Fazio*,[62] three partners incorporated their preexisting plumbing supply business. Each structured $2,000 of their contribution as equity. Two of them also took back promissory notes from the corporation, one for $43,000 and the other for $4,000. The appellate court held it error not to have subordinated the shareholder debt, as the corporation "was grossly undercapitalized." The plumbing supply business's previous existence in partnership form was held to have demonstrated what level of capitalization was "adequate."

Shareholders persist in structuring their contributions in this way because interest paid with respect to debt is an expense, and therefore, for income tax purposes, a deduction to the corporation. Conversely, money paid out with respect to shares will likely be treated as profit, taxed once at the corporate level, and then again at the shareholder level as dividends (albeit at only a 15% rate for the shareholders after tax reform in 2003). Secondarily, shareholders structure some of their contribution as debt, hoping that, in the event of business failure, they will be able to recover a portion at least of their contribution as creditors.[63] These aims are permissible in moderation. Too much debt in comparison to equity increases the risk that in the event of bankruptcy, the shareholder-creditors will be "subordinated."

Subordination is not limited to formal debt incurred at incorporation or capitalization. In *Pepper v. Litton*,[64] Justice Douglas noted the power of bankruptcy courts, "essentially courts of equity," "to sift the circumstances of any claim to see that injustice or unfairness is not done in administration of the

---

[62] 256 F.2d 903 (9th Cir. 1958).

[63] Use of debt is discussed in the chapter dealing with financing the corporation, see the discussion in Chapter 4.

[64] 308 U.S. 295 (1939).

bankruptcy estate." The Court upheld the trial court's subordination of salary claims by Litton, the sole shareholder and officer of the Dixie Splint Coal Company.

Getting "deep rocked" is not the worst of possible worlds. Shareholders lose all of their contribution to the corporation but not their personal assets (individual investments, automobiles, home). By contrast, when under the related doctrine the corporate veil is pierced, shareholders' personal assets are "on the line" for satisfaction of judgment creditors' claims.

Courts have pierced the veil in bankruptcy. *Stone v. Eacho*[65] involved Tip Top Tailors, a Delaware corporation headquartered in New Jersey which had nine sales outlets in various states. Its Virginia outlet was incorporated in Virginia, with three shares of stock issued for $3. Virginia Tip Top employees measured clients for suits, showed bolts of cloth to customers, but forwarded orders to New Jersey for manufacture. The New Jersey office received all funds and paid all the expenses of Virginia Tip Top and recorded the excess of charges over receipts on the books of the Virginia outlet as open account indebtedness to New Jersey Tip Top. In bankruptcy, the trial court subordinated ("postponed") Tip Top New Jersey.

The Fourth Circuit agreed that "claims of a parent corporation against a subsidiary should thus be postponed where the subsidiary, as here, in reality has no separate existence, is not adequately capitalized and constitutes a mere instrumentality of the parent corporation."

"But in a case such as this," the court continued, "where both corporations are insolvent . . . and where the subsidiary has no real existence whatever, there is no reason why the courts should not face the realities of the situation and ignore the subsidiary for all purposes." The court disregarded Tip Top Virginia's "corporateness," ordering the bankruptcy proceeding of the two corporations consolidated.[66]

Stone v. Eacho also previews the grounds upon which a court may premise a decision to subordinate shareholder debt. Courts are receptive to a creditors' committee motion to subordinate when intermixture of affairs has occurred. For example, a court may consolidate when, as with Tip Top, the subsidiary has no independent purpose other than as an instrumentality of the shareholder or parent, or where the owners manipulate the corporation in an attempt to defraud creditors, as in *Pepper v. Litton*. As with piercing the corporate veil, there seems to be a reluctance to subordinate shareholders claims based upon undercapitalization alone.[67] On the other hand, thin or inadequate capitalization does weigh

[65] 127 F.2d 284 (4th Cir. 1942).

[66] A similar case in which the court consolidated bankruptcies of affiliated corporations is *In re Seatrade Corp.*, 255 F. Supp. 696 (S.D.N.Y.), *affirmed sub nom, Chemical Bank New York v. Kheel*, 369 F.2d 845 (2d Cir. 1966).

[67] *See, e.g., Friedman v. Kurker*, 438 N.E.2d 76 (Mass. 1982) ("undercapitalization alone, unaccompanied by inequitable conduct, will not provide a basis for subordination of claims for advances to a corporation which later becomes bankrupt"). *Accord In re Branding Iron Steak House*, 536 F. Supp. 299 (9th Cir. 1976).

heavily in matrix of factors applicable to a decision on whether to subordinate.[68]

§ 3.05   PIERCING THE CORPORATE VEIL: PROCEDURAL CONTEXTS

Procedural matters may be affected by the determination of whether affairs have been intermixed or whether corporate formalities have been observed. Courts may hold, for example, that territorial jurisdiction and service of process over an in-state subsidiary is good as against an out-of-state parent corporation. A slight variant of that occurred in *Empire Steel of Texas v. Superior Court*.[69] A California contract claimant served an officer of a California subsidiary who also was an officer of a Texas parent corporation. The parent corporation had not done business in California. Nonetheless, because in-hand service occurred in California, the California court held jurisdiction and service good as against the Texas entity.

Other variants include successful service on a New Jersey subsidiary as good against Canadian parent and English grandparent corporations.[70] Service on an in-state parent corporation has been held sufficient to hail into the state three out-of-state subsidiaries operated as "part of the parent and fully controlled by it."[71]

Courts that accept the argument in a procedural context are careful to add a caveat. Just because a litigant has been able to pierce the corporate veil for purposes of territorial jurisdiction or service of process does not mean that an attempt will succeed to pierce the corporate veil "on the merits."

§ 3.06   STATUTORY LIABILITY UNDER ENVIRONMENTAL LAWS

Two areas in which piercing the corporate veil, or piercing-like concepts, are utilized are products liability and environmental liability.[72] Under CERCLA, an "owner" or an "operator" of a hazardous waste site is made liable for "response costs" such as cleanup and monitoring.[73] Courts hold a corporation liable for the response cost for a subsidiary's hazardous waste activity in situations in which piercing the corporate veil is warranted. Thus, federal law borrows heavily from state law to determine when indirect owners such as parent corporations will be

---

[68] *See, e.g.*, Note, *Equitable Subordination of Shareholder Debt to Trade Creditors: A Reexamination*, 61 B.U. L. Rev. 433 (1981).

[69] 56 Cal. 2d 823, 17 Cal. Rptr. 150, 366 P.2d 502 (1961).

[70] *TACA Int'l. Airlines Inc. v. Rolls Royce Ltd.*, 201 A.2d 97 (N.J. 1964).

[71] *Frazier v. Alabama Motor Club, Inc.*, 349 F.2d 456 (5th Cir. 1965). *Cf. Botwinick v. Credit Exchange, Inc.*, 213 A.2d 349 (Pa. 1965) (inability to reach out-of-state parent by service on in-state subsidiary because subsidiary carefully maintained separate existence).

[72] *See* 42 U.S.C. §§ 9601–9675 (1980), the Comprehensive Environmental Response, Compensation and Liability Act (CERCLA).

[73] Of course, the former owner at the time of release of the hazardous material, as well as the actual generator or transporter of hazardous waste, also are held liable.

held liable as an "operator" or as an "owner."

In *United States v. Best Foods*,[74] Best Foods' predecessor, Corn Products Corp. (CPC), owned Ott Chemical of Muskegon, Michigan, from 1965 to 1972. Later, Ott's plant property was declared a Superfund site. In 1989, the United States sued Best Foods, as well as prior and subsequent owners and operators, for tens of millions of dollars in cleanup costs. In his opinion, Mr. Justice Souter approved of federal courts' extensive use of state law piercing the corporate veil and instrumentality theories to flesh out when a parent corporation will be held liable as an "operator."

As a technical matter, under CERCLA, the liability of the operator may be direct rather than derivative when the parent corporation is itself a participant in the wrongdoing. Nonetheless, Mr. Justice Souter's opinion is an excellent summary of the general law on the subject of veil piercing and instrumentality theories in the parent subsidiary context. He states that "[t]he question is not whether the parent operates the subsidiary, but rather whether it operates the facility" which the subsidiary owns. The former is permissible and involves normal relationships between a parent and a subsidiary growing out of the parent's status as a shareholder/investor. These would involve exercise of democracy rights, such as electing directors, appointing principal officers, and having joint directors and officers ("directors and officers holding positions with a parent and its subsidiary can and do 'change hats,' " notes Justice Souter).

Even some operation of the facility, rather than the subsidiary, is permissible. "Activities that involve the facility but which are consistent with the parent's investor status, such as monitoring of the subsidiary's performance, supervision of the subsidiary's finance and capital budget decisions, and articulation of general policies and procedures, should not give rise to direct liability" or veil piercing.

By contrast, when the parent sends it its own employees to participate in day-to-day or week-to-week operating decisions, or otherwise attempts directly to dictate or influence those decisions, the parent may lose its limited liability, or be directly liable if the interference relates to the activity from which the liability emanates. The latter was the case in *Best Foods*. The parent had sent its governmental and environmental affairs director, a Mr. G.R.D Williams, to Muskegon. While on the ground there, Mr. Williams had "played a conspicuous part in dealing with the toxic risks emanating from the operation of the plant."

A case in which a court found both owner and operator liability is *United States v. Kayser-Roth Corporation*.[75] The court found Kayser-Roth liable for its defunct textile mill subsidiary's pollution of the local aquifer and water supply. The subsidiary had dumped trichloroethylene used to remove dirt and oil from newly woven fabric. "To be held directly liable as an operator," the court observed, "courts have considered a number of factors including: whether the person or corporation had the capacity to discover in a timely fashion the release of hazardous substances; whether the person or the corporation had the power

---

[74] 524 U.S. 51 (1998).

[75] 724 F. Supp. 15 (D. R.I. 1989).

to direct the mechanisms causing the release [of hazardous waste]; and whether the person or corporation had the capacity to prevent and abate damage." The court deduced the presence of those factors from the parent's total monetary control of the subsidiary, approval requirements for all subsidiary real estate dealings, capital expenditures over $5,000 and subsidiary-governmental dealings, and the placement of Kayser-Roth personnel in almost all subsidiary officer and director positions.

§ 3.07 SUCCESSOR CORPORATION LIABILITY IN PRODUCTS LIABILITY

A products liability tort victim of a defunct corporation may attempt to reach the assets of the entity that acquires the product line or which assumes the liabilities of the previous entity.

In *Tift v. Forage King Industries, Inc.*,[76] plaintiff was injured using a farm implement known as a chopper box. A sole proprietor had produced the product. The proprietorship had subsequently become a partnership and then a corporation. Seven months before the plaintiff's accident another corporation, Tester, Inc., acquired Forage King. The question in such cases is whether the injured person can reach through time to reach the assets of the later appearing entities (Forage King/Tester). The Wisconsin Supreme Court's list of cases in which it would find such "successor liability included "(1) when the purchasing corporation expressly or impliedly agreed to assume the selling corporation's liability; (2) when the transaction amounts to a consolidation or merger . . . (3) when the purchaser corporation is a mere continuation of the seller corporation; or (4) when the transaction is entered into fraudulently to escape liability for such obligations." The court found the Forage King/Tester successors liable as "in substance the identical organization manufacturing the same product."

Nissen Corp. v. Miller involved an injury to plaintiff while using an exercise treadmill he had purchased 5 years earlier.[77] The defendant corporation later purchased the treadmill firm's assets but expressly excluded assumption of liabilities. The court refused to expand the "mere continuation" prong of successor liability to a broader "continuity of the enterprise" prong used in California and Michigan. "[S]elling replacement parts, performing contracts, retaining some employees, honoring existing 90-day warranties, and serving customer accounts" does not result in liability for the successor corporation. A successor company may only be liable if it continued manufacture and selling. For one thing, if a successor who has not manufactured or sold the defective product, causation is lacking. A causal relationship between sale or manufacturer and the injury is, according to the Maryland court, a "bedrock requirement."

Ex ante mergers and acquisitions attorneys must be knowledgeable in the successor liability area. Attorneys are frequently asked to structure an acquisition so as to best minimize successor liability. For that reason, law school courses in mergers and acquisitions may cover the area of products liability successor

---

[76] 322 N.W.2d 14 (Wis. 1982).

[77] 594 A.2d 564 (Md. 1991).

liability, as well as CERCLA liability, in greater detail than a corporate law class.

§ 3.08   PIERCING THE CORPORATE VEIL — STRUCTURAL SETTINGS

There are at least three corporate settings, two involving groups of related corporations, in which a plaintiff may invoke the doctrine.

[A]   Personal Shareholder Liability

The most common setting for piercing the corporate veil involves a plaintiff who prevails in a lawsuit but finds the defendant's corporate assets potentially insufficient to satisfy the judgment. In this instance, the, plaintiff seeks to pierce the veil, reaching the pockets of individual shareholders.

Shareholder   Shareholder

↑

Corporation

↑

Plaintiff

When the veil is pierced, the owners (shareholders) are held liable, and not the directors or officers of the corporation. In most cases, however, a significant overlap exist between the two groups.[78] When the corporate veil is pierced it may be pierced as to all the shareholders, relatively innocent and culpable alike. The logical consequence of the metaphor, "piercing the veil," may be thought to be that when the veil or shroud drops all standing behind it become exposed.

In a famous California case,[79] two promoters formed a corporation to lease a swimming pool and operated it on a shoestring. When a young girl drowned in the pool, her survivors sued for wrongful death, and in a second lawsuit, sought to pierce the corporate veil to reach the estate of the attorney who had formed the corporation. The attorney had taken a qualifying share (an arrangement often utilized in the days in which three or more shareholders were necessary to

---

[78] In *Freeman v. Complex Computing Co., Inc.*, 119 F.3d 1044 (2d Cir. 1997), the court recognized piercing the veil to hold liable an "equitable owner." Because Columbia University would not license software to a corporation of which the defendant was an owner, the defendant used an acquaintance as a "dummy" shareholder. As the real party in interest, the defendant received the vast majority of the revenues, was the sole signatory on the corporation's bank account, and used his apartment address as the corporation's address. The court allowed that the plaintiff Freeman (a software salesperson) could reach the defendant's pocket if, on remand, he could establish that defendant "used his control over C3 to commit a fraud or other wrong that resulted in unjust loss or injury to Freeman."

[79] *Minton v. Cavaney*, 56 Cal. 2d 576, 15 Cal. Rptr. 641, 364 P.2d 473 (1961).

form a corporation) and had also acted a director and corporate secretary, probably as an accommodation to his clients. His estate was held liable.[80]

Two corollaries flow from the proposition that when the veil is pierced, it may be pierced as to all.[81] First, in a small corporation, the shareholders become each others' keepers. The more passive shareholders must nonetheless deal with issues such as adequacy of capital, observation of the corporate formalities, and the like. Second is that, from an observational rather than doctrinal perspective, the veil is rarely if ever pierced in larger or even medium size corporations. The reason is that in such cases, too many innocent shareholders become potentially liable, far outnumbering those who may bear some culpability. Judges are far less likely to lift the protections of limited liability in cases involving a larger number of shareholders.[82]

Further, judges are also aware that if the veil is lifted, the personal assets of real human beings are on the line. State statutes expressly permit citizens to incorporate for the purpose of limiting personal liability.[83] Limitation of personal liability has become a central purpose of incorporation. Ergo, it should be difficult to pierce the corporate veil to reach the pockets of individual shareholders who have sought to limit their liability.

Thus, some courts look for the elements of fraud, deception, or extreme abuse of the corporate form, before allowing creditors to reach shareholders' personal assets. For example, in *Perpetual Real Estate Service, Inc. v. Michaelson Properties, Inc.*,[84] plaintiff and defendant Aaron Michaelson had entered into two separate joint ventures involving the conversion of apartment buildings into condominium associations. Before dealing with his co-venturer, Mr. Michaelson took the precaution of forming a corporation (defendant Michaelson Properties, Inc.) which he then caused to enter into the joint venture arrangements on his behalf. After paying breach of warranty claims by condominium purchasers, plaintiff Perpetual attempted to hold Aaron Michaelson personally liable since his corporation had long since distributed the profits of the condominium conversion transactions.

Surveying Virginia law, Judge Wilkinson of the Fourth Circuit found that Virginia courts "lift the veil of immunity only in 'extraordinary' cases." Previously, he observed that "Virginia courts have long recognized the basic proposition that a corporation is a legal entity separate and distinct from its

---

[80] 364 P.2d at 475 (citations omitted).

[81] A small number of cases hold that a purely passive shareholder will not be held liable when the veil is lifted. *See, e.g., Zubrik v. Zubrik,* 384 F.2d 267 (3d Cir. 1967) (controlling shareholder who did not participate in the running of the business not liable); *Segan Construction Corp. v. Nor-West Builders, Inc.,* 274 F. Supp. 691 (D. Conn. 1967) (liability limited to shareholder "who is the real actor").

[82] In his study, Professor Thompson, *supra* note 4, found that of 1423 cases, only 9 involved veil piercing allegations in cases of publicly held corporations and none of the 9 efforts succeeded. By contrast, courts permitted plaintiffs to reach individual shareholder assets in 49.64 % of the one-person and 46.22 % of the two/three person corporation cases.

[83] "[T]he law permits the incorporation of a business for the very purpose of escaping personal liability." *Bartle v. Home Owners Co-operative, Inc.,* 309 N.Y. 103, 127 N.E.2d 832 (1955).

[84] 974 F.2d 545 (4th Cir. 1992) (Virginia law).

shareholders" and "[a] fundamental purpose of incorporation is to 'enable a group of persons to limit their liability in a joint venture.' " Flowing from these strongly held views was the doctrinal result that in Virginia, in addition to traditional proofs of intermixture of affairs or lack of formalities, a "plaintiff must also establish 'that the corporation was a device or sham used to disguise wrongs, obscure fraud or conceal crime.' " Because "Virginia adheres to a rigorous standard requiring proof that the defendant used the corporation to 'disguise' some legal 'wrong,' " and such proof was lacking here, Perpetual could not recover from defendant Michaelson, even though the result left Perpetual bearing the entire burden of the breach of warranties.

There are jurisdictions that require lesser showings. For example, in *Kinney Shoe Corp. v. Polan*,[85] another panel of the Fourth Circuit applied West Virginia law. As in *Perpetual Real Estate*, rather than entering into a transaction himself, the defendant utilized a thinly capitalized corporation to enter into a lease and then re-leased the premises to another corporation owned by the defendant for a cheaper rent. The court held that under West Virginia law, a plaintiff need only show "a unity of interest and ownership such that the separate personalities of the corporation and the individual shareholder no longer exist" and that "an [in]equitable result [would] occur if the acts are treated as those of the corporation alone." The court found that corporate formalities had not been observed (shareholders bought no stock, kept no minutes, elected no officers) and that the corporation was merely a "transparent shell," with no capital, set up never to be viable, piercing the veil to hold defendant Polan liable.

Nonetheless, no matter what the jurisdiction, a central tenet of the defense against any veil piercing allegation is that the law permits a person to incorporate for the precise purpose of limiting liability to whatever sum has been invested in the corporation.

[B]   Parent-Subsidiary Settings

Another group of cases concerns corporate pockets ultimately belonging to another corporation rather than an individual person. It is conceivable that a plaintiff could face piercing the veil twice, first reaching from subsidiary to parent corporation and, second, reaching from parent corporation to grandparent corporation or individual shareholders:

---

[85] 939 F.2d 209 (4th Cir. 1991).

Individual Shareholder

↑

Parent Corporation

↑

Subsidiary Corporation

↑

Plaintiff

Commentators observe that it should be easier to pierce the corporate veil when the only result will be the liability of a second corporation rather than a human being. The reasons include the ease with which funds can be shuffled between related corporations, the consequent ability to keep the subsidiary relatively poor by upstreaming profits and cash flow to the parent, and the absence of personal, individual liability.[86] A famous commentary about subsidiaries remarks that some subsidiaries "had, to begin with, nothing, made nothing, and could only end up with nothing."[87]

Nevertheless, some corporations follow a segmentation strategy. They allocate their business to a number of related corporations so that liability of one does not impact the assets of several others. The related corporations pursue the same business but in different states or regions. An alternate strategy is to isolate riskier portions of corporate business to separate subsidiaries. A forest products company, for example, could segment its higher risk transportation activities into a corporation separate from its timberlands.[88] Pursued in moderation, and when each subsidiary has a measure of functional independence and adequate capital, a segmentation strategy may be legitimate.[89]

Larger corporations continue to follow the strategy perhaps because, contrary to what commentators say should be the case, courts may be more hesitant to pierce the veil to reach the assets of a parent corporation.[90] Professor Robert Thompson has mused over the question:

---

[86] *See, e.g.,* Jonathan M. Landers, *A Unified Approach to Parent, Subsidiary, and Affiliate Questions in Bankruptcy,* 42 U. Chi. L. Rev. 589, 596–97 (1975) (creditors of a subsidiary corporation face greater risks than do other creditors, thus justifying increased willingness to pierce); Easterbrook & Fischel, *supra* note 8, at 111 ("Allowing creditors to reach the assets of parent corporations does not create unlimited liability for people").

[87] E. Latty, SUBSIDIARIES AND AFFILIATED CORPORATIONS 138.

[88] These strategies have long been pursued. *See* William O. Douglas & Carrol M. Shanks, *Insulation from Liability Through Subsidiary Corporations,* 39 Yale L. J. 193 (1929).

[89] On the issue of a subsidiary's functional independence, see the discussion of *United States v. Best Foods,* § 3.06, *supra.*

[90] Thompson, *supra* note 4, at Table 2, finds that courts reach parent corporation assets in 36.79 % of the cases but 49.64 % in one-person and 46.22 % in two-person corporation cases.

The continuing puzzle is why courts remain so willing to provide limited liability to parent corporations in tort cases . . . . Even if piercing would be harsh to a passive parent corporation that did not participate in the wrongful action, it would seem to be outweighed by the harshness to those injured.[91]

Bartle v. Home Owners Cooperative[92] is a parent-subsidiary case often studied because of its dissent. The Home Owners Cooperative had as its members returning veterans of World War II. In the post war housing shortage, the cooperative was unable to obtain the services of a builder so it formed a subsidiary building corporation, Westerlea Builders, Inc. After the homes had been built, Westerlea filed for bankruptcy. The trustee then attempted to pierce the veil to hold liable Home Owners Cooperative for the substantial debts of the subsidiary. The trial court refused to pierce the veil. The Appellate Division and Court of Appeals affirmed.

Judge Van Voorhis dissented, finding the structure to be the very case Professor Latty had described. "This set-up is often, though not necessarily, found in combination with a scheme whereby the corporation cannot possibly make profits." Judge Van Voorhis's conclusion was that "Westerlea was merely an agent of Home Owners to construct houses at cost for Home Owners stockholders, and therefore Home Owners is rendered liable for Westerlea's indebtedness."

[C]   Brother-Sister (Sibling) Corporation Settings

Sibling corporations are those with a common owner, which may be a parent corporation with multiple (brother-sister) subsidiaries. In other cases, the multiple corporations' common owner may be an individual or group of individuals.

The paradigmatic sibling corporation cases involve taxi cabs. In *Walkovszky v. Carlton*,[93] the same individual owner divided his twenty taxi fleet among ten corporations, two cabs to each corporation. Each cab was mortgaged to the hilt and each corporation carried but the minimum $10,000 liability insurance required by law. Plaintiff Walkovszky, was badly injured by one of the taxis and its driver. His damages far exceeded the meager assets of the corporation which owned the taxi that struck him.

Other sibling corporation cases involve similar factual scenarios. In *Mangan v. Terminal Transportation System*,[94] a parent corporation owned sixty percent each of four corporations owning taxi cabs and 100 percent of Terminal, the

---

[91] Robert Thompson, *Unpacking Limited Liability: Direct and Vicarious Liability of Corporate Participants for Torts of the Enterprise*, 47 Vand. L. Rev. 1, 40 (1994). A reason may be that subsidiaries may be incorporated and advised by more sophisticated attorneys, who make doubly certain that the subsidiary's capital is adequate and affairs separate from those of the parent corporation.

[92] 127 N.E.2d 832 (N.Y. 1955).

[93] 223 N.E.2d 6 (N.Y. 1966).

[94] 284 N.Y.S.2d 183 (1935), *affirmed*, 286 N.Y.S.2d 666 (App. Div. 1936).

corporation that hired cab drivers, dispatched the taxis, and performed other administrative duties. Other sibling corporation cases involve businesses other than taxi cabs. For example, in *My Bread Baking Co. v. Cumberland Farms, Inc.*,[95] a common shareholder owned a dairy which supplied five retail stores, each incorporated as a separate entity, making six sibling corporations all together.

In sibling corporation cases, rather than piercing the veil vertically (↑) to reach the pocket of the common shareholder, the plaintiff may attempt to pierce the veil horizontally (→), dropping the veil that exists between sibling corporations. Plaintiff may allege that in reality, all of the sibling corporations are one unified or largely unified enterprise. For example, in *Mangan*, all taxis had the same name and logo and the terminal company serviced and dispatched all of the cabs out of one garage.

In these cases, plaintiffs argue that the assets of all should be available to satisfy liability to a tort or contract claimant of any one of the siblings:

Common Shareholder (Individual or Parent Corporation)

↑

Siblings: Corporation → Corporation → Corporation → Corporation → Corporation

↑

Plaintiff

The taxi cab cases have mixed results. In *Mangan*, the plaintiff was able to reach the assets of the operating corporation since all of the taxis had its logo (Terminal) on the door, operated out of the same garage, and had many common attributes. In *Walkovszky*, the court allowed that it might be easier for a plaintiff to plead and prove "enterprise liability":[96]

> [I]t is one thing to assert that a corporation is a fragment of a larger corporate combine which actually conducts the business. It is quite another to claim that the corporation is a "dummy" for its individual stockholders . . . . Either circumstance would justify treating the corporation as an agent and piercing the corporate veil to reach the principal but a different result would follow in each case. In the first, only a larger *corporate* entity would be held financially responsible while, in the other, the stockholder would be personally liable.

In *Walkovszky*, the court upheld the dismissal of the complaint, finding that Walkovszky had failed to allege sufficiently particularized facts that "the defendant Carlton and his associates were actually doing business in their individual capacities, shuttling their personal funds in and out of the corpora-

---

[95] 233 N.E.2d 748 (Mass. 1968).

[96] Citing Adolf Berle, *The Theory of Enterprise Liability*, 47 Colum. L. Rev. 343 (1947).

tions, 'without regard to formality and to suit their immediate convenience.' " Walkovszky's complaint thus fell "short of adequately stating a cause of action against the defendant Carlton in his individual capacity."[97]

On remand, despite the Court of Appeals strong hint that a "horizontal" piercing might be easier, Walkovszky took the more difficult path. He plead additional facts on "the theory that [Carlton] and others were conducting business of the taxi cab fleet in their individual capacities." Those allegations survived a motion to dismiss.[98] The case settled thereafter.

In the *My Bread Baking Co.* case, the court found an agency or similar relationship among entities having a common owner. Justice Cutter found that reasoning appropriate "(a) when there is active and direct participation by the representatives of one corporation, apparently exercising some form of pervasive control, in the activities of another and there is some injurious or fraudulent consequence of the intracorporate relationship, or (b) when there is a confused intermingling of activity of two or more corporations engaged in a common enterprise with substantial disregard of the separate nature of the corporate entities . . . ." Paraphrasing himself, the Justice stated that "[w]hen there is common control of a group of separate corporations engaged in a single enterprise, (a) failure to make clear which corporation is taking action in a particular situation and the nature and extent of that action, or (b) to observe with care the formal barriers between the corporations with a proper segregation of their separate businesses, records, and finances, may warrant some disregard of the separate entities . . . ."

Another wrinkle is added by cases such as *Sea-Land Services, Inc. v. Pepper Source.*[99] Gerald Marchese owned all the shares of Pepper Source, as well as five other corporations. He owned a half interest in a sixth corporation which the court found he "treated . . . like all his other corporations; he 'borrowed' over $30,000 from Tie-Net; money and loans flowed freely between Tie-Net and the other corporations." Pepper Source had "stiffed" Sea-Land on a substantial freight bill for the importation of Jamican sweet peppers. The court permitted Sea-Land to reach from Pepper Source to Marchese, a vertical pierce, and thence back down, in a "reverse pierce," to Pepper Source's six sibling corporations.[100]

---

[97] The *Walkovszky* court also rejected thin capitalization as being alone a sufficient ground upon which to pierce the corporate veil: "The corporate form may not be disregarded merely because the assets of the corporation, together with the mandatory insurance coverage of the vehicle which struck the plaintiff, are insufficient to assure him the recovery sought."

[98] 287 N.Y.S.2d 546 (App. Div. 1968).

[99] 941 F.2d 519 (7th Cir. 1991), *after remand,* 993 F.2d 1309 (1993).

[100] Applying Illinois law, the court required that Sea-Land prove both "unity of interest and ownership" in the corporations, which was easily done, and "circumstances . . . such that adherence to the fiction of separate corporate existence would sanction a fraud or promote injustice," which proved more difficult and necessitated a remand. Use of multiple corporations to promote a fraud, the court noted, "would be quite difficult on summary judgment," involving as it does proof of mental state (intent). Use of multiple corporations to "promote an injustice," the other prong upon which Sea-Land relied, had to mean more than mere non-payment of a debt or judgment. "The prospect of an unsatisfied judgment looms in every veil piercing action: why else would a plaintiff bring such an action?"

K.C. Roofing Center v. On Top Roofing, Inc.[101] is a case in which a defendant used sibling corporations over time in order to minimize exposure to creditors. Imagine, for example, in the cyclical construction business, an earth moving company which needs bulldozers, excavators, dump trucks and other equipment. Suppose the shareholders own the equipment and lease it to the corporation. The corporation has some assets and the owners carefully segregate their affairs from those of the corporation. When an economic downturn is on the horizon, the owners cause the equipment leases to lapse. They simply lock the doors of the construction corporation, throwing the keys to the creditors. When an economic upturn is on the horizon, the owners form a new corporation, lease the equipment to it, and commence business anew. Over time, the owners use several different corporations to minimize liabilities in economic downturns.

In *On Top Roofing*, the shareholders used at least four different corporations over a twelve year period.[102] Trade creditors of a predecessor entity were able to pierce the veil to reach the assets of the individual owners and a subsequent corporation. The owners had kept the same business location (614 South Main), the same Yellow Pages Listing (On Top Roofing), and had otherwise failed to separate the affairs of the various corporations. The strategy pursued could work for an enterprise in a cyclical industry, if the corporations were capitalized properly and the affairs of a successor corporation strictly segregated form predecessor entities.[103]

The dissent in *Minno v. Pro Fab*[104] argued that horizontal piercing, as it were, was improper between sibling corporations. According to the dissent, the plaintiff, a steel worker who had fallen off a 19 feet wall, should be put through a "triangular piercing" exercise, that is, a pierce upward from the subsidiary to the parent corporation and then a "reverse pierce," back down to the sibling

---

On the second appeal, the Seventh Circuit accepted as proof of injustice "unjust enrichment" on Marchese's part through "obtaining countless benefits at the expense of not only Sea-Land, but the Internal Revenue Service and other creditors as well." Injustice also resulted from Marchese's use of multiple corporations as his " 'playthings' to evade responsibilities to creditors." He used the corporations' funds to pay alimony, child support, educational expense for his children, maintenance of his personal automobiles, "health care for his pet — the list goes on and on. Marchese did not even have a personal bank account! (With 'corporate' accounts like these, who needs one?)."

[101] 807 S.W.2d 545 (Mo. Ct. App. 1991).

[102] Russell Nugent Roofing, Inc.; On Top Roofing, Inc.; RNR, Inc.; DBA Tops N Roofing; and RLN Construction, Inc.

[103] That was the case in *J. F. Anderson Lumber Co. v. Myers*, 206 N.W.2d 365 (Minn. 1973). Plaintiff supplied lumber to a home remodeling business, Richard T. Leekley, Inc. After trial but before judgment was entered, Leekley formed a new corporation, Leekley, Inc. The second corporation paid the first corporation $1,788.58 for two trucks and other equipment, which amount was made available to the creditors of the first corporation. The three employees of the first corporation were hired by the second corporation. The court did not permit the creditor to reach through the veil into the second corporation: "[T]he motive of Leekley and his wife in forming the second corporation was to avoid paying the debts of the first corporation, particularly the judgment in question. However, such a motive no more forms the basis for requiring the second corporation to assume the debts of the first corporation than it serves as a basis for an objection to a discharge in bankruptcy . . . ."

[104] 2007 Ohio App. LEXIS 5724 (Dec. 7, 2007).

corporation.[105] The majority permitted a more direct route, a "sideways" pierce from one sibling to the other sibling corporation, but did so using an ill-fitting parent-subsidiary template. One subsidiary (Pro Fab), which had insurance, successfully bid on a contract to do steel work on construction of a new school building. Pro Fab then subcontracted the work to a sibling corporation (See Ann) which had no insurance. Besides common ownership, the two entities shared officers, business address, and corporate business and purpose.[106]

[D]   Enterprise Liability

Courts and commentators sometimes refer to cases of horizontal veil piercing, as in the taxi cabs cases, as enterprise liability. Over the last twenty years or so, however, the doctrinal offshoot of enterprise liability has taken on additional dimensions.[107] When a group of corporations (brother-sister subsidiaries, parent, grandparent and even great-grandparent) are under common control, and contribute to a collective endeavor, they may be held all to be one single enterprise. Multiple corporate veils are thus disregarded. Usually such cases involve use of the same corporate logo, interchange of corporate personnel, operation out of common offices, and similar factors.

An example involves the wreck of the oil tanker Amoco Cadiz on the French coast in 1978. The U.S. court held not only the owner of the ship, Amoco Tankers, Inc., but also Amoco International Oil Co. (sister), Amoco Transport (parent), Amoco (grandparent), and Standard Oil of Indiana (great-grandparent), liable for the massive cleanup costs. The court held the various corporations to be elements of an integrated international enterprise to be treated as one for liability purposes.[108]

The court in *Gardenal v. Westin Hotel Co.*[109] recognized the theory, which it called "the single business doctrine," but refused to hold Westin Hotels and Westin Mexico to be so integrated so as to support application of the theory. Plaintiff's decedent had drowned when a rogue wave hit him while he was walking in the beach at Westin's Mexican resort. Plaintiff sued not only Westim Mexico but Westin as in reality one enterprise.

---

[105] *See* the discussion of reverse piercing § 3.08[E], *infra*.

[106] Upon review, the Ohio Supreme Court agreed with the dissent. *Minno v. Pro Fab*, 905 N.E.2d 613 (Ohio 2009), holds that no "sideways" piercing can take place without control and control means by virtue of share ownership. Thus in Ohio, simple brother-sister corporation liability cannot exist.

[107] *See, e.g.*, Phillip O. Blumberg, *The Increasing Recognition of Enterprise Principles in Determining Parent and Subsidiary Corporations Liabilities*, 28 Conn. L. Rev. 295 (1996). *See also* Phillip I. Blumberg, *Accountability of Multinational Corporations: the Barriers Presented By Concepts of the Corporate Juridical Entity*, 24 Hastings Int'l & Comp. L. Rev. 297 (2001).

[108] *See In the Matter of the Oil Spill by Amoco Cadiz Off the Coast of France*, 954 F.2d 1279 (7th Cir. 1992). A similar state court case is *Las Palmas Associates v. Las Palmas Center Associates*, 235 Cal. App. 3d 1220, 1 Cal. Rptr. 2d 301 (1991) ("single enterprise theory of liability" used to hold grandparent and parent as well as subsidiary corporation liable).

[109] 186 F.3d 588 (5th Cir. 1999).

Advocates of expanded enterprise liability term it "honest bookkeeping."[110] Large multinational corporations should not be able to upstream most of the cash and all of the profits to corporate headquarters while at the same time bottling up the liability (and the moral responsibility) in a third or fourth tier subsidiary operating in some distant location. Increasingly, activists are seeking to hold large multinational corporations responsible for international human rights violations and environmental degradation committed by their subsidiaries and their subcontractors by utilizing enterprise liability principles.

[E]   Reverse Piercing

In a reverse pierce, a contract or tort claimant, or a judgment creditor, finds her judgment unsatisfied (because the defendant has insufficient assets), or predicts that such could be the case. She then attempts to pierce downward to reach the assets of a corporation in which the defendant is a shareholder. Commentators sort some reverse piercing cases into "inside claims," in which a controlling shareholder seeks to have himself regarded as one and the same as the corporation so that he can avail himself of corporation privileges or of corporate claims against third parties. Most reverse piercing claims are "outside claims." A creditor of the human shareholder seeks to reach the corporation's assets.[111]

Courts must be wary of reverse piercing because, if successful, a reverse pierce represents a reach through the backdoor, resulting in the exhaustion of corporate assets, leaving legitimate creditors empty handed, standing at the front door, so to speak. In the usual case, the corporation's assets should remain available for claims by persons who extended credit to the corporation in the normal course.

In re Phillips[112] allows for reverse piercing by trial courts, at least in outside reverse pierce cases. A trustee in bankruptcy sought to reach real estate the debtor had placed in a shell corporation prior to bankruptcy. The Supreme Court of Colorado hedged its conclusion with several safeguards: (1) the remedy should be "granted sparingly"; (2) the reverse pierce must "contribute to an overall equitable result"; and (3) "the individual and the corporation must be alter egos of one another."

We usually regard veil piercing, including reverse piercing, as an adverse development from the corporate shareholder's viewpoint. In *Cargill v. Hedges*[113] the Supreme Court of Minnesota allowed an "insider reverse pierce" that benefitted the shareholder. The court allowed a farmer's spouse, who was a sole shareholder and the family farm corporation to be considered one and the same, disregarding the corporate veil between them. The spouse could thus

---

[110] *See* Anita Bernstein, *Conjoining International Human Rights Law with Enterprise Liability for Accidents*, 40 Washburn L. Rev. 383, 403 (2001).

[111] *See* Gregory Crespi, *The Reverse Pierce Doctrine: Applying Appropriate Standards*, 16 J. Corp. L. 33, 37 (1990).

[112] 139 P.3d 639 (Col. 2006).

[113] 375 N.W.2d 477 (Minn. 1985).

protect from creditors 80 acres of the farm under her personal homestead exemption. A corporation, being a fictional being, needs no place to live and has no homestead exemption but an individual shareholder does need the exemption. Under the bankruptcy code, federal courts borrow from state law to determine the parameters of the homestead exemption.

The farmer and his spouse operated the corporate held farm on their own, lived there, had no lease, and paid no rent. For a reverse pierce in Minnesota there must be "a close identity" between the person and the corporation. Moreover, a reverse pierce will be allowed in only the most carefully limited circumstances."

[F]   Summary

A creditor or tort claimant plaintiff may plead facts attempting to reach the pockets of individual shareholders; parent corporations as shareholders; both parent and grandparent corporations; or parent corporation and individual shareholders in the parent. This section has discussed all of the foregoing instances as examples of "vertical piercing." A claimant may also attempt "horizontal piercing," claiming that a group of brother-sister corporations are a single enterprise, all of the assets of which should be available to satisfy her claim.

Still another variant in structural setting is the "reverse pierce." The claimant pierces vertically to reach the pocket of the individual or corporate owner of the corporation. Finding insufficient assets to satisfy her claims, the claimant may try to reach down to the assets of another corporation which is the sibling of the corporation first sued. *Sea-Land Services, Inc. v. Pepper Source*[114] demonstrates the reverse pierce, as do the *Phillips* and *Cargill v. Hedges* cases.

Plaintiff may also seek to pierce the veil forward, through time, as in the products liability cases. For example, in *Tift v. Forage King Industries, Inc.*,[115] an injured worker sought to reach forward from the time of the equipment's manufacture to a successor entity that had taken over trademarks, patents, and other items of the original manufacturer.

Finally, a plaintiff may attempt to reach back or forward through time to a succession of incorporated entities, such as when a series of corporations are used to shield assets from creditors or when a new corporation is formed to evade a contract signed by a predecessor entity.[116] Understanding the various relationships that may exist among affiliated owners and corporations may be as important to understanding piercing the corporate veil as is a thorough understanding of the various grounds upon which a court may disregard a corporate entity.

---

[114] 941 F.2d 519 (1991), *after remand*, 993 F.2d 1309 (7th Cir. 1993). *See* the discussion at the conclusion of § 3.4[C], *supra.*

[115] 322 N.W.2d 14 (Wis. 1982). *See* the discussion in § 3.07, *supra.*

[116] *K.C. Roofing Center*, 807 S.W.2d 545 (Mo. Ct. App. 1991). See, for example, the discussion of the fictitious case of *Bypass, Inc.*, in which the party sought to evade a contract requirements contained in an agreement with Raskin and Bobbins, Inc., in § 3.03[E], *supra.*

One new and potentially explosive application of veil piercing, agency and enterprise liability concepts is to reach upward in large, multi-layered multinational corporations for alleged human rights, environmental, and other claims. The U.S.'s Alien Tort Claims Act confers subject matter jurisdiction on U.S. courts for certain torts committed anywhere in the world. Foreign plaintiffs have brought claims in U.S. courts against Royal Dutch Shell for alleged human rights violation in Nigeria, Texaco for environmental claims in Ecuador, Unocal for human rights abuses in Myanmar, Coca Cola, Exxon, Dole Foods, Del Monte, and others. The first issue plaintiffs confront in such cases is the need to pierce through multiple corporate veils, or devise some other means to reach upward in a corporate organization (enterprise liability, agency, joint venture). This application of ages old corporate law concepts to new contexts illustrates well the concept of "old wine in new bottles."

Chapter 4

FINANCING THE CORPORATION

§ 4.01 INTRODUCTION

All businesses need capital to function. Capital is raised in primarily two ways: through borrowing (which creates debt) and through the investment of funds by owners (which creates equity).[1] Lending creates a debtor/creditor relationship in which the debtor (borrower) promises to pay back the principal and interest for use of the funds to the creditor (lender) at a certain date and on a regular basis. Creditors have priority over equity holders and must be paid interest on the money borrowed before dividends are paid to shareholders. In a dissolution of the corporation, creditors receive their principal before equity holders receive anything. Failure of the borrower to pay either the interest or the principal when due allows the creditor to sue and collect. The creditor may force the debtor into bankruptcy if the debtor is unable to pay or to work out another arrangement with the creditor.[2]

Equity in a corporation are represented by the shareholders. Shareholders may be paid dividends by the corporation when there are profits and when the board of directors determines that dividends should be paid. Shareholders have no right to the return of their invested funds from the corporation unless there is a dissolution of the corporation or the directors offer to buy back the shares. Thus, shareholders have no right to payments from the corporation and unlike creditors, a failure to pay them will not force the business into bankruptcy.

Shareholders in a publicly traded corporation may sell their shares in the stock market but the price depends on the success of the business. If the corporation is successful, the common shareholders benefit by the increased value while creditors are usually just entitled to their princial. Thus, compared to creditors, the shareholders have greater risk (lower priority than creditors) but also the potential for greater return (increased profits benefit the shareholders).

---

[1] Retained earnings also constitute a major source of capital. Retained earnings are profits held by the business and not paid out in dividends to the shareholders.

[2] Generally, interest paid to creditors by a business is tax deductible and has the effect of reducing the taxable income reported, and thus the amount of tax paid. For example, if a corporation has taxable income of $80,000 and interest of $10,000, the deduction for interest reduces the income to $70,000 from which taxes are paid. If the tax rate was 25% the corporation would pay $17,500 in taxes instead of $20,000 on the $80,000 and that would save the corporation $2500 in taxes.

§ 4.02 SECURITIES

In terms of long term investments in the corporation, publicly held corporations issue securities that can be broadly described as debt, common and preferred shares. Generally, each security carries with it attributes relating to 1) the risk of loss of the investment; 2) the power to control the business; and 3) the ability to share in success of the enterprise. Investment in the different securities depends upon the purchaser's willingness to trade the risks associated with each security with its return. In order to induce investors to turn their capital over to a business, investors need an expectation of some return. The return should compensate for inflation (the fact that money loses value over time, i.e., a dollar today is more valuable than a future dollar), for risk (the fact that any investment except United States government guaranteed securities have the risk of nonpayment) and for lost opportunity (that investment in one business means the funds cannot be used for other investments). The interest rate that creditors are paid on their loans and the dividends paid and expected to be paid to equity reflect this compensation. Since all business investments involve inflation[3] and lost opportunities, risk is the primary factor to be weighed against potential return in deciding among business investment opportunities. Because all the securities described involve long term investment, there is additional risk resulting from the duration of the investment.

There must be some exercise of control by all investors to protect their investment. Creditors often contract to protect their investment while shareholders, with the most at risk, elect the directors who manage the corporation for their benefit.

[A] Debt

Long term debt instruments are often denominated as bonds or debentures. Bonds are usually secured by specific assets, which means that in the case of default, the bondholders may usually claim payment from specific assets of the business (similar to a bank holding a mortgage on a home). Debentures involve unsecured debt. Holders of debentures have a general claim to assets with other unsecured creditors.

The relationship between the creditor and the corporation is contractual. There may be contractual provisions that limit corporate activities to protect the loan and may give the creditors some limited control. If the debt is sold to the public, the contract is called an indenture and a trustee may be selected to represent the interests of the public debt holders.[4] Since debt has priority over equity for both interest and payment of principal, it generally has less risk of loss than equity. Creditors are concerned with the success of the business because it will help to insure repayment of interest and principal. However, creditors do not usually receive more if the business is successful.[5]

---

[3] Debt can be issued with an inflation adjustment provision that protects the holder from rising inflation by adjusting the interest rate.

[4] *See* Trust Indenture Act of 1939, 15 U.S.C. §§ 77aaa-bbb, 53 Stat. 1149.

[5] If the corporation agrees to allow a creditor to convert their debt to common shares, creditors

Generally, the greater the risk, the more return or contractual control the creditors demand. For example, if a corporation is able to sell 10-year secured bonds, offering 5% interest, it would need to offer a higher rate of interest, such as 7%, if at the same time it was selling a 10-year unsecured debenture.[6] The higher rate of interest compensates the debenture holders because of the difference in risk between secured and unsecured debt.[7]

[B]   Common Shares

Common shareholders have been described as residual claimants in the corporation because they have a claim to receive the income and assets of the corporation after all other claims have been satisfied.[8] The common shareholders are directly concerned with the success of the business enterprise because their return is directly linked to the corporation's profitability. Conversely, claims of creditors and preferred shareholders are usually fixed. Once fixed claims have been paid, all remaining value is for the benefit of the common shareholders. Thus, as the value of a firm increases, so does the value

---

would enjoy a greater return if the corporation flourishes. This type of debt, called a convertible, allows for a fixed return but with option to convert to shares if their value increases. A convertibility feature allows the holder of a security the right to convert his or her debt to common stock, usually at a fixed conversion price. For example, if the common stock is selling at $20 a share, the corporation could contract with a debenture holder (issued at $1000 which is the norm for publicly traded debt) to convert at a conversion price set at a premium over the market price, such as $25. The conversion would allow the debenture holder to receive 40 shares for the $1000 debenture ($1000 debt ÷ $25 conversion price). If for example, the stock later moved to $40, then the $1000 convertible investment would have appreciated to at least $1600 (40 shares if converted × $40). If the stock never goes higher than $25, the debenture holder would probably remain a creditor and not benefit from the conversion right. Generally, when convertible debt is sold, the creditor accepts a lower interest rate than the rate she would have been paid if the debt was nonconvertible.

[6] Debt can be sold privately or in a public offering and be publicly traded. After debt is issued at a fixed interest rate that reflects the realities at the time of sale, its market value may vary during its life as inflation or risk changes. For example, assume a company issued a $1000 10 year bond at 5% (predicted inflation was 3% at the time and the 2% was for risk and opportunity costs) which was sold to investors. If, after one year, inflation rises from the expected 3% to 5% such that interest rates go up in general, the value of the bond will decline in the market because of the change. The holder of the $1000 debt is still getting only 5% but overall interest rates have risen from the earlier 3% assumption. A new purchaser in the market would now buy the bond at less than $1000 in order to get a higher return than 5% because a new purchaser would want to be compensated for the increased inflation. The same would be true if after a year, the business developed financial problems which increased the risk that the debt would not be paid in 10 years. The increased risk would also lower the market price of the bonds because a purchaser would no longer be willing to pay $1000 for a 5% $1000 bond given increased risk. For example, the 5% $1000 bond could sell for around $870 if rates go up (inflation from 3% to 5%) after a year. The lower bond price means the purchaser of the bond will earn more than 5% because she has paid less than $1000 (e.g. $870) but will receive 5% of $1000 each year ($50 in interest) and at the end of the term, the full principal ($1000). At the same time, if inflationary expectations went down from 3% to 2%, the bond would trade at a higher price because it still pays 5% on $1,000.

[7] However, the creditor could accept a lower interest rate in return for other rights, such as a convertibility option, and would trade off the lower interest for the possibility of an increased return if the shares appreciate. *See* note 5, *supra.*

[8] *See* Model Bus. Corp. Act Ann. § 6.03(c) (4th ed. 2008) (there must be outstanding shares that have unlimited voting rights and that are entitled to receive the net assets of the corporation upon dissolution).

of the common stock. For example, a corporation that is valued at $1000 which has $300 in debt and $200 in preferred shares leaves $500 in value for the common shareholders. If the corporation increases in value to $2000 the common stock is now worth $1500 since the increased value goes to the common shareholders.[9] The amount owed the creditors and preferred shareholders and their interest or dividends do not usually change unless they have contracted for a greater return.

Common shares have lower priority and greater risks of loss than other securities but have the potential for greater return than other investments. Because of the risk and expectations, common shareholders are usually given significant control of the corporation, through voting rights, to select the board of directors to manage the corporation with the goal of increasing its value.

[C]   Preferred Shares

Preferred shares are equity authorized by state corporate statutes. Preferred shares are usually authorized in the articles of incorporation which also contain their contract rights. In most cases, preferred shareholders are paid fixed dividends after the creditors are paid their interest but before the common shareholders are paid dividends. Since preferred shares are considered equity, their holders have no right to be paid like creditors. Rather, preferred shareholders are paid when the board of directors authorizes payment (that is, declares dividends).[10] In liquidation, the preferred shareholders are paid their liquidation preference after the creditors but before the common shareholders. Therefore, preferred shareholders have higher risk than creditors in receiving a return and repayment but less risk than common shareholders. On the other hand, they usually do not have the rights of the common shareholders to vote and control the corporation[11] or share in the increased return if the corporation is successful.[12]

Preferred shares are an unusual security which has the disadvantages of both debt (little direct control or potential for increased return) and common shares (lower priority and greater risk) without any of their respective advantages. One may ask why there is a market for preferred shares? Preferred shares attract

---

[9] The common stock benefit from this increase either by an appreciation in market value or by increased dividend payments.

[10] Most preferred stock contracts provide that dividends are cumulative. This means that failure to pay a dividend creates a credit for the unpaid amount which must be paid before the common stockholders receive any dividends. If the preferred stock is noncumulative, the unpaid dividends usually do not cumulate and need not be paid prior to the payment of dividends to the common stockholders.

[11] The contract may provide that a failure to pay a dividend over several quarters may allow the preferred shareholders to elect a number of directors, giving them some potential control over the corporation. Some statutes give preferred shareholders the right to vote, particularly when an action affects them, such as a merger. Model Bus. Corp. Act Ann. § 11.04(f) (4th ed. 2008).

[12] Their contract can provide for increased return for participating preferred shares, which provide greater dividends if the common shares receive higher dividends. They could also contract for a convertibility option. *See* note 5, *supra.*

investors because they tend to pay higher dividends.[13] In addition, since dividend payments to corporate shareholders are partially nontaxable, there is a market for preferred shares among corporate investors.[14]

§ 4.03 LEVERAGING AND CAPITAL STRUCTURE

Businesses usually finance operations with both debt and equity. The use of debt creates leverage by allowing debtors to put creditors' funds at risk, requiring a smaller investment of equity from the common shareholders (i.e. using creditors' money to make money). Thus, if the business fails, the shareholders have invested less and lose less. If the business is successful, the owners make a greater return on the amount they invested. For example, a business capitalized by $100 of owner's equity which earns $20 the first year (not considering taxes), has earned 20%. Conversely, if the $100 initial capital was comprised of a loan for $60 at 10% interest, plus only $40 invested by owners as equity, the $20 earnings would have to be reduced by $6 (the interest payment to the creditor), leaving $14 of earnings. The owners, having invested only $40 instead of $100, now earn $14, which is a 35% return on their $40. In addition, interest on debt is also tax deductible (dividends are not) which creates a tax benefit when financing with debt.[15] Leveraging with debt can create benefits for owners by investing less of their money, getting a tax deduction and using other's to make money.[16]

The problem with leveraging is that failure to pay interest on debt can trigger a default with possible bankruptcy ramifications. For example, if the business which borrowed $60, earned only $1 but had to pay $6 interest to a creditor, there would be a $5 deficiency and a possible default if the interest is not paid. However, if there were more equity in the business, the threat of bankruptcy

---

[13] For example, if a corporation could sell its debt at 10% but decided to sell preferred shares instead, it would have to offer a dividend rate of more than 10% to compensate for the increased risk, such as 12%. There are advantages to the corporation as well. Preferred shares are equity so they have lower priority than creditors and provide a cushion for creditors who are more willing to lend. If a business is in trouble, it need not pay the dividends. The issuance of the preferred stock does not dilute the common shareholders' claims if the business is successful.

[14] Generally, seventy percent of the dividends received by a corporate shareholder are not taxed. This minimizes triple taxation where corporate profits are taxed and then the dividend to the corporate shareholder could be taxed again and the dividend paid to the shareholders of the corporate shareholder could be taxed a third time. The significant tax free status of dividends may encourage corporations to buy preferred for the dividend. I.R.C. § 243 (1988). For a discussion of the double taxation of dividends, see § 1.05[A], *supra.*

[15] If taxes are considered, the return would be even greater. Assume that the business had made taxable income of $30 and paid taxes of $10 (assuming a 33.3% tax rate) reducing the profit to $20. If the corporation now pays interest on a loan of $6 (tax deductible), the taxable income would be reduced to only $24. Assuming a 33.3% tax rate, the business would pay only $8 in taxes instead of $10 (a $2 tax benefit because the interest deduction reduced taxable income from $30 to $24 and thus reduced the tax liability). As a result there would be a profit of $16 or a 40% return on the owner's $40 investment. Thus, leveraging with debt can also be beneficial for its tax savings and its use of other peoples money to make a greater return than for the corporation than available from traditional borrowing.

[16] The use of preferred shares can also have a leveraging effect except, unlike interest on debt, the dividends are not tax deductible.

would diminish because unlike debt, equity does not require the payment of dividends. Thus, if the business earned $1 and was financed with $100 in equity the business would not be as concerned with default. When a business is flourishing, leverage benefits the owners by increasing the return on equity. However, when a business has poor earnings and interest is due to creditors, leveraging creates a greater risk of default and bankruptcy.

While it would appear the use of debt has advantages, all businesses need some equity. Although State corporate law requires that shares must be issued, there is no requirement of any minimum equity. In practice, a reasonable amount of equity will be required to encourage reasonable lending.[17] Substantial investments of equity also signals creditors that the owners have their own money at risk, a factor which encourages lending. Since a creditors' principal must be paid before the equity receives a return of its capital, the existence of equity reassures creditors.[18]

A variety of factors influence the choice of capital structure. Capital structure includes the amount of debt and equity as well as the type of debt and equity.[19]

§ 4.04   LEGAL CAPITAL RULES

State corporate law statutes regulate the issuance or sale of shares and provide rules designed to protect both shareholders and creditors of the corporation. The statutes provide that the number of shares (both common and preferred) authorized (available for sale) must be stated in the articles of incorporation.[20] The articles must also indicate if different classes of shares are authorized and their relative rights and preferences.[21] There is usually a requirement that there be at least one class of shares with voting rights and a residual claim on the corporate assets.[22]

Corporations usually have authorized more shares than they plan to sell. Unsold shares are retained for future use. If additional shares are not authorized in the articles of incorporation, shareholders would have to amend the articles to provide for authorization in the event additional shares were needed.

---

[17] The amount of equity may be a factor in whether the shareholders could be liable for corporate obligations under the piercing the corporate veil doctrine. For a discussion of piercing, see Chapter 3.

[18] Generally, the larger the amount of equity, the lower the risk to creditors. A corporation with $100 in capital with $50 debt and $50 in equity is less risky than one with $80 debt and $20 in equity. In the case of the former, the value of the business would have to decline to below $50 before the creditors would be in jeopardy while in the latter, a value below $80 would put the creditors at risk. Thus equity provides a cushion for creditors.

[19] Some economic theorists argue that aside from tax reasons and in a world without transactions costs, the amount of debt or equity is irrelevant to the value of the firm. *See* Franco Modigliani &Merton H. Miller, *The Cost of Capital, Corporation Finance and the Theory of Investment*, 28 AMER. ECON. REV. 261 (1958).

[20] Model Bus. Corp. Act Ann. § 2.02(a)(2) (4th ed. 2008).

[21] Model Bus. Corp. Act Ann. § 6.01(a) (4th ed. 2008).

[22] Model Bus. Corp. Act Ann. § 6.03(c) (4th ed. 2008).

At the outset, the incorporator issues shares to the initial shareholders. Shares that are already authorized in the articles but not issued can be subsequently issued at the discretion of the board of directors. When the shares are sold, they are considered authorized, issued and outstanding when held by the shareholders. Shares that are repurchased from shareholders at a later date by the corporation are sometimes called treasury shares and are considered authorized and issued, but no longer outstanding. Some statutes have eliminated the concept of treasury shares.[23]

[A] Preemptive Rights

A shareholder's ownership interest depends on the number of shares issued and not the number of shares authorized for sale. For example, if a corporation has authorized 1000 shares but 400 shares are sold and issued equally to four shareholders, then each owns 100 shares and 25% of the corporation. If the remaining 600 shares are later issued equally to all four shareholders, the percentage of ownership remains the same. However, if only three shareholders receive the remaining 600 shares, then the one shareholder owning only 100 shares is now a 10% owner because her interest has been diluted by the actions of the other three.

The shareholder holding the diluted shares may be protected by preemptive rights. Preemptive rights require that each shareholder be offered the right to purchase a proportionate number of shares in order to maintain the percentage of ownership and voting control.[24] In our example, each shareholder would have the right to buy 150 shares. If all four shareholders purchased the new shares, they would each retain their 25% interest in the corporation. Generally, preemptive rights must be provided for in the articles of incorporation.[25] Publicly traded corporations do not provide preemptive rights. Shareholders of a publicly traded corporation are less concerned with preemptive rights because they are usually passive investors and have no expectation of maintaining their percentage ownership. In addition, the mechanics of first offering newly issued shares to many shareholders would be unduly burdensome if the shares provided preemptive rights. If they desire more shares they can purchase them in the stock market. Thus preemptive rights may be important in a closely held corporation.

---

[23] *See* Model Bus. Corp. Act Ann. § 6.31 (official comment) (4th ed. 2008). Corporations are not permitted to vote either their authorized shares which have not be issued or repurchased shares. To allow these shares a vote could transfer voting control from the actual shareholders holding issued shares to the directors controlling the corporation. The repurchased shares are generally available for future sale.

[24] Even if there are no preemptive rights, if a distribution of shares excludes some shareholders and involves oppression by the majority shareholder towards the minority, there may be a breach of fiduciary duty. For a discussion of oppression, see § 11.07[G], *infra*.

[25] Model Bus. Corp. Act Ann. § 6.30(a) (4th ed. 2008). Some statutes grant preemptive rights automatically to shares unless restricted in the articles. There may also be restrictions in the statute on the automatic right so that preemptive rights may not apply to certain issuances. For example, preemptive rights may not apply to shares issued within six months of incorporation. Model Bus. Corp. Act Ann. § 6.30(b)(3)(iii) (4th ed. 2008).

[B]   Par Value

The board of directors usually sets the price for shares. Many state statutes set forth what constitutes valid consideration. For example, MBCA § 6.21(b), provides that the consideration must be "any tangible or intangible property or benefit to the corporation, including cash, promissory notes, services performed, contract for services to be performed or other securities of the corporation."[26] The directors' determination of the adequacy of consideration is usually conclusive.[27]

While the board of directors may set the price at which the shares are sold, some states require that when shares are originally authorized in the articles of incorporation, a certain value must be assigned. This value is known as par. Par value is the minimum price for which shares may be sold. Failure to sell shares for at least the par value results in the issuance of "watered" stock[28] and creates liability.[29] Today, either low par or no par shares are usually issued. Therefore, almost all common shares are now issued for prices above par.

In the past, par was the price the corporation set for selling its shares. In an age in which corporations were generally closely held and shares were sold to different individuals over time, the par price assured that all purchasers bought at the same price. With the advent of full disclosure as required by federal and state securities law, shareholders are necessarily informed of the prices paid by others and par no longer provides disclosure.

Another rationale for par was to protect creditors by assuring that the par amount would be available as a cushion for creditors. The amount of par paid to the corporation was often called stated capital. State corporation law statutes generally precluded a corporation from paying this stated capital amount to shareholders, either through a dividend payment or by repurchasing shares. In reality, the amount paid in as par was not set aside for the creditors but were used in the business. Creditors found other ways to protect themselves from overpayments to shareholders by restricting dividends through contract, or by using fraudulent conveyance law or bankruptcy law to attack preference payments made by an insolvent corporation. As a result, the MBCA and some states such as California, have eliminated the concepts of par and stated capital. Even in states in which par is codified, corporations have avoided legal capital

---

[26] Some states are more restrictive and may preclude the issuance of shares for future services or promises to pay.

[27] *See* Model Bus. Corp. Act Ann. § 6.21(c) (4th ed. 2008). The purchaser of the shares is liable for failure to pay the consideration or the amount agreed to in a share subscription agreement. *See* Model Bus. Corp. Act Ann. § 6.22 (4th ed. 2008).

[28] For illustrative purposes, consider a corporation which has authorized 1000 shares of $10 par. If the shares are issued for no consideration, the stock is called bonus stock. If the cash paid is less than $10,000 for the 1000 shares it is called discount stock. If some non-cash consideration is paid but its true value is less than par, (the shares are issued for $5000 worth of equipment) it is watered stock.

[29] Shareholders who purchase stock for less than par may be liable to corporate creditors. The courts have developed three theories on enforcing the obligation to pay par. An early theory was that par created a trust fund for the creditors. Later, courts used a "holding out" theory based upon a representation that the funds had been paid. Some courts created liability based upon the statutory obligation to pay par. *See* Bayless Manning, LEGAL CAPITAL 50–57 (1990)

difficulties by issuing low par stock or no par stock.[30] Thus, the concept of par is practically obsolete, but because some states continue the concept it is important to understand.

[C]   Dividends and Repurchases of Shares

Dividends are payments to shareholders which represent a current return on investment.[31] Dividends are paid at the discretion of the directors.

As an alternative to paying dividends, the board of directors may decide to have the corporation buy back or repurchase shares. This repurchase is another means by which shareholders may receive funds from the corporation. For example, if 1000 issued and outstanding shares are owned by two equal shareholders, there are $2000 in funds to pay out. The corporation could either issue a $2 dividend per share (that is, $1000 to each) or the corporation could buy an equal number of shares from each shareholder, (say 100 shares at $10 a share) to equal $1000 from each. In each case, the economic result would be similar. Each shareholder receives $1000 and maintains its 50% ownership.

Dividend policy or repurchases involve many issues.[32] In a publicly traded corporation, the decision of the directors to pay a dividend or repurchase shares is rarely challenged. In a closely held corporation, there are tax considerations associated with the decision.[33] Also, minority shareholders face possible oppression by the majority which may limit dividends, denying the minority a return.[34]

The legal requirements for the payment of dividends and repurchase of shares (sometimes called "distributions") vary among states. The basic principle is not to permit payment of dividends in cases where the payment will adversely impact investors or creditors. If dividend payments deplete a company's capital, creditors and future shareholders could be harmed.[35] Most statutes do not allow payment of dividends when the corporation is equitably insolvent, that is, if after

---

[30] Even in the case of no par stock, the statute may require some allocation of the consideration to the stated capital account. *E.g.*, N.Y.B.C.L. § 506(b).

[31] Although shareholders often profit by the increased market value of the shares, some economists view that increase in value reflects the market estimate of future dividends. Dividends provide actual return to the shareholders.

[32] Economic theorists argue that a corporation's dividend policy is irrelevant to the value of the shares since the retained earnings are reflected in the increased value of the shares. *See* Merton Miller & Franco Modigliani, *Dividend Policy, Growth and the Valuation of Shares*, 34 J. BUSINESS 411 (1961).

[33] Shareholders may attempt to elude double taxation by avoiding dividends and either retaining the earnings for corporate use or paying salaries in place of dividends. The Internal Revenue Service may attack the retention of earnings or the salaries as unreasonable and an illegal attempt to avoid double taxation. This is more likely to occur in a closely held corporation. For a discussion of the avoidance of double taxation in the corporation, see § 1.05[A], *supra.*

[34] Challenges to dividend policy are more likely in a closely held corporation. The lack of dividend payments could precipitate a claim for breach of fiduciary duty for oppression of the minority shareholders. For a discussion of oppression, see § 11.07[G], *infra.*

[35] Directors are usually liable for improperly paying dividends by not complying with the legal requirements of the statute. *See, e.g.*, Model Bus. Corp. Act Ann. § 8.33 (4th ed. 2008). The directors

the payment, the corporation cannot meet its obligations as they become due. The traditional approach for statutes that use par is to require that the dividend payments be from either earned surplus (the net profits retained in the business) or surplus comprised of both earned and capital surplus (excess amount paid for shares over par).[36]

The modern approach treats the rules that govern par and legal capital as formalistic and eliminates the concepts. For example, the MBCA no longer requires par and instead focuses on a balance sheet test for distribution. After a distribution, remaining assets must exceed the sum of liabilities and the total amount that would have to be paid on liquidation to any senior preferred shares.[37] The corporation must also be able to pay its debts as they mature (i.e., not equitably insolvent).

§ 4.05 VALUATION

To a potential creditor or investor, the value of the business is significant information. Creditors look to the value of the business to determine how much to lend and to evaluate the risks associated with making the loan. Owners need to know the value of the business if they decide to buy or sell their ownership interests.

Valuation is also an important issue in a legal context. For example, major transactions such as mergers often trigger valuation issues. The law sometimes allows shareholders who oppose a merger to seek an independent valuation of shares in a judicial proceeding called an appraisal.[38] The value of a business may also be important in a context unrelated to corporate law such as in a divorce proceeding in which the value of a spouse's business may be determined in order to properly divide the assets.

For a simple example of valuation, consider a window washing business that earns $100,000 a year in reported profits after deducting expenses. The business has operated for several years and has good prospects for continued similar profits. The owner seeks to sell the business and finds an interested buyer. The parties must then decide how to value it.

---

can sue a shareholder who knowingly received the improper payment. Model Bus. Corp. Act Ann. § 8.33(b) (4th ed. 2008).

[36] For example, assume a corporation issues 10,000 shares of $1 par stock and sells them to the public at $20. Then, the corporation has a stated capital of $10,000 and a capital surplus of $190,000. In a state which allows dividends or stock repurchase out of capital surplus, the entire $190,000 can be used, so long as the corporation is not equitably insolvent. In some states, a corporation may also be able to pay dividends out of current earnings, even when there is a deficit in the surplus account. This is called the nimble dividend test. See, e.g., Del. G.C.L. § 170(a).

[37] Model Bus. Corp. Act Ann. § 6.40(c)(2) (4th ed. 2008). California has also eliminated par. In place of par, California limits dividends and repurchases to the extent of retained earnings, provided certain ratios are maintained after the distribution. See Calif. Corp. Code § 500.

[38] For a discussion of appraisal, see § 6.06, infra. Courts may also need to value shares when the control group of a corporation wants to eliminate the minority shareholders in a freezeout transaction (see § 10.03, infra) or minority shareholders of a closely held corporation claim oppression by the majority under a statute allowing for a buy out (see § 11.07[G], infra).

[A]   Liquidation Value

One way to value a business is to look at its liquidation value. Liquidation value is the amount for which the assets could be sold minus the liabilities owed. The assets of this business include pails, soap, sponges, uniforms and a building which houses the business. There is a $25,000 mortgage liability on the building. At an auction, all the assets may sell for $60,000. Subtracting the $25,000 liability, the business would have a $35,000 liquidation value. Obviously this $35,000 liquidation value does not reflect business potential or its value to a buyer since the business earns $100,000 annually in profits.

[B]   Book Value

Another method of valuation is based upon analysis of the corporation's financial statements as prepared by accountants. One of those statements is called the balance sheet. The balance sheet lists the assets of the business on one side and the liabilities and equity on the other side (Assets + Liabilities = Equity). The balance sheet captures the corporate financial accounts on one day, usually the last day of the corporation's fiscal year. For example the balance sheet of this business would be:

Assets		Liabilities	
Current Assets		Mortgage	$25,000
Cash	$5,000		
Accounts Receivable	10,000		
Fixed Assets			
Equipment	5,000	**Equity**	
Building	90,000	Shares	5,000
Depreciation	(−30,000)	Retained Earnings	50,000
Total	$80,000	Total	$80,000

If one subtracts the liabilities ($25,000) from the assets ($80,000), the equity remains ($55,000) (Equity = Assets − Liabilities). Equity represents the ownership interest in the business and may be referred to as the book value (amount paid for the shares plus retained earnings).

Valuing a business based on its balance sheet and book value has several limitations, including the need to use cost based accounting methods, the depreciation of certain fixed assets and the exclusion of certain intangible assets from the balance sheet. In addition, the value of a business based on its earnings is not really considered.

[1]   Cost Based Accounting

Although the balance sheet is useful in understanding the financial condition of a business, it has shortcomings for valuation purposes. Under generally accepted accounting principles ("GAAP")[39] assets must be listed on the balance sheet at their cost or at a lower amount if the asset has decreased below cost. Thus, if an asset was purchased many years ago but has appreciated in value, the increase in value would not be reflected. For example, if a corporation owns a building acquired for $90,000, the balance sheet would reflect the purchase price, minus $30,000 for depreciation, and would indicate a building value of $60,000. Of course, the fact that the building cost $90,000 does not mean its current market value is the same. For example, if the market value is *lower* (e.g., $30,000), then the balance sheet must reflect the loss in value and the building written down to $30,000. If the building has appreciated, GAAP would not allow the increase in value to be reported in the balance sheet.[40]

The cost based accounting method is conservative. It is thought to redress concerns that corporations may overvalue assets in the course of adjusting them to their market value. This practice, if left unchecked, could result in overvaluation of assets and a fraud upon creditors and purchasers of securities.

[2]   Depreciation

The second limitation involves depreciation. In our example, assume the window washing company's building, was purchased years ago for $90,000. The company may now report on its balance sheet a net value for the building of $60,000, because $30,000 in depreciation was subtracted from the original $90,000.

When the building was purchased, it was listed on the balance sheet at its cost of $90,000. While the purchase of the building was a corporate expense, the $90,000 was not immediately claimed as a current expense because the asset would help the business for many years. Rather, the purchase price was spread out over the building's useful life in the business, that is, depreciated. If the building cost $90,000 and will last 30 years, then each year, the business may take an amount reflecting the building's use in the business as an expense against income. Here, the $90,000 cost was divided by 30 years (assuming there is no value at year 30) to provide $3000 a year as a depreciation expense in determining income. At the same time as it serves as annual $3000 expense reducing income, the value of the building on the balance sheet is also reduced by $3000 annually. Since the building has been in use for 10 years, its accumulated depreciation over that period is $30,000 ($3000 a year times 10 years) which reduces the figure on the balance sheet to $60,000.

---

[39] Generally accepted accounting principles are rules which indicate how financial information should be reported. They are required by the SEC to be used by publicly traded corporations.

[40] Another way to value a business is to look at the replacement value of the assets, subtracting liabilities. While this may produce a higher value than book value, it does not reflect the value generated from business operations through earnings.

As illustrated by the example of the depreciated building, figures on the balance sheet for certain fixed assets often do not reflect the actual market value (if the value has increased) but may be further undervalued because of depreciation.

[3] Intangible Assets

Certain valuable assets such as trade names, patents or trademarks are not purchased but are developed over time. These assets may be very valuable. However, they are not usually represented at their market value on the balance sheet. For example, if a business develops an excellent reputation and its trade name is well known, the market value of the corporate trade name would not be listed as an asset on the balance sheet.[41] Thus, the book value of the corporation reflected in the equity figure does not usually represent the real value of the business because the market value of intangible assets might be missing from the balance sheet under accounting rules.

[C] Earnings Approach

Book value and liquidation value focus on the value of corporation's individual assets minus liabilities. Most investors do not seek to purchase the company's particular assets but rather intend to use them as part of a business to make money. The ability of an investment to generate earnings produces value. In the window washing business, investors are interested in the company's ability to earn $100,000 a year and not in the value of its assets. If our business did not generate sufficient earnings, then the value of the assets would be significant in liquidating the business.

In valuing an investment based upon earnings, an investor looks to the future. Predictions of the future are uncertain and valuation is not an exact process but is often a best guess.

According to the earnings approach, a business may be valued by finding the present value (or the amount one will pay currently) for a future expected return. Thus, one must determine the future expected return, its duration and the economic and business conditions under which the future return may be expected. Since investment usually involves the loss of immediate use of one's money in return for future payments, there must be some compensation to reflect that a future dollar (the return) is subject to inflation and is worth less than a current dollar (the inflation). Also, an investment represents a lost opportunity to participate in other investments (opportunity cost). Finally, if the investment involves a risk of not receiving the return, that risk must also be compensated (the risk). Thus, investors should be compensated for inflation, lost opportunity and risk. These factors are used to calculate a rate of return of an investment.[42]

An example of the interplay between the return, the duration of the investment and the rate of return may be seen if an investor is a creditor.

---

[41] The cost of developing the trade name can be included as an asset but not at its market value.

[42] For a discussion of the rate, see § 4.05[C][3], *infra.*

Assume that a corporation wants to borrow $1000 by issuing a bond for 10 years. The corporation will negotiate with the creditor over the term (duration), the contract terms (bears on risk), and the interest rate (rate of return). Whether an investor will agree to pay (i.e., loan) its set value ($1000) depends upon the interest rate offered. The interest rate reflects a best guess estimate on future inflation, the risk of the debtor's default and other opportunities foregone during the period of the loan. For example, if inflation for the 10 year period is predicted to be 3%, then the bond must offer more (such as 5%) to cover risk and opportunity costs. The higher the risk for the loan, the higher the interest would be required to induce the loan. Once the loan is agreed to and the interest rate set, then at the time the loan is entered into, the $1000 is the present value of both the future interest payments plus the return of the $1000 in principal at the end of ten years.

[1]   Capitalization of Earnings

More often, businesses are valued based on future returns. This method involves calculating the present value of the future returns by predicting how much one expects to earn from the business in the future. Risk, inflation and lost opportunity of the investment are factors that help to determine the appropriate rate of return. In addition, the duration of the business is also important. If we assume that the business will last far into the future, then we value it based upon perpetuity, which simplifies the calculation. In finding the present value of a future return in perpetuity we are capitalizing earnings.[43]

Using our window washing business as an example, how would one calculate the value of the business if income was predicted to total $100,000 a year in perpetuity and the risks, inflation and lost opportunities were estimated to result in an expected rate of return of 20%? In other words, how much would be needed to invest now (or the present value of) to earn $100,000 a year forever at 20%? The answer is $500,000 (because $500,000 invested at 20% will generate $100,000 a year in perpetuity). The formula is:

$$\text{P (present value \$500,000)} = \frac{\text{A (annual return \$100,000)}}{\text{R (rate of 20\%)}}$$

Assuming a $100,000 per year return forever at a 20% rate, the value of this investment is calculated by the deriving the reciprocal of 20% (100 ÷ 20 which gives us a multiplier of 5) times $100,000, that is, $500,000 earning at 20% a year forever produces $100,000 a year. Thus, the present value or the amount one needs to invest now to earn $100,000 a year forever at 20% is $500,000. If the rate of return were 25%, the multiplier would be 4 (100 ÷ 25) and the present value would be $400,000. With that rate, a purchaser would be willing to pay 4 times the earnings. The higher the rate, the lower the value (if a higher rate reflects more risk and inflation, then a lower value would follow). This method of valuation in

---

[43] If the valuation of our business was based on a shorter, finite period (e.g., five years), we would find the present value of our earnings each year for five years producing a discounted present value. Discounting is finding the present value over a finite period. *See* William A. Klein & John C. Coffee, BUSINESS ORGANIZATION AND FINANCE 306–327 (10th ed., 2007).

perpetuity is called capitalizing the earnings of a business to calculate its value. Thus, in order to value we need earnings, duration (assume perpetuity in this example) and the rate.

[2]   Cash Flow as Earnings

The earnings approach to valuation more truly reflects the purpose of investing, which is to earn a return on an investment. In the financial world, sophisticated methods and models can be used to determine both the rate and earnings for valuation purposes. To calculate future earnings, one could look at the corporation's financial statements to look at past earnings of the business and then try to predict its future earnings. Many analysts (and, as we will see, some courts) are more sophisticated and look not at earnings reported in the financial statements but instead look at the actual cash the corporation received annually. For example, the income statement of the window washing business looks as follows:

Income	$250,000
Expenses	−112,000
Depreciation	−3,000
Profit (gross)	135,000
Taxes	−35,000
Net Profits (reported earnings)	$100,000

When a corporation prepares its income statement under generally accepted accounting principles, it reports its gross income minus its expenses (which includes depreciation), resulting in the reported gross profit. After taxes are paid on the profit, net profits or reported earnings remain. Some of the expenses used to lower profits (and taxes) such as depreciation do not involve actual cash payments but are paper expenses that reduce profits, taxes and net profits. As discussed earlier, depreciation represents the allocation of the original cost of a fixed asset over its useful life.[44] In our example, the building cost $90,000. Each year $3000 was used to depreciate it on the balance sheet and as an expense on the income statement. While this depreciation reduced income (resulting in lower taxes paid) and the reported profit, the depreciation was not an actual cash expense for the business because the $90,000 used to purchase the building was expended many years ago. Thus, depreciation reduces reported earnings but does not decrease actual cash in the business. That is why investors, in valuing the business, look to actual cash generated, that is, the "cash flow" of the business.

Thus, in the window washing business, the reported profits were $100,000 but the actual cash flowing in the business was $103,000 (reported earnings plus depreciation which was not paid out). This is the cash flow of the business: the amount the owner would have for their actual use. The cash flow of the business, if it represents the future return, should be considered in determining the return on the investment and the value of the business.

---

[44] For a discussion of depreciation, see § 4.05[B][2], *supra.*

If the business is to operate over time then it is necessary to factor into our cash flow figure used in valuation the need to repair or replace fixed assets to generate the future cash flow. If, in our window washing business, we need to use $1000 each year to repair or replace the assets, then for valuation purposes our cash flow would be $102,000 (reported profit of $100,000 plus $3000 in depreciation minus $1000 to repair or replace assets).[45]

[3]   The Rate

As we have seen in valuating a business, one needs to come up with a figure representing the future return (sometimes based upon the cash flow and the numerator A in the formula), its duration (assume perpetuity), and apply a rate to that return (the denominator R in the formula). In our window washing business, we assumed the business will operate in perpetuity and its cash flow will be $102,000 (reported earnings plus depreciation and minus the amount needed to replace assets). For our formula of P = A/R we now have A (the predicted cash flow of $102,000) and the duration (perpetuity) but need R (the rate) in order to come up with P (the present value). The formula determines the present value (P) of the future return (A) in perpetuity at a given a rate (R). Thus the present value (P) of our business if the rate (R) was 20% and the cash flow (A) was $102,000 a year forever would be $510,000. This is another way of saying that if we invested $510,000 at 20% forever, we would earn $102,000 per year.

The rate we use is intended to reflect the fact that the value of any dollars earned in the future from the business may be adversely affected by future inflation and the risk of not receiving the return. If we decided to invest our money in United States treasury bonds, the interest rate we would earn would compensate for future inflation and lost opportunities to use the money elsewhere but not for risk. Since bonds issued by the government are considered risk free.[46] If the long term U.S. bonds were paying 8% then we would expect a higher rate of return from our business because there is greater risk compared to the risk-free return of the bonds. Calculating the rate for a given business or investment can be very complex.[47] One method that is often used compares our business to how other similar businesses are valued. For example, one can see how the stock market values those comparable businesses, assuming they are public companies. If other service-type businesses like our window washing business are traded, then by looking at those companies' stock market prices as compared to their earnings we can find a multiplier. For example, if a similar business has a market price of $100 with earnings per share of $20 then the stock market may be valuing the shares at 5 times the earnings

---

[45] Warren Buffet, *The Essays of Warren Buffet: Lessons for Corporate America*, 19 CARDOZO L. REV. 1, 180–87 (1997).

[46] Investors give up the current use of their money for consumption or other investments so they need to be compensated for that opportunity cost. The rate received by investment in United States treasury bonds are considered to be risk free so that rate will compensate investors for opportunity cost and inflation.

[47] The Dividend Discount Model and Capital Asset Pricing Model can also be used to help determine a rate. William Bratton, CORPORATE FINANCE 63–110 (6th ed. 2007).

per share, or a price earnings (P/E) ratio of 5. If our business is comparable, we could use that P/E multiplier to apply to the earnings of the window washing business.[48] A multiplier of 5 suggests a rate of 20% since the multiplier is the inverse of the rate.[49] In our window washing business, at a 20% rate, the business will be valued at 5 times the cash flow.[50]

$$P\ (\$510,000) = \frac{A\ (\$102,000)}{R\ (20\%)}$$

[48] If our business is closely held and the comparable business is publicly traded, there may need to be a marketability discount applied to the valuation of a closely held corporation because there is no liquid market for the shares. Discounts can come up in appraisal proceedings. See § 6.06, note 33, *infra.*

[49] In order to divide R (a fraction) into A we use its reciprocal, e.g., R of 20% is 1/5 and its reciprocal is 5 (our multiplier).

[50] If we apply the P/E ratio which was derived from the market price and reported earnings (not the cash flow) of the comparable business to the cash flow of the window washing business that could be a problem unless the cash flow and earnings were similar in both businesses.

Chapter 5

THE LEGAL MODEL AND CORPORATE GOVERNANCE: THE ALLOCATION OF POWER UNDER STATE LAW

§ 5.01   INTRODUCTION

Under traditional corporate theory, control of a corporation is vested in the board of directors elected by the shareholders. In turn, these directors choose the officers to run the business. Although various constituencies or stakeholders, such as creditors or employees, are affected by how corporations are governed, the primary relationship which has shaped corporate law is between the managers (the officers and directors) and the owners (the shareholders).[1] The possible mismanagement or self dealing by those in control of the corporation is the focus of corporate governance. Issues of corporate governance in publicly traded corporations look to how to minimize this bad behavior. Those issues have often revolved around the shareholders' right to a voice in corporate matters and the monitoring of the managers versus the managers' power to operate the business without shareholder interference. A balance must be struck between the need of shareholders to monitor management's power and the need of the managers to take risks and operate the business effectively.[2]

In publicly traded corporations, different corporate governance issues arise depending on the types of ownership that exist.[3] Many publicly traded corporations have widely dispersed ownership in which no large group of shareholders exercises any control over the selection of the directors. As a result, the directors often manage the corporation with little accountability or direct oversight by the shareholders, thus the control of the corporation is separated from the ownership.[4] This context raises significant issues about how to allow managers to run the business while protecting the shareholders from opportunistic behavior and poor management.

Other publicly traded corporations have a concentration of shareholders that act together to control the business through the election of directors. In these

---

[1] For a discussion of other constituencies, see § 5.02[A] *infra.*

[2] *See generally* Douglas M. Branson, CORPORATE GOVERNANCE (1993); Arthur R. Pinto, *Corporate Governance: Monitoring the Board of Directors in American Corporations*, 46 AM. J. COMP. L. 317 (Supp. 1998).

[3] In closely held corporations, a group of shareholders often controls the corporation by virtue of its ownership and ability to select the directors (that is, the control group). In that context, the issue of governance involves the protection of the minority shareholders from overreaching by the control group, a topic which will be discussed in Chapter 11, *infra.*

[4] For a discussion of separation of ownership from control, see § 5.02[E][1], *infra.* The increasing role of institutional investors in corporate governance arguably has resulted in greater accountability. See § 5.02[E][2], *infra.*

corporations, public shareholders are in a minority position. Some publicly traded corporations are primarily owned by one family (for example, the New York Times Co.). Other publicly traded corporations, called subsidiaries, are controlled by another corporation, called the parent. In both contexts, corporate governance involves protection of minority shareholders from possible self dealing by those in control.[5]

Due to a variety of situations in which the shareholders may be harmed by either acts of the managers or by a control group, some means must be available to protect the shareholders Such protection is not only fair but necessary if corporations are to continue to attract outside equity capital from investors. Without some protection investors would be wary of buying stock. In many cases, market mechanisms may restrain the activities of those who control the business.[6] In addition, there are legal devices that may be used to try to protect shareholders. They include fiduciary duty obligations of managers and control groups, shareholder litigation that enforces the duty, proxy fights to change management or influence policy, hostile tender offers to remove managers, information rights and disclosure requirements which may affect behavior, and an appraisal remedy or dissolution remedy which may be available to permit a cash exit in certain circumstances. There are also monitors designed to protect shareholders such as independent directors, independent accountants, lawyers, investment bankers, the stock markets, and the Securities and Exchange Commission (the "SEC").

§ 5.02   THEMES

This Chapter initially discusses several major themes that relate to the study and development of corporate law and corporate governance. In the study of corporate law, several topics influence legal developments, including the focus of corporate governance, importance of public trading markets, the impact of the Efficient Capital Market Hypothesis, the separation of ownership from control, the role of ownership and the rise of institutional ownership of corporations, the role of independent directors and gatekeepers, the interplay between state and federal law, and the need to adapt the law to both closely held and publicly held corporations.[7] There are also different theories of the firm that will be high-lighted.

A discussion then follows regarding the allocation of power within the corporation, as determined by state law. The Chapter will conclude with a discussion of the Sarbanes-Oxley Act of 2002 passed by Congress in reaction to numerous corporate financial scandals such as Enron and Worldcom.[8]

---

[5] For a discussion of controlling shareholders, see Chapter 10, *infra.*

[6] For a discussion of market mechanisms, see § 5.03[C][2], *infra.*

[7] These themes have also influenced the development of law outside of the United States. *See* Arthur R. Pinto, *The European Union's Shareholder Voting Rights Directive from an American Perspective: Some Comparisons and Observations*, 32 FORDHAM INT'L L.J. 587 (2009) (compares proxy voting in the European Union law to the U.S. and the influences of share ownership, federalism and focus of corporate law).

[8] See the discussion of the Sarbanes-Oxley Act of 2002 at § 5.08, *infra.*

[A] Focus of Corporate Governance and Stakeholders

Because of the importance of publicly traded corporations in society there is a debate over the focus of corporate governance, how power should be allocated and the role of corporate law.[9] The publicly held corporation can be viewed in purely economic terms as a means by which capital is raised from a large number of public savers and used by businesses. Under that focus, corporate governance may focus on the suppliers of capital (creditors and shareholders) and the managers or those who control management. Since shareholders are owners, this view usually gives them primacy.[10] But given the economic significance of these corporations, a broader view has long been advocated by some because the governance of these large economic units have an impact on other interests who do not supply capital to the business, e.g., stakeholders including labor (who invests human capital) and the society where the business operates.[11]

Concern for stakeholders other than shareholders may involve lower profits for the business. In a variety of contexts, courts have identified the primary purpose of the corporation as the making of profits. For example, in *Dodge v. Ford Motor Co.*,[12] ("*Ford*") Henry Ford, who controlled Ford Motor Co. (a closely held corporation), wanted to benefit society by lowering the price of cars and sharing the profits with consumers. He cut back the dividend paid to the shareholders. The court ordered the payment of a dividend to the shareholders, a rare outcome, because such decisions are normally protected by the business judgment rule which limits courts in second guessing business decisions.[13] The court would allow incidental expenditures to benefit society but a corporate

---

[9] *See* Christopher M. Bruner, *The Enduring Ambivalence of Corporate Law*, 59 ALA. L. REV. 1385 (2008) (describes the ambivalence of different theories of shareholder and board power). The focus also relates to different theories of the firm discussed at § 5.03 *infra.*

[10] When a corporation is insolvent, the fiduciary duty shifts to the creditors because insolvency means that there is no equity and the creditors become the owners. The Delaware courts have recognized that there may be some obligation to creditors even prior to actual insolvency but near it. *Credit Lyonnais Bank Nederland, N.V. v. Pathe Communications Corp.*, 1991 WL 277613 (Del. Ch. 1991); 17 Del. J. Corp. L. 1099 (Dec. 30, 1991).

[11] *E.g.*, Organization for Economic Co-Operation and Development, *Principles of Corporate Governance*, 11–13 (2004). The role of stakeholders can be viewed from an external or internal perspective. An external perspective sees stakeholders as outside the internal corporate governance and may suggest that their interests be protected by the concept of corporate social responsibility. In addition, corporations should also be accountable and to account to society for the implications of corporate actions. Cynthia Williams, *Corporate Responsibility in an Era of Economic Globalization*, 35 U.C. DAVIS L. REV. 705, 712–720, 722–724. An internal perspective will look to include stakeholders more directly in corporate governance. *E.g.* Kent Greenfield, *The Place of Workers in Corporate Law*, 39 B.C.L. REV. 283 (1998). Some scholars have suggested viewing the corporation as a team production model where the board serves as a mediating hierarchy among all interests. Margaret Blair & Lynn Stout, *A Team Production Theory of Corporate Law*, 85 VA. L. REV 247 (1999). *See* Amir Licht, *The Maximands of Corporate Governance: A Theory of Values and Cognitive Style*, 29 DEL. J. CORP. L. 649 (2004) (a good discussion of the history of the United States stakeholder debates).

[12] 170 N.W. 668 (Mich. 1919).

[13] For a discussion of the business judgment rule, see § 8.03[B], *infra.*

general purpose to benefit society would be improper.[14] The court emphasized that corporations should be run to generate profits for shareholders. Given the espoused view of Mr. Ford and the failure to argue that potential profits that could result because lowering prices would increase demand, the decision was predictable.[15]

In *Shlensky v. Wrigley*[16] a minority shareholder brought a derivative suit (an action on behalf of the corporation) claiming that the directors of the Chicago Cubs had breached their fiduciary duty because they had not installed stadium lights so that more profitable night baseball games could be played. Plaintiff tried to rely on the *Ford* case claiming that Wrigley, the controlling shareholder, was motivated by his beliefs on what was good for baseball and the neighboring community, not the interests of the shareholders in maximizing profits. Unlike *Ford*, in which the court emphasized the need to make profits and benefit the shareholders, the Illinois court saw the issue as matter of business policy which was untainted by fraud, illegality or self dealing. Further the concerns for the neighborhood could possibly benefit the baseball park and the corporation in the long term. The court recognized that while the decision may be wrong, there was no dereliction of duty (no self dealing or negligence in directors making the decision). It was not up to the courts to second guess directors because their legal decisions are presumed to be in good faith. The Ford case may be distinguished from *Shlensky* because in *Ford* the large amount of money was being withheld as dividends and the problems of the minority shareholders in a closely held corporation, needing a return on their investment.[17] However, the tone of the *Shlensky* case gives directors broad discretion in making business decisions and in considering interests other than those of the shareholders.

Over the years, there have been attempts by groups to change the board of directors to include representatives of different constituencies or the public interest. Rarely have these attempts made any progress.[18] Attempts by stakeholders like labor to change or modify corporate activities have been more successful when they act as shareholders and have submitted proposals on social

---

[14] Some corporations go public with an announced social policy and investors know in advance when deciding to invest. For example Ben and Jerry's ice cream company donated 7.5% of its profits to philanthropy and supported local Vermont farms. http://www.benjerry.com/our_company.

[15] It is also possible to view Mr. Ford's activity as ultra vires because the purpose of a corporation was to make profits. For a discussion of ultra vires, see § 1.10 *supra*.

[16] 237 N.E.2d 776 (Ill. 1968).

[17] When a controlling shareholder treats minority shareholders unfairly in a closely held corporation courts may be more likely to scrutinize the business. For a discussion of heightened scrutiny in closely held corporations see § 11.07[B] *infra*.

[18] There may be some labor representatives on boards where employee stock ownership (ESOP) is significant. *See* The National Center for Employee Ownership, *A Comprehensive Overview of ESOPs, Stock Options, and Employee Ownership* (2005), *available at* http://www.nceo.org/library/overview.html. Labor has not generally sought representation on the board. A rare example is when Chrysler had a labor representative on its board as a result of its precarious financial situation in the 1970's. Eventually labor wanted to be off the board and preferred collective bargaining with management. When Daimler-Benz, a German company, merged with Chrysler, a representative of American labor was placed on their Supervisory Board where German labor under German law has one half the seats. Allowing labor on the board in Germany is called co-determination.

issues through the federal proxy rules.[19] Even in that context, a proposal needs to be within the power of the corporation to effectuate.

When some publicly traded corporations have been subject to a hostile takeover (because directors oppose the takeover)[20] the directors have argued that in considering the takeover, there should be consideration of the impact of the takeover on other constituencies, such as creditors and employees who may be harmed by the reorganization or financing of the corporation after it is acquired. As a result, the managers should be given greater power to oppose the takeover. Others view these arguments as an attempt to protect the directors from losing their jobs rather then protecting constituencies. The Delaware Supreme Court had expressed concern for these other constituencies but also has indicated that while "concern for various corporate constituencies is proper when addressing a takeover threat, that principle is limited by the requirement that there be some rationally related benefit accruing to the shareholders." However, such concern for non-stockholder interests is inappropriate when an auction among active bidders is in progress, and the object no longer is to protect or maintain the corporate enterprise but to sell it to the "highest bidder."[21]

Many states have gone further and enacted statutes which attempt to broaden the fiduciary duty of directors to consider other constituencies in exercising their power. The impact of these statutes remains uncertain because it is unclear whether they will be broadly or narrowly interpreted and used.[22]

It is interesting to note that other well developed capitalist systems have a different attitude toward stakeholders other than shareholders. For example, in Germany, employee participation in corporate decision making is the norm. German law requires labor representation on a corporation's supervisory board.[23] In Japan, lifetime employment for workers affects business decisions which may not be directly beneficial to the shareholders.[24] In the United States

---

[19] If anything labor's role in corporate governance is through their pension funds acting as shareholders. *See, e.g.*, Mary Williams Walsh and Jonathon D. Glater, *Pension Fund Trustees Taking Aim at Safeway*, N.Y. TIMES, March 26, 2004, at C4. For a discussion of shareholder proposals, see §§ 5.05[C][3] and 7.05, *infra*.

[20] A hostile takeover may often start as a hostile tender offer where the bidder offers to buy the shares directly from the shareholders. For a discussion of hostile tender offers and fiduciary duty, see § 12.05, *infra*.

[21] *Revlon Inc. v. MacAndrews & Forbes Holdings, Inc.*, 506 A.2d 173, 183 (Del. 1985).

[22] Some of these enactments only apply when there is a change of control and the managers are allowed to consider these other interests in that context. Other statutes are applicable in broader contexts. *See generally* Roberta Karmel, *Implications of the Stakeholders Model*, 61 GEO. WASH. L. REV. 1156 (1993); Lawrence Mitchell, *A Theoretical Framework for Enforcing Corporate Constituency Statutes*, 70 TEX. L. REV. 579 (1992). These statutes may be more about protecting management from a hostile takeover than about protecting shareholders. For a discussion of state statutes and hostile tender offers, see § 12.07, *infra*.

[23] In Germany there are two boards: a supervisory board and a management board. The former has few management functions but does select and supervise the management.

[24] *See generally* Mark J. Roe, STRONG MANAGERS AND WEAK OWNERS (1994).

public corporations are concerned about issues of social responsibility[25] but shareholder primacy greatly influences policy, theories of the firm and the law.[26]

[B]   Publicly Held Corporation

The United States has the largest number of publicly traded corporations in the world. The style of ownership of many corporations, particularly larger corporations, consists of numerous widely dispersed shareholders who trade their shares in the stock markets. In addition to a public market for shares, there are also public markets for corporate debt. As a result, corporations can borrow from the public as an alternative to bank lending. Having a public market provides corporations with an alternative to private financing of the business.

While the vast majority of business entities in the United States are either sole proprietorships, partnerships or closely held corporations,[27] the publicly held corporation remains a significant economic actor in the United States economy.[28] As of the end of 2003, there were approximately 6,900 publicly held corporations traded on the three major United States stock markets with a market capitalization of more than $14 trillion.[29] These corporations are not only major employers and taxpayers with a significant impact on the United States economy, but also are an important repository for the savings of United States citizens. More than half — 51.9 percent — of households owned stock as of 2001.[30]

[C]   The Stock Markets

Given the number of publicly held companies and shareholders, there is an extensive market for the trading of shares. For example, in 2002, there were more than 2,700 corporations listed on the New York Stock Exchange, the largest and most significant centralized trading market in the United States. During 2003, more than 350 billion shares were traded annually with a daily volume of approximately $39 billion.[31] There are also over-the-counter markets

---

[25] For a discussion of corporate social responsibility, see § 1.10[A] *infra.*

[26] For a discussion of the influential law and economics approach to law see § 5.03[C] *infra.*

[27] In 2004, there were about 5.5 million corporations doing business in the United States. *See Statistical Abstract of the United States, Table 721, Number of Returns, Receipts, and Net Income by Type of Business,* 1990–2004 (2008).

[28] Corporations during 2001 accounted for 60 percent of U.S. gross domestic product (GDP). The Economic Report of the President (2003) at 73.

[29] Information from the NASDAQ (www.NASDAQ.com) and New York Stock Exchange (www.NYSE.com) websites. Based on SEC filings, there may be close to 16,000 public corporations. *See* text at note 19, § 7.02, *infra.*

[30] The Economic Report of the President (2003) at 73 Fewer than one-third of U.S. households (31.6 percent) owned corporate stock directly or indirectly in 1989. By 1992 that number had grown to 36.7 percent. "The greatest percentage-point increases in household stock ownership appear to have occurred in groups where it was lowest at the start of the decade, for example among households with moderate rather than high levels of income." *Id.*

[31] New York Stock Exchange, *Fact Book Data* (2003).

in which trading is done between dealers acting for customers or for their own accounts.[32]

All of these trading markets are called secondary markets. Secondary markets involve trading among investors and do not usually involve sales by the corporation itself. The sale of shares by corporations to the public is usually accomplished through direct sales by the corporation using underwriters to sell to investors.[33] These secondary markets provide liquidity for investors (that is, the ability to sell quickly when the need for cash arises or conditions change), which reduces their risk. Investors who know that they can easily liquidate their investment because there is a ready market are more likely to purchase securities. In addition the lower risk to investors means the corporations can sell their shares at higher prices. This facilitates the raising of capital for corporations.[34]

The development of publicly traded corporations in America and the growth of the stock markets may be viewed as a natural result of economic growth. As the nation expanded and technology grew, capital was needed to finance this expansion. Instead of raising capital from private lenders, companies sold debt and shares to the public (i.e., went public).[35] Businesses were operated by professional managers who supplied expertise while the public passively supplied capital.[36] Politics may have also limited large private institutions such as banks and insurance companies from owning large amounts of shares.[37]

---

[32] The NASDAQ is the primary over-the-counter market. The over-the-counter market is a dealers' market in which the dealers compete with each other to make the market by offering to buy or sell shares. Customers' orders are designed to go to the dealer offering the best price. The New York Stock Exchange was traditionally an auction market where customers' orders are handled centrally through specialists responsible for keeping the trading orderly (similar to an auction). *See generally* Norman Poser, *Restructuring the Stock Market: A Critical Look at the SEC's National Market System*, 56 N.Y.U. L. Rev. 884 (1981). The NYSE now operates both with a specialist system and electronic trading side by side.

[33] For a description of the process see § 7.03, *infra*.

[34] The public market can also lower the cost of raising money. *See* note 42, *infra*.

[35] Companies may also go public by selling shares of the original investors, entrepreneurs and workers who have built the company, allowing the initial investors to cash in on their investment. With the liquidity of the stock markets, investors can sell their shares more easily, gaining a return on their investment. When a corporation offers to sell its own shares to raise capital that is called a primary offering while the sale of the shares of others is a secondary offering.

[36] This specialization can be beneficial. For a discussion on separation of ownership from control, see § 5.02[E][1] *infra*.

[37] Mark J. Roe, STRONG MANAGERS, WEAK OWNERS 3–8 (1994). Professor Roe has argued that political considerations limited large financial institutions such as banks, mutual funds and insurance companies from owning large stakes in corporations. Thus, there was a need to raise capital from the public markets. Analysis of the history of American corporations also uncovers other reasons for the creation of public markets. *See* Michael C. Jensen, *Eclipse of the Public Corporation*, 67 HARV. BUS. REV. 61 (1989).

[1]   Benefits of Stock Markets

Public markets provide numerous investment choices, allowing the public to purchase shares in different companies. This makes diversification of investment possible and discourages concentrated ownership. Diversification is beneficial because investors reduce their risks by buying a portfolio of different investments, rather than concentrating ownership.[38] By not owning a large percentage of shares of any one corporation, the shareholders remain passive investors. These shareholders are unlikely to want to incur expenses related to monitoring managers if they do not own a significant amount of shares in that corporation.[39]

The sale of securities to the public provides corporations with significant capital for modernization or expansion. In 2003, approximately $2.7 trillion was raised in public security offerings of debt and equity.[40]

The ability to raise capital from the public provides corporations an alternative to private funds which may provide greater flexibility in financing. For example, if a business needs to raise capital, it may borrow or issue equity. The business may also choose to sell securities privately, or to sell to a large number of public investors in a public offering. If it is an initial public offering then it results in a trading market for the security. The public markets benefit corporations because the corporation's cost of selling securities through a public offering may be lower than through a private sale. While transaction costs increase in the public sale,[41] the corporation's overall cost of its public debt or equity is generally lower than it would be in a private sale because the trading market provides investors with liquidity. Liquidity lessens the risk to investors. An investor who buys an investment privately knows she cannot easily sell it. She can expect to be compensated for that greater risk by a greater rate of return. A business which can offer investors a trading market in which investments can be easily sold need not compensate investors for that risk. This could result in lower costs to the company which lowers its cost of capital compared to private financing.[42] But markets have the disadvantage of being

---

[38] By buying different shares, one reduces one's risk since different shares move in different directions. For example, owning shares in both an umbrella company and a suntan lotion manufacturer reduces the risk that either a rainy or sunny period will ruin one's investment. This risk which can be diversified away is called unsystematic risk or unique risk. If fully diversified in different shares, the only risk for the investor is overall market performance, which is called systematic or market risk.

[39] For a discussion of passivity and the collective action problem, see § 5.05[C][4], *infra.*

[40] Andrew Sorkin, *Merger Renaissance a Good Possibility in the Coming Year*, N.Y. TIMES, Jan. 1, 2004 at C1.

[41] Such costs include the expenses of lawyers, accountants and underwriters required under the Securities Act of 1933. For a discussion of the process of going public, see § 7.03, *infra.*

[42] For example, assume a corporation needs to borrow funds. Assume a bank will charge 12% interest after considering the risk, future inflation and opportunity costs of the loan. If the corporation could sell its debt to the public, it may be able to lower its interest rate to 11%, an amount public lenders in the market may be willing to accept and which reflects the lower risk assumed by the lenders considering their ability to more easily sell the debt in the market, i.e., liquidity. Without liquidity and investor will require to be compensated for the increased risk which in our example means 12%. The savings to the corporation in selling publicly traded securities lowers its cost of

volatile and at times may not provide capital.[43]

[2]   Shareholder Protection and Stock Markets

In addition to providing liquidity which encourages public investment, the trading markets also protect shareholders. The markets, such as the New York Stock Exchange and the National Association of Securities Dealers ("NASD," which runs the over-the-counter market, called "NASDAQ") enact rules and enforce them on issues involving both corporate governance and trading such as disclosure, fair-trading practices, fraud, market manipulation and insider trading for corporations listed on those markets. For example, an important corporate governance rule requires most corporations listed on the New York Stock Exchange or NASDAQ to have a majority of independent outside directors (that is, who are not full time employees of the corporation).[44] In addition, there must be a separate auditing committee of the board, (which selects the accounting firm that prepares the financial statements and reviews those statements), a compensation committee, and a nominating committee, all made up of independent directors.[45]

[D]   The Efficient Capital Market Hypothesis

The stock markets are also significant because the active trading of shares provides a market mechanism to monitor the running of the business. The share price set by the market can be a benchmark for the performance of the business and its management. In order for the share price to serve that purpose, the shares must trade in an efficient market, that is, the share price reflects all available information. The Efficient Capital Market Hypothesis ("ECMH") postulates that the numerous active traders in the stock market react quickly and efficiently to information.[46] Thus, whenever new information is available about a company, it is immediately reflected in the price of the shares.[47]

---

capital for example from 12% to 11% which saves the corporation money.

[43] Capital markets often have a short term perspective and can be volatile and create speculative bubbles. The high tech boom of the 1990s in the United States and subsequent market crash is an example. But the markets also can respond quickly and adapt easier. Bank centered finance can take a longer term view and provide capital in times when markets are volatile. But banks can be subject to political influence, overinvest and can also not react as quickly to changes in assets market value. The Asian financial crisis in the 1990s is an example. *When Capital Markets Rule* THE ECONOMIST, May 3 2001.

[44] New York Stock Exchange, *Listed Company Manual* § 303A (2003). For a discussion of independence, see § 5.02[F] *infra*.

[45] *Id.* Some of these and other requirements were the result of recent scandals. *See* § 5.08, *infra*.

[46] *See* James H. Lorie, Peter Dodd & Mary Kempton, THE STOCK MARKET: THEORIES AND EVIDENCE 55–87 (2d ed. 1985); *see also* Christopher Paul Saari, *The Efficient Capital Market Hypothesis, Economic Theory and the Regulation of the Securities Industry*, 29 STAN. L. REV. 1031 (1977). It would be like having an auction involving the sale of a Rembrandt painting, and every expert is in the room bidding on the Rembrandt. The price of that Rembrandt would be an efficient price because all available information about that Rembrandt would be there and reflected in the price.

[47] Economists describe the markets as having different degrees of efficiency. The weak form indicates that the price of shares reflects all past information. The semi-strong form of the market argues that both past and present public information is reflected in the price. The strong form

According to the ECMH, the only factor that will change the value of a company's shares is new information because the current share price contains all currently available information.[48] Thus, the share price in an efficient market can reflect how well a corporation is run.

There are many arguments against the usefulness of the ECMH.[49] Some attack the studies underlying the ECMH as inconclusive. Others view the ECMH as applying only to shares that are widely traded and followed.[50] There have also been certain trading strategies with which investors have beat the market on a regular basis — something that, according the the ECMH, should not consistently happen if the market is truly efficient. Although the market is also made up of rational profit maximizers under ECMH, behavioral finance studies have pointed out that the market can be influenced by psychological factors and often moves irrationally where investors act with the flow of the market like a "herd" or by irrational "noise" trading.[51] Another argument states that even though the markets may be efficient in the trading of shares, the resulting price of the shares from daily trades does not necessarily reflect the value of the corporation as a whole.[52]

---

suggests that past, present and private information is reflected in the price. Empirical evidence has generally supported the semi-strong theory. For an excellent discussion of ECMH, *see* Richard A. Brealey and Stewart C. Myers, PRINCIPLES OF CORPORATE FINANCE, 354–376 (6th ed. 2000).

[48] Since available information is already reflected in the share price and moves only on new information, prices move randomly, that is, the past cannot predict the future movement. Thus, attempts to predict future share price movements by studying past trends or information should be unsuccessful. *See* Burton G. Malkiel, A RANDOM WALK DOWN WALL STREET (9th ed. 2007); J. Lorie & M. Hamilton, THE STOCK MARKET: THEORIES AND EVIDENCE 70–97 (1973).

[49] *See generally* William Bratton, CORPORATE FINANCE 149–171 (2003).

[50] *See* William K. S. Wang, *Some Arguments That The Stock Market Is Not Efficient*, 19 U.C. DAVIS L. REV. 341 (1986); Lynn A Stout, *The Unimportance of Being Efficient: An Economic Analysis of Stock Market Pricing and Securities Regulation*, 87 MICH. L. REV. 613 (1988).

[51] *See* Robert Schiller, *Do Stock Prices Move Too Much to be Justified by Subsequent Changes in Dividends?* 71 AM. ECON. REV. 421 (1981). A new approach too finance looks to psychology to demonstrate that people are not always rational in their decisions. *See, e.g.,* Andrei Shleifer, INEFFICIENT MARKETS: AN INTRODUCTION TO BEHAVIORAL FINANCE (2000).

[52] *See* Louis Lowenstein, *Pruning Deadwood In Hostile Takeovers: A Proposal For Legislation*, 83 COLUM. L. REV. 249, 274–76 (1983). Some theorists argue that the stock market may be speculatively efficient (that by trading, one cannot beat the market, i.e., there are no bargins) but not necessarily allocatively efficient (that the price reflects the true value and creates the right investment of funds, i.e., prices react correctly). *See* Jeffrey Gordon & Lewis Kornhauser, *Efficient Markets, Costly Information, and Securities Research*, 60 N.Y.U. L. REV. 761 (1985).

The ECMH has had a significant impact on corporate law issues[53] and monitoring mechanisms[54] and has been influential in the debate over what corporate governance rules are best. For example, some commentators argue that a hostile takeover monitors bad management by removing it. Assume that a corporation's shares are trading at $15 a share in an efficient market. An outsider offers to buy the corporation for $20 a share, a substantial premium over the market price. The managers refuse the offer, possibly for fear of losing their jobs if the ownership shifts, or because they generally believe the price to be unfair. The outsider may offer to buy the shares from the shareholders directly in a hostile tender offer. If the $15 price in an efficient market truly reflects the current value of the company, then the business should be sold for the higher price of $20 a share.[55] However, if the market is not so efficient, or the daily pricing of shares does not reflect the value of the corporation as a whole, then it may be ultimately more valuable not to sell the company. Thus, how one views hostile tender offers may depend upon the impact of the ECMH.[56]

[E]   Role of Ownership

Share ownership is a significant influence on the development of corporate law and publicly traded corporations. There are three particular aspects of share ownership that can play a role. They are the separation of ownership from control in many corporations, the increased role of large institutional investors and the political significance of share ownership.

[1]   The Berle-Means Corporation-Separation of Ownership from Control

In many publicly traded corporations, there are a large number of widely dispersed shareholders so there is no large shareholder to monitor the business.[57] Professors Berle and Means, in their landmark book THE MODERN

---

[53] For example, an efficient market in which information is quickly assimilated into the price of shares also suggests that investors are unable to beat the market on a consistent basis. Thus, shareholders should buy a portfolio of shares to diversify and maximize their return. Diversification is discussed in § 5.02[B][1] *supra.* If owning a diversified portfolio is the norm, some would argue that this reality should be considered in making corporate rules which might be fashioned to maximize the value of the portfolio and overall corporate interests as opposed to shareholder interests in a specific corporation. *See generally* Frank Easterbrook & Daniel Fischel, *Proper Role of Target's Management in Responding To a Tender Offer*, 94 HARV. L. REV. 1161, 1165–74 (1981).

[54] For a discussion of market mechanisms including the stock market to monitor, see § 5.03[C][2], *infra.*

[55] The $5 premium could reflect the increased value the outsider can bring to the business or a control premium for the ability to control the business.

[56] For a discussion of hostile tender offers, see Chapter 12, *infra.*

[57] The United States story is more complex. There are significant publicly traded corporations in which there is a control group and the public are minority shareholders. They range from traditional family owned businesses like the major newspapers (New York Times and Washington Post) to high tech companies (Microsoft and Google) where control remains in the original owners. It may be more accurate to describe the Unite States publicly traded corporation as a mixture of both dispersed and concentrated owners. *See* Ronald Anderson & David M. Reeb, *Founding Family Ownership and*

CORPORATION AND PRIVATE PROPERTY (1932), studied the publicly traded corporations at that time. They found that many publicly traded corporations had a dispersion of ownership in which no single shareholder owned a large number of shares, which meant a "separation of ownership from control."[58] Ownership usually implies control, but without a concentration of ownership in shares,[59] managers who control corporate assets, information and the voting mechanisms are in de facto control of the corporation with little oversight by the owners, i.e., the shareholders. Because of the vacuum created by the separation of ownership from control, management of many large corporations has become self perpetuating.[60]

The separation of ownership and control is beneficial when the managers operate the business in ways that benefit the shareholders. The idea is that managers serve as specialists who use their expertise to increase the value of the firm while the shareholders are passive investors who are diversified and supply large amounts of capital and seeking the gains from increases in value of the business.[61] On the other hand, if managers unfairly self deal or mismanage the business, the shareholders may suffer losses or insufficient gains. Much of corporate law in the United States focuses on balancing the costs and benefits of this separation and utilizing the different monitoring devices available to protect shareholders from losses resulting from the separation of ownership from control.[62]

Firm Performance: Evidence from the S&P 500, J. FIN. (forthcoming), *available at* http://papers.ssrn.com/sol3/papers.cfm?abstract_id=365260 (significant family ownership and presence in about 1/3 of the S & P 500 firms); Ronald Anderson, Augustine Duru & David M. Reeb, *Founders, Heirs, and Corporate Opacity in the U.S.*, J. FIN. ECON. (JFE) (forthcoming), *available at* http://papers.ssrn.com/sol3/papers.cfm?abstract_id=1142346 (in 2,000 largest industrial U.S. firms, founder and heir ownership in 22% and 25% of these firms, respectively).

[58] For example, in 1986 General Motors repurchased the shares of its largest shareholder at the time, H. Ross Perot, who owned shares representing only .08% of its common shares. *Grobow v. Perot*, 539 A.2d 180, 184 (Del. 1988).

[59] There are legitimate reasons why shareholders choose not to concentrate their ownership or be actively involved in management. Shareholders often limit their investment in one corporation in order to diversify their investment and lessen the risk that any one investment may not prove successful. Shareholder passivity and the difficulty of collective action further contributes to the power managers have over the corporation. *See* the discussion at § 5.05[C][4], *infra*. Aside from economic reasons, there may be legal and political reasons why concentration of ownership is not favored. For example, legal rules that restrict share ownership by large financial institutions such as banks and insurance companies. *See generally* Mark Roe, STRONG MANAGERS, WEAK OWNERS (1994).

[60] For a discussion of the collective action problem of shareholders, see § 5.05[C][4], *infra*.

[61] For a discussion of passivity and diversification, see § 5.02[C][1], *supra*.

[62] While in the United States the separation of ownership from control is significant, in most countries where there are publicly traded corporations, one finds a controlling shareholder so that the public shareholders are in the minority. The explanations for the difference are many, including different legal systems, cultural differences and politics. *See* Arthur R. Pinto, *Globalization and the Study of Corporate Governance*, 23 WIS. INT'L. L.J. 477 (2005) This difference has an impact on the legal rules established. *See generally* THE LEGAL BASIS OF COMPARATIVE CORPORATE GOVERNANCE IN PUBLICLY-HELD CORPORATIONS (Arthur R. Pinto and Gustavo Visientini eds. 1998).

[2]   Institutional Investors

For most of this century the ownership of shares of publicly traded corporations was primarily in the hands of private individuals. Corporate law was influenced by and recognized this primacy. In the last several decades, the ownership of shares has shifted to large institutions consisting of private and public pension funds, insurance companies, foundations, hedge funds,[63] universities, brokerage firms, bank trust companies and mutual funds.[64] This trend is very significant for corporate governance. While the Berle-Means model of widely dispersed owners continues, institutional ownership means that those owners now hold a larger number of shares representing a big dollar investment (albeit a small ownership percentage) compared to individuals. If these institutions act collectively, they can influence their corporations.

In the past, shareholders disappointed with their investment would follow the "Wall Street Rule" and sell their shares rather than try to influence corporate behavior i.e., choosing exit over voice. With the concentration of ownership, certain large institutional investors (particularly public pension funds) have become more active in the corporations whose shares they own.[65] Large investors may also find that exiting through quick sales may be difficult. They may also find that more active influence may be more profitable if they can influence managers to increase share value.[66] Generally union and public pension funds and some hedge funds are considered the most active institutions on corporate governance issues.[67] This development has already had an impact on many of the issues discussed and will continue to influence the development of corporate law.[68]

---

[63] A hedge fund is a private investment fund that has different strategies to try to earn a greater return than other investment vehicles. The idea of a hedge is to take positions to offset your risk but many of these funds do not hedge. Some funds have a strategy of pressuring corporations to implement changes to increase share value.

[64] U.S. institutional investors as a whole have increased their share of U.S. equity markets to 51.4% of total U.S. equities in the year 2000 then to 61.2% of total U.S. equities in 2005. The Conference Board, U.S. *Institutional Investors Continue to Boost Ownership of U.S. Corporations* (Jan. 22, 2007).

[65] *See* Bernard S. Black, *Agents Watching Agents: The Promise of Institutional Investor Voice*, 39 U.C.L.A. L. Rev. 811 (1992). The control of institutions also raises issues of agency costs and the ability to monitor the monitors. *Id.* at 850–52.

[66] While increased monitoring may lower agency costs, there are costs to both the shareholders and the corporation associated with the exercise of influence. For example, management fears that too much shareholder involvement will adversely affect their freedom to manager and take risks and thus hurt the business. There is also a concern that if institutions become too involved in the management of the company, they could be liable for either violating insider trading rules or as a control person under federal securities laws.

[67] *See* Thomas W. Briggs, *Corporate Governance and the New Hedge Fund Activism: An Empirical Analysis*, 32 Iowa J. Corp. L. 681 (2007) (discusses the increased activism of hedge funds).

[68] In 1992 the SEC modified the proxy rules to facilitate communications between institutional investors without full compliance with the proxy rules. See § 7.04[C][2], *infra*; Thomas W. Briggs, *Shareholder Activism and Insurgency Under the Proxy Rules*, 50 Bus. Law. 99 (1994). See § 8.03[B], *infra*. The Private Securities Litigation Act of 1995 provided for a lead plaintiff provision with the idea that institutions with large shareholdings should exercise control over class action litigation. *See*

There has been some discussion of relational investing, which recognizes the possibility of a long term relationship between a corporation and large shareholders. But the growth of institutional ownership does not mean that any one institution is likely to dominate the ownership of a corporation. There are a large number of these institutions, many of which are not interested in either increased activity or ownership, because it would mean increased costs that might not produce benefits.[69]

Some large institutional investors try to influence corporate decisions through voting, meetings with managers and exerting pressure for change on independent directors. For example, shareholder proposals supported by institutional investors have suggested that directors modify or drop anti-takeover devices, change compensation policy or strengthen corporate governance mechanisms.[70]

[3]   Political Significance of Share Ownership

The political voice of shareholders can play a significant role in the development of corporate law. A large number of households own shares directly or indirectly.[71] The savings and pensions of a substantial number of people are dependent upon the stock markets.[72] As a result of the greater financial stake of US families in share ownership, issues of corporate governance in the US can become significant political issues and an impetus for regulation. For example, the corporate scandals at Enron, Worldcom and other public corporations led to the quick federal passage of Sarbanes-Oxley[73]

---

generally Jill E. Fisch, *Class Action Reform: Lessons from Securities Litigation*, 39 Ariz. L. Rev. 533 (1997).

[69] *See generally* Ian Ayres & Peter Crampton, *Relational Investing and Agency Theory*, 15 Cardozo L. Rev. 1033 (1994); Jill Fisch, *Relationship Investing: Will It Happen? Will It Work?*, 55 Ohio St. L. J. 1009 (1994).

[70] For a discussion of proxy fights to change policy, see § 5.05[C][3], *infra*. *See* John C. Coffee, Jr., *The Bylaw Battlefield: Can Institutions Change the Outcome of Corporate Control Contests?*, 51 U. Miami L. Rev. 605 (1997) (discussion of whether institutional investors can mandate action on issues involving corporate control contests).

[71] *See* note 30 *supra; e.g.*, Profile of Mutual Fund Shareholders (ICI) (2008), 4, http://www.ici.org/stats/res/rpt_profile08.pdf (". . . at the end of 2007, more than two in five U.S. households own mutual funds, representing more than 88 million individual fund shareholders. Furthermore, mutual fund holdings represent a significant component of the savings and investments of many American households, with mutual fund assets now accounting for more than one-fifth of all U.S. households' financial assets."). "The largest percentage of mutual fund-owning households, 80 percent, own equity funds." *Id.* at 1.

[72] *E.g.* The National Center for Employee Ownership,. *New Data Show Widespread Employee Ownership in U.S.*, (2007) http://www.nceo.org/library/widespread.html ("New data from the General Social Survey show that 20 million American workers own stock in their company through a 401(k) plan, ESOP, direct stock grant, or similar plan, while 10.6 million hold stock options. That means that 17% of the total workforce, but 34.9% of those who work for companies that have stock, own stock through some kind of benefit plan, while 9.3% of the workforce, but 18.6% of those in companies with stock, hold options."). *The US Retirement Market 2007*, ICI Research Fundamentals, vol. 17 number 3, http://www.ici.org/stats/mf/fm-v17n3.pdf (over half of Americans retirement savings are held in IRAs and Defined contribution plans representing 52% of retirement assets compared to 39% in 1990).

[73] For a discussion of Sarbanes-Oxley, see § 5.08 *infra*.

reflected the importance of shareholder protection from both a political and economic perspective.

[F]   Independent Directors

Many of the recent corporate governance proposals have centered around proposals to strengthen boards of directors through the use of independent directors.[74] State corporate law does not require independent directors. Publicly traded corporations have inside directors who are also officers of the corporation, and now must have a majority of independent outside directors under stock market rules.[75] Advocates hope that a truly independent, board of directors will function to monitor managers and protect the public shareholders.[76] There have been examples in the past of independent directors acting to make major changes, including the replacement of the president or chief executive officer and creation of standards of conduct for the board.[77] But there are also many examples of the independent directors' failure to monitor.[78]

Independent directors are not only important as monitors to protect shareholders but have an important legal role to play under state law because their involvement may affect how courts scrutinize board activities.[79] Boards have both inside and outside directors. When referring to independent directors it usually means that they are outside (i.e., do not work full time for the

---

[74] Jeffrey N. Gordon *The Rise of Independent Directors in the United States, 1950–2005: Of Shareholder Value and Stock Market Prices* 59 STAN. L. REV. 1465 (2007).

[75] Stock market rules require a majority of independent directors for publicly traded corporations without a 50% or more controlling shareholder. *E.g.*, NYSE, Inc., Listed Company Manual § 303A.02 (2004). The rules have specific tests on what constitutes independence, although the board is required to make a general determination that directors are independent, Section 303A(2)(b) lists several relationships that would prevent a director from being independent. *See also* § 5.02 *supra.* Prior to this requirement of a majority of independent directors, some public corporations had them anyway. There are several explanations for this phenomenon. Investors may prefer corporations with some independent directors and corporations may use these directors to attract investors (that is, a bonding cost under agency theory). In addition, independent directors may change the legal standard used when courts apply standards of fiduciary duty. For an example of the use of independent directors and judicial scrutiny, see note 79, *infra.*

[76] *See* Ira M. Millstein, *The Professional Board*, 50 BUS. LAW. 1427 (1995); James M. Tobin, *The Squeeze on Directors — Inside Is Out*, 49 BUS. LAW. 1707 (1994).

[77] In the early 1990s, heads of several major corporations, including General Motors, Kodak, American Express, Sears, Westinghouse and IBM, were replaced by the directors. This unusual development involved pressures from institutional investors. Mark J. Roe, STRONG MANAGERS WEAK OWNERS: THE POLITICAL ROOTS OF AMERICAN CORPORATE GOVERNANCE vii-ix (1994).

[78] The corporations involved in the scandals that took place in 2001 usually had independent directors. Enron had a majority of seemingly well qualified independent directors which failed to monitor. For a discussion of the scandals, see § 5.08, *infra.*

[79] For example, the deferential business judgment rule which limits judicial scrutiny would not apply if a majority of the directors are either interested in the transaction or lacked independence. For a discussion of the rule, see § 8.03[C], *infra.* Other contexts where the role of independent directors may affect judicial scrutiny will be discussed in different chapters and include interested directors transactions and other conflict of interest issues (see § 9.03[B], *infra*), control transactions (see § 10.04[A], *infra*), responses to hostile tender offers (see § 12.05[A][2], *infra*), and the demand requirement and special litigation committees used in derivative suits (see §§ 14.05, 14.06, *infra*).

corporation),[80] disinterested (i.e., receive nothing from the transaction at issue different from what the shareholders or the corporation receive) and independent (i.e., no relationship to the interested director that would make him or her unable to be impartial).[81] Under Delaware law independence is factual and contextual requiring an inquiry of whether a particular director is controlled by another either through domination or control. Domination can result from personal or familial ties, force of will or when a director is beholden to the interested party.[82] In many cases the courts give a presumption of independence that may be difficult to overcome without strong evidence of bias.[83] But even with a director meeting all the legal tests of independence, it does not necessarily mean that the director will in fact act independently. That raises issues of who ends up on boards and the group dynamics that limit a real independent role by directors.[84]

The problems with reliance on an independent board to monitor are that independent directors are often identified for election by the inside directors and challenges to elections are rare. Thus, there may be personal or professional relationships that do not create a legal conflict of interest but can create bias. Other problems with reliance on an independent board include the control of corporate information by insiders, a lack of economic incentive to further the financial well-being of the corporation, and the limitations of part time status. These issues limit the independence of board members or infringe on their ability to truly monitor insiders.

Reform proposals have focused on increasing the involvement of independent directors, using a lead independent director who may have the power to convene

---

[80] The A.L.I. recognizes that some directors may be outside directors but not independent. Directors that have a "significant relationship" with the senior executives of the corporation will not be considered independent for purposes of some of their rules. Former employees, family members, recipients of commercial payments in excess of $200,000, legal advisors, etc. are included. A.L.I Corp. Gov. Proj. § 1.34.

[81] *Orman v. Cullman*, 794 A.2d 5 (Del. Ch. 2002). Independence means that the director's decision is based upon the merits and not on extraneous considerations or influences. The director must not be beholden or controlled by the interested director. The fact a director is nominated or elected by the controlling shareholder does not mean a lack of independence when dealing with the controlling shareholder. *Aronson v. Lewis*, 473 A.2d 805 (Del. 1984). Delaware requires a subjective test, i.e., an actual director as opposed to reasonable director standard, in determining whether a particular director's interest was material to a transaction or lacked independence for being controlled by the interested party. *Cinerama v. Technicolor*, 663 A.2d. 1156 (Del. Sup. Ct. 1995).

[82] *Orman, supra.* One may be beholden if the controlling shareholder has the unilateral power to decide if the director receives a material benefit which may be financial or otherwise material to him or her and that its loss may create a reason to question whether he or she can objectively consider the transaction at issue. *Id.*

[83] The reluctance to use non-economic factors to compromise independence may stem from the need for boards to act cohesively and collegially. Courts may be hesitant to substitute their judgment for the shareholders who elected the directors. *See generally* Leo Strine, *Derivative Impact? Some Early Reflections on the Corporation Law Implications of the Enron Debacle*, 57 BUS. LAW. 1371 (2002) (discusses how Delaware courts deal with independence and suggest the need for more careful scrutiny post Enron and other corporate scandals).

[84] Behavioral economics may have a role to play in determining legal standards for directors. See § 5.03[C][5], *infra.*

the independent directors in executive session.[85] Some proposals envision the separation of the position of the chief executive officer from the chairman of the board, who should be an independent director,[86] and increased share ownership and compensation (including stock options) for independent directors, in hopes of aligning their interests with the shareholders.[87]

[G]   Gatekeepers

In addition to legal and market mechanisms intended to limit mismanagement or fraud, the regulatory system also relies on outside parties or gatekeepers who may vouch for the corporation or specific transactions. The principal gatekeepers are independent accountants, credit rating agencies,[88] investment banks and outside counsel. Since these gatekeepers have their reputations to uphold, it is believed that they will not sacrifice that reputation to assist a client in wrongdoing. Corporate scandals beginning with Enron called into question the effectiveness of these gatekeepers.[89] One of the aims of the Sarbanes-Oxley Act of 2002 was to strengthen the role of these gatekeepers.[90]

The role of independent accountants is very important in publicly traded corporations. All such corporations are required to have their financial statements audited by an independent accountant, who certifies to their validity in order to protect investors. While the accountants must rely to a great extent on the corporation for the information, the auditing process requires them to check to a certain extent the accuracy of the information. In that process, they must disclose any material problems and ultimately give their opinion on the financials.

Investment banks also have a role to play. Whenever corporations sell securities to the public, the Securities Act of 1933 imposes liability on the underwriters (usually investment banks and brokerage houses) who sell the securities to the public. The underwriters involved in the preparation of documents which are intended to provide full disclosure to investors and may be liable for failure to do their due diligence, i.e., an investigation of the

---

[85] Under market rules passed as a result of scandals, the boards must now meet in executive session without the inside directors. See § 5.08, *infra.*

[86] *See* Report of the NACD Blue Ribbon Commission, *Director Professionalism* (1997).

[87] *See generally* Warren F. Grienenberger, *Institutional Investors and Corporate Governance,* 970 PLI/Corp. 371 (1997); It is not clear whether the use of independent directors has in fact been effective. *See* Laura Lin, *The Effectiveness of Outside Directors as a Corporate Governance Mechanism: Theories and Evidence,* 90 Nw. U. L. Rev. 898 (1996).

[88] The credit agencies (e.g., Moody's) generally rely on corporate and market information to rate a corporation's securities. Their ratings are important to the corporations and their investors. These agencies are paid by the corporations they rate. There is little competition since there are very few credit agencies. *See generally* Arthur R. Pinto, *Control and Responsibility of Credit Rating Agencies in the United States,* 54 Am. J. Comp. L. 341 (Supp. 2006).

[89] John Coffee, *Understanding Enron: "Its About the Gatekeepers Stupid",* 57 Bus. Law. 1403 (2003).

[90] For a discussion of Sarbanes-Oxley and legislative changes in the role of these gatekeepers, see § 5.08, *infra.*

corporation.[91] In addition, stock analysts who work for stock brokerage firms cover an industry, play a role in advising their public clients on their view of a corporation's securities.

The role of lawyers is more complicated because their work often is not directed to the public and they do not vouch for the corporation. Attorneys are advocates and assist the corporation in a variety of transactions. But investors may rely on the attorneys acting to help prevent fraudulent activity. The relationship of an attorney to the client can limit the attorney's ability to blow the whistle if the attorney discovers wrongdoing. Lawyers clearly may not act in furtherance of a client's fraud but whether they should disclose such fraud to outsiders raises difficult public policy issues. If disclosure is required by attorneys then there is a fear that it will stifle free and frank discussion between the client and the lawyer. Yet lawyers are considered to be officers of the court and when working for the corporation owe their duty to all constituent parties including the shareholders.[92]

[H]   Federalism

Another major theme in American corporate law is the interplay between federal law and state law. Federalism raises the issue of whether there needs to be a uniform federal law as opposed to the law of each state. Every state has a corporate law statute that provides the corporate rules and a common law that interprets the statutes. Generally, the law of the state of incorporation supplies those rules.[93] The federal securities laws are also extremely important in governing corporations, particularly those corporations which are publicly traded.[94]

Federal securities law and state corporate law coexist so long as federal law allows. If Congress wished to establish a single body of federal corporate law applicable to companies in interstate commerce, it could do so under the Commerce Clause of the United States Constitution.[95] In the past, there have been calls for Congress to mandate federal incorporation and uniform rules for large companies.[96] However, the enactment of such federal legislation has never been a serious possibility. Thus, state law usually provides the rules and regulations governing the relationship between the managers and the shareholders, as owners of the company. Delaware remains the dominant state in providing corporate law for publicly traded corporations.[97]

---

[91] For a discussion of underwriters and public offerings, see § 7.03[C], *infra.*

[92] For a discussion of changes for attorneys as a result of Sarbanes-Oxley, see note 270, *infra.*

[93] For a discussion of choice of law, see § 1.09 *supra.*

[94] *See* Chapters 7, 13, *infra. See generally*, Robert B. Thompson & Hillary A. Sale, *Securities Fraud as Corporate Governance: Reflections upon Federalism*, 56 VAND. L. REV. 859 (2003) (federal securities law and enforcement via securities fraud class actions today have become the most visible means of regulating corporate governance).

[95] U.S. Const. Art. I, § 8, cl.3.

[96] *See* Ralph Nader, Mark Green & Joel Seligman, CONSTITUTIONALIZING THE CORPORATION (1976).

[97] Some argue that Delaware competes with other states to create its law while some have

Federal securities law deals primarily with disclosure of material information to the shareholders. That dichotomy does not seem to create a conflict, but the line between disclosure and regulation is often unclear. The requirement that a company make certain kinds of disclosures will affect its behavior. For example, excessive compensation of managers is usually an issue of state corporate law involving the fiduciary duty of the managers. Yet the disclosure of compensation as required under federal securities law may influence the amount of compensation authorized. In addition the enactment of Sarbanes-Oxley Act of 2002 has further expanded the federal presence in corporate law issues.[98]

[I] Publicly Held vs. Closely Held Corporations

State corporate law provides most rules for all corporations. There are, however, different types of corporations and the rules may not be appropriate for universal application. For example, there are corporations that are publicly held and those that are closely held. Closely held corporations have fewer shareholders which are not traded in a stock market. Some of these shareholders may be family members or friends of the founder. Shareholders of closely held corporations are often active in the management of the business. Thus, the law may recognize a certain informality in determining whether there has been compliance with corporate rules that may be inappropriate in other types of corporations.[99] In addition, the closely held corporation may use contracts to govern relationships among shareholders and the directors.[100] The law may recognize these private arrangements as a substitute for legal rules.

As for closely held corporations, there is also no stock market to provide liquidity and easy exit from investment. Therefore, minority shareholders may end up locked into a situation in which a control group acts for its own benefit.[101] As will be discussed in Chapter 11, some courts recognize that these closely held corporations are like incorporated partnerships to which courts may apply higher standards for fiduciary duties to the participants which are inapplicable in publicly traded corporations.

On the other hand, a publicly held corporation that has a large number of widely dispersed shareholders may increase the need for formalities and

---

suggested that Delaware really competes with the federal government. For a discussion of Delaware's dominance, see § 1.09[A], *supra.*

[98] For example, the Sarbanes-Oxley Market rules dictate that publicly traded companies trading in their markets have independent directors and certain required committees. Sarbanes-Oxley Act of 2002, § 301, 15 U.S.C. § 78j-1(m) (Supp. IV 2004); NYSE, Inc., Listed Company Manual § 303A.02 (2004). For a discussion of Sarbanes-Oxley, see § 5.08, *infra.*

[99] For example, must the board of directors have a meeting in order to make decisions? See § 5.06[B][1], *infra.*

[100] For a discussion of contracting in closely held corporations, see § 11.03, *infra.* For a discussion of nexus of contracts in publicly traded corporations, see § 5.03[C][3], *infra.*

[101] In some publicly held corporations, a shareholder group such as a family or parent corporation controls the majority of the shares, leaving public shareholders in the minority. In this context, there are issues relating to the extent to which the law should modify its rules to restrain the control group in its ability to use control for its own benefit. For a discussion of controlling shareholders, see Chapter 10, *infra.*

compliance with rules. The dispersion also makes it difficult for the shareholders to act together, making contractual arrangements sometimes inappropriate.[102] In addition, certain market mechanisms are available to protect investors in publicly held corporations which are not available in a closely held corporation.[103] Shareholders of publicly held corporations have the opportunity to exit by selling their shares in the stock market.

§ 5.03 THEORIES OF THE FIRM

Legal scholars have studied the Berle and Means thesis regarding the separation of ownership from control in publicly traded corporations.[104] They have debated its implications and the extent to which the law should deal with it. The issues raised concern both the focus of corporate governance and the allocation of power within the corporation. This debate has produced different theories of the firm and corporate law models for publicly traded corporations.

[A] Regulatory Approach

The traditional view sees the need for a regulatory approach. This approach views managers as unaccountable and likely to take advantage of the shareholders and not necessarily protect other stakeholders. Thus, the traditional approach asks for stronger state law protection of shareholders and an increased federal presence through an expansion of the reach of federal securities law[105] or, in the past, federal incorporation of large publicly traded corporations.[106] Given the failure of markets and passivity of shareholders when acting collectively, certain corporate rules must be made mandatory to assure minimal standards to protect shareholders. The regulation resulting from corporate scandals and the enactment of the Sarbanes-Oxley Act has increased the role of federal regulation in corporate governance.[107]

[B] Management Approach

The management approach favors laws which give managers tremendous latitude in their activities. This model is premised on the idea that managers will protect the interests of shareholders because they have a mutual interest in protecting the corporation.[108] Although managers do not own large numbers of shares, their livelihood depends upon a successful company. Thus, the shareholders and managers share the similar goal of corporate advancement. In addition, managers are often in the best position to consider the different demands on the corporation and are thus well suited to advance corporate

---

[102] For a discussion of contracting problems in the public corporation, see § 5.03[C][4], *infra*.

[103] For a discussion of market mechanisms, see § 5.03[C][2], *infra*.

[104] See § 5.02[E][1], *supra*.

[105] *See* Joel Seligman, *The New Corporate Law*, 59 Brook. L. Rev. 1 (1993).

[106] See discussion of Delaware's dominance at § 1.09[A], *supra*.

[107] For a discussion of Sarbanes-Oxley, see § 5.08, *infra*.

[108] The use of stock options as compensation is an attempt to align the interests of managers with shareholders. For a discussion of stock options, see § 9.04[A], *infra*.

interests and consider other constituencies such as labor and the community.[109]
However, there are often conflicting ways in which managers seek corporate
advancement. For example, one manager might see expansion or enlargement
of the corporation as being in the company's best interest, but that may not be
beneficial to the shareholders.[110] Concerns about the lack of management
accountability have lead some to argue for increased shareholder power[111] and
easier mechanisms to replace them.[112]

[C]   Law and Economics Approach

Since the 1980s, the dominant theory of the firm has been the law and
economics approach or contractual model. This approach views the separation of
ownership from control as beneficial because the passive investors provide
capital in return for the managers maximizing profits for shareholders. Under
this approach, managers should run the business and abuse by managers would
be controlled privately with market based solutions as opposed to government
regulation. Wealth maximization for shareholders is its primary focus.[113]

[1]   Agency Costs

Financial economists look at the corporation and describe the relationship
between the shareholders and managers as an agency relationship.[114] In any
such relationship, the agent (managers in the corporate context) do not always
act in the best interests of the principal (shareholders). Thus there are certain
costs associated with the relationship called agency costs. Agency costs include
monitoring expenditures (costs of supervising the agent),[115] bonding
expenditures (the agent attempts to assure the principal that the costs will be

---

[109] A team production theory model sees the corporation requiring inputs from a large number
of different stakeholders constituting a team and looks to the board as mediating between
stakeholders who look out for their concerns. Margaret Blair and Lynn Stout, *Director Accountability and the Mediating Role of the Corporate Board*, 79 WASH. U.L.Q. 403 (2001).

[110] The "empire building" of managers could justify higher compensation even when the larger
enterprise did not produce gains for shareholders.

[111] *See Shareholder Democracy Battling for Corporate America*, THE ECONOMIST, Mar 9th 2006 (a
good discussion of some of the current issues).

[112] *See generally* Lucian Arye Bebchuk, *The Case for Increasing Shareholder Power*, 118 HARV.
L. REV. 833 (2005); Lucian Arye Bebchuk, *The Myth of the Shareholder Franchise and Related
Essays* 93 VA. L. REV. 675 (2007); Stephen M. Bainbridge, *Director Primacy and Shareholder
Disempowerment*, 119 HARV. L. REV. 1735 (2005) (concerned that increased shareholder power will
hurt the corporation and the need for director primacy).

[113] Much of the empirical work on firm value looks to stock market pricing and other indicia of
shareholder value *See* Jill E. Fisch, *Measuring Efficiency in Corporate Law: The Role pf
Shareholder Primacy*, 31 Iowa Journal of Corporate Law 638 (2006) (critiques the embrace of law
and economic scholarship on shareholder value which is not equivalent to firm value nor takes into
account stakeholder or societal interests).

[114] Jensen & Meckling, *Theory of the Firm: Managerial Behavior, Agency Costs and Ownership
Structure*, 3 J. FIN. ECON. 305, 308 (1976). The law would not describe the relationship in terms of
agency. For a discussion, see § 5.05, *infra.*

[115] For example, an employer would incur costs to check the employee before hiring. Once hired,
the employer would try to make sure the employee is working at her best.

minimized)[116] and residual loss (there will inevitably be some cost to the principal).[117] From this analysis, it is generally beneficial to have a system that will reduce these agency costs to the lowest possible level. Corporate law and rules are often analyzed with this agency cost perspective using a cost/benefit analysis.

[2]   Markets

The law and economics approach views a market oriented approach as the optimal way of looking at the firm and for lowering agency costs. Markets present a more efficient (cost less and benefit more) means to monitor the agency relationship than government regulation. For example, the stock market for public companies provides a significant mechanism to monitor managers. Assuming a stock exchange is an efficient market[118] and reflects the value of the company, then a decline in value or low price indicates poor management. A lower share price hurts the company, the shareholders and the managers. For example, a low share price requires the company to sell a greater number of shares to raise the same amount of equity capital and raises the costs of doing business.[119] There is also a market for corporate control where a low share price may encourage shareholders to challenge directors in a proxy fight or induce the bidder to try to buy the corporation.[120] Therefore, management in response to these markets will attempt to manage efficiently to keep the share price high.[121] In addition, monitoring functions are performed by other markets. If the company is run poorly and its products do not compete in that market, the company could fail and the managers would lose their jobs. The market for managers encourages managers to work efficiently because it enhances their ability to move to another job. As discussed earlier, there is even a market which involves attracting companies to incorporate in a particular state.[122] In light of the monitoring of the markets, the law and economics model argues that

---

[116] For example, an employee prepares materials such as a resume to get hired and agrees to do things to remain hired.

[117] For example, an employee may take long lunch breaks or use corporate supplies for personal use. Thus, the employee shirks responsibilities (an issue of duty of care) or acts opportunistically by self dealing (an issue of duty of loyalty).

[118] The economic theory on which a stock market functions as a monitoring mechanism is based upon the Efficient Capital Market Hypothesis ("ECMH"). See § 5.02[D], *supra*.

[119] If a corporation needs to raise $10 million and its shares trade at $20, it will need to sell 500,000 shares. But if a share trades at $10 because of poor management, the corporation must sell one million shares, which dilutes existing shareholder control and raises the cost of raising capital. Raising money more expensively hurts the corporation by raising it costs and because companies compete with other companies that may be able to raise capital more cheaply.

[120] For a discussion of proxy fights, see § 5.05[C], *infra*. For a discussion of hostile tender offers, see Chapter 12.

[121] Another example of the stock market inducing good management is that managers are often compensated with options to buy shares at a fixed price. If managers run the company well, the price of the shares will rise in the efficient market over the option price and increase the managers' compensation. In theory this aligns the interests of the managers with the shareholders in seeking to raise the stock market price. For a discussion of stock options, see § 9.04[A], *infra*.

[122] For a discussion of this market for corporate charters, see § 1.09[A], *supra*.

law should only facilitate market mechanisms or provide rules when markets fail.[123]

[3]　Nexus of Contracts

Law and economics theorists conceptualize the corporation in terms of contract law. A corporation can be viewed as a nexus of contracts through which various claimants such as creditors, workers, shareholders, and consumers enter into agreements. Private contracts are viewed as an efficient means to lower costs in the agency relationship between the shareholders and managers. One can view the articles of incorporation and the bylaws as a contract between the shareholders and the managers setting out the rules governing their relationship.[124] This private ordering through contracts allows the parties to provide rules to maximize value and minimize costs. Under this view, corporate law should provide the basic terms of these contracts (that is, default rules), but the shareholders and the managers should be allowed to change the terms, thus providing an optimal and mutually agreeable system.[125]

[4]　Critics of Contractual Approach

While many corporate law rules can be waived or modified because the statutes explicitly allow for it,[126] critics of this approach argue that some minimal protection and regulation is needed, and some of these rules should not be changed so easily.[127] The ability to fairly contract depends upon the characteristics of the parties, their knowledge, the process and the realities of the business world.[128] In addition, markets can fail (for example, because of fraud) and may not be able to constrain managerial behavior. One of the most convincing arguments against all rules being subject to contractual modification is that a publicly traded company with thousands of shareholders cannot have any real bargaining over the terms of the contract. Management controls the

---

[123] *See generally* Daniel Fischel, *The Race to the Bottom Revisited: Reflections on Recent Developments in Delaware's Corporation Law*, 76 Nw. U. L. Rev. 913 (1982).

[124] *See* Symposium, *Contractual Freedom in Corporate Law*, 89 Colum. L. Rev. 1395 (1989).

[125] *See generally* Frank Easterbrook & Daniel Fischel, The Economic Structure of Corporate Law (1991). For a critique, *see* William Bratton, *The Economic Structure of the Post-Contractual Corporation*, 87 Nw. U. L. Rev. 180 (1992).

[126] For example, shareholders can amend the articles of incorporation to modify the requirements for voting such as supermajority voting. That type of modification is less controversial than contractual changes in fiduciary duty law. For a discussion of the elimination of damages for duty of care cases by contract, see § 8.05, *infra*.

[127] *See* Douglas M. Branson, *Assaults on Another Citadel: Attempts To Curtail The Fiduciary Standard Applicable to Corporate Directors*, 57 Fordham L. Rev. 375 (1988). *But see* Henry Butler & Larry Ribstein, *Opting Out of Fiduciary Duties: Response to the Anti-Contractarians*, 65 Wash. L. Rev. 1 (1990). Contractualists support the right of the majority to modify the voting rules and agree to a more optimal system. Critics view the change as disenfranchising shareholders who are unable to protect their interests and need legal protection by only a majority vote of those actually voting.

[128] *See* Robert Charles Clark, *Agency Costs Versus Fiduciary Duties* in Principles and Agents: The Structure of Business (Pratt & Zeckhauser eds. 1985).

structure and timing of the process while shareholders are widely dispersed, unable to act collectively.[129]

Although the contract theory has not been adopted for all corporate rules, it remains influential and does provide a framework for analyzing those rules. Courts and legislatures have taken the theory into account in fashioning rules.

[5]   Behavioral Economics

The field of behavioral economics reflects the use of cognitive and social psychology applied to economics. The traditional law and economics view and its impact on corporate law has been based on the rational profit maximizing individual. Yet psychological and social psychologists observe that human behavior is often not rational, and that decision-making is subject to persistent biases and thinking "shortcuts."[130] The use of behavioral economics undermines some of the classic law and economic approach and is having an impact on the future development of corporate law. For example, group biases that bind members of a group, blind them to the failings of its members and could call into question the independent directors serving on a board of directors.[131]

§ 5.04   THE LEGAL MODEL

A state's corporate statute (hereinafter "the statute") is the usual source of the statutory rules that allocate power within the corporation. The governing structure of a corporation is composed of the shareholders as the owners of the company, and the board of directors who oversee the management of the company For example, § 8.01 of the MBCA provides that "the business and affairs of the corporation [will be] managed by or under the direction, and subject to the oversight, of its board of directors . . . ."[132] The board of directors is usually elected by the shareholders at an annual meeting. The annual

---

[129] Often, the management of the company presents a proposal to the shareholders and the shareholders vote without negotiation. Shareholders are often passive and rationally apathetic and do not possess perfect information about the corporation. For a discussion of the collective action problem in shareholder voting, see § 5.05[C][4], *infra.*

[130] Donald C. Langevoort, Symposium, *The Legal Implications of Psychology: Human Behavioral Economics and the Law: A Literature Review*, 51 VAND. L. REV. 1499 (1998).

[131] The Delaware Supreme Court discussed bias among directors who serve on a special litigation committee of the board reviewing litigation against other directors who were a majority of the board. *Zapata Corp. v. Maldonado*, 430 A.2d 779 (Del. 1981). For a discussion of *Zapata* and structural bias, see § 14.06[D], *infra. See* James Fanto, *Whistleblowing and the Public Director: Countering Corporate Inner Circles*, 83 OREGON L. REV. 435 (2004) (using social psychological theory to argue for the need for boards having at least 1/3 independent directors selected from a pool of candidates not usually serving as directors and picked by a public oversight board whose members are selected by the SEC). Another example is the presence of irrational or noise traders have raised issues about the efficiency of the stock markets. For a discussion of the efficient market theory, see § 5.02[D], *supra.*

[132] Model Bus. Corp. Act Ann. § 8.01(b) (4th ed. 2008). The statute allows for limitations on board power in the articles, which require both a shareholder vote and board authorization. Model Bus. Corp. Act Ann. § 10.03 (4th ed. 2008). Shareholders may try to limit board power in other ways. In publicly traded corporations, shareholders have tried to use changes in the bylaws (which only require a shareholder vote) to restrict board power. *See* note 171, *infra.* In closely held corporations, there may be shareholder agreements that restrict board power. *See* § 11.03, *infra.*

meeting is often required by state statute.[133] In a publicly held company, the board of directors sets policy and selects the officers who manage the business. The board of directors monitors the officers (the board and officers can be viewed as the "managers"). This legal model recognizes that, unlike most partnerships where participation by the partners in management is the norm, the shareholders are not necessarily on the board and thus do not run the business. Rather, the business is managed by a distinct group of professionals. This model is beneficial when managers are effective, but is problematic when they fail to do so or engage in self dealing. The legal model allocates to directors and officers the authority to manage while it provides the shareholders, as owners, with some ability to monitor the managers' performance.

§ 5.05 SHAREHOLDERS

The common shareholders, as owners of the corporation, are viewed as residual claimants because their claim on assets (upon liquidation) and profits follows creditors and preferred shareholders, who usually have fixed claims with priority. All amounts above those fixed claims are for the benefit of the common shares. Thus, as the value of a firm increases, so does the value of the common shares.[134]

A significant issue in corporate law is the allocation of power between the shareholders and the directors and officers. The primary source for the allocation of power within a corporation is state law.[135] Although the common shareholders are owners who select the directors to act on their behalf, the relationship between them is not legally an agency/principal relationship. In an agency relationship, the law requires the agent to act for the benefit and under the control of the principal. In the corporate context, the principals (the shareholders) do not control the decisions of the agent (the directors).[136] Once elected, the directors must act on behalf of the corporation and all of the shareholders, not for the group that elected them.[137] This system makes economic sense if one views owners as the suppliers of equity capital and passive

---

[133] *See* Model Bus. Corp. Act Ann. § 7.01 (4th ed. 2008).

[134] For a discussion of common shareholders' financial rights, see § 4.02[B], *supra.*

[135] State corporate law statutes have many different rules, some of which are mandatory, some enabling and others supplementary. Mandatory rules must be applied and cannot be altered. Other rules are enabling and may be applied if the corporation chooses to do so. Still other rules are supplementary and must be used but can be altered. Supplementary rules may also be called default rules. *See* Melvin Eisenberg, *The Structure of Corporation Law*, 89 COLUM. L. REV. 1461, 1480–85 (1989).

[136] From a financial economic perspective, the managers work on behalf of the owners and view the relationship in terms of agency. For a discussion of agency costs, see § 5.03[C][1], *supra.*

[137] In *Charlestown Boot & Shoe Co. v. Dunsmore*, 60 N.H. 85 (1880), a majority of shareholders selected a committee to work with directors to close up business. The directors refused and even contracted for more debt and the delay in closing the business resulted in losses. There was also an uninsured loss caused by fire. The shareholders sought damages from the directors for failure to follow the committee's advice. The Supreme Court of New Hampshire viewed the statutory framework as providing that the directors manage and thus the shareholders' actions were unavailing. The court found no evidence of directors' negligence in not procuring insurance. For a discussion of directors acting as agents for the benefit of controlling shareholders, see § 10.02, *infra.*

investors and the managers as the investment specialists.

[A]   Right to Vote

In terms of the allocation of power between the shareholders and the board of directors, the state statutes are explicit on certain voting issues. The general scheme is for ordinary business decisions to be made by the board while certain structural and governance decisions are for the shareholders (although sometimes the board may also be involved in those decisions).[138] Shareholders are given explicit power to vote on such issues as the election of directors, and amendments to the bylaws and articles of incorporation (under state statutes, amendments to the bylaws usually can be done by the shareholders without board approval while article amendments require both directors and shareholder approval).[139] In addition, shareholders vote on certain major structural issues such as mergers or liquidation and sale of substantially all of the assets.

There are times, however, when a court will find a shareholder's right to vote even without explicit statutory authorization.[140] The usual voting required for shareholder action is a plurality vote (a majority of the quorum) although some states require a majority vote for certain actions.[141] There must be a quorum (a minimum number of shares voting) which is usually established in the bylaws.[142] The articles or in some cases the bylaws can also require an absolute majority[143]

---

[138] In some cases, state statute permits the board to act on matters which are primarily a shareholder right but allow the shareholders to override the action. For example, the bylaws may give the board power to amend the bylaws but may also provide the shareholders with the power to change the result. *See* Model Bus. Corp. Act Ann. § 10.20 (4th ed. 2008).

[139] As a result the by laws are where the shareholders try to enhance their power because they can act without prior board approval. For a discussion of the use of by laws, see § 5.05[C][3], *infra.*

[140] For a discussion of the right of expression, see § 5.05[A][2], *infra.* The stock markets also have rules that require shareholder voting rights in order for a corporation to keep its listing. For example, the New York Stock Exchange mandates shareholder voting when new shares are issued and the new shares significantly dilute share value. New York Stock Exchange Listed Company Manual § 312.03. Post Sarbanes-Oxley Act, the stock markets changed their listing requirements requiring shareholder approval of all equity compensation plans, including stock option plans, and material revisions to such plans. *E.g.*, N.Y. Stock Exch. Listed Co. Manual § 303A.

[141] A statute may require an absolute majority vote for certain transactions (e.g., Del. Gen. Corp. Law § 251(c), shareholder vote on mergers).

[142] Most state statutes provide default or supplemental rules when the bylaws or articles do not cover a subject. For example, MBCA § 7.25(a) provides that a majority will be a quorum for the shareholders unless the articles provide otherwise. Model Bus. Corp. Act Ann. § 7.25 (4th ed. 2008). Under Delaware law the by-laws or certificate of incorporation can set the quorum but in no event can it be less than one third of the shareholders. Del. Code Ann. tit. 8, § 216.

[143] Generally directors only need a plurality to win election which means a win if you get the most votes cast. Shareholders wanting to express unhappiness over certain directors without having to run a candidate could withhold their votes. *See* note 167, *infra.* But since a withheld vote is not cast or counted, the director could get elected with very few positive votes. For example if a corporation has 1 million shares issued and at the meeting 600,000 are present by proxy (a quorum) and 525,000 are unhappy with a director and do not vote for her, the director wins with 75,000 votes out of 525,000 at the meeting (not even a majority vote of the quorum). This lead to shareholder activists seeking to amend corporate bylaws to require that a director receive a majority vote of the quorum. A number of corporations responded to this movement by effectuating such a change. Delaware

or super majority vote or super majority quorum.[144]

Generally, there must be at least one class of shares with voting rights. The norm for most publicly traded corporations is to have one class of common shares with each share having one vote.[145] The articles of incorporation may provide for more than one class of shares with voting rights and those rights may vary among classes.[146] The shares held by the corporation in itself or held in a subsidiary cannot usually be voted otherwise it would undermine the voting rights of the shareholders.[147]

---

responded by amending its statute to provide that directors cannot amend or repeal any bylaw amendment adopted by shareholders that specifies the votes necessary for election of directors. Del. Code Ann. tit. 8, § 216 (Supp. 2006).

[144] Statutes generally allow for a corporation to select greater voting requirements by including such requirements in the articles of incorporation. *See, e.g.*, Model Bus. Corp. Act Ann. § 7.27 (4th ed. 2008). Some public corporations may have a supermajority provision that could give veto power to a significant shareholder. Supermajority requirements are more likely to be found in closely held corporations as a means of protecting the minority shareholders. See § 11.05[B], *infra.*

[145] One of the most controversial defensive tactics developed to avert hostile takeovers was the attempt by target managers to change the one share-one vote rule by reclassifying shares into two classes. The reclassification required a shareholder vote to amend the articles of incorporation to reallocate the shares. One of the new classes of shares created more significant voting power and was largely owned by managers, while the other class had dividend rights and lesser voting rights and was owned by the public shareholders. The result of this dual classification was that managers had enough votes in their super voting class of shares to thwart a hostile tender offer. This tactic was controversial because the change in voting rights was implemented when the company's one class of common shares was already widely held by public shareholders. If the two classes were provided initially when the corporation went public, it would have allowed investors to decide not to buy the shares with lesser voting rights. But reclassifying into two classes while a publicly traded corporation initially had only one class was viewed as a disenfranchisement of public shareholders and the process of change raised questions of fairness. Jeffrey N. Gordon, *Ties that Bind: Dual Class Common Stock and the Problem of Shareholder Choice*, 76 CAL. L. REV. 3, 40–41 (1988). But the tactic did require a shareholder vote and arguably, may have even encouraged the managers with voting power to increase shareholder value. Ronald J. Gilson, *Evaluating Dual Class Common Stock: The Relevance of Substitutes*, 73 VA. L. REV. 807, 811–23 (1987). The voting for the recapitalization could involve coercion. See the discussion of *Lacos Land Co. v. Arden Corp.*, 517 A.2d 271 (Del. Ch. 1986), at § 10.01, *infra.* The SEC reacted to the New York Stock Exchange's attempt to change its one share-one vote requirement for its listed companies in order to continue to list companies after a dual-class recapitalization. The SEC enacted 1934 Act Rule 19c-4 which barred all regulated markets from listing companies that adversely changed existing voting rights. Ultimately, the courts found that the S.E.C. did not have the authority to promulgate this rule, and indicated that voting rights are traditionally matters of state corporate law. The court did allow for the markets to establish their own rules. *Business Roundtable v. SEC*, 905 F.2d. 406 (D.C. Cir. 1990). In fact, the markets adopted rules that are very similar to what the S.E.C. had proposed. *See New York Stock Exchange Listed Company Manual* § 313. *Williams v. Geier*, 671 A.2d 1368 (Del. 1996), discussed at § 5.05[D], notes 198–200, *infra*, involved a form of dual class voting. The change of voting structure is an example of the nexus of contract theory which permits corporations to change the rules that apply to them through shareholder voting. For a discussion of the nexus of contracts, see § 5.03[C][3], *supra.*

[146] By creating different classes, a corporation may provide representation on the board of directors for different shareholder groups. This may be important in a closely or a publicly held corporation in which a family or large shareholder group is involved. The articles of incorporation or state statute may also provide certain limited voting rights for specific purposes. For instance, preferred shares could be given the right to vote for directors if they fail to receive dividends. Under some state statutes, preferred shares may also be allowed to vote on issues that adversely affect preferred shareholder rights. *See, e.g.*, Model Bus. Corp. Act Ann. § 10.04 (4th ed. 2008).

[147] *E.g.*, Del. Gen. Corp. Law § 160 (c) In *Speiser v Baker*, 525 A2d 1001 (Del. Ch. 1987), the court

[1]   Cumulative Voting

The normal shareholders voting procedure is that each shareholder votes his or her shares for a particular issue. A plurality of the vote wins. This procedure is followed with regard to the election of directors. If a group of shareholders own a majority of the shares, under this "straight voting" scheme, the group will elect all the directors.

There are means by which shareholders with less than a majority interest can have some representation on the board. Cumulative voting permits shareholders to collect their votes and allocate them any way they choose. For example, consider an election in which shareholders must elect 6 directors. If Shareholder A owns 60 shares and Shareholder B owns 40 shares, under straight voting, A would elect all six directors. Under cumulative voting B would be able to use all her votes (40 votes per director times 6 directors=240 total votes) in any way she decided. In order to determine if she is able to use those votes and cumulate them to elect any directors, she would calculate using the following formula:

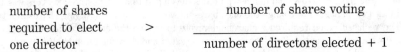

$$\text{number of shares required to elect one director} \quad > \quad \frac{\text{number of shares voting}}{\text{number of directors elected} + 1}$$

Thus, in the example the minimum number of shares necessary to elect one director (assuming no fractional shares outstanding) would be 15 shares:

$$15 \text{ shares} \quad > \quad \frac{100 \text{ shares voting}}{6 \text{ directors elected} + 1} \qquad [14.28]$$

Here, the number of shares (100) divided by seven (six directors to be elected, plus 1) would equal 14.28, i.e., 15 shares needed to elect a director.[148] Thus, 15 shares, each with six votes to cumulate because there are six directors being elected, means that 90 votes are needed for one candidate to win. Thus if B (with a total of 240 votes) voted at least 90 votes for each of two candidates, she would elect two directors. A would elect the remaining 4 directors, so long as she cast at least 90 votes for each candidate. To use the cumulative voting formula, one must know how many shares will actually be voted at the meeting.[149] While

___

interpreted the provision to reach not only a majority held subsidiary holding shares of the parent but other corporations without majority ownership that could be viewed as holding shares belonging to the parent. The court looked to the effect of the arrangement which was "to muffle the voice of the public shareholders."

[148] Since fractional shares do not vote, the number would be rounded upward.

[149] The majority may try to undercut cumulative voting by taking steps to limit its usefulness. For example, reducing the number of directors, staggering the election of directors so that they have longer terms usually for three years and each year 1/3 of the board is up for election (which has the effect of reducing the number up for election) or increasing the number of shares the majority owns will affect the formula and make it harder for minority shareholders to have enough votes to elect any directors. If the majority has the right to remove a director elected by the minority without cause, that could also limit the right of the minority. Thus, in closely held corporations a contract may be

cumulative voting may be useful as a means of providing for minority representation in a closely held corporation, it is infrequently used in publicly traded corporations.

Cumulative voting must be set forth in the articles of incorporation.[150]

[2] Right of Expression

As discussed, the statutes generally indicate those issues on which the shareholders can vote. But significant case law has provided shareholders with additional voting rights. In *Auer v. Dressel*,[151] the New York Court of Appeals decided several issues raised by a dissident group of shareholders who were upset about the current management of the corporation. This group owned more than 50% of the Class A shares, which elected 9 out of 11 directors (common shareholders elected the other 2). Since the annual meeting was not approaching, they requested a special shareholders' meeting pursuant to the bylaws. There were several purposes for the meeting, including the removal of four Class A directors and their replacement with new directors favored by the majority. The group also sought endorsement of the former president who had been removed by the current directors.

The company refused to call a meeting, claiming that the purposes were improper under state corporate law. The endorsement was considered improper because only the directors can select officers and the shareholders have no right to express their views on a subject which is in the purview of the directors. Thus the shareholder resolutions, even if adopted, would be purely advisory. But the court found that the shareholders should have the right to express themselves even on issues that under the statutes they have no right to vote on. Such advisory votes will put directors on notice of their desires before the next election. This right of expression, which is not contained in the statutes but is based upon principles of shareholder democracy, is an important right. However, the right may cause problems such as where to draw the line on what is proper for shareholder consideration under this principle. Shareholders often use SEC 34 Act Rule 14a-8 to put shareholder proposals recommending actions in the corporation's proxy statement.[152]

---

useful to protect minority shareholders from such undercutting by the control group.

[150] In most states, since the articles must specifically provide for cumulative voting, the shareholders effectively elect the system. *See* Model Bus. Corp. Act Ann. § 7.28(b) (4th ed. 2008). In some states, cumulative voting is required for all corporations in order to facilitate minority representation. In those states, there is a concern that methods of undercutting cumulative voting undermine the mandatory requirement. *See Wolfson v. Avery*, 126 N.E.2d 701 (Ill. 1955) (use of classified boards with different terms for different directors violated the constitutional requirement of cumulative voting). *See also* note 149, *supra*, on the different methods that undercut cumulative voting.

[151] 306 N.Y. 427, 118 N.E.2d 590 (1954).

[152] For discussion of SEC Rule 14a-8, see § 7.05, *infra*. For a discussion of this right to try to change policy, see § 5.05[C][3], *infra*.

[B]   Proxy Voting

Annual shareholder meetings are required by statute, at which the directors are elected and other issues may be voted upon.[153] Special meetings prior to the annual meeting can also be called if action needs to be taken before the next annual meeting.[154] Procedural issues of notice, record dates[155] to vote and quorum are usually found in the bylaws of the corporation. The statutes usually provide default rules to be used when the bylaws do not specify a rule.

In publicly traded corporations, the voting actually occurs prior to the shareholder meeting because the shareholders generally do not wish to incur the costs of attending the meetings. To facilitate voting in this situation, the state statutes permit the use of proxies. Proxies allow shareholders to vote on certain matters prior to a meeting or assign the voting right to another person who will be present at the meeting. Delaware law and other state laws also permit shareholders to act without a meeting through the use of written consents or consent solicitation. The consent solicitation seeks the requisite vote without a meeting and once obtained, the action is approved.[156] However, even the consent mechanism may not be used to replace the annual meeting.[157] The internet provides opportunities to change the voting process.[158] For example, Delaware allows the participation in shareholder meetings using remote

---

[153] MBCA § 7.02 authorizes 10% of the votes entitled to be cast to call for a special meeting. Many states leave special meetings to be dealt with by the bylaws or articles of incorporation. Model Bus. Corp. Act Ann. § 7.02 (4th ed. 2008). *See* Del. Gen. Corp. Law § 211(d) (1997).

[154] Model Bus. Corp. Act Ann. § 7.01 (4th ed. 2008).

[155] States use a record date as the means of establishing the ownership of shares entitled to vote at meetings. *E.g.* Del. Code Ann. tit. 8, § 213.

[156] *See* Del. Gen. Corp. Law § 228. At a shareholder meeting, a majority of the quorum is required i.e. a plurality, but for consent vote, a majority of all shares are needed in most cases. In *Datapoint Corp. v. Plaza Securities Co.*, 496 A.2d 1031 (Del. 1985), the Delaware Supreme Court was faced with an attempt by a challenger to replace the directors through the consent mechanism. The directors tried to limit consents by enacting a bylaw delaying the effectiveness of any consent. The challenger claimed that the board had no authority to enact the bylaw while the board argued that the bylaw was a reasonable internal corporate regulation. The court found the bylaw to be an arbitrary and unreasonable delay of shareholder action giving the board time to try to defeat the action. The court did not, however, preclude all bylaws affecting consents, especially those that would be viewed as a ministerial review of the consent mechanism. This view is consistent with the Delaware courts' generally strong support for shareholder democracy and concern with boards interfering with the right to vote. For a discussion, see § 5.05[D], *infra*.

[157] In *Hoschett v. TSI International Software, Ltd.*, 683 A.2d 43 (Del. Ch. 1996), the court emphasized the importance of the annual shareholder meeting in corporate governance and thus viewed it as mandatory under the state statute. Such meetings may be beneficial in forcing management's attention and providing discipline. Although arguably impractical when there is a control group which does not need minority shareholder votes, the court found that the impracticality argument could be used even when there is no control group in large publicly traded corporations. In addition, shareholders should be able to raise issues at a meeting and provide a forum for discourse consistent with the notion of corporate democracy. While the right to use proxies is provided by state law, federal securities law also regulates their use by providing rules on the mechanics and the disclosure associated with proxy voting in publicly traded corporations. For a discussion of the proxy rules, see Chapter 7, *infra*.

[158] For a discussion of Internet voting under federal securities laws, see § 7.04[E], *infra*.

communications or the use of online meetings.[159] In addition a shareholder can designate the proxy holder by electronic means.[160]

Managers send out proxies to the shareholders requesting their votes for issues to be voted on at the shareholder meeting. Managers need to solicit proxies in order to have a quorum at the meeting and to be reelected and remain in power. One would assume that given the need to obtain shareholder votes, managers would always be concerned with their reelection and retention. But managers have control over corporate information and the corporation's proxy materials, and solicitations are at corporate expense. In addition, shareholders in publicly traded corporations are viewed as passive with a preference to exit by selling rather than using their voice to challenge management.

If there exists a group which opposes management, that group may send out its own proxy material which results in a "proxy fight."

[C] The Proxy Fight

The right to vote for directors is the most significant right that the shareholders of publicly traded corporations possess especially when there is no control group. But the rights to amend the by laws to try to mandate changes and to propose precatory proposals for change are also significant. If there exists a group which opposes management for election or their views, that group may send its own proxy material which results in a "proxy fight."[161]

Proxy fights are not the norm but can occur in three situations. They can involve (1) a challenge to the current directors by replacing them with new directors (change management); (2) changing the directors with new directors who will support an acquisition of the corporation (change directors to facilitate an acquisition); and (3) not challenging the election of directors but seeking shareholder votes on a policy issue or corporate governance rules that the directors oppose (change policy). In some cases the shareholders may try to mandate the change through amending the by laws and other times pressure for change using precatory proposals.

---

[159] *See* Del. Code Ann. tit. 8, § 211(a)(2). The statute establishes certain requirements for online shareholder meetings to protect their integrity and requires corporations to take reasonable steps to ensure that those who attend online meetings have "a reasonable opportunity to participate" and to vote. Corporations, therefore, must give online attendees the chance to follow the meetings in real-time. There is also a duty on corporations to keep records of shareholders' and proxy votes and actions at meetings that take place through remote communication to prevent potential fraudulent voting. *See,* Daniel Adam Birnhak, *Online Shareholder Meetings: Corporate Law Anomalies or the Future of Governance?,* 29 Rutgers Computer & Tech. L.J. 423,427–29 (2003). Concerns over internet only meetings contributed to the defeat of a bill in Massachusetts to change its corporate law. Some shareholder activists "condemn[ed] it as a backdoor effort to insulate company executives from unhappy shareholders." *Id.* At 443–444.

[160] Del. Code Ann. tit. 8, § 212(c)(2).

[161] *See generally* Lisa M. Fairfax, *Making the Corporation Safe for Shareholder Democracy,* 69 Ohio St. L.J. 53 (2008) (argues that increased shareholder democracy could also favor other stakeholders).

[1]   Change Management

If a corporation is not being run effectively then an outside group could initiate a proxy fight to replace the directors with a view to changing management or having a voice in the running of the business. This remedy through private action by the insurgent shareholders creates a market mechanism to monitor managers.

Proxy fights, along with hostile tender offers, are part of the market for corporate control.[162] According to proponents of this market mechanism, it can serve as a monitoring device because managers, fearful of losing their positions, will try to maximize value for the shareholders and thereby win reelection and preclude a takeover by an outside group. Proxy fights often raise legal issues such as compliance with federal proxy rules and state law issues resulting from the incumbent directors trying to insure their election.

Proxy fights to change the directors (that are not intended to facilitate an acquisition of the corporation) are more difficult to win. In these cases, shareholders must be convinced to vote against incumbent management and expect that the new managers will be more effective. Shareholders in a proxy fight are neither offered nor guaranteed any increase in the value of their shares. There are also substantial costs in a proxy fight which may not be reimbursed.[163]

[2]   Change Directors to Facilitate an Acquisition

If someone wants to acquire a corporation and the incumbent directors are opposed, there may be a proxy fight to replace those directors with a new board that will favor the acquisition. The need for a proxy fight is usually because the directors may have implemented a defensive tactic that would deter the acquisition and thus requires the board to remove it first.[164] This proxy fight may be easier to win because the insurgents have announced their willingness to buy the corporation in the proposed acquisition for a premium price over the market price. The costs of this proxy fight will be high because of the expenses of the fight and the costs of buying the corporation if successful. But if the insurgents prevail and the acquisition is successful they will be compensated by increasing the value of the corporation they had bought.

---

[162] If the corporation is run poorly, then an outside group will initiate a proxy fight or tender offer to replace managers. This remedy through private action creates a market mechanism to monitor manager. For a discussion of markets as monitors, see § 5.03[C][2], *supra.* For a discussion of hostile tender offers, see Chapter 12, *infra.*

[163] For a discussion of proxy expenses, see § 5.05[C][5], *infra.*

[164] Some defensive tactics cannot be removed by the board if the bidder buys shares over a certain threshold. For example, if the threshold is 15% then the bidder would buy 14.9% and commence a proxy fight for a new board to remove the tactic that blocks the acquisition. For a discussion of defensive tactics and poison pills, see § 12.04[B][1], *infra.*

[3]   Change Policy

In seeking to change policy shareholders have the option of using management's proxy statement to propose resolutions pursuant to SEC Rule 14a-8[165] or to solicit proxies using their own proxy materials which are not subject to the limitations of the rules.[166] Shareholders may try to mandate change by trying to amend the by laws or influence change by sponsoring votes on precatory resolutions. Shareholders can also try to influence by opposing incumbent directors[167] or urge shareholders to vote against an issue proposed by management. It may be easier to convince shareholders to vote for or against a proposal then to change management by replacing the current directors in a proxy fight. Often the changes sought are recommendations to the board of directors and not binding. The issues raised can involve issues relating to important social issues involving the corporation or issues of improving corporate governance. While many of these proposals do not receive majority support,[168] they are a means of influencing the managers to make changes.

---

[165] For a discussion of SEC 34 Act Rule 14a-8, see § 7.05, *infra.* For example, in 1996 some investors of RJR Nabisco solicited proxies in a consent solicitation for a proposal calling for the split of the corporation into separate tobacco operations and food operations. The idea was that as two separate corporations, the food business would trade at a higher value so the two parts would be more valuable than the combined corporation. The shareholders needed to comply with the federal proxy rules but when they used their own proxy materials they were not asking that their proposal be included in management's material pursuant to SEC Rule 14a-8. At the same time a group of priests also submitted a shareholder proposal recommending a similar split up but used SEC 34 Act Rule 14a-8. Glenn Collins, *SEC Allows Priests' Bids For Vote on Nabisco Spinoff,* N.Y. Times, Jan. 3, 1996, at D3. For a discussion on Rule 14a-8, see § 7.04, *infra.* The corporation did not act immediately as a result of the vote but eventually did decide to split the corporation as suggested.

[166] Policy could also be changed by trying to elect some directors to the board to increase voice. In some cases the threat of a contested election resulted in the corporation agreeing to add new directors. Both the NY Times and Yahoo have recently done so. Some have argued that some directors (not a majority) should be allowed to be nominated through SEC 34 Act Rule 14a-8 in management's proxy statement and run against other directors. This would avoid the costs of preparing their own proxy materials and arguably give their claim some legitimacy. Some have expressed concern that such a proposal would be disruptive and undermine the collegiality of the board. Others have argued it as a means to enhance shareholder voice. The SEC at one point had a proposal favoring such nominations. 17 C.F.R. Parts 240, 249, 274 It then withdrew it. At the same time shareholders tried to amend the by laws to implement a procedure for direct nominations but that raised an issues of whether such proposal should be excluded as an improper shareholder proposal because it related to an election under Rule 14a-8. For a discussion of this issue see § 7.05[H], *infra.* In 2009, Delaware added Gen. Corp. Law § 112 which allows bylaws to provide for a solicitation for election of directors to be included in management's proxy statement.

[167] Shareholders can oppose the election of certain directors and may not have to comply with the requirements of the proxy rules if it is not viewed as a solicitation. For a discussion of solicitation and the 1992 revisions, see § 7.04[C][2], *infra.* Recently, institutional shareholders have actively asked shareholders to withhold votes in favor of certain directors as an expression of protest. In 2004, approximately 43% of the shareholders withheld votes for Michael Eisner, the chief executive officer and chairman of the board of Disney. Although elected as a director, the board decided to replace him as board chairman given the protest withheld votes. The shareholder action was motivated by Eisner's hiring and firing of his friend Michael Ovitz which resulted in litigation in Delaware. For a discussion of the *Disney* case see § 8.06[A] *infra.* For a discussion of the majority vote movement, see note 143, *supra.*

[168] Corporate governance issues are usually more successful in receiving majority shareholder support and often has institutional shareholder involvement.

Shareholder attempts to amend the bylaws that require action as opposed to recommending raises issue of the allocation of power between the board of directors and the shareholders. The bylaws are the focus of shareholder action because the power to amend the articles require both shareholder and board approval.[169] The power to amend the bylaws is given to the shareholders and usually to the directors.[170] The issue raised by a shareholder initiated bylaw are whether the proposed bylaw improperly interferes with the power of the board or whether the issue is one of shareholder power.[171]

In *CA, Inc. v. AFSCME Employees Pension Plan*[172] the Delaware Supreme Court dealt with two questions raised by a proposed bylaw[173] that raised the issue of the allocation of power between the board of directors and shareholders. The proposed bylaw would have required reimbursement of reasonable proxy expenses if a shareholder group was successful in running a slate of directors and at least one director was elected to the board.[174] The questions were whether the proposal was a proper subject for shareholders under Delaware law and, if the proposal was adopted, would it violate any Delaware law. The court found that the proposal was a proper subject but that, if adopted, it would violate the law. In answering the first question, the court found the power of shareholders to amend the bylaws is not identical or co-extensive with the board's concurrent power. The court did not adopt any bright line test for determining how far the shareholders could go in using the bylaws. The court did focus on the use of the bylaws for process-oriented issues that establishes or

---

[169] *E.g.*, Del. Gen. Corp. Law § 242.

[170] For example, Del. Gen. Corp. Law § 109 (a), allows the board to amend or repeal the bylaws if given the power in the certificate of incorporation. In most publicly traded corporations this power is given to the board.

[171] Under Del. Gen. Corp. Law § 109 (b), the bylaws may contain any provision not inconsistent with law. Del. Gen. Corp. Law § 141(a) gives the board the power to manage. Whether an amendment to the bylaws gives the shareholders the power to act and restrict the board's power depends upon the state statutes, attitude toward corporate governance and allocation of power within the corporation. *See Int'l Bhd of Teamsters Gen. Fund v. Fleming Cos.*, 975 P.2d 907 (Okla. 1999) (shareholders have the power to amend the by laws to allow for a shareholder vote on poison pill plans used to fight a hostile tender offers and implemented by the board). The validity of mandatory bylaws for shareholder voting on poison pills in Delaware is unresolved. The Delaware Supreme Court's strong statement about board power in managing the corporation (*see Mentor Graphics Corp. v. Quickturn Design Systems, Inc.*, 721 A.2d 1281 (Del. 1998), discussed in § 12.04[B][1], note 54, *infra*), may suggest that shareholders' power is limited. In *General DataComm Industries, Inc. v. State of Wisconsin Investment Board*, 731 A.2d 818 (Del. Ch. 1999), the court left the issue open as not ripe and allowed a vote on an amendment to the bylaws to give the shareholders the right to vote on changes in the stock option plans when the exercise price is lowered. In an early case, *SEC v. Transamerica*, 163 F.2d 511 (3d Cir. 1947), the court indicated the shareholders had the power to amend the bylaws for the shareholders to select the auditors. Interestingly, in Delaware, the board can be given, and usually is, the power to repeal a bylaw approved by shareholders, which may mean the directors could immediately repeal a shareholder-approved bylaw. Del. Gen. Corp. Law § 109.

[172] 953 A.2d 227 (Del. 2008).

[173] The questions had been certified to the court by the SEC under a new procedure of certification allowed under the Delaware Constitution. Under SEC Rule 14a-8, a proposal submitted in management's proxy statement must be proper under state law and certification allows the SEC to ask the Delaware Supreme Court to make that decision. See the discussion of SEC Rule 14a-8 at § 7.05, *infra*.

[174] For a discussion of reimbursement of proxy expenses, see § 5.05[C][5], *infra*.

regulates a process for substantive decision-making (as opposed to mandating the decision itself) and that the bylaw dealt with the process of elections which was not unduly intrusive and thus permissible. As to the second question, the court found that the bylaw, if enacted, could force the board to pay expenses in a case which would be precluded normally under fiduciary duty principles.[175] For example, if the proxy contest involved promotion of personal and not corporate interests. Thus the bylaw would violate Delaware law.[176]

[4] Collective Action Problem

Proxy fights are infrequent and often fail because shareholders are passive. The passivity of widely dispersed shareholders, their failure to exercise their voting rights, and their inability to network even if they desire to do so has been described as involving a "collective action" problem. This passivity can be viewed as rational apathy. First, there is an issue of whether the cost of activity is greater than the benefits. For example, if one owns shares in a company in which managers have stolen 10 dollars and it will cost 15 dollars to enforce shareholder rights, then the shareholder will do nothing because the cost of recovery exceeds the benefit. A rational profit maximizer will not spend the money. Even if it cost five dollars to avoid losing 10 dollars, choosing not to act may still be justified by the shareholder's rational apathy. Although the benefits exceed the cost, a rational profit maximizer would rather let someone else, particularly a larger shareholder, enforce rights on its behalf and thus "free ride." Free riding is a problem because it raises an issue of fairness.[177] This collective action problem contributes to the separation of ownership from control by allowing the managers to control both the corporate proxy and information and thereby retain control.[178]

[5] Proxy Expenses

Management has an advantage in proxy solicitation because corporate funds pay the expenses of the proxy solicitation. Proxy battles can be expensive because they involve not just the printing and mailing of proxy materials but also the use of professional firms to convince shareholders (especially institutional shareholders) to support management's position.[179]

---

[175] Delaware courts have not looked favorably on contracts that limit or undermine fiduciary duties. For example, in the *QVC* case, the Delaware Supreme Court invalidated a contract that limited the directors' ability to find the best price for the shareholders. *See* § 12.05[A][5], *infra*.

[176] Delaware enacted a new provision in Del. Gen. Corp. Law, § 113, to allow bylaws that provide for reimbursement to shareholders in soliciting proxies in connection with an election of directors subject to conditions and procedures established in the bylaws.

[177] Robert Clark, CORPORATE LAW 390–96 (1986).

[178] The increasing number of large institutions that own shares may reduce the collective action problem if they act together and share the costs. See § 5.02[E][2], *infra*.

[179] In an unusual proxy battle surrounding the merger of Compaq and Hewlitt-Packard, Walter Hewlitt a director used his own money in a proxy fight to oppose the merger. He failed in a close vote. It was reported that the proxy fight cost over $100 million total and approximately $30 million was attributed to Mr. Packard's unsuccessful fight which he had to pay for. Joann S. Lublin, *Corporate Funding For Shareholder Activism? Critics Cite Strategic Issues, But Backers See Fairer Game;*

In *Rosenfeld v. Fairchild Engine & Airplane Corp.*,[180] the New York Court of Appeals considered the policy regarding reimbursement of expenses for both the defeated incumbent managers and the successful insurgents in their solicitations. The court allowed for reimbursement of both. The incumbents were entitled to be reimbursed so long as there was an issue of policy at stake and not just their reelection. This distinction is virtually impossible to make since one can always convert a power play into a policy argument. Further, the court allowed funds to be used for solicitation by the incumbents. Solicitation encompasses more than merely giving notice to the shareholders. The court placed the burden of proof on the complaining shareholders to specify which expenses were unreasonable. In terms of the insurgents, the court looked to a substantial shareholder vote approving the payment (16 to 1).[181] The result is that management has an easy time being reimbursed, so long as it couches its campaign as an issue of policy. Insurgents, on the other hand, may need shareholder approval for reimbursement.[182]

[6]   Fiduciary Duty

In proxy fights, the incumbent directors may try to implement tactics that will defeat the insurgents. In hostile tender offers, the directors may also take actions to defeat the bidder.[183] When those actions are challenged, plaintiffs claim that the directors breached their fiduciary duty.[184] Three levels of judicial scrutiny may apply — duty of loyalty, duty of care (including the business judgment rule) and the modified business judgment rule (a proportionality test).

Plaintiffs argue that these defensive actions are subject to the duty of loyalty because there is a conflict of interest (that is, the directors want to protect their positions). In those loyalty cases involving a conflict of interest the burden shifts to the defendant to prove fairness. The court looks at both the process and the substance of the transaction.[185] The defendants prefer to argue that the directors met their duty of care and that the decision is protected by the business judgment rule, which then places the burden on the plaintiff to prove that the defendants were negligent (grossly negligent in Delaware) in the decision-making process. Courts will not generally look at the substance of the

---

Judge Offers a Compromise, WALL ST. J., July 3, 2006, at B3.

[180]   309 N.Y. 168, 128 N.E.2d 291 (1955).

[181]   The dissenting judges argued that the burden should be on the defendants to prove that their expenditures were reasonable and that they should only be reimbursed for giving notice to the shareholders. Previously, expenditures did not exceed $28,000 while this battle cost $133,966. In addition, the dissent argued that the insurgents should not be reimbursed because they have no obligation to the corporation and payments to them would be ultra vires, requiring a unanimous shareholder vote. *Id.* The concurring and swing opinion relied primarily on the lack of proof by the plaintiff.

[182]   There are times when management has agreed to pay the proxy expenses of other unsuccessful parties, especially when the challenge resulted in positive changes in the governance of the corporation.

[183]   For a discussion of defensive tactics, see § 12.04[B], *infra.*

[184]   For an overview of fiduciary duty, see § 8.01[A], *infra.*

[185]   For a discussion of the duty of loyalty and conflicts of interest, see Chapter 9, *infra.*

decision but just the process ifr the business judgment rule applies.[186] Delaware has developed a third intermediate level of scrutiny applicable in reviewing actions taken by directors in implementing defensive tactics. The standard of judicial review established in *Unocal Corp. v. Mesa Petroleum*[187] is a modified business judgment rule, or proportionality test, that initially places the burden on the defendant to justify its actions. The directors must show that there were reasonable grounds for believing in a threat to corporate policy. Their response must have been reasonable in relation to the threat posed (that is, proportionate). Here, the court scrutinizes both process and substance but not as closely as a fairness review under the duty of loyalty.

[D]   Shareholder Democracy

At times, directors have tried to thwart voting by shareholders, usually by limiting or precluding the vote in a contest for control (proxy fight or hostile tender offer). The actions taken are usually unilateral by the directors.[188] In a series of Delaware cases, the courts have shown a willingness to treat voting rights cases with greater scrutiny. In *Schnell v. Chris-Craft Industries, Inc.*[189] incumbent management, fearing a proxy challenge, changed the date of the annual meeting to an earlier time which would make it more difficult for the insurgents. Under the bylaws, the board had the legal right to change the date. However, the court indicated that inequitable conduct is not permissible simply because it is authorized under the bylaws and thus seemingly legal. The management's attempt to perpetuate their offices constituted inequitable conduct contrary to principles of corporate democracy. The original meeting date was reinstated. The court viewed the actions of the directors as perpetuating themselves in office and undermining shareholder democracy.

---

[186] For a discussion of the business judgment rule, see § 8.03[B], *infra.*

[187] 493 A.2d. 946 (Del. 1985). For a discussion of the *Unocal* test, see § 12.05[A][2], *infra.*

[188] In *Unilever Acquisition Corp. v. Richardson-Vicks, Inc.*, 618 F. Supp. 407 (S.D.N.Y. 1985), the directors issued a convertible preferred stock to existing shareholders which gave the holders additional voting rights (one share of preferred stock was issued for each five shares of common and each preferred had 25 votes compared to one vote per common share). The additional voting rights of the preferred initially had no effect since all the shareholders had both common and preferred status. However, upon transfer of the preferred shares, the purchaser acquired reduced voting rights for three years (from 25 to 5 votes). Thus existing shareholders, all of which received the preferred, had equivalent voting rights but when those shares were sold, the new holder had the decreased voting rights and remaining shareholders increased voting. power. This structure was intended as a takeover defense because a large shareholder group which owned as little as one third of the shares could have majority voting rights if they held their shares while public shareholders sold to a bidder who would have reduced voting. The bidder could have a majority of the shares but would have to wait three years to attain full voting rights. This would prevent the immediate transfer of control and deter a bidder. The directors issued the preferred shares without a shareholder vote. Normally, the issuance of shares that are authorized in the articles do not require a shareholder vote. The court found that the plan violated Delaware law. Although the statute did not preclude the issuance of the preferred stock, the limitation on future voting rights restricted transferability and affected voting rights, which appeared to violate the statute on restricted voting.

[189] 285 A.2d 437 (Del. 1971).

In *Blasius Industries v. Atlas Corp.*,[190] an insurgent group used the shareholder consent mechanism (solicited proxy votes on a matter directly from the shareholders without the necessity of calling a shareholder meeting) to expand the board and elect new directors for the new positions.[191] The consent would have expanded the board from 7 to 15 and the insurgents would have elected 8 new members, shifting the power to them. The expanded board, with the insurgents in the majority, would vote in favor of recapitalizing the company opposed by the directors.[192] In response, the incumbent board used its power under the bylaws to expand the board by an additional two directors (now a total of 17). The incumbent board filled those two vacancies so they would constitute nine directors out of the 17 to thwart the shift in power sought by the insurgents. Plaintiffs relied on *Schnell* and argued that there was a breach of duty of loyalty because of a conflict of interest by the directors in perpetuating themselves. The defendant directors argued that they were protected by the business judgment rule and acted for the interest of the corporation to protect it from the recapitalization plan of the insurgents.

The court recognized the importance of protecting shareholder voting. The court found that the board's action of expanding the number of directors thwarted the insurgents and the primary purpose was to interfere with shareholder voting. Therefore, the action was not protected by the business judgment rule, which restricts judicial scrutiny.[193] While rejecting a perse rule that would never allow a board to thwart shareholder voting, the court, in order to provide flexibility for future situations, used a strict duty of loyalty standard. This standard provides for close judicial scrutiny which shifts the burden to the directors and, given the importance of shareholder voting, requires a "compelling justification" of their actions. Thus under *Blausius*, when the primary purpose of the directors' actions is to impede or interfere with shareholder voting the compelling justification test applies.[194]

---

[190] 564 A.2d 652 (Del Ch. 1988).

[191] For a discussion of consent mechanism, see the text at note 156, *supra*.

[192] The plan would have the company borrow funds and use the loan proceeds to pay large dividends to the shareholders. Such increased borrowing is a form of leveraging. For a discussion of leveraging, see § 4.03, *supra*.

[193] The rule protects the substance of board decisions from review by the courts so long as the decision making process was proper. For a discussion of the business judgment rule, see § 8.03[C], *infra*.

[194] In *State of Wisconsin Investment Board v. Peerless Systems Corp*, 2000 Del. Ch. LEXIS 17 (Jan. 24, 2000), the corporation adjourned the shareholder meeting because there were insufficient votes cast to authorize an increase in the stock option plan. The chairman adjourned the meeting and closed voting on other resolutions that had passed but kept the polls open on the stock options increase. The reason that the other proposals passed was because under NYSE rules brokers who hold shares can vote those shares for routine matters unless instructed differently by the shareholders. The stock option issue was not routine so the shareholders had to vote their shares. During the adjournment there was no disclosure about the postponed vote. The managers then solicited sufficient votes to pass the resolution. Plaintiffs argued for a Blausius review while defendants argued the business judgment rule. Because of the lack of disclosure there was no evidence that the defendants were trying to enhance shareholder voting by increasing participation. The court applied *Blausius* and the subsequent passage of the proposal could only serve as a ratification if the vote was fair. For a discussion of ratification and voting, see § 9.06, *infra*.

Both *Schell* and *Blausius* indicated that there would be close judicial scrutiny and intervention when voting rights were implicated. This close scrutiny will also apply to voting issues in other contests for control, such as a hostile tender offer.[195] Subsequent cases have modified this scrutiny by looking closely at the particular context in which the issue is raised and whether the shareholders voted in favor of the changes. In *Stroud v. Grace*,[196] certain amendments to a corporation's bylaws and certificate regarding qualifications of directors and nomination procedures were proposed by the control group. These amendments could have had the effect of entrenching existing management. The company was a closely held corporation and there was fully informed shareholder approval of the actions. The court found no inequitable conduct to manipulate corporate voting. Unlike *Schnell* or *Blasius* in which there were unilateral board actions to frustrate or completely disenfranchise voting, in *Stroud* fully informed shareholders approved the changes. Thus, because of a "full and fair opportunity to vote", a stringent rule was not applied and the burden was on the plaintiff to show an improper purpose and unfairness and not just hypothetical abuse.[197] The court seemed to suggest that it would look to the actual use of the amendments in practice to see if they abused the minority.

In *Williams v. Geier*,[198] a plan was proposed by the control group to recapitalize the shares through amendments to the articles of incorporation. Under the plan, existing shareholders would have 10 votes per share (creating super voting shares) while new shareholders would have only one vote for their first three years, after which they would then have super voting (that is, 10 votes). The plan further entrenched the control group because any bidder in a hostile takeover (a takeover opposed by management) would have to buy shares having only one vote for three years, delaying an acquisition for at least 3 years.[199] The control group, which was less likely to sell than public shareholders, would have the super voting shares.[200]

The plaintiff wanted the court to apply the compelling justification standard of *Blasius*, which shifts the heavy burden on to the defendants. The trial court applied a standard of judicial review established in *Unocal Corp.*, which involved

---

[195] The *Unocal* modified business judgment rule usually applies in cases of directors initiating defensive tactics but the compelling justification test applies when shareholder voting is involved. For a discussion of these two tests and shareholder voting issues in tender offers, see § 12.05[A][7], *infra.*

[196] 606 A.2d. 75 (Del. 1992).

[197] 606 A.2d 75 (Del. 1992). The court utilized a fairness inquiry, which meant that it would look at the substance of the decision. The case is in line with other cases dealing with shareholder ratification when controlling shareholders were involved. *See* § 10.03[C][2][a][ii], *infra; see also In Re Wheelbrator Technologies Shareholder Litigation*, 663 A.2d. 1194 (Del. Ch. 1994) (the Delaware Chancery Court viewed the shareholder voting in *Stroud* as shifting the burden on fairness). *But see Williams v. Geier*, 671 A.2d 1368 (Del. 1996) (court suggested that fairness may not be an issue).

[198] 671 A.2d 1368 (Del. 1996).

[199] The fact that there may be an entrenchment effect does not mean that it was intended. Here, there was evidence of a good faith belief that it would enhance long term corporate planning.

[200] Although management and a family group controlled more than 50% of the shares, the plan would allow them to potentially sell some shares and own less than 50% but still retain control. There are also times when a control group can split up into different factions with one group wanting to sell. Under the plan a minority group which did not sell could then retain control.

a modified business judgment rule that initially placed the burden on the defendants to justify their actions.[201] The Delaware Supreme Court in *Williams* rejected the *Blasius* rule as one to be rarely applied[202] and the *Unocal* test as inapplicable because there was no unilateral board action because the shareholders voted for the proposals. Instead, the majority applied the business judgment rule (a presumption that the directors acted independently with due care and in good faith) to the decision of the directors, who were considered independent.[203] There was no evidence of self interest or motivation of entrenchment by the majority of directors, and all shareholders were treated equally (although there was no obvious benefit to them).

In *Williams* there was a shareholder vote because it was required by the statute for amendments to the articles of incorporation and was not a case of optional voting such as a shareholder ratification.[204] Since the shareholders' vote was fully informed and without fraud, waste or inequitable conduct, the vote was dispositive.[205] Although a majority of the minority shareholders failed to approve of the plan, that was not significant because approval was not conditioned on such approval and there was no statutory requirement for it.[206] The fact that the majority shareholder voted in favor of the plan was also not significant since shareholders may vote their own self interest so long as they do so without breaching their fiduciary duty. *Williams* suggests that there will be less judicial scrutiny when shareholders vote to authorize potential defensive tactics, especially when the statute authorizes the particular action taken.

---

[201] 493 A.2d 946 (Del. 1985). See discussion of the *Unocal* test at § 12.05[A][2], *supra*. The dissent in *Williams* would have used both *Unocal* and *Blasius* analysis because the plan had a clear benefit for the control group. The majority shareholders had indicated they would vote in favor (the minority shareholders could not have stopped the plan). A failure to get a 2/3 vote would have resulted in delisting under New York Stock Exchange Rules. This put the public shareholders in a bind because if they voted against the plan, it could have meant their shares would not trade on the New York Stock Exchange. This vote had potential for coercion in a publicly-held corporation with minority shareholders, while *Stroud* involved a closely held corporation. The dissent believed that the plan's primary motivation was entrenchment with a substantial effect on voting rights, requiring stricter judicial scrutiny.

[202] For a discussion of *Blausius* and *Unocal*, see § 12.05[A][7], *infra*.

[203] That there was a control group with a majority of shares did not mean that the directors were not independent. The plaintiff must show by particularized facts that there is lack of independence. For a discussion of independence see § 5.02[F], *supra*. On the effect of independent director approval and interested directors transactions, see § 9.03, *infra*.

[204] For a discussion of shareholder ratification, see § 9.06, *infra*.

[205] Here the vote was dispositive even when there was a controlling shareholder who voted in favor. If there was no rational corporate purpose or if the vote was primarily for entrenchment, the result would be different. The court distinguished this from cases invoking an entire fairness standard (such as freezeouts) where the votes of minority shareholders may be relevant to judicial scrutiny. Here an amendment to the articles with shareholders voting complied with the statute and thus no entire fairness inquiry. Full and fair disclosure was required. But see *Stroud*, which suggested that fairness remains an inquiry with the burden on the plaintiff.

[206] There are cases in which such approval does effect judicial scrutiny. For a discussion of shareholder ratification generally, see § 9.06, *infra*, and in freezeouts, see § 10.03[C][2](a)(ii), *infra*.

[E]   Vote Buying

When shareholders vote, they usually may vote as they please. However, if the voting of the shares involves coercion[207] or some breach of fiduciary duty by a controlling shareholder,[208] or vote buying, there may be limitations on that right to vote. Vote buying can occur when pursuant to an agreement, a shareholder receives consideration that divorces discretionary voting power from her shares.[209] Some courts may view vote buying as illegal perse because its purpose is to defraud or disenfranchise other shareholders or because shareholders rely on other shareholders to use their independent judgment. The modern view is less strict and looks at the voting agreements in light of their object or purpose.

Voting arrangements among shareholders in which votes are restricted or transferred are often important ways to structure share holdings in closely held corporations.[210] On the other hand, courts faced with charges of vote buying will look at the substance of the transaction and its object to determine if it will defraud or disenfranchise shareholders unfairly.[211]

[F]   Right to Information

In addition to the power to vote, shareholders are granted the right to receive some information. This right is conferred by both federal securities laws and state law.[212] For example, when public shareholders vote, they must receive information about the issue under both state corporate law and federal securities law. The corporate financial statements are an important source of information given to shareholders. In publicly traded corporations, federal securities laws require that financial statements and other important

---

[207] For an example of coercion by controlling shareholders, see § 10.03[C][2](c), *infra*, and the *Kahn* case.

[208] For a discussion of controlling shareholders, see Chapter 10, *infra*.

[209] *See* Henry T. C. Hu & Bernard Black, *The New Vote Buying: Empty Voting And Hidden (Morphable) Ownership*, 79 S. CAL. L. REV. 811 (2006) (discusses new forms of vote buying through the use of derivatives that decouple voting and argues for disclosure).

[210] For example, shareholders are permitted to use irrevocable proxies in different situations that does separate voting rights from ownership. For a discussion of shareholder agreements and irrevocable proxies in closely held corporations, see § 11.02[C], *infra*.

[211] In *Schreiber v. Carney*, 447 A.2d 17 (Del. Ch. 1982), there was a loan from the corporation to its controlling shareholder. The shareholder had threatened to block a proposed merger of the corporation if the loan was not made. The loan was attacked as vote buying and a conflict of interest transaction. The vote buying was valid because the agreement to favor the merger for the loan was intended to benefit all the shareholders and not to defraud or disenfranchise shareholders. Although the loan transaction was voidable because of a conflict of interest, it was negotiated by independent directors unaffiliated with the controlling shareholder and was approved by the disinterested directors and shareholders after full disclosure, which precluded judicial inquiry. *See* discussion of shareholder ratification at § 9.06, *infra*, and disinterested directors' approval at § 9.03[B], *infra*. *See also* discussion of *Lacos* at § 10.01, note 9, *infra*.

[212] The state statutes do not usually require significant disclosure, but fiduciary duty rules established by the courts can provide full disclosure. For a discussion of the fiduciary duty of disclosure see § 8.07, *infra*.

information be provided to public investors and to the stock markets.[213] The financial statements must be prepared by independent public accountants who are obligated to the investors to use their best efforts to provide full disclosure and thereby inhibit fraud. The use of accountants in the preparation of the financial statements is a significant monitoring device for publicly traded corporations.[214]

Under state law, shareholders may be able to inspect the books and records[215] or the list of shareholders, so long as there is a proper purpose.[216] The shareholder list is very important if a group of shareholders would like to communicate with other shareholders or challenge management in a proxy contest.[217] The inspection of books and records may be important for finding wrongdoing, to communicate with directors about reform, to assist shareholder litigation[218] or to help value the shares.[219] The response to a demand for books and records depends on which documents the shareholders seeking to inspect[220] and the purpose for the inspection.[221]

---

[213] For a discussion of mandatory disclosure for publicly traded corporations under federal securities laws, see § 7.02, *infra*. For disclosure and fiduciary duty under state law, see § 8.07, *infra*.

[214] *See* Louis Lowenstein, *Financial Transparency and Corporate Governance: You Manage What You Measure*, 96 Colum. L. Rev. 1335 (1996). For a discussion of gatekeepers and monitoring, see § 5.02[G], *supra*.

[215] Since closely held corporations are not covered by mandatory disclosure under federal securities law, the right of inspection is particularly important in that context.

[216] The right often existed under the common law as a result of equitable principles and is now covered by statute. *See* Model Bus. Corp. Act Ann. § 16.02 (4th ed. 2008). Directors usually have the right to inspect books and records that relate to their duties. *See* Del. Gen. Corp. Law § 220 (d).

[217] Federal law provides management with the choice of providing the list or mailing the materials for the insurgent group. *See* SEC Rule 14a-7. Shareholders prefer the list in order to have direct contact with the shareholders. Since state law provides greater rights such as direct access to the list, it would prevail over federal law. This is not a case where federal law would preempt state law because the proxy rules were intended to protect shareholders. Thus, greater rights under state law would foster federal policy. In a tender offer, access to the shareholder list should be viewed as a proper purpose. In *Crane Co. v. Anaconda Co.*, 39 N.Y.2d 14 (1976), the New York Court of Appeals allowed for the shareholder list and rejected the argument that a tender offer did not relate to the business of the corporation.

[218] In the litigation in the *Disney* case the plaintiffs original complaint was dismissed and the court advised the plaintiffs to use their inspection rights to gather more information. The plaintiffs did so and refiled their complaint which was not dismissed. For a discussion of the *Disney* litigation see § 8.06[A], *infra*.

[219] In *Thomas & Betts Co. v. Leviton Mfg. Co.*, 681 A.2d 1026 (Del. 1996), The court found that the need to inspect for purposes of valuation of the shares was permitted so long as the plaintiff showed that the records sought were essential and sufficient for that purpose. The court also indicated that a shareholder seeking inspection of books and records for claims of waste and mismanagement has a normal burden of proof on proper purpose and must present credible evidence that will show the mismanagement or waste.

[220] For example, MBCA § 16.02(a) makes it easier to inspect certain records like the bylaws and shareholder minutes than accounting records, board minutes or shareholder lists. Model Bus. Corp. Act Ann. § 16.02(a) (4th ed. 2008). The latter would require a proper purpose described with reasonable particularity. Model Bus. Corp. Act Ann. § 16.02(b)(c) (4th ed. 2008). *See* note 219, *infra*.

[221] In *Saito v. McKesson HBOC, Inc.*, 806 A.2d 113 (Del. 2002), the Delaware Supreme Court allowed inspection of documents created prior to becoming a shareholder even though if a derivative suit was brought by the shareholder there would be no standing for prior acts. To bring a derivative

In deciding these issues, courts look to both the common law right of inspection and the corporate statutes. In either case, there is usually a requirement of proper purpose for the inspection. The burden of proving proper purpose depends on the circumstances. Proper purpose and the burden of proof issues are intended to deal with the tension between the shareholders' legitimate right to be informed and right to communicate with other shareholders and the possible harassment of managers and abuse of the information. Generally, the shareholder list[222] is easier to obtain while an inspection of books and records may involve confidential information and may be more difficult to obtain.[223] Under Delaware law if the shareholders are seeking information because of alleged wrongdoing then the shareholder must provide some evidence to establish it by a "credible basis."[224]

In *State ex. rel. Pillsbury v. Honeywell, Inc.*,[225] a shareholder of Honeywell requested the shareholder list and other corporate records under Delaware law. He wished to communicate with other shareholders about his opposition to the

---

suit, a shareholder must own the shares at the time of the wrongdoing. That date does not control inspection rights. The key question is whether the documents are necessary and essential to a proper purpose. Access by a shareholder of a parent to a subsidiary's books required a showing of fraud or no real separate existence (see Chapter 3 on piercing the corporate veil). The legislature modified the requirement for inspection of subsidiary corporations if the parent had actual possession or could obtain the information through exercise of control. Del. Gen. Corp. Law § 220 (a)(2).

[222] In publicly traded corporations, most of the shares are not actually held by the individual shareholders but in "street name" on deposit with major depositories. The holding of shares by depositories facilitates the transfers of shares when sold because the shares need not be physically signed over by the owner. The shares are registered in the names of the brokerage houses representing the shareholders (called the "CEDE list" after Depository Trust Co., the largest depository). Without the true names of the owners, it is difficult to contact the actual owners. As a result, brokers are required under S.E.C. Rules to send the names of the beneficial owners to the corporation so long as those own ers do not object ("NOBO" rules, that is, non-objecting beneficial owner). In *Sadler v. NCR Corporation*, 928 F.2d 48 (2d Cir. 1991), the court ordered the inspection of the NOBO list under New York law, even though a Delaware case had indicated that if the preparation of that list takes time and could be burdensome, it need not be produced. The Delaware court had ordered the production of only the "CEDE," which are not as complete because they usually do not include a breakdown of individual owners.

[223] The courts have wide latitude in determining the scope of any inspection and can tailor the inspection to its purpose. *See Marathon Partners L.P. and Furtherfield Partners L.P. v M & F Worldwide Corporation*, 2004 Del. Ch. LEXIS 101 (the court allowed access to some corporate information concerning the board granting permission for purchases of the corporate stock but subjected the access to a confidentiality agreement.).

[224] In *Seinfeld v. Verizon Communications, Inc*, 909 A2d 717 (Del. 2006) the Delaware Supreme Court affirmed the use of the credible basis standard and the need for some evidence to support the claim. The court was concerned with a "fishing expedition" that would not benefit the shareholder. While the plaintiff has the burden of proof, they are not required to prove wrongdoing but only by a preponderance of evidence a credible basis which could infer wrongdoing. That could be showed through documents, logic, testimony or otherwise, The court viewed this a low standard although the plaintiff would have preferred just presenting "some evidence" without the requirement of credible basis which the Court rejected as mere suspicion. In *Security First Corp. v. United States Die Casting and Development Co.*, 687 A.2d 563 (Del. 1997), the Delaware Supreme Court indicated that a shareholder seeking inspection of books and records must show by a preponderance of evidence a credible basis of probable wrongdoing, not actual proof of its occurrence. But in seeking particular records, the plaintiff must be precise and show that it is essential to her purpose.

[225] 291 Minn. 322, 191 N.W.2d 406 (1971).

company's manufacture of munitions used in the Vietnam War. The company refused him the shareholder list, claiming that it was an improper purpose to promote his political views. The shareholder had purchased his 100 shares for the avowed purpose of challenging the manufacture of munitions. Since Honeywell was a Delaware corporation, the Minnesota court applied its view of Delaware law because the issue involved the internal affairs of the corporation.[226] Applying Delaware law, the court found the request to be an improper purpose, citing plaintiff's insignificant number of shares and the fact that his motivation for ownership was to change the policy was political rather than economic.[227] While the court was concerned with the possibility of harassment, it took a narrow view of shareholder interests and the right of shareholders to communicate with each other on important issues that at least were related to the corporation and its business.[228]

The decision seemed contrary to Delaware law because Delaware's courts tend to allow inspection, especially of the shareholder list, if the primary purpose is to solicit proxies and communicate with shareholders. The courts recognize that secondary purposes might exist but usually should not preclude access to the list.[229] In addition, the Delaware statute distinguishes between a request to inspect the shareholder list versus a request to inspect corporate books and records. In seeking the shareholder list, the burden of proof is on the defendant corporation to prove improper purpose.[230] For a request to inspect books and records, the plaintiff shareholder has the burden of proof on proper purposes.[231]

---

[226] See discussion of the choice of law and internal affairs doctrine at § 1.08, *supra*.

[227] This is similar to the arguments used against Henry Ford in *Dodge v. Ford Motor Co.*, 170 N.W. 668 (Mich. 1919), discussed at § 5.02[A], *supra*.

[228] For a discussion of a similar case involving SEC 34 Act Rule 14a-8 in, *Medical Committee v. Dow*, see § 7.05[E], *infra*.

[229] *See Credit Bureau Reports, Inc. v. Credit Bureau of St. Paul, Inc.*, 290 A.2d. 91 (Del.1972) (criticizing *Pillsbury*). *See also Conservative Caucus v. Chevron Corp.*, 525 A.2d 569 (Del. Ch. 1987) (finding a proper purpose when a nonprofit corporation owning 30 shares of Chevron sought list to communicate about risks of doing business in Angola, which might have affected the value of shares). In *General Time Corp. v. Talley Industries, Inc.*, 240 A.2d 755 (Del. 1968), the court found that the primary purpose for the list, to solicit proxies, was proper since it was reasonably related to the shareholder interest and any secondary purpose was irrelevant.

[230] An improper purpose could be inferred from an inability to verbalize the purpose for which the list is needed. In such a circumstance, the request may be viewed as a fishing expedition, idle curiosity or a plan to sell the list. In *Compaq Computer Corp. v. Horton*, 631 A.2d. 1 (Del. 1993), the Delaware Supreme Court found a proper purpose where a shareholder list was sought to enable a class action lawsuit against the corporation. It was sufficient that the shareholder had a single proper purpose related to the role as a shareholder.

[231] *See* Del. Gen. Corp. Law § 220(c). Under the statute proper purpose means "a purpose reasonably relates to such person's interest as a stockholder." Del. Gen. Corp. Law § 220(b).

§ 5.06   BOARD OF DIRECTORS

The board of directors in publicly traded corporations must give managers flexibility to run the business, while monitoring them to limit self dealing and mismanagement.[232] Most of the legal monitoring devices are aimed at trying to get the board to monitor managers without too much interference from shareholders.

Since the board of directors is not legally the agent of the shareholders, the board can act within its power to run the corporation, even if the majority of the shareholders disapprove.[233] If the shareholders want change, they may elect different directors at the next annual meeting or try to remove the directors by calling a special meeting prior to the annual meeting.[234] Once elected, directors act as fiduciaries to the corporation. This means that they must serve the "best interests of the corporation," including all its shareholders and not merely the interests of those who elect them.[235]

[A]   Board Structure

The unitary or single board of directors is the statutory norm for American corporations. The number of directors is usually set out in the bylaws or articles, and the directors are elected by the shareholders at their annual meeting, usually for a one year term.[236] The board acts for the corporation as a group and traditionally takes actions at meetings, usually by a majority vote. Individual directors who are not officers have no authority to act except through the board.

---

[232] A.L.I. Corp. Gov. Proj. § 3.02 provides that the directors of publicly traded corporations should: 1. Select or replace and compensate senior executives; 2. Oversee the business and evaluate it; 3. Review and if appropriate approve the financial objectives; 4. Review and if appropriate approve the accounting and auditing principle; 5. Perform other functions provided bylaw or under corporate standards. The board also has power to initiate and adopt corporate plans and actions, initiate and adopt changes in accounting practices, provide advice to officers, instruct others to review actions, make recommendations to shareholders, manage the business and act as to all matters not requiring shareholder approval.

[233] *See People ex rel. Manice v. Powell*, 94 N.E. 634 (N.Y. 1911). Shareholders have tried to amend the bylaws to require the directors to take certain actions. Shareholders can also express their views to the directors to change policy. See § 5.05[C][3], *supra.*

[234] The statutes generally allow for removal of directors for cause. They also may provide for removal by the shareholders without cause. Model Bus. Corp. Act Ann. § 8.08 (4th ed. 2008). Prior to the statutory enactments on removal, courts found an inherent right to remove directors for cause because shareholders, as owners, had the right to protect the corporation. *See Auer v. Dressel*, 118 N.E.2d 590 (N.Y. 1954). *See also Campbell v. Loew's, Inc.*, 134 A.2d 852 (Del. Ch. 1957). In *Campbell*, the court required a showing of cause for removal. While lack of cooperation and desire to take control was insufficient to constitute cause, charges of harassment and obstructive behavior by a director could be grounds for removal. The court did require some fair process such as service of specific charges, adequate notice and full opportunity to respond.

[235] That the shareholders cannot force the directors to act does not mean that they cannot influence them. For a discussion of the right of expression, see § 5.05[A][2], *supra.*

[236] Shareholders can opt to stagger the election of the board so that directors have terms longer than a year. The terms can be up to three years, in which case only one third of the directors are elected at the annual meeting. Such an arrangement may make it more difficult for someone wanting to challenge a board to gain immediate control. Usually the articles must authorize the staggered term. *E.g.*, Model Bus. Corp. Act Ann. § 8.06 (4th ed. 2008).

The actual role of the board will depend on many factors, including its makeup. There are generally no state legal requirements that establish any particular norm for either board makeup or function. Those rules are more the result of stock market requirements. In general, public companies must now have a majority of independent directors who are not directly affiliated with the corporation. They must also have committees of the board composed exclusively of independent members such as the audit, compensation and nominating committees.[237] This is the result of corporate governance rules which the markets themselves have initiated after the enactment of the Sarbanes-Oxley Act of 2002.[238]

Statutes generally permit boards to establish committees. Committees are given particular tasks and make recommendations to the whole board. In some cases, committees are delegated the power to act for the board.[239] For example, most publicly traded corporations have executive, nominating, audit and compensation committees. These and other committees allow for fewer directors to focus on important issues.[240]

[B]   Meetings

The board traditionally acts at a duly called meeting. Rules on voting, notice and quorums are usually set out in the bylaws pursuant to the requirements of the corporate statute. The statute often sets default rules which can be modified by the corporation, either through the bylaws or the articles. For example, the usual requirement is for a majority vote on most matters, so long as a quorum is present. Both the vote and quorum can be modified.[241] The more important the issue, the more likely the requirement that it be done by amending the articles of incorporation,[242] which requires a shareholder vote and a public filing, usually with the office of the State's Secretary of State.

[1]   Actions Without A Meeting

There has been some debate in the context of closely held corporations about whether the board may only act at a meeting, as opposed to more informal arrangements. The statutes generally provide for either unanimous written consent of the directors to act without a meeting, or teleconference. In closely

---

[237] For a discussion of the use of independent directors, see § 5.02[F], *supra.*

[238] For a discussion of Sarbanes-Oxley, see § 5.08, *infra.*

[239] *See, e.g.,* Model Bus. Corp. Act Ann. § 8.25 (4th ed. 2008). There are some limitations on the ability of the board to delegate certain important functions to committees. *See* Model Bus. Corp. Act Ann. § 8.25(e) (4th ed. 2008).

[240] For example, sometimes a special litigation committee may be appointed to deal with shareholder litigation. For a discussion of these committees, see § 14.06, *infra.*

[241] *See, e.g.,* Model Bus. Corp. Act Ann. § 8.24 (4th ed. 2008).

[242] Under MBCA § 10.03, the board recommends and shareholders vote on most amendments to the articles of incorporation. Model Bus. Corp. Act Ann. § 10.03 (4th ed. 2008). While amendments to the bylaws are usually voted on by the shareholders, the directors are sometimes given the power to amend. Shareholders can always repeal a board amendment to the bylaws and preclude the board from acting on that bylaw. Model Bus. Corp. Act Ann. § 10.20 (4th ed. 2008).

held corporations, informality is common and there may not be a conventional meeting called. There may also be absentee directors. Some courts take a strict view and require a meeting on the theory that since individual directors have no authority, only the board acting as a group can act for the corporation.[243] A meeting also provides the forum in which to express and change one's views. In reality, in many closely held corporations, directors act informally without proper meetings.

An early case, *Baldwin v. Canfield*,[244] made a strong statement against informal action in a corporation. A deed was executed seriatim by the directors of the Minneapolis Agricultural and Mechanical Association. Despite the signatures of each and every director, the court held the conveyance not to have been properly authorized. According to the court, the management of the corporation was vested in the board of directors. Thus, directors were to manage *as a board*, and not otherwise. Therefore, the directors had no authority to act, except when assembled at a board meeting.

Shareholders and directors of closely held and small corporations do act informally. Either they act at meetings without the requisite formalities, such as notice, minutes, and the like, or they act without meetings altogether, by seriatim agreement, as in *Baldwin v. Canfield*. In some cases, less than the whole number of shareholders or directors may act, without a meeting or any other formality, but with the acquiescence of the others.

There is a long history of corporate law finally coming to terms with the reality that directors and shareholders of closely held corporations do not observe the formalities statutes envision, either because they neglect the formalities required,[245] do not want to pay their attorney additional fees, or cannot assemble in the way envisioned because of the press of time and other responsibilities. The modern view will take these considerations into account and look at substance over form.

---

[243] Individual directors are not agents unless they are officers. Their authority depends upon their officer position, not their directorship.

[244] 26 Minn. 43 (1879).

[245] In *Bayer v. Beran*, 49 N.Y.S. 2d 2 (Sup.Ct. 1944) the corporation was publicly traded and the directors approved of an advertising campaign where the wife of the president and director of the company would benefit by performing. The plaintiffs asserted a conflict of interest claiming that was the motivation for the contract and approval was illegal because of the informal process (no formal meeting or resolution), In terms of the process, the court accepted the fact that this particular board acted informally on a regular basis and the corporation was successful so the lack of formality was not an issue. It did suggest that in the future it should act less informally. For a discussion of the conflict of interest, see § 9.03 note 14, *infra*.

§ 5.07   OFFICERS

The daily operation of business is usually delegated to the corporate officers, who are appointed by the board of directors.[246] The appointment of an officer may be for a term. Officers may be removed by the directors at will, even if no cause exists.[247] The designation of officers is usually done by the corporation through the board or by designation in the bylaws.[248] Often one finds a president, one or more vice presidents, a treasurer and a secretary. Officers have a fiduciary duty to the corporation since they are corporate agents. Officers often serve as directors, in which case they are known as "inside directors."

[A]   Authority

An officer's power originates from the board of directors.[249] Statutes usually say little about the actual power of an officer. Determining the power of the officers to bind the corporation is an important issue that is usually based upon agency law principles. Officers are agents of the corporation and the corporation as an artificial entity can only operate through its agents. In order for an agent to have the power to bind the principal, there must be either a grant of authority from the principal or other policy considerations that dictate the result.[250]

There are three significant ways that an agent may bind the principal — express, implied and apparent authority. In each case the authority comes from the principal (i.e., the corporation). Express actual authority is present where the principal expressly endows the agent with authority. For example, express authority exists when the board or president tells a manager of one of its stores to hire employees. Implied actual authority exists where the principal implicitly gives the agent authority to act. This implication can result from the manager's title or by the behavior of the principal. For example, the manager may purchase goods for a store to sell even though the manager was not expressly told to do so. If store managers in her position usually have authority to buy goods to sell, the authority is implied by the principal having given her the position. If the store manager acts and the principal acquiesces in the actions, authority may also be implied. The owner would be bound by the manager's purchases. Apparent authority is created when the principal manifests to third parties that the agent has authority to act (express and implied results from the manifestation from the principle to the agent). In most cases of apparent authority, an implied authority may coexist. In naming someone as manager, the

---

[246] Some states permit the articles to allow for shareholders to elect officers. Officers elected by shareholders may only be removed by them. *See, e.g.*, N.Y.B.C.L. § 715. This would be used in a closely held corporation.

[247] *See, e.g.*, Model Bus. Corp. Act Ann. § 8.43(b) (4th ed. 2008).

[248] Model Bus. Corp. Act Ann. § 8.40 (4th ed. 2008).

[249] Some powers cannot be delegated to officers. For example, under state statutes, certain fundamental transactions, such as the approval of mergers, require board approval and cannot be delegated. *See, e.g.*, Model Bus. Corp. Act Ann. § 11.03(b) (4th ed. 2008).

[250] A principal may be bound by an agent even though the principal has done nothing to create authority. For example, if an agent injures someone while in the course of employment, the principal may be liable, even though she never authorized the act, under vicarious liability. *See Croisant v. Watrud*, 248 Or. 324, 432 P.2d 799 (1967).

principal creates implied authority to the manager with the authority that managers are expected to possess and similarly through apparent authority to third parties who would reasonably assume she had the authority of a manager. However, if the owner had told the manager not to order goods but she did so anyway and the third parties did not know of her lack of authority, the owner could still be liable under the concept of apparent authority even though there was no implied actual authority. There is liability because it is reasonable for third parties to assume that the manager had the authority and to rely on that assumption. While the agent may be liable in that case to the principal for exceeding her authority, third party transactions are protected.[251]

If an officer exceeds her authority, the principal may ratify the authority either expressly, or implicitly, as for example by accepting the benefits with knowledge of the consequences.[252] For example, if an employee buys goods for a store without authority and the owner retains the goods with knowledge and later sells those goods, the owner has ratified the purchase of the employee.

In the corporate context determining authority may not always be clear. Express authority may be found in the bylaws, corporate resolutions made by the board, or properly approved employment contracts. Senior officers will usually have the power to create authority in other employees. The implied authority will depend on the position held and customs. When questions arise as to whether an agent has authority to act on behalf of a corporation particularly on a significant decision, one should make sure the corporation agrees to be bound by his or her acts. To do so, the party may seek a board resolution certified by the secretary, a writing signed by someone authorized to give authority or an opinion of the corporate attorney that there was proper authorization.

While the legal model described allows flexibility in board structure and officer power, the usual management structure of publicly traded corporations centralizes power in the chief executive officer and senior officers. While concerns have been expressed over this power and the need to strengthen the

---

[251] Sometimes there is no implied or apparent authority but the principal is liable because of inherent agency power. In that case, no authority was manifest by the principal but the power to bind the principal stems from the agency relationship and the need to protect third parties. The acts must be usual for the agent and third party reasonably believes agent has the authority and is without notice of the lack of authority. Restatement of Agency 2d § 161 For example, inherent agency can create liability for a principal if the contract is the kind made by a general agent (one authorized to conduct a series of transactions involving a continuity of service) but in fact there is no authority to contract or manifestation of that authority to the third party. *See Nogales Service Center v. Atlantic Richfield Co.*, 613 P.2d 293 (Ariz. 1980). *See also Menard, Inc. v. Dage-Miti, Inc*, 726 N.E.2d 1206 (Ind. 2000) (the court found that a president who was not authorized to purchase land had the inherent power to bind the corporation because it was in the usual scope of authority and in the past the president wielded significant power and the seller could reasonably believe based upon the president's positions, statements that he had the authority, involvement of the corporate attorney and the contract itself indicated the authority).

[252] The acceptance of acts done by promoters of the corporation prior to formation cannot be ratified because at the time the promoter acted, there was no corporation in existence. In order to have a ratification, the principal must exist at the time the act was done. Thus the corporation in accepting an act of a promoter is an adoption rather than a ratification. An adoption does not relate back to the time the promoter acted. For a discussion of promoter liability, see § 2.02, *supra.*

independent directors' monitoring[253], this structure will remain the norm given the business necessity of full time insiders managing the company.

§ 5.08   THE SARBANES-OXLEY ACT OF 2002

Major corporate scandals have influenced the development of regulation to try to limit the ability of managers or controlling shareholders to harm the public shareholders. In the 1920s there was a stock market boom where prices of shares seemed to be going only in one direction. The euphoria associated with that kind of market has been described by some economists as a market bubble.[254] The stock market crash of 1929 burst this bubble which was later followed by the Great Depression. The election of Franklin Roosevelt in 1932 and his New Deal legislation that tried to address the market crash. Many believed that the rise and eventual fall of the stock market were due to frauds in the stock markets and by many publicly traded corporations and self dealing in the financial industry. As a result there was sweeping reforms on the federal level with the passage of federal securities laws.[255] The major focus of the legislation in terms of corporate governance was full disclosure to investors, regulation of proxies, anti fraud and insider trading rules, the role of independent accountants and reforms of the stock markets including insider trading rules.[256]

In the 1990s, the stock market boomed again lead by enthusiasm for the technology, telecom and high tech sector and the rise of the Internet. There was again a euphoria about investing in the stock market and its continued rise. Predictions of a new age of stock valuation seemed to attract investors. The market was over valued and was due for a fall and the bubble burst again beginning in 2001.[257] As the market declined, corporate scandals began to unfold which further hastened the market downward. The various scandals made investors concerned about the management of large corporations and the reliability of their financial statements.

The first major scandal was the fall of a company called Enron, followed by other corporate scandals. Enron began its existence as a pipeline company and ended up as a trading company and a financial intermediary. At one point it ranked as the seventh largest company in the United States in terms of market capitalization and its shares hit a high of $90 and was widely admired on Wall Street and in the press. All was not well with Enron. It turns out that it had tried to make its balance sheet and income statement look better through numerous transactions with supposedly independent entities (some of which were in fact

---

[253] In some publicly traded corporations the position of the Chief Executive Officer and Chairman of the Board has been split or there has been an appointment of a lead outside director in order to strengthen the independent directors.

[254] Robert Shiller, IRRATIONAL EXUBERANCE (2000).

[255] For a discussion of the federal securities law, see Chapters 7 and 13, *infra*.

[256] Joel Seligman, THE TRANSFORMATION OF WALL STREET (1982).

[257] In 1994, the Dow Jones Average (a stock composite for blue chip stocks) was around 3,600 and it rose to around 11,700 in 2000. But by 2002, the Dow declined to close to 7,500. Basic economic indicators were not close to tripling during the period. By any traditional measures the market was overvalued.

not independent of Enron). Many of these transactions were illegitimate and designed to remove liabilities from its balance sheet and increase its revenues and profits on its income statement. In essence, Enron was committing accounting fraud in order to increase the value of its shares. That increasing value justified increasing salaries and bonuses for managers and enabled them to cash in on the higher market price through their stock options. Some executives were involved in conflicts of interests being on both sides of the transactions with Enron and these entities and personally profited from their activities.[258] All this was done while Enron's independent directors and gatekeepers i.e., accountants, outside lawyers, rating agencies[259] and investment bankers who were supposed to protect the shareholders failed to prevent the fraud.[260] Upon discovery of the fraud, Enron went bankrupt, wiping out the shareholders and many employees' pensions that were invested in Enron shares. Arthur Andersen, Enron's independent accountant, was criminally indicted and convicted at the trial level of obstruction of justice and document destruction which lead to the firm's demise.[261]

Enron was soon followed by other financial frauds such as WorldCom, Adelphi Communications, Imclone and Tyco. The frauds included improper insider trading, false financial statements, excessive compensation, unfair self dealing transactions and improper use of corporate funds. There were numerous cases of unfair dealing by the managers and mismanagement by the outside directors who were supposed to monitor the managers and be sure the financial statements were accurate. Ultimately, investment depends on trust, and the pessimistic public mood was reflected in the decline of the stock markets and in opinion polls.

The scandals raised several questions.[262] Was the market bubble the creation of fraud or overly enthusiastic investors, or both? Were the scandals a reflection of a few bad companies committing fraud, or was there a systemic problem that needed correction?[263] Were the systems intended to protect investors really effective and where were those who were supposed to protect shareholders and investors? Did the extensive use of stock options create incentives for financial

---

[258] William Bratton, *Enron and the Darkside of Shareholder Value*, 76 TUL. L. REV. 1275 (2002). *See also* Bethany McClean & Peter Elkind, THE SMARTEST GUYS IN THE ROOM: THE AMAZING RISE AND SCANDALOUS FALL OF ENRON (2003).

[259] Under Sarbanes-Oxley, the SEC was required to study the role of the rating agencies and recommend any needed reforms.

[260] John Coffee, *Understanding Enron: "Its About the Gatekeepers Stupid,"* 57 BUS. LAW. 1403 (2003). Criminal, civil and private litigation has been brought against various participants in the fraud. Both Citigroup and JP Morgan Chase settled with the SEC, paying large penalties after they was accused of participating in the fraud.

[261] The Supreme Court unanimously reversed the conviction based upon faulty jury instructions that should have required proof it know it was breaking the law. *Arthur Andersen LLP v. United States* 543 U.S. 1042 (2005) Arthur Andersen was also the accountant for numerous corporations guilty of financial fraud including Worldcom, Sunbeam and Waste Management.

[262] *See generally* Symposium, *Lessons From Enron: How did Corporate and Securities Law Fail?*, 48 VILL. L. REV. 989–1280 (2003).

[263] Douglas Branson, *Enron — When All Systems Fail: Creative Destruction or Roadmap to Corporate Governance Reform?*, 48 VILL. L. REV. 989 (2003).

manipulation that really benefitted the managers and not the shareholders?[264] Was the problem a reflection of the United States corporate governance system and a failure of markets to protect investors?[265]

The bust of the stock market bubble created large losses for the public shareholders. One significant difference between the recent downturn and the crash of 1929 is the increased ownership of shares by the public though personal savings or retirement funds, which clearly raised the political stakes over corporate governance issues. Corporate governance became a major news story and political issue with calls for actions by Congress and pressure on the Bush administration. As a result of these scandals there were several reactions. Congress enacted quickly and with bipartisan support the Sarbanes-Oxley Act of 2002 ("Sarbanes-Oxley").[266] The law deals with among other things accounting, corporate governance issues, increased disclosure[267] and conflicts of interest in the securities business. In terms of accounting, a new Public Company Accounting Oversight Board was established to set auditing, quality control and ethics standards for public accounting firms. In the past many of these functions were done with self policing by private bodies. This new board consists of full time independent members which have the power to investigate and impose sanctions.

The new law dealt with other accounting issues. While the independent accountant's role is to audit the financial statements, many public accounting firms had also supplied the corporations they audit with other services which were often more lucrative to the accountants. The variety of roles accountants play had raised issues of whether the auditing function is compromised by the desire to perform consulting services. Although some critics called for a complete ban on consulting, Sarbanes-Oxley does not ban those activities but strengthens the independence of auditors by limiting the scope of consulting activities accountants can undertake while also auditing the financial statements. In addition, the lead partner on the audit must now be rotated after five years (some critics called for the entire firm to be rotated). The accountants also must report directly to the board of directors and to its audit committee, which must consist of independent directors.

---

[264] *See* Roger Lowenstein, ORIGINS OF THE CRASH (2004) (arguing that poorly structured stock options create perverse incentives). For a discussion of stock options, see § 9.04[A], *infra*.

[265] Corporate governance systems overseas have been described as less of a market driven system and one that relies more on large debt and equity holders (family groups or banks) to monitor the business. Yet there were financial scandals such as Elan in Ireland, Vivendi in France, Parmalat in Italy and Ahoud in the Netherlands.

[266] Sarbanes-Oxley Act of 2002, Pub. L. No. 107-204, 116 Stat. 745 (codified in sections of Titles 11, 15, 28, and 29 of the U.S. Code). The Sarbanes-Oxley Act of 2002 was passed by the United States House of Representatives by a vote of 423-3 and by the United States Senate by a vote of 99-0. Stephen Labaton, *Corporate Conduct: Accounting; New Rules on Accountants, but Also Questions*, N.Y. TIMES, July 26, 2002 at C1.

[267] Sarbanes-Oxley also increased fraud and criminal penalties. The civil penalties cannot be reimbursed under directors and officer insurance policies or from indemnification. For a discussion of reimbursement, see § 14.11, *infra*.

In terms of corporate governance, Sarbanes-Oxley tries to increase the monitoring of the business and responsibilities of managers.[268] The law seeks a strengthened audit committee of the board to hire the accountants and review accounting issues. The accountant's responsibility is to the board of directors, not the managers. The audit committee is also required to implement procedures for whistle blowers to be able to report their concerns without retaliation. The chief executive officer and chief financial officer of the corporation must now certify that the financial statements and disclosure fairly present the operations and financials with the possibility of criminal penalties if not the case. Further, if the corporation materially restates its financials then managers may have to forfeit some compensation. Section 302 of Sarbanes-Oxley mandates a set of internal procedures designed to ensure accurate financial disclosure and a certification that they have been designed to ensure that material information relating to the company is made known. Section 404 requires management and the external auditor to report on the adequacy of the company's internal control over financial reporting which must be attested to by the accountants.[269]

Loans from the corporation to directors or executive officers are now generally barred. The SEC was also given the power to bar certain persons from serving as directors or officers. Sarbanes-Oxley also recognized the role of attorneys in protecting shareholders and authorized the SEC to issue rules of professional conduct.[270] Some of the civil penalties paid when the SEC brings an action can now be used as part of a fund to benefit harmed investors.

In terms of increased disclosure, Sarbanes-Oxley requires disclosure of insider trading transaction promptly (i.e., by the second day after the transaction) under § 16(a) of the Exchange Act.[271] A public corporation must also disclose whether it has a code of ethics for its financial officers and if not, it must explain why not. In addition, corporations must disclose if their audit committee has at least one member who is considered to be a financial expert.[272] Material changes in the operations or financial condition must be made in a rapid and current basis.

---

[268] Lyman P.Q. Johnson & Mark A. Sides, *Corporate Governance and the Sarbanes-Oxley Act: The Sarbanes-Oxley Act and Fiduciary Duty*, 30 WM. MITCHELL L. REV. 1149 (2004). For a discussion of monitoring, see § 8.03[A], *infra.*

[269] Internal controls relates to duty to monitor. See § 8.03[A], *infra.*

[270] Section 307 of Sarbanes-Oxley required the SEC to set minimum standards for attorneys who practice before the SEC. The rules provide that attorneys who become a ware of credible evidence of a material violation to report such evidence "up the ladder" of the corporation (the audit committee, another committee of independent directors or full board). The issue of whether the attorney should at some point make a "noisy withdrawal" and contact the SEC about wrongdoing was not in the rules but that issue remains a possibility for the future. 17 C.F.R. Part 205. The concern of the rules and possibility of whistle blowing by attorneys may be contrary to the rules of Professional Responsibility in some states which may preclude any disclosure by attorneys. The American Bar Association, responding to the SEC proposal and corporate scandals, changed its Model Rule of Professional Responsibility 1.13 "Organization as Client" to require reporting up the organization as opposed to the old rule which made it optional.

[271] For a discussion of § 16 liability for short swing trading, see § 13.06, *infra.*

[272] The chairman of Enron's audit committee was an accounting professor from Stanford, which did not seem to matter.

In addition to the corporate governance issues, other scandals emerged. Several investment analysts and stock brokers were found to have been recommending to their customers and the public the purchase of shares of certain corporations. It turned out that their employer (the stock brokerage house or investment banking firms) had other relationships with those corporations such as underwriting or advisory work. Those positive recommendations were often not based on a true belief but designed to please the corporation and facilitate those relationships. Sarbanes-Oxley requires the SEC and the National Association of Securities Dealers to issue rules designed to deal with the conflicts.[273]

Both the New York Stock Exchange and NASDAQ (over the counter market) have also made changes to their listing standards some of which were motivated by Sarbanes-Oxley and the scandals. Both now require a majority of directors to now be independent.[274] Only independent directors can serve on the audit, compensation and nominating/corporate governance subcommittees of the board.[275] The independent board must meet in executive session without the inside directors. The rules also provide that most stock option plans and significant changes in those plans must now be approved by the shareholders.

From a corporate governance perspective, Sarbanes-Oxley does several things. First, the crisis (like the crash of 1929) demanded a federal response notwithstanding the prominent role of state law in corporate governance. Many of the changes required by Sarbanes-Oxley are traditional state law issues (e.g., board makeup and meeting procedures, loans, compensation, etc.). Second, the increased use of criminal penalties to enforce fiduciary type duties is a shift away from the traditional use of civil remedies in corporate law.[276] Third, Sarbanes-Oxley was not trying to fundamentally change the system but make changes within the current system. Fourth, the scandals and the need for a regulatory response suggest a failure of some market mechanisms to protect investors. Fifth, the regulatory requirements will increase the cost of compliance for public corporations.[277] Finally, the effectiveness of the law remains unclear and further

---

[273] Norman Poser, Broker Dealer Law and Regulation § 1.02[C] (3rd ed. 2004 & Supp.). In some cases, investment banks were providing managers of corporations with a preferred allocation of shares in their hot public offerings in order to win corporate business. This allowed those managers to buy the shares at the offering price and make a quick profit when the shares rose in the first few days of trading. See the *Ebay* case discussed at § 9.05[D], note 144, *infra*.

[274] The market rules provide that the independent directors have no material relationship directly or indirectly with the corporation. The rules specify what particular positions or relationship will not qualify as independent.

[275] Corporations with a controlling shareholder holding more than 50% of the voting power need not comply with the requirement of independent directors except for the audit committee. They are required to disclose why they have decided not to select a majority of independent directors in their annual proxy statement.

[276] For a discussion of enforcement of fiduciary duty through shareholder litigation, see Chapter 12, *infra*.

[277] The increased costs could result in fewer corporations deciding to go public, or even in some publicly traded corporations deciding to go private. There are also concerns that smaller publicly traded corporations must bear substantial costs to comply with the law.

reforms may be necessary.[278]

---

[278] *See generally* J. Robert Brown, Jr, *Criticizing the Critics: Sarbanes-Oxley and Quack Corporate Governance* 90 MARQ. L. REV. 309 (2006) (discusses the critics).

Chapter 6

MERGERS AND ACQUISITIONS

§ 6.01 INTRODUCTION

Corporations may choose to expand through acquiring other companies.[1] From an economic perspective, the reason a corporation would seek to acquire another business is to increase the overall value of the firm. Thus, if Corporation A ("A") is valued at $4 and Corporation B ("B") is valued at $3, then the potential combination of firms A and B ("AB") should be worth more than $7. Otherwise, the combination would not be worthwhile to the shareholders of AB or beneficial to the economy.[2] Not all acquisitions are successful.[3] Some acquisitions may involve a bad business decision. Others may be motivated by management's desire to expand the business to justify higher compensation or to satisfy its ego without regard to increasing the value of the firm. Some acquisitions may be motivated by a control group which tries to take advantage of its position by engaging in self dealing and by acquiring another firm under its control at an unfair price.[4]

There are a variety of ways one can acquire another corporation. All methods involve the exchange of consideration in the form of securities, cash or a combination of consideration. The three primary methods of acquisition are the merger, sale of assets and the tender offer.

§ 6.02 MERGERS

A merger or consolidation is when two firms are combined. The statutory merger occurs where A Inc. acquires B Inc. by B Inc. merging into A Inc. The statutory merger is accomplished by the formulation of a plan of merger which

---

[1] In 2007, in the United States, approximately $1.6 trillion of transactions were announced. Worldwide, the amount was $4.5 trillion. Matthew Karnitschnig, *For Deal Makers, Tale of Two Halves — Private Equity Feels Pinch, Attracting Corporate Buyers*, WALL ST. J., Jan. 2, 2008, at R10.

[2] Some acquisitions are horizontal in that the corporations involved are in the same line of business. For example, the merger of Chrysler and Daimler Benz involved two auto manufacturers. Other acquisitions are vertical in that they involve businesses that are connected, such as a supplier and a manufacturer. There are also conglomerate combinations where the businesses are unrelated but the expectations are that excellent management can run the business well. General Electric is an example of a well run conglomerate. General Electric owns a media company, appliance and jet engine manufacturers and a finance business.

[3] *See, e.g.*, James Fanto, *Braking the Merger Momentum: Reforming Corporate Law Governing Mega-Mergers*, 49 BUFF. L. REV. 249 (2001).

[4] For a discussion of freeze-outs by controlling shares, see § 10.03, *infra*.

is approved initially by the boards of directors of both companies, followed by a vote of both shareholder bodies.[5] After the filing of the articles of merger with the Secretary of State, B Inc. loses its separate corporate existence.

MERGER

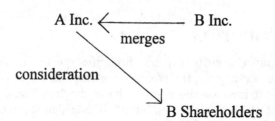

B merges into A and B loses its existence

In a consolidation, which is form of merger, both A Inc. and B Inc. merge into a new company, C Inc. A Inc. and B Inc. both lose their separate existence. This can happen when both A Inc. and B Inc. have significant identities and want to combine to form a new company.

CONSOLIDATION

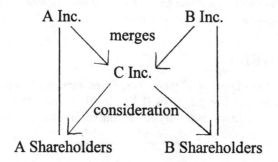

C Inc. remains, while A Inc. and B Inc. lose their existence

---

[5] Many state statutes require a majority shareholder vote. *E.g.*, Del. Gen. Corp. L. § 251(c). Model Bus. Corp. Act Ann. § 11.04(e) (4th ed. 2008) only requires a majority of the quorum. Corporate statutes sometimes do not require a shareholder vote. Under Model Bus. Corp. Act Ann. § 11.04(g) (4th ed. 2008) a vote may not be required by the acquiring corporation's shareholders in a merger into it of there is a share exchange. As discussed, in a triangular, reverse triangular or short form merger, the acquired corporation's shareholders do not usually vote.

[A]   Triangular Merger

In a triangular merger, the acquiring party ("A Inc.") forms a wholly owned subsidiary (A^S) and B Inc. merges into A^S. B Inc. shareholders receive consideration in exchange for their B shares. Shares of A^S owned by A Inc. are unaffected:

TRIANGULAR MERGER

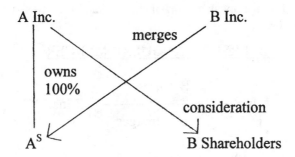

After the transaction:

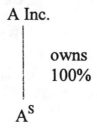

The merger into A^S eliminates B Inc.

A^S is still wholly owned by A Inc. If former shareholders of B Inc. are offered A^S shares, they become shareholders of A^S along with A Inc., as the parent. If B shareholders are offered shares of A Inc., then A^S remains a wholly owned subsidiary of A Inc. If B shareholders are offered cash or debt, it could be viewed as a freezeout transaction.[6]

The triangular merger is used when A Inc. wishes to keep the assets acquired from B Inc. in a separate corporation. One common reason to do this occurs when B Inc. is in a business fundamentally different from A Inc. and wants to avoid combining the assets, liabilities and income of the two businesses. There may also be contingent liabilities (for example the possibility of some tort liability) from B Inc. that A Inc. wants to keep separate. In a straight merger between A Inc. and B Inc., A Inc. would usually assume all of the liabilities of B Inc. In addition, since A^S is acquiring B Inc. through a merger, the shareholders of A

---

[6] For a discussion of freezeouts and controlling shareholders, see § 10.03 *infra.*

Inc. do not have the right to vote on the merger because they are not the shareholders of A^S.[7] The shareholder of A^S is A Inc. and A Inc.'s board votes those shares that represent ownership of A^S.

[B]   Reverse Triangular Merger

A reverse triangular merger may be necessary if, for some reason, it is critical that the corporate entity of B Inc. remains intact. For example, if B Inc. is a publisher and has copyright permissions which will not survive a merger in which B Inc. is the disappearing corporation, it may wish to structure a reverse triangular merger.

REVERSE TRIANGULAR MERGER

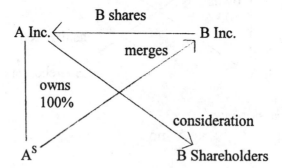

Thus, A^S merges into B Inc. with B Inc. as the surviving corporation. The plan of merger provides that the shares of A^S (all owned by A Inc.) will be converted into shares of B Inc. The shares of B Inc. which were outstanding before the merger will be exchanged for consideration from A Inc. to the B shareholders, leaving A Inc. as the 100% owner of B Inc. After the merger:

---

[7] The avoidance of a shareholder vote by A Inc. not only saves costs of holding the shareholder meeting and issuing proxy statements but may preclude the shareholders from seeking their right to an appraisal, which usually requires a vote. For a discussion of the appraisal right, see § 6.06, *infra.* Even if state law does not allow voting, there are times when the rules of the stock markets may provide for voting if the corporation's shares trade in that market. For example, if as a result of the transaction, a significant number of A Inc. shares will be issued, A Inc. shareholders will have the right to vote under New York Stock Exchange rules. *See* NYSE Listed Company Manual § 312.03. Under Model Bus. Corp. Act Ann. § 6.21(f) (4th ed. 2008), if shares are used to acquire another corporation and those shares carry more than 20% of voting power, then a shareholder vote would be required by the acquiring corporation issuing the shares. It may also be possible to argue that a given transaction is a de facto merger under state law which could result in voting rights. *See* § 6.07, *infra.*

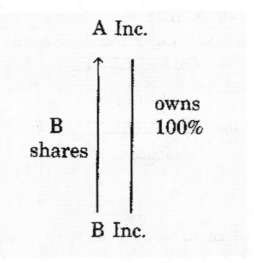

[C]   Short Form Merger

State statutes permit a parent corporation (usually owning 90% or more of the shares of the subsidiary) to merge the subsidiary out of existence without the formal requirements of a board or shareholder vote by the subsidiary. The subsidiary can be merged into the parent or into another subsidiary as a triangle merger.[8]

---

[8] Model Bus. Corp. Act Ann. § 11.05 (4th ed. 2008). The shareholders of the subsidiary are required to receive notice after the merger and usually have the right to seek appraisal. Model Bus. Corp. Act Ann. § 13.02(a)(1) (4th ed. 2008). In a short form merger in Delaware that freezes out the minority shareholder from their ownership, the remedy for any unfairness will be appraisal not entire fairness which looks at both fair dealing and fair price. The short form merger statute eliminates the process associated with regular mergers making process not the important issue. *Glassman v. Unocal Exploration Corp.*, 777 A2d 1182 (Del. 2001) For a discussion of entire fairness see § 10.03[B] *infra.*

§ 6.03   SALE OF ASSETS

A Inc. can just decide to acquire substantially all of the assets of B Inc.

SALE OF ASSETS

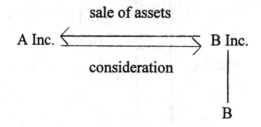

sale of assets

A Inc. ⟵⟶ B Inc.

consideration

B

At the end, the two corporations will remain extant:

A Inc.   B Inc.

A Inc. has the assets of B Inc. and B Inc. has the consideration paid for the assets (stock, cash or other securities). Thereafter, there are two options. B Inc. may remain in existence as a holding company, keeping the consideration and its shareholders. Another possibility is that B Inc. is liquidated with the consideration received from A Inc. distributed to the B Inc. shareholders in liquidation.

State law usually provides that, in a sale of assets, the boards of both corporations must approve of the sale. In general, only the shareholders of B Inc. have the right to vote on the sale when the sale involves all or substantially all of B Inc.'s assets.[9]

§ 6.04   TENDER OFFER

The tender offer,[10] or takeover bid, involves A Inc. (the bidder) making an offer directly to the shareholders of B Inc. (the target) to buy their shares. If A Inc. is able to purchase at least 51% of the shares, A Inc. will control B Inc. through its selection of B Inc.'s directors. As a consequence, B Inc. will be a subsidiary of A Inc.[11] The tender offer usually takes place when B Inc. is a

---

[9] If a corporation is just selling an important but independent branch of its business or engaging in a major restructuring, a shareholder vote is not required. Sometimes, courts must determine if a transaction meets the statutory standard for sale of *substantially all* of the assets and thus require a shareholder vote. In *Gimbel v. Signal Companies, Inc.*, 316 A.2d. 599 (Del. Ch. 1974), the court viewed the statutory right to vote as protecting shareholders from fundamental change which would destroy the means to accomplish the corporate purposes. Thus, if a sale is quantitatively vital to corporate operations, out of the ordinary and substantially affects corporate purposes, a shareholder vote will be required. Model Bus. Corp. Act Ann. § 12.02 (4th ed. 2008) provides for a vote whenever the transaction would leave the corporation without a "significant continuing business activity" (defined as at least 25% of total assets and income).

[10] The shareholders are invited to tender their shares if they wish to accept the offer; thus the term "tender offer."

[11] Parent and subsidiary corporations may raise conflict of interests, see § 10.02[B], *infra.*

publicly traded corporation. If B Inc. were a private corporation, the offer to buy B Inc.'s shares would probably involve a privately negotiated sale. The tender offer requires the board approval of A Inc. to make the offer but requires no board approval from B Inc., since the offer is made directly to the shareholders. A Inc.'s shareholders do not usually vote[12] and B Inc.'s shareholders can either accept or reject the offer.

This acquisition technique is the only one where the corporate statutes do not require the approval of B Inc.'s board and allows for an acquisition that they oppose. Thus, some tender offers may be classified as hostile in the sense that B Inc.'s management disapproves or resists the offer. Whether B Inc.'s directors can try to stop the offer is discussed in Chapter 12.

TENDER OFFER

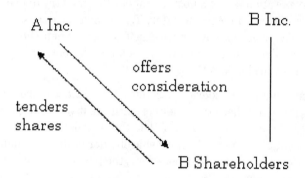

If B shareholders tender enough shares to give A Inc. control, then after the transaction:

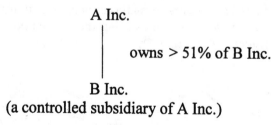

If A Inc. wants to own 100% of B Inc.'s shares, then A Inc. will make a tender offer for all the shares. In a publicly traded corporation there will always be some holdouts and so 100% will not tender. Thus, A Inc. will do a second step merger (usually triangular) after the tender offer to acquire the remaining shares that were not tendered. This second step involves a freeze-out merger (the remaining shareholders' equity interest will be eliminated by the merger) and because A

---

[12] A Inc. may need the vote of the shareholders for other reasons. For example, if A Inc. wants to acquire B Inc. using its shares and there are not enough shares authorized in the articles of incorporation, A Inc.'s shareholders would have to vote to amend the articles to authorize more shares.

Inc. now controls B Inc. as a result of the tender offer, fiduciary duties are raised.[13]

§ 6.05 OTHER LEGAL ISSUES

Acquisitions raise significant legal issues unrelated to corporate law such as issues related to taxation, labor law, antitrust, environmental law, pension law and contract law. In terms of corporate law, state statutes regulate the role of the board of directors, notice requirements and shareholder voting. In many states, shareholders are also given the right to dissent from the acquisition and to seek a proceeding called appraisal pursuant to which a court determines the cash value of the shares.[14] There are also fiduciary duty issues. The directors must act in good faith and in an informed manner in making the decision whether to sell the corporation. Otherwise, the directors may breach their fiduciary duty.[15] Managers of a corporation facing a hostile tender offer may try to keep the public shareholders from responding to the offer. This sometimes causes a breach of fiduciary duty.[16] Acquisitions may involve self dealing when the managers or controlling shareholders use their power to acquire the corporation and eliminates the minority shareholders.[17]

Acquisitions also implicate federal securities laws. If the acquiring corporation is issuing securities to purchase the other corporation, it will have to comply with the requirements of the Securities Act of 1933 that regulate the offer and sale of securities in interstate commerce.[18] Since shareholder voting is usually required for acquisitions, in publicly traded corporations, the parties must comply with the federal proxy rules under the Securities and Exchange Act of 1934.[19] If the acquisition involves a public tender offer, the parties must comply with the tender offer provisions in the Securities Exchange Act of 1934 (these provisions are called the "Williams Act") and Securities and Exchange Commission rules.[20] If certain individuals have access to material, nonpublic information about an acquisition and then trade in securities using the information, there may be a violation of the insider trading rules.[21]

---

[13] The second step involves the duty of loyalty (see Chapter 9) as a conflict of interest transaction because the controlling shareholder is on both sides of the transaction and thus not at arms' length. For a discussion of freezeouts, see § 10.03, *infra*.

[14] For a discussion of appraisal, see § 6.06, *infra*.

[15] For an example of Delaware's approach in *Smith v. Van Gorkom*, see § 8.04, *infra*.

[16] For a discussion of fiduciary duty in tender offers, see § 12.05, *infra*.

[17] For a discussion of freeze-outs by controlling shareholders, see § 10.03 *infra*.

[18] For a discussion of the process of going public, see § 7.03, *infra*.

[19] For a discussion of federal proxy rules, see § 7.04, *infra*.

[20] For a discussion of federal securities regulation and tender offers, see § 12.06, *infra*.

[21] For a discussion of insider trading, see Chapter 13, *infra*.

§ 6.06   APPRAISAL REMEDY

The state statutory scheme may allow for those who object to the merger to dissent and seek an appraisal as a remedy.[22] Early American law required a unanimous vote when mergers were proposed. The idea was that all of the shareholders should agree when there were major changes in the focus of the business such as those brought on by a merger. Such changes affected shareholders' expectations. The rule may have made sense when most corporations were closely held. The unanimous rule was also consistent with legislative suspicion of large business. But as industry grew and attitudes changed, mergers and expansion became more important. Legislatures lowered the unanimity requirement, providing shareholders who dissent from the merger an appraisal remedy.

Historically, mergers involved the use of securities as consideration, usually exchanging shares for shares. Appraisal gave shareholders who objected to major structural changes and the securities being offered, the right to dissent and seek a judicial decision on the fair value[23] of their shares which would be paid in cash.[24] Thus, appraisal was an exit strategy designed to protect shareholders by providing liquidity and an independent review of fair value. It was also meant as a check, or a monitoring device, to regulate those in control and to offer the shareholders a fair deal.[25]

There are considerable problems and limitations with appraisal. There are procedural requirements which usually oblige the shareholders to dissent from the merger by voting against it and by serving notice of their election to seek appraisal.[26] When a shareholder seeks appraisal, she must bear the initial costs of attorneys, consultants and expert witnesses such as appraisers and investment bankers. Class actions are not usually allowed in an appraisal proceeding which limits appraisal to shareholders with major interests given the costs. In addition, the proceeding often takes a long time during which the shareholders may not have the use of their money[27] and the amount of interest they receive

---

[22] Appraisal may also be available for other actions taken by the corporation. For example, under New York law, an amendment to the articles which adversely affects shares in certain ways may allow for appraisal (e.g., alters or abolishes preferential rights or rights of redemption of preferred shares). N.Y.B.C.L. § 806(b)(6).

[23] Under Model Bus. Corp. Act Ann. § 13.01(4) (4th ed. 2008), fair value is determined immediately before the event that triggered appraisal.

[24] *See* Stephen Schulman & Alan Schenk, *Shareholders' Voting and appraisal Rights in Corporate Acquisition Transactions*, 38 Bus. Law. 1529 (1983). *See also* Melvin Eisenberg, The Structure of the Corporation § 7 (1976).

[25] There may be attempts to structure a transaction to avoid appraisal. For example the triangular merger discussed in § 6.02[A], *supra*, could avoid appraisal consequences because the acquiring corporation is a subsidiary and the parent corporation votes in favor of the merger not the shareholder of the parent. In some states (e.g., Delaware), the sale of substantially all of the assets does not allow for appraisal but such a sale can sometimes be, in reality, a merger. For a discussion of the defacto merger doctrine, see § 6.07, *infra.*

[26] *See* Model Bus. Corp. Act Ann., ch. 13(b) (4th ed. 2008).

[27] In some jurisdictions, if a shareholder elects appraisal, the acquirer must offer some payment in cash as soon as the corporate action is consummated or upon demand. The payment must represent the corporation's good faith judgment as to the fair value. If the proceeding results in a

is often uncertain.[28] Because valuation is not a science, but a prediction based upon the future,[29] a judicial determination of value creates uncertainty as to the result and even the risk that the shareholders could receive less than what was offered in the merger.

Whether an appraisal remedy makes sense in a publicly traded corporation is an issue. Since shares are traded in stock markets, there is liquidity and an exit for shareholders.[30] In addition, in an arms' length bargain merger with no conflict of interest, shareholders are protected by the directors negotiating a fair price.[31]

Another issue is, even if there is an appraisal remedy, is it the appropriate Remedy in all mergers? For example, should appraisal be the exclusive remedy in a merger case which involves a conflict of interest (that is, a control group is on both sides of transaction) where minority shareholders received cash or other forms of non-equity securities in a freezeout transaction? The payment of cash provides liquidity, but are the minority shareholders protected from opportunistic behavior by appraisal? Minority shareholders may seek other remedies to avoid appraisal and get a higher price.[32]

[A]   Delaware Block Approach

Even outside of Delaware, courts have traditionally used a valuation methodology called the "Delaware block approach" to determine the fair value of the shares of the dissenting shareholders. In appraisal, the court should value what was taken from the shareholders, i.e., the proportionate interest in the going concern value of the corporation. This approach determines the value of shares by looking primarily at three different components. The idea is that shareholders value shares for several reasons including whether it trades in a stock market,[33] has assets or produces earnings (that is, market value, net asset

---

higher price, the shareholder will receive the difference. *See, e.g.*, Model Bus. Corp. Act Ann. § 13.24 (4th ed. 2008).

[28] Interest is intended to compensate the dissenters for the lost use of their money during the proceedings. The amount of interest and whether it compounded can make a significant difference in the amount received and is often at the discretion of the court. *See In Re Valuation of Common Stock of McLoon Oil Co.*, 565 A.2d.997 (Me. 1989) (awarding compound interest).

[29] For a discussion of valuation, see § 4.05, *supra.*

[30] For a discussion of the stock market exception, see § 6.06[B], *infra.*

[31] Shareholders could sue the directors for breaching their duty of care or a lack of good faith. See Chapter 8, *infra.*

[32] For a discussion of remedies in freeze-outs and whether appraisal is exclusive, see § 10.03[C], *infra.*

[33] Appraisal can occur in a closely held corporation where the shares do not trade in any stock market. In that context, the controlling shareholders argue that the lack of a market and lack of liquidity should affect the fair value of the shares and may be used to discount the value. In addition, the value should be further discounted because those shares represent a minority interest in the corporation which carries limited rights. While the market and minority discounts are often used in other valuation proceedings such as estate tax or divorce proceedings, many courts have held them inapplicable to appraisal proceedings. Since appraisal results from the involuntary change from a merger, shareholders are entitled to their proportionate share of the business as a whole. The court will value the business as a whole and then prorate it among the shares. Otherwise, the use of

value and earnings value).[34] Since corporations differ, the relative weight of these components will differ when valuing in appraisal. One court indicated that the "weighting of these interdependent elements of fair value is more akin to an artistic composition than to a scientific process. A judicial determination of 'fair value' cannot be computed according to any precise mathematical formula."[35]

The case of *Piemonte v. New Boston Garden Corp.*[36] is an example of the traditional Delaware block approach to appraisal. The dissenting shareholders of Boston Garden Arena, which owned the Boston Garden and professional hockey league franchises, sought appraisal after a merger. The trial court set the fair value of each share at $75.27 by determining the components of value and assigning them a weight of market value (10%), earnings value (40%) and net asset value (50%). The Supreme Judicial Court of Massachusetts agreed with this approach but remanded because the trial court, in some of its determinations, did not exercise its own judgment on valuation but merely accepted an expert's opinion. The opinion reflected the limitations of the Delaware block approach. First, the court did not fully explain why it used the particular weights it did. While it did recognize that the limited trading of the stock meant that the market price should have had a low weight (10%) there is no real explanation of how weights should be determined.[37] Second, the valuation on earnings was based on an average of the past five years reported earnings and a multiplier of 10. While the court recognized that those past earnings must be adjusted for extraordinary gains and losses, the court assumed that the past would be indicative of the future. Valuation of investment assets is generally based on future return, not past. In addition, reported earnings are based upon accounting figures and may not reflect the actual cash flow of the business.[38] Use of an average figure over the past five years also may not reflect the trend in earnings.[39] In addition, there was no real discussion of

---

discounts would provide an incentive for those in control to freeze out the minority and receive a windfall. *In Re Valuation of Common Stock of McLoon Oil Co.*, 565 A.2d.997 (Me. 1989). The use of discounts also adds speculation on the factors involved and imposes a penalty for lack of control. *Cavalier Oil Co. v. Hartnett*, 564 A.2d 1137 (Del. 1989). *See also* Model Bus. Corp. Act Ann. § 13.01(4)(iii) (4th ed. 2008) (inappropriate in most circumstances). For a discussion of the issue of discounts in the context of buyouts in lieu of dissolution in a closely held corporation, see § 11.07[H], *infra*.

[34] In some cases, a component of value has been based upon dividend pay out. In most cases, it is not treated as a separate component since earnings value should also reflect dividend value.

[35] *Valuation of Common Stock of Libbey, McNeill &Libby*, 406 A.2d 54 (Me.1979).

[36] 387 N.E.2d 1145 (Mass. 1979). The Massachusetts courts had adopted the Delaware block approach.

[37] The weighing of the components should reflect how each contributes to fair value in a given corporation. This, in a service business with limited assets, earnings should have a higher weight.

[38] Many shares trade in the stock market but the issuing corporation has no reported earnings. This may reflect that the investors are valuing those shares by their expected future earnings or valuing the corporation's positive cash flow as opposed to no reported earnings. The lack of reported earnings could also be the result of corporate write offs including depreciation. For a discussion of cash flow and valuation see, § 4.05[C][2], *supra*.

[39] For example if a corporation's past five year earnings each year were as follows: $2, $4, $6, $8 and $10, the average would be $6. That figure does not reflect the upward trend in earnings growth

why the multiplier of 10 was used.[40] Third, valuation of net asset value begins with the figures on the balance sheet which are conservative and based upon the historical cost of an asset, as opposed to its market value.[41] While a court may adjust the figures, the use of the balance sheet tends toward a conservative approach to valuation. Fourth, any gains from the merger that go to the controlling shareholders will not be reflected in appraisal.[42]

[1]   The New Delaware Methodology

In *Weinberger v. UOP*,[43] the Delaware Supreme Court expanded the Delaware block approach and recognized some of the limitations of the traditional appraisal remedy. According to the court, the Delaware block approach will no longer exclude valuation techniques generally acceptable in the financial community such as analysis of comparative takeover premiums or valuation based upon discounted cash flow.[44] Thus, elements of future value susceptible to proof are allowed but not speculative elements of value from the accomplishment or expectation of the merger.[45] This new expanded "Delaware

---

and would be conservative. If the earnings over the past five years were as follows: $6, $6, $7, $5 and $6, then an average of $6 may be more realistic.

[40] For a discussion of the multiplier and the rate in valuation, see § 4.05[C][3], *supra*.

[41] For a discussion of book value and its limitations, see § 4.05[B], *supra*.

[42] The case of *Valuation of Common Stock of Libbey, McNeill & Libby*, 406 A.2d 54 (Me.1979), is a good example of the court recognizing the limitations of appraisal and the factors that influence the weighing. Initially, the court rejected the use of the stock market price as a check against the price set by the merger because it is not a perfect market. However, the court used investment value (earnings value) and net asset value to compute price. In looking at earnings value, it recognized the subjective nature of determining a capitalization rate or multiplier and applying them to erratic earnings. It also recognized the use of book value for net asset value as being suspect. The court eventually agreed with the appraiser as having exercised sound judgment in the value (even though it was less than the shareholders were offered in the merger). The court criticized the trial court's disagreement with is appraiser over the weight assigned to each component. The trial judge had assigned more weight to asset and investment value than market value because it felt that unsophisticated shareholders had an image of ownership that focused on part ownership of the assets. The Maine Supreme Court rejected the idea that appraisal should compensate for psychological injury or because of any special benefits the acquirer receives. Instead, appraisal should be based upon a reasonable and objective view of the intrinsic value of the shares.

[43] 457 A.2d 701 (Del. 1983). For a discussion of *Weinberger* and the Delaware courts' scrutiny of freeze-outs, see § 10.03[C], *infra*.

[44] For a discussion of cash flow and valuation, see § 4.05[C][2], *supra*. New York legislatively took a similar approach in N.Y.B.C.L. § 623(h)(4). *See also* Model Bus. Corp. Act Ann. § 13.01(4)9(ii) (4th ed. 2008). The *Weinberger* approach to appraisal still has limitations because it allows the continued use of the Delaware block approach with the modern valuation techniques and still involves time and expense for minority shareholders. In addition appraisal actions cannot be brought as a class action.

[45] In *Cede & Co., Inc. v. Technicolor*, 684 A.2d 289 (Del. 1996), the Delaware Supreme Court indicated that the plans of the controlling shareholder in acquiring the business were susceptible of proof and non-speculative. The limitation on viewing the accomplishment of the merger is narrow, excluding pro forma date or speculative projections, but known elements of value can be used in appraisal. In *Cede* the controlling shareholder acquired control in a first step tender offer and then later did a second step freezeout merger to gain 100% ownership. Prior to the merger the controlling shareholder's plans began to be implemented and thus susceptible to proof. Gains to the acquirer from a merger will be more easily considered if plaintiffs could avoid appraisal and go to equity allowing the court to look at recissory damages. For a discussion of possible equitable relief in

block approach" will be the norm in appraisal.[46]

The MBCA has attempted to modernize its remedy called dissenters' rights. While judicial appraisal is available, the statute tries to encourage the parties to settle their dispute. Dissenting shareholders must make a demand for payment and the corporation must pay the dissenter the amount it estimated as the fair value, plus interest. A dissenter who disagrees with the valuation must notify the corporation of the "correct" estimated fair value. If the estimate is unreasonable, the dissenter runs the risk of being assessed litigation expenses. Generally, the costs of appraisal are assessed against the corporation. However, counsels' fees and expenses can be assessed against either party. The discretionary nature of costs and attorney fees tends to encourage parties to act in good faith and settle without a judicial appraisal.[47]

[B]   Stock Market Exception

Appraisal developed when stock markets were not well developed and thus provided some liquidity for dissenting shareholders. Some jurisdictions now eliminate the shareholder right to seek appraisal if the shares trade in the stock markets.[48] In effect, the market value set by the stock market substitutes for a judicial determination of fair value. In a truly efficient market, all information is reflected in securities prices and the price set may reflect the fair value of the corporation. However, the value set in the market is for the trading of individual shares and not the value of the corporation as a whole.[49] Reliance on the market may also not provide protection since the merger transaction itself could lower the price of the stock or may encourage many shareholders to sell as a result of the change, further depressing the market value.

In some mergers, the elimination of appraisal may be fair. If the merger is between two unaffiliated corporations (that is, there is no self dealing) and the directors are subject to the duty of care, then the absence of an appraisal remedy may not be problematic. However, when a merger involves a lack of good faith or a conflict of interest and self dealing, the elimination of appraisal would be a problem if there were no other remedy available to the minority shareholders.[50] But often the stock market exception does not apply to conflicts of interest mergers or freeze-outs.[51]

---

freezeout mergers with controlling shareholders see § 10.03[C][1], [2], *infra*.

[46] In *Rapid-American Corp. v. Harris*, 603 A.2d 796 (Del. 1992), the Delaware Supreme Court, using the new appraisal approach and included in its valuation of the shares of the parent corporation the control premium the parent corporation had in its subsidiaries.

[47] *See* Model Bus. Corp. Act Ann., ch. 13. In addition fair value is determined using customary and current valuation concepts used for similar businesses in the context that required appraisal. Model Bus. Corp. Act Ann. § 13.01(4)(ii) (4th ed. 2008).

[48] *E.g.*, Model Bus. Corp. Act Ann. § 13.02(b)(1) (4th ed. 2008). The stock market exception requires a liquid market.

[49] For a discussion of the limits of the efficient market theory, see § 5.02[D], *supra*.

[50] For a discussion of minority shareholders' right to seek equity in freeze-outs, see § 10.03[C][1], [2], *infra*.

[51] Under Delaware law, if the consideration paid in the merger is cash, the stock market exception is inapplicable. Del. Gen. Corp. L. § 262(b)(2). *See also* Model Bus. Corp. Act Ann. § 13.02(b)(4)(4th

§ 6.07 DEFACTO MERGERS

At times, an acquisition tries to preclude shareholder voting or appraisal rights.[52] For example, Delaware and some states provides appraisal rights for mergers but does not allow it for sale of substantially all of the assets. Assume an acquisition is structured as an asset sale with the acquiring corporation also assuming the liabilities and issuing its shares to the selling corporation which will dissolve and then distribute the shares to its shareholders. If viewed as a sale of assets in Delaware, then the selling corporation's shareholders will not have appraisal rights available in the event valuation is challenged.[53] As a result, shareholders of the selling corporation may argue that the transaction was more like a merger, that is a "defacto merger." They will ask a court to look at the transaction and determine if the substance of the transaction, as opposed to its form, is in effect a merger with the right of appraisal for the shareholders. Given that appraisal was to protect shareholders, when the combination means the corporation loses its essential nature and alters the original fundamental relationships of the shareholders then appraisal rights may be found.[54]

This potential judicial review protects shareholders' statutory rights by not allowing clever attorneys to structure transactions in a way that technically avoids a merger. Thus, the court looks at the intent of the legislature in protecting shareholders and will not allow the use of one statutory provision (that is, sale of assets) to undercut another designed to protect shareholders (that is, merger provisions).[55] Other states, including Delaware, view their statutory scheme differently. Instead, each statutory rule has independent legal significance and thus stands on its own. So long as a transaction technically complies with the statutory provision, it is irrelevant that it undermines the protections of another statutory provision. For example, a sale of assets that looks like a merger need only comply with the statutory provisions dealing with

---

ed. 2008) (on cash mergers conflicts of interest mergers, where the stock market exception is inapplicable).

[52] The A.L.I. approach does not look to the form of the transaction but instead treats all similar transactions equally by extending the shareholders voting rights and appraisal. For example, if there is a transaction in control (defined in A.L.I. Corp. Gov. Proj. § 1.38) then A.L.I. Corp. Gov. Proj. § 6.01 allows for shareholder voting. However, if the shareholders of a corporation end up owning a large proportion of the new corporation (that is they suffered little dilution of their power), then there may not be voting (if they own 75% of the new corporation [A.L.I. Corp. Gov. Proj. § 1.38(b)(3)]) or appraisal rights (if they own 60% of the new corporation [A.L.I. Corp. Gov. Proj. § 7.21(a)]).

[53] The facts are similar to *Hariton v. Arco Electronics, Inc.*, 182 A.2d.22 (Del. Ch. 1962), *aff'd*, 188 A.2d 123 (Del. Ch. 1963). Under Model Bus. Corp. Act Ann. § 13.02(a)(3) (4th ed. 2008), shareholders have a right to dissent and appraisal when they authorize any significant disposition of assets under Model Bus. Corp. Act Ann. § 12.02 (4th ed. 2008).

[54] In *Farris v. Glen Alden Corporation*, 143 A2d, 25 (Pa. Sup 1958), the reorganization involved a sale of assets from List to Glen Alden and an assumption of liability. The plaintiff shareholders of Glen Alden the survivor found themselves to be in a very different corporation. The new List Alden corporation would be much larger more diversified business, owning a much smaller percentage of the new company, control passing to the other company and a significant decrease in their book value from $38 to $21 per share. The court using the de facto merger doctrine awarded appraisal rights. Subsequently the Pennsylvania legislature took away the de facto merger doctrine.

[55] *See, e.g., Applestein v. United Board and Carton Corp.*, 159 A.2d 146 (N.J. Supr. Ct.), *aff'd*, 161 A.2d 474 (N.J. 1960).

the sale of assets, even if the substance of the transaction looks like a merger. Thus, Delaware rejects the defacto merger doctrine so long as the statute is complied with.[56]

---

[56] *See Hariton v. Arco Electronics, Inc.*, 182 A.2d 22 (Del. Ch. 1962), *aff'd*, 188 A.2d 123 (Del. Ch. 1963).

Chapter 7

INTRODUCTION TO FEDERAL REGULATION AND THE PROXY RULES

§ 7.01 INTRODUCTION AND OVERVIEW

Corporations are creatures of state law. State statutes govern the birth of corporations, as well as their adolescence, mid-lives, and deaths. Corporations are formed when a promoter files articles of incorporation with a particular jurisdiction's secretary of state or comparable official.[1] During a corporation's mid-life, other issues may arise in the form of transactions, such as the legality of dividends or other distributions,[2] the election or removal of directors, shares' eligibility to vote, directors' and officers' fiduciary responsibilities,[3] derivative suits and other corporate litigation,[4] mergers and sales of assets,[5] and so on. Finally, state law provisions govern corporate death, that is, the voluntary and involuntary dissolution of corporations.

Over the body of predominantly state law which governs corporate life exists a federal law overlay which is the subject of this chapter. The overlay affects small and closely held corporations through federal regulation of securities, proscriptions on insider trading, general antifraud rules which apply to the actions of "*any* person . . . in connection with the purchase or sale of *any* security,"[6] and the reorganization and liquidation provisions of the federal bankruptcy laws.

For publicly held corporations, the federal overlay is much more extensive. That overlay includes not only regulation of securities issuance and insider trading but also of takeover bids (tender offers) for the shares of public corporations, the Securities and Exchange Commission's (SEC) continuous disclosure system, the so-called short swing profits provision, the regulation of solicitation of proxies in public corporations, and other provisions.

Federal regulation dates from the Great Depression and the presidency of Franklin Delano Roosevelt. The first plank in the platform of regulatory reform is the Securities Act of 1933 ("the 1933 Act"), which, roughly speaking, governs the initial issuance of securities by corporations themselves. The 1933 Act

---

[1] For a discussion of formation, see § 1.07, *supra.*

[2] See the discussion of dividends and distributions in § 4.04[C], *supra.*

[3] For a discussion of fiduciary duties, see Chapters 8 and 9.

[4] For a discussion of corporate litigation, see Chapter 14.

[5] For a discussion of mergers and sales of assets, see Chapter 6.

[6] Securities Exchange Act of 1934 § 10(b); SEC Rule 10b-5 (emphasis added). For a discussion of insider trading, see Chapter 13.

mandates preparation and filing of an extensive registration statement for the sale of securities, unless the seller fits within an exemption from registration, and delivery to investors of a prospectus describing the securities offered, the corporation's products or services, its principal plants and facilities, its management, and its finances. The 1933 Act also contains liability provisions applicable to public offerings of securities, to other oral and written offers to sell, and to registration violations.

By contrast, the Securities Exchange Act of 1934 ("the 1934 Act") governs, *inter alia*, subsequent trading and other activities respecting securities. The 1934 Act is not as monolithic as is the 1933 Act. The 1934 Act deals with a host of diverse topics, including registration and regulation of stock exchanges and other self-regulatory organizations (SROs); regulation or self-regulation of broker-dealers; regulation of margin trading;[7] prohibition of manipulation of share prices and securities markets; penny stock fraud;[8] private securities litigation "reform;"[9] takeover bids; continuous reporting and disclosure by public companies; short swing profits provisions; proxy solicitation; several antifraud rules[10] that are applicable to takeover bids, proxy solicitations, and broker-dealers;[11] creation of the so-called National Market System; and more.

Regulatory reform of the depression era ended with a number of specialized but important federal statutes such as the Trust Indenture Act of 1939, which requires a corporate trustee to act as a sort of "guardian ad litem" for scattered debt holders in debt offerings of over $10 million.[12] The Indenture Act also requires the corporate trustee to furnish a lengthy document called an indenture which outlines the responsibilities of the trustee and the issuing corporation. The

---

[7] Margin trading involves the purchase of securities using borrowed funds. In this situation, the very securities that are being purchased serve as the security for the loan. Excessive margin trading was thought to be a principal cause of the 1929 market collapse. For that reason, the 1934 Act made it illegal either for an investor to borrow or for a broker-dealer, bank or other entity to lend excessive amounts. The limits are set by the Federal Reserve. For many years, investors could borrow no more than fifty or sixty percent of the security's value. Moreover, investors would face "margin calls," requiring them to post additional cash when the value of the security fell, or face forced liquidation of their positions. Regulation of margin trading has been greatly relaxed in recent years and borrowing of up to ninety percent of market value is now permitted.

[8] Penny stocks are defined as those that sell for less than (often much less than) $5 per share. The market for penny stocks has always involved fraudulent practices. One fraudulent scheme involves the purchase of shares for a penny each by unscrupulous promoters who change the company name, purchase a few assets in the company name, maybe promulgate press releases and trade shares back and forth among each other to create the appearance that the stock is actively traded. After increasing the price, the shares are sold in a "pump and dump" scheme and the promoters disappear. Public investors are left holding shares in a worthless "shell" corporation. In 1990, Congress passed the Penny Stock Reform Act, amending the broker-dealer provisions of the 1934 Act to deal with the problem.

[9] See § 14.09, *infra*.

[10] *See, e.g.*, Securities Exchange Act § 10(b); SEC Rule 10b-5 pursuant thereto.

[11] *See, e.g.*, Securities Exchange Act § 14(a); SEC Rule 14a-9 pursuant thereto (proxy solicitations); § 7.05[B], *infra;* Securities Exchange Act § 14(e) (takeover bids); § 12.06[D], *infra*.

[12] Trust Indenture Act of 1939 § 4(a)(9) (as amended by the Trust Indenture Improvements Act of 1990). A bond is nothing more than a promise to pay — a promissory note issued by a corporation, customarily with a $1000 face value. For a discussion of various debt instruments and their characteristics, see § 4.02, *supra*.

Investment Company Act of 1940 regulates the governance and sales practices of investment companies, the most ubiquitous of which is the open end investment company, commonly known as the mutual fund. The Public Utility Holding Company Act of 1935 (repealed) was enacted to simplify the practice of pyramiding utility company holdings and endows the SEC with broad powers to free the operating utility companies from their holding companies. The Investment Advisers Act of 1940 requires registration by and regulates the practices of persons and firms who provide investment advice (including mutual fund advisors) that is not ancillary to provision of another service, such as brokerage.

The delicate balance between state and federal roles was radically altered in July 2002, when Congress enacted and the president signed into law the Sarbanes-Oxley (SOA) of 2002.[13] In signing the legislation, President Bush hailed the act as the most far reaching reforms of American business practices since the days of Franklin Delano Roosevelt. More importantly, for purposes of this chapter, SOA represents the first pervasive incursion of federal legislation into the internal affairs and governance of corporations, traditionally matters of state law. Prohibitions on loans to senior managers, structure and conduct of audit committees, potential lifetime bars on service as officers and directors of public corporations, codes of ethics for corporate officers, "reporting up" responsibilities for corporate attorneys, and a dozen or so other provisions, regulate matters that until 2002 had been left to state law.

§ 7.02   SEC JURISDICTION AND PERIODIC REPORTING BY PUBLICLY HELD CORPORATIONS

[A]   SEC Jurisdiction

This chapter explains the provisions of general federal law applicable to corporations and their officers and directors, rather than more specialized laws applicable to banks, broker-dealers, utility holding companies, investment companies, investment advisers, or stock exchanges.

The question that thus arises is "To what categories of companies do these myriad provisions (takeover, continuous reporting, proxy solicitation, short swing profits) apply"? As originally conceived, the 1934 Act extended its reach only to those corporations with a class of securities "registered on a national securities exchange."[14] These corporations are referred to as "12(b) corporations" after the section of the act requiring their registration by filing with the relevant exchange and with the SEC.

A little-noted but watershed event occurred in 1964, when Congress extended those 1934 Act provisions to a large segment of the over-the-counter market.[15]

---

[13] Pub. L. 107-204, discussed in detail in § 5.08, *supra.*

[14] Securities Exchange Act of 1934 § 12(b). The New York Stock Exchange is such an exchange.

[15] The over-the-counter market is often characterized as predominantly a dealer market, in which various broker-dealer firms (market makers) maintain and trade from inventories of shares, much as would a hardware store which maintains an inventory in more tangible goods. The OTC market has no centralized location but is instead made up of an amorphous network of wires, telephone and

Today, corporations which have a class of equity securities held by 500 or more persons[16] and over $10 million in assets, so-called "12(g) corporations,"[17] must register with the SEC and, in doing so, commence their governance by various provisions of the Securities Exchange Act of 1934.[18]

Approximately 3,300 corporations have a class of shares traded on one of the national stock exchanges. In 1964, Congress added section 12(g) to the 1934 Act. Today, due to this amendment, an additional 12,000 to 13,000 corporations whose shares are traded over-the-counter are a part of the SEC system.[19] The 1964 amendments, adding 12(g) corporations to the mix, constitute a vast expansion of the SEC's jurisdiction and coverage of the 1934 Act.[20]

[B]   Periodic Reporting — An Overview

Once corporations reach 12(b) or 12(g) status, they must file annual 10-K and quarterly 10-Q reports with the SEC. The 10-K is a thick gray document prepared in addition to the glossy annual report corporations send their

---

computer connections. By contrast, an exchange market has a central location (the trading floor in New York or San Francisco) where trading is done through a specialist and is supposedly characterized by the predominance of agency trading. Rather than buying from or selling to inventory of a dealer, an investor buys from or sells to another investor, who may be located in a distant corner of the country. She does so through the intermediary of her broker and the other party's broker, agents entitled to be on the trading floor by virtue of ownership of a stock exchange seat. The person with whom the investor actually deals is technically not the broker but the registered representative of the broker, although the uniform layperson practice is to call him "my broker."

[16] Securities Exchange Act of 1934 § 12(g)(1)(B). That is, not 500 shareholders. A corporation with 400 holders of its preferred shares and 450 different holders of its common shares has over 500 shareholders but would not have a class of equity securities held by 500 or more persons. That corporation would still not fall within the ambit of the various 1934 Act provisions.

[17] SEC Rule 12g-1. The act speaks simply in terms of "assets," not in terms of *net* assets (assets minus liabilities) or net worth. A corporation with $10 million in assets but $7 million in liabilities falls nonetheless under the various 1934 Act provisions.

[18] Technically speaking, corporations register classes of securities with the SEC, and do not register the corporation itself. The A.L.I. Securities Code, once promulgated by the American Law Institute, would have changed to company, rather than security, registration.

[19] In 2002, 16,200 corporations filed annual reports with the SEC. *See, e.g.,* SEC, *Framework for Enhancing the Quality of Financial Information,* 67 Fed. Reg. 44,999 (July 5, 2002). If one subtracts the number of corporations with a class of securities registered on an exchange (3,300), the total number of corporations registering a class of securities pursuant to § 12(g) is approximately 12,900. In recent years, the total number has been estimated to drop to 16,000, or lower, as the requirements (and costs) of compliance with the Sarbanes-Oxley Act have caused a decrease in the number of registrations as well as withdrawals by foreign issuers especially. Due to mergers, initial public offerings (IPO), and "going private" activity, the number fluctuates greatly.

[20] Corporations enter the system when they reach 12(g) size, or if they go public pursuant to a registration statement. First, corporations must comply with the SEC's continuous disclosure system by filing a thick annual report-like document called Form 10-K. Thereafter, each year, the corporation must file another Form 10-K. After each calendar or fiscal year quarter, 12(b) and 12(g) corporations must also file Form 10-Q with the SEC. Last of all, ten days after the end of the month in which any of specified list of events has occurred (change of control, sale of principal business, change of outside auditors, etc.), corporations must file Form 8-K with the SEC. Corporations remain subject to this disclosure system until such time as the number of holders of the registered class of securities falls below 300.

shareholders in the annual proxy solicitation process. The corporation must send a copy of the 10-K (which contains much valuable information) but only to shareholders who request the document in writing.

Public corporations file 10-Qs shortly after the end of each calendar quarter. The 10-Qs contain unaudited financial results. These SEC filings contain valuable information but have been criticized because they are filed only after the reporting period has concluded rather than in anything approaching real time.

The third broad category of periodic reports required by the SEC comes closer to real time reporting. Traditionally, public corporations had to file form 8-K within 10 days following the end of any month in which certain listed events had occurred. For a few of those events, corporations had to file immediately after the occurrence. The list of triggering events for 8-K filings was relatively short, confined to rather episodic events such as a change in control, bankruptcy, resignation or dismissal of the outside auditors, and so on (many corporations, however, voluntarily file 8Ks much more frequently, which the SEC has encouraged them to do).

While Congress was considering SOA, the SEC had under consideration greatly expanded mandatory 8-K filings by public corporations, through electronic reporting and on a near real time (within 5 days) basis. The SEC proposals have now been implemented. New SEC regulations list 12 specific events, which include many "sub items," which will trigger an obligation on behalf of corporations to file 8-Ks, including resignation of a directors, amendments or waivers of corporate codes of ethics, and blackout periods when no trading may be allowed under 401(k) and other employee benefit plans.[21]

[C]   Certifications, Code of Ethics Disclosure, and Penalties for Earnings Restatements

One burdensome requirement, especially for smaller public companies, is the certification system put in place by SOA. Section 302 requires the corporation's chief executive officer (CEO) and its chief financial officer (CFO) to certify no less than nine statements with regard to each quarterly and annual report. By their signatures, they certify that they have reviewed the report; it contains no material omissions; putting generally accepted accounting principles (GAAP) aside, the reports "fairly present in all material respects the financial condition and results of operation of the issuer [the corporation]"; and that in the preceding 90 days they have reviewed the issuer's internal financial and accounting controls and what that review revealed to them.[22]

Section 404 requires the CEO and CFO to make an additional certification on an annual basis. They must (1) state the responsibility of management for establishing and maintaining internal controls; (2) assess the effectiveness of

---

[21] *See* General Instructions to SEC Form 8-K (2002).

[22] The act directs the SEC to implement the certification requirement by rule, which the Commission has done. *See* SEC Rules 13a-14; 15d-14 (2002).

those controls in their corporation; and (3) obtain and include the attestation by the outside auditors as to management's assessments.[23]

Smaller corporations may not have internal staff sufficient to carry out these tasks. For many of those tasks, managers must depend on outside law firms and accountants whose fees, post SOA, have more than doubled in many instances. Predictions are that these added costs, alone or in combination with the angst of senior managers, will cause more public corporations to "go private" and cause other corporations to think twice before becoming publicly held in the first place.

The SEC has leveled charges of violation of the certification requirements in recent prosecutions of corporate officials for financial and accounting irregularities. For example, in the HealthSouth debacle, the SEC procured a guilty plea from a HealthSouth CFO, based upon alleged false or reckless certifications. Predictions are that the SEC will use this tool much more in the future.[24]

A punitive SOA position requires that CEOs and CFOs forfeit any incentive based or equity compensation received in the last year if a restatement of corporate earnings is necessary and the restatement was due to "misconduct" either by them or them subordinates. The forfeiture includes profits on the sale of stock received upon exercise of stock options.[25] It was estimated that, had the provision been in effect in 2001, the Enron CEO and CFO would have had to forfeit well over $200 million following Enron's October, 2001 earnings restatement.

One last SOA disclosure requirement illustrates the often fine line between mere disclosure and substantive ("do's" and "don'ts") regulation. Public corporations must disclose if they do not have in place a code of ethics for senior financial officers. The code must "promote honest and ethical conduct, including the ethical handling of actual and apparent conflicts of interest." The code must also "promote compliance with applicable governmental rules and regulations."[26] It is doubtful whether any public corporation will be so brazen as to disclose that it has neither a code of ethics nor any intention of adopting one.

---

[23] *See* SEC Rules 13a-14; 15d-14 (2002).

[24] *See* Chad Terhune & Carrick Mollenkamp, *Ex Finance Chief of HealthSouth to Plead Guilty*, Wall St. J., at A-24 (April 22, 2003). *See also* John Wilke, Chad Terhune & Carrick Mollenkamp, *Scrushy May Be Indicted Today*, Wall St. J., at A-3 (Nov. 4, 2003) (similar false certification charges against HealthSouth's former CEO). *But see HealthSouth Corp. — Scrushy Lawyers to Challenge Flaws in Sarbanes-Oxley Act*, Wall St. J, at C-15 (Dec. 10, 2003) (Constitutional challenge to be mounted).

[25] Sarbanes-Oxley Act § 304.

[26] Sarbanes-Oxley Act § 406

[D]　Private Securities Litigation Reform Act (PSLRA) Safe Harbor for Forward Looking Statements

In an earlier era (1995), PSLRA created a safe harbor for predictions of future economic performance or other forward looking statements, provided the statements are accompanied by "meaningful, cautionary language."[27] So, in addition to certifications such as those SOA requires, many corporate documents and filings to contain, several paragraphs of cautionary language under the heading "Safe Harbor for Forward Looking Statements" will also be evident.

[E]　Management Discussion and Analysis (MD&A)

A central portion of any disclosure document, including reports on SEC forms 10-Q and 10-K, is "Management's Discussion and Analysis of Financial Conditions and Results of Operations," known as MD&A.[28] This section of any report is intended to let investors and shareholders see the corporation's performance "through management's eyes."

In *In the Matter of Caterpillar, Inc.*,[29] the SEC chose Caterpillar's MD&A disclosure to send a message to all SEC reporting companies about the importance the SEC attaches to MD&A disclosure. In 1989, only five percent of Caterpillar's revenues but 25 percent of its profits came from its Brazilian operation, CBSA. Due to hyper-inflation, Brazilians were investing inordinately in heavy equipment of the type Caterpillar manufactures, which provides a hedge against inflation. Thus 1989 had been a stellar year for CBSA.

The election and inauguration of a new Brazilian president heralded a new austerity and monetary control regime in Brazil which would make CBSA's results a drag on 1990 Caterpillar earnings, a complete turnaround from events in 1989. MD&A is to "discuss the liquidity, capital resources, and results of operations" of the corporation, including for individual lines of business or subsidiaries if appropriate to the understanding of a particular line of business.

Caterpillar's directors had wrestled with whether or not or in how much detail the turnaround in Brazil should be discussed in MD&A. The SEC obtained board minutes and, very unfairly, used the discussion in those minutes to build its case against Caterpillar, which, discretion being the better part of valor, settled with the SEC. The points are that MD&A is an important part of the SEC regulatory schematic and is to be taken seriously by corporations

---

[27] In 1978, the SEC adopted Rule 175, intended to encourage issuers to make projections and other forward looking statements, provided that they stated all assumptions. Issuers did not utilize the rule much, perhaps because it was only a rule, but it paved the way for enactment of a statutory safe harbor 18 years later. The PSLRA safe harbor, 1934 Act § 21E, is discussed, *inter alia*, in § 13.02[F], *infra*.

[28] Outlined and required by Item 303, SEC Regulation SK. Regulation SK is the master regulation which informs interested parties as to the form of presentation and the content of all documents filed with the Commission (registration statements, periodic reports [8Ks, 10Qs, and 10Ks], proxy statements, and so on).

[29] SEC Release No. 34-30532 (1992).

which file reports with the SEC. An ancillary teaching is the way in which the SEC may use an individual corporation, such as Caterpillar, as the vehicle whereby it sends a message to lawyers, accountants, senior managers, and corporations under the SEC's jurisdiction.

[F]   Earnings Management and Revenue Recognition Issues

Since the dot.com boom of the mid 1990s, a hot button issue with the SEC has been illicit earnings management by SEC reporting corporations. Tens of millions of investors and analysts watch closely the performance of public corporations. In particular, they note the quarterly and annual consensus earnings estimates made by analysts and complied by organizations such as Thompson First Call. Falling a few pennies short of consensus earnings estimates may mean a drop as much as 15 or 20 percent in a corporation's stock price. By contrast, meeting or slightly exceeding consensus estimates quarter after quarter and year after year is as near an assured path to robust stock price performance as may be imagined. Corporations announce their quarterly results in conference telephone calls with securities analysts, announcing the "earnings conference calls" well in advance and permitting the public to listen.

This current milieu leads to tremendous pressure on corporate executives to "smooth out," earnings (if not to fabricate them, which has also happened with regrettable frequency). Corporations may judge that they have been too successful in a particular quarter or year. They establish "cookie jar reserves" which may be drawn upon as a rainy day fund in some future quarter in which earnings fall short. Even a paragon of muscular earning capacity, Microsoft Corp., was charged by the SEC with, and admitted to, "cookie jar" earnings management tactics.

Other corporations frantically seek to make up expected shortfalls from analysts' projections of earnings, through a variety of improper revenue recognition tactics. At HealthSouth Corp., these frantic endeavors were termed "digging up the dirt to fill the hole."

In the Matter of Informix Corp.,[30] an SEC proceeding, describes a mix of such tactics. The company, a database software manufacturer from California, had to restate its earnings for 1994, 1995, 1996 and the first quarter of 1997. Management, employees, and sales persons had engaged in a variety of practices that inflated annual and quarterly revenues and earnings, including:

(1)   backdating license sales agreements;

(2)   entering into side agreements granting rights to refunds and other concessions to customers;

(3)   recognizing revenue on transactions with reseller customers that were not creditworthy;

---

[30] SEC Release No. 34-42326 (Jan. 11, 2000).

(4) recognizing amounts due under software maintenance agreements as software license revenues;

(5) recognizing revenue on disputed claims against customers.

Among other things, the SEC faulted the company for its lack of "sufficient internal accounting controls" which would have curtailed, if not eliminated, many of the improper practices.

Today, especially in industries such as software design and manufacturing, in which customers may delay payments until they are insured that the product is not vapor ware and performs adequately the tasks for which it was purchased, outside auditors expend considerable amounts of effort establishing proper revenue recognition practices and then closely auditing accounts with those practices in mind.

§ 7.03 SECURITIES ISSUANCE

[A] The Federal Disclosure Philosophy

Mr. Justice Brandeis observed that "sunshine is the best disinfectant, electric light the best policeman."[31] The Congressional drafters of the Securities Act of 1933 seized upon Brandeis's observation, incorporating in that act what has come to be known as the full and fair disclosure philosophy. The full disclosure philosophy states that issuers of securities may do whatever they wish, so long as the registration statement and prospectus (Part I of the registration filed with the SEC) fully and fairly disclose what it is that they propose to do. Beyond requirements for filing and for prospectus delivery, federal securities regulation (pre SOA) contains few substantive commands, "Thou shalt's," or "Thou shalt not's." In theory, an issuer's business plan could have no rational basis ("it is the intention of the issuer to utilize proceeds of the offering to monopolize world trade in lettuce") or could be venal in the extreme ("it is the intention of the issuer to utilize proceeds of the offering to purchase homes in Palm Springs, yachts, and luxury automobiles for the principal executive officers of the issuer"). If the registration fully discloses that plan, the SEC cannot prevent the scheme from going forward.[32] On the few occasions the SEC has ventured beyond the full and fair disclosure mandate without explicit congressional authorization, courts have upheld challenges to the SEC's actions.[33]

The fifty states and other United States jurisdictions have their own securities acts, the first of which was adopted by Kansas in 1911, preceding the federal enactments by several decades. Known as blue sky laws, based upon

---

[31] Louis D. Brandeis, OTHER PEOPLE'S MONEY AND HOW BANKERS USE IT 92 (1914).

[32] Staff at the SEC's Division of Corporate Finance may wage a war of attrition, requiring amendment after amendment until the registration statement virtually bludgeons investors with the stupidity or venality of the scheme.

[33] *See, e.g., The Business Roundtable v. Securities and Exchange Commission*, 905 F.2d 406 (D.C. Cir. 1990) (under 1934 Act, SEC had no power to invade the province of corporate governance, imposing upon stock exchanges and corporations a "one share, one vote" rule). For a discussion, see § 5.04[A], *supra.*

their objective of curbing "speculative schemes which have no more basis than 'so many feet of blue sky,' "[34] these statutes also incorporate a full and fair disclosure philosophy.[35] However, a handful of states go beyond disclosure requirements, engaging in so-called merit regulation. In these states, the securities commissioner may block an offering in the state, despite full and fair disclosure, on grounds that the offering would work or would tend to work a fraud or inequity upon the citizens of the state, or under a requirement that offerings be "fair, just and equitable."[36]

The purpose of disclosure is said to be twofold: to provide information to enable investors to make well-informed investment decisions and to prevent fraud. Obviously, disclosure statutes prevent fraud because the essence of fraud is non-disclosure, half truth, or disclosure in a misleading way. Disclosure requirements are also intended to operate in more subtle ways. They are intended to curb highly speculative acts and practices, sharp dealing, and dubious schemes. The notion is that if a promoter or issuer is forced to disclose just how speculative or dubious the scheme is, the promoter will modify or even abandon those aspects of the business plan that make it speculative or dubious. Alternatively, "hit them between the eyes" disclosure causes the scheme to fail in the marketplace. Disclosure makes deficiencies so obvious that no one will invest.

[B]   Registration Requirements

Before a single share or unit of participation is offered for sale, there must be registration, or an exemption therefrom, both on the federal level and, traditionally, in each state in which the security will be offered for sale. The Securities Act of 1933 imposes strict liability for registration violations by entities who sell unregistered securities.[37] There are also criminal penalties which are enforced.

The National Market Improvements Act of 1996, however, removed from the states their plenary power to regulate issuances of "covered securities." There are several categories of "covered securities" but the most important are issuances by SEC reporting corporations and issuances that are part of a fully

---

[34] *Hall v. Geiger-Jones Co.*, 242 U.S. 539, 550 (1917).

[35] Approximately 40 states have adopted one of two versions (1956 or 1985 revision) of the Uniform Securities Act promulgated by the Commissioners on Uniform State Laws, although through local modification the statute has become more of a model rather than uniform act. *See* Douglas M. Branson, *Chasing the Rogue Professional After the Private Securities Litigation Reform Act of 1995*, 50 SMU L. Rev. 91, 116 (1996); Branson, *Collateral Participant Liability Under State Securities Laws*, 19 Pepp. L. Rev. 1027, 1038 (1992). In 2003, the Commissioners promulgated a third version of the act which may eventually be adopted by states.

[36] *See generally* Conrad Goodkind, *Blue Sky Law: Is There Merit In the Merit Requirements?*, 1976 Wis. L. Rev. 79. Many states with merit regulation do not apply it to large national corporations. They may, for instance, exempt from regulatio corporations with shares listed on a national stock exchange.

[37] "Any person who . . . offers or sells a security in violation of section 5 [registration and prospectus delivery requirements] . . . shall be liable to the person purchasing such security from him . . . ." Securities Act of 1933 § 12(a).

registered SEC public offering. Under the Act, states may require only a brief notification form. They may also collect the fees (sometimes very large) that they formerly collected. Invoking the Commerce Clause of the U.S. Constitution, however, Congress has decreed that states securities commissions may no longer require the filing of disclosure documents, much less documents that conform to varying state requirements or engage in merit regulation, with regard to covered securities.

The state-federal boundary thus marked, it is important to warn that securities law is a highly technical, demanding area of law that has ruined the careers of many young lawyers who practiced in the area without proper preparation and experience.[38]

Securities law, especially violation of the registration provisions, is a favorite vehicle of the white collar crime divisions of prosecutors' offices and of civil litigators who represent plaintiffs in commercial litigation. Because the legal definition of a security encompasses much more than traditional stocks and bonds, the registration provisions apply to a wide range of investments and instruments,[39] including "investment contracts." Many unorthodox investment schemes may be viewed as securities under the catchall "investment contract" contained in the statutory definition of a security.

In *SEC v. W.J. Howey Co.*,[40] the United States Supreme Court found an investment contract to be "an investment of money with the expectation of profits solely from the efforts of promoters or third parties." Thus, the Supreme Court upheld a finding that sale of interests in Florida orange groves with accompanying services contracts constituted an investment contract rather than the mere sale of a fee simple interest in real property. The issuer thus could be strictly liable to purchasers because it had not, and probably had not even thought about, registering under the securities laws.

Smith v. Gross[41] involved an unorthodox investment scheme. There, the plaintiffs purchased earthworms with an ancillary agreement that the promoters would repurchase the Smiths' output of worms for $2.25 per pound. The worms did not multiply as represented ("double in quantity every sixty days") and the seller did not repurchase. The plaintiffs sued, alleging that they purchased not only worms but also an investment contract. The Ninth Circuit applied prior precedent[42] which "held that despite the Supreme Court's use of the word 'solely,' the third element of the *Howey* [investment contract] test is 'whether the efforts made by those other than the investor are the undeniably significant ones, those essential managerial efforts which affect the failure or

---

[38] *See, e.g., SEC v. Spectrum, Ltd.*, 489 F.2d 535 (2d Cir. 1973) (young lawyer found liable for permitting unregistered sale of securities; Judge Friendly observed that "[i]n our complex society . . . the lawyer's opinion can be an instrument for inflicting pecuniary loss more potent than the chisel or the crowbar"); *Florida Bar v. Calvo*, 630 So. 2d 548 (Fla. 1993), *cert. denied*, 513 U.S. 809 (1994) (upholding disbarment of young lawyer who assisted registration violations).

[39] Securities Act § 2(1).

[40] 328 U.S. 293 (1946).

[41] 604 F.2d 639 (9th Cir. 1979).

[42] *SEC v. Glenn W. Turner Enterprises, Inc.*, 474 F.2d 476, 482 (9th Cir. 1973).

success of the enterprise.'" In the case at bar, no matter how diligently the Smiths raised and trained their worms the scheme would fail unless seller Gross fulfilled his responsibilities. Gross's efforts were "the undeniably significant ones." The court found Gross liable for the unregistered sale of a security.

By contrast, in a true franchise, the efforts of the franchisee-investor are significant. An investor must expect actively to participate in the business venture as a partner with the franchisor. Many franchise agreements spell out the involvement required of the franchisee, such as number of hours to be spent on the premises, education requirements, and so forth. Although under state law a franchise may have to be registered under the franchise act, true franchises are not securities.[43]

There are literally thousands of state and federal cases determining whether various items or schemes, often with a "get rich quick" aspect, are investment contracts, and therefore securities.[44] Interests in worm farms, mink ranches, chinchilla farms, airplanes, over-the-road trucks, condominiums, cemetery plots, warehouse receipts for scotch whiskey or Bordeaux wines, wheat farms, cattle, race horses, vineyards, rare coins, gold bars, Christmas tree farms, ornamental shrubbery farms, limited partnerships of all descriptions, and certain general partnerships have been found to be securities.[45] On a number of occasions, the United States Supreme Court has entered the fray, deciding whether particular items are securities pursuant to the investment contract catchall, or otherwise.[46]

The consequences of an item being found to be a security are several: (1) the item must be registered or have met the requirements for registration;[47] (2) the securities laws' general antifraud rules apply to statements made and

---

[43] *See, e.g., Bitter v. Hoby's Int'l, Inc.,* 498 F.2d 183 (9th Cir. 1974).

[44] Investment contracts involve (1) investment of money; (2) in a common enterprise; (3) with the expectation of profits or other economic benefit; (4) arising solely (primarily?) from the efforts of others.

[45] Many states apply an alternative "risk capital" definition to expand the notion of a security to include interests in which the expectation is for social or athletic rather than purely economic benefits. There the purchaser's membership or other fee is found to be the "very risk capital of the venture." The seminal case is *Silver Hills Country Club v. Sobieski,* 55 Cal. 2d 811, 361 P.2d 906 (1961) (Traynor, J.).

[46] *See* SEC v. Edwards, 540 U.S. 389 (sale and leasebacks of pay telephone held an investment contract); *Reves v. Ernst & Young,* 494 U.S. 56 (1990) (promissory notes may be securities, depending upon their "family resemblance" to longer term investment transactions or shorter term commercial transactions, such as the installment purchase of a refrigerator or an automobile; investment contract definition not to be applied to list of items in statutory definition); *Landreth Timber Co. v. Landreth,* 471 U.S. 681 (1985) (shares of stock in a closely held corporation are still stock subject to securities laws; rejecting "economic realities" approach and "sale of business doctrine" in favor of a literal approach (stock is stock is stock)); *Marine Bank v. Weaver,* 455 U.S. 551 (1982) (bank certificate of deposit not a security because holders "abundantly protected under the federal banking laws"); *International Brotherhood of Teamsters v. Daniel,* 439 U.S. 551 (1979) (compulsory pension plan not an investment contract because not "investment of money"; "an employee is selling his labor primarily to obtain a livelihood, not making an investment for the future"); *United Housing Found. Inc. v. Forman,* 421 U.S. 837 (1975) (although purchase of co-op apartment involves purchasing shares of stock, economic reality is that purchaser obtains housing rather than a pure investment).

[47] Usually, the item is not registered since the promoters did not likely consider the item to have been a "security."

allegations of nondisclosure; (3) the person who sold the item may be classified as a broker-dealer and may be required to have been registered as such; and (4) any credit extended to the purchaser to facilitate the acquisition may be subject to the margin rules laid down by the various regulatory authorities.

[C]   The Registration Process

Section 11 of the Securities Act of 1933 is a tough (called Draconian by many) express liability provision governing any "untrue statement of a material fact" or material omission "in any part of the registration statement" filed with the Commission. Defendants under the section include the issuer, every person who signed the registration statement (the principal executive officer, chief financial officer, comptroller or other chief accounting officer, and a majority of directors *must* sign), every person who was a director, those named as becoming a director, and every accountant, engineer, appraiser or "other person whose profession gives authority to a statement made by him" who "expertises" or certifies a portion of the registration statement. The issuer is strictly liable.

The other defendants have a "due diligence" defense. An individual may escape liability if he or she proves that "he had, after a reasonable investigation, reasonable grounds to believe and did believe . . . that the statements made therein were true and that there was no omission of a material fact." The due diligence defense is a little easier to prove if the misstatement or omission was contained in an expertised portion of the statement.[48] Early court decisions reinforce beliefs as to just how "tough" § 11 is.[49]

Attorneys should advise issuers to retain a well-respected accounting firm which will credibly audit and certify financial statements. Issuers should also retain an attorney to examine the corporation's good standing in all jurisdictions in which it does business, examine all conflict of interest transactions with senior executives or principal shareholders, review all the corporation's principal contracts, and perform a myriad of other housekeeping chores. All persons connected with the corporation should be warned about premature offers to sell securities, or any attempts to condition the market to a forthcoming offer to sell securities before a registration statement has been filed. Such attempts are known as "gun jumping." They violate section 5(c) of the act and traditionally have been considered a major violation in securities practice.

In preparing a draft of the registration statement, the attorney must follow a detailed series of items and instructions. Some of the items include:

- a description of the company's business;

---

[48] *See* Securities Act § 11(b)(3)(C) ("did not believe that the statements therein were untrue"). Expertised portions are those "certified" by an expert, such as accountants with respect to financial statements, or tax or patent counsel with respect to legal opinions included in the prospectus.

[49] *See Escott v. BarChris Construction Corp.*, 283 F. Supp. 643 (S.D.N.Y. 1968), in which Judge McLean held that the attorney for the issuer who quarterbacks the preparation of the registration statement cannot be held liable as one who expertises any portion of it. Section 11 makes no mention of attorneys. Yet, if an attorney serves in a secondary capacity, e.g., as a director or corporate secretary, the counselor will jump ahead of all the other potential defendants and may face the highest due diligence burden of all.

- a financial summary;

- an analysis of competition;

- a statement defining the proposed use of offering proceeds; and

- a description of the securities being sold.

Counsel must ensure that all material information is disclosed. The attorney may also assemble a due diligence file in which to collect corroboration of every substantive statement contained in the registration statement. The due diligence file will support a due diligence defense if a suit is brought later.

Once the registration statement has been filed, the "waiting period" or filing period begins. During this time, broker-dealers in the underwriting syndicate may make oral (but not written) offers to sell but actual sales may not take place. Also, during this time, the preliminary prospectus (also known as the "red herring" prospectus) is circulated to investors. Any necessary amendments to the registration statement are prepared and filed. Once the registration becomes effective then actual sales may occur. The final, or statutory prospectus, must also be delivered to purchasers when the sale is confirmed or the security delivered, whichever occurs first.

The process is expensive. Typically, large, high-priced law firms are retained. Printing, registration and auditing costs are very high.[50] Many small corporations simply cannot afford to pay these high fees.[51]

Since registration costs are so high, attorneys representing small and startup corporations focus on identifying an exemption from the registration requirements and work with the issuing corporation or other entity to qualify for that exemption.[52]

Two features of the registration landscape that had been firmly in place since 1933 gave way in 2005. One was the absolute prohibition against "jump jumping," any statements or actions before a registration statement had been

---

[50] In 2003, average out-of-pocket costs for a public offering were $940,000.

[51] Even if the corporation can afford the cost, another significant bottleneck is finding an underwriter willing to do a public offering. Almost all public offerings in the United States are done on a firm commitment underwriting basis. This means that the underwriter or underwriting syndicate is firmly committed to paying to the issuing company, at closing (3 to 5 days after the registration "goes effective"), the offering proceeds (price times number of shares) less the spread (that is, the difference between the selling price and the proceeds due the issuer) by which the syndicate is compensated. Underwriters fear having a "sticky offering" that they are unable to sell while in the meantime they have pay off the issuing corporation. Those fears make underwriting firms extremely selective about which issues they will underwrite. To be contrasted to firm commitment is "best efforts" underwriting. There the underwriter merely agrees to act as a selling agent, doing the best that they are able to do. By and large, best efforts underwriting is confined to small exempt offerings of securities.

[52] The process has been simplified for proven companies which are already public companies by "integration" of the 1933 Act disclosure requirement and the 1934 Act continuous disclosure system. Corporations that participate in the system may bring securities to market with SEC Form S-2, a simpler registration form that incorporates by reference information already on file in 1934 Act reports. Larger corporations with a strong track record may use an even more simplified registration form, SEC Form S-3.

filed that could be construed as conditioning the market to a forthcoming offering. Two was the absolute prohibition on delivery of promotional or similar products ("free writings") before a final prospectus had been delivered to the purchaser or prospective purchaser. Now at least Well Known Seasoned Issuers (WKSIs, a new term introduced by the 2005 rule changes) can be engaged in relatively unrestricted oral and written offers even before they have filed a registration.[53] Following the filing of a registration statement, printed information supplemental to the preliminary prospects, known now as "free writing prospectuses," may be used.[54] These changes seem radical to experienced securities practitioners but are not that radical, as the securities law antifraud provisions, especially Rule 10b-5, continue to apply.[55]

[D] Exemptions From Registration

[1] Scope

Detailed treatment of the various exemptions to registration is a broad topic best covered in material devoted exclusively to securities regulation. The following discussion can only present an overview of the most widely used exemptions, namely, the intrastate exemption, the private offering or private placement exemption, and the various small issue and limited offering exemptions under the SEC safe harbor known as Regulation D.

[2] The Intrastate Exemption

The intrastate exemption has five requirements, several of which may be gleaned from the face of the statutory section:[56]

(1)   the issuer must be incorporated in the state;

(2)   the issuer must be doing business principally within the state;

(3)   the security may be offered and sold only to bona fide residents of the state;

(4)   the proceeds of the offering must be by and large used within the state; and

(5)   there can be no immediate resales of the security across state lines.

Attorneys often combine reliance on the federal intrastate exemption with a registration with state authorities, often using a simpler fill-in-the-blanks registration form known as ULOR (Uniform Limited Offering Registration). Given its demanding requirements, policing or conducting a large intrastate offering is well-nigh impossible. By its very nature, the intrastate exemption is useful only in the context of smaller offerings.

---

[53] *See, e.g.*, SEC Rule 163.

[54] *See* SEC Rules 164 & 433.

[55] Rule 10b-5 is discussed in §§ 13.01–02 *infra*.

[56] Securities Act of 1933 § 3(a)(11).

[3]   The Private Offering Exemption

The Securities Act of 1933 exempts from registration and prospectus delivery requirements "transactions by an issuer not involving a *public* offering."[57]

From 1947 to 1952, when little guidance about the exemption was available, Ralston Purina offered and sold $2 million of stock to employees who inquired about purchasing shares. Ralston had some 7,000 employees but only 1244 persons participated in the program over the six years it existed. Ralston claimed that the offering was limited to "key" employees, key in the sense of energy and loyalty, rather than seniority or levels of the company's organizational chart. In *SEC v. Ralston Purina Co.*,[58] Mr. Justice Clark found that the limitation to key employees did not result in a private offering. The Court quoted a federal appeals court judge's ruminations about the meaning of "public":

> [M]anifestly an offering of securities to all redheaded men, to all residents of Chicago or San Francisco, to all existing stockholders of General Motors . . . is no less "public," in every realistic sense of the word, than an unrestricted offering to the world at large. Such an offering is none the less "public" in character . . . .[59]

Justice Clark turned to the statute, finding that "[t]he natural way to interpret the private offering exemption is in light of the statutory purpose." An offering was private if none of the offerees needed the sort of protection a registration statement would afford. That would be true if all offerees were shown "to be able to fend for themselves" and if they also were shown to have "access to the kind of information which registration would disclose."

Mr. Justice Clark declined the SEC's invitation to put a numerical limit on the number of offerees in a private offering, observing only that "[i]t may well be that offerings to a substantial number of persons would rarely be exempt."

In subsequent years, courts attempted to supply rough numerical limits and to flesh out other elements of the exemption. Twenty-five offerees represented a rough upper limit. However, the limit could relax significantly if the risk was low and the offeree group homogenous. The example given was placement of high quality debt securities by a well-known issuer with 70 insurance companies.

Each and every offeree was required to be sophisticated and knowledgeable enough to evaluate the merits of the offering. Since the exemption's availability depended upon who was offered the item and not merely those who purchased, a certain amount of pre-screening was needed to ensure that each and every offeree possessed the requisite sophistication.

Some practitioners limited private placements to those who had significant financial resources as well, finding that those with means had enhanced ability to evaluate an offering. Also, securities were required to be "placed," that is, there

---

[57]   Securities Act § 4(2) (emphasis added).

[58]   346 U.S. 119 (1953).

[59]   Quoting Denman, J., in *SEC v. Sunbeam Gold Mines Co.*, 95 F.2d 699 (9th Cir. 1938).

could be no resale until either a later registration, the passage of time (two years was a good guess), or a "change of circumstances." Personal wealth also lessened the likelihood of a need to resell. Finally, limitations on resale also prevented use of private placements to "go public by the back door."[60]

Soon, in the hands of several federal courts of appeal, compliance with the requirements for the private placement exemption became nearly impossible. The Fifth Circuit held that each and every offeree had not only to possess the type of information a registration would disclose but also to have access to further information and sources of verification "tantamount to [those of] an insider."[61]

Subsequent cases retreated from extreme interpretations. For example, in *Doran v. Petroleum Management Corp.*,[62] the Fifth Circuit upheld the offer to eight and the sale to four investors of oil well interests in Wyoming. The plaintiff had a net worth of over $1 million and a degree in petroleum engineering. He clearly possessed the needed sophistication. The court made clear that in its view, the informational requirement was disjunctive:

> [o]n remand . . . the district court must keep in mind that the 'availability' of information means either disclosure of or effective access to the relevant information." When, however, the issue relies upon access rather than provision of formal disclosure documents it must be "effective" access, not merely some gratuitous offer by the issuer. The issuer "must show that the offerees occupied a privileged position relative to the issuer that afforded them an opportunity for effective access to the information registration would otherwise provide.

Securities practitioners may have found it easier to live under the aegis of cases such as *Doran* but compliance with the private offering exemption was nonetheless very difficult. The difficulty also went beyond the opaque judicial interpretation of the private offering exemption.

In an influential law review article, Professor Rutherford Campbell of the University of Kentucky School of Law pointed to "the pervasive vagueness that boggles the keenest legal minds" existent in the case law, the "unmanageable levels of ambiguity," the "exorbitant costs," the "unworkable resale provisions," and other factors that affected small issuers. His piece, *The Plight of Small Issuers Under the Securities Act of 1933: Practical Foreclosure From the Capital Market*,[63] finally spurred the SEC into action.

---

[60] To inhibit resale, investors signed "investment letters" agreeing not to attempt resale. The stock was also "lettered." The margin of the stock certificate would have typed thereon words such as: "These shares have been issued pursuant to an exemption under the Securities Act of 1933 and may not be resold, or offered for resale, without the written opinion of the corporation's counsel."

[61] *SEC v. Continental Tobacco Co.*, 463 F.2d 137 (5th Cir. 1972).

[62] 545 F.2d 893 (5th Cir. 1977).

[63] 1977 Duke L. J. 1139.

[4]   Regulation D Exemptions

In the late 1970s, the SEC promulgated experimental safe harbor rules, which added certainty to the process of working with so-called transaction exemptions from registration.[64] Deeming the experiment a success, in 1981, the SEC promulgated Regulation D.[65] Regulation D contains three exemptions from registration that have become the most widely used exemptions under the federal securities laws.[66]

Rule 504 permits the issuer to engage in a general solicitation, that is, to contact persons with whom the issuer or selling agents have no pre-existing relationship and who have not been pre-screened in any way, if the issuer utilizes a disclosure document pursuant to state law. The issuer is limited to raising up to $1 million. Rule 505 permits sales to up to 35 persons plus an unlimited number of "accredited investors." Accredited investors are offerees who have been screened and found to have income of $200,000 ($300,000 jointly), or a net worth in excess of $1 million, or to be eligible financial institutions. The issuer must prepare and provide purchasers with a formal disclosure document. The rule exempts offerings of up to $5 million.

Rule 506 is the private placement safe harbor. It permits the issuer to sell to up to 35 purchasers plus an unlimited number of accredited investors. Each and every purchaser "either alone or with his purchaser representative(s) [must have] such knowledge and experience in financial and business matters that he is capable of evaluating the merits and risks of the prospective investment." The sophistication requirement is more relaxed than that required for the common law exemption. Sophistication is tested as to all purchasers and not as to each and every offeree, as at common law, and a purchaser who is unsophisticated may retain an agent to represent her or to aid her in evaluating the offer. For example, many professional athletes, rock stars, and movie actors who have been asked to subscribe to private offerings use a purchaser representative. The rule has no dollar limit on the amount that an issuer may raise.

If any unaccredited investors are present in the transaction, the issuer must prepare and distribute a disclosure document, usually titled "Private Placement Memorandum," or PPM. A typical PPM has financial statements, copies of all contracts, partnership agreements, and other documents appended to it. PPMs are often thicker than the telephone directories of a medium-sized city.

The exemptions from registration may not be utilized to evade the registration requirement. An issuer who offered $5 million pursuant to rule 505 with offerings in alternative months, and who thereby sought to raise $30

---

[64] *See, e.g.*, SEC Rule 142.

[65] Regulation D consists of rules 501–508 under the Securities Act of 1933. Subsequently, under the guidance of the North American Securities Administrators' Association (NASAA), most of the states have adopted a parallel set of exemptions known as the Uniform Limited Offering Exemption (ULOE).

[66] All the "ins and outs" of Regulation D practice are beyond the scope of a work such as this. Indeed, at least one treatise devotes itself wholly to the topic. *See* William J. Hicks, LIMITED OFFERING EXEMPTIONS: REGULATION D (rev. ed. 1997). *See also* Hicks, EXEMPTED TRANSACTIONS UNDER THE SECURITIES ACT OF 1933 (rev. ed. 1997) (in 5 volumes).

million per year, may find that the allegedly "exempt" transactions were "integrated," resulting in the loss of any exemption. Integration aims at a pattern of using the same or different exemptions to reach a result that properly should be reached by means of full-blown registration.

Regulation D exemptions are "non-exclusive safe harbors." An issuer out of technical compliance with a provision applicable to rule 506 may nonetheless be able to "fall back" on the common law private placement exemption. A small issuer that runs afoul of some provision of the rule 504 safe harbor may find that it meets all the requirements of the intrastate exemption and defend on that basis any suit alleging a registration violation.[67]

§ 7.04 PROXY REGULATION

[A] Introduction

A proxy is a species of agency relationship. The agency is limited to allowing another to vote one's shares in a corporation for issues on which the shareholders have the right to vote, such as the election of directors, merger proposals, amendment of articles of incorporation, and so on.[68] The shareholder is the principal, referred to as the "proxy giver." The document creating, and perhaps limiting the scope of, the agency, is the "proxy." The agent is the "proxy holder," often referred to as the "proxy" as well.[69]

As with any other agency relationship, the agent/proxy holder owes a fiduciary duty of obedience and loyalty to the principal and the agency is revocable — by a later-dated proxy to someone else, by an instrument of revocation, by the proxy giver's attendance and vote at the shareholders' meeting for which the proxy was intended, and, in any case, under many state corporation laws by the passage of time.[70]

Proxy voting is sometimes utilized in closely held, small, and quasi-public corporations. In publicly held corporations, proxy voting is used extensively (indeed, in nearly every corporation and on at least an annual basis). Frequently, in a large corporation, only a few shareholders attend the annual meeting or special meetings that may be called at times other than the annual meeting. Prior to the meeting, the incumbent management of the corporation solicits proxies from shareholders. Those proxies authorize two or three of the incumbent managers to vote the shareholder's shares at the annual meeting,

---

[67] Any reader who has read merely the portions of this volume regarding securities issuance, or the analogous sections in a law school corporations casebook, is ill-prepared to represent clients in the complex arena of securities regulation. A little knowledge is not only dangerous to clients and investors but, given the criminal penalties and very real prospect of civil liability, very dangerous to attorneys.

[68] For a discussion of the state law rules applicable to shareholder voting, see § 5.05, *supra.*

[69] The terminology can become confusing. For that reason, the Model Business Corporation attempts to introduce new terminology, calling the document "the appointment form" rather than "the proxy." *See* MBCA § 7.22.

[70] *See, e.g.*, MBCA § 7.22 (an "appointment is valid for 11 months unless a longer period is expressly provided for in the appointment form").

principally for election of the slate of directors nominated by incumbent management but also for other items listed on the proxy card (appointment of auditors and approval of stock option plans for management are two frequent items) and on "such other business as may properly come before the meeting or any adjournment thereof."[71]

Thus, in the United States, several weeks prior to the annual meeting of a publicly held corporation, shareholders receive a large envelope containing an annual report for the previous year, management's discussion and analysis of the previous year, and financial statements. Also included is the proxy statement, which also may double as the notice of meeting required by state law.[72]

The annual proxy statement speaks directly to the issues to be voted upon at the meeting. Because one of those issues will be election of some (in the case of a staggered, or classified, board) or all of the directors, the statement will disclose background information on directors, their shareholdings, and their compensation. Under SEC regulations, the proxy statement must contain in tabular form detailed disclosure as to the cash and non-cash compensation of the five most highly compensated officers of the corporation.[73] The latter is one of the most widely read items in the proxy solicitation process.

Last of all, the envelope will contain the proxy card itself, previously discussed. The shareholder marks the proxy card "yea" or "nay" as to the various items, dates and signs the card, and places the card in the enclosed small envelope for posting back to the corporation or proxy soliciting firm.

This process, involving publicly held corporations, is highly regulated. The Securities Exchange Act of 1934 contains a broad mandate for the Securities and Exchange Commission (SEC) to regulate proxy voting. That act makes it "unlawful for any person . . . in contravention of such rules and regulations as the Commission may prescribe as necessary or appropriate in the public interest or for the protection of investors, to solicit or to permit the use of his name to solicit any proxy or consent or authorization in respect of any security . . . registered pursuant to section 12 of this title."[74] SEC regulation is in fact so pervasive that, as has perhaps already been revealed by the discussion thus far, the very structure of the proxy solicitation process is not

---

[71] The SEC's regulations provide that if management knows that a certain item will come before the annual meeting the proxy solicitor must include on the proxy card the item and space for the shareholders to vote "yea" or "nay" as to that item. SEC Rule 14a-4(a), (c).

[72] An example reads:

> We [the Norfolk Southern Corporation] will hold our annual meeting of Stockholders at The Kimball Theater, 428 West Duke of Gloucester Street, Williamsburg, Virginia, on Thursday, May 14, 2009, at 10:00 A.M. Eastern Standard Time, for the following purposes. . . .
>
> By order of the Board of Directors,
> HOWARD D. McFADDEN
> Corporate Secretary

[73] SEC Schedule 14A, Items 7, 10. Schedule 14A is titled "Information Required in a Proxy Statement."

[74] Securities Exchange Act § 14(a).

only informed but dictated by SEC regulation. It is that process, the regulations applicable to it, and court cases interpreting those regulations, as well as recent extensive changes to it,[75] to which this section of the instant chapter is devoted.

[B]   A Proxy Solicitation Hypothetical

Perhaps the most efficient manner in which to discuss the regulatory structure and to place it in context is with a hypothetical:

> A number of Northern Pines, Inc., shareholders, who are all active members of the Save Our Forests' Topography (SOFT) organization, are in your law office. The Northern Pines annual shareholders' meeting is four months hence. The SOFT shareholder group wants to force Northern Pines to amend its articles of incorporation to prohibit clear cutting and cease construction of logging roads that seriously alter topography in the areas in which Northern Pines harvests timber.
>
> Alternatively, the SOFT shareholders want to force a merger of Northern Pines with Ecological Logging, Inc., a forest products company which engages in selective harvesting of timber tracts, utilizing soft tired vehicles and other environmentally friendly techniques.
>
> Northern Pines is publicly held, with 1100 holders of its common stock, and traded in the over the counter market. SOFT represents about 3 percent of the common stock but is very militant. SOFT has said to you, "We're going to make them do this whether they like it or not."
>
> Advise the SOFT representatives what their alternatives might be, with a short cost benefit analysis of each alternative.[76]

Before detailed discussion of the alternatives most relevant to this section and chapter of this volume, it might be helpful briefly to discuss and dismiss a few other alternatives and make a few preliminary observations.

The SOFT shareholders could sue, seeking a preliminary and then final injunction against clear cutting and road construction. That alternative seems unattractive because, by statute, it is the board of directors which manages the corporation's business and affairs. By their lawsuit, the SOFT shareholders would be seen as attempting to control management decisions and would run into the business judgment rule.[77]

Alternatively, the SOFT shareholders could purchase additional shares, via the over-the-counter market or by a takeover bid made directly to fellow shareholders, or both. Two observations may be made. First, the purchase of shares is only the penultimate step. SOFT wants shares so as to obtain votes. In turn, votes will enable them to remove the incumbent directors or, better yet,

---

[75] *See* Lisa M. Fairfax, *Making the Corporation Safe for Shareholder Democracy*, 69 Ohio St. L. J. 53 (2008) (discussing changes and non-traditional uses to which the system has been put by shareholder activists and others).

[76] Based upon problem Number 88, in Douglas M. Branson, Questions and Answers on Business Organizations (LexisNexis 2004).

[77] For a discussion of the business judgment rule, see § 8.03, *infra.*

elect a competing slate of directors who are sympathetic to or share SOFT's agenda. Second, the purchase of a sufficient number of shares will be expensive, perhaps beyond SOFT members' ability to finance, either directly or through borrowing.[78]

A third alternative for the group is to wage a proxy contest, proposing for election to the board of directors a slate of directors who are opposed to clear cutting and sympathetic to other items on the SOFT agenda. The SOFT group would follow nomination with proxy solicitation aimed at obtaining votes in favor of their slate. The SOFT group could also wage its own proxy solicitation in favor of a shareholder proposal that reflects its position and tries to get majority shareholder approval to support its views. Treatment of the SOFT hypothetical now turns to proxy contests, to be followed by discussion of a fourth alternative, a shareholder proposal in the corporation's own annual proxy solicitation, as opposed to their own solicitation pursuant to SEC Rule 14a-8.

[C]   Proxy Contests

[1]   The Shareholder's Role

In the hypothetical posed, the SOFT shareholder group wants to force Northern Pines to amend its articles of incorporation to prohibit clear cutting. Alternatively, the SOFT shareholders want to force a merger of Northern Pines with Ecological Logging. Any attorney advising them, however, must tell them that they cannot do so, at least directly.

By law, formal amendment of the articles of incorporation must begin with a proposal by the board of directors.[79] Similarly, a merger may begin only with directors' formulation and approval of a plan of merger or share exchange.[80] If the Northern Pines board will not propose an amendment or a merger, then the shareholders who desire amendment or merger must mount an effort to elect a board of directors who will. This process (nomination and attempted election of a slate of insurgent directors) is known as a "proxy contest" or "proxy fight."

[2]   Inadvertent Solicitation and Other Problems

Mounting a proxy fight in a publicly held corporation is expensive, in part because of costs imposed by SEC regulation. Printing, paper, and mailing costs may be extensive. Legal representation must be relatively sophisticated and,

---

[78] Extensive market purchases of shares and partial takeover bids often are used in conjunction with a proxy solicitation, or "proxy fight" (a solicitation in competition with management's solicitation usually with the goal of control of the board of directors). In the 1980s takeover boom, takeover players such as T. Boone Pickens often used market and direct purchases of shares (partial takeover bid) as a prelude or adjunct to a proxy solicitation. For a discussion of these tactics, see § 6.04, *supra*.

[79] *See, e.g.*, MBCA § 10.03 ("A corporation's board of directors may propose one or more amendments . . . . For the amendment to be adopted . . . the board of directors must recommend the amendment . . . .").

[80] *See, e.g.*, MBCA § 11.01 ("One or more corporations may merge into another corporation if the board of directors of each corporation adopts and its shareholders . . . approve a plan of merger"). For a discussion of mergers, see § 6.02, *supra*.

therefore, expensive.[81] In hard-fought battles, both the incumbents and the insurgents retain proxy solicitation firms to solicit and re-solicit shareholders, entailing still more fees for professional services.[82]

Navigating various regulatory obstacles is difficult even if it is not expensive. The regulations define very broadly the terms "solicit" and "solicitation" to include "[a]ny request for a proxy," "[a]ny request to execute or not to execute, or to revoke, a proxy," and "[t]he furnishing of a form . . . or other communication under circumstances reasonably calculated to result in the procurement, withholding or revocation of a proxy."[83] In turn, proxy is defined to include "*every* proxy, consent or authorization" relating to shares.[84]

In *Studebaker Corp. v. Gittlin*,[85] Gittlin solicited authorizations from other shareholders to enable him to inspect the shareholder list so that he could study the feasibility of a proxy fight. New York law gave a five percent shareholder group an absolute right of inspection. The court held that the solicitation of authorizations to conduct a preliminary feasibility study was itself a solicitation, requiring pre-filing with the SEC. The court upheld an injunction against Gittlin. While the SEC urged that solicitation should "include authorizations to inspect shareholder lists, even in cases where obtaining the authorizations was not a step in a planned solicitation of proxies," Judge Friendly instead relied upon *SEC v. Orkin*,[86] which held that "a letter which did not request the giving of any authorization was subject to the Proxy Rules if it was part of a 'continuous plan' intended to end in a solicitation."

This broad view of what conduct is subject to SEC regulation has ducked challenges on First Amendment free speech and free press grounds. The SEC filing and other requirements, along with the SEC's unilateral definition of what is misleading, are argued to be prior restraints on speech, subject to heightened scrutiny under the First Amendment.[87] In *Long Island Lighting Co. v. Barbash*,[88] a candidate for Nassau County (New York) county executive was an advocate of public power. He also held 100 shares in Long Island Lighting (LILCO), the private electric utility serving the area. The political advocacy group with which he was affiliated published newspaper advertisements encouraging citizens to support replacement of LILCO with a state-run utility. LILCO argued that advertisements were proxy solicitations covered by SEC

---

[81] For a discussion of reimbursement of proxy contest expenses, see § 5.05[C][5], *supra.*

[82] Since any proxy may be revoked by a subsequent proxy or by a shareholder's attendance at the meeting itself, solicitation may continue until the last possible minute, including at the door of the meeting room.

[83] SEC Rule 14a-1(*l*)(1).

[84] SEC Rule 14a-1(f).

[85] 360 F.2d 692 (2d Cir. 1966).

[86] 132 F.2d 784 (2d Cir. 1943).

[87] *Cf.* Arthur R. Pinto, *The Nature of Capital Markets Allows a Greater Role for the Government*, 55 Brook. L. Rev. 77 (1989) (arguing SEC mandatory disclosure does not violate the First Amendment because securities, which have no independent value that is separate from the information supplied by the firm, therefore require greater government oversight and protection).

[88] 779 F.2d 793 (2d Cir. 1985).

rules while Barbash argued First Amendment protection.

The appellate court did not decide the issue and held that the trial judge had not given LILCO sufficient opportunity to demonstrate that the political ads were part of or themselves were a solicitation, subject to the proxy rules, noting that "[the] rules apply not only to direct requests . . . but also to communications which may indirectly accomplish such a result or constitute a step in a chain of communication designed ultimately to accomplish such a result."

Judge Winter dissented on grounds that the advertisements were "addressed solely to the public," and were "sheer political advocacy and would be so recognized by any reasonable shareholder." He thought that the majority's disposition of the case, along with "LILCO's claim" that a proxy solicitation had taken place, raised "a constitutional issue of the first magnitude" and "asks nothing less than that a federal court act as a censor." Judge Winter would have held that "[w]hen advertisements are critical of corporate conduct but are directed solely to the public . . . I would construe the federal proxy regulation as inapplicable, whatever the motive of those who purchase [the advertisements]."

In 1992, the SEC revised the proxy rules to permit a small increase in communication among shareholders without regulatory compliance. The Commission did so not by revision of the definition of solicitation but through broadening the categories of solicitations that are exempt from filing and other regulatory burdens. Pre-existing exemptions included the "pass-through" to clients by brokers of proxy solicitation materials relating to securities which those clients hold in nominee or street name, if the pass-through is accomplished without recommendation on how to vote, and "any solicitation made otherwise than on behalf of the registrant where the total number of persons solicited is not more than ten."[89] The 1992 amendments added an exemption for communications between shareholders that do not solicit proxy voting authority and that are sent by persons who have no material economic interest in the outcome of a solicitation or proxy fight.[90] This exemption for "unilateral voting announcements" is intended to permit institutional investors and shareholder activists to communicate with one another as to how they intend to vote.[91] The 1992 amendments also eliminated pre-filing requirements for speeches, advertisements, and other communications. In that manner, the amendments lessened, if they did not eliminate, many of the First Amendment "prior restraint" objections alluded to earlier.

---

[89] SEC Rule 14a-2(a)(1), (b)(2).

[90] SEC Exchange Act Release No. 34-31326 (1992).

[91] *See, e.g.*, John C. Coffee, Jr., *The SEC and the Institutional Investor: A Half Time Report*, 15 CARDOZO L. REV. 837, 840–41 (1994) (characterizing the 1992 revisions as radical). *Cf.* Carol Goforth, *Proxy Reform as a Means of Increasing Shareholder Participation in Corporate Governance: Too Little, But Not Too Late*, 43 AM. U. L. REV. 379 (1994). *See also* Robert S. Frenchman, *The Recent Revisions to Federal Proxy Regulations: Lifting the Ban on Shareholder Communication*, 68 TUL. L. REV. 161 (1993); Jill A. Hornstein, *Proxy Solicitation Redefined: The SEC Takes an Incremental Step Toward Effective Corporate Governance*, 71 WASH. U. L.Q. 1129 (1993). For a discussion of institutional investor activism, see § 5.02[E], *supra*.

Despite the increased freedom to communicate posed by the 1992 amendments, shareholder activists such as the SOFT group need to be warned to take great care. Any press release, mass mailing, or other communication that may be construed even as conditioning the shareholder group to a forthcoming solicitation is itself a solicitation, however inadvertent it may have been. Northern Pines, or any other public corporation, along with the powerful law firm likely to represent it, may, and probably will, seek an injunction on the grounds that a solicitation has occurred and that, because regulatory compliance is not in place, the solicitation is an unlawful one. The SOFT group will find its resources and attention diverted to a court fight. Often, that diversion will derail altogether the shareholder activist effort, at least for that proxy season.

[3]   Regulatory Burdens and Costs

The SEC rules provide that "[n]o solicitation subject to . . . regulation shall be made unless each person solicited is concurrently furnished or has been previously furnished with a written proxy statement" meeting SEC requirements.[92] In order to do that, an insurgent group such as SOFT must first comply with complex SEC rules regarding the information to be furnished to shareholders, the form of proxy, and the form and presentation of information in the proxy statement.[93] The SOFT insurgents must then pre-file with the SEC: regulations provide that "[f]ive preliminary copies of the proxy statement and form of proxy shall be filed with the Commission at least 10 calendar days prior to the date definitive copies of such material are first sent."[94] Pre-filing entails several costs. One is that sophisticated legal representation may be necessary to put material into proper format. Another is that despite legal representation, the SEC may find the material deficient, requiring amendment that in turn entails delay.

[4]   Proxy Contest Procedures and Further Costs

When SOFT has completed its solicitation materials, the options then belong to Northern Pines. Within five business days, Northern Pines may either furnish SOFT with a copy of its shareholder list or, if it does not wish to give up a copy of its shareholder list, offer to mail the proxy materials for SOFT. There is, however, no free ride. In the latter instance, SOFT must advance "the estimated cost of mailing a proxy statement, form of proxy, or other communication"[95] and, after the fact, reimburse the corporation for any further cost. Paper, printing, legal and mailing costs may easily run into several hundreds of thousands of dollars, even in a small publicly held corporation such as Northern Pines.

---

[92] SEC Rule 14a-3(a).

[93] SEC Rules 14a-3-14a-5.

[94] SEC Rule 14a-6(a).

[95] SEC Rule 14a-7(a). If SOFT has greater rights to the shareholder list under the law of Northern Pines's state of incorporation, SOFT should opt for obtaining the list in order to be able to communicate directly with shareholders. SEC Rule 14a-7 was not designed to preempt state law.

In the 1992 reforms, the SEC did loosen its rigid requirements. In a case in which a security holder or the corporation is opposing a solicitation by another relating to an election or to removal of directors, that is, in cases of election contests, the person may communicate with shareholders without pre-filing, provided that no form of proxy is sent and that "a written proxy statement meeting the requirements of [the] regulation is sent . . . at the earliest practicable date."[96]

In cases other than election contests, such as merger, amendment of articles of incorporation, and so on, opposition may also be mounted without pre-filing with the SEC. Solicitation may be made "prior to furnishing security holders a written proxy statement . . . if the solicitation is made in opposition to a prior solicitation, or an invitation for tenders or other publicized activity, which if successful, could reasonably have the effect of defeating the action proposed." No form of proxy may be sent, however, and the soliciting person must simultaneously file with the SEC eight copies of its material "no later than the date such material is published, sent or given to any security holders."[97]

Recent years have seen attempts by shareholder activists to promote bylaw amendments at publicly held corporations.[98] A number of those proposed bylaws would require corporations to reimburse insurgents' proxy contest expenses, or reasonable expenses, even in cases in which insurgents had lost. In *CA, Inc. v. AFSCME Employees Pension Plan*,[99] while opining that the proposal under consideration was illegal, the Supreme Court of Delaware left open a comparatively wide field of play for such amendment proposals in the future.

The picture that emerges is that a proxy contest should not be lightly undertaken. The costs are considerable even before considering the effect of the SEC's general antifraud rule (SEC Rule 14a-9) applicable to proxy solicitations which will be discussed later in the Chapter. That rule gives rise to a cause for action for mere negligence in the solicitation of proxies. A group such as SOFT that complies with all other SEC requirements may nonetheless find itself in court, with Northern Pines seeking a preliminary injunction on grounds that, in its shareholder communications, SOFT has disclosed some material in a misleading way or has omitted material facts. SOFT's defense of "mistake" or merely "a slip of the pen" may be insufficient. For an activist shareholder group such as SOFT, however, there does exist a more practical and less costly alternative to strategies such as litigation, a takeover bid, or a full-fledged proxy fight. Before considering the general antifraud rule in more detail, then, we will detour a bit in our treatment of the SOFT hypothetical in order to describe such

---

[96] SEC Rule 14a-11. Significantly, shareholders now communicate with each other without fear of it being a solicitation under SEC Rule 14(a)-2(b) if they do not seek proxy voting and have no material economic interest in the issue. This was designed to encourage institutional investors to communicate with each other.

[97] SEC Rule 14a-12.

[98] Discussed in § 7.05[H] & [I] *infra*.

[99] 953 A.2d 227 (2008), discussed in § 7.05[I] *infra*.

an alternative.[100]

[D]   Use of Shareholder Consents

Many states allow the use of shareholder consents in lieu of a meeting. Several states, most principally Delaware, but also including Illinois, Nevada, and California, allow valid shareholder consent action to be by majority rather than unanimous vote.[101] Recent amendments to the MBCA allow use of majority consents, at least in cases in which the articles of incorporation authorize use of the procedure.[102]

Consents and consent solicitations are markedly different than proxies and proxy solicitations. While a proxy appoints some one else as an agent for the voting of shares a consent is self implementing, somewhat in the nature of an absentee ballot. It is itself a vote. Consents have several advantages: (1) no shareholders meeting is required, thus saving considerable expense, and (2) secrecy is possible, as no meeting is required and nothing need be filed until on or before the 60th day after the first consent has been signed, when the insurgents present the consents all at once to the corporation. A big disadvantage is that to be successful a consent solicitation must obtain an absolute numerical majority (50% plus 1) rather than a majority of those present at a meeting, given the presence a quorum (as low as 25% plus 1 in the typical case). Corporate officials and others have criticized consents as means of "sneak attacks" and "corporate hijacking."

The Supreme Court of Delaware, however, has been especially vigilant in voiding corporate bylaw amendments and other arrangements designed to negate use of the consent procedure in particular corporations.[103]

[E]   The Internet and the "Notice and Access" Proxy Regime

Delaware begin the movement of corporate law into the Internet age. In 2000, the Delaware legislation authorized the conduct of virtual meetings in which the forum may be an Internet chat room rather than a physical place such as a hotel ballroom.[104] Further legislative enactments authorized electronic delivery of proxies or consents by means such as email. In place of authentication by signature, the old way, the new provision directs proxy or consent solicitors and election inspectors to accept such filings "provided that such [electronic transmissions] . . . either set forth or are submitted in such a

---

[100] Discussion of SEC Rule 14a-9 is thus postponed and treated more fully in § 7.06, *infra.*

[101] *See, e.g.* Del. Gen. Corp. L. § .228; Cal. Corp. Code § .603; Ill. Bus. Corp. Act § 7.10; Nev. Rev. Stat. § .78.320.

[102] MBCA § 7.04(b).

[103] *See, e.g., Frantz Mfg. Co. v. EAC Ind.,* 501 A.2d 401 (Del. 1985) (measures to restrict use of consent procedure held invalid); *Empire of Carolina, Inc. v. Deltona Corp.,* 501 A.2d 1252 (Del. Ch. 1985) (same); *Datapoint Corp. v. Plaza Securities Corp.,* 496 A.2d 1031 (Del. 1985) (modifications to statutory consent procedure must be in charter rather than bylaws).

[104] Del. Gen. Corp. L. § 211(a)(2).

form from which it can be determined that the telegram, cablegram or other electronic transmission was authorized by the shareholder."[105] The MBCA followed with similar provisions.[106]

In 2007, the SEC rolled out the final version of its Notice and Access proxy rule, part of its "access equals delivery" initiative.[107] The new delivery method is available for all but solicitations seeking approval of business combinations. Forty days or more before a meeting, issuers send out a notice of where proxy materials may be obtained (that is, where on the Internet) and a post card which can be used by those who still desire written materials. By 2009, the SEC will require all corporations registered with it to have an electronic version of their proxy materials posted on the web. Instead of receiving a thick envelope containing notice of meeting, proxy statement, proxy or voting instruction form, and annual report, shareholders will receive thin envelopes containing two single page items.

The first year of the program saved corporations an estimated $143 million in paper, printing and postage costs. Environmentalists note that the program saved 180,000 trees which would have been harvested to manufacture the needed paper.[108]

Another new Internet initiative consists of rules enabling shareholders to conduct Electronic Shareholder Forums (ESFs).[109] Both companies and shareholders may establish ESFs with communications exempt from the otherwise broad SEC definition of solicitation (any communication which may be construed as seeking a consent or authorization, or the withholding of a consent or authorization from another). At least if the communications take place 60 days or more before a meeting, or the notice of the meeting plus 2 days, whichever occurs later, even though similar to a solicitation, shareholder communications will not trigger application of the SEC's costly filing and other requirements. Commentators predict that ESFs will become forums for shareholder activists and will be used, *inter alia*, by activists seeking to garner support for SEC Rule 14a-8 proposals.[110] The SEC adopted the rule with surprisingly little opposition from corporations and other would-be opponents.[111]

---

[105] Del. Gen. Corp. L. § 212(c)(2).

[106] MBCA §§ 7.04(1) (consents) & 7.22(b) (proxies).

[107] *See* SEC Release 34-55146 (Jan. 22, 2007, eff. March 30, 2007) (adding new Rule 14a-16 and amending, *inter alia*, Rules 14a-1, 14a-3, 14a-4 and 14a-7).

[108] Mark A. Sargent & Dennis R. Honaback, Proxy Rules Handbook 895 (2008–09 ed.); *see generally id.* at 883–99.

[109] SEC Release No. 34-57172 (Jan. 18, 2008).

[110] Discussed in § 7.05 *infra.*

[111] *See, e.g.,* Sargent & Honaback, *supra*, at 897–99.

§ 7.05   THE SEC SHAREHOLDER PROXY PROPOSAL RULE: SEC RULE 14a-8

[A]   Proposals

The student of corporate law must distinguish carefully between a proxy contest or other full-fledged proxy solicitation, to elect directors or support a shareholder proposal, which may be a costly (even gigantic) undertaking, and submission of a single proposal and supporting statement (together limited to 500 words), to be included in corporate management's own annual solicitation.[112] The latter is a far more modest undertaking done in several hundred publicly held corporations each annual proxy season. An SEC Rule 14a-8 proposal under SEC Rule 14a-8, also known as the "town meeting" rule, may be ideal for achievement of some or all of the goals of the SOFT shareholder group.

Historically, shareholder proposals fall roughly into two main groups: corporate social responsibility proposals and corporate governance proposals. The former include proposals relating to product safety, employment discrimination, affirmative action, environmental pollution, nuclear power, and so on. Other social responsibility proposals have been more topical: for example, tobacco and anti-smoking, (non) participation in the Arab boycott of Israel, cessation of operations in South Africa during the apartheid era, and divestment from Northern Ireland. Some seasonal topics, such as requests for disclosure on or safeguards against illegal campaign contributions or foreign payments (topical in the 1970s and early 1980s) shade over into the governance area.

The volume of social responsibility proposals increased rapidly around 1970 with Earth Day and Campaign General Motors. The latter was a highly publicized effort by law students at Georgetown University to include in the General Motors proxy statement requests that General Motors disclose, among other things, its record regarding automobile safety. Although the student proposals garnered only 2.73 and 2.44 percent of the vote respectively, General Motors eventually did make the requested disclosures.[113]

Church groups have been very active in the social responsibility area. Groups range from the American Episcopal Church and other major denominations to small orders of Roman Catholic nuns such as the Sisters of Our Lady of Perpetual Hope. An umbrella organization, the Interfaith Center on Corporate Responsibility, has 250 or so members, including religious communities, pension funds, healthcare systems, dioceses of various religious denominations, and the like. The ICCR provides "how to" advice and tracks activity in the shareholder proposal area. In 1997, 100 ICCR religious members submitted 191 resolutions to 137 corporations. The ICCR made proposals to RJR Nabisco to end "Joe Camel Ads anywhere in the world," to General Electric to "no longer to seek

---

[112] For a discussion of proxy contests, see § 5.05[C], *supra*.

[113] *See* Donald Schwartz, *The Public Interest Proxy Contest: Reflections on Campaign GM*, 69 MICH. L. REV. 419 (1971).

new nuclear fuel sales abroad," and to 40 companies to endorse the CERES Principles for Public Environmental Accountability.[114]

Governance proposals were prevalent in the 1950s and 1960s, often propounded by corporate gadflies such as Evelyn Davis or the Gilbert brothers, individuals who owned small numbers of shares in a great many corporations. Their proposals related to traditional issues such as cumulative voting, selection of auditors, location of shareholder meetings, requirements that corporations issue reports of annual meeting proceedings, and executive compensation.[115] For much of the 1970s and well into the 1980s, the social responsibility proposals eclipsed the governance ones. Although those social responsibility proposals seldom garnered significant votes, they did significantly affect the culture in many publicly held corporations and reflected more general activism on the issue in question.

Today, corporate governance proposals match in number, and far exceed in success, social responsibility shareholder resolutions. Current governance perennial favorites include executive compensation proposals, requests for secret voting by shareholders, replacement of classified boards with annual election of all directors, and redemption or recession of poison pill antitakeover defense plans. In 1994, the poison pill initiatives were adopted in five of nine cases and received on average 37 percent of the votes cast in the efforts which failed. Proposals to institute confidential shareholder voting passed in two of nine cases, and received over 40 percent of the votes in two others. Almost 30 public corporations held votes on annual election of directors with success in two cases.[116] By contrast, social responsibility proposals are considered to have done well if they receive four or five percent of the vote.

Today, with systematic involvement of church and religious groups in the social responsibility area, and institutional investor involvement in the corporate governance area, corporations take shareholder proposals very seriously.

---

[114] 25 The Corporate Examiner, Nos. 7–8, at 8–10, 14 (1997). In the 1994 proxy season, one study found that 232 social policy resolutions were presented to United States corporations. Of those, 118 were included in corporate proxy statements and voted upon. Only 10 of those 118 received a vote of more than 15 percent; none passed. See A. Bradley, How Institutions Voted on Social Policy Shareholder Resolutions (IIRRC 1994).

[115] See, e.g., SEC v. Transamerica Corp., 163 F.2d 511 (3d Cir. 1947) (court orders inclusion of three proposals by Gilbert brothers as proper subjects for shareholder action under Delaware law: (1) to have corporation's independent auditors elected by the shareholders; (2) to eliminate bylaw requiring all bylaw changes to be contained in notice of meeting approved by management; and (3) to require a report of the proceedings at the annual meeting be sent to all shareholders).

[116] See generally Bradley, supra note 114. In 1998, the top three governance proposals were redeem or vote on poison pills (58.1 %), repeal classified board (47.9 %), and confidential shareholder voting (47.3 %). The three least successful were restrict executive compensation (9.6%), pay directors only in stock (13 %), and board diversity (14.4 %). Kenneth Bertsch, Voting on Corporate Governance Shareholder Proposals — 1998 (IIRRC 1999).

[B]   Eligibility and Procedure

Pursuant to SEC regulation, the proponent of a proposal to be printed and circulated in a corporate management's proxy statement must have been a record or beneficial owner of shares for at least one year. The market value of shares owned by the proponent must exceed $2,000 or, if less, must equal at least one percent of the shares entitled to vote on the proposal.[117] The proponent must continue ownership of those shares through the date upon which the shareholders' meeting is held. She must represent that she, or her representative, will attend the meeting in order to present the proposal. If either of the latter two representations is violated, the shareholder is then in the "penalty box." This means that the corporation may exclude any proposals by the proponent "for any meetings held in the following two calendar years."[118]

In her proposal, the proponent must provide her name, her address, the number of shares she holds, the date(s) upon which shares were acquired, and an indication whether the shares are held in "street" or nominee name. The proponent must also provide "documentation to support a claim for beneficial ownership." The proponent then submits the requested information, proposal, and supporting statement to the corporation "not less than 120 calendar days before the date of the company's proxy statement [for] . . . the previous year's annual meeting."[119]

[C]   Background on the Nature of the Proposals

While SEC Rule 14a-8 facilitates communication among shareholders, state corporation law defines a shareholder's right to propound proposals in the first place. Under state statutes, shareholders have power only with respect to a very limited range of matters: amendment of articles of incorporation, mergers, sales of all or substantially all of the corporation's assets, dissolution, and election and removal of directors. Shareholders have still less power of initiative. Shareholders may only initiate removal of directors and nomination and election of directors. All other evolutions (merger, amendment of articles and so on) begin with an initiative by directors.[120] Shareholder power is only the power to react to what the board of directors has done or proposes to do.

---

[117] SEC Rule 14a-8, Question 2. The regulation has been formatted into an easily followed question and answer format. *See, e.g.,* 17 CFR § 240.14a-8 (2002).

[118] SEC Rule 14a-8, Question 8.

[119] SEC Rule 14a-8, Question 5.

[120] *See Continental Securities Corp. v. Belmont,* 99 N.E. 138 (N.Y. 1912).

> As a general rule, shareholders cannot act in relation to the ordinary business of the corporation. The body of stockholders have certain authority conferred by statute- . . . but except for certain authority conferred by statute . . . they have no express power given by statute. They are not by any statute in this state given general power of initiative in corporate affairs. Any action by them relating to the details of the corporate business is necessarily a request in the form of an assent, request, or recommendation. Recommendation by a body of stockholders can only be enforced . . . indirectly through the authority of the stockholders to change the personnel of the directors at a meeting for the election of directors.

Id. at 141. *See also* discussion of basic governance model in § 5.04, *supra.*

How, then, are shareholders enabled to submit proposals regarding Joe Camel advertising, affirmative action, nuclear power, and so on? The answer lies in a well-known New York Court of Appeals decision and in the manner in which educated scriveners of such proposals frame them. In *Auer v. Dressel*,[121] the court held that shareholders could propound and vote upon resolutions which, even if adopted, would be purely advisory.

Auer v. Dressel is an important case and one which the SEC seems to assume, without ever directly so stating, to be the correct model of the corporation under state law. The *Auer v. Dressel* view seems subsumed in the fabric of the SEC shareholder proposal rule which permits shareholders to propound and vote upon resolutions which, even if adopted, are purely advisory in a technical sense.

One other implication of the model is that, when shareholders propound a resolution as to a matter in which they have no power of initiative, they ordinarily must phrase the resolution as a request or recommendation to the repository of direct power in the matter, namely, the board of directors. Thus, most proposals are framed in advisory language: "RESOLVED, that the shareholders recommend that the board of directors of Northern Pines, Inc. cause the corporation and its officers and employees to cease clear cutting of timber tracts located on the corporation's land."

If shareholders fail to utilize language of request or recommendation (advisory language), the corporation may exclude the proposal on the grounds that the proposal is "not a proper subject for action by shareholders under the laws of the jurisdiction of the company's organization."[122] The result may then be that a shareholder group such as SOFT will have to cool its heels, waiting an entire year to rephrase and then resubmit its proposal.[123] This necessity of utilizing advisory language in the phrasing of most shareholder proposals is another offshoot of the received state law model of corporate governance set out in *Auer v. Dressel* and other cases.

[D]   Mechanics of the Shareholder Proxy Proposal Process

Episodes involving employment practices at Cracker Barrel Old Country Store, Inc., and Wal-Mart Stores, Inc., illustrate both the process and the standard of judicial review applicable to it. The cases are *New York City Employees' Retirement System v. Securities and Exchange Commission*[124]

---

[121] 118 N.E.2d 590 (N.Y. 1954). For a discussion of *Auer v. Dressel*, and of shareholders' roles in governance, see § 5.05, *supra.*

[122] SEC Rule 14a-8, Question 9.

[123] For that reason, a cautionary "NOTE" inserted in the text of Rule 14a-8, Question 9(1), reads in part: "Depending on the subject matter, some proposals are not considered proper under state law if they would be binding on the company if approved by shareholders. In our experience, most proposals that are cast as recommendations or requests that the board of directors take specified action are proper under state law."

[124] 45 F.3d 7 (2d Cir. 1995).

(Cracker Barrel) and *Amalgamated Clothing and Textile Workers Union v. Wal-Mart Stores, Inc.* (Wal-Mart).[125]

A shareholder proponent makes a timely submission of her proposal with supporting information and documentation. If the corporation decides to include the proposal in the proxy statement, effectively that is the end of the matter. If the proposal garners less than three percent of the vote, then the corporation may omit not only it but all similar proposals for the next five years.[126] If on the second go-around a proposal garners less than six percent, the corporation may omit it, or similar proposals, for the next five years. To survive on the third try, a proposal must receive a ten percent vote.[127] So there is some wisdom, and a potential benefit, in following the path of least resistance by including the proposal, but fewer corporations do so than one might surmise.

If the corporation wants to omit a proposal, the corporate general counsel or secretary requests that the SEC issue a "no-action letter," a written determination by the SEC staff that if the facts are as the corporation has stated them to be, and the corporation omits the proposal, the SEC staff will recommend to the Commission that "no-action" be taken. By contrast, if the SEC staff believes the corporation should include the proposal, the SEC issues a letter, also known as a no-action letter (that really is the converse) to that effect.[128]

One case of particular note involved Cracker Barrel, a restaurant chain, which announced that it would no longer employ gay and lesbian persons. The announcement set off a furor, with Cracker Barrel rescinding its policy, but refusing to rehire the employees who had been terminated as a result of the objectionable policy. Three pension plans which held Cracker Barrel shares, including the New York City Employees' Retirement System (NYCERS), submitted to Cracker Barrel a Rule 14a-8 proposal, recommending that shareholders propose to the directors an express prohibition on discrimination on the basis of sexual orientation.

Cracker Barrel proposed, and the SEC staff agreed via a no-action letter, that the proposal could be excluded as a proposal "that deals with a matter relating to the conduct of the ordinary business operations."[129]

---

[125] 821 F. Supp. 877 (S.D.N.Y. 1993).

[126] SEC Rule 14a-8, Question 9(12).

[127] *Id.*

[128] Even if the SEC agrees with the corporation, the shareholders can challenge the view by bringing an implied private cause of action under Rule 14a-8. *Roosevelt v. E.I. Du Pont de Nemours & Co.*, 958 F.2d 416 (D.C. Cir. 1992). See § 7.05[C], *infra.* Knowledge of the SEC's view as reflected in the no-action letters is helpful. Although dozens of court cases exist, thousands of no-action letters (really no-action and "action" letters) are published. Counsel intent on learning the "ins and outs" of practice under SEC Rule 14a-8, do so by accessing no-action letters, available on searchable databases such as Lexis or Westlaw.

When a proposal is omitted by a corporation, often after receipt of a no-action letter, the aggrieved shareholder or shareholder group such as SOFT usually sues the corporation, and not the SEC. *Cf. Roosevelt v. E.I. Du Pont de Nemours & Co.*, 958 F.2d 416 (D.C. Cir. 1992) (shareholder has an implied cause of action against the corporation to challenge an SEC no-action letter).

[129] SEC Rule 14a-8, Question 9(7).

In 1976, the SEC revised the Rule, attempting to tighten up the exclusion for "ordinary business operations." It wanted to permit corporations to exclude "routine day-to-day matters relating to the conduct of ordinary business operations" but not if the proposals regarded ordinary business operations "which have significant policy, economic or other implications inherent in them."[130]

With the Cracker Barrel proposal, the SEC staff decided to reverse course, agreeing with Cracker Barrel that the proposal "related to employment policies and [these] fell with the ambit of 'ordinary business operations.' " The staff no-action letter read:

> [T]he Division has determined that the fact that a shareholder proposal concerning a company's employment policies and practices for the general workforce is tied to a social issue will no longer be viewed as removing the proposal from the realm of ordinary business operations of the registrant.[131]

NYCERS went immediately to court, alleging that this sudden SEC staff policy shift amounted to rulemaking, subject to the notice, comment and other provisions of the Administrative Procedure Act. The court held that the Cracker Barrel and other no-action letters are "interpretive because they do not bind the SEC, the parties, or the courts." For example, a "no-action letter does not affect a shareholder's right to institute a private action" and "[h]ere, the plaintiffs have an effective alternative to suing the SEC. They can sue Cracker Barrel."

In *Wal-Mart*, the plaintiffs fared better.[132] Along with the National Council of Churches of Christ, the Unitarian Universalist Society, and the Literary Society of Saint Catherine of Siena, the Amalgamated Clothing Workers submitted a proposal that Wal-Mart prepare and distribute reports about its equal employment and affirmative action programs, including descriptions of steps taken to increase the number of minority managers and to purchase goods from minority-and female-owned businesses. Judge Kimba Wood, while finding that "[a]n individual no-action letter by itself is not an expression of agency interpretation to which the court must defer," found that courts do trace and defer to no-action letters evincing "the consistency of the SEC's staff's position and reasoning on a given issue." She traced the SEC policy relating to employment practices proposals through its various permutations but declined to apply the most recent permutation, the Cracker Barrel no-action letter, which was available to her at the time she rendered her decision:

> The court does not defer to the SEC's position in *Cracker Barrel* and is not persuaded by its reasoning, because the reasoning in *Cracker Barrel* sharply deviates from the standard articulated in the 1976 Interpretive Release [and subsequent no-action letters] . . . . That release interpreted Rule 14a-8(c)(7) as permitting the exclusion of

---

[130] SEC Exchange Act Release No. 12,598 (July 7, 1976).

[131] 45 F.3d at 10.

[132] *Amalgamated Clothing v. Wal-Mart Stores*, 54 F.3d 69, 71 (2d Cir. 1995).

"proposals that are mundane in nature *and* do not involve any substantial policy or other considerations."

Cracker Barrel fails to apply both parts of the Release's conjunctive standard.[133]

Earlier, Judge Wood had noted that the "SEC has until recently recognized that the issues of EEO and affirmative action raise policy issues elevating them above excludable day-to-day issues," such as "employee health benefits, general compensation issues not focused on senior executives, labor-management relations, employee hiring and firing, conditions of employment, and employee training and motivation."

Wal-Mart Stores did not appeal, including the Amalgamated Clothing Workers' proposal in Wal-Mart's 1993 proxy solicitation. The plaintiffs then moved for, and were awarded attorneys' fees, based upon a common benefit rationale. Wal-Mart resisted on the ground that 90 percent of the shares voted against the proposal. The Second Circuit upheld a fee award, observing that "[t]he percentage of shares voted against a proposal is insignificant because the right to cast an informed vote, in and of itself, is a substantial interest worthy of vindication."[134]

Cracker Barrel and *Wal-Mart* are not reconcilable. However, it is not necessary to reconcile the two decisions. The SEC has reverted to the position that employment-related matters that also implicate social concerns are proper matters for Rule 14a-8 proposals. They are not automatically excludable under the ordinary business, "management functions" exception.[135] Now the Commission once again deals with such proposals on an *ad hoc* basis. *Cracker Barrel* and *Wal-Mart* are nonetheless instructive as to the mechanics, politics and administrative law setting surrounding SEC no-action letter practice and the field of shareholder Rule 14a-8 proposals.

[E]   The 14a-8, Question 9(7) Ordinary Business Operations Exclusion

Cracker Barrel and *Wal-Mart* illustrate the administrative and procedural context in which corporations attempt to exclude shareholder proposals. Several other well-known cases deal more directly with the most frequently invoked ground for exclusion, that the proposal relates to the "ordinary business operations" of the issuer.

A famous case is *Medical Committee for Human Rights v. SEC*.[136] Throughout the 1960s, Dow Chemical Company continued to manufacture napalm for the United States Department of Defense. Much of that napalm was used in the Vietnam war. Dow continued manufacture even though it lost money on the product line. More seriously, Dow's public image suffered greatly. When

---

[133] 821 F. Supp. at 890.

[134] *Amalgamated Clothing v. Wal-Mart Stores*, 54 F.3d 69, 71 (2d Cir. 1995).

[135] *See* SEC Exchange Act Release No. 40018 (May 28, 1998).

[136] 432 F.2d 659 (D.C. Cir. 1970).

Dow recruiters appeared on college campuses, they were blocked by protesters. Many universities barred Dow from recruiting altogether.

Medical Committee first submitted a proposal requesting the Dow board of directors to adopt a resolution setting forth an amendment to articles of incorporation "that napalm shall not be sold to any buyer unless that buyer gives reasonable assurance that the substance will not be used on or against human beings." Dow proposed to exclude the proposal as relating "to the conduct of the ordinary business operations of the issuer." Dow's argument went something like this: "if the amendment were adopted, each of our napalm sales persons would have to obtain certificates from each napalm customer relating to prospective use of the napalm ordered." Dow claimed that such a requirement is too specific and interferes with day-today business activity.

Medical Committee went back to the drawing board. It submitted a proposal recommending that articles be amended to prohibit manufacture of napalm altogether. Dow then proposed to exclude that proposal on the additional grounds that it was too general and had been submitted "primarily for the purpose of promoting general economic, political, racial, religious, social or similar causes."[137]

The court recognized that Dow was attempting to whipsaw the Medical Committee between two exclusions and between the overly specific and the overly general. The court grafted onto the "general economic and political" exclusion the requirement that the proposal also involve a matter with no specific relation to the corporation's business. With Dow, by contrast, "the [Medical Committee proposal to cease manufacture] related solely to a matter that is completely within the accepted sphere of corporate activity and control."

The court noted that Dow made the decision to continue napalm manufacture "not *because* of business considerations, but *in spite of* them . . . that management in essence decided to pursue a course of activity which . . . actively impaired the company's public relations and recruitment activities because management considered this action morally and politically desirable."[138] Dow was ordered to include the Medical Committee proposal in its proxy statement for presentation at the 1971 annual meeting.[139] While decisions on what products a corporation manufactures are usually ordinary business

---

[137] Former SEC Rule 14a-8(c)(2). Today, the comparable exclusion, reflecting the outcome in *Medical Committee*, permits exclusion if the company "would lack the power or authority to implement the proposal," meaning a matter of general economic, political, racial, religious or social import. SEC Rule 14a-8, Question 9(6).

[138] The Court continued:

> We think that there is a clear and compelling distinction between management's legitimate need for freedom to apply its expertise in matters of day-to-day business judgment, and management's patently illegitimate claims of power to treat modern corporations with their vast resources as personal satrapies implementing personal political or moral predilections. It could scarcely be argued that management is more qualified or more entitled to make these kinds of decisions than shareholders . . . .

432 F.2d at 681.

[139] The proposal received the support of less than three percent of the shareholders. *See* 404 U.S. 403 (1972) (vacating grant of writ of certiorari on grounds of mootness).

decisions, napalm's significance to the corporation and its business was relevant to the issue of exclusion.[140] A similar and less weighty shareholder proposal case is *Lovenheim v. Iroquois Brands, Inc.*[141] Iroquois imported pate de foie gras (goose liver) from France into the United States. Shareholder Lovenheim requested the directors "to form a committee to study the methods by which its French supplier produces pate . . . [and report] on whether this production method causes undue distress, pain or suffering to the animals involved." Iroquois invoked former SEC Rule 14a-8(c)(5), which permitted exclusion "if the proposal relates to operations which account for less than 5 percent of the issuer's total assets at the end of its most recent fiscal year, and for less than 5 percent of its net earnings and gross sales . . . and is not otherwise significantly related to the issuer's business." Iroquois had annual revenues of $141 million (pate sales of $78,000) and assets of $78 million (pate assets of $34,000).

Iroquois attempted to distinguish *Medical Committee* as involving both political or social motivation and economics. By contrast, Lovenheim's motivation was political or social but economically insignificant.[142] The court found no basis in the history of the rule "to limit the determination to the economic criteria" (five percent of sales, profits or assets). Finding the proposal to have a "significant relationship to the issuer's business," and also to have "ethical and social significance," the court granted a preliminary injunction ordering Iroquois to include the proposal in its proxy statement.[143]

The most feasible method for the SOFT group would be to submit to Northern Pines, Inc., a shareholder proxy proposal together with supporting statement. The proposal should be framed in advisory or precatory language

---

[140] In *NYCERS v. Dole Foods Co.*, 795 F. Supp. 95 (S.D.N.Y.), *appeal dismissed as moot*, 969 F.2d 1430 (2d Cir. 1992), the court characterized ordinary business matters as matters "mundane in nature and [which] do not involve any policy or other considerations." It ordered Dole to include a proposal recommending a committee of the board to evaluate the effects of various national health care reform proposals then being considered in the political arena. Rather than ordinary business matters, the proposal related to "significant strategy decisions as to" daily business matters.

[141] 618 F. Supp. 554 (D.D.C. 1985). Still another "ordinary business operations' case is *Apache Petroleum v. NYCERS*, 2008 U.S. Dist. LEXIS 32955 (S.D. Tex. Apr. 22, 2008). Five New York public employee pension plans submitted a resolution recommending that Apache "management implement equal employment opportunity policies based upon [10 listed] principles." In listing those principles, the proponents had over-reached, listing anti-discrimination rules which the court found interfered with day-to day business (human resources) operations at Apache. Principles such as "[t]here shall be no discrimination in the allocation of employee benefits," "Corporate advertising policy will avoid the use of negative stereotypes," "there will be no discrimination in corporate advertising," and the like doomed the proposal. The devil truly was in the details. Too much detail can cause a proposal to be intrusive, running afoul of the ordinary business operations exclusion.

[142] In truth, napalm was not a significantly profitable product for Dow Chemical Corporation either.

[143] A court did find the difference between an issuer and a proponent to be so insignificant as to be excludable under the "ordinary business operations" provision. In *Roosevelt v. E.I. Du Pont de Nemours & Co.*, 958 F.2d 416 (D.C. Cir. 1992), Friends of the Earth Society submitted a proposal that Du Pont phase out production of chlorofluorocarbons harmful to the atmosphere. Du Pont had already decided upon such a phase-out, over five years. Friends desired a phase-out over one year. The court held that such a matter involved "implementation of a policy" rather than adoption of the policy in the first place, a distinction that may prove useful in future cases.

("request", "recommend"). Last of all, to avoid the "ordinary business operations" exclusion, the proposal should take the form of a recommendation that the articles of incorporation be amended to restrict clear cutting and logging road construction by the corporation.

Thus, a shareholder may propound resolutions that have important social, environmental or political implications but the proposal also must have a significant relationship to the business of the issuer corporation.

[F]   Other Rule 14a-8 Exclusions

Corporations may exclude proposals if they "relate to an election to office."[144] The reasoning is obvious. If shareholders, such as the SOFT group, wish to elect individuals to the board, rather than merely have shareholders vote on a proposal, the shareholders must wage a proxy contest, usually an expensive proposition.

Issues arise concerning the exclusion. In *Rauchman v. Mobil Corp.*,[145] a shareholder proposed that "the bylaws of the corporation are amended to read as follows: Citizens of countries belonging to OPEC are not qualified for election to, or membership on, the Corporation's Board of Directors." At the time, Mobil had on its board a Saudi Arabian citizen, Mr. Olayan. The court agreed with the SEC staff that the proposal could be excluded as "a form of electioneering which Mobil was not required to include in its proxy statement." On its face, the proposal related to the manner of election, which under the rule would be a proper subject for a proposal (as opposed to the election or non-election of specific individuals). In reality the proposal "would force the shareholders to choose between ratifying the proposal and reelecting Olayan . . . which could clearly be viewed as an 'effort to oppose management's solicitation on behalf of' Olayan's reelection."

Other key exclusions under SEC Rule 14a-8 include:

- If the proposal, if implemented, would cause the company to violate any state, federal, or foreign law to which it is subject . . . .[146]

- If the proposal relates to the redress of any personal claim or grievance against the company or any other person, or if it is designed to result in a benefit to [the proponent] or to further a personal interest . . . .[147]

- If the proposal relates to specific amounts of cash or stock dividends.[148]

In its current reincarnation, the rule has 13 exclusions.[149]

---

[144] SEC Rule 14a-8, Question 9(8).

[145] 739 F.2d 205 (6th Cir. 1984).

[146] SEC Rule 14a-8, Question 9(2).

[147] SEC Rule 14a-8, Question 9(4).

[148] SEC Rule 14a-8, Question 9(13).

[149] SEC Rule 14a-8, Question 9(1)–(13).

Threading one's way through the maze of exclusions must be undertaken with great care.

While not without its critics, especially in the ranks of corporate managers, the SEC shareholder proposal rule seems here to stay. Accordingly, any corporate practitioner must have more than passing familiarity with it.

[G]   Proposals to Amend Corporate Bylaws

Self implementing (mandatory) resolutions are not a proper matter for consideration by shareholders. Thus self implementing proposals may be excludable as "not a proper matter under state law." It is for the board of directors, not the shareholders, to formulate a plan of merger, or propose an amendment to articles of incorporation, and so on. An exception to that normal rule is amendments to the bylaws. Shareholders have either power to initiate bylaw changes in some states, or a veto power over bylaw amendments in others. In recent years, shareholder activists have seized upon shareholders' power to initiate bylaw changes and upon SEC Rule 14a-8 to attempt to implement governance changes in publicly held corporations.

Fo example, Harvard law professor Lucien Bebchuk attempted to put before shareholders of software company CA, Inc., a bylaw amendment which would restrict adoption of poison pill plans.[150] Under the proposed bylaw, directors would have to be unanimous to adopt a poison pill plan. Moreover, the bylaw contained a sunset provision: any plan directors adopted would expire 1 year later, unless shareholders had approved it.

The SEC staff declined to take a position on whether the proposal was excludable or not (in Rule 14a-8 parlance, refused to issue a no action letter, despite having been requested to do so). CA maintained that such a bylaw unduly tied directors' hands and thus was illegal under Delaware law. Bebchuk went to court for a declaratory judgment on the bylaw's legality. He wasted his time and money.

Vice-Chancellor Lamb held the issue not ripe for determination, dismissing Bebchuk's case. Bebchuk had not sufficiently forced the issue. After the SEC refused to issue a no-action letter, Bebchuk should have insisted that CA include his proposal in CA's annual proxy statement. If CA refused, Bebchuk should then have gone to court, but for a different firm of relief: an order that CA include the proposal. Only after CA had included the bylaw proposal, and the shareholders had adopted it, would the legality of the bylaw be ripe for adjudication by a court in Delaware. Bebchuk's efforts were for naught.

A 14a-8 bylaw amendment bylaw proposal achieved more success in *American Federation of Sate, County & Municipal Employees v. American International Group, Inc.*[151] Distinguish between two proposals, one that resolves that Bluebird Airlines adopt a bylaw providing that 2 of 11 directors be

---

[150] *Bebchuk v. CA, Inc.*, 902 A.2d 737 (Del. Ch. 2007). Poison pill plans are discussed in § 12.04[B][1] *infra.*

[151] 462 F.3d 121 (2d Cir. 2006).

members of the pilot group, and another which goes further, providing that the nominees for those positions be captains Smith and Jones. The latter had always been thought to be excludable because it "relates to an election."[152] If activists wish to elect captains Smith and Jones, the activists should spend their own money to wage a full-fledged proxy contest.

The former type proposal has had a more checkered history. Under one view, the proposal related to the manner of an election ("the procedures") rather than to an election itself, and was a proper matter for the proxy statement. Under another view (the SEC's), such procedural changes were preludes to election contests in the future, fomenting the very situation (a "contested election") the exclusion sought to funnel out of 14a-8 and into the arena of full blown proxy contests, with dueling slates of directors each filing their own materials with the SEC, and so on.

The court sided with AFSCME, adhering to the first view and requiring insurance giant AIG to include in its own proxy materials bylaw amendments establishing a procedure whereby shareholders could nominate candidates for director that would have to be included on the corporate ballot. Following the case, the SEC adopted amendments to Rule 14a-8(i)(8) attempting to reverse the outcome: "The principal purpose of the [amendment] is to make clear, with respect to corporate elections, that Rule 14a-8 is not the proper means for *conducting campaigns or effecting reforms* in elections . . . ."[153]

[H]   *CA, Inc. v. AFSCME Employees Pension Trust*[154]

At issue was a proposed bylaw, propounded pursuant to SEC Rule 14a-8, which would require CA to reimburse insurgents' proxy contest expenses, similar to proposals activists have advanced in many public corporations ("the board of directors shall cause the corporation to reimburse a stockholder . . . for reasonable expenses in connection with nominating one or more candidates in contested elections of directors"). CA's law firm said that the bylaw proposal "was not a proper subject for shareholder action." AFSCME's lawyers, from another prominent Delaware law firm, said the proposal was legal. The SEC declined to take a position on whether or not the proposal was excludable under Rule 14a-8. But rather than merely throwing up its hands, the SEC had an alternative available to it. Under a new procedure, in addition to federal courts, the SEC itself could certify questions to the Supreme Court of Delaware.[155]

The Supreme Court held that (1) at least process oriented additions, deletions or amendments to corporate bylaws, which this was, were a proper subject for

---

[152] The election exclusion in incorporated in SEC Rule 14a-8(i)(8).

[153] SEC Release No. 34-56914 (Dec. 6, 2007). New Del. Gen. Corp. Law §§ 112–13 (2009) expressly enable corporate bylaws to (1) provide for inclusion of shareholder director nominees in corporate proxy materials and (2) reimburse shareholder proxy solicitation expenses. *See generally* § 5.05[C], *supra*. Proposals advocating adoption of such bylaws arguably contradict SEC Rule 14a-8 exclusions, as they have traditionally been interpreted.

[154] 953 A.2d 227 (Del. 2008).

[155] Del. Constitution, Art. IV, § 11(8); Supreme Court Rule 41.

shareholder action; and (2) due to its mandatory character, the particular bylaw addition would unduly handcuff present and future boards of directors and therefore was illegal.

Justice Jacobs first balanced the tension between 2 statutory sections. Del Gen Corp. L § 109(a) provides that while giving directors power to adopt, amend or repeal bylaws, the section also provides that "that such power has been conferred upon the directors . . . shall not divest the shareholders of the power . . . nor limit their power." By contrast, Del Gen Corp L § 141(a) provides that a corporation's business and affairs "shall be managed by or under the direction of a board of directors." Delaware courts have never roughed out a line of demarcation between the 2 sections, as various commentators have noted.[156]

Justice Jacobs marked out a line. "[T]he proper function of bylaws is not to mandate how the board should decide specific substantive decisions, but rather, to define the processes and procedures by which those decisions are made." "[B]ylaws that regulate the process by which the board acts are statutorily authorized."[157] Bylaws such as those which fix the number of directors, require directors' meetings for valid action, set vote requirements, and the like are "procedural, process-oriented bylaws" which do not interfere with the statutory mandate that it is the board of directors which manages or supervises management. Even though it was a "substance-sounding mandate," the AFSCME proposed bylaw had "both the intent and the effect of regulating the process of electing directors." It was a proper matter for stockholder action under state law.

But it was illegal. Citing two well-known Delaware cases striking down contract or certificate provisions which unduly restrict boards of directors,[158] the court turned to the argument that as framed the proposed enactment violated the proviso that any bylaw be "not inconsistent with law."[159] Proponents argued that the bylaw mandated only reimbursement of reasonable expenses and that the board of directors would make the reasonableness determination. Thus, the bylaw would not unduly restrict or handcuff the board.

That was not enough for the court: the bylaw should have prefaced itself with "In the board's discretion," or Subject to what their fiduciary duties might

---

[156] *See, e.g.*, Lawrence A. Hamermesh, *Corporate Democracy and Shareholder-Adopted Bylaws: Taking Back the Street?*, 73 Tul. L. Rev. 409, 416 & 444 (1998); William W. Bratton & Joseph A. McCahery, *Regulatory Competition, Regulatory Capture, and Corporate Self-Regulation*, 73 N.C. L. Rev. 1861, 1932 (1995).

[157] Quoting *Hollinger Intern. Inc. v Black*, 844 A.2d 1022 (Del. Ch. 2004) (shareholders could adopt a bylaw eliminating a committee the board had created).

[158] *Paramount Communications, Inc. v. QVC Network, Inc.*, 637 A.2d 34 (Del. 1994) ("no shop" provision in contract with a favored bidder was invalid to "the extent that [as] a contract it purports to require a board to act or not act in such a fashion as to limit the exercise of its fiduciary duties"); *Quickturn Design Sys., Inc. v. Shapiro*, 721 A.2d 1281 (Del. 1998) ("no hand" or "delayed redemption" poison pill plan would "impermissibly deprive an newly elected board of its statutory authority to manage . . . and its concomitant fiduciary duty pursuant to that statutory mandate"). *Paramount v. QVC* is discussed in § 12.05[A][5] *infra*; *Quickturn* is discussed in § 11.03[D] *infra*.

[159] Del. Gen. Corp. L. § 109(b).

require." The bylaw must allow the board enough wiggle room so that it may disallow reimbursement: "[I]n situations where the proxy contest is motivated by personal or petty concerns or to promote interests that do not further, or are adverse to, the board's fiduciary duty could compel that reimbursement be denied altogether."[160]

In this important case, the Supreme Court of Delaware left a large field of play for shareholder-initiated proposals to amend or repeal corporate bylaws. Further, although dooming the proposal at issue, the court set out a roadmap directing proponents how to draft such proposals in the future.

§ 7.06 THE PROXY RULES' GENERAL ANTIFRAUD RULE: AN INTRODUCTION TO GENERAL DISCLOSURE LAW CONCEPTS

[A]   Introduction

Distributed throughout the securities laws and regulations are antifraud rules. These rules prohibit any statement "which, at the time and under the circumstances under which it is made, is false or misleading with respect to any material fact."[161] The rules also prohibit any statement, written or oral, "which omits to state any material fact necessary in order to make the statements therein not false or misleading." The antifraud rules are catchalls. Thus, an issuer of securities who complies with an item-and-answer SEC form may still run afoul of the applicable antifraud rule if there exist material omissions or misleading statements. To some uncertain extent, the antifraud rules are also intended to relax somewhat the strict common law state fraud rules that otherwise might apply to a plaintiff's case.

Some federal antifraud rules are statutory. One such rule applies to omissions or misleading statements "in connection with any tender offer or request or invitation for tenders, or any solicitation of security holders in opposition to or in favor of any such offer, request, or invitation."[162] Another, the general antifraud rule, Rule 10b-5, is a regulation the SEC adopted in 1943 pursuant to powers granted the Commission under section 10(b) of the Securities Exchange Act. The SEC and private plaintiffs have developed the federal insider trading prohibition from this opaque rule but its coverage is much broader. Rule 10b-5 prohibits material omissions or misleading statements in any form, whether in merger documents, brokerage research reports, or even face-to-face dealings in the shares of a closely held corporation, as the rule applies to omissions or misleading statements "in connection with the purchase or sale of *any* security."[163]

---

[160] 953 A.2d at 240. For example, "if a shareholder group affiliated with a competitor of the company were to cause the election of a minority slate of candidates . . . ." *Id.*

[161] SEC Rule 14a-9(a).

[162] Securities Exchange Act § 14(e), discussed in the chapter on hostile tender offers, § 12.06[D], *infra.*

[163] SEC Rule 10b-5 and the law of insider trading are the subject of Chapter 13.

Securities Exchange Act of 1934 section 14(a) contains a broad grant of authority to the SEC to regulate the solicitation of proxies "as necessary or appropriate in the public interest or for the protection of investors." Pursuant to that grant, the SEC has adopted many of the detailed rules described in this chapter. Added to that mix of rules is the general antifraud rule applicable to "any proxy statement, form of proxy, notice of meeting, or other communication, written or oral" in the proxy field.[164]

SEC Rule 14a-9 introduces the reader to antifraud rules and disclosure concepts generally, such as implication of private rights of action to sue for violation of the rules; standing to sue; materiality of omitted or misleading statements and information; the required state of mind, also known as the scienter requirement; reliance, or so-called transaction causation; causation, often distinguished from reliance as "loss causation"; and remedies for violation of some of the rules. These concepts are introduced here but some of them are also treated with detail elsewhere in this volume.[165]

The best manner in which to put in context the SEC anti-fraud rule is to compare it with the state law that otherwise would apply. The elements of common law fraud (state law) are materiality, falsity, privity, knowledge or intent to deceive, intent that the other party rely, justifiable reliance, loss causation, and damages.[166] Under federal antifraud rules, federal courts have had to determine if Congress intended courts to depart from common law standards and, if so, by how much.

[B]   SEC Rule 14a-9

In a contested corporate election, one or the other side, or both, often claims that their opponent is attempting to achieve victory through innuendo, misleading statements, misrepresentations, nondisclosure or outright fraud practiced upon the shareholders. The losing side may make those claims in a lawsuit, after the fact, but more often the contending factions will seek to enjoin the alleged offending statements and to enjoin the use of any proxies already obtained.

In publicly held corporations, the plaintiffs would do so under SEC Rule 14a-9, which provides that "[n]o solicitation subject to this regulation shall be made by means of any proxy statement, form of proxy, notice of meeting, or other form of communication, written or oral, containing any statement which, at the time and in light of the circumstances under which it is made, is false or misleading with respect to any material fact, or which omits to state any material fact necessary to make the statements made therein not false or misleading . . . ." By contrast, if the corporation is not a section 12(g)

---

[164] SEC Rule 14a-9.

[165] See the discussion in Chapter 13. The rule itself does not deal with these issues. Rather they are a matter of judge-made law developed pursuant to this and other antifraud rules.

[166] *See, e.g., McAnally v. Gildersleeve,* 16 F.3d 1493, 1497 (8th Cir. 1994). *See generally* Douglas M. Branson, *Securities Litigation in State Courts — Something Old, Something New, Something Borrowed,* 76 Wash. U. L.Q. 509 (1998).

corporation under the Securities Exchange Act (that is, not publicly traded), the losing side must make out its disclosure claims under state law.

Federal law is stringent. In *SEC v. May*,[167] a stockholder group demanded disclosure from management, asking questions such as "are we not entitled to know how much is made . . . in major [product] lines?" and "[w]hy are not the stockholders informed of the purchases and sales of capital assets?" The Second Circuit agreed that the statements made were misleading and unlawful under SEC Rule 14a-9:

> Appellants' fundamental contention appears to be that stockholder disputes should be viewed in the eyes of the law just as are political contests, with each side free to hurl charges with comparative unrestraint, the assumption being that the opposing side is then at liberty to refute and thus effectively deflate the "campaign oratory" of its adversary. Such, however, is not the policy of the Congress as enacted in the Securities Exchange Act. There Congress has clearly entrusted to the Commission the duty of protecting the investing public against misleading statements made in the course of a struggle for corporate control.

Contemporaneous state court pronouncements take almost exactly the opposite position: "[a] certain amount of innuendo, misstatement, exaggeration and puffing must be allowed as a natural by-product of a bitter campaign," stated a New York court.[168] A Delaware court opined that, in contested state elections, "as in other types of campaigns, the verbal niceties are not always observed" and "there is almost necessarily an area of what might be called permissible puffing."[169]

The wide gulf between outcomes may be explained because federal and state law differ in the state of mind, or fault they require. Congress has given the SEC an open-ended mandate to regulate the solicitation of proxies in publicly held corporations and to require full and fair disclosure.[170] Implementing that broad mandate, the SEC has adopted a broad antifraud rule that on its face does not require a plaintiff to prove any degree of fault on a defendant's part but which courts have determined requires a showing of lack of reasonable care.[171] On the other hand, state courts require that the losing side in an election prove that any misleading statement, exaggeration or innuendo is the product of intentional or reckless conduct (that is, scienter). The standard usually articulated is "fraud."[172]

---

[167] 229 F.2d 123, 124 (2d Cir. 1956).

[168] *Matter of R. Hoe & Co.*, 137 N.Y.S.2d 142, 147–48 (1954).

[169] *Kerbs v. California Eastern Airways, Inc.*, 94 A.2d 217, 218 (Del. Ch. 1953).

[170] *See* Securities Exchange Act § 14(a) (SEC given power to adopt "such rules and regulations as the Commission may prescribe as necessary or appropriate in the public interest or for the protection of investors").

[171] *See* the discussion in § 7.05[F], *infra*.

[172] *See Maybrown v. Malverne Distributors, Inc.*, 393 N.Y.S.2d 67 (App. Div. 1977) ("The record is devoid of any showing of fraud which would justify the setting aside of the election").

The stringent federal standard has been criticized, on First Amendment and other grounds.[173] And a few states have moved in the direction of the federal standard. In *Brown v. Ward*,[174] the Supreme Court of Alaska held that, despite a statute expressly holding federal proxy rules inapplicable, the spirit of those rules should inform election of directors in Alaska Native corporations. However, the majority of state courts adhere to a fraud standard or something like it, reluctant as they are to intervene in what they view as an internal matter of a corporation.[175]

Seinfeld v. Bartz[176] may be an example of a federal court going the other way, relaxing the standard of what is material and therefore within the scope of Rule 14a-9. In its annual solicitation of proxies, Cisco, the networks hardware company, disclosed that it paid directors an annual retainer of $32,000. It also disclosed that it granted new directors options on 20,000 Cisco shares and made annual grants of shares of 10,000 and upwards per director. Plaintiff claimed that Cisco's failure to value, using the well known Black-Scholes formula, such options and disclose in the proxy statement violated 14a-9. Plaintiff alleged that the value could be up to $365,000; Cisco maintained that the option's value could be zero. Following 4 other courts which had decided similar issues, the district court held that the omitted facts were not material, dismissing the plaintiff's Rule 14a-9 complaint.

[C]   Implication of Private Rights of Action

Various SEC rules and federal statutes make unlawful certain forms of conduct, such as publication of misleading statements or material omissions in connection with proxy solicitations, tender offers or "in connection with the purchase or sale of any security." The SEC may bring suit to redress violations of those rules. The question that arises is whether private parties may bring suit for injunctive relief or for damages based upon allegations that defendants have violated federal statutes or rules in cases in which the statute does not give an express remedy.

The first major cases arose in the proxy solicitation area. Section 14(a) provides no express cause of action for those injured by a violation of the

---

[173] *See generally* Henry M. Butler & Larry E. Ribstein, *Corporate Governance Speech and the First Amendment*, 43 Kan. L. Rev. 163 (1994); Symposium, *The First Amendment and Federal Securities Regulation*, 20 Conn. L. Rev. 261 (1988).

[174] 593 P.2d 247 (Alaska 1979).

[175] Three states, Alaska, Illinois and South Carolina, have adopted state law versions of SEC Rule 14a-9. No state has *affirmative disclosure requirements* similar to the SEC and state courts have refused to move in that direction. *See, e.g., Stroud v. Grace*, 606 A.2d 75 (Del. 1992) (only disclosure Delaware requires is the date, hour and place in notice of shareholders' meeting); *In re Portland Gen. Elec.*, 362 P.2d 766 (Or. 1961) (refusal to adopt affirmative disclosure requirement); *Bresnick v. Home Title Guar. Co.*, 175 F. Supp. 723 (S.D.N.Y. 1959) ("[I]t may well be that the standards laid down by [the SEC] are higher than those necessarily required for a full and frank disclosure by a corporation [under state law]"). Under fiduciary standards, as opposed to fraud, Delaware and some other courts are evolving an after-the-fact requirement of candor or of "complete candor." For a discussion of the duty of candor, see § 9.06, *infra*.

[176] 2002 U.S. Dist. LEXIS 2547 (N.D. Cal. Feb. 8, 2002).

section: if one exists, it must be judicially implied. The Supreme Court did so in *J.I. Case Co. v. Borak*.[177] As a J.I. Case Co. shareholder, Borak complained that a proposed merger with American Tractor Corp. involved self-dealing by Case managers and that the proxy statement failed to disclose self-dealing and the unfair treatment of minority shareholders, thereby rendering it "false and misleading."

In a sweeping opinion, perhaps long on rhetoric and short on statutory analysis, Mr. Justice Clark noted that "[w]hile [section 14(a)'s] language makes no specific reference to a private right of action, among its chief purposes is the 'protection of investors,' which certainly implies the availability of judicial relief where necessary to achieve that result." While the trial court held that a private action existed only for purposes of prospective or declaratory relief, that is, an injunction or a ruling on the law, the Supreme Court swept away any limitation, holding that a plaintiff under SEC Rule 14a-9 need not post security for expenses under state law[178] and could pursue a claim for damages as well by allowing both a derivative (that is, on behalf of the corporation) and direct cause of action:

> The damage suffered results not from the deceit practiced on [the shareholder] alone but rather from the deceit practiced on the stock-holders as a group . . . . Private enforcement of the proxy rules provides a necessary supplement to Commission action. As in antitrust treble damage litigation, the possibility of civil damages or injunctive relief serves as the most effective weapon in the enforcement of the proxy regulations. The Commission advises that it examines over 2,000 proxy statements annually and each of them must necessarily be expedited. Time does not permit an independent [SEC] examination of the facts set out in proxy material . . . .

> We, therefore, believe that under the circumstances here it is the duty of the courts to be alert to provide such remedies as are necessary to make effective the congressional purpose.

> For several years following *Borak*, the Supreme Court assumed the existence of private rights of action.

For example, in *Mills v. Electric Auto-Lite Co.*,[179] the Court assumed a private right of action under section 14(a), and praised *Borak* and the "corporate therapeutics" private actions would produce. Similarly, in *Superintendent of Insurance of the State of New York v. Bankers Life & Casualty Co.*,[180] the Court assumed a private right of action under its mandate that "[s]ection 10(b) [and SEC Rule 10b-5] be read flexibly, not technically and restrictively," an assumption some lower courts had been making for some time.[181]

---

[177] 377 U.S. 426 (1964).

[178] See the discussion of security for expense statutes in derivative suits in § 14.04[C], *infra*.

[179] 396 U.S. 375 (1970), discussed at length in § 7.05[A], *infra*.

[180] 404 U.S. 6 (1971).

[181] A federal court first implied a private right of action under SEC Rule 10b-5 in *Kardon v. National Gypsum Co.*, 69 F. Supp. 512 (E.D. Pa. 1946).

Ten years passed. The era of the Burger Court was then well underway and views of access to the courts by litigants were more limited. A unanimous Supreme Court refused to imply a private right of action under the Federal Election Campaign Law which makes illegal corporate contributions to partisan political contests. In *Cort v. Ash*,[182] the Court refused to allow a Bethlehem Steel Corporation shareholder to sue to recover illegal contributions the corporation had made to the 1972 presidential campaign. The Court announced a four factor test: (1) Is the plaintiff one of the class for whose special benefit the statute was enacted? (2) Is there any indication of legislative intent, explicit or implicit, either to create or deny the private remedy? (3) Is it consistent with the underlying purpose of the legislative scheme to imply such a remedy? and (4) Is the cause of action one traditionally relegated to state law in an area basically the concern of the states?

The Court revisited the federal securities area in *Touche Ross & Co. v. Redington*.[183] The Securities Investors Protection Corporation had commenced an action against the accounting firm of Touche Ross, which had been auditors of a failed brokerage firm. Even though the court found the statute[184] to be for the benefit of investors, the court focused solely on the second *Cort* factor, legislative intent. It found no evidence of congressional intent that investors might sue for violations of the section. The court subsumed the third and fourth *Cort* factors as part of determining legislative intent while at the same time expressly disavowing the remedial analysis of *Borak*.[185] The Court did, however, grandfather in a private right of action under SEC Rule 10b-5, in footnote 19 indicating the Court's acquiescence "in the 25 year-old acceptance by the lower federal courts of an implied action under § 10(b)."

Surprisingly, the Court has never reversed *Borak*, leaving intact a private right of action for section 14(a) and Rule 14a-9 violations. In a Rule 10b-5 case, *Herman & MacLean v. Huddleston*,[186] the Court held that the existence of express causes of action does not necessarily exclude implied and cumulative causes of action. The Court compared the express remedy under Securities Act section 11 with the implied remedy under SEC Rule 10b-5, thereby cementing its acceptance of a private right of action under the Securities Exchange Act antifraud rule.

The older implied private rights of action under securities laws' antifraud rules thus seem safely grandfathered, preserved if not frozen through time. Wholly new implied private rights of action will not be created absent strong evidence of legislative intent to create them. In between those extremes, the continuing availability of newer implied rights of action, such as that under Securities Exchange Act section 14(e), which is an antifraud rule that applies to tender offers, is mixed.

---

[182] 422 U.S. 66 (1975).

[183] 442 U.S. 560 (1979).

[184] Securities Act of 1933 § 17(a). The section is a general anti-fraud rule.

[185] *See generally* Robert H. A. Ashford, *Implied Causes of Action Under Federal Laws: Calling the Court Back to* Borak, 79 Nw. U. L. Rev. 227 (1984).

[186] 459 U.S. 375 (1983).

In *Piper v. Chris-Craft Industries, Inc.*,[187] a losing bidder sued the winning bidder alleging that misstatements and fraudulent conduct had cost the plaintiff the opportunity to acquire the valuable target corporation. Applying the *Cort v. Ash* factors, the Court found that the losing bidder had no section 14(e) implied right of action. By contrast, the Court assumed without deciding that target corporation shareholders would have such an action.

Implied private rights of action exist but probably will not expand in the federal securities area. Defense interests will also continue attempts to chip away at the existent rights, probably with little success. The area of implication of private rights of action is quiet now but the flurry of activity from *Borak* to *Piper* and beyond has left us with an uneven and mixed picture.

[D] Standing to Sue

The person who brings any lawsuit must have standing, that is, they must be damaged or threatened with damage and that damage must arguably be of a type cognizable under the laws they invoke. Sometimes courts fashion standing rules to govern certain areas of law. A plaintiff's inability to come within a standing rule does not mean that she has not been injured. It does mean that the probabilities are that her damage is not cognizable in that area of law.

In securities law, the most well-known standing rule is that, in order to get past the courthouse door with a Rule 10b-5 claim, the plaintiff must have purchased or sold securities "in connection with" the defendant's fraud or other activity. Courts have often visited the Rule 10b-5 purchaser-seller standing rule. For that reason, it is discussed at length elsewhere in this volume.[188]

In cases involving proxies and tender offers, a plaintiff's standing usually seems obvious. The person who brings the antifraud rule claim is a shareholder whose vote was sought by means of the offending proxy or the tender of whose shares was sought by the bidder's offer to purchase. One issue the defense raises is that, because the plaintiff has brought suit, they have no injury. They detected the alleged omission or misleading statement; otherwise they would not be in court.

Despite the apparent lack of damages, courts find standing nonetheless. The plaintiff shareholder can establish injury if the omission or offending statement misleads a sufficient number of fellow shareholders. The *Borak* Court noted as much when it stated that "[t]he damage suffered results not from the deceit practiced on [the stockholder] alone but rather from the deceit practiced on the stockholders as a group."

A lower court echoed those sentiments in *Cowin v. Bresler*.[189] "The injury the [shareholder] alleges was not caused by his individual reliance on deceptive proxy solicitations." "Rather," the court noted, "his claim is that other

---

[187] 430 U.S. 1 (1977). For a discussion of § 14e, see § 12.06[D], *infra.*

[188] See the discussion in § 13.02[B], *infra.*

[189] 741 F.2d 410, 427 (D.C. Cir. 1984).

shareholders elected appellees as directors because they were misled by the proxy materials."[190]

[E]   Materiality of the Omission of the Misleading Statement

Not every omission or half-truth is actionable. The omission or statement must be misleading to a hypothetical reasonable investor and also must have a propensity at least to affect the reasonable investor's thought process (but not necessarily conduct) in deciding how to vote, whether to tender, or whether to purchase or sell securities. This concept is known as materiality. To be actionable, the offending omission, half truth or misrepresentation must be "material."

In the 1960s, lower federal courts relaxed the standard of what statements were material, by holding that if the omitted fact or statement "might" affect a reasonable investor, the materiality standard was satisfied. Even the Supreme Court inadvertently adopted the relaxed standard, in a case involving issues of reliance. The Court noted in passing that "[a]ll that is necessary is that the facts be material in the sense that a reasonable investor might have considered them important in the making of his decision."[191] One federal judge rejected the "might" standard as "too suggestive of mere possibility, however unlikely" that an omitted or misstated fact would influence an investor or shareholder decision.[192]

The Supreme Court shared that observation in *TSC Industries, Inc. v. Northway, Inc.*,[193] a Rule 14a-9 case which has become the leading materiality case in federal securities law. In the case, National Industries proposed to acquire the assets of TSC. In the proxy statement soliciting the votes of TSC shareholders, National disclosed that it owned 34 percent of the TSC shares, that no one else owned more than 10 percent, and that 5 out of 10 TSC directors were National nominees, but National did not go further to disclose that it controlled TSC. The Supreme Court agreed with the district court that the omission was not material, using the opportunity to firm up considerably the standard of materiality under federal law:

> [A]n omitted fact is material if there is a substantial likelihood that a reasonable shareholder would consider it important in deciding how to vote . . . . It does not require proof of a substantial likelihood that disclosure of the omitted fact would have caused the reasonable investor to change his vote. What the standard does contemplate is a showing of a substantial likelihood that, under all the circumstances, the omitted

[190] In *Gaines v. Haughton*, 645 F.2d 761 (9th Cir. 1981), a Ninth Circuit panel held that a shareholder who did not give a proxy in reliance on an alleged misleading proxy solicitation lacks standing under Rule 14a-9. Later Ninth Circuit decisions limit, or effectively reverse, the holding. *See Western District Council v. Louisiana Pacific Corp.*, 892 F.2d 1412, 1414 (9th Cir. 1989); *Stahl v. Gibraltar Financial Corp.*, 967 F.2d 335 (9th Cir. 1992).

[191] *Affiliated Ute Citizens v. United States*, 406 U.S. 128, 154 (1972).

[192] *Gerstle v. Gamble Skogmo, Inc.*, 478 F.2d 1281, 1302 (2d Cir. 1973).

[193] 426 U.S. 438 (1976).

fact would have assumed significance in the deliberations of the reasonable shareholder. Put another way, there must be a substantial likelihood that the disclosure of the omitted fact would have been viewed by the reasonable investor as having significantly altered the "total mix" of information made available.[194]

In *TSC*, the addition of express disclosure that National controlled TSC would not have significantly altered the "total mix." The proxy statement contained ample indications that such was the case; the proxy material just did not say so expressly.

Under *TSC*, the test of materiality is a substantial likelihood "whether a reasonable [person] *would* attach importance to the fact misrepresented or omitted in determining his [or her] course of action." The reasonable investor is defined in *SEC v. Texas Gulf Sulphur Co.*,[195] a case under Rule 10b-5. A contention could be made that the reasonable investor is the conservative investor purchasing common stocks for medium-to long-term performance. In *Texas Gulf Sulphur*, TGS employees exploring in Northern Ontario, Canada, had unearthed drill cores showing possible extensive mineral deposits to a great depth. The employees, who had then secretly bought TGS shares, argued that a drill core does not a mine make and that chemical assay of the drill core would give a more reliable estimate. They thus argued that the information upon which they had traded was not material.

Speculators in mining company shares would, however, find drill core mineralization highly relevant to an investment decision. "The speculators and chartists of Wall and Bay Streets[196] are also 'reasonable' investors entitled to the same legal protection afforded conservative traders," observed the *TGS* court. The materiality determination must take into account what recognized investment schools or regular followers of a corporation's performance would regard as important in making decisions to buy, sell, tender, or vote.

[F]   State of Mind (Fault) Required

While *TSC Industries* has been taken to establish a uniform standard of materiality, in the federal securities law area the amount of fault required depends upon the antifraud rule or statutory provision involved. Plaintiffs and regulators argue for low states of mind such as negligence or, indeed, near strict liability. Defendants, including corporations and corporate officials, argue that plaintiffs must prove knowing or intentional conduct. The middle ground is gross negligence, or recklessness, which itself may have gradations, ranging from error-riddled sloppy behavior to conscious disregard of the effect one's conduct may have on others.

Securities Act of 1933 § 11 makes the issuer of securities strictly liable for omissions or misstatements in registration statements filed with the SEC. Other persons, such as the chief executive and financial officers, directors and

---

[194] 426 U.S. at 449.

[195] 401 F.2d 838 (2d Cir. 1968) (en banc), *cert. denied*, 394 U.S. 976 (1969).

[196] The Toronto Stock Exchange is on Bay Street.

accountants who sign or expertise a portion of the registration are liable unless they are able to sustain a due diligence defense: that, after a reasonable investigation, they had reason to believe, and did in fact believe, that the statements made in the registration were true. Early decisions interpreting the provision were hard on corporate executive directors, underwriters and accountants and set the standard for interpreting the provision as requiring proof only of slight negligence.[197]

By contrast, under Rule 10b-5 the Supreme Court has held that proof of negligence is insufficient either to ground a damages recovery or an SEC injunction.[198] In a footnote in one of those cases, the Court left open the question of whether, under certain circumstances, proof of recklessness would suffice. In subsequent decisions, all courts of appeal have held that recklessness would suffice, at least if it was of the high "conscious disregard" variety. Defense counsel and conservative judges call fault the "scienter" element of a Rule 10b-5 case while plaintiffs and plaintiffs' counsel use the blander term "state of mind."[199]

The wording of the statute, Securities Exchange Act section 10(b) ("manipulative or deceptive device or contrivance"), defined the permissible scope of SEC Rule 10b-5, requiring that plaintiffs prove a high state of mind under any rule the SEC might adopt under the section.[200] In the proxy area no such limiting statutory language exists. Section 14(a) gives the SEC a broad mandate to regulate the solicitation of proxies "as necessary or appropriate in the public interest or for the protection of investors." The SEC has always interpreted the antifraud rule, Rule 14a-9, as requiring proof only of negligence.

The courts have agreed. In the leading case of *Gerstle v. Gamble Skogmo, Inc.*,[201] the Second Circuit held that negligence sufficed to establish liability under Rule 14a-9. The court held that plaintiffs, shareholders who had been the targets of a misleading proxy statement, "are not required to establish any evil motive or even reckless disregard of the facts."

On its face, Rule 14a-9 may be read as providing for strict liability. In *Shidler v. All American Life & Financial Corp.*,[202] in its proxy statement, the corporation stated that Iowa law required two-thirds approval of all classes of shares, common and preferred, voting together. Later the Iowa Supreme Court held that Iowa law required a two-thirds vote class by class. A disgruntled shareholder sued. The Eighth Circuit upheld dismissal of the claim on grounds that Rule 14a-9 required at least proof of negligence, while all the facts demonstrated was a good faith mistake as to an undecided point of Iowa law:

[197] The leading case in *Escott v. BarChris Construction Corp.*, 283 F. Supp. 643 (S.D.N.Y. 1968).

[198] *Ernst & Ernst v. Hochfelder*, 425 U.S. 185 (1976) (negligence insufficient to ground damage recovery); *Aaron v. SEC*, 446 U.S. 680 (1980) (same — SEC injunctions).

[199] The scienter, or state of mind, required in a Rule 10b-5 case is discussed in § 13.02[D], *infra*.

[200] It was irrelevant that Rule 10b-5's wording may not require scienter because it is the statute that Congress enacted and the SEC Rule may not exceed the scope of the statute. *Ernst & Ernst v. Hochfelder, supra*.

[201] 478 F.2d 1281 (2d Cir. 1973).

[202] 775 F.2d 917 (8th Cir. 1985).

The purpose of section 14(a) is to "prevent management or others from obtaining authorization for corporate action by means of deceptive or inadequate disclosure in proxy solicitation." A strict liability rule would impose liability for fully innocent misstatements. It is too blunt a tool to ferret out the kind of deceptive practices Congress sought to prevent in enacting section 14(a).

An argument may be made that, in the proxy rule area, the public would be better served by a higher standard such as one requiring proof of recklessness. A negligence standard frequently permits a resource rich corporation to tie up a shareholder activist or group which makes a misstatement or fails to make full disclosure. Nonetheless, the negligence state of mind, or fault requirement, under SEC Rule 14a-9 is well-established.

[G]   Causation

Causation in securities cases falls into two categories. The first is transaction causation, more frequently termed reliance. An allegation of reliance states that not only a hypothetical reasonable person, but the actual plaintiff, would have considered the omitted fact important in the making of her decision and that the omission or misleading statement did in fact cause or affect her purchase, sale, tender or vote (transaction causation). The second type of causation is loss causation. In an antifraud rule claim, the plaintiff alleges that the defendant's omissions or misleading statements caused the damage to the plaintiff.[203]

In a Rule 10b-5 case, court opinions often separately discuss the two types of causation.[204] On the other hand, proxy Rule 14a-9 opinions blend their discussion of the two elements.

The early leading case is *Mills v. Electric Auto-Lite Co.*[205] Mills, a shareholder of Auto-Lite, had been asked to vote on a merger proposed between Auto-Lite and Mergenthaler Linotype Company. For two years previous, Mergenthaler had owned over 50 percent of the outstanding Auto-Lite common shares. The Auto-Lite proxy statement told the Auto-Lite shareholders that their board of directors recommended approval of the merger. The proxy statement did not, however, disclose that all eleven of the Auto-Lite directors were the nominees of Mergenthaler and were under the "control and domination of Mergenthaler." Also, because the relevant state law required two-thirds approval of the merger, even though Mergenthaler owned more than 50 percent, it and Auto-Lite still had to solicit additional proxies to vote in favor of the merger.

The plaintiff's complaint was that he was damaged by the merger, or by a merger for insufficient consideration. The Seventh Circuit held that if Auto-Lite and Mergenthaler could show "by a preponderance of the probabilities, that the merger would have received a sufficient vote even if the proxy statement had not been misleading, [plaintiff Mills] would be entitled to no relief of any kind."

---

[203] *See Schlick v. Penn-Dixie Cement Co.*, 507 F.2d 374 (2d Cir. 1974).

[204] See the separate discussions of reliance and of loss causation in Chapter 13.

[205] 396 U.S. 375 (1970).

The Seventh Circuit held further that the corporation could make that showing "by a preponderance of probabilities" if they could demonstrate that the terms of the merger were in fact fair. If the merger terms were fair, the reasoning went, there would be no loss and therefore no loss causation.

The Supreme Court disagreed, noting that "[u]se of a solicitation that is materially misleading is itself a violation of law." The Court seemed also to allow room for shareholders to reject a merger whose terms were fair if they did not like the manner in which the merger was proposed, believed they had been lied to, and so on:

> The decision below, by permitting all liability to be foreclosed on the basis of a finding that the merger was fair, would allow the stockholders to be bypassed . . . a judicial appraisal of the merger's merits could be substituted for the actual and informed vote of the stockholders.

> The result would be to insulate from private redress an entire category of proxy violations — those relating to matters other than the terms of the merger. Even outrageous misrepresentations in a proxy solicitation, if they did not relate to the terms of the transaction, would give rise to no cause of action under § 14(a).[206]

The Court's rejection of the Seventh Circuit approach, however, required that it fashion its own approach to these thorny questions.

As has been seen in the discussion of standing, in a proxy solicitation case, the plaintiff has not relied on the misleading material. She has seen through the alleged omissions or deception and brought suit alleging that it is her fellow shareholders who may have relied on the misleading statements.[207] The loosening of the requirement of proving actual reliance is also based upon the difficulty of proving reliance. In a case of omission and in class actions with numerous plaintiffs, positive proof of reliance then cannot be required of the plaintiff.

In *Mills*, the Court permitted materiality to substitute for reliance, or probable reliance. It further dealt with the loss causation issue by not requiring plaintiffs to demonstrate actual monetary loss (that is, that the merger terms were actually unfair) but injury to corporate suffrage rights (a material misrepresentation had occurred and the shareholder voting thereby affected was an "essential link" in the transaction for which defendants sought approval). The relevant passage in the opinion states:

> Where the misstatement or omission in a proxy statement has been shown to be "material" . . . that determination itself indubitably embodies a conclusion that the defect was of such a character that it might [would — *TSC*] have been considered important by a reasonable shareholder who was in the process of deciding how to vote. This requirement that the defect have a significant *propensity* to affect the

---

[206] 396 U.S. at 381–82.

[207] Contrast the Rule 10b-5 case in which the standing rule requires that a plaintiff have purchased or sold securities. If the shareholder plaintiff alleges that her fellow shareholders have been tricked, but she has not, then not only has she not relied, she has not purchased or sold. She has not even a semblance of a case.

voting process is found in the express terms of Rule 14a-9 itself . . . .

There is no need to supplement this requirement, as did the Court of Appeals, with a requirement of proof of whether the defect actually had a decisive effect on the voting. Where there has been a finding of materiality, a shareholder has made a sufficient showing of causal relationship . . . if, as here, he proves that the proxy solicitation itself, rather than the particular defect in the solicitation materials, was an essential link in the accomplishment of the transaction.[208]

Mills's reasoning may be difficult to take in on a first reading, although the conclusion is readily understandable: a plaintiff alleging proxy violations must demonstrate materiality of the omission, need not demonstrate reliance, and, on the remaining causation issue, need only demonstrate that the misleading solicitation was an "essential link" in accomplishing the result about which plaintiff complains.[209] *Mills* also seemed a victory for shareholder rights and plaintiffs, although the victory turned out to be a pyrrhic one.[210]

The "essential link" turned out to be missing in *Virginia Bankshares, Inc. v. Sandberg.*[211] First American Bankshares (FAB), through its subsidiary Virginia Bankshares, Inc. (VBI), already owned 85 percent of the target First American Bank of Virginia. FAB decided to acquire the remaining 15 percent through a freeze-out merger of First American into VBI.[212] FAB caused First American to solicit proxies for the merger, even though it was not required to do so as it controlled 85 percent of the votes. In the proxy materials, First American directors stated that the offer of $42 per share represented an opportunity for the minority shareholders to achieve a "high" value, which they also described as a "fair" value. However, the evidence at trial indicated that $60 would have been a fair value.

The Court first found that statements of opinion or belief are actionable under Rule 14a-9 if those statements misstate the reasons for that belief. The directors

---

[208] 396 U.S. at 384–85 (footnote omitted).

[209] *Mills* also permits awards of attorneys' fees from the corporate treasury if the plaintiff shareholder has conferred "a substantial benefit" on the corporation and fellow shareholders. The benefit need not be monetary, as in creation of a common fund. When a shareholder's action is of the sort that "involve[s] corporate therapeutics," the court may award fees. *See* 396 U.S. at 389–97. In a subsequent case, *Alyeska Pipeline Serv. Co. v. Wilderness Soc'y,* 421 U.S. 240 (1975), the Court severely limited the ability of lower federal courts to shift attorneys' fees, absent statutory authority, but notably preserved the *Mills* rule. The *Alyeska* Court cited *Mills* as an example of the "historic power of equity to permit the trustee of a fund or property, or a party preserving or recovering a fund for the benefit of others in addition to himself, to recover his costs, including his attorneys' fees."

[210] On remand from the Supreme Court, the district court held the merger terms unfair, awarding $1,233,918.35 in damages and $740,000 in prejudgment interest. On appeal, the Seventh Circuit reversed, holding that the merger terms were fair and plaintiffs therefore were not entitled to damages. 552 F.2d 1239 (7th Cir.), *cert. denied,* 434 U.S. 922 (1977). The Seventh Circuit further held that on remand no corporate therapeutics (common benefit) component existed. Any attorneys' fees would have to be based upon creation of a common fund, which, given the reversal, the attorneys had failed to produce. No fees were allowed. 552 F.2d at 1249–50.

[211] 501 U.S. 1083 (1991).

[212] Freeze-out mergers are discussed in detail in § 10.03, *infra.*

had not acted for the reasons stated (that the price was "fair" or a "high" value) but for other reasons (they were doing what the parent corporation told them to do).

Despite that victory, the plaintiffs lost the case. The majority of five justices found the offending proxy solicitation had not been an "essential link" in the accomplishment of the transaction. Instead, the solicitation was gratuitous. FAB, through VBI, owned sufficient shares to vote the merger through by itself.[213]

The case pointed to a second means whereby proxy plaintiffs in a solicitation case may prove causation. Damage is caused to the plaintiff and her fellow shareholders if an offending statement in a proxy solicitation caused them to forgo a state law remedy. The statement by First America directors that $42 was "fair" and "high" value may have put the target shareholders off the trail of an appraisal remedy in which a Virginia state court might have found the shares' worth to be $60 or even more. By evading the issue, the Court hinted at an alternative route to proving causation, other than by the essential link route:

> The case does not . . . require us to decide whether § 14(a) provides a cause of action for lost state remedies, since there is no indication in the law or the facts before us that the proxy solicitation resulted in any such loss. The contrary appears to be the case.

The overwhelming majority of merger cases presents the possibility that director misstatements may have put shareholders off the scent of seeking a state court appraisal,[214] or from seeking equitable relief based upon a violation of fiduciary duty, such as the duty of candor.[215] Indeed, the misleading statements, if they lead a shareholder to vote for the merger rather than abstain, would foreclose the state law remedy. Dissenters' rights statutes forbid a shareholder who voted for an action from later dissenting and seeking appraisal of her shares.

Virginia Bankshares is a rare case. The Virginia bank merger statute did not bestow upon dissenters a right to seek appraisal of their shares, something of a rarity. Moreover, later federal court cases have taken the hint as to proof of causation other than by essential link proofs. They have answered the question *Virginia Bankshares* raises in the affirmative.

In *Wilson v. Great American Industries, Inc.*,[216] and in *Howing v. Nationwide Corp.*,[217] the vote of target shareholders was not necessary to accomplish a merger. In one of the cases (*Howing*), however, as in *Virginia Bankshares*, the corporation solicited the minority shareholders' proxies anyway. In the other

---

[213] *Virginia Bankshares* thus presents the case the common law abhorred: a wrong without a remedy. In dissent, Mr. Justice Stevens said as much: "The case before us today involves a merger that has been found by a jury to be unfair, not fair. The interest in providing a remedy to the injured minority shareholders therefore is stronger, not weaker, than in *Mills*."

[214] See the discussion of dissenters' rights and appraisal in § 6.06, *supra*.

[215] For a discussion of such duties, see Chapter 9. There may also be a state cause of action to enjoin the freeze out for violating fiduciary duty. See §§ 8.01[C]; 10.03[B], [C], *infra*.

[216] 979 F.2d 924 (2d Cir. 1992).

[217] 972 F.2d 700 (6th Cir. 1992), *cert. denied*, 507 U.S. 1004 (1993).

case, the corporation did not solicit proxies but distributed an information statement, as Securities Exchange Act section 14(c) requires them to do even if they do not solicit proxies. In both cases, despite the inability of plaintiffs to offer "essential link" proofs as to causation, the plaintiffs' Rule 14a-9 claims were allowed to proceed. Minority shareholders had a Rule 14a-9 cause of action because misleading statements or omissions may have caused them or fellow shareholders to forego the state law remedy commonly present in merger situations, namely, the right to dissent (vote "no") and then seek appraisal of their shares in state court.

In Rule 14a-9 proxy solicitation cases, plaintiffs need only prove materiality and not reliance. On the loss causation issue, two avenues are open to plaintiffs. They may prove that the solicitation of proxies was an "essential link" in the accomplishment of the defendant's objective. Or, they may prove that the defendants' misleading statements or omissions foreclosed or caused then to forego state law remedies they may otherwise have pursued.

[H]   Remedies

In SEC Rule 14a-9 cases, involving allegations of misrepresentation or omission in proxy solicitation activities, a prospective remedy is often sought. The party who alleges misrepresentation, frequently the corporation, seeks an injunction — or three injunctions: an injunction against the offending statements; an injunction against solicitation of further proxies; and an injunction against use of any of the proxies thus far obtained.[218]

In a case under the Securities Exchange Act provisions applicable to tender offers, the Supreme Court held that an issuer corporation had to make the traditional equitable showings, as well as demonstrate that a federal regulatory scheme such as the securities laws has been violated. In *Rondeau v. Mosinee Paper Corp.*,[219] the Court refused to uphold orders enjoining shareholder Rondeau from voting shares, or from acquiring further shares, and for divesting shares he already had acquired, simply because he had filed an extremely late Schedule 13D with the SEC.[220] The court held that in order to obtain an injunction or preliminary injunction, a plaintiff must demonstrate a probability of success on the merits, the threat of irreparable harm, the inadequacy of a remedy at law, and a balancing of the hardships (the hardship on the plaintiff if the injunction is not granted will exceed the hardship on the defendant if the injunction is granted). The Court did not limit its holding to the tender offer provisions. Presumably, *Rondeau* could apply across the spectrum of federal securities law, including the proxy solicitation area.

---

[218] *See, e.g., SEC v. May*, 229 F.2d 123 (2d Cir. 1956) (also ordering that the shareholders' meeting be postponed to allow time for resolicitation).

[219] 422 U.S. 49 (1975).

[220] For a discussion of Section 13d, see § 12.06[B], *infra.*

Chapter 8

INTRODUCTION TO FIDUCIARY DUTY: THE DUTY OF CARE, THE BUSINESS JUDGMENT RULE AND GOOD FAITH

§ 8.01 INTRODUCTION

The law imposes on certain individuals the responsibility of being a fiduciary. While there is no explicit definition of a fiduciary relationship, it is generally created when one is given power that carries a duty to use that power to benefit another.[1] The label of a fiduciary is applied to a variety of relationships, such as trustees with the beneficiaries of trusts, among partners or agents and principals, but once it is established, the responsibilities imposed may differ in each context. The often quoted statement by Justice Frankfurter sums this up when he wrote "to say that a man is a fiduciary only begins analysis; it gives direction to further inquiry. To whom is he a fiduciary? What obligations does he owe as a fiduciary?"[2]

Much of corporate law is about fiduciary duties and its parameters. In the corporate context, directors and officers are in a fiduciary relationship to their corporation and to the shareholders. Controlling shareholders may also be characterized as fiduciaries.[3]

The primary problems faced by shareholders are mismanagement of the business or unfair self dealing by those in control.[4] The requirement and enforcement of fiduciary duty serves as a monitoring device to limit those harms. In the context of the publicly held corporation when there is separation of ownership from control, fiduciary duty can help monitor managers by maintaining their accountability to the public shareholders.[5] In those publicly traded corporations, in which there is no separation of ownership from control because a shareholder or group of shareholders controls the corporation, the public minority shareholders may need protection from self-dealing by the shareholders in control. In the closely held corporate context, majority shareholders may use their power to oppress the minority shareholders denying them a return or

---

[1] J. Shepherd, Law of Fiduciaries 97 (1981).

[2] *SEC v. Chenery Corp.*, 318 U.S. 80, 85–6 (1943).

[3] In *Gantler v. Stephens*, 2009 Del. LEXIS 33 (Jan. 27, 2009), the Delaware Supreme Court held that officers like directors owe fiduciary duties of care and loyalty the same as directors. For a discussion of controlling shareholders, see Chapter 10, *infra*.

[4] Economists refer to mismanagement as shirking and unfair self dealing as opportunistic behavior.

[5] For a discussion of corporate governance and separation of ownership from control, see § 5.02[E][1], *supra*.

forcing them to sell their shares.[6] In all of these contexts, fiduciary duty tries to limit the potential abuse of those in positions of control.

[A]   Overview of Duty of Care and Loyalty

The characterization of someone as a fiduciary generally means that the individual has to obey certain duties and look our for the interests of whoever is owed the duty. Most of the duties have been developed by the common law. They are generally bound by a duty of care, and duty of loyalty. The duty of care requires directors to perform their duties with the diligence of a reasonable person in similar circumstances which vary depending on the context. As will be discussed, directors can be liable for both malfeasance and nonfeasance. Most decisions involving the duty of care are protected under the business judgment rule, which creates a presumption (or safe harbor) that limits courts in questioning business decisions. The focus of any judicial inquiry will usually be on the decision making process not the decision. Thus, the plaintiff usually has the burden of proof on the issue of breach of duty and courts rarely look at the substance of the decision. The business judgment rule does not protect nonfeasance, lack of good faith, or an irrational or wasteful decision.[7]

The duty of loyalty requires a fiduciary to act for the best interests of their corporation and in good faith. A lack of good faith can involve actual intent to harm the corporation or an intentional dereliction of duty and a conscious disregard for one's responsibilities.[8] The duty of loyalty also focuses on conflicts of interest where the fiduciary's (or those associated with her) personal interests may be advanced over corporate interests.[9] Generally, the court will scrutinize a conflict of interest transaction to determine if it is fair. The court may not only shift the burden of proof to the directors to show fairness but will inquire as to both the process and substance of the decision (i.e., entire fairness). Thus, in duty of loyalty cases involving a conflict of interest, there is more judicial involvement and scrutiny than in duty of care or good faith cases.[10] The difference is justified because, in a duty of care case, the courts want to protect business decisions that are intended to enhance corporate gain, while in a duty of loyalty involving a conflict of interest case the directors may be motivated by personal gain.[11]

---

[6] For a discussion of fiduciary duty in the closely held corporation, see Chapter 11, *infra*.

[7] When an irrationality or waste is alleged there is some limited judicial scrutiny of the substance of the transaction to determine if the allegations support such a claim but the burden of proof remains on the plaintiff. The waste standard generally means that what the corporation received in a transaction was so inadequate in value that no person of ordinary sound business judgment would deem it worth what the corporation paid. In essence, waste would involve an exchange for consideration so disproportionately small that it is beyond what a reasonable person would trade. *Michelson v. Duncan*, 407 A.2d 211, 224 (Del. 1979). For a discussion of waste, see § 9.04[C], *infra*.

[8] For a discussion of good faith under Delaware law, see § 8.06[B], *infra*.

[9] For discussion of duty of loyalty and conflicts of interest, see Chapter 9, *infra*.

[10] *See generally* Ahmed Bulbulia & Arthur R. Pinto, *Statutory Responses to Interested Directors' Transactions: A Watering Down of Fiduciary Standards?*, 53 Notre Dame L. Rev. 201 (1977).

[11] For a discussion of duty of loyalty, see Chapter 9.

[B] Sliding Scale

While fiduciary duty is usually described in terms of two categories of care and loyalty, there is in fact a sliding scale of fiduciary duty rules. Some cases fall between those duties because the legal standards and burdens may differ in a given case from traditional loyalty and care. As the Delaware Supreme Court indicated in *Guth*, fiduciary duty is subject to "no fixed scale."[12] The courts, in establishing the legal rules of fiduciary duty, attempt to balance the need of the fiduciary to act and transact with the protection of the shareholders. There is a tension between the judicial "hands off" approach reflected by the business judgment rule and the extensive judicial scrutiny of a fairness inquiry. Thus, the extent of judicial scrutiny is the key issue in these cases with plaintiffs seeking extensive judicial scrutiny and defendants seeking minimal judicial scrutiny. Plaintiff shareholders would prefer the courts to use a loyalty analysis of conflicts of interest because the defendants have the burden of proof and there is active judicial scrutiny of both the fairness of substance and process. Defendants, on the other hand, seek limited judicial involvement under the protection of the business judgment rule (which places the burden on the plaintiff to prove that the rule should not apply).

The courts find that some situations do not fit easily within either analysis and attempt to balance shareholders' and managers' interests and establish a range of fiduciary duty rules along this sliding scale between the traditional duties of care and loyalty. This may involve modifying the legal standard used by the courts or shifting the burden of proof.[13] In studying fiduciary duty cases, it is helpful see where the court places the case on this sliding scale. This is determined by what standards the court applies to scrutinize the transaction (e.g., the business judgment rule or fairness or lack of good faith or waste) and how it allocates the burden of proof (i.e., who has the burden and whether it shifts). In trying to understand the cases and the sliding scale, it is important to study the standards applied, as well as the placing of the burden and the rationale for doing so.[14] For example, in a conflict of interest, self dealing

---

[12] *Guth v. Loft*, 5 A.2d. 503 (Del. 1961). In *McMullin v. Beran*, 765 A.2d 910 (2000), the Delaware Supreme Court described fiduciary responsibility as contextually specific.

[13] For example, the Delaware courts, as well as other courts following their lead, has developed a different level of scrutiny applicable in reviewing some actions taken by directors in implementing defensive tactics implicating control. An intermediate standard recognized that battles for control involve both important business decisions affecting the corporation and possible conflicts of interests by directors protecting their positions. Thus, the standard of enhanced judicial review established in *Unocal Corp. v. Mesa Petroleum*, 493 A.2d. 946 (Del. 1985) is a modified business judgment rule or proportionality test that unlike the duty of care initially places the burden on the defendant to justify its actions. The directors must show that there were reasonable grounds for believing there was a danger to corporate policy and the response must also be reasonable to the threat posed which allows scrutiny on substance but unlike loyalty it is not a fairness inquiry. Thus on this sliding scale the modified business judgment or proportionality test allows for more judicial scrutiny than duty of care but less than duty of loyalty. For a discussion of *Unocal*, see § 12.05[A][2], *infra.*

[14] As some cases may indicate, the level of scrutiny, and thus where it is placed on the sliding scale, may be dependent upon three different factors. First, the type of transaction involved may be important. For example, is it an ordinary normal business decision or does it involve self-dealing and what kind of self-dealing? Second, what is the context of the transaction or what is the type of corporation with which we are dealing? For example, is the corporation publicly traded or is there a

transaction, the court may initially place the burden of proof on the defendant to prove fairness of process and substance under the traditional duty of loyalty rule. But if an independent board of directors approves of the transaction, some courts may shift the burden to the plaintiff to prove fairness or may even decide to apply the business judgment rule.[15] By doing so it has changed the judicial scrutiny (the burden and legal standard) and moved these cases along that sliding scale.

§ 8.02 POLICY ISSUES

There are views that the directors' fiduciary duty should not only be to the shareholders, but it should also be to other stakeholders in the business such as labor, creditors or consumers.[16] Generally, the duty is to the corporation and shareholders and the shareholders have the right to enforce it through litigation.[17] Those who manage and control corporations need flexibility to make business decisions and take risks that hopefully will benefit the corporation and the shareholders (a rationale for the business judgment rule).[18] In addition, in publicly traded corporations there is a need to attract outside directors which may be discouraged by litigation and the possibility of liability and paying damages. Shareholders, who have enough votes to control the corporation, also have some right to use their control for their own personal benefits. Not all self-dealing is necessarily unfair to the shareholders, but there needs to be some check on the power of those who control the business because all of the shareholders' money is at risk. In most situations, the interests of the managers or control persons and the owners are aligned because a successful business benefits everyone. But there are times when those who manage or control the corporation will not act diligently or will seek to self deal unfairly.[19]

The debate over corporate fiduciary duty involves whether litigation is the best means of enforcing the duty and the extent to which the courts should scrutinize transactions. Those who owe fiduciary duties tend to argue that judicial scrutiny should be limited to allow for flexibility and reduce or avoid unnecessary litigation costs. Those who argue for shareholder interests favor increased judicial scrutiny through litigation and strengthening of various legal rules and monitoring devices. Litigation may not only produce damages but even if damages are limited it can still potentially deter bad behavior.

---

control group? Third, the procedure that was undertaken to either authorize or ratify the transaction may also be significant. For example, are the directors who approved it disinterested or was there shareholder approval? Thus, the level of judicial scrutiny is influenced by transactional, contextual and procedural factors.

[15] For a discussion of when procedure may change judicial scrutiny in interested director's transactions See § 9.03[B], *infra.*

[16] A violation of fiduciary duty may be raised when the directors appear to be acting for interests other than the shareholders. For more on this subject, see § 5.02[A], *supra.*

[17] *See* Chapter 14, *infra.*

[18] For a discussion of the reasons for the business judgment rule, see § 8.03[B], *infra.*

[19] For a discussion of conflicts of interest and the duty of loyalty, see Chapter 9, *infra.*

Civil penalties and criminal law are also used to enforce fiduciary duties, especially violations of federal securities laws, but such enforcement will depend on the willingness of prosecutors and regulators to bring such action.[20]

[A] Law and Economics Approach

To some extent, the debate about fiduciary duty rules reflects the differences in theories of and approaches to corporate law.[21] Some commentators who approach corporate law from the law and economics perspective view the relationship between the shareholders and managers as a matter of contract.[22] Fiduciary duty rules are among the terms of the contract. Under this view, investors could actually contract for this obligation, but the law instead imposes this responsibility because it would be expensive and time consuming to negotiate detailed contracts delineating managers' obligations. Thus, the law eliminates the need to actually enter a contract and provides standardized rules which lower transaction costs of actually contracting. Given the need for managerial flexibility, these fiduciary rules are rarely detailed. At the same time, since they are based on contract, these rules are like default rules and should be able to be modified by the parties in order to allow for efficient private ordering. Thus, under this view, legal rules, and particularly fiduciary duty, can be contracted away.[23] If needed, there are market mechanisms available that are more effective in enforcing fiduciary duty.[24]

The contract view has been attacked from different perspectives. Some view fiduciary duty as fundamental legal rules necessary to protect investors. Critics of the contractual approach argue that some minimal protection and regulation is needed, and some of these rules should not be changed so easily. In a publicly traded company with thousands of shareholders, there is likely to be no real bargaining over the terms of the contract and informational disparities would distort the process if any bargaining did occur. Management controls the structure and timing of the process. Shareholders are widely dispersed and not in a position to negotiate and unable to act collectively.[25] Further, there is a moral perspective that comes into play when there is a duty of loyalty issue.[26]

---

[20] There have also been actions brought by state attorneys general and local district attorneys. For example, the Manhattan District Attorney charged two Tyco executives with theft of corporate property, enterprise corruption and securities fraud involving $600 million. Mark Maremont, *Kozlowski's Defense Strategy: Big Spending was no Secret*, WALL ST. J., A1 (Feb. 9, 2004).

[21] For a discussion of these theories, see § 5.03, *supra*.

[22] For a discussion of the law and economics view and the nexus of contracts, see § 5.03[C], *supra*.

[23] *See generally* Frank Easterbrook & Daniel Fischel, THE ECONOMIC STRUCTURE OF CORPORATE LAW (1991). States have adopted this view by allowing corporations to have provisions in their articles to eliminate monetary damages in duty of care cases. See § 8.05, *infra*.

[24] *See* Kenneth Scott, *Corporation Law and the American Law Institute Corporate Governance Project*, 35 Stan. L. Rev. 927 (1983) (arguing for elimination of the duty of care as harming entrepreneurs and preferred the use of market mechanisms to deal with the issue). For discussion of the market mechanisms, see § 5.03[C][2], *supra*.

[25] For discussion of the problems of contracting in publicly traded corporations, see § 5.03[C][3], [4], *supra*.

[26] For discussion of morality and duty of loyalty, see § 9.02, *infra*.

§ 8.03 DUTY OF CARE

Traditionally liability under the duty of care required finding duty, breach, proximate cause and loss. The directors' fiduciary duties have developed primarily through case law although the duty of care is often described in some state statutes.[27] The traditional statutory provision indicates that directors must discharge their duties in good faith, with the care an ordinarily prudent person in a like position would exercise under similar circumstances, and in manner reasonably believed to be in the best interest of the corporation.[28] The MBCA had previously used this standard but has changed it to now require, in § 8.30(a), that each director act in good faith and in a manner the director reasonably believed[29] to be in the best interest of the corporation and, in subsection (b), that the board discharge its duty with the care a person in a like position would reasonably believe appropriate under the circumstances. The change does several things. First, it separates the standard of care of each director in subsection (a) from the general duty of the board (as opposed to the director itself) in subsection (b).[30] In addition, subsection (b) does not refer to the "ordinary prudent person" standard, but uses "a person in a like position." The concern of the drafters of the MBCA was that the use of the "ordinary prudent person" standard from torts and negligence law might suggest that directors should act with caution when, in fact, directors need to take risks in order to create gains.[31]

The courts will determine, in a given case, the parameters of fiduciary duty. Generally, the directors acting in the corporation's interest must not be negligent in their duties.[32] The fiduciary duty imposed upon directors is not the same duty imposed upon other fiduciaries such as trustees. The law recognizes that fiduciary duties vary according to the nature and circumstances of the relationship. For example, it is recognized that when money is placed into a trust, trustees are under strict duties as to how they can invest that money. These duties are measured under by a "prudent person" standard, which requires great care when investing. The same rule is inapplicable in the corporate context since, unlike trustees, directors are hired to take risks because greater profits require risk and shareholders seek risk and profits in buying stock. The courts recognize

----

[27] Delaware does not have a statutory standard for the duty of care.

[28] *E.g.*, N.Y.B.C.L. § 717.

[29] The reasonably believed standard is subjective when looking at the belief, but objective in looking at whether it was reasonable. Model Bus. Corp. Act Ann. § 8.30 (official comment) (4th ed. 2008).

[30] The standard in subsection (b) focuses on the context of the a director's dealing with the board's decision making and oversight. The standard is designed to apply to both individual action and the degree of care to be collegially used in performing their functions. Model Bus. Corp. Act Ann. § 8.30 (official comment) (4th ed. 2008).

[31] Model Bus. Corp. Act Ann. § 8.30 (official comment) (4th ed. 2008).

[32] The standard in Delaware appears to be gross negligence, at least in a case of malfeasance when the business judgment rule is at issue. *Smith v. Van Gorkom*, 488 A.2d 858 (Del. 1985). For a discussion of *Smith*, see § 8.04, *infra*. *See also Aronson v. Lewis*, 473 A.2d 805 (Del. 1984) ("under the business judgment rule director liability is predicated on concepts of gross negligence"). *But see Rabkin v. Philip A. Hunt Chemical Corp.*, 1987 Del. Ch. LEXIS 522 (suggesting that ordinary negligence is the test in neglect or nonfeasance cases).

the responsibilities of fiduciaries in different contexts and necessarily impose different rules.[33]

The "ordinary prudent person" in similar circumstances, and "a person in a like position," are objective standards. The standards are interpreted to mean not what a director personally believes she should do, but what a reasonable person would do in similar circumstances.[34] The courts, in determining liability, will usually distinguish between directors who are insiders (that is, managers) and those that are outsiders. Directors that are insiders are held to a higher standard of care.[35] This reflects the reality that insiders will always be more involved and aware of the business. It is also often justified by the need to attract outside independent directors who would be unwilling to serve if their liability were the same as that of insider directors. In addition, if certain directors are placed on the board for their particular skills, their performance may be tested by a different standard measured by their expertise.[36] For example, a director who is also a lawyer may be obligated to pay more attention to legal issues when the board makes a decision involving that expertise. The kind of corporation and the business will also influence the standards that will apply. Directors are also able to rely on officers, employees, professionals (such as lawyers and accountants) and board committees, so long as it is reasonable to do so.[37]

Directors make decisions important to the business, but they also monitor the business. Issues of breach of duty of care can arise in two kinds of situations: when (1) there is a decision made in a negligent manner (i.e., malfeasance) and (2) there is a failure to act or monitor where a loss could have been prevented (i.e., nonfeasance).

[A] Nonfeasance

The duty of care requires directors to undertake certain responsibilities. In *Francis v. United Jersey Bank*,[38] the New Jersey Supreme Court set out a model of how directors should generally act. *Francis* was a case of nonfeasance involving a family owned and closely held corporation which operated as a reinsurance broker. These brokers arrange for the sale among insurance companies of some of their risks under their policies thus facilitating the diversification of that risk. In these transactions, the reinsurance broker held

---

[33] *Joy v. North*, 692 F.2d 880, 885-6. (2d Cir. 1982), *cert. denied sub nom, Cititrust v. Joy*, 460 U.S. 1051 (1983).

[34] There used to be a standard widely found in state law that did not look at the ordinary prudent person in similar circumstances but instead, looked at the ordinary prudent person acting in his own affairs. That was viewed to be a much higher test of responsibility for directors because it was thought that a person will spend more time and attention taking care of his own affairs than those of another person. Most states changed the standard to the current one and focus on what an ordinary prudent person would do in similar circumstances. Interestingly, in § 11 of the Securities Act of 1933, which deals with the responsibility of directors in preparing the documents used when selling securities, directors are held to the older and higher standard.

[35] *See Bates v. Dressler*, 251 U.S. 524, 40 S. Ct. 247, 64 L. Ed. 388 (1920).

[36] James Cox, et al., CORPORATIONS 188 (1997).

[37] *See* Model Bus. Corp. Act Ann. § 8.30(b) (4th ed. 2008).

[38] 432 A.2d 814 (N.J. 1981).

funds for the insurance companies and industry practice required segregation of those funds. In *Francis*, however, the Pritchard sons, who ran the reinsurance brokerage, commingled the various insurance companies' funds in a single account and then personally "borrowed" from the account without subsequent repayment (i.e., they stole funds). Unfortunately, Mrs. Pritchard, their trusting mother, who was a grieving widow and was drinking heavily, was a director who never became involved in the business. She was sued by the trustee in bankruptcy[39] for breach of her duty of care.

In analyzing whether Mrs. Pritchard's nonfeasance amounted to negligence, the court spelled out what is expected of directors. Generally they should have some understanding of the business, keep informed on activities, perform general monitoring including attendance at meetings, and have some familiarity with the financial status of the business as reflected on the financial statements.[40] While the court rejected the idea that a director could be a "dummy director" serving merely as an ornament, it recognized that the responsibilities will vary. In addition, the court acknowledged that generally, the duties of directors of publicly traded corporations are greater than that of closely held corporations.[41] But here, the business was the reinsurance business in which the practices of holding other peoples' money in a trust-like situation (segregation of funds was industry practice) required greater care of the directors.[42] Given Mrs. Pritchard's total lack of involvement and failure to monitor the managers, it was easy to find her negligent for nonfeasance.[43] But even with a finding of negligence, there still may be a requirement of causation which links the negligence with the losses.[44]

---

[39] The trustee in bankruptcy represents the creditors who normally are not owed a fiduciary duty. But when a corporation is insolvent and there is no equity, the creditors become the owners of the corporation.

[40] In *Bates v. Dresser*, 251 U.S. 524 (1926), the Supreme Court found the President of a bank liable for the failure to discover the theft of an employee. Although the fraud was a novelty, he had sufficient warnings of lost money and the employee living beyond his means. Thus, if there are warnings, there is a duty to inquire. Interestingly, the outside directors were free of liability because of the novelty of the fraud and reasonable reliance on the President. The court recognized that the responsibilities of outside directors are different from insiders.

[41] In publicly traded corporations, the directors may be held to a higher standard. There is the separation of ownership from control where shareholders are more passive and rely more on the directors. In addition, the large amount of capital invested by the public and the importance of creating confidence to attract investors may require higher duties of directors.

[42] Cases involving banks, where not only shareholders' money is at risk but public deposits as well, generally hold directors to a higher standard of care. *See, e.g., Litwin v. Allen*, 25 N.Y.S.2d 667 (1940).

[43] In many small family run closely held corporations the model set out may not be realistic. Often family members serve on a board with no real involvement in the business. Whether the model set out in the *Francis* case would apply when there is no special situation involving holding other peoples' money is unclear.

[44] For a discussion of causation and *Francis*, see § 8.03[C], *infra*.

[B] Malfeasance and the Business Judgment Rule

Due care for directors requires that they be informed and deliberate when making a decision. When directors are accused of violating the duty of care, by making a negligent or ill advised decision which can even involve a decision not to act, then they are accused of malfeasance. Those decisions are subject to review under a judicial principle called the business judgment rule which is a tool of judicial review.[45] The duty of care sets a standard of conduct while the business judgment rule limits judicial inquiry into business decisions and protects directors who are not negligent in the decision making process.[46] Under the rule, the courts will usually not review the substance of a director's decision, even if it is a wrong or poor decision, but only review the process.[47]

In Delaware, the business judgment rule provides a presumption that in making a decision directors were informed, acted in good faith and honestly believed that the decision was in the best interests of the corporation.[48] The business judgment rule is both a procedural guide and a substantive rule of law. Procedurally, it is a rule of evidence placing the initial burden of proof on the plaintiff. If the plaintiff fails, then the business judgment rule protects the decision and the courts will not review the decision. If the rule is rebutted, under Delaware law the burden shifts to the defendant to prove "entire fairness" (i.e., fair dealing and fair price).[49]

---

[45] *See generally* Dennis J. Block, Nancy E. Barton & Stephen A. Radin, THE BUSINESS JUDGMENT RULE (1998). The rule protects the directors from personal liability and the courts from scrutinizing the decision. It has been suggested that the business judgment rule protects directors and the business judgment doctrine protects decisions, but generally both are subsumed under the business judgment rule.

[46] In *Shlensky v. Wrigley*, 237 N.E.2d 776 (Ill. 1968), the decision to protect neighborhood interests that could have hurt profits was allowed because it was viewed as matter of business policy which was untainted by fraud, illegality or self dealing. For a discussion of corporate governance and stakeholders see § 5.02[A] *supra.*

[47] There are some suggestions that the decision must also be rational. *See* A.L.I. Corp. Gov. Proj. § 4.01(c)(3) (directors must rationally believe the business judgment is in the best interest of the corporation). Arguably, a rationality standard allows a court to look at substance and second guess an irrational decision which undercuts the protection of the business judgment rule. But rationality is an easy enough standard to meet and it would be a rare case in which an informed process resulted in an irrational decision. Some would suggest that only the process should be scrutinized and never the substance of a decision. *See also In Re Caremark International Inc. Derivative Litigation*, note 96, *infra* (duty of care requires looking at good faith or rationality of process not the decision even if "stupid," "egregious" or "irrational"). The business judgment rule, however, does not protect a decision that is wasteful which may require at least some minimal substantive scrutiny. If waste is alleged, the court may determine if what was received in a transaction was so inadequate that no person of ordinary sound business judgment would deem it worth what was paid. For a discussion of waste, see § 9.04[C], *infra.*

[48] *Aronson v. Lewis*, 473 A.2d 805 (Del. 1984). The rule gives deference to the directors requiring greater evidence to overcome it. The ALI treats the rule as safe harbor and provides that a director or officer, when making a business judgment in good faith, fulfills her duty of care if there is no interest in the transaction, she is informed and she rationally believes that it is in the best interests of the corporation. A.L.I. Corp. Gov. Proj. § 4.01(c).

[49] *Cinerama, Inc. v. Technicolor, Inc.*, 663 A.2d 1156 (Del. 1995). *See* discussion of causation at § 8.03[D], *infra.*

As a result of the business judgment rule, the courts will defer to the directors' decision which will not be second guessed by the courts. The courts believe they do not have the expertise, and it is not their role to make business decisions. Directors must be able to make business decisions without fear of a lawsuit because shareholders want directors to make decisions and to take risks to produce gain even though mistakes may lose money. The idea of a court second guessing business decisions and then creating liability for directors could make directors overly cautious, resulting in reduced shareholder value.[50]

In *Kamin v. American Express Co.*,[51] the court found no liability for directors of American Express who decided to distribute to its shareholders as a dividend the shares of another corporation it owned. By distributing those shares (valued at $4 million), American Express avoided selling those shares at a loss because the current value had declined from the original purchase price. If American Express had decided to sell the shares instead of distributing them as a dividend to its shareholders, it would have had been able to take the loss on the sale as an offset against other taxable income. Thus by reducing taxable income, American Express would benefit by paying less taxes (a $8 million tax benefit). But its sale at a loss would have also reduced American Express' reported profits and the stock market could react to the loss by reducing its share price.

Plaintiffs argued in a derivative suit that the sale of the shares at a loss would be more beneficial than the dividend because it would result in lower taxes paid. They also suggested that some of the directors were concerned about the sale lowering the stock price, which could hurt their compensation, but those directors were in the minority. The court found no self-dealing and that dividend decisions are usually business decisions left to the board of directors' discretion. Even if the decision was imprudent or a mistake, it was not for the court to question because the judicial scrutiny in a breach of duty of care focuses on neglect of duty (malfeasance or nonfeasance) not the decision itself. Here the board was not negligent in its process of making its decision because it acted in an informed manner after consideration of the alternatives. In addition, the court took note of the fact that a majority of the directors who made the decision were outside directors without any conflicts of interest.

There are situations in which the business judgment rule does not apply. The plaintiff shareholder must overcome the presumption of the rule. The rule protects mistakes but not negligence in making a decision.[52] Thus, if plaintiff can prove malfeasance, the business judgment rule presumption is rebutted and does not protect the directors. Attacks on the substance of the decision are

[50] The rule arguably makes sense since shareholders undertake the risks of bad business judgments by buying shares as opposed to other less risky investments. In addition, after the fact litigation cannot replicate the situation that took place when the decision was made. Risk also has its rewards because of the possibility of greater profits. If shareholders want, they can reduce risk by diversifying their holdings. *Joy v. North*, 692 F.2d 880, 885-6. (2d Cir. 1982), *cert. denied sub. nom.*, *Cititrust v. Joy*, 460 U.S. 1051 (1983).

[51] 383 N.Y.S. 2d. 807, *aff'd*, 387 N.Y.S.2d 993 (1st Dept. 1976).

[52] The Delaware courts suggest that gross negligence is the standard used in determining whether a business judgment was an informed one. *See* note 32, *supra*.

difficult given the court's reluctance to look at substance. But the court will sometimes look at the substance if there are sufficient allegations that the business judgment rule is inapplicable. For example, if the decision had no business purpose, or was irrational[53] or created a no-win situation.[54] In addition actions that were ultra vires[55] or constituted waste are not protected.[56] The business judgment rule is also inapplicable if there is a duty of loyalty claim that a majority of the directors had a conflict of interest by being interested or lacking independence.[57] or a lack of good faith with actual intent to harm the corporation or an intentional dereliction of duty.[58] Furthermore, it does not protect nonfeasance like the *Francis* case or a prolonged failure to exercise supervision or a failure to act. Finally it is inapplicable if there was fraud, bad faith or illegality in the decision.[59] But once the business judgment rule is rebutted, there is still the issue of causation.

[C] Causation

The fact that a director breaches her duty and is negligent does not often end the inquiry, because traditionally, for there to be liability, the negligence must be the proximate cause of the loss. There needs to be a finding of causation in fact that the defendant's actions or omissions were a necessary antecedent of the loss. The plaintiff usually has the burden of proof and must show the amount of loss or damages caused by the negligence. Finding a link between negligence and damage is difficult, but it is particularly so in a case of nonfeasance where the director failed to act. In malfeasance, there are actual actions to relate to the losses,[60] while in nonfeasance one needs to prove that if the director had done her duty there would not be damage (that is causation in fact). Because there is no certainty what would have occurred if the fiduciary had acted differently, the issue is whether it is reasonable to conclude that the failure to act was a substantial factor in producing a particular result. Thus, courts faced with an allegation of nonfeasance would have to determine the reasonable steps a director would have taken and would it, as a matter of common sense, have averted the loss.

---

[53] *But see* note 47, *supra.*

[54] In *Litwin v. Allen*, 25 N.Y.S.2d. 667 (1940), directors of a bank had agreed to purchase securities with the option of the seller to buy it back after 6 months at a fixed price. The result according to the court was that bank was at risk if the securities declined in value but would not gain if they rose. The court viewed the transaction as so improvident and risky as contrary to prudent banking practices and left the bank in a no-win situation.

[55] For a discussion of ultra vires, see § 1.10, *supra.*

[56] If waste is alleged, the court may determine if what was received in a transaction was so inadequate that no person of ordinary sound business judgment would deem it worth what was paid. For a discussion of waste, see § 9.04[C], *infra.* Issues of compensation may raise duty of care and duty of loyalty issues. See § 9.04, *infra.*

[57] For discussion of independence, see § 5.02[F], *supra.*

[58] For a discussion of good faith, see § 8.06, *infra.*

[59] For a discussion of the duty to act lawfully, see § 8.08, *infra.*

[60] For example, in *Smith*, discussed at § 8.04, *infra*, the negligence of the directors in selling the corporation for $55 per share caused damage if the value of the corporation was greater than $55 per share.

In the *Francis* case,[61] Mrs. Pritchard was found to be negligent. But the plaintiff had to also prove that her negligence caused the harm and the extent of the damage. While her sons were responsible for the theft, her nonfeasance was a substantial factor in the loss. She was not monitoring them and according to the court "they spawned their fraud in the backwater of her neglect." Mrs. Pritchard could claim that even if she had done her duty and discovered the thefts, her protestations or resignation would not have stopped the thefts and therefore there was no causation. The court recognized that proof of causation was difficult yet found that it can still be inferred if the director's negligence (nonfeasance here) was a substantial factor in the loss. In *Francis*, the court believed that her resignation might have stopped the illegal loans but went even further, indicating that Mrs. Pritchard should have taken steps to stop the conversion, including hiring an attorney and threatening to sue. This expanded responsibility was related to the nature of the reinsurance business where funds are being held in a trust like situation and may not hold true in other closely held corporations. Thus, the extent of the duty imposed on directors will depend on factors including the nature of the business.

Although causation was found in *Francis*, its proof is difficult. In *Barnes v. Andrews*,[62] Judge Learned Hand found an outside director negligent for his inattention[63] but not liable for damages. Plaintiff had failed to show how the director's lack of performance would have avoided the loss and what actual loss would have been avoided. A business can fail for many reasons and thus, imposition of liability depends on proof of causation.[64] The decision also expressed the concern of attracting outside directors to serve if they were held liable without proof that their negligence caused harm.

The Delaware Supreme Court has taken a more limited view of who has the burden on causation in cases of malfeasance. If plaintiff can prove a breach of duty of care, in making a decision, there is a prima facie case of liability even without causation and a showing of injury. In *Cede v. Technicolor*,[65] the court indicated that requiring proof of injury by the plaintiff was unnecessary and undermined the business judgment rule that placed the initial burden on the

---

[61] See § 8.03[A], *supra.*

[62] 298 F.2d. 614 (S.D.N.Y. 1924).

[63] The director, a friend of the President, paid little attention to the business and attended only one of two meetings. At the time there were business problems that led to the demise of the business, including production delays and conflicts between personnel.

[64] The *Barnes* decision also appeared to suggest no liability for an inattentive director unless the board would have followed her lead. Since each director is only one member of the board, it may be difficult to connect her role to the losses. But that would allow a director an excuse for her lack of due care. Instead, if the board as a whole violated its duty of care and there is causation in fact, each director remains liable. *See* A.L.I. Corp. Gov. Proj. § 7.18(b), which provides that the plaintiff proves legal cause if (i) the breach was a substantial factor in the loss and (ii) likelihood of injury would have been foreseeable to an ordinary prudent person in like position of the defendant and in similar circumstances. The directors cannot avoid liability by pointing to others, claiming their conduct was less significant than others. It would not be a defense to liability if damage to the corporation would not have resulted but for the acts or omissions of others. *Id.*

[65] 634 A.2d 345 (Del. 1993). Whether the *Cede* standard in a malfeasance case applies in a case of failure to monitor or nonfeasance is not clear. In a nonfeasance case it would be difficult to prove fair dealing.

plaintiff to prove that the rule did not apply. If proof of injury were also required by the plaintiff before the burden shifted to the defendant, then the effect would be to replace the business judgment rule's use of a burden-shifting process to an adjudication of liability. The fact that the plaintiff has proven enough to rebut the business judgment rule does not mean the plaintiff has won. It merely shifts the burden and the defendants may still be able to prove entire fairness by presenting evidence of the cumulative manner in which she discharged her duties. Damages are determined after it is found that the transaction was not entirely fair.[66]

§ 8.04 THE *SMITH v. VAN GORKOM* CASE

A significant duty of care case decided by the Delaware Supreme Court was *Smith v. Van Gorkom*.[67] The facts are complex and will be described briefly. The company was profitable and had a market price of approximately $38 a share. The company had tried to figure out ways to raise the price of the stock but no action was taken. Mr. Van Gorkom, the Chairman of the Board and Chief Executive Officer who was close to retirement, decided to contact Mr. Pritzker, an investor known to be interested in purchasing companies. Van Gorkom did so without consulting the board of directors or other officers. He met with Pritzker who agreed to offer to buy the company for $55 a share. Van Gorkom had suggested the price to Pritzker. This price was almost 40% higher than the current market price and the stock highest price in the previous 5 years was $39.50. Although there was some opposition to the offer from some of the officers, Van Gorkom called a meeting of the board of directors. They had no prior notice of the Pritzker offer. The board of directors had 5 outside directors, who were unaffiliated with the company, and 5 directors who were employees of the company. Van Gorkom presented the offer. After a two hour meeting, the board voted to accept the offer and to present it to the shareholders for a vote. They received limited advice from the financial officers of the company and no opinion from any investment banker that the price was fair. The board had the impression that under the merger agreement they could accept a higher offer from another bidder which could compete with the Pritzker offer (the "market test"). The directors never read the merger documents in this initial approval of the deal to determine if there was a market test.

The Delaware Supreme Court concluded that the directors breached their duty of care at this meeting on the initial approval and were not protected by the

---

[66] In *Cinerama, Inc. v. Technicolor, Inc.*, 663 A.2d 1156 (Del. 1995), the directors had previously been found to have violated their duty of care and were grossly negligent in not having a market check on the value of the corporation when it was sold. That finding of gross negligence did not create liability, but rebutted the presumption of the business judgment rule. The directors had to prove entire fairness, i.e., fair dealing and fair price in the sale. Fair dealing looks at the process and fair price at economic and financial factors. The test is not bifurcated, so all aspects of fairness must be examined. Since the majority directors were disinterested and not dominated by an interested director or shareholder, the entire actual conduct in discharging its duties was relevant to meeting its fair dealing and fair price obligations. Here, the directors were able to prove entire fairness weighing other conduct by the directors, and the price obtained was the highest reasonably available. *Id.* For discussion of entire fairness in freezeouts, see § 10.03, *infra*.

[67] 488 A.2d 858 (Del. 1985).

business judgment rule. The court used the concept of gross negligence as "the proper standard for determining whether a business judgment reached by the board of directors was an informed one."[68] The directors were grossly negligent in being uninformed on the intrinsic value of the company or Van Gorkom's role in forcing the sale and establishing the price and approving the sale after 2 hours without prior notice or reason to act so swiftly.

The directors claimed that they were not grossly negligent for several reasons. First, there was the magnitude of the premium offered over the market price. Second, the merger contract allowed a market test so that another offer could be made for the corporation. Third, the board had extensive experience and knowledge about the business. Fourth, the board had relied on counsel's advice that failure to accept the offer would result in shareholder litigation for failure to accept it.

That there was a substantial premium ($55 versus around $38 market price) did not excuse the directors because they had no other information on the value of the company. A premium over the stock market price without other valuation information was insufficient to judge a fair price. This was especially true when the directors knew the stock price was undervalued. In addition, reliance on the stock price may not be appropriate because the price of the shares in the stock market values trading in individual shares and not the value of the corporation as a whole.[69] The court indicated that the use of an investment banker and a fairness opinion was not required so long as the directors have sufficient information. Given the decision, the directors would now be foolish not to consult with investment bankers when selling the company.

The court also found no real market test was provided for in the initial agreement because there was no evidence the agreement provided for such a test or that a test was permitted to occur. The written merger agreement was not even produced. The lack of valuation inquiry and market test undermined the directors' claim of experience and sophistication to overcome their negligence in approving the sale. The directors also claimed that the corporate attorney warned them that failure to accept the offer would result in shareholder litigation for breaching their duty to benefit the shareholders. But that advice was not legal advice that entitled the directors to make an uninformed decision on the sale of the corporation. Thus, the directors breached their duty of care in the initial meeting approving the sale by being uninformed and acting too hastily. Their decision was not protected by the business judgment rule because of the faulty decision making process.

The directors also claimed that subsequent events after the initial approval of the sale cured their breach of the duty of care. After some opposition was raised

---

[68] While the Delaware Supreme Court appeared to use a gross negligence standard there is some uncertainty over the use of gross negligence in all duty of care cases or just when the focus is on the business judgment rule. Thus, ordinary negligence may be the test on cases involving nonfeasance. *See* note 34, *supra.*

[69] The court rejected the idea that the stock market price will reflect the value of the corporation as a whole, which some law and economics commentators have advocated. For discussion of the efficient market theory, see § 5.02[D], *supra.*

among senior management to the initial agreement, there were changes in the merger agreement that were approved by the board at a second board meeting. The amended agreement now allowed solicitation of competing offers, i.e., a market test. But now, in order to avoid the Pritzker agreement, there had to be either a consummated sale or a definitive contract with greater consideration than Pritzker's offer, not just a better offer. In addition, the time frame was narrowed for the competing bid. It appeared that the board did not understand these restrictions when they approved the amended agreement and thus were uninformed again about the market test. The actual problems that occurred when other possible bidders appeared (Van Gorkom was also hostile to these bids) indicated that the contract restrictions were inconsistent with the board's concept of a free market test. Thus, there was no cure of the directors' initial breach of the duty of care by these subsequent actions.

The directors also tried to rely on the fact that approximately 70% of the shares approved of the merger and only 7.25% voted against it. The court found that a shareholder vote to ratify a transaction required full disclosure.[70] The burden to prove full disclosure is on the directors, and here the shareholders did not know what happened in the directors' meeting or subsequently. Thus, the case was remanded to determine the fair value of the shares based upon the intrinsic value.[71]

Smith was a controversial decision with 3 of the 7 judges dissenting (a rare occurrence in Delaware). The dissent criticized the majority because the shareholders were receiving a high price and the directors were experienced and knew a great deal about their company. The dissent suggested that if the directors had not accepted the offer, the shareholders could have sued them for breach of fiduciary duty. The majority decision emphasized that the selling of a company is the most important decision the board could make and thus required an informed decision. None of the directors inquired about the fairness of the price.

§ 8.05 THE DEMISE OF THE DUTY OF CARE

Plaintiffs bringing duty of care cases are rarely successful. Generally, they have to prove some form of negligence and in some cases causation. If the case involved allegations of malfeasance then the business judgment rule will limit the judicial inquiry into the decision making process and not the substance of the decision. In addition, the directors are sometimes permitted to prevent the litigation from going forward if a plaintiff is required to first make a demand to the board and a majority of disinterested directors conclude that the litigation is not in the best interests of the corporation.[72]

---

[70] For a discussion of shareholder ratification, see § 9.06, *infra*.

[71] The case was settled with an additional payment to the shareholders of over $23 million. If the case had been decided by the trial court it would have looked at entire fairness after finding a breach of the duty of care. *See Cede & Co. v. Technicolor, Inc.*, 634 A.2d 345 (Del. 1993). *See* note 66, *supra*.

[72] For a discussion of the demand refused requirement, see § 14.05[B], *infra*.

[A] Delaware General Corporation Law § 102(b)(7)

The aftermath of the *Smith* case further limited the viability of the duty of care case. The business community was upset by the case. They saw directors (including independent directors) being liable even though they had arranged for the sale of the corporation for a substantial premium over the market price. One could isolate the *Smith* case as rare because the directors had acted quickly on the most important decision to be made (the sale of the business) without advice. But Delaware was also concerned that the corporations incorporated in the State would fear the ruling and reincorporate elsewhere.[73] This prompted the state legislature to enact a new provision, § 102(b)(7), to its corporate statute that allows Delaware corporations to amend their certificate of incorporation to eliminate monetary damages for duty of care cases.[74] Now companies whose shareholders amend the articles of incorporation can effectively eliminate most duty of care cases.[75]

With the enactment of § 102(b)(7), plaintiffs needed to find ways to avoid it by limiting its application. Without the possibility of damages, plaintiffs attorneys would be less willing to bring duty of care cases since their fees may be paid from those damages.[76] Since damages for both duty of loyalty[77] and acts or omissions not in good faith[78] are explicitly excluded from the statutory limitation on damages, plaintiffs would try to allege either to avoid the limitation on damages.[79] Intentional ignorance or willful blindness to problems may be sufficient to show a conscious disregard of fiduciary duty and thus bad faith.[80] If the complaint properly states breach of the duty of loyalty or bad faith, the claim will not be barred by the article's provision limiting damages. But if the complaint fails to allege well pleaded facts to support those actions and all that is left is a duty of care claim for damages then the lawsuit will be dismissed.[81]

---

[73] For a discussion of Delaware's dominance as the state where most publicly traded corporations incorporate, see § 1.08[A], *supra*. After *Smith*, premiums on directors and officers liability insurance (D & O) increased adding to the pressure for a response.

[74] Del. Gen. Corp. L. § 102 (b)(7). *See also* Model Bus. Corp. Act Ann. § 2.02(b)(4) (4th ed. 2008).

[75] Even if the articles have a provision to eliminate damages, one can still bring an action for equitable relief such as an injunction and duty of loyalty and bad faith cases are unaffected by most of these statutes.

[76] For a discussion of attorney fees in shareholder litigation, see § 14.08[B], *infra*.

[77] For a discussion of duty of loyalty, see Chapter 9, *infra*.

[78] For a discussion of good faith, see § 8.06, *infra*.

[79] Claims under the duty of disclosure (*see* § 8.07, *supra*) and the modified business judgment rule in hostile takeovers (see § 12.05[A][2], *infra*) will usually come under the exclusion of damages under § 102(b)(7). *McMillan v. Intercargo Corp.*, 768 A.2d 492 (Del.Ch. 2000). *See also Zirn v. VLI Corp.*, 621 A.2d 1050 (Del. 1996) (no bad faith and loyalty claim in a duty of disclosure breach, so § 102(b)(7) applied). But knowingly witholding information may implicate the duty of loyalty. *Johnson v. Shapiro*, 2002 Del. Ch. LEXIS 122 (2002).

[80] *McCall v. Scott*, 239 F.3d 808, *modified*, 250 F.3d 997 (6th Cir. 2001) (interpreting Delaware law). *See also In re The Walt Disney Company Derivative Litigation*, discussed in § 8.03[C][1], *supra* (bad faith was alleged with sufficiency to suggest neither protection of the business judgment rule or a § 102(b)(7) provision).

[81] *Malpiede v Townson*, 780 A.2d 1075 (Del. 2001).

But once passed the pleading stage the use of a § 102(b)(7) provision becomes an affirmative defense where defendants bear the burden of establishing the protection of the statute.[82]

The ability of corporations to amend their articles is an example of the law-in-economics view of corporate law as primarily contractual in nature. Here the statute permits the majority of shareholders to change the legal rules they find unnecessary. This may be beneficial in eliminating unnecessary litigation, attracting directors and preferring other monitoring devices. At the same time, it is a strange situation when a fiduciary may commit gross negligence in Delaware and not be liable for damages.[83] Most states have passed similar legislation to protect directors and most public companies have placed this provision in their articles.[84]

§ 8.06   GOOD FAITH

Plaintiffs have tried to avoid the limitation on damages in a duty of care case as a result of exculpatory provisions from statutes like Delaware's Section 102 (b)(7) by arguing that the defendants did not act in good faith. The Delaware courts had indicated that in order to rebut the business judgment rule, plaintiffs must provide evidence that the decision breached one of the "triad of fiduciary duties, loyalty, good faith or due care."[85] What remained unclear was how good faith differed from the duty of care or loyalty and whether good faith was itself an independent fiduciary duty. Two Delaware Supreme Court cases discussed below (the *Disney* and *Stone* cases) clarified those issues. Lack of good faith is now clearly a duty of loyalty violation.

---

[82] *Emerald Partners v. Berlin*, 726 A.2d 1215 (Del. 1999). In *Emerald Partners v. Berlin (II)*, 787 A.2d. 85 (Del. 2001), the Delaware Supreme Court indicated that whenever entire fairness is at issue, the court must first determine if there was unfairness before determining if the directors are exculpated from liability under § 102(b)(7). Entire fairness can involve the duty of loyalty in conflicts of interest and in duty of care if the plaintiffs can prove that there was no business judgement rule protection. *See* § 8.03[C], *supra.* But if the court does not find a lack of entire fairness and the liability is based only upon a duty of care claim, then under the § 102(b)(7) provision in the certificate there will be no monetary damage.

[83] Arguably, if the provision was a problem for shareholders they would not approve the amendment. But in publicly traded corporations there is the collective action problem in voting. For a discussion of shareholder passivity, see § 5.05[C][4], *supra.* Over 90% of a sample of Delaware corporations passed these amendments. Roberta Romano, *Corporate Governance in the Aftermath of the Insurance Crisis*, 39 EMORY L.J. 1155 (1990).

[84] Other states passed related statutes to decrease duty of care liability. *E.g.*, Ohio Gen. Corp. L. § 1701.59 (requires plaintiff to prove liability with clear and convincing evidence and proof of scienter by the defendant's conduct). States also changed their indemnity provisions making it easier for directors to be indemnified. *See, e.g.*, N.Y.B.C.L. § 721 (one can contract with the corporation for greater indemnification rights than the statute provides so long as the acts were not in bad faith or the result of active and deliberate dishonesty. For a discussion of indemnity, see § 14.11, *infra.*

[85] *Cede & Co v. Technicolor Inc.*, 634 A.2d 345, 361 (1993).

[A] *Disney* Litigation and Good Faith

The *Disney* litigation involved Walt Disney ("Disney") and the lucrative employment contract and severance for Michael Ovitz. The case dealt with the issues of good faith and the business judgment rule.[86] Ovitz received approximately $130 million in compensation and severance after serving only fourteen months as President. The deal was orchestrated by his friend, Disney's Chief Executive Officer, Michael Eisner. The first complaint filed had been dismissed earlier for failure to sufficiently allege particularized facts supporting the cause of action and was affirmed by the Delaware Supreme Court.[87] The plaintiffs then used their right to inspect the books and records of Disney to gather more information for litigation and to have more particularized facts for a complaint.[88] and a new complaint was filed and was not dismissed.

In the subsequent trial[89] it turned out that Ovitz and Eisner were unable to manage Disney together and the hiring was problematic from the start. Plaintiffs attacked the large of amount of the compensation for such a short tenure claiming a breach of fiduciary duty of care, good faith and waste.[90] Approximately $92 million of the $130 million was the result of stock options Ovitz was able to keep so long as his termination was not for cause. This was a case of malfeasance. The court found that the process failed to meet best practice standards, where the documentation should have indicated that the compensation committee of the board understood the potential compensation under different scenarios including the magnitude of the severance package for termination without cause. But the court found that there was sufficient evidence to find that they acted in an informed manner and thus no violation of the duty of care.

Plaintiffs also argued that the directors had acted in bad faith. The Delaware Supreme Court affirmed the lower court decision and the view that bad faith needed to be more then acting without information and inadequate deliberation which was essentially a due care analysis,[91] The court held that good faith was distinguishable from duty of care and would require more proof than a duty of

---

[86] For a discussion of executive compensation, see § 9.04, *infra.*

[87] *Brehm v. Eisner,* 746 A.2d 244 (Del. 2000). The Supreme Court seemed troubled by the case but pointed out that dismissal was based on the need to allege violations of standards of liability which are not the same as ideal corporate governance practices to which directors should aspire. In *McMullin v. Beran,* 765 A.2d 910 (Del. 2000), the court indicated that a motion to dismiss required a two step analysis. First, take the facts alleged as true with all inferences in a light most favorable to plaintiff. Second, determine with reasonable certainty under any set of facts if proven the plaintiff would succeed in rebutting the presumption of the business judgment rule.

[88] For a discussion of shareholder right to information, see § 5.05[F], *supra.*

[89] *In re the Walt Disney Company Derivative Litigation* 907 A.2d 693 (Del. Ch. 2005). The court found no breach of fiduciary duty notwithstanding the fact that the board did not follow best practices. The court indicated that aspirational ideals do not equate with what is required under fiduciary duty.

[90] Waste was not found because it is very difficult to prove and happens in the rare case where he directors irrationally give away assets. For a discussion of waste, see §. 9.04[C], *infra.*

[91] *Brehm v. Eisner (In re the Walt Disney Company Derivative Litigation),* 906 A.2d 27 (Del Sup 2006).

care violation. The court found support for that idea from the fact that the legislature in Section 102 (b)(7) allowed for exculpation for duty of care damages but made an exception for actions not in good faith.[92] Thus to get damages for a lack of good faith, would require more than a duty of care violation. Since there was no lack of due care in *Disney* there could not be a lack of good faith.

Notwithstanding the lack of good faith in *Disney*, the Delaware Supreme Court decided to discuss good faith in order to clarify its parameters and show how it differed from the duty of care and gross negligence. According to the court a lack of good faith would include conduct motivated by subjective bad intent and by an actual intent to harm the corporation. In addition, an intentional dereliction of duty and a conscious disregard for one's responsibilities would also constitute a lack of good faith because it shows more culpability (a malevolent intent) than the gross negligence of duty of care. The Delaware Supreme Court cited with approval the trial court's examples of lack of good faith. They were: 1. an intentional act in not advancing the corporation's best interest; 2. an intent to violate positive law; 3. intentionally failing to act in face of a duty to act i.e., a conscious disregard of duty. What the Delaware Supreme Court did not clarify was whether good faith was an independent theory of fiduciary duty liability.

[B] *Stone v. Ritter* and the Duty to Monitor

The issue of liability for failure to monitor raised by the *Francis*[93] case takes on significance in large enterprises where board's policy is implemented by officers and employees. In the Delaware case of *Graham v. Allis-Chalmers Mfg. Co.*,[94] the directors failed to prevent antitrust violations by employees. Plaintiffs claimed that the directors should have known about the liability and that they had a duty to implement compliance with the law, especially since the corporation had agreed to a consent order 20 years earlier to not violate the antitrust laws. The Delaware Supreme Court found no duty of care liability and in broad language indicated that unless they had reasons to suspect the existence of a violation, directors have no obligation to install a system of monitoring or reporting (that is, a duty of inquiry). They are entitled to rely on the honesty and integrity of the employees. This was especially true given the large size of the corporation.

The modern view is that directors should implement procedures and programs to assist in their monitoring role.[95] Over the years, courts have recognized the importance of the role directors play and their duty to keep themselves informed. Since the *Graham* case, there has also been expanded criminal liability of corporations under federal statutes. Federal sentencing

---

[92] The court also found support for distinguishing lack of good faith from duty of care claims in Del. Corp. Code § 145 which does not allow indemnification for bad faith but will allow it for a breach of duty of care.

[93] For discussion of *Francis*, see § 8.03[A], *supra.*

[94] 188 A.2d 125 (Del. 1963).

[95] A.L.I. Corp. Gov. Proj. § 4.01 comment. For a discussion of the duty to monitor and the issue of good faith, see § 8.06[B], *infra.*

guidelines have provided for lesser sentences to corporations that have implemented compliance programs. Thus directors do have some responsibility to implement appropriate reporting or monitoring systems.

The Delaware Chancery Court decision *In Re Caremark International, Inc. Derivative Litigation*[96] recognized the trend and viewed the *Graham* case more narrowly. In *Caremark*, the corporation had paid $250 million in fines and damages because the employees had violated the law applicable to the health care industry. A derivative suit was brought against the directors for breach of their duty of care by a failure to monitor the employees. The case involved an approval of the settlement of the suit by the court. In reviewing the fairness of the settlement, the court looked to the viability of the claims. Even though huge civil and criminal penalties were imposed on the corporation, the court found no breach of the duty of care. There was no evidence of lack of good faith in monitoring or a knowing violation of the law. But contrary to the broad reading of *Graham*, the court found that directors have a responsibility to assure that an adequate system exists for receiving corporate information and reporting, including compliance with relevant statutes and regulations. Thus, even if there is no reason to suspect a lack of compliance, some monitoring system must be in place in order to satisfy the obligation that directors need to be informed for both legal compliance and decision making. According to the court, directors would be liable if there is a sustained or systematic failure to exercise oversight sufficient to indicate a lack of good faith (for example, if there was ignorance of liability and an utter failure to attempt to assure a reasonable information and reporting system exists). But the court indicated that this test of liability is high because a demanding test of liability is necessary to attract outside directors while still providing a stimulus to good faith performance. Further, the level of detail appropriate for the system is itself a question of business judgment. Again the court did not clarify whether good faith was distinct fiduciary duty.

In *Stone v Ritter*[97] the Delaware Supreme Court was faced with a *Caremark* type claim of a failure to monitor and the issue of good faith. The case concerned a bank which failed to file reports aimed at possible money laundering and was subject to $40 million in fines and $10 million in civil penalties. No fines or penalties were imposed on the directors. The regulators had concluded that the compliance program in place was "materially deficient". As part of the bank's deferred prosecution agreement with the government, they hired a consultant (KPMG) to review the bank' compliance program and to make recommendations for changes.

Because the litigation was a derivative suit (i.e., shareholders are bringing an action on behalf of their corporation which alleged a breach of fiduciary duty that essentially harms the corporation), the plaintiff shareholders are required to make demand on the board of directors prior to filing the cause of action. Plaintiffs tried to avoid the demand requirement which could end their litigation by claiming that such a demand on directors who are accused of the fiduciary

---

[96] 698 A.2d 959 (Del. Ch. 1996).

[97] 911 A.2d 362 (Del. Sup. 2006).

duty breach should be excused as futile.[98] The plaintiffs were required to allege with particularity that the directors were incapable of handling the litigation. There was also a § 102(b)(7) exculpation of duty of care damages in the bank's certificate of incorporation, so plaintiffs seeking damages needed to allege conduct that would not be covered by duty care such as a failure to act in good faith in order to excuse the demand. Given the allegations were a failure to exercise oversight, the court adopted *Caremark's* view of *Graham* and that oversight responsibility was an issue of good faith. The court also reiterated the *Disney* examples of the failure to act in good faith as: 1. an intentional act in not advancing the corporation's best interest; 2. an intent to violate positive law;[99] or 3. intentionally failing to act in face of a duty to act i.e., a conscious disregard of their duty.[100] All of these examples require some form of intent or scienter.[101]

Both *Caremark* and *Stone* dealt with the third example which implicates oversight liability. This can involve either an utter failure to implement a reporting system or a system was created but the directors consciously failed to monitor or oversea it thus limiting their ability to be informed. Either situation requires the directors knowing of the failure to act when there was a duty to act, i.e., a conscious disregard. In *Stone* the bank was accused of the second failure because there was system in place. But there was no allegation of "red flags" raising awareness that the system was inadequate and would result in illegal activity because the board did nothing. While the illegal activity was harmful to the bank and the result of inadequate internal controls, the fact that there were substantial fines does not alone establish bad faith. Directors cannot be held liable just because employees have done something wrong There needs to be a sustained or systematic failure to exercise oversight such as an utter failure to attempt to assure a reasonable information and reporting system exists, The court quoted Caremark's concern that this test needed to be high in order to attract the kind of directors needed to monitor and protect the corporation. Given the KPMG report of a system in place *ex ante* was reasonable, the failures

---

[98] Under Delaware law demand is excused when the allegations raise a reasonable doubt that either the majority of the board was disinterested and independent or the transaction could have been an exercise if business judgment. For a discussion of the demand requirement and futility in derivative litigation, see § 14.05, *infra*.

[99] To what if any extent will the court look at this issue from a cost/benefit analysis and will it make distinctions between different violations of law remains unclear. For example is there a lack of good faith in a conscious decision to illegally park because parking tickets cost less than the cost of late delivery. *See* Stephen M. Bainbridge, Star Lopez & Benjamin Oklan, *The Convergence of Good Faith and Oversight* 55 UCLA L. Rev. 559 (2008) (argues that maybe the distinction should be between *malum prohibitum* laws and *malum in se* where the former violate a statute and not natural law.) *But see Desimone v. Barrows* 924 A.2d 908, 935 (Del. Ch. 2007) ("directors have no authority knowingly to cause the corporation to become a rogue, exposing the corporation to penalties from criminal and civil regulators. Delaware corporate law has long been clear on this rather obvious notion, namely, that it is utterly inconsistent with one's duty of fidelity to the corporation to consciously cause the corporation to act unlawfully").

[100] The court leaves open the possibility of other examples of a failure to act in good faith.

[101] It remains unclear how if the courts will define culpability as actual intent or reckless disregard sufficient? In *Disney* the Supreme Court mentioned in its footnote 111 prior case law indicating a lack of good faith included "reckless indifference". 906 A.2d 27,110. For a discussion of scienter in the context of federal securities law, see § 13.02[E], *infra*.

and resultant large fines do not equate with bad faith and the court should not second guess *ex post*.

Stone also indicated that the failure to act in good faith does not itself impose liability but does so because good faith is "a subsidiary element, i.e., a condition of the fundamental duty of loyalty." Thus good faith is not an independent fiduciary duty but the lack of good faith means that the directors are not acting in the best interest of the company and they are breaching their duty of loyalty.[102]

It is unclear how significant *Stone* and its notion of good faith will be. Proving good faith will be difficult since it must be conduct motivated by subjective bad intent and with an actual intent to harm the corporation or an intentional dereliction of duty and a conscious disregard for one's responsibilities.[103] The enactment of the Sarbanes-Oxley Act of 2002 in the wake of corporate scandals has tried to enhance monitoring by directors and a firm's internal controls to avoid illegal activities.[104] The increased federal regulations aimed at publicly traded corporations plus the fears of criminal prosecution and liability will probably be the main impetus for directors to monitor.

The lack of good faith also has a role to play in corporations with controlling shareholders.[105] In a post *Stone* case, the Delaware Chancery Court, in *ATR-Kim Eng Fin. Corp. v. Araneta*,[106] found liability for directors of a closely held corporation who allowed the controlling shareholder to basically self deal by transferring assets unfairly and impoverishing the company. While the controlling shareholder breached his duty of loyalty, the other directors who were not self dealing but who did nothing were found to be liable. The court described them as "stooges" with these directors having no regard for their obligations as directors. They consciously acted as a tool for the controlling shareholder as opposed to trying to make decisions for the best interests of the corporation. According to the court, directors in order to act loyally (i.e., in good faith) must make a genuine good faith effort to do their job and assure an adequate information and reporting system exists. Here there were no systems nor were there any board meetings. The directors did nothing to make

---

[102] Traditionally the duty of loyalty involved conflicts of interest where there is some form of self dealing by the fiduciary. By making good faith part of the duty loyalty it remains unclear what aspects of traditional duty of loyalty will apply to a claim of lack of good faith. *Stone* seems to keep the burden of proof on the plaintiff unlike traditional duty of loyalty and does not seem inclined to adopt the traditional fairness test. While loyalty usually meant more judicial scrutiny, the high burden of proving lack of good faith actually means less scrutiny. But loyalty may permit the court to fashion "broad, discretionary and equitable remedies." *Gotham Partners. L.P. v Hollywood Realty Partners L.P.*, 817 A.2d 160, 175 (Del. 2002) For a discussion of duty of loyalty in conflicts of interest transactions see § 9.03, *infra*.

[103] Lack of good faith has been raised in cases involving changes in stock option plans which created favorable treatment for the recipients. *See* discussion § 9.04[B], *infra*.

[104] For example, management is required to be responsible for and assess its internal controls. For a discussion of Sarbanes-Oxley, see § 5.08, *supra*.

[105] For a discussion of controlling shareholders see Chapter 10.

[106] 2006 Del. Ch. LEXIS 215 (Dec. 21, 2006).

themselves aware of the problem or try to stop it.[107] Even though they themselves did not self deal they were found to consciously breach their fiduciary duty and were held jointly liable.

§ 8.07   DUTY OF DISCLOSURE

While disclosure has always been an important aspect of fiduciary duty. The obligation usually comes up in the context of a request for shareholder action like voting on an issue.[108] In addition the primary objective of federal securities law is full disclosure not only aimed at shareholder actions but the needs of the stock markets. It was thought that federal securities laws and not state law would be the law which governed dissemination of information to the markets. But the Delaware Supreme Court in *Malone v. Brincat*[109] indicated that the directors have a fiduciary duty to communicate honestly with the shareholders in all communications. The court held that "directors who knowingly disseminate false information that results in corporate injury or damage to an individual stock- holder violate their fiduciary duty, and may be held accountable in a manner appropriate to the circumstances." This obligation is not limited to situations where the directors are seeking shareholder action, such as a vote, but applies to all communications including dissemination of information even through SEC filings. The court indicated that it will not replicate causes of actions permitted under federal securities laws, but there was still a role to play such as in the facts of the case which involved no shareholder voting.[110] Thus there may be a derivative claim or a cause of action for damages[111] or equitable relief under

---

[107] It is unclear from the case why the court focused on the good faith issue when the nonfeasance raised a duty of care issue and there does not seem to be a § 102(b)(7) exculpation provision limiting duty of care damages. It is possible that loyalty allowed the court to shift attorney fees on the defendant. This case of nonfeasance seems similar to the *Francis* case discussed at § 8.03[A], *supra.*

[108] State statutes do not usually require full disclosure but the courts have established disclosure rules through fiduciary duty. In actions involving lack of disclosure in this context plaintiffs must show materiality but may not be required to prove reliance, causation or actual damages. *See generally* Lawrence Hammermesh, *Calling Off the Lynch Mob: A Corporate Director's Fiduciary Disclosure Duty*, 49 VAND. L. REV. 1087 (1996).

[109] 722 A.2d 5 (Del. 1998). The directors of the publicly traded corporation for several years were accused in a class action of knowingly and intentionally misleading the shareholders in public filing with the SEC and communications to the shareholders and as a direct result the corporation lost its value. In addition their accountants were accused of aiding and abetting the breach.

[110] There are times when the federal securities rules will not apply to a private lawsuit when there is a lack of disclosure. For example in *Brincat*, the shareholders were not purchasers or sellers and would not have a claim under SEC Rule 10b-5. See § 13.02[B], *infra.*

[111] Damages may be difficult to prove in these circumstances. In addition, monetary damages can be eliminated if the breach of duty of disclosure is a violation of the duty of care and damages exculpation was provided for in the certificate of incorporation under Del. Gen. Corp. Law § 102(b)(7). In *Malone* the court refers to the violation as potentially involving duty of care, good faith and loyalty. To get damages it would need to involve lack of good faith or loyalty. See § 8.05[A], *supra.* In *Loudon v. Archer-Daniels-Midland*, 700 A.2d 135 (Del. 1997), there were claims of lack of disclosure in a case involving action by the shareholders and the election of directors. The Delaware Supreme Court indicated that the duty of disclosure means shareholders should have all material information reasonably available when they act. Liability will depend on the nature of the action and the nondisclosure. There was no *per se* rule of damages unless a deprivation of the shareholder's

238 INTRODUCTION TO FIDUCIARY DUTY CH. 8

state law based upon the breach of the disclosure duty.[112]

In order to provide full disclosure, especially when a shareholder vote is requested, the directors are required to provide disclosure of material facts. According to *Malone* they must "provide a balanced, truthful account of all matters disclosed in the communication with the shareholders."[113] Materiality requires disclosure of all facts that under the circumstances would have assumed actual significance to a reasonable shareholder which is similar to the standard used in federal securities laws.[114]

§ 8.08 DUTY TO ACT LAWFULLY

Directors are also required to act in a lawful manner.[115] Delaware seems to suggest that a failure to act lawfully implicate a lack of good faith and the duty of loyalty[116] but other states may view it as an independent duty. In *Miller v. American Telephone and Telegraph Co.*,[117] the directors were sued by shareholders for their breach of the duty of care in failing to collect a debt from the Democratic National Committee. While generally an issue of debt collection should be a business decision protected by the business judgment rule, the lack of action could have been viewed as a contribution which violated federal criminal law. Since the allegations involved illegal activity, public policy required that the business judgment rule not protect the decision even if the activities were beneficial to the corporation. The court did look at the purpose of the criminal statute when deciding that there was no business judgment rule protection. The particular criminal statute in the case was designed to limit corporate influence and protect shareholders, which further supported the breach of fiduciary duty claim.

The case was allowed to go forward on whether there was in fact an illegal contribution made under the statute. The court placed the burden on the shareholder plaintiffs to establish the elements that will comprise a violation of

---

economic interest or impairment of voting rights are implicated. Injunctive relief or corrective disclosure may be the appropriate remedy.

[112] But a class action would be difficult under *Malone* if reliance had to be proved for each plaintiff since Delaware has rejected the fraud on the market theory, which presumes reliance. For a discussion of fraud on the market, see § 13.02[G], *infra*. Even though Congress preempted many claims brought under state law involving false and misleading statements, there are two important exceptions — if the claim was derivative in nature and where state courts had previously recognized such an action under fiduciary duty ("Delaware carve-outs"). *See* Securities Litigation Uniform Standards Act of 1998 § 16(d)(1)(a).

[113] *Malone*, 722 A.2d at 10.

[114] *Arnold v. Society Bancorp.*, 650 A.2d 1270 (Del. 1994). The court quotes the *Northway* case where the Supreme Court articulated a materiality test for proxy violations. For a discussion of materiality and federal securities law, see § 7.06[E], *infra*.

[115] In some situations the directors or officers may be criminally liable when the statute specifically holds them responsible or when for policy reasons they are responsible parties for the act of the corporation's agents.

[116] An intent to violate positive law will violate the duty of loyalty because it is a lack of good faith. For a discussion of good faith, see § 8.06, *supra*.

[117] 507 F.2d 759 (3d Cir. 1974) (interpreting New York law).

the statute. As part of that proof the plaintiff must show that there were not legitimate business justifications for failure to collect the debt.

Chapter 9

THE DUTY OF LOYALTY AND CONFLICTS OF INTEREST

§ 9.01 INTRODUCTION

As discussed in Chapter 8, if one does not act in good faith, it can implicate the duty of loyalty.[1] The duty of loyalty requires a fiduciary to act in the best interests of the corporation.[2] Traditionally, the duty of loyalty was raised when the fiduciary (or those associated with him or her) had a conflict of interest with the corporation, suggesting that personal interests may be advanced over corporate interests.[3] Conflicts of interest usually involve some form of self-dealing where the fiduciary is on both sides of a transaction and in a position to receive a benefit unavailable to other shareholders or the corporation generally.[4] Generally, when the duty of loyalty in a conflict of interest applies, there is a duty of complete candor; the burden of proof shifts to the directors; and, there is greater judicial scrutiny of both the fairness of the process and the substance of the transaction (sometimes described as entire fairness). In addition, under a duty of loyalty analysis, the defendants are not afforded the protection of the business judgment rule with its presumption of a proper decision.[5] Thus, a plaintiff will often try to characterize the activity of a defendant as a breach of the duty of loyalty in order to take advantage of greater judicial scrutiny.[6]

---

[1] For a discussion of good faith, see § 8.06, *supra*.

[2] This objective has not been defined with any precision. Such an interest is largely congruent to, but not always identical to, shareholders' best interests. A violation of fiduciary duty may be raised when the directors appear to be acting for interests other than the shareholders. For a discussion of the *Ford* and *Shlensky* cases and the focus of corporate governance and stakeholder interests other than shareholders, see § 5.02[A], *supra*. A director who is not independent and is acting under the domination of the interested director will not be acting in the corporation's best interest. For a discussion of independent directors, see § 5.02[F], *supra*.

[3] Some have suggested the increased institutional shareholder involvement should mean that fiduciary duties apply to them and that self-interested shareholder activism should similarly trigger shareholder loyalty duties. Iman Anabtawi & Lynn Stout, *Fiduciary Duties for Activist Shareholders*, 60 STAN. L. REV. 1255 (2008).

[4] *Aronson v. Lewis*, 473 A.2d 805 (Del. 1984). Self interest may also occur when a corporate decision will have a materially detrimental impact on a director but not on other shareholders or the corporation. *Rales v. Blasband*, 634 A.2d 927 (Del. 1993). The ALI has adopted rules for directors, officers and controlling shareholders when they act with an interest in a matter affecting the corporation. Since the courts have used duty of loyalty in both pecuniary and non-pecuniary conflict of interest contexts, the ALI used the term "duty of fair dealing" in the pecuniary context. *See* A.L.I. Corp. Gov. Proj. Part V (Introductory Note).

[5] For a discussion of the business judgment rule, see § 8.03[B], *supra*.

[6] For a discussion of duty of care and loyalty, see § 8.01[A], *supra*.

As will be discussed in this Chapter, the context in which the conflict of interest arises can affect the level of judicial scrutiny. Self-dealing that may involve controlling shareholders will be dealt with at Chapter 10, while possible conflicts of interest in tender offers will be dealt with in Chapter 12. Insider trading also raises an issue of conflict of interest and discussed in Chapter 13.

§ 9.02 POLICY

The duty of loyalty is different from the duty of care in that it seeks to prevent directors from acting against the best interests of the corporation or self dealing in such a way as to reap a personal benefit unavailable to other shareholders. The duty of care, on the other hand, involves poor decision making or lack of attention, but no personal benefit. Self-dealing raises the specter of corruption and personal profit at the expense of shareholders. When personal benefits are at stake, a director's incentives and motivation for a transaction change. For example, the person who is self-dealing seeks to avoid disclosure and detection. Therefore, self-dealing may be difficult to detect. While self-dealing transactions are sometimes beneficial to the corporation, it may also have no real business purpose other than to provide personal benefits at the expense of the sharehold-ers.[7] Even the "law and economics" approach to corporate law, which prefers to rely on market forces instead of a litigation system to influence corporate behavior, recognizes that markets may be unable to effectively restrain this form of opportunism.[8] For example, managers may use their power for a one time significant personal benefit that far exceeds the penalty of the markets.[9] Thus, the fiduciary duty rules on the duty of loyalty are stricter than other rules, such as the duty of care, and may not be appropriate for allowing the parties to modify the legal rules through amendments to the articles of incorporation.[10]

There is a strong moral basis for imposition of fiduciary responsibility in loyalty situations and some cases reflect this attitude. The traditional view is that fiduciary duty means that the fiduciary is responsible for someone else and should consider the other person's interest over their own. A line in the New Testament is sometimes quoted in duty of loyalty cases: "No servant can serve two masters: for either he will hate the one and love the other; or else he will hold to the one, and despise the other."[11] Another often quoted opinion, *Meinhard v. Salmon*, by Judge Cardozo reflected this view:

---

[7] *See* Alison Anderson, *Conflicts of Interest: Efficiency, Fairness and Corporate Structure*, 25 UCLA L. Rev. 737 (1975).

[8] For a discussion of the law and economics approach and fiduciary duty, see § 8.02[A], *supra.*

[9] For example, if there is a market for managers that provides employment, managers will do their best so that they can move to other employment for better positions and compensation. If they self-deal, they hurt their marketability. But if the value of the self-dealing exceeds their market value, they will self-deal and the market will not constrain them. *See, e.g.,* Henry N. Butler, *The Contractual Theory of the Corporation*, 11 Geo. Mason L. Rev. 99 (Summer 1989).

[10] When many state legislatures allowed the articles of incorporation to provide for no monetary damages in duty of care cases they exempted duty of loyalty cases from the rule. For a discussion of these statutes, see § 8.05[A], *supra.* For a discussion of the contractual approach to the fiduciary duty, see § 5.03[C][3], *supra.*

[11] Luke 16:12 (King James).

Many forms of conduct permissible in a workaday world for those acting at arm's length, are forbidden to those bound by fiduciary ties. A trustee is held to something stricter than the morals of the market place. Not honesty alone, but the punctilio of an honor the most sensitive, is then the standard of behavior. As to this there has developed a tradition that is unbending and inveterate. Uncompromising rigidity has been the attitude of the courts of equity when petitioned to undermine the rule of undivided loyalty by the 'disintegrating erosion' of particular exceptions [citation omitted]. Only thus has the level of conduct for fiduciaries kept at a level higher than that trodden by the crowd. It will not consciously be lowered by any judgment of this court.[12]

Because duty of loyalty cases raise issues of self-dealing in a variety of transactions and corporations, fiduciary duty rules tend to differ. In many cases, process issues may be significant in setting those rules. The procedural issues will look at disclosure and the approval process by either disinterested directors or shareholders. Courts will need to decide the extent to which process will be a substitute for substantive issues of fairness.

§ 9.03   INTERESTED DIRECTOR TRANSACTIONS

The classic duty of loyalty defendant is a fiduciary[13] (a director or officer or in some cases controlling shareholders) who contracts or transacts unfairly with her own corporation,[14] receiving a benefit that is not equally shared with the

---

[12] 249 NY 458, 464 (1928). The case involved a partnership where Salmon, the partner who managed the real estate venture, took for himself the opportunity to enter into another venture that involved extending and expanding the venture when it expired. Salmon was contacted by the real estate owner and did not know that Meinhard was a silent partner. Even though the partnership was for a limited time and purpose (that is, a joint venture) and arguably the duty should not have extended beyond the joint venture, the court found that Salmon should have at least disclosed the extension to the other partner, Meinhard allowing him to compete. The court awarded Meinhard a 49% interest in the new corporate venture. Although he was a 50% owner of the joint venture, Salmon was the managing partner of the prior venture and was thus given control of the new one with a 51% interest. Although fiduciary duty in partnerships are often greater than in corporations (one reason is the unlimited liability among partners) this quote can be frequently found in corporate cases. It is usually a signal that the fiduciary is in trouble.

[13] The contract may be with close associates of the fiduciary such as relatives. The law is mindful of the ingenuity of contracting parties and will treat such associates as if they were fiduciaries. *See, e.g.*, A.L.I. Corp. Gov. Proj. § 5.08 (the fiduciary fails to meet her duty of fair dealing if she knowingly advances the pecuniary interest of an associate in a manner that would fail to comply with the rules if the fiduciary had acted for herself). Under § 1.03, "associate" is broadly defined. *But see* note 59, *infra* (MBCA limits associates).

[14] In *Bayer v. Beran*, 49 N.Y.S. 2d 2 (Sup.Ct. 1944), the corporation contracted for advertising on a radio show where the wife of the president and director of the company would benefit by performing. The plaintiffs asserted a conflict of interest claiming that was the motivation for the contract. The court found that the decision to advertise appeared to have been reasonable and would normally have business judgment rule type protection but the issue of the wife's participation raised a duty of loyalty issue and thus subject to closer scrutiny. Notwithstanding the fact that the directors appeared to not know of the wife's participation until they approved of the advertising and the informal process of approval (no formal meeting or resolution), the court concluded no breach of duty. While the wife may have gained from the program her compensation was fair, i.e., what other singers would have been paid, and there was no evidence that it was designed to promote her. In terms of

other shareholders and thereby creating a conflict of interest. There are a variety of circumstances in which such self-dealing can occur.[15] For example, an officer or director may sell personal property to the corporation or buy corporate property. A conflict of interest would also arise where a fiduciary's corporation contracts with another corporation or business entity in which the fiduciary has a significant financial interest. For example, Corporation A sells property to Corporation B and a director of A is the controlling shareholder of B. Another example is when a parent corporation contracts with its subsidiaries (that it controls) and the subsidiary has other shareholders.[16] There may also be conflicts of interest when two corporations have common directors (also called "interlocking directors") but they have no significant financial interest in either.[17] These transactions (which will be called "interested director transactions") can involve a variety of exchanges such as loans to or from the corporation or purchases and sales of property or services.

Early courts adopted a prophylactic rule and often found such transactions void to remove any temptation to overreach. The courts feared that the fiduciary would take advantage of the corporation and recognized that other directors could be influenced by the self-interested director. Although the director could, in theory, avoid participation in any corporate decisions under which she stood to gain a personal benefit, the courts reasoned that this would deny the corporation the benefit of all of its directors' judgments and so would constitute only a different type of harm to the corporation. Although a void rule had advantages for being easy to administer, such a rule also had disadvantages. In fact, such interested contracts could be very valuable to a corporation. For example, the services, property or funds of the director may be necessary to expand or continue the corporation's operations. In addition, as publicly traded corporations developed, there was increasing use of outside directors who would serve on several boards and those corporations contracted with each other (that is interlocking directors). Courts recognized that contracting between companies with common directors could be advantageous to both companies and their shareholders. In addition such contracting could be a common occurrence such as the contracting between a parent corporation and its subsidiaries.

In recognition of changed corporate practices, the courts moved from a void standard to a voidable standard.[18] Under this approach, the courts generally

---

the process, the court accepted the fact that this particular board acted informally on a regular basis and the corporation was successful so the lack of formality was not an issue. For a discussion of the formality of board process, see § 5.06[B][1], *infra.*

[15] *See* Robert Clark, CORPORATE LAW 159 (1985).

[16] For a discussion of conflicts in that setting, see § 10.02[B], *infra.*

[17] In this context, there is less concern about the conflict of interest if the common director has no large financial interest in one corporation and was not actively involved in the negotiations. *Cf.* A.L.I. Corp. Gov. Proj. § 5.07 (if two contracting corporations have only common directors or senior executives, it does not implicate the loyalty rules if they did not participate in the negotiations or cast the necessary vote to approve it).

[18] *See* Harold Marsh Jr., *Are Directors Trustees-Conflicts of Interest and Corporate Morality*, 22 BUS. LAW. 35 (1966). *But see* Norwood P. Beveridge, *The Corporate Director's Fiduciary Duty of Loyalty: Understanding the Self-Interested Director Transaction*, 41 DEPAUL L. REV. 655 (1992) (different view of the history finding contracts were voidable not void).

focused on the fairness of the process of approval and the substance of the transaction.[19] The process often would require full disclosure and approval by either disinterested directors or shareholders.[20] The contract itself would need to be fair and the burden of proof would generally be placed on the fiduciary.[21] If self dealing is found the usual remedy are restitutionary in nature with recisiion of the unfair contract or seeking the gains made by the fiduciary. But loyalty claims also allows the court to fashion "broad, discretionary and equitable remedies."[22] This general approach to interested director transactions (as well as other conflicts of interests) varied depending upon the circumstances and the availability of a relevant statutory provision. Thus, a variety of rules existed. In approaching the cases and the statutory provisions dealing with interested director transactions, three issues should be kept in mind. First, what are the legal procedural requirements in terms of voting, quorum and disclosure? Second, how does compliance with those requirements affect the level of judicial scrutiny applied to the transaction (business judgment rule, fairness, waste or some other test) or the burden of proof? Third, if there is a failure in the procedure, does that void the contract or have some other effect, such as increasing the level of judicial scrutiny or shifting the burden of proof?

[A] Common Law

In an early common law case, Judge Cardozo established a high standard for interested director transactions. In *Globe Woolen Co. v. Utica Gas & Electric Co.*,[23] Utica Gas had a contract to supply energy to Globe Woolen's textile mills. Utica Gas and Globe Woolen had a common director named Maynard. He was the mills' chief shareholder and the chairman of the executive committee of the utility (he had 1 share in the utility). The contract to provide electricity to the mills had a guarantee of savings that proved to be very expensive for the utility

---

[19] For a critique of the fairness test as a weak check on self-dealing, *see* Lawrence E. Mitchell, *Fairness and Trust in Corporate Law*, 1993 Duke L.J. 425.

[20] In some cases, the mere voting or attendance by the interested fiduciary could invalidate the contract. *See, e.g., Teft v. Schaefer*, 239 P.2d 837 (Wash. 1925).

[21] *See generally* Ahmed Bulbulia & Arthur R. Pinto, *Statutory Responses to Interested Directors' Transactions: A Watering Down of Fiduciary Standards?*, 53 Notre Dame L. Rev. 201 (1977). In *Lewis v. S.L. & E. Inc.*, 629 F2d 764 (2d Cir 1980), the court placed the burden of proof on the defendants to prove fairness under New York law in a derivative suit brought on an alleged unfair lease contract. There were two family owned corporations consisting of LGT, which ran a tire dealership, and SLE, which owned the property where the dealership was located. After the father, who founded both corporations, distributed the shares among his children, some of the children owned LGT while all owned SLE. The lease between the companies had set a rent which over time was not raised to reflect higher costs thus harming SLE. There was a shareholders' agreement that required that the shareholders of SLE sell their shares for book value to LGT. The plaintiffs claimed that because the rent was unfair SLE did not receive a fair rental, which had the effect of lowering the book value. Because the defendants did not prove the rental was fair (i.e., an arms length bargain price by looking at comparable rentals), the plaintiffs were not required to sell their shares without an adjustment to reflect a fair rental value. The defendants unsuccessfully argued that LGT could not afford a higher rent. Whether the result would have been different if defendants could have proven that the father had wanted SLE to act on LGT's behalf and to subsidize is unclear.

[22] *Gotham Partners. L.P. v Hollywood Realty Partners L.P.*, 817 A.2d 160,175 (Del. 2002).

[23] 224 N.Y. 483, 121 N.E. 378 (1918).

because there was a miscalculation based upon the projected future use of electricity. While Maynard negotiated for the mills, his subordinate represented the utility. The directors of the utility approved the contract knowing that Maynard had a conflicting interest, but Maynard remained silent and did not vote.

The court voided the contract. Maynard's abstention from the vote gave the contract a presumption of propriety but did not excuse Maynard of his responsibility. Maynard had a dominating influence[24] which meant that he had a duty to warn, that is, provide full disclosure of both his interest and the details of the contract itself.[25] The court went further, however, holding that disclosure alone was insufficient because the contract must also be fair. Here, the idea of fairness was that the contract have "some reasonable proportion between the benefits and burdens," that is, equivalent to an arm's-length bargain.[26]

Cases generally follow the view that the process of approval and the terms of the transaction itself must be fair, with the burden of proof on the fiduciary. This rule protects shareholders from exploitation and permits flexibility in corporate dealings.[27] In determining substantive fairness, courts look to factors such as the value of what is received; the market value; the value of the bargain compared to what it could have obtained from others; the need for the property; the ability to finance the transaction; the existence of a detriment; the quality of the disclosure; and the possibility of corporate gains being siphoned off by the directors.[28] Some cases suggest that lack of disclosure itself is a grounds for voiding a contract without regard to its fairness.[29] But even a fair contract in terms of disclosure and its terms the contract must be in the best interests of the corporation.

---

[24] Domination of the directors by the party to the transaction can also affect the independence of the other directors. Under Model Bus. Corp. Act Ann. § 8.62(d) (4th ed. 2008), a person would not be considered qualified to vote if she has a familial, financial, professional or employment relationship with an interested director which would reasonably be expected to exert an influence on her. For a discussion of how the MBCA deals with these transactions, see § 9.03[B][3][b], infra. For a discussion of independent directors, see § 5.02[F], supra.

[25] In Talbot v. James, 190 S.E.2d 759 (S.C. 1972), even though James acted as the building contractor and received no more than what similar contractors would have received (i.e., fair price), the contract was voidable for failure to disclose (i.e., unfair dealing).

[26] There is language in the opinion that suggests that the contract could be tested on its fairness, not only at its formation, but also in its performance. Generally, courts look at the time of formation.

[27] In Shlensky v. South Parkway Building Corp., 19 Ill. 2d 268 166 N.E.2d 793 (1960), the court rejected placing the burden on the plaintiff because it would further separate corporate management from the shareholders and encourage "sharp practices" by directors.

[28] Id. Substantive fairness can accommodate a range of results and is not solely measured by the best or highest price. Since fairness may not always be easy to ascertain, the procedural context can be important in the judicial review. See also Victor Brudney, Contract Law and Fiduciary Duty in Corporate Law, 38 B.C. L. Rev. 595 (1997) (comparing contract concepts with duty of loyalty and fairness concepts).

[29] State ex rel. Hayes Oyster Co. v. Keypoint Oyster Co., 391 P.2d 979 (Wash. 1964). In Talbot v. James, 190 S.E.2d 759 (1972), the court not only voided the contract for lack of disclosure but required the fiduciary to return corporate funds received, which included not only his profit but normal overhead expenses attributed to the work done by the defendant. See also A.L.I. Corp. Gov. Proj. § 5.02 (contract voidable for failure to disclose).

[B]   Statutory Responses

Many states have enacted statutory provisions that deal with interested director transactions ("interested director statutes"). Many of these statutes do not codify the duty of loyalty, but provide mechanisms that may create presumptions or deal with the burden of proof or act as safe harbors that limit or preclude any judicial review.

California was the first state to enact a statutory provision that dealt with interested director transactions. Accordingly, the California statute became a model for other states ("the California model") and provided, in effect, that such a transaction would not be void solely because of a conflict of interest, or the voting and presence of an interested director, if:

1. the transaction was approved by the disinterested directors with disclosure of the conflicting interest; or

2. disclosure was followed by shareholder approval; or

3. the contract was just and reasonable at the time of approval (i.e., fair).[30]

The statute also dealt with procedural issues by allowing the interested director to be part of the quorum and indicating that a vote of the disinterested directors was needed for board approval.

The statute used the disjunctive "or" between the different requirements, which suggested that one needed only one of these requirements to validate the contract. Thus, if either the disinterested board[31] or majority of shareholders approved of the transaction then the contract need not be fair. Alternatively, if the contract was fair, there was no need for either disinterested board or shareholder approval.[32] Thus this interpretation of the California statute, and similar interested director statutes would look at process or substance. This

---

[30] Civil Code § 311 (1931) replaced in 1947 by § 820 of the Corporations Code. For a discussion of the current § 310 of the California Corporations Code, see § 9.03[B][2][b], *infra*.

[31] The concept of disinterested directors is important. The idea is that approval of the transaction requires a neutral decision making body. Aside for those who are actually contracting, there is generally no *per se* rule even for family members and business associates but whether it was reasonably expected that those directors exercise of independent judgment would be compromised. *Shapiro v. Greenfield*, 764 A.2d 270 (Md. 2000). Generally, a director must be both disinterested and independent. For a discussion of these concepts, see § 5.02[F], *supra*. A.L.I. Corp. Gov. Proj. § 1.23 indicates that interest goes beyond directors or officers as parties to the transaction. Associates (broadly defined in A.L.I. Corp. Gov. Proj. § 1.03) of the director or officer who are parties to a transaction can create an interest. Interest also includes parties or persons with a material pecuniary interest to the transaction who have familial, business and financial relationships with the directors which would reasonably be expected to affect the director's judgment in a manner adverse to the corporation. Directors could also be interested if subject to a controlling influence which could reasonably be expected to affect their judgment in a manner adverse to the corporation. For a discussion of the MBCA requirements, see § 9.03[B][3][b], *infra*.

[32] It is interesting to note that while many of the statutes do not explicitly require approval by a majority of disinterested shareholders, the courts will require such approval under the theory that the vote served as a ratification of the transaction which usually requires disinterested shareholder voting. For a discussion of shareholder ratification, see § 9.06, *infra*. In addition, the good faith requirement of the statute could be read to require disinterested shareholder approval.

view represents a dramatic change from the common law that looked at both process and substance for fairness.

The primary issue of compliance with the interested director statutes is the effect on judicial scrutiny on the transaction when approved by disinterested directors. If the common law is retained, a fairness inquiry allows a court to look at both the process and substance with the burden of proof on the defendant. Another view is that compliance with the interested director statute retains a fairness inquiry but shifts the burden of proof to the plaintiff. Yet another possibility is that statutory compliance means that the business judgment rule applies, with the burden of proof on the plaintiff to prove that the rule should not apply and with courts generally looking only at the process. These are the three primary approaches to reconciling the implications of compliance with interested director statute with the common law doctrine. They can be described as weak form, semi-strong form, and strong form statutes.

A weak form view of the statute is that compliance with the interested director statute was not intended to change the common law, which places the burden of proof on the fiduciary and requires fairness in process and substance.[33] This would mean that the statutes only removed the taint of the conflict of interest or dealt with procedural issues, and like the common law, transactions were still voidable, as opposed to void. Close judicial scrutiny should still be required.[34]

A semi-strong view of the interested director statute is that compliance with disinterested board approval shifts the burden of proof to the plaintiff. Under this view, fairness would always remain an issue when the disinterested directors approve the transaction (that is, no business judgment rule protection). With a fairness inquiry the court can look at process and substance. The rationale for retaining a fairness inquiry, rather than the business judgment rule rests on the possible influence the interested director could have on the other disinterested directors and the difficulty of detecting the effects of that influence on the judgments of the disinterested directors. The collegial atmosphere of the board could preclude close scrutiny by the disinterested directors. In addition, disinterested directors who do not have a pecuniary interest in the transaction could have other relationships or connections that would not automatically disqualify the director but could raise an issue of impartiality. The continued use of a fairness test allows the court the flexibility to ensure that the process of approval and substance was fair.

---

[33] *Id.* In *Scott v. Multi-Amp Corp.*, 386 F. Supp. 44 (D. N.J. 1974), the court viewed compliance with New Jersey's interested director statute as retaining a fairness standard with the burden of proof remaining on the defendant. The only effect of the vote would have been to change defendant's burden of proof from a clear and convincing evidence standard to a preponderance of evidence. The court also required compliance of all three statutory requirements (board approval, shareholder approval and fairness) notwithstanding the disjunctive nature of the statute.

[34] *See* Ahmed Bulbulia & Arthur R. Pinto, *Statutory Responses to Interested Directors' Transactions: A Watering Down of Fiduciary Standards?*, 53 NOTRE DAME L. REV. 201 (1977), (suggesting that the statutes were designed to deal with procedural fairness issues and not substantive fairness).

A strong form view of the interested director statute is that approval of the disinterested board would generally limit judicial scrutiny. Disinterested board approval not only shifts the burden of proof to the plaintiff, but removes a fairness inquiry. There still must be full disclosure, but the decisions of the disinterested directors are now protected by the business judgment rule (i.e., no substantive review), which must be rebutted.[35] The rationale for the use of the business judgment rule is that the disinterested directors act for the corporation's best interests and therefore, a lessened scrutiny is in order.

In terms of disinterested shareholder approval under the interested director statutes, the general view is that with full disclosure such approval should validate the transaction and limit judicial scrutiny to the issue of whether the transaction amounted to waste.[36] As a result, scrutiny would be rare because the plaintiff must prove that value of what was received in the transaction was so inadequate that no reasonable person would deem it worth what the corporation was paid (i.e., no real consideration).[37] But the interested director has the burden of proof on whether there was full disclosure to the shareholders when voting. The rationale for such limited scrutiny is that courts should generally not review decisions made by disinterested shareholders which ratify the transaction.[38] A majority of disinterested shareholders are less likely to be tainted by the interested director than disinterested directors who may be independent under the law but still influenced by the interested director since they serve on the board together.[39] If the transaction is with controlling shareholders, then the Delaware courts will scrutinize the transaction under a fairness test even when there is a majority of the minority shareholder ratification of the transaction.[40]

[1]   Weak Form Approach

In *Remillard Brick Co. v. Remillard Dandini Co.*,[41] the California Supreme Court determined the effect of its statute at the time. The majority shareholders of a closely held manufacturing corporation arranged for a contract with their wholly owned sales company. The contract had the effect of removing the sales function from the manufacturing corporation. The majority shareholder claimed that the contract was validated since there was full disclosure of the conflict of

---

[35] For a discussion of the business judgment rule, see § 8.03[B], *supra*.

[36] In New York there is case law that suggests shareholder approval shifts the burden of proof and retains a fairness review. *See* note 47, *infra*.

[37] But see *Harbor Finance Partners v. Huizenga*, 751 A.2d 879 (Del. Ch. 1999) (where the court suggests that disinterested shareholder approval with full disclosure should preclude judicial scrutiny and waste should no longer be used in this context), discussed in text at notes 113–16, *infra*. For a discussion of waste, see § 9.04[C], *infra*.

[38] For a discussion of shareholder ratification, see § 9.06, *infra*.

[39] The semi-strong form view of the statutes would only shift the burden of proof and retain a fairness review if the transaction was approved by the disinterested directors. The strong form would use the business judgment rule if there was disinterested directors approval.

[40] For a discussion of shareholder ratification and controlling shareholders, see § 10.03[C][2][a][ii], *infra*.

[41] 214 P.2d 66 (Cal. 1952). The statute was essentially the California model.

interest and the shareholders (that is, the majority shareholders with the conflict of interest) had approved of the contract pursuant to the statute. The statute did not explicitly require disinterested shareholder approval. The court did not view literal compliance with the statute as precluding a fairness inquiry. The court seemed to suggest that the purpose of the statute was only to remove the taint of the involvement of the interested director in approval (that is, the idea that involvement by the interested director voided the transaction). The common law rule of fairness remained, with the burden of proof on the interested director.

In *Cookies Food Products, Inc. v. Lakes Warehouse Distributing, Inc.*,[42] the Iowa court took an approach similar to *Remillard*. Herrig, a director and controlling shareholder of a closely held food company, had a contract for the exclusive distribution and storage of the company's products. Herrig also received compensation from a royalty agreement for a product he developed and as a consultant for work done on behalf of the corporation. The corporation had become very successful through his efforts. Nevertheless, the minority shareholders challenged these contracts as interested director transactions and a violation of his duty of loyalty.[43] The Iowa statute was similar to other disjunctive statutes, such as the California model which seemingly validates interested director contracts based upon full disclosure and either shareholder or board approval. But the court viewed the Iowa statute as merely removing the taint of the conflict of interest. The court essentially followed the common law approach by requiring that such contracts be fair, with the burden of proof on the fiduciary. Thus, even with statutory compliance, the burden of proof remained on Herrig to prove that the contract was fair. The majority of the court found that he had met the burden and the contracts were valid.[44]

[2] Semi-Strong Approach

A more common view is that statutory compliance with disinterested director approval shifts the burden of proof from the defendant to the plaintiff but retains a fairness test. Generally, under this approach, the fairness of the transaction will remain a consideration (that is, courts can view both the procedure and the substance) if the approval is by the disinterested directors.[45]

---

[42] 430 N.W.2d 447 (Iowa 1988).

[43] It appeared that although the corporation was doing well, no dividends were paid. The minority shareholders were not receiving a present return on their investment and that may have been a reason to bring the action and pressure the controlling shareholder. There are times when not paying a dividend could violate the fiduciary duty of the majority to the minority, but this was not such a case. For a discussion of the oppression of minority shareholders by the majority in closely held corporations, see § 11.07[G], *infra.*

[44] There was a strong dissent which agreed with the legal analysis of the effect of the statute, but felt that Herrig had not proven fairness. The dissent accused the majority of focusing on the success of the business rather than the issue of whether the contracts were equivalent to arm's-length bargain contracts, i.e., fair.

[45] A.L.I. Corp. Gov. Proj. § 5.02 has focused on the approval process to distinguish the extent of judicial inquiry. First, lack of disclosure itself is a ground for voiding the contract. Second, if there is disclosure but no disinterested directors' or shareholders' approval, then the common law rule applies and fairness remains an issue with the burden of proof on the fiduciary. Third, if there is

If the disinterested shareholders approve of the transaction, however, a waste[46] test will often apply instead of a general inquiry into the underlying fairness of the transaction, making it more difficult for the plaintiff to prove a breach of the duty of loyalty.

[a]   The New York Approach

Some state statutes have attempted to elucidate the effect of either shareholder or disinterested director approval. For example, section 713(b) of the New York Business Corporation Law clearly indicates that failure to get either shareholder or board approval pursuant to the statute means that the fiduciary has the burden of proof on the fairness of the transaction. Unfortunately, the statute is not explicit on what happens if there is either board or shareholder approval although courts suggest that compliance with the statute (particularly disinterested board approval) merely shifts the burden, without precluding a further inquiry into fairness.[47]

[b]   The Current California Approach

Section 310(a) of California General Corporation Law appears to validate the contract if approved in good faith by the disinterested shareholders.[48] By contrast, under the statute, approval by the disinterested directors only shifts the burden to the plaintiff and retains a fairness test. Lack of either disinterested board or shareholder approval like the common law places the burden on the defendant to prove the contract is just and reasonable (that is, fair). If the contract involves a transaction in which there are only interlocking common directors on both sides and there is no material financial interest in either corporation, than either disinterested board or shareholder approval removes a fairness inquiry under section 310(b).

---

disinterested shareholder approval, the contract must amount to corporate waste in order to be voided, with the burden of proof resting on the plaintiff. Fourth, if there is disinterested director approval, the burden is on the plaintiff to show the directors could not have reasonably concluded that the transaction was fair to the corporation (a sort of hybrid fairness test somewhere between the business judgment rule and traditional fairness allowing for some scrutiny of the substance).

[46] Approval by a majority of disinterested shareholders is less likely to be tainted or influenced by the interested director than disinterested directors who serve together on the board with the interested director. For a discussion of the waste test, see § 9.04[C], *infra*. Some courts suggest that even with disinterested shareholder approval, fairness remains an issue, especially if controlling shareholders are involved. For a discussion of shareholder ratification and controlling shareholders, see § 10.03[C][2][a][ii], *infra*.

[47] *See Cohen v. Ayers*, 596 F.2d. 733 (7th Cir. 1979) (suggesting that compliance with the New York statute shifted the burden but retained a fairness inquiry). *But see Aronoff v. Albanese*, 85 A.2d. 3 (N.Y. 1982) (finding that under New York's statute (NYBCL § 713) shareholder ratification shifts the burden of proof and limits the judicial inquiry of the substance unless the plaintiff can prove waste).

[48] Arguably, the statute would validate a wasteful transaction, upon disinterested shareholder approval, unless the good faith requirement would preclude that result. In *Harbor Finance Partners* (discussed at § 9.04[C][1], *infra*), the court felt if highly unlikely that disinterested shareholders would approve a wasteful transaction.

[3]   Strong Form Approach

The strong form approach precludes or severely limits judicial inquiry if there has been statutory compliance, including independent directors approval.

[a]   Delaware Approach

Delaware has an interested director statute similar to the California model, but in addition to disclosure of the conflict of interest, it requires disclosure about the transaction itself. The Delaware courts' application of the statute, however, has been somewhat confusing. In *Fleigler v. Lawrence*,[49] the Delaware Supreme Court faced a situation similar to the one in *Remillard* because there was shareholder approval of the conflict of interest transaction by the majority shareholders with the conflict of interest. The transaction was an option agreement that allowed the corporation to acquire the stock of another corporation controlled by common directors and officers. The defendants argued that shareholder ratification, under the Delaware General Corporation Code section 144 (the interested director statute), had shifted the burden of proof to the plaintiff. The court rejected the argument because there was no ratification by a disinterested majority of shareholders.[50] The court was, therefore, unwilling to read the statute as precluding a judicial inquiry as to fairness, at least in that context. According to the court, the statute "merely removes an 'interested directors' cloud when its terms are met and provides against invalidation of an agreement 'solely' because such director or officer is involved. Nothing in the statute sanctions unfairness . . . or removes the transaction from judicial scrutiny." The case seems to follow a weak form approach in line with other cases, such as *Remillard*, and *Cookies* that allowed fairness to remain an issue even with statutory compliance.

Later, however, in *Marciano v. Nakash*,[51] the Delaware Supreme Court seemed to suggest a different approach. It followed *Fleigler* by indicating that compliance with Delaware General Corporation Code section 144 removed the taint of the conflict of interest. The failure to secure either disinterested directors' or shareholders' approval under the statute did not void the contract as long as it was fair as required by the common law. But the court, in dictum, indicated that compliance with the statute (by either disinterested shareholder or board approval) not only shifted the burden to the plaintiff but also afforded the defendants the protection of the business judgment rule, thus precluding a fairness inquiry and essentially endorsing a strong form approach.[52] In order to overcome the business judgment rule, the plaintiff must attack the process of

---

[49] 361 A.2d 218 (Del. 1976).

[50] The statute has no requirement of disinterested shareholder approval, but it can be read into the statute, either because the statute requires good faith approval or because, by analogy, a shareholder vote is like a ratification of the interested transaction, which would require a disinterested vote. For a discussion of shareholder ratification, see § 9.06[B], *infra*.

[51] 535 A.2d 400 (Del. 1987). The ownership of the corporation was split evenly between two family groups which meant the transaction could not be approved by either a majority of independent directors or shareholders.

[52] 535 A.2d 400, 405n.3 (Del. 1987). *See also Oberly v. Kirby*, 592 A.2d 445 (Del. 1991) (under § 144, a transaction will be sheltered from challenge if approved by independent directors or shareholders).

approval (lack of fair dealing), or the disinterested directors really were not independent,[53] or the decision itself was on grounds not protected by the business judgment rule such as waste.[54] Finally in *Benihana of Tokyo, Inc. v. Benihana, Inc*[55] the Delaware Supreme Court clarified that compliance with disinterested director approval meant that the business judgment rule applied and thus Delaware seems to have adopted the strong form approach to interested director transactions. But if the conflict of interest transaction is with a controlling shareholder, Delaware seems to take a semi strong approach where the courts shift the burden but retain a fairness standard with either disinterested board approval[56] or shareholder ratification.[57]

[b]   The MBCA Approach

Subchapter F of the Model Business Corporation Act (called "Directors' Conflicting Interest Transactions") has tried to clarify the effect of statutory compliance on interested director's transactions. The statute takes a strong form view by limiting judicial scrutiny of fairness if there is either disinterested board or shareholder approval.[58] First, a contract involving a "conflicting interest" will not be voidable if approved by disinterested shareholders or directors or if the interested director proves fairness.[59] In terms of the approval

---

[53] For a discussion of independent directors, see § 5.02[F], *supra.*

[54] For a discussion of other grounds to attack the business judgment rule, see § 8.03[B], *supra.*

[55] 906 A.2d 114 (Del. 2006). Benihana Inc was in need of financing to modernize its restaurants. Its investment advisor, Fred Joseph of Morgan Joseph & Co, developed different financing options. He recommended financing with a convertible preferred share sale (could convert it to common shares which could dilute existing shareholders). Abdo, a board member who had access to Joseph's plans, contacted Joseph and negotiated a financing transaction using convertible preferred on behalf of BFC which was 30% owned by Abdo. The board was presented with the transaction with BFC. Because the transaction could dilute the ownership (upon conversion of the preferred to common) of Aoki the company founder and his family, Aoki objected and wanted other financing pursued. A committee of independent directors reviewed other proposals and concluded that the BFC was better. Plaintiffs claimed a failure to comply with § 144 (a)(1) because the board did not know of Abdo's involvement, but that was not the case because they were informed. The fact the Abdo had confidential information as a board member about the financing was not important because there was no evidence it was used to favor Abdo. There was give and take in the negotiations, Benihana succeeded in getting much of what it wanted, and Abdo did not set the terms, deceive the board, nor dominate it. Even though the result was to dilute the voting power of one group, the action was not taken for the primary purpose of entrenchment.

[56] For a discussion of independent committee of the board approval in control transactions, see § 10.03[C][2][a][i], *infra.*

[57] For a discussion of shareholder ratification in control transactions, see § 10.03[C][2][a][ii], *infra.*

[58] In terms of contracts with controlling shareholders or parent corporations and their subsidiaries, Subchapter F does not apply and should be decided under the duty of controlling shareholders established by case law. *See* Official Comment.

[59] Model Bus. Corp. Act Ann. § 8.61(b) (4th ed. 2008). Unlike the ALI approach (*see* note 41, *supra*), the statute seems to validate a fair transaction under MBCA § 8.61(b)(3) even if there is a lack of full disclosure. Model Bus. Corp. Act Ann. § 8.61(b)(3) (4th ed. 2008). But the Official Comment suggests that the behavior of the director (including disclosure) could affect the inquiry on fairness, suggesting fairness is relevant to both substance and process.

of disinterested directors (called "qualified directors"),[60] their approval must comply with the standards of conduct requiring good faith and acting in the best interests of the corporation; and if so, there is no fairness inquiry.[61] The MBCA also uses a bright line test to determine which transactions are covered by the statute[62] and only those transactions are subject to review under the statute.[63]

§ 9.04 EXECUTIVE COMPENSATION

Compensation paid to executives and directors may raise both duty of care and duty of loyalty issues.[64] More recently, executive compensation in publicly traded corporations has also raised public policy issues given the large amounts.[65] Compensation policy is generally established within the ordinary course of business, in order to retain and reward those who manage the business. Proper form and amounts of compensation can align the interests of the managers with those of the shareholders by encouraging maximization of

---

[60] Under MBCA § 8.61(d), a qualified director means a person who has no conflicting interest in the transaction and has no familial, financial, professional or employment relationship with the interested director that reasonably could be expected to exert influence on him or her. Model Bus. Corp. Act Ann. § 8.61(d) (4th ed. 2008).

[61] Model Bus. Corp. Act Ann. § 8.30(a) (4th ed. 2008).

[62] Under MBCA § 8.60(1), conflicting transactions include directors who are a party to the transaction or when a related person to the director has a beneficial financial interest in or closely linked to the transaction and it is of such financial significance that the interest would reasonably be expected to exert an influence of the director's judgment if she was to vote on it. Model Bus. Corp. Act Ann. § 8.60(1) (4th ed. 2008). Related persons are limited to immediate family members. Model Bus. Corp. Act Ann. § 8.60(3) (4th ed. 2008).

[63] Only transactions covered by the definitions of MBCA § 8.60 are covered and if a transaction does not come within those definitions then a court is precluded from viewing it as a conflict of interest transaction under the statute. Model Bus. Corp. Act Ann. §§ 8.60 & 8.61(a) (4th ed. 2008). For example, if the corporation enters into a transaction with a cousin (even a kissing cousin) of a director, there is no conflicting interest transaction, since a cousin is not covered under the "bright line" test of related persons under MBCA § 8.60(3). Model Bus. Corp. Act Ann. § 8.60(3) (4th ed. 2008). The ALI approach (*see* note 31, *supra*) does not use a bright line test but would allow a court to determine if the relationship would reasonably be expected to affect the judgment in a manner adverse to the corporation.

[64] Historically, directors were not compensated for their work but today statutes generally provide that directors can set their compensation. *E.g.*, Model Bus. Corp. Act Ann. § 8.11 (4th ed. 2008).

[65] In the United States, chief executive pay was 531 times the employee average compared to 57 times in Britain and 10 times in Japan. Gretchen Morgensen, *Explaining (or Not) Why the Boss is Paid so Much*, N.Y. Times, Jan. 25, 2004, at sec. 3, p. 1. *See* Mark J. Loewenstein, *The Conundrum of Executive Compensation*, 35 Wake Forest L. Rev. 1 (2000) (CEOs are not overpaid, citing shareholder proposals on compensation that receive little support). A number of corporate scandals were driven by the managers' manipulation of the financials to justify high compensation and high stock prices in order to increase the value of their stock options. Under the Sarbanes-Oxley Act of 2002, if the corporation restates its financials due to material noncompliance and misconduct, the CEO and CFO must reimburse their bonuses and share-based compensation and profits from share sales for that period. In addition Sarbanes-Oxley, Section 402 banned most corporate loans to its directors or officers because of the practice of giving loans on highly favorable terms and in some case forgiving them. For a discussion of the scandals and Sarbanes-Oxley, see § 5.08, *supra.* For a discussion of stock options, see § 9.04[A], *infra.*

shareholder returns, thereby lowering agency costs.[66] In that sense, compensation issues are the kind of decisions that should be protected by the business judgment rule and not be subject to direct judicial scrutiny.[67] But compensation can also be a form of self-dealing where those who manage reward each other excessively, at the expense and exclusion of the shareholders. However, because compensation is a common business decision, even if it involves self-dealing, it differs from other interested director transactions which may not be in the usual course of business.[68]

Compensation issues can differ in the closely held corporation. Large payments of compensation to those in control can eliminate funds available to pay dividends to the minority shareholders.[69] In that context, the decision may be part of a plan to oppress the minority, eventually forcing them to sell out at a low price to the control group.[70] Then, it is likely that the minority shareholders will try to seek judicial review using fiduciary duty claims. In the context of a closely held corporation, courts may be more likely to evaluate compensation policy under the stricter standards of the duty of loyalty.[71]

---

[66] For a discussion of agency costs, see § 5.03[C][1], *supra.* The press has reported a number of examples where an executive received a large amount of compensation even though during the periods the corporation performed badly. For example, Robert Nardelli served 6 years as head of Home Depot. During that period the company grew through expansion but that stock rose 6% (versus its competitor Lowes rose 230%) and Mr. Nardellis earned approximately $360 in compensation and stock options (he received a severance package valued at $210 million. Del Jones and Matt Krantz, *Home Depot Boots CEO Nardelli*, USA Today, Jan. 4, 2007.

[67] Even if compensation is authorized by disinterested directors there needs to be actual consideration for its authorization. In *Adams v. Smith*, 153 So. 2d 221 (Ala. 1963), payments to the widow of the deceased president were improper and ultra vires because they were granted after the death of the president. The payments were not a pension since the president could no longer perform services and were not justified as a charitable contribution. In *Osborne v. Locke Steel Chain Co.*, 218 A.2d. 526 (Conn. 1966), however, an agreement to pay the former president and chairman of the board compensation was for consideration. Although the agreement seemed to be for past services, there was a promise by the retiring officer to consult and not compete. In *Zupnick v. Goizueta*, 698 A.2d. 284 (Del. 1997), the court found no cause of action based upon stock options granted even though it was argued that they were wasteful because they were granted for past services and the officer could resign immediately after receipt of those options. The options were approved by independent directors and given Mr. Goizueta's service (Coca Cola's shares increased by $69 billion during his tenure), the grant was not unreasonable in view of past services. Thus, past consideration can serve as consideration if implied or reasonable in view of past services.

[68] The A.L.I. distinguishes between interested director transactions and compensation when there is disinterested director approval. *Compare* A.L.I. Corp. Gov. Proj. § 5.02(a)(2)(B)(C) (interested directors' contract valid if it "could reasonably have concluded the transaction was fair"), *with* A.L.I. Corp. Gov. Proj. § 5.03(a)(2) (compensation subject to the business judgment rule).

[69] The payment of high levels of compensation can also be intended to eliminate profits to avoid double taxation. For a discussion of the double taxation, see § 1.05[A], *supra.*

[70] For a discussion of oppression, see § 11.07[G], *infra.* This can also happen in smaller publicly traded corporations where there is a control group which pays itself high compensation that drives the stock market price down to enable the group to acquire the minority at a discount in a freeze out transaction. *See Berkowitz v. Power/Mate Corp.*, 342 A.2d. 566 (N.J. Ch. Div. 1975).

[71] Even in closely held corporations, courts do not like to second guess decisions on compensation because even those in control have the right to be compensated. In *Mlinarcik v. E.E. Wehrung Parking, Inc.*, 620 N.E.2d 181 (Ohio 1993), the court placed the burden on the minority to prove the unreasonableness of the compensation. There was no evidence of oppression by the majority and the minority was receiving dividends. The annual reports they received also informed them of the

In the publicly traded corporation, in which there may be separation of ownership from control, the amount of compensation may be excessive.[72] In most publicly traded corporations, compensation is approved by the board's compensation committee which is made up of independent directors.[73] But the selection of outside directors is greatly influenced by the insiders which may limit their ability to closely monitor the compensation. In addition, many of them are also officers of their own corporation where they are seeking compensation and will be sympathetic to paying high compensation. Generally, there is little judicial scrutiny of salary and bonuses[74] although stock options have been subject to some review. The approval by the independent directors makes it difficult to attack the compensation as a breach of fiduciary duty. In addition most of these corporations have Section 102(b)(7) provisions in their certificate to eliminate damages for a duty of care case.[75] As a result plaintiffs have to find a basis to attack the compensation that could subject the defendants to damages. Thus allegations of a lack of good faith[76] or that there was waste[77] is often how the plaintiff must proceed.

Because the litigation will be a derivative suit (i.e., shareholders are bringing an action on behalf of their corporation which alleged a breach of fiduciary duty that essentially harms the corporation), the plaintiff shareholders are required to make demand on the board of directors prior to filing the cause of action. Plaintiffs will try to allege sufficient facts to avoid the demand requirement (which could end their litigation) by claiming that such a demand should be

---

compensation which was approved in 1982 but was not challenged until 1989.

[72] *See* Lucien Bebchuk, Jessie Fried & David Walker, *Managerial Power and Rent Extraction in the Design of Executive Compensation*, 69 U. CHI. L. REV. 751 (2002) (discussing how executives influence their compensation).

[73] Stock market rules now require most publicly traded corporations to have a majority of independent outside directors and the compensation committee of the board must be composed of only independent directors. For a discussion of independent directors, see § 5.02[F], *supra.*

[74] While courts do not like to be involved in compensation decisions, an early example of judicial involvement were the bonus payments paid by American Tobacco. became so large that it appeared to be wasteful. In 1912, the shareholders had approved a by-law amendment that allowed for bonus payments to officers based upon net profits. By 1930, the payments to the President were $842,507 (a significant amount of money at that time). The Supreme Court, in *Rogers v. Hill*, 289 U.S. 582 (1933), found that the while percentages were not *per se* unreasonable, the amounts became so large as to suggest fraud and waste because there was no reasonable relationship of the amount to the employment. A bonus needs to relate to the value given to the corporation. In later litigation, a New York court recognized the difficulty the judiciary has in determining what is reasonable compensation because of the difficulty in determining and comparing it to other compensation in the world outside of business. While recognizing that courts will not allow waste or misuse of corporate assets, it placed the ultimate responsibility on the shareholders. *Heller v. Boylan*, 29 N.Y.S.2d 653 (Sup. Ct. 1941) *aff'd. mem.* 32 N.Y.S.2d 131 (1st Dept. 1941). The reasonable relation test may still be applied by some courts.

[75] For a discussion of Section 102(b)(7), see § 8.05[A] *supra.*

[76] In *Walt Disney*, the $130 million compensation and severance package for its president who resigned after serving 14 months raised issues of whether there was a breach of the duty of care or a lack of good faith approval by the directors. The Delaware court found that there was sufficient evidence to find that they acted in an informed manner and thus no violation of the duty of care or lack of good faith. For a discussion of the Disney litigation and good faith, see § 8.06[A], *supra.* For a discussion of good faith and stock options, see § 9.04[B], *infra.*

[77] For a discussion of waste and compensation, see § 9.04[C], *infra.*

excused as futile because the board violated the duty of loyalty by not acting in good faith in making the compensation decision or the decision itself was wasteful and not protected by the business judgment rule.[78] Compensation is more likely to be affected by forces outside of fiduciary duty law. Various market mechanisms could be used to limit compensation.[79] The use of independent directors is supposed to select compensation schemes that are beneficial.[80] Compensation policy may also be influenced by institutional or large investors who push their agenda on compensation.[81] Public pressures have influenced law and regulation[82] and pushed the SEC to change disclosure rules on compensa-

---

[78] Under Delaware law demand is excused when the allegations raise a reasonable doubt that either the majority of the board was disinterested and independent or the transaction could have been an exercise if business judgment. For a discussion of the demand requirement and futility in derivative litigation, see § 14.05[D], *infra*. Plaintiffs also must allege (prior to discovery) sufficient facts with sufficiency to avoid a motion to dismiss. *See* note 91, *infra*.

[79] For a discussion of market mechanisms that enforce fiduciary duty, see § 5.03[C][2], *supra*. For example, if directors award excessive compensation there could be a proxy fight or voting to influence or replace them. At Walt Disney in 2004 43% of the shareholders in a reaction to the excessive compensation dealt with in the *Disney* case, withheld their vote for the re-election of the CEO Michael Eisner who was elected by a plurality vote. As a result he resigned as chairman of the board but remained as CEO. Paul R. La Monica, *Eisner out as Disney chair*, CNN Money.com (March 4, 2004). For a discussion of the campaign to withhold votes and majority voting, see § 5.05[D] *supra*. For a discussion of the *Disney* case and good faith, see § 8.06[A] *supra*.

[80] The compensation paid to outside directors raises issues of their independence. Large payments or benefits may align these directors with the interests of the chief executive officer who plays a significant role in their selection and retention. It has been suggested that payments in shares would be preferable in that it would align their interests more with the shareholders. *See* Charles Elson, *The Duty of Care, Compensation and Stock Ownership*, 63 U. CINN. L. REV. 649 (1995).

[81] Shareholders have used shareholder proxy proposals to try to influence compensation in a variety of ways. For a discussion of shareholder proxy fights and proposals, see §§ 5.05[C] and 7.05, *supra*. *See* Mark J. Loewenstein, *The Conundrum of Executive Compensation*, 35 WAKE FOREST L. REV. 1 (2000) (CEOs are not overpaid, citing shareholder proposals on compensation that receive little support). Recent shareholder proposals that deal directly or indirectly with compensation issues have been more successful. For example in 2007 the AFL CIO submitted several precatory shareholder proposals at Verizon on a variety of compensations issues involving golden parachutes, compensation consultants and a nonbinding shareholder vote on compensation ("say on pay" proposal). Close to 50% of the shareholders voted in favor. American Federation of Labor — Congress of Industrial Organizations, *Record Shareholder Votes on CEO Pay at Verizon Meeting Send Powerful Message that Shareholders are Fed Up with the Status Quo*, http://www.aflcio.org/mediacenter/prsptm/pr05032007a.cfm (May 3, 2007). In the United Kingdom shareholders vote annually on an advisory vote on compensation and U.S. shareholders have tried to implement such a system through shareholder proposals under the proxy rules. *See* Jeffrey N. Gordon *"Say on Pay": Cautionary Notes on the UK Experience and the Case for Muddling Through*, http://papers.ssrn.com/sol3/papers.cfm?abstract_id=1262867 (argues to hold on the "say on pay" idea to see if SEC disclosures rules have an affect and suggest that changes in tax law may be the better solution).

[82] The financial crisis of 2008 resulted in the need for government funding of some financial institutions. Because of the high compensation paid to a number of executives of these institutions including large severance packages and public outrage, when Congress enacted the Emergency Economic Stabilization Act of 2008 to assist these institutions it mandated limits on executive compensation for those institutions that participate in the funding. Another example, high executive compensation also became a campaign issue in 1992 and President Clinton proposed and Congress enacted changes in the tax law that tied the deduction of compensation in excess of $1 million for top executives to corporate performance. I.R.C.§ 162(m) (1995).

tion federal securities laws.[83]

[A]   Stock Options

Compensation may take different forms, including salaries, bonuses, pensions, fringe benefits, restricted stock (shares that cannot be sold immediately), severance packages, golden parachutes[84] and stock options (or other plans intended to compensate based upon stock performance). Because stock options can produce very high compensation, controversy has centered on publicly traded corporations that offer stock options as compensation. Stock options allow the recipient to elect to buy the shares of the corporation for a period of time at a set price. For example, if the president of the corporation is granted an option to buy 10 million shares at the exercise price of $20 for 5 years (the market price can be the same $20 or a lower or higher than the exercise price, which could affect the tax consequences of the granting of the option). If the market value of the shares moves to $60, she can exercise the options (pay $20 per share), then sell the shares with a $400 million pre-tax profit.[85] Some would argue that this is an inexpensive way to compensate because there is no direct payment from the corporation. In addition, stock options can be viewed as performance-based compensation although geared to

---

[83] A few years ago, the SEC tried to deal with concerns about excessive compensation by increasing disclosure. Its proposals generated over 20,000 comments, which was the most ever for a SEC regulatory issue. U.S. Securities and Exchange Commission, *SEC Votes to Adopt Changes to Disclosure Requirements Concerning Executive Compensation and Related Matters*, http://www.sec.gov/news/press/2006/2006-123.htm (July 26, 2006). In 1992, for example, President Bush visited Japan to pressure the Japanese to open their markets and was accompanied by some corporate executives. The result of the visit was embarrassing for Mr. Bush because it was revealed that these American executives who were complaining about the Japanese, received compensation that was extremely high in comparison to their Japanese counterparts. American chief executive officers were paid 150 times more than the average American worker whereas Japanese executives were paid 17 times the ordinary Japanese worker. *See* Byrne, *How CEO Paychecks Got So Unreal*, BUSINESS WEEK, Nov. 18, 1991, at 20. The public outrage about the high compensation influenced the SEC to submit a proposal to require companies to disclose more information about executive compensation. The SEC also changed its position and now allows shareholders to make recommendations about compensation to the board of directors under the federal proxy rules. *See Regulation of Communications Among Security Holders*, Exchange Act Release No. 34-30849 (June 24, 1992) (revision of proposed rules on proxy proposals concerning executive compensation).

[84] Golden parachutes are usually designed to reward executives with significant compensation when there is a change of control.

[85] In some cases, when the market has declined, directors have repriced the options, lowering the exercise price. Thus, in our example, after 2 years the market price declined from $20 to $10 while the exercise price of the option was $20. The market price of the stock looks like it will not exceed the exercise price of the option so the directors lower the exercise price to $10 or new options are issued at $10. Such repricing appears unfair because the employees are now benefitting from the decline in share price; however, the repricing can also be viewed as creating incentives for future service. See *Cohen v. Ayers*, 596 F.2d 733 (7th Cir. 1979), the court found that repricing alone would not constitute waste (that is, giving added value without consideration) when the market price is declining, because there may be no added value to the option holder for the new lower priced options. Even if there were added value, there may be future consideration (for example, continued service) for the change. Thus, a decline of the market price from $20 to $10 and an equivalent decline in the option price in theory gives the option holder nothing new. However, if the price of the shares is rising and the option price is lowered, then there is a possibility of waste because of the lack of consideration. Stock market rules may now require a shareholder vote to reprice options.

the stock market. The employee will work to enhance the value of the shares which will benefit shareholders.[86] However, there is a cost to this form of compensation because additional shares must be available when the options are exercised. In addition under current accounting rules the value of most options is treated as an expense like other forms of compensation and will reduce reported income.[87] Corporations must either issue more shares, which increases the number of shares outstanding and results in a dilution of existing shares, or use corporate funds to repurchase shares to fund the exercise of the options. The tying of compensation to stock price may not necessarily reflect added value to the corporation since the stock market may be influenced by many factors not related to employee efforts. In addition, some managers may take inappropriate actions to influence the share price, including fraudulent manipulation of financial information to cash in on their options.

Most states require that the granting of stock options need not be approved by shareholders and require only board approval.[88] But current stock market rules now require shareholder approval for most stock option plans and material changes in those plans.[89] Once the options are authorized, the directors usually have the power to grant the options. While consideration is necessary for the options, the judgment of the directors as to the consideration is usually conclusive.[90]

Just as in other fiduciary duty cases, plaintiffs challenging the granting of options (or other excessive compensation schemes) try to have the courts apply a fairness test, while defendants argue for the business judgment rule or a waste standard. If a majority of the directors are voting compensation for themselves, then there is self-dealing with fairness as the standard and the burden of proof on the defendants.[91] When there is an independent board or

---

[86]

[87] In the past stock options were not expensed which meant that their use did not have an immediate impact on earnings which encouraged their use. There were concerns expressed about the difficulty in valuing the options, But post Sarbanes-Oxltey Act and the concerns raised about high compensation, US accounting rules were changed to the current requirement of expensing. For a discussion of Sarbanes-Oxley § 5.08, *supra*.

[88] Del. Gen. Corp. L. § 157; Model Bus. Corp. Act Ann. § 6.24 (4th ed. 2008) (no shareholder vote required). If there are insufficient shares authorized in the articles then a shareholder vote will be needed for those shares.

[89] Post Sarbanes-Oxley Act, the stock markets changed their listing requirements requiring shareholder approval of all equity compensation plans, including stock option plans, and material revisions to such plans. In addition, equity compensation plans and amendments not subject to shareholder approval must be approved by the company's independent compensation committee or a majority of the company's independent directors. *E.g.*, N.Y. Stock Exch. Listed Co. Manual § 303A.

[90] Del. Gen. Corp. L. § 157. *Cf.* Model Bus. Corp. Act Ann. § 6.24 (4th ed. 2008) (the board shall determine the terms and consideration).

[91] But even with the advantages to the plaintiff of a fairness standard and shift of burden of proof, the complaint can still be dismissed if the allegations of unfairness are conclusory and not factually based. Thus allegations that compensation was excessive without more will not be sufficient. There needs to be excessiveness on its face or facts supporting a claim of wrongdoing or waste. *Marx v. Akers*, 666 N.E.2d 1034 (N.Y. 1996). However, what are well-pleaded facts or mere conclusions is often unclear and gives courts leeway on a motion to dismiss the complaint for failure to state a cause of action. Allegations of unfairness and waste are factual and may need discovery. If the factual

disinterested shareholder ratification of the self-dealing compensation, then courts must decide what standard applies. Courts will often look at the case law and statutes dealing with interested director transactions for guidance. There has been some confusion over the extent of judicial scrutiny. Compliance with interested director statutes requiring disinterested director or shareholder approval generally shifts the burden of proof but the standard used to evaluate the stock option policy may vary (business judgment fairness or waste).[92] Generally, in compensation cases, the business judgment rule will apply when the disinterested directors approve and a waste test will apply when the shareholders approve.[93] Not retaining a fairness standard and thus lessened scrutiny may be justified because compensation differs from other interested transactions. The compensation decision is a necessary ordinary business decision while other conflict of interest transactions are often substitutes for arms length bargain transactions.

[B]   Good Faith and Compensation

In Delaware a lack of good faith, which violates the duty of loyalty, requires conduct motivated by subjective bad intent with an actual intent to harm the corporation or an intentional dereliction of duty and a conscious disregard for one's responsibilities.[94] The lack of good faith has become an issue in the way some stock options were granted. It turned out that some publicly traded corporations were issuing stock options on often more favorable terms then the stock option plans approved by the shareholders called for and shareholders and regulators were mislead about their issuance. Some option grants were

---

allegations are so far from satisfying the legal standard of waste, then dismissal would be appropriate. *See Lewis v. Vogelstein* 699 A.2d 327 (Del. Ch. 1997).

[92] For a discussion of shareholder ratification, see § 9.06, *infra.* For a discussion of the different approaches to interested director transactions, see § 9.03[B], *supra.*

[93] *See Beard v. Elster*, 160 A.2d 731 (Del. 1960). A.L.I. Corp. Gov. Proj. § 5.03 uses the business judgment rule for disinterested board approval of compensation and a waste standard for disinterested shareholder approval. *Cf.* A.L.I. Corp. Gov. Proj. § 5.02 (applies a modified fairness standard for disinterested board approval of interested director transactions). Some courts will shift the burden of proof to the plaintiff but retain the fairness standard which allows the court to examine process and substance to see if it is an arm's-length bargain. In *Cohen v. Ayers*, 596 F.2d 733 (7th Cir. 1979), the corporation's shares had declined so that the market price was significantly less than the option price (that is the option was "underwater"). The directors canceled the options and replaced them with a smaller number of new options with a lower option price. The shareholders overwhelmingly voted to ratify the board's actions. Plaintiffs brought a derivative suit alleging, among other things, waste. Since the directors granted themselves the options there was clearly self-dealing. The court applied New York law and indicated that under N.Y.B.C.L. § 713 (interested director statute), compliance with the statutory requirement of full disclosure and ratification by a disinterested board or shareholders shifts the burden of proof to the plaintiff. The court at one point indicated that the plaintiff would have to prove unfairness, but the court also indicated that ratification means the business judgment rule applies (that is, fairness was not an issue). The court actually used a waste test which is more difficult for a plaintiff to prove than unfairness. Waste may be the appropriate test because plaintiff had alleged waste and the test may be proper when there is shareholder ratification as opposed to director approval. The mere fact that option price was lowered with new options does not necessarily prove waste since it could be viewed as maintaining the options value and compensating for future services. *See* note 85, *supra.*

[94] Lack of good faith was the issue in the awarding of compensation in the *Disney* case, discussed at § 8.06[A], *supra.*

"backdated" in that some corporations would issue stock options on one date but then provided fraudulent documentation to show that they were issued earlier when the market price was lower.[95] Others were "spring loaded" where a corporation was about to announce some positive news that would probably raise the market price, but stock options were awarded based upon the current lower market price and then the recipients would gain when the price rose on the announcement. Options granting also involved "bullet dodging" because the compensation committee would wait until negative news was announced and then would grant the options when the market price declined.[96]

These actions raise an issue of lack of good faith. Since the plans are usually approved by the shareholders, the granting of the options has to be authorized by the plan.[97] In the derivative suits, the plaintiff shareholders are required to make demand on the board of directors prior to filing the cause of action unless excused as futile because they did not act in good faith in making the decision.[98]

In *Ryan v Gifford*[99] the court viewed the backdating of the options as providing a windfall to the recipients because the shares were trading at a higher price than the earlier lower market price that was used. If the board had no discretion under the shareholder-approved plan and could only issue the options at the fair market price and the shareholders in approving the plan were assured of such an issuance, then allegations of backdating will raise the issue of lack of good faith by a knowing and intentional violation of the option plan. In addition, the defendants mislead the shareholders[100] when disclosing information about the granting of the options.

---

[95] For example, on March 1 the market price was $25 and the options issued that day would usually be based on that price but on February 15 the market price was $20. So on March 1 the options would be backdated to reflect the February 15 price.

[96] Bullet dodging does not raise the same concerns as the other issuances because the issuance takes place after the market has absorbed the negative news and that is not as problematic because the options were at least issued at the fair market price. But bullet dodging will be problematic if the directors have other non public information that will result in a market price increase after the issuance. Bullet dodging can be part of a breach of fiduciary duty if there are other facts suggesting waste such as the size of the grant being egregious or unfair self-dealing when the directors were dominated or controlled by the option recipients. *Desimone v. Barrows*, 924 A.2d 908 (Del. Ch. 2007).

[97] Thus if the issuance clearly violates the plan they are arguably ultra vires and invalid for that reason. But courts may prefer to use a fiduciary duty analysis so courts can look at each situation flexibly to see if there is a reasonable justification for not holding the directors liable. For a discussion of ultra vires, see § 1.10, *supra*.

[98] Under Delaware law demand is excused when the allegations raise a reasonable doubt that either the majority of the board was disinterested and independent or the transaction could have been an exercise if business judgment. For a discussion of the demand requirement see § 14.05 *infra*

[99] 918 A.2d 341 (Del. Ch 2007) The court excused demand in this case of backdating because of allegations that more than half the directors knowingly violated the plan and was not a valid business judgment. In the alternative there were sufficient allegations that the directors faced a substantial likelihood of damages for breaching their duty of loyalty for a lack of good faith and thus were not disinterested or independent.

[100] Even if a backdating issuance below fair market did not itself violate the plan, the directors often represent to the shareholders, markets and regulatory authorities that they were issued at fair market value. The lack of full disclosure could result in federal securities law liability and has implications for accounting and tax treatment, which may require the corporation to recognize the options as an expense and need restate prior reported income. These can be violations of positive law

In re Tyson Foods, Inc. involved spring loading the option and the court viewed that differently from backdating which by its nature involves a lie about the date of the issuance. The granting of spring loaded options at a favored price is not necessarily a breach of duty because the directors usually under the plan can decide when to issue the options. But there is a more subtle deception associated with the issuance prior to the announcement of positive news and can raise an issue duty of loyalty to act fairly and honesty with the shareholders in a lack of good faith. Even if directors follow exactly what the shareholder approved plan required (for example, issuance at the market price at the time of issuance), the grant of stock options cannot undermine the objectives of the plan that they be issued at a fair market price. When a director is authorized to issue stock options at the fair market price, knows that the shares are worth more and intentionally uses inside information to benefit employees, that demonstrates a lack of good faith.[101]

But not all issuance of backdated or spring loaded options will result in liability and could depend on a variety of issues such as whether the plan allowed for below market issuance, what was disclosed about the issuance, and how involved and what knowledge did the entire board of directors have in the issuance. Plaintiff will need to allege sufficient facts to have demand excused by a reasonable doubt of the board's ability to deal with the litigation because of their lack of independence or good faith or their interest in the options.[102]

---

that implicates a lack of good faith if culpability can be established. *Desimone v. Barrows* 924 A.2d 908, 935 (Del.Ch. 2007) ("directors have no authority knowingly to cause the corporation to become a rogue, exposing the corporation to penalties from criminal and civil regulators. Delaware corporate law has long been clear on this rather obvious notion, namely, that it is utterly inconsistent with one's duty of fidelity to the corporation to consciously cause the corporation to act unlawfully").

[101] 919 A.2d 563 (Del. Ch 2007). Demand was excused because of sufficient allegations creating a reasonable doubt that the directors could act independently from those who received the options. The court indicated that plaintiff is required to allege that the options were shareholder approved and were issued with material inside information and intended to circumvent shareholder approved restrictions. If shareholders had allowed such actions in the approved plan, there would be no cause of action.

[102] In *Desimone v. Barrows*, 924 A.2d 908, 935 (Del. Ch. 2007), the Delaware chancery court dealt with two different shareholder approved stock option plans. One plan was directed at employees and officers while the other at the outside directors. The plan directed at employees and officers did not require issuance at a fair market price and allowed the issuance to be done by executives and not the board. There were allegations of back dating for the employees and officers plus spring loading and bullet dodging for the officers. But plaintiff needed to allege facts allowing for demand to be excused and there were insufficient facts suggesting that the entire board (which did not issue or receive these options) could not decide either because they were interested or lacked independence or faced a threat of personal liability by acting with a lack of good faith. A claim of lack of good faith needed factual allegations of the requisite state of mind (i.e., culpability). The options granted to the outside board raised different issues because the option plan provided for issuance at a fair market price. It was alleged that they were timed to benefit the recipients. Since a majority of the board was interested because they received the options, demand could be excused. The complaint could not withstand a motion to dismiss, however, because their options were scheduled to be issued on an automatic basis on the date of the annual shareholders meeting and there were no allegations of any manipulation of those dates.

[C] Waste

There are times when the courts, in scrutinizing a transaction, apply a waste standard. A waste of corporate assets is never protected by the business judgment rule. The waste standard generally means that what the corporation received in a transaction was so inadequate in value that no person of ordinary sound business judgment would deem it worth what the corporation paid.[103] In essence, waste would involve an exchange for consideration so disproportionately small that a reasonable person would not make the trade. Waste can also involve transfers for an improper or unnecessary purpose. Thus, to be wasteful, the transaction would have to be a gift, or for no real consideration, or unnecessary. It would be a very rare occurrence for disinterested directors to approve of a wasteful transaction. Given the high standard for waste, plaintiffs have a difficult burden of proof.[104] But a claim of waste has the advantage of rarely being dismissed before trial by summary judgment and requires some scrutiny of the substance.[105] Because waste is not protected by the business judgment rule, in executive compensation cases plaintiffs will often allege waste.

[1] Delaware's Waste Standard

Delaware courts have generally held that shareholder ratification of stock options has the effect of limitng judicial review of the compensation under a waste standard with the burden of proof on the plaintiff.[106] While the waste standard would seem to mean minimal scrutiny, the Delaware courts, in some earlier decisions, created confusion about what kind of scrutiny was available when applying the waste test. These decisions looked carefully at the consideration for the options and used a two-prong test. First, there needed to

---

[103] *Michelson v. Duncan*, 407 A.2d 211, 224 (Del. 1979). In the *Disney* case the plaintiffs claimed in addition to a lack of good faith a claim of waste. The court indicated that such claims rarely arise, and are limited to "unconscionable cases where directors irrationally squander or give away corporate assets" *Brehm v. Eisner*, 746 A.2d 244, 263 (Del. 2000).

[104] *See Lewis v. Vogelstein*, 699 A.2d 327 (Del. Ch. 1997). Courts of an earlier era have found compensation to be wasteful. The bonus payments paid by American Tobacco became so large that it appeared to be wasteful. In 1912, the shareholders had approved a by-law amendment that allowed for bonus payments to officers based upon net profits. By 1930, the payments to the President were $842,507 (a significant amount of money at that time). The Supreme Court, in *Rogers v. Hill*, 289 U.S. 582 (1933), found that the while percentages were not *per se* unreasonable, the amounts became so large as to suggest fraud and waste. A bonus needs to relate to the value given to the corporation. In later litigation, a New York court recognized the difficulty the judiciary has in determining what is reasonable compensation because of the difficulty in determining and comparing it to other compensation in the world outside of business. While recognizing that courts will not allow waste or misuse of corporate assets, it placed the ultimate responsibility on the shareholders. *Heller v. Boylan*, 29 N.Y.S.2d 653 (Sup. Ct. 1941) *aff'd. mem.* 32 N.Y.S.2d 131 (1st Dept. 1941).

[105] *Michelson v. Duncan*, 407 A.2d 211 (Del. 1979).

[106] Failure to have either disinterested director or shareholder approval means that the burden is on the directors *see Bryne v. Lord* 1995 Del. Ch. LEXIS 131 (defendant failed to prove that the stock options would benefit the corporation under the second prong because the defendants had resigned before the plan was approved and thus did not have reasonable safeguards that the corporation would receive the benefit of retaining directors). For a discussion of the effect of shareholder ratification, see § 9.06, *infra*.

be a reasonable relationship between the value of consideration flowing both ways, and second, there had to be a determination that a benefit to the corporation was received.[107] These cases suggested that the courts were using the waste standard but at the same time scrutinizing compensation more closely when they applied the two-prong test. The courts seemed to be using an intermediate review (between fairness and business judgment rule) that would look at substance and assess the reasonableness of consideration (that is, a proportionality test).[108] In the later case of *Beard v. Elster*,[109] the Delaware court still looked at consideration, but its focus shifted away from the two-prong test. Instead, its main focus was on the process of approval rather than assessment of whether the corporation had received proportionate value.

In *Lewis v. Vogelstein*,[110] the Delaware Chancery Court finally moved away from the two-prong test, indicating that a more modern view would be that stock options with disinterested shareholder ratification implicate the traditional waste standard for judicial review. In order to ratify, the shareholders need full disclosure both under federal proxy rules and fiduciary duty standards.[111] The court held that if there was an informed, uncoerced and disinterested shareholder ratification of an interested director transaction, such as compensation, then waste is the only basis for judicial review. The court partially justified the use of a waste test because there is more shareholder activism among institutional shareholders so voting has become more important.[112]

At least one Delaware court has called into question the use of a waste test when there is a majority of disinterested shareholders (i.e., no controlling shareholder) voting to ratify a transaction. In *Harbor Finance Partners v. Huizenga*,[113] the Delaware Chancery Court in dicta questioned whether a waste standard was really necessary when disinterested shareholders constituting the majority of shares and with full disclosure approved of a transaction.[114] Although waste is very difficult to prove, the use of the test still allows some judicial scrutiny of substance. The rationale for the waste test is that shareholders cannot ratify a wasteful transaction.[115] A wasteful transaction was

[107] *E.g.*, *Kerbs v. California Eastern Airways*, 90 A.2d 652 (Del. 1952).

[108] This test is similar to the *Unocal* modified business judgment rule or proportionality test used in hostile takeovers. For a discussion of that test, see § 12.05[A][2], *infra*.

[109] 160 A.2d 731 (Del. 1960). *See also Michelson v. Duncan*, 407 A.2d 211 (Del. 1979).

[110] 699 A.2d 327 (Del. Ch. 1997).

[111] For a discussion of the federal proxy rules, see § 7.04, *supra*. For a discussion of the duty of disclosure, see § 8.08, *supra*.

[112] For a discussion of the role of institutional shareholders, see § 5.02[E][2], *supra*. The court also recognized the collective action problem faced by shareholders of publicly traded corporations, discussed at § 5.05[C][4], *supra*.

[113] 751 A.2d 879 (Del. Ch. 1999).

[114] The court recognized that if the corporation was transacting with a controlling shareholder, then a majority of the minority shareholder approval means the burden of proof shifts to the plaintiff, but a fairness review is the standard and not waste. For a discussion of shareholder ratification in that context, see § 10.04[B], *infra*.

[115] For a discussion of shareholder ratification, see § 9.06, *infra*.

traditionally viewed as a void transaction (such as illegal, fraudulent, or ultra vires)[116] and thus not subject to ratification by shareholders. The court suggested that it is highly unlikely a majority of disinterested shareholders with full disclosure would ever ratify a wasteful transaction. The shareholders are further protected by the requirement that those seeking ratification must prove that the vote was fair, fully informed and uncoerced. Thus, shareholders can always challenge the vote on that basis. The court felt that the use of a waste standard in this context did not really protect shareholders but may allow unnecessary litigation to proceed. The court found it hard to imagine that a majority of the disinterested shareholders would ever ratify a transaction that no person of ordinary sound business judgment would find to be a fair exchange (i.e., waste) and called for a reexamination of the use of the waste test in this context.

In summary, executive compensation cases in publicly traded corporations are difficult. The use of independent directors in setting compensation will usually mean the business judgment rule will apply and shareholder approval of stock option plans results in the waste test. Both tests put a difficult burden on the plaintiff to overcome. In addition, plaintiffs have to satisfy procedural requirements, such as the demand requirement in a derivative litigation, that make it difficult to bring an action. And most publicly traded corporations have exculpatory provisions in their articles that eliminates damages in duty of care cases.

§ 9.05 CORPORATE OPPORTUNITY AND ABUSE OF POSITION

Unlike an interested director transaction where the fiduciary is contracting with her corporation, abuse of position and corporate opportunity usually involves the fiduciary taking advantage of her position. A corporate fiduciary should not be able to unfairly profit from her corporate role. If an investment opportunity is viewed as belonging to the corporation, (that is, a corporate opportunity), the corporation should be given the chance to invest in it. While this idea seems simple, its application has resulted in differing legal tests to determine which opportunities are corporate opportunities and which opportunities the directors or officers may properly take advantage of personally.

A broad concept of corporate opportunity would limit fiduciaries from taking the investment and could stifle entrepreneurs interested in improving their outside business or developing a new business which could discourage competition.[117] A narrow concept of a corporate opportunity could encourage fiduciaries to devote less energy to their corporation and take advantage of their positions to profit in other ventures while denying their corporation any gains. But within the corporation there are also different fiduciaries that will be affected by whatever rule is established. Many publicly traded corporations have indepen-

---

[116] For a discussion of ultra vires, see § 1.10, *supra.*

[117] *See generally* Pat K. Chew, *Competing Interests in the Corporate Opportunity Doctrine,* 67 N.C. L. REV. 435 (1989) (courts have inadequately looked at the effect on the fiduciaries and competition).

dent directors that are not full-time employees. A broad rule could discourage their membership on the board.

If a corporate opportunity is found, the inquiry does not end. The issue of whether the corporation in some way rejected or failed to take the opportunity allowing the fiduciary to take it instead can still arise. It may be that the corporation could not afford to undertake the investment or the third party may not have wanted to deal with the corporation.[118] But if it is a corporate opportunity and there are no defenses, courts can order damages or a constructive trust over the investment in favor of the corporation.[119]

[A]   Legal Tests

There are several different tests that have been used to determine if there is a corporate opportunity.[120] These tests include the interest or expectancy test, the line of business test, and the fairness test; some courts apply a combination of these tests. In addition, a test developed by the American Law Institute has also been used by courts.

[1]   Interest Test

The interest or expectancy test focuses on circumstances that indicate that the corporation had a special or unique interest in the opportunity. For instance, if the corporation had been negotiating to acquire the opportunity or the corporation needed the particular investment, but the fiduciary ended up taking the opportunity.[121] The test can be viewed narrowly by looking at the corporation's specific or unique interest in the investment.[122] This test is also fact-sensitive and difficult to apply. A general interest in expansion would usually not be covered by this doctrine.

In *Farber v. Servan Land Company, Inc.*,[123] Servan Land ("Servan") was formed to build a golf course and country club and, accordingly, land was purchased. Nine years later, at the shareholders meeting, it was announced that an additional 160 acres of abutting land was available but no action was taken.

---

[118] Generally, a defense that the third party would not deal with the corporation will fail if the corporation is not told and at least given the opportunity to try to make the investment. *See Energy Resources Corporation, Inc. v. Porter*, 438 N.E.2d 391 (Mass. 1982).

[119] It is interesting that Delaware permits corporations to renounce corporate opportunities by placing a provision in its certificate. Del. Gen. Corp. L. § 122(17). This is another example of the contractual approach to corporate law which allows the corporation to opt out of certain rules. For a discussion of the nexus of contracts, see § 5.03[C][3], *supra*. The statute also permits the board to renounce opportunities.

[120] *See generally* Victor Brudney and Robert Charles Clark, *A New Look at Corporate Opportunities* 94 Harv. L. Rev. 997 (1981).

[121] *Litwin v. Allen*, N.Y.S.2d 667 (1940).

[122] In *Lagarde v. Anniston Lime &Stone Co.*, 28 So. 199 (Ala. 1900), the court indicated that a corporate opportunity involved "an interest already existing, or in which it has an expectancy growing out of an existing right, or . . . where the officer's interference will in some degree balk the corporation in effecting the purposes of its creation."

[123] 662 F.2d 371 (5th Cir. 1981).

Two years later, at the shareholders meeting, it was acknowledged that two officers and shareholders owning a majority of shares had purchased the 160 acres of land on their own. Two years later, the majority shareholders and the corporation together sold all of the land as a package deal to a purchaser. Plaintiff brought a derivative action claiming that the purchase by the majority shareholders of the 160 acres was a theft of corporate opportunity. The defendants claimed there was no corporate opportunity. Further, they claimed that even if it were a corporate opportunity, the shareholders had failed to act and thus declined the opportunity. Moreover, the defendants argued that the purchase was ratified by the shareholders and the purchaser's requirement of the package deal for purchasing both properties together rectified any wrong from the initial purchase.

The court found for the plaintiff. Applying Florida law, the court indicated that a corporate opportunity is a business opportunity in which the corporation has an active interest. The court noted that there had been discussions by Servan shareholders about the need for and possible acquisition of land. In addition, it was revealed that, in the past, other land had been purchased by Servan from the seller. Thus, the opportunity to acquire the land was advantageous and fit into a present, significant corporate purpose and ongoing corporate policy.

The failure of the shareholders to vote to purchase the land was not considered to be a rejection of the corporate opportunity. Since one of the purchasers was the president and an active director, the shareholders would have relied on him to exercise his executive function and act on the property. There was some dispute over whether the shareholders had voted to ratify the purchase by the officers. The court did not decide whether ratification could end the derivative suit because the vote of the interested shareholders would not serve as a ratification.[124] That there was a benefit to selling the properties together was irrelevant because if there was a corporate opportunity both properties would belong to the corporation.

[2]   Line of Business Test

The line of business test is similar to but broader than the interest test. Like the interest test, it is factually sensitive. The test applies if the opportunity embraces "an activity as to which [the corporation] has fundamental knowledge, practical experience and ability to pursue, which, logically and naturally is adaptable to its business having regard for its financial position[125] and is one that is consonant with its reasonable needs and aspirations for expansion . . . ."[126] The test focuses on how closely related the opportunity is to the existing business. A director or officer personally taking advantage of an opportunity that meets this test would essentially be competing with the corporation.

---

[124] For a discussion of shareholder ratification, see § 9.06[B], *infra.*

[125] The test raises the issue of financial ability to undertake the investment. For a discussion of this issue, see § 9.05[B], *infra.*

[126] *Guth v. Loft,* 5 A.2d 503, 514 (Del. 1939).

In *Broz v. Cellular Info Sysytems, Inc.*,[127] Broz was the president and owner of a corporation which competed with Cellular Information Systems ("CIS"). Broz served on the board of CIS. Broz purchased cellular telephone licenses in Michigan. Prior to the purchase he had contacted several officers and directors about his acquisition and was told CIS had no interest. The licenses were never offered to CIS because it had emerged recently from bankruptcy and was thought not to be able to financially undertake the licenses. It turned out another corporation, PrimeCellular, wanted to purchase the licenses and had an option do so but Broz offered a higher price. PrimeCellular was planning to acquire CIS and when they did they then sued Broz to recover the licenses, claiming that Broz had usurped a corporate opportunity. According to the Delaware Supreme Court, Broz became aware of the opportunity not as a CIS director. It held that determining a corporate opportunity may depend on whether the corporation can financially exploit it; from its nature it is within the line of business and is of practical advantage to it; there is a corporate interest or expectancy; and the taking of it places the fiduciary in a position inimicable to the fiduciary's duties. Thus, the fiduciary can take the opportunity if it was presented to her in an individual capacity; the opportunity is not essential to the corporation; there is no corporate interest or expectancy; and there is not wrongful use of corporate resources. These guidelines are considered together and no one factor is dispositive. Even though the licenses are within the line of business of CIS, there was no expectancy there because CIS was divesting its licenses and there were financial issues since CIS had emerged from bankruptcy. In addition, Broz was not liable because he comported himself correctly and pursued the license when he knew CIS had no interest. Broz was not required to formally go to the board of CIS to reject the license in order for him to acquire it so long as the factors indicated that it was not a corporate opportunity. The fact that PrimeCellular eventually acquired CIS did not mean Broz had a duty to them prior to their acquisition of CIS.

The line of business standard could be viewed as too restrictive in cases where the opportunity is not closely related but would still be of interest to the corporation. The test could also be overly expansive if the view is that a corporation may always be interested in any opportunity for expansion.

[3]   Fairness Test

The fairness test is more open-ended because it looks at the total circumstances to see if there is unfairness and if the interests of the corporation call for protection.[128] Given the broad parameters of a fairness inquiry, the test does not provide sufficient practical guidance. Some courts have combined the fairness and line of business test to try to avoid the vagueness of each test. Thus, a court would look at whether it was in the line of business and then look at the circumstances to see if its acquisition by the fiduciary was unfair.[129] Far from correcting any deficiencies in the individual tests, however, this combined

[127] 673 A.2d 148 (Del. Ch. 1996).
[128] *Durfee v. Durfee Canning, Inc.*, 80 N.E.2d 522 (Mass. 1948).
[129] *Miller v. Miller*, 222 N.W.2d 71 (Minn. 1974).

approach only compounds the uncertainty.

[4]   The ALI Test

The ALI tries to clarify the definition of a corporate opportunity and when a fiduciary can invest. Several courts have adopted their view.[130] In defining an opportunity, the ALI distinguishes between directors and senior executives. There is a corporate opportunity if the opportunity to engage in a business activity is presented to either the directors or senior executives under circumstances that (1) would reasonably lead them to believe that the opportunity was intended for the corporation or (2) would require that they use corporate information and it would reasonably be expected to be of interest to the corporation. If the defendant is a senior executive, there is a third test for the corporate opportunity which includes any opportunity that she knows is closely related to the business in which the corporation is engaged or expects to be engaged.[131] Notice that the first two tests focus on the opportunity resulting from the corporate position or use of corporate information or property and thus applies to a wider group. The third test which is limited to senior executives who would be expected not to be able to take advantage of investments that are closely related to the corporation for which they work full time.

In *Northeast Harbor Golf Club, Inc. v. Harris*,[132] Harris, the president of a country club with a golf course, acquired property adjacent to the golf course at two different times. The real estate agent testified that the first property was offered to Harris as president, with the thought that the club would be interested. Years later, she acquired additional property that was adjacent to the golf course. In both cases, she informed the board after the fact. The board took no action as a result of the purchase. Later, Harris divided the real estate into parcels for building. For several years, the board took an ambivalent position towards the development. Years later, after a substantial change in board membership, a cause of action was instituted based upon her usurpation of a corporate opportunity.

The trial court found no theft because the property was not in the line of business of the country club, the financial difficulty of the club made it unable to purchase the property, and Harris had exhibited good faith. In reversing, the Maine Supreme Court rejected the line of business test as being difficult to apply, particularly in this case where the club was not in the business of purchasing land, but could have been interested in limiting adjacent development. In addition, the court was concerned about the presence of a financial inability element in this test. The court noted that the director or officer taking advantage of the opportunity is also often the one who is in a position to solve the corporation's financing problems. Allowing the fiduciary to make a personal gain creates a strong disincentive for the fiduciary to do her job. The court also rejected the fairness test because it is too open-ended and provides no real guidance to fiduciaries. The court further noted that the

---

[130] *See, e.g., Klinicki v. Lundgren*, 695 P.2d 906 (Or. 1985).

[131] A.L.I. Corp. Gov. Proj. § 5.05(b).

[132] 661 A.2d 1146 (Me. 1995).

combination of the fairness and line of business test results only in combining the problems of both tests.[133] Instead, the court chose to use the ALI test.

In addition to setting forth a test for identifying a corporate opportunity, the ALI established a procedure for what to do if the business venture meets the ALI definition of corporate opportunity.[134] First, the directors must offer the opportunity to the corporation with disclosure as to the conflict of interest and the opportunity. Failure to make such disclosure creates liability *per se*.[135] Second, the corporation must reject the opportunity before the fiduciary may take advantage of it. Rejection by the disinterested directors means the business judgment rule would apply to any challenge to the board action. Rejection by disinterested shareholders means a waste test would apply. But if the rejection is not by a disinterested board or shareholders, then the rejection must be fair to the corporation and the burden of proof rests on the defendant.[136] Because the trial court had not used the ALI test, the case was remanded for further proceedings in light of the new test.

[B] Financial Inability

The financial inability of the corporation to take advantage of the corporate opportunity has resulted in a variety of outcomes. In *Irving Trust Co. v. Deutsch*,[137] a contract to acquire shares of another corporation was taken over by some of the directors. Their defense was that they believed that their corporation did not have the funds or access to funds to make the purchase. The court rejected the argument, fearing that fiduciaries would refrain from using their efforts on behalf of the corporation to obtain financing. While it was unclear that the corporation lacked the ability to raise the funds,[138] the court relied on a rigid rule providing that as long as the corporation was solvent, financial inability would not be a defense to taking an opportunity.

Other cases view financial inability as a relevant consideration to the question of whether or not the investment will be defined as a corporate opportunity in the first place. For example, under the line of business test used in Delaware there is an inquiry which determines if the opportunity is in the line of business and if the opportunity is in the line of business, they then consider the financial ability. The burden of proof is on the plaintiff to prove it is an opportunity under the interest test and that there is financial ability to exploit it. Thus, even if the investment is in the line of business there is no corporate opportunity if there is no financial ability to undertake it. The ALI approach is that financial ability is

---

[133] For a discussion of these tests and their problems, see § 9.05[A][2] and [3], *supra*.

[134] A.L.I. Corp. Gov. Proj. § 5.05(a)(c).

[135] A good faith failure to disclose can be cured by ratification by the board, shareholders or decision maker that initially rejected the opportunity. A.L.I. Corp. Gov. Proj. § 5.05(d).

[136] For example, if the opportunity was disclosed but rejected by an interested board, the fairness test would apply. A delayed offering because of a good faith belief that the activity was not an opportunity may still be rejected it if is fair. A.L.I. Corp. Gov. Proj. § 5.05(e).

[137] 73 F.2d 121 (2d Cir. 1934).

[138] One of the directors had a note with the corporation although he claimed he had a defense to its collection. No effort was made to collect on the note.

not relevant to the definition of corporate opportunity but can be considered in looking at fairness after rejection by the corporation.[139]

[C]   Multiple Boards

There are times when directors serve on different boards and are shareholders of different corporations in similar businesses.[140] In *Burg v. Horn*,[141] three shareholders (Mrs. Burg, George and Max Horn) formed a corporation which purchased a rental building. The corporation sold the property and purchased other property over the years. At the same time the Horns had also purchased properties individually and through other corporations. Plaintiffs sought a constructive trust on these other properties as a corporate opportunity. The court first rejected the opportunities as not being ones in which the corporation had either an interest or tangible expectancy. It also rejected a broad reading of the line of business test. The Horns were not full-time employees of the corporation and had made other real estate investments prior to the formation of this company.[142] Thus, there needed to be some evidence of an expectancy, or understanding or agreement between the parties that these other investments belonged to the corporation.[143]

---

[139] *See Klinicki v. Lundgren*, 695 P.2d 906 (Or. 1985) (discussing the different theories but adopting the ALI view). For a discussion of the ALI treatment of corporate opportunities, see § 9.05[A][4], *supra.*

[140] A similar problem exists when there are parent and subsidiary corporations or corporations with controlling shareholders. In recognizing the importance of context, the ALI has taken a different approach to corporate opportunities. A corporate opportunity exists when it is developed or received by the corporation (the subsidiary or controlled corporation) or comes to the parent or controlling shareholders by virtue of its relationship with the controlled corporation. A corporate opportunity also exists if it is held out to the subsidiary's shareholders as being within its scope of business (i.e., looking at expectations). If it is a corporate opportunity there is no requirement of prior disclosure to or rejection by the subsidiary. The parent or controlling shareholder can take the corporate opportunity if it is rejected by the disinterested shareholders (and not wasteful) or the taking is deemed to be fair (burden on the parent). A.L.I. Corp. Gov. Proj. § 5.11.

[141] 380 F.2d 897 (2d Cir. 1967).

[142] The court also rejected the argument that the Horns were illegally competing with the corporation for similar reasons and that the corporation was not harmed by the ownership and operations of the other properties.

[143] The dissent believed that it was up to the fiduciary to show that there was an agreement that they could take the related business opportunities. The dissent cited to oft-quoted Judge Cardozo principle from *Meinhard v. Salmon* and found in the text at note 12, *supra.* In *Meinhard*, Salmon was the managing partner of a real estate venture that leased premises. Less than four months before the lease ended, the owner of the building approached Salmon, whom he had been dealing with since Meinhard was a silent partner. He offered him a new lease that would cover more property than the original parcel. Salmon did not notify Meinhard and Meinhard sued claiming a breach of fiduciary duty and theft of a partnership opportunity. Even though the partnership was a joint venture that was limited as to the original lease, the court found Salmon liable. Since there was nexus between the old lease and the new one it was a partnership opportunity. At a minimum, he should have disclosed the new lease to Meinhard so he could have bid for it although the court suggested that may not be sufficient. As the managing partner, Salmon had a higher fiduciary duty.

[D]   Use of Information and Competition

As discussed, a corporate fiduciary cannot improperly take a corporate opportunity. In addition, a corporate fiduciary cannot use corporate information, a corporate position[144] or assets unfairly for personal profit[145] and may not be able to compete with the corporation.[146] All three principles (corporate opportunity, unfair use of position or assets and unfair competition) are distinct duties but can overlap. For example, a fiduciary could use corporate information to acquire another business closely connected to her other business that competes with it.

[E]   Undisclosed Profits

Even with no usurpation of a corporate opportunity, improper use of information or competition, a corporate fiduciary could be liable for secret profits gained in a transaction on behalf of the corporation. In *Hawaiian International Finances, Inc. v. Pablo*,[147] the president of the Hawaiian corporation traveled to California on behalf of the business to purchase real estate. In California, the selling brokers paid the president a commission because he was a real estate broker. The commissions were not disclosed to the Hawaiian corporation. A corporate fiduciary cannot engage in a transaction for the corporation and retain an undisclosed profit. Arguably, there was no harm to

---

[144] In *In re Ebay*, 2004 Del. Ch. LEXIS 4 (Feb. 11, 2004), the court refused to dismiss a derivative suit against the officers and directors of Ebay who were given the opportunity to buy shares from Ebay's investment banker in hot initial public offerings (in the first day of trading the hot IPO shares can move up dramatically). The plaintiff alleged this was a corporate opportunity because it was given to the defendants as a reward or appreciation for Ebay's business. The court used the factors in *Broz v. Cellular Info Sysytems, Inc.*, 673 A.2d 148 (Del. Ch. 1996), in deciding not to dismiss the litigation (discussed in the text at note 127, *supra*). Ebay had in the past invested in marketable securities and this it could have been an opportunity for the company. Even if it was not a corporate opportunity, the court indicated that there may also be a claim based upon an agent's duty of loyalty to account for profits obtained in connection with transactions related to the corporation. The reason these officers may have been given the opportunity to buy these shares could be to induce a continuation of Ebay's business with the investment bankers. *See also Reading v Attorney-General* [1951] App.Cas. 507 (H.L.) (a sergeant in the Royal Army in his uniform facilitated transport for payments. The Army successfully sued for the payments on the theory of unjust enrichment since the agent's using his position was the reason for his profit and it was irrelevant on whether the Army had actually lost anything).

[145] A.L.I. Corp. Gov. Proj. § 5.04. The improper use of information or assets to develop a business opportunity that does not fit in any of the tests for corporate opportunity could still be viewed as an opportunity because of the misappropriation. That could apply to use of both hard and soft assets (such as corporate time to develop the investment). While hard assets are often easier to relate to the opportunity, the connection of soft assets may be less clear. Thus, in order for the fiduciary to be estopped from the investment it must involve a significant use of assets and a direct and substantial nexus with the creation, pursuit and acquisition of the business opportunity. *See Rapistan Corp. v. Michaels*, 511 N.W.2d 918 (Mich. 1994).

[146] Generally, employees may be able to do some preparation and then leave their employment to compete with their business if there is no contract that restricts competition. Directors and officers are often held to a higher standard that limits their ability to compete when employed by their corporation. *See* A.L.I. Corp. Gov. Proj. § 5.06 (forbids competition by directors and senior executives that creates a disadvantage to the corporation unless authorized and with full disclosure).

[147] 488 P.2d 1172 (Haw. 1971).

the corporation in *Hawaiian International* because it was not entitled to a real estate commission. But the court would not allow the fiduciary to claim ultra vires because the corporation was not a broker and take the profit. If the corporation had known of the profit, it could have negotiated a lower selling price with the seller, net of commission, or even given the fiduciary compensation.

§ 9.06   SHAREHOLDER VOTING AND RATIFICATION

When shareholders vote on a transaction, an issue arises as to the effect of that vote. In some cases, a shareholder vote is not optional but a statutory requirement, such as voting on amendments to the articles of incorporation or to effectuate a merger or fundamental transaction (i.e., required voting). In other cases, the shareholder vote is not required but is sought for other reasons (i.e., optional voting). For example, a shareholder vote may take place under a particular statute that allows for voting but is optional, such as under the interested director statutes.[148] Other times, there is no statutory provision but the optional shareholder vote is sought for other reasons, such as to minimize the level of judicial scrutiny. Whenever there is shareholder voting, it should be fair, without coercion and with full disclosure, otherwise the vote is inoperative.

Sometimes the shareholder voting is to ratify a transaction. The idea of shareholder ratification derives from agency principles. Unauthorized acts of an agent may be ratified and validated by the principal so long as the principal has knowledge of all material facts. Shareholder ratification, however, may be different from this traditional ratification. In a publicly traded corporation, no single individual is acting as principal, but rather a collective body of shareholders (in which some of the shareholders may have a conflict of interest) is acting as principal.[149] Often, the shareholder ratification will not be directed at a lack of authority in the agent but as a result of some conflict of interest by a fiduciary.[150] The shareholders' vote may be sought to sanitize the transaction by trying to limit judicial scrutiny. In that case, the interested director statutes may have a bearing on the effect of the shareholder vote.[151]

[A]   Required Voting

There are times when shareholders take an action that requires their vote under a particular provision of the statute. In that case, the voting is not to validate the transaction as much as it is to authorize it, because without the shareholder vote, the action could not be taken. Such voting is not a ratification.

---

[148] For a discussion of these statutes, see § 9.03[B], *supra*

[149] For a discussion of collective action problems and shareholder voting, see § 5.05[C][4], *supra.*

[150] Sometimes the fiduciary is the controlling shareholders who have sufficient votes to try to ratify the transaction. For a discussion of shareholder ratification in the context of control transactions, see § 10.03[C][2][a][ii], *infra.*

[151] *Lewis v. Vogelstein*, 699 A.2d 327 (Del. Ch. 1997). For a discussion of the interested director statutes and shareholder voting, see text at notes 36–40, *supra.*

In *Williams v. Geier*,[152] a plan was proposed by the control group to recapitalize the shares that could have the effect of keeping the control group in power. In *Williams*, a shareholder vote was required by the statute for the recapitalization through amendments to the articles of incorporation. As long as there was compliance with the statutory requirements, and absent fraud, waste, manipulative or inequitable conduct, or breach of fiduciary duty, a controlling shareholder had broad powers to vote its shares. Shareholders could vote as they pleased, even if they voted their own self-interest. There was no general requirement that called for the votes of a majority of the minority (non-controlling shares) to implement the changes.[153] The court indicated that the shareholder vote, which included the votes of the controlling shareholders, was dispositive.[154]

[B]   Optional Shareholder Voting and Ratification

In cases in which the shareholder vote is optional, the effect of seeking a shareholder vote may be viewed as a ratification. Ratification can also occur when there is required voting. For example, a freezeout merger with a controlling shareholder requires a majority vote and the controlling shareholders have the requisite majority, but opt to condition the merger on the affirmative vote of a majority of the minority shareholders. This is not required but an option that may be elected to try to change the judicial scrutiny of the transaction.[155] Thus, shareholder ratification is not a statutory requirement but tends to occur when the shareholder vote is sought to affect how the law will treat the transaction and what amount of judicial scrutiny will be involved. Courts sometimes distinguish between acts that are void (for example fraudulent, illegal, ultra vires or wasteful transactions) with those that are voidable (for example, unfair conflicts of interests). The former generally cannot be ratified unless there is unanimous shareholder approval. The latter, which

---

[152] 671 A.2d 1368 (Del. 1996). For a discussion of *Williams* and corporate democracy, see § 5.05[D], *supra*.

[153] *Id.* If the corporate action has no rational purpose or is designed to entrench, then fiduciary principles would apply to the voting by the control group. *Id.*

[154] *But see Stroud v. Grace*, 606 A.2d. 75 (Del. 1992). In *Stroud*, the shareholders (including the vote of the control group) had amended the certificate and bylaws with provisions that could adversely affect future shareholder voting (they gave the board more power on selection of directors), but it was not found to be the primary purpose. As a result, the shareholder voting shifted the burden, but the court retained a fairness inquiry which meant that it would look at the substance of the decision. This case is in line with other cases dealing with shareholder ratification when controlling shareholders were involved. *See In Re Wheelabrator Techs. Shareholder Litig.*, 663 A.2d. 1194 (Del. Ch. 1994) (the Delaware chancery court viewed the shareholder voting in *Stroud* as shifting the burden on fairness). The court in *Williams* cited *Stroud* favorably but, unlike *Stroud*, did not suggest that, upon shareholder approval, fairness would remain an issue, but viewed the vote as dispositive.

[155] There are cases in which such approval does effect judicial scrutiny. For example, although mergers require shareholder voting and the statute does not require a majority of the minority approval, controlling shareholders may seek such a vote to limit judicial scrutiny of the conflict of interest. Generally, approval by the majority of minority shareholders in a control transaction will shift the burden of proof to the plaintiff but retain a fairness test. For a discussion of shareholder ratification in control transactions, see § 10.03[C][2][a][ii], *infra.*

can involve a transaction being challenged as a breach of fiduciary duty, may be affected by the shareholder vote, depending on the circumstances. In order for shareholder ratification to have an effect, it must involve full disclosure and the approval of disinterested shareholders.[156] Generally, the party relying on ratification must prove full disclosure and no coercion in the voting.

If a transaction or decision was subject to ratification, an important issue is what the effect of the shareholder vote is on any challenge to it. One possibility is that ratification precludes all judicial scrutiny of the disputed acts and extinguishes all claims. A second possibility is that ratification replaces the traditional fairness test for conflicts of interest transactions (judicial scrutiny of the process and substance of the transaction, with the burden of proof on the defendants) with the business judgment rule (i.e., burden of proof on the plaintiff and judicial scrutiny of the process) or a waste test (i.e., a gift of corporate property). A third possibility is that shareholder ratification only shifts the burden of proof to the plaintiff but retains a fairness test which allows greater judicial scrutiny of the substance of the act. A fourth possibility is that shareholder ratification has no effect on judicial scrutiny perhaps because in publicly traded corporations, the voting process has problems. There is a collective action problem and rational shareholder apathy when widely dispersed public shareholders are voting.[157]

In the case of *In Re Wheelabrator Technologies Litigation*,[158] the Delaware Chancery Court indicated its view of Delaware law on shareholder ratification. In *Wheelabrator*, Waste Management wanted to buy control of Wheelabrator. Waste already owned 22% of the shares. Waste's purchase was to be accomplished by a stock for stock merger in which Wheelabrator would end up owning 55% of Waste. While the merger statute required a majority vote of the shareholders, the parties agreed that approval of the merger would require a majority vote of the disinterested shareholders of Wheelabrator. Plaintiffs challenged the merger, claiming breaches of the duty of care and loyalty. Since the merger was approved with full disclosure by the majority of disinterested shareholders, the court had to decide the effect of the shareholder ratification on these issues.

In terms of the duty of care claim, the court found that a fully informed, disinterested shareholder vote extinguished that claim. The failure of the board to act in an informed and non-negligent manner was a voidable act that could be cured by a shareholder vote.[159]

---

[156] Often to try to lessen judicial scrutiny, an interested director will seek disinterested shareholder approval under the interested director statute even though such a vote is not explicitly required under the statute. For a discussion of these statutes, see § 9.03[B], *supra.*

[157] *See Lewis v. Vogelstein*, 699 A.2d 327 (Del. Ch. 1997). For a discussion of collective action, see § 5.05[C][4], *supra.*

[158] 663 A.2d 1194 (Del 1995).

[159] The court cited *Smith v. Van Gorkom* which is discussed at § 8.04, *supra.* The court indicated that the only other time a shareholder vote would extinguish a claim would be in a case where the board exceeded its *de jure* authority. For example, if the by-laws restricted the board's power to enter into certain contracts, a shareholder vote to approve the transaction would extinguish the claim.

In duty of loyalty claims, the court made a distinction between interested director transactions where there was no controlling shareholder and transactions with a controlling shareholder. In the former case, shareholder ratification turned the loyalty case into an issue under the business judgment rule and the plaintiff had the burden to show that the transaction was wasteful and unprotected by the rule.[160] But according to the court, when the transaction involved a controlling shareholder, more judicial scrutiny was required. The approval of the majority of the minority had the effect of shifting the burden of proof to the plaintiff to prove unfairness. This allowed some scrutiny of the substance of the transaction under a fairness standard. The rationale used to distinguish these two situations was that, with controlling shareholders, there was the possibility of process manipulation in the voting and the presence of the controlling shareholder in the transaction might influence the vote.[161]

In *Wheelabrator*, Waste Management was not a controlling shareholder since it had neither *de facto* nor *de jure* control.[162] Thus, the shareholder voting meant the duty of care claim was extinguished and the duty of loyalty claim was viewed under the business judgment rule.[163]

---

[160] The court cited *Marciano v. Nakash* and its discussion of Del. Gen. Corp. L. § 144(a)(2). For a discussion of *Marciano*, see § 9.03[B][3][a], *supra*. But see the discussion of *Harbor Financial Partners* in the text at note 113, *supra* (suggesting the waste test is unnecessary if the transaction is approved by a majority of disinterested shareholders and there was no controlling shareholder).

[161] Delaware courts recognized that the controlling shareholders will continue to control the corporation after the transaction. Their relationship has the potential to influence the voting by the minority. Even without actual coercion, the minority might perceive some retaliation from their voting against the majority. Thus, a court could not be certain that the transaction will fully approximate an arm's-length bargain. For a discussion of shareholder ratification in the context of control transactions, see § 10.03[C][2][a][ii], *infra*.

[162] For a discussion of *de facto* and *de jure* control, see § 10.01. *infra*.

[163] The involvement of independent directors can also affect judicial scrutiny. For example, use of independent directors to negotiate for the minority shareholders in a freeze-out transaction may shift the burden of proof from the controlling shareholder to the minority shareholder but does not remove a fairness inquiry. See *Kahn v. Lynch Communication Sys.*, 638 A.2d 1110 (Del. 1994). For a discussion of disinterested directors approval in freeze-outs, see § 10.03[C][2][a][i], *infra*. In other interested directors transactions, where there is no controlling shareholder, the effect of disinterested directors approval may vary. See § 9.03[B], *supra*.

Chapter 10

CONTROLLING SHAREHOLDERS

§ 10.01 INTRODUCTION

If a shareholder or group acting together own a majority or 51% or more of the voting shares of a corporation, it usually means de jure control for most shareholder decisions, including the selection of the directors.[1] In a publicly traded corporation with widely dispersed shareholders, owning less than a majority may also provide a shareholder or group of shareholders acting together with de facto or so-called working control because no other shareholders have a competing significant ownership interest. In some situations, ownership of significantly less than a majority of shares may be the largest shareholding.[2] The percentage needed to have this control will depend on a number of factors including how widely dispersed are the other shareholders. Thus one who owns less than a majority can be a controlling shareholder based upon their exercise of actual control over the business.[3] The control group may either be a number of shareholders acting together (such as a family or investment group) or it may be another corporation owning control creating a parent and subsidiary situation.

There are advantages and disadvantages for shareholders in a corporation with a control group. Because of their large investment, the control group is less diversified than other shareholders and the fortunes of the business have a greater impact on them. A significant advantage is that the control group will closely monitor potential mismanagement to assure that the managers are running the business effectively. Thus, the corporation may be more efficiently run and monitoring costs may be reduced because of the lack of separation of ownership from control. A significant disadvantage occurs when there is a

---

[1] There are ways in which the minority shareholders can have representation on the board of directors through cumulative voting or creation of different classes of common shares. Such provisions are more likely to be used in closely held corporations when the minority contract for that right. See discussion at § 11.02[E], [F], *infra*. If there is a supermajority requirement in the articles for shareholder actions, that could also limit the power of the majority. See discussion at § 11.05[B], *infra*. In a publicly traded corporation with widely dispersed shareholders, a supermajority requirement could give a large minority block veto power.

[2] For example, 10% equity owners are subject to the short swing profit rules of Section 16b of the Federal Securities Exchange Act of 1934 discussed at § 13.06, *infra*. The theory is that a 10% shareholder of a publicly traded corporation is presumptively a controlling shareholder with access to information.

[3] Potential control is insufficient to establish a controlling shareholder. But the fact that a large shareholder selects board members or even has veto power does not by itself make the shareholders controlling shareholders without more actual use of the power or other significant powers. *Williamson v Cox Communications, Inc.*, 2006 Del. Ch. LEXIS 111 (June 5, 2006).

conflict of interest transaction (i.e., self dealing) between the control group and the other shareholders. Many of the monitoring devices available when there is separation of ownership from control are not available. When there is a control group the possibility of either a proxy fight[4] or a hostile takeover[5] to take over control is diminished.[6] Truly independent directors are less likely to serve on the board.[7] Instead the minority shareholders must rely more on disclosure and fiduciary duty rules to protect them from self dealing.[8]

Generally a shareholder has no fiduciary duty when voting her shares because pursuing one's economic self interest is the usual reason why one invests in shares. But controlling shareholders are not merely shareholders because they may use their control and position in the corporation unfairly for their own self interest.[9] The fiduciary duty of controlling shareholders may come up in a variety of contexts as will be discussed in this chapter. Those shareholders may be involved in a self dealing transaction where they use their control so that they dominate the actions by the board of directors to favor their interests and treat the minority shareholders unfairly.[10] They sometimes use their control to eliminate the minority shareholders in freeze-out transactions and treat the minority unfairly. There are also times when the control group sell their shares

---

[4] For a discussion of proxy fights, see § 5.05[C], *supra*.

[5] For a discussion of hostile tender offers, see Chapter 12, *infra*.

[6] If the control group owns less than 51% there is a possibility of battle for control. Even with 51% ownership or control by a group, the group can split up. Rupert Murdoch was able to buy Dow Jones and the Wall Street Journal because his offer appealed to enough members of the Bancroft family, the controllong shareholders, to buy control. Sarah Ellison & Matthew Karnitschnig, *Murdoch Wins His Bid for Dow Jones Bancroft Family Agrees To $5 Billion Offer After Deal on Fees, A New Owner for Journal*, WALL ST. J., Aug. 1 2007, at A1.

[7] While stock market rules require a majority of independent directors, corporations with controlling shareholders are exempt from that rule except for the audit committee which must have independent directors. For a discussion of the use of independent directors, see § 5.02[F], *supra*.

[8] For a discussion of fiduciary duty, see § 8.01, *supra*. The problems of minority shareholders in a publicly traded corporation that has a control group are similar to those in a closely held corporation where the control group takes advantage of the minority shareholders. In the publicly traded corporation at least there is a trading market to provide for exit, which is unavailable to closely-held shareholders.

[9] For a discussion of a shareholder's right to vote when voting is required in order to take corporate action and the *Williams* case, see § 5.05[D], *supra*. In *Lacos Land Co. v. Arden Corp*, 517 A.2d 271 (Del. Ch. 1986), there was a proposal to reclassify the corporation's equity into two classes in which one class would have super voting rights. (For a discussion of this tactic, see § 5.05[A], note 145, *supra*.) The proposal was supported by the largest shareholder (21%). That shareholder had explicitly threatened to vote against future transactions that could be in the best interests of the corporation unless the proposal was approved. Plaintiffs challenged the vote on the reclassification claiming coercion because of the threat. The court viewed the threat as coercive but in doing so focused on the shareholder's role as a director and officer creating a fiduciary duty and not just on the fact that the shareholder was the largest shareholder. As a fiduciary, he had no right to take that position no matter what the motivation. Compare *Shreiber v. Carney*, discussed in § 5.05[E], note 211, *supra* with *Kahn v. Lynch Communications Sys., Inc.*, discussed in § 10.03[C][2][a][i], *infra* (both cases dealt with coercion; in the former there was no liability, but in the latter, the coercion was an element of fair dealing).

[10] In *Pepper v. Litton*, 308 U.S. 295, 306 (1939), the Supreme Court indicated that dominant and controlling shareholders hold their powers in trust and that their transactions with the corporation are subject to rigorous scrutiny with the burden on them to prove good faith and inherent fairness.

to another, receiving a substantial premium over the market price and the action harms the corporation or the minority shareholders. If the duty of loyalty applies to any of these transactions as a conflict of interest then a fairness inquiry may be applied with the burden of proof usually on the controlling shareholder to prove entire fairness, i.e., both fair dealing and fair price. As will be discussed, the controlling shareholders may try to change the level of judicial scrutiny by using independent directors to approve the transaction or by having the transaction ratified by the disinterested shareholders.

§ 10.02   USE OF CONTROL

[A]   The *Zahn* Case

Controlling shareholders may not use their control to self deal unfairly with the assets of the corporation. The case of *Zahn v. Transamerica Corporation*[11] involved Axton-Fisher Tobacco Company ("AF") and 2 classes of shares (Class A and Class B)[12] whose rights were found in its articles. The Class B functioned as the common shares and the Class A were similar to preferred shares. Under the articles, the Class A was entitled to $3.20 in dividends annually that were cumulative if not paid (that is, the corporation would owe the shareholders the dividend arrears). The Class A was also entitled in liquidation to receive twice as much as the Class B in the remaining assets. The Class A could also convert into Class B shares on a one for one basis. But the Class A could be redeemed (that is, bought back) by the corporation at any time so long as the Class A received 60 days' notice and $60 plus all dividends owed. Class A had also been given voting rights along with Class B (the articles provided Class A with such rights since no dividends were paid for four quarters).

Transamerica Corporation had acquired control of the company through purchases of both Class A and B shares. It turned out that AF owned leaf tobacco which was a valuable asset but listed on its books for its cost of more than $6 million. It was actually worth about $20 million.[13] Transamerica decided that it would acquire the tobacco by having the board eliminate the Class A shareholders by redeeming those shares for $60, plus accrued dividends as permitted by the articles. Transamerica would then liquidate the corporation and appropriate the tobacco. The redemption required the vote of the directors of AF who were selected by Transamerica. There was no disclosure to Class A shareholders of the plan to liquidate the corporation and use of the tobacco.

The Class A shareholders brought a class action lawsuit claiming that Transamerica, through the directors, had breached its duty of loyalty (with the burden on the defendant to prove fairness to them) by the redemption. The actions of the directors precluded the Class A from its 2:1 liquidation right and

---

[11]   162 F.2d 36 (3d Cir. 1947).

[12]   There were actually 3 classes of equity, including the preferred stock, which was not involved in the case.

[13]   An example of cost based accounting where assets are listed at their cost and not fair market value. For a discussion of accounting principles, see § 4.05[B][1], *supra.*

receiving its share of the value of the tobacco favoring Transamerica. The plaintiffs argued that the directors should not favor Transamerica over the Class A shareholders. Transamerica argued that the redemption was permitted under the articles and protected by the business judgment rule and could be effectuated at any time and for any purpose by the directors.

The court recognized that shareholders may act as they please when voting as shareholders. But there was a breach of the duty of loyalty by Transamerica because it was not acting solely as a shareholder, but through its control of the directors. Directors must act for all shareholders, and here they were not independent (described as being in a "puppet-puppeteer relationship" with Transamerica)[14] in redeeming the Class A shares.[15]

The remedy that the court initially seemed to favor was for the Class A to share in the value of the tobacco as it would in liquidation (that is, receive twice as much as Class B). This result was a strict view of fairness but would harm Class B by favoring Class A's liquidation rights. Ultimately the remedy was to allow Class A to receive what it would have been entitled to if there had been disclosure of the liquidation plan and they converted to Class B (that is, share equally with Class B).[16] The idea was that an independent board would consider the interests of both Class A and B shareholders and would have disclosed the true value of the tobacco and the future liquidation of the company prior to redemption. Thus permitting the Class A either to convert to Class B or accept the redemption payment of $60 plus dividends.

[B] Parent-Subsidiary Dealings

Controlling shareholders may find themselves contracting with their corporation. The result is a conflict of interest transaction similar to interested directors' transactions and the application of the duty of loyalty.[17] Generally, the duty of loyalty in conflicts of interest requires a shifting of the burden of proof and the use of a fairness standard, allowing the court to look at both the process and substance of the decision.

In some parent and subsidiary contexts, the parent corporation has chosen not to own 100% of the shares of the subsidiary so that there are other shareholders. As a result, transactions between the two corporations may involve conflicts of interest because of the existence of minority shareholders. In *Sinclair v. Levien*,[18] Sinclair, an oil company, owned 97% of the shares of Sinven, which operated as an oil company in Venezuela. The directors of Sinven

---

[14] Directors who consciously act as a tool for the controlling shareholder as opposed to trying to make decisions for the best interests of the corporation may themselves be liable for a duty ofloyalty claim based upon their lack of good faith. *ATR-Kim Eng Fin. Corp. v. Araneta* 2006 Del. Ch. LEXIS 215 (Dec. 21, 2006). For a discussion of good faith, see § 8.06, *supra*.

[15] In *Jones v. H.F. Ahmanson*, 406 P.2d 464 (Cal. 1969), the California Supreme Court found liability for controlling shareholders independent of their control of the directors. For a discussion of *Jones*, see § 10.04[C], *infra*.

[16] *Speed v. Transamerica*, 235 F.2d 369 (3d Cir. 1956).

[17] For a discussion of interested directors transactions, see § 9.03, *supra*.

[18] 280 A.2d 717 (Del. 1971).

were not viewed as independent from Sinclair. A derivative action was brought by minority shareholders of Sinven claiming that dividend policy was established to favor Sinclair, that Sinclair had seized corporate opportunities away from Sinven, and that a contract between Sinclair and Sinven was unfairly administered.

The Supreme Court of Delaware found that as a controlling shareholder, Sinclair was required to meet an intrinsic fairness test whenever a conflict of interest existed. The judicial scrutiny involved a shift of the burden of proof and an inquiry into whether the transaction was fair (i.e., a review of the substance of the decision).[19] While the decision seemed to be a strong statement of fiduciary principles, consistent with the duty of loyalty, the result can be viewed as more limited. Contrary to the conclusions of the trial court,[20] the large dividend payments did not violate any duty or involve self-dealing since all shareholders received them (that is, the minority was not excluded). That there was a policy of paying out large dividends financially to assist Sinclair was not significant because, although Sinclair received a large sum of money, it did not receive a proportionally larger amount than the minority as the amount paid per share was the same.

The plaintiff was also unable to point to any corporate opportunities that were taken from Sinven and there was again no exclusion and self-dealing. Sinclair had a policy of exploiting its oil properties through subsidiaries in those countries where the properties were located. The opportunities belonged to Sinclair and the allocation to different subsidiaries was a matter of their business judgment. As with the dividend claim, the controlling shareholder had not received a benefit to the exclusion and detriment of the minority shareholders.

The court did find liability for Sinclair as a result of its contract between Sinven and another Sinclair subsidiary. The contract was breached by failure to make timely payments to, and minimum purchases from, Sinven. As a result, the intrinsic fairness test required Sinclair to prove that its breach of the contract was fair. But this holding may be different from other interested transactions if the plaintiff must prove self dealing as defined. The court defined self-dealing in a parent-subsidiary setting as requiring an exclusion (that is, the parent receives a benefit not received by the minority through the contract) and an additional showing of detriment (that is, harm which in this case was the breach of the contract).[21] In other interested directors' transactions, all that is

[19] In transactions with controlling shareholders, the Delaware Supreme Court now uses an entire fairness test that looks at both fair dealing and fair price. *See Kahn v. Tremont*, 694 A.2d 422 (Del. 1997). For a discussion of entire fairness, see § 10.03[C], *infra.*

[20] *Levien v. Sinclair Oil Corporation*, 261 A.2d 911 (Del. Ch. 1969). The trial court focused on how Sinclair took as much money out of the subsidiary as possible leaving it is a cash poor position which precluded it from investing in other business opportunities that allegedly were taken by Sinclair.

[21] In *Case v. New York Central R.R.*, 15 N.Y.2d 150 (1965), the parent (which had losses) had a contract with its subsidiary (which had profits) to allocate the tax benefits the subsidiary received by using the parent's losses to reduce its taxes. While the contract produced greater benefits to the parent as a result, there was no breach of fiduciary duty. The court indicated that for a breach there needs to be an advantage to the controlling shareholder which was to the disadvantage of the

usually required for a conflict of interest is a showing of an unfair exclusion in that the fiduciary was on both sides of the transaction.[22] If this definition means plaintiff must prove both exclusion and detriment before intrinsic fairness applies then arguably it makes duty of loyalty cases more difficult in this context (parent-subsidiary).[23] Even if all that is required is pleading these elements, there may be a need for greater acts by the parent to support the claim of exclusion and detriment. But the result of more difficult pleading or proof may be justified because in this context the shareholders as investors expect contracting between a parent and its subsidiary as a normal part of business which may not be true of conflicts of interests in other contexts.

[C] Sale of Corporation

When a corporation is sold, fiduciary duties come into play. Generally, in an arm's length bargain transaction involving a sale of the business, there is the duty of care and disclosure.[24] In a sale of the entire company, the directors should focus on securing the best value reasonably available to all shareholders.[25] When controlling shareholders are in the picture, the judicial scrutiny may be heightened. If the controlling shareholder is itself buying the corporation and eliminating the minority shareholders, then it is a viewed as a freeze-out transaction, which will be discussed later in this Chapter.[26] But even if the corporation is being sold to a third party, the transaction may not be completely at arm's length. In *McMullin v. Beran*,[27] the Delaware Supreme Court was faced with allegations that the sale of the corporation to a third party was at the behest of the controlling shareholders. The controlling shareholders were accused of pursuing their interests in the sale as they were involved in the

---

minority. Here, the court found an advantage to the parent, but no disadvantage to the subsidiary (even though the parent had a greater advantage). Without the parent's losses there would have been no tax benefits to the subsidiary and thus the subsidiary did not lose anything. The court was also unable to determine what a fair allocation would be under the circumstances.

[22] For a discussion of interested directors' transactions, see § 9.03, *supra.*

[23] When a parent corporation uses its power to freezeout or eliminate the minority shareholders, the standard is entire fairness which results in greater judicial scrutiny. For a discussion of freeze-outs, see § 10.03, *infra.*

[24] For an example of a breach of duty of care in an arm's length bargain acquisition, see the discussion of *Smith v. Van Gorkom* at § 8.04, *supra.*

[25] The methods could include an auction or canvassing the market but there is no single method required. For a discussion of this duty in the context of a hostile tender offer and the *QVC* case, see § 12.05[A][5], *infra.*

[26] For a discussion of freeze-outs, see § 10.03, *infra.*

[27] 765 A.2d 910 (Del. 2000). In this case, the Delaware Supreme Court reversed the lower court's dismissal of a cause of action against the directors who were accused of breaching their fiduciary duty in the sale of the corporation to a third party at the behest of the controlling shareholder who needed cash. There were sufficient allegations to rebut the business judgment rule. The complaint alleged potential violations of due care (rushed a decision to approve the sale to accommodate the controlling shareholders need for cash); duty of loyalty (8 of the 12 directors were not independent but controlled because they were either employed or had prior affiliations with the controlling shareholder); an improper delegation of the negotiation of the merger to the controlling shareholders; and lack of full disclosure (usually a mixed question of law and fact requiring discovery).

negotiations and timing of the transaction.[28] Because of the majority shareholders' control, there may be no real expectation of an alternative competing transaction. The minority shareholders are usually left with no choice but to accept the deal negotiated by the controlling shareholder or seek appraisal.[29] But in such a situation the directors cannot abdicate their responsibility to the corporation and let the shareholders decide by their vote on the merger[30] since they still have a fiduciary duty to the minority shareholders to be informed and determine whether the transaction is fair. Thus, directors may have to make a critical assessment of the merger and make an independent determination of whether it maximizes value for all shareholders.

§ 10.03 FREEZEOUTS

Freezeouts involve controlling shareholders forcing the minority shareholders to relinquish their equity position in the corporation. Usually, the shareholders receive cash for their shares but they also may receive other non voting securities. In a publicly held corporation, the result is usually that the corporation becomes a privately held corporation.[31] While the courts and state legislatures were initially hostile to such freezeouts, the law today is generally permissive.[32] Many of the freezeouts involve the practice of using large amounts of debt to finance the freezeout and are described as leverage buyouts.[33]

The mechanics of freezeouts may vary but the common means is to use a shell corporation A^s, which is set up as a wholly owned corporation of the controlling shareholder (e.g., A Inc.), which in turn controls the public corporation (B Inc.). A Inc. uses its control of the board of directors of B Inc. to enter into a merger agreement where by B Inc. then merges into A^s. A Inc. votes their controlling shares in favor of the merger. The plan of merger provides that the minority shareholders of B Inc. receive cash or debt securities for their shares, resulting in elimination of their ownership of B Inc.[34]

---

[28] The court indicated that the controlling shareholders could have sold their shares but once they tried to sell the whole corporation their duty changed to try to maximize the value.

[29] For a discussion of appraisal, see § 6.06, *supra.*

[30] Under Del. Gen. Corp. L. § 251(b), directors are required to approve any mergers. If the transaction is a tender offer where directors are not statutorily involved, than the scrutiny may be different. See § 10.03[C][2][c], *infra.*

[31] After the freezeout, the corporation will either be owned by private investors or wholly owned by a publicly traded parent corporation. There can also be a freezeout in a closely held corporation where the control group eliminates the minority shareholders.

[32] *See generally* Elliott Weiss, *The Law of Take Out Mergers: A Historical Perspective*, 56 N.Y.U. L. Rev. 624 (1981) (traces of development of merger statutes and judicial approach to them).

[33] Given the high rate of interest for much of the debt and because the corporation often increased its debt/equity ratio, the debt used to finance have been popularly described as junk bonds (or high yield debt). Junk bonds have also been used to finance large hostile takeovers. See § 12.02, *infra.*

[34] For a discussion of this triangular merger, see § 6.02[A], *supra.* Another method would be for B Inc. to sell its assets to A Inc. for cash or other securities which then would be distributed to the minority shareholders of B Inc. In a closely held corporation, the controlling shareholders of B Inc. would set up another corporation that they would wholly own (i.e., 100%). The controlling

FREEZEOUT MERGER

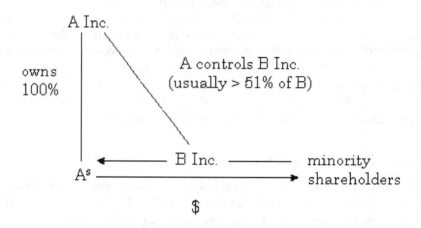

After the merger, A Inc. owns 100% of B Inc.

[A] Policy Issues

Freezeouts of public shareholders raise significant policy issues. Many commentators view freezeouts as beneficial both to the shareholders and society as a whole. The shareholders who are frozen out benefit, because they usually receive a premium over the current market price of their stock and are arguably better off than they were before the freezeout. For example, if the market price of the corporation is $15 before the transaction and the selling price is $20 (that is, a $5 premium over the market) the shareholders receive a greater return.[35] The premium reflects the anticipated higher value as a result of the acquisition which is beneficial to society as whole. The group paying $20 would arguably only do so if they thought they could make the business worth more than $20.[36]

Eliminating minority ownership saves costs that must be incurred by public corporations (i.e., agency costs)[37] such as the costs of compliance with SEC requirements. If management has a major equity position in the acquiring corporation, managers will now have a strong incentive to run the company more efficiently because they have more at stake in the success of the business.

---

shareholders would use the wholly owned corporation to acquire B Inc. and freezeout the minority shareholders of B Inc.

[35] The premium will be beneficial so long as the shares trading in the market reflect the fair value of the shares. Thus, the efficiency of the market is an important issue. See § 5.02[D], *supra.*

[36] *See* Frank Easterbrook & Daniel Fischel, *Corporate Control Transactions,* 93 YALE L.J. 698, 705–708 (1982). The authors argue against a fiduciary principle that requires equal treatment of all shareholders by sharing any and all premiums paid for corporation. They see most control transactions as being beneficial by increasing the value of the corporation's assets. So long as minority shareholders are as well off after the transaction as before, the law should not impose restraints. *Id.* at 708–14. The argument is premised on stock market price reflecting fair value and is similar to the arguments used by proponents of hostile tender offers. *See* § 12.03[A], *infra.*

[37] For a discussion of agency costs, see § 5.03[C][1], *supra.*

The leveraging that often results in freezeouts means that the corporation has to be run more efficiently to avoid defaulting on the increased debt. If the freezeout is the result of a parent corporation taking over a subsidiary, there may be economies of scale in the acquisition. Without minority shareholders, there is more flexibility in decision-making and no concern for conflict of interest transactions being challenged.

Others have viewed freezeouts by controlling shareholders in traditional fiduciary terms, involving a conflict of interest and potential unfairness to shareholders. Freezeouts may involve the insider taking advantage of a corporate opportunity, non-public information, or the future growth potential of a company, at a time when the market may not accurately reflect the true potential of the corporation. The control group is, in effect, using its insider status to misappropriate the corporation's future. The control group chooses the timing and that choice will always favor them over the public shareholders. Freezeouts are seen as coercive because shareholders may receive less than the value they assign to their shares and have no real choice because of their minority status.[38] The control group may also take steps to keep the market price of the shares low so that the premium offered is not really beneficial to the minority public shareholders.[39] The shareholders often are forced to pay taxes on any gains when they are receiving cash.

While freezeouts involve the forced elimination of common stock ownership, not all freezeouts are conducted in the same manner. The particular context may affect the amount of judicial scrutiny of the transaction.[40] In some cases, the freezeout has been the result of an acquisition of control of B by A through an initial arm's length purchase, or public tender offer, in which the freezeout was intended to acquire the remaining shares in a second step transaction.[41] If the price offered in the second step to the minority in the freezeout is the same price at which the acquiror purchased the majority in the first step, then there may be less concern over fairness. Since it was initially at arms length presumedly the directors of A negotiated a fair price for the acquisition. But if the price offered to the minority in the second step is less than that paid to acquire control, this may be unfair.[42]

---

[38] See generally James Vorenberg, Exclusiveness of the Dissenting Stockholder's Appraisal Rights, 77 HARV. L. REV. 1189 (1964); Victor Brudney & Marvin Chirelstein, A Restatement of Corporate Freezeouts, 87 YALE L.J. 1354 (1978).

[39] For example, if the control group reduced dividend payments or increased its compensation and thereby reduced earnings, the market price could be negatively affected so that the premium over the market price offered in the freezeout seemed fair. See, e.g., Berkowitz v. Power/Mate Corp. 342 A.2d 566 (1975) (controlling shareholders used large bonuses to reduce reported earnings and depress the market price of the shares).

[40] See Ed Greene, Corporate Freeze Out Mergers: A Proposed Analysis, 28 STAN. L. REV. 487 (1976); Brudney & Chirelstein, note 38, supra.

[41] Freezeouts may result after a takeover if the bidder wants 100% ownership but acquires less in the tender offer due to the inevitable holdouts. This is known as a two — tier offer, a tender offer followed by a freezeout transaction. See, e.g., Singer v. Magnavox Co., 380 A.2d 969 (Del. 1977).

[42] In the context of a hostile takeover there was a strategy called the front-loaded two-tier tender offer where a higher price was offered in the tender offer to the public to gain 51% control but the public was informed that once control was acquired there would be a second step freezeout merger

Some cases involve a parent corporation, as a controlling shareholder, deciding to eliminate the minority shareholders in its subsidiary to avoid conflicts of interests with intra corporate transactions and reduce agency costs. Arguably these transactions serve a useful business purpose for the parent but may still be unfair to the minority shareholder requiring close judicial scrutiny.[43]

There have also been transactions in which a control group of a publicly traded corporation, such as a family, has decided that it no longer wanted to be a public corporation and has then taken the corporation private (sometimes called "going private").[44] Sometimes, the control groups had taken advantage of a strong stock market to go public and then later took advantage of a weak stock market to eliminate the minority public shareholders and go private. Some of these corporations that went private in this manner subsequently went public again. Former SEC Commissioner A.A. Sommer Jr. has described going private as: ". . . serious, unfair, and sometimes disgraceful, a perversion of the whole process of public financing, and a course that inevitably is going to make the individual shareholder even more hostile to American corporate mores and the securities markets than he already is."[45]

In management buyouts ("MBOs"), the managers, who controlled the operations of the corporation but did not have control through large ownership, decide to take the corporation private by offering the public shareholders a premium for their shares.[46] Usually this required borrowing (often using the assets of the corporation as collateral) to finance the purchase (i.e., a leveraged buyout).[47] Many MBOs occurred in the 1980s and were a response to hostile tender offers. Management decided that if an outside bidder could come in and buy the corporation by borrowing against the assets, then management should

---

at a lower price. This tactic was highly controversial and viewed as coercive and is rarely used now. For a discussion, see § 12.04[A], *infra.*

[43] *See, e.g., Weinberger v. UOP, Inc.,* 457 A.2d 701 (Del. 1983), discussed at § 10.03[C][1], *infra.*

[44] Going private can also describe all freezeouts of publicly traded corporations because the result is a public corporation becoming private.

[45] A.A. Sommer Jr., *Going Private: A Lesson in Corporate Responsibility,* BNA Sec. L. Rep. No. 278, at D-1 (Nov. 20, 1974). Professors Brudney and Chirelstein, note 38, *supra,* argue that these different contexts require different rules. The going private transaction should be prohibited, the parent-subsidiary merger should be subject to a fairness test, and the two-step merger (where the second-step freezeout is at the same price as the first step purchase), subject to the business judgment rule. The courts have not generally adopted their analysis and apply an entire fairness test to most freezeouts. Professors Fischel and Easterbrook, note 36, *supra,* reject any rule that would prohibit or restrict control transactions so long as there is a premium over the market price paid to the shareholders.

[46] *See generally* Deborah DeMott, *Puzzles and Parables: Defining Good Faith in the MBO Context,* 25 WAKE FOREST L. REV. 15 (1990).

[47] The increased indebtedness and the large payouts to shareholders raised an issue of whether the transactions were fraudulent conveyances (i.e., transfers made for inadequate consideration while insolvent) that harmed the existing corporate creditors if the leveraged buyout failed and went into bankruptcy. The issue was not whether there was actual intent to defraud creditors, but constructive fraud in that the payments to shareholders were for inadequate consideration leaving the corporation either insolvent or with unreasonably small capital. *See generally* Douglas Baird *Fraudulent Conveyance, Agency Costs, and Leveraged Buyouts,* 20 J. LEGAL STUDIES 1 (1991).

be able to do the same.[48] Like other freezeouts, shareholders would benefit by the premium they receive. To some, management buyouts were justified by the premium offered and the increased efficiency in the business because management would have greater incentives because of their increased ownership.[49] Yet the question arises, if management has a fiduciary duty, why shouldn't they be operating the business more efficiently when it was a public corporation? At least in a management buyout, the managers proposing the buyout do not own enough shares to control the outcome and have to offer a fair enough price to get the approval of the majority of shareholders and independent directors. In addition, the management buyout may induce other competing bidders.[50]

[B]　State Law

In order to facilitate a freezeout, the control group must comply with a state's statutory scheme of regulation for mergers and case law on fiduciary obligations. The statutory requirements for a merger involve approval by the board of directors and a shareholder vote.[51] Corporate statutes permit the use of cash or securities other than common stock as consideration, resulting in a freezeout merger. When a vote is required, most statutes require a majority vote, which is easily obtainable for those in actual or de facto control of the corporation. The short form merger provisions require no shareholder vote when the control group owns a large percentage of stock, usually 90% or more.[52]

In the 1960s the states began to amend their merger statutes to allow the use of cash (as opposed to securities which usually meant shares) as consideration in mergers. When cash became available as consideration, the freezeout merger

---

[48] Some management buyouts were a direct response to a hostile tender offer from an outside bidder. Generally the directors cannot play favorites when both are bidding and should seek to maximize shareholder value. *See Mills Acquisition Co. v. Macmillan, Inc.*, 559 A.2d 1261 (Del 1989). For a discussion of the need to auction the corporation when the corporation is viewed as up for sale, see § 12.05[A][3] and [5], *infra.*

[49] Some commentators have argued that the use of debt in many of these freezeouts is an important incentive that forces managers to be more efficient because they must pay their debts or lose the business. This restricts their opportunities to waste money. *See* Michael Jensen, *Agency Costs of Free Cash Flow, Corporate Finance and Takeovers*, 76 AMER. ECON. REV. 323 (1986).

[50] *Cf.* A.L.I. Corp. Gov. Proj. § 5.15 (if there is market test and disinterested board and shareholder approval than a waste standard as opposed to fairness applies to the transaction). In 1988, the managers of R.J.R Nabisco, Inc. proposed a management buyout of the company for $17 billion (the market price equaled about $13 billion). But instead of precluding a tender offer it created a bidding war for the company in which management ultimately lost but the company sold for over $20 billion, at that point the largest corporate control transaction ever. *See* Bryan Burroughs & John Helyar, BARBARIANS AT THE GATE (1990) (an excellent recount of the events surrounding this takeover). If there is a control group that owns more than 50% then the fact that an outsider responds to the freezeout by offering to buy the corporation for a higher price does not mean that the control group has to sell or give up the freezeout. *See Mendel v. Carroll*, 651 A.2d 297 (Del. Ch. 1994), discussed at note 132, *infra.*

[51] For a discussion of the legal requirements for mergers, see § 6.02, *supra.*

[52] E.g., Model Bus. Corp. Act Ann. § 11.04 (4th ed. 2008). For a discussion of the short form merger, see § 6.02[C], *supra*

became more prevalent.[53] Freezeouts result from the control group eliminating the public shareholders from future ownership, usually by paying cash.[54]

In general the courts will scrutinize freezeouts by control groups as a duty of loyalty issue requiring entire fairness (fair dealing and fair price) and in some cases requiring a business purpose for the transaction. Approval of an unfair transaction can also create liability for the directors who approve of the merger.[55] Given the conflict of interest, an issue arises as to whether an appraisal (a statutory right shareholders may have in mergers that entitles them to seek judicial review of the fair value of their shares) is the appropriate and exclusive remedy for the minority shareholders, or whether the courts may fashion other remedies based upon fiduciary principles? Minority shareholders have attempted to avoid the appraisal procedure because of its limitations.[56] Generally the minority shareholders would prefer using shareholder litigation through the federal securities laws or state fiduciary duty doctrine to enjoin the transaction or seek damages greater than the limited appraisal remedy. Through litigation, they hope to force the control group to offer a higher price.[57] Some courts have used their equitable powers to closely scrutinize the transaction and either enjoin the transaction or award higher damages or other

---

[53] A shareholder could also be frozen out through the use of securities when they receive debt or preferred shares.

[54] With common shares of the acquiror, the shareholders would at least be able to retain an equity interest in the acquiring corporation. But the transaction would still involve a conflict of interest.

[55] In *In re Emerging Communications, Inc, Shareholders Litigation*, 2004 Del. Ch. LEXIS 70 (May 3, 2004), the court found unfair dealing and awarded the plaintiffs a higher price than offered in the freezeout merger (also awarded the same price to those who were in appraisal). Because there was an exculpatory provision for duty of care damages in the certificate pursuant Delaware's § 102(b)(7), liability needed to be based upon duty of loyalty or lack of good faith not duty of care. In order to claim protection under that exculpatory provision the defendants must prove that it applies to the case i.e. their breach did not involve loyalty or good faith. For a discussion of § 102(b)(7), see § 8.05[A], *infra*. The controlling shareholder was liable for a breach of duty of loyalty and the court also found some of the directors liable for loyalty violations based upon a lack of good faith. One director actively assisted the controlling shareholder and his economic interest was tied to that shareholder. Another director did not actively assist the breach but voted to approve the transaction knowing or having a strong reason to know it was unfair. That director had special expertise and should have acted on it by opposing the merger. The lack of good faith could be explained either because his loyalty was with the controlling shareholder to further other business interests or he consciously and intentionally disregard his fiduciary duty. These defendants were held jointly and severally liable for the fair value of the shares. As to other directors there may have been a duty of care violation but there was no lack of good faith based upon intentional conduct so any possible damages from them were exculpated. For a discussion of good faith, see § 8.06, *infra*.

[56] For a discussion of appraisal and valuation, see § 6.06, *supra*. *See generally* Note, *Valuation of Dissenters' Stock Under Appraisal Statutes*, 79 HARV. L. REV. 1453 (1966) (general discussion of traditional valuation and various factors to be considered). In equity, there exists the possibility of rescissory damages, allowing a plaintiff to recover any increase in the value of stock resulting from its acquisition by the control group. *See Lynch v. Vickers Energy Corp.*, 429 A.2d 497, 501 (Del. 1981).

[57] Class actions may have advantages over an individual appraisal. Attorneys will bring litigation on a contingency basis and if successful or settled, receive fees, which are paid by the entire class. Actions in appraisal are brought by individual shareholders and not usually as a larger class action, thus limiting who pays attorney fees to those seeking appraisal. Attorneys' fees are discretionary in appraisal. Appraisal may also take longer compared to a settlement of litigation. For a discussion of shareholder litigation, see Chapter 14, *infra*.

equitable relief. Other courts have only allowed for the use of an appraisal but have expanded and modernized that remedy.[58]

[C]   Cases

Prior to 1977 it was unclear how Delaware courts would treat freezeouts and whether appraisals would be the exclusive remedy. The Supreme Court of Delaware in *Singer v. Magnavox*[59] held that a majority shareholder who eliminated the minority shareholders in a freezeout merger for the sole purpose of eliminating the minority must meet the burden of proving entire fairness. The court also required a business purpose to the merger, other than the elimination of the minority shareholders. It allowed a class action for all shareholders in equity against the controlling shareholders without having to seek appraisal. This was a strong statement of fiduciary duty principles by the Delaware Supreme Court that may have reflected criticisms at that time of Delaware concerning its lack of protection for shareholders. *Singer* may have also been a reaction to the attempts around that time to federalize corporate law for large publicly traded corporations which would have taken away Delaware's franchise.[60]

[1]   The *Weinberger* Case

In 1983 the Delaware Supreme Court, in *Weinberger v. U.O.P. Inc.*, moved away from *Singer*, eliminating the requirement of a business purpose[61] and limiting the use of equitable relief in freezeouts. The court found the business purpose test was not useful because creating a business purpose in an interested transaction was unnecessary and not difficult for creative lawyers. Instead, the court focused on the concept of entire fairness. Entire fairness in this context meant fair dealing and fair price.[62]

In 1975, Signal Oil Co. had acquired majority control of UOP in a friendly tender offer at $21 a share (the market price was $14). Six of the thirteen UOP directors were nominees of Signal and later Crawford, the president and chief executive officer, was designated by Signal. Three years later, Signal decided to acquire the remaining shares of UOP. Signal eventually offered $21, which was a 50% premium over the market price. In a matter of 4 days, UOP's investment bankers had issued a fairness opinion indicating that the offer was a fair price. Signal also agreed that the merger would be subject to a requirement of a positive vote of the majority of the minority shareholders.[63] The independent

---

[58] For a discussion of the new appraisal, see § 6.06[A][1], *infra*.

[59] 380 A.2d 969 (Del. 1977).

[60] For a discussion of Delaware's interest in protecting its preeminent position, see § 1.09[A], *supra*.

[61] 457 A.2d 701 (1983). See Herzel & Colling, *Squeeze-Out Merger in Delaware — The Delaware Supreme Court Decision in* Weinberger v. UOP, Inc., 7 Corp. L. Rev. 195, 203–04 (1984).

[62] For a discussion of the use of entire fairness as the standard used when the directors are not protected by the business judgment rule, see § 8.03[B], *supra*.

[63] There is no statutory requirement for approval of a majority of the minority. Usually the majority can effectuate a merger. This approval by the minority was an attempt to limit judicial

directors of UOP met privately and agreed to the merger. The shareholders approved the merger, which received the positive vote of the minority.

Some minority shareholders brought an action under *Singer* claiming a lack of entire fairness in the freezeout with a controlling shareholder. The Delaware Supreme Court in *Weinberger* first analyzed fair dealing, indicating that it involves more than full disclosure by the control group. Fair dealing includes other process issues such as timing, initiation, negotiations and structure of the merger. In *Weinberger*, the court found a lack of fair dealing. A feasibility study prepared by 2 directors of UOP (who also served as Signal directors) indicated that a price up to $24 would be a good investment for Signal. That report was never disclosed to the independent directors or shareholders of UOP. Since UOP directors worked for Signal and prepared the report with UOP information, it was unfair dealing and a lack of complete candor in the failure to disclose the report to the other UOP directors and the shareholders. In addition, Signal's insistence on a quick approval, the time constraints faced by UOP and the lack of any real negotiations (none of which were disclosed to the shareholders) added to the unfairness of the dealing. In effect the court was looking for the earmarks of arm's length bargaining. The court suggested in a footnote that, while perfection is not expected, the use of an independent negotiating committee would affect the result.[64]

According to the court in Weinberger, fair price relates to all the relevant factors which affect the value of the shares. The court recognized some of the limitations of the traditional appraisal remedy and decided that, the traditional "Delaware block approach" used in appraisal needed to be updated. That approach will no longer exclude valuation techniques generally acceptable in the financial community, such as looking at comparative takeover premiums or valuation based upon discounted cash flow.[65] Thus, in this new appraisal elements of future value susceptible to proof will be allowed (but not speculative elements of value from the accomplishment of the merger). The new appraisal expanded the "Delaware block approach" and has become the norm. in appraisal.[66] The fairer the course of dealing the less likely the courts are to find

---

scrutiny of the conflict of interest. For a discussion of shareholder ratification, see § 10.03[C][2](a)(ii), *infra.*

[64] 457 A.2d at 709–10 n.7. For a discussion of the use of independent directors in freezeouts, see § 10.03[C][2](a)(i), *infra.*

[65] New York legislatively took a similar approach in N.Y.B.C.L. § 623(h)(4). Under the MBCA fair value is determined using customary and current valuation concepts used for similar businesses in the context that required appraisal. Model Bus. Corp. Act Ann. § 13.01(4)(ii) (4th ed. 2008). A.L.I. Corp. Gov. Proj. § 7.22(a) also allows for modern financial methods. The A.L.I. distinguishes between arms-length and control transactions in appraisal. The former would allow for the valuation negotiated by the independent board unless plaintiff could show by clear and convincing evidence that the fair value was otherwise. § 7.22(b) In control transactions, appraisal should award the highest realistic price a willing buyer would have paid for the corporation. § 7.22(c).

[66] The *Weinberger* approach to appraisal still has limitations because it allows the continued use of the "Delaware block approach," the inability to bring a class action and the time and expense for minority shareholders. For a discussion of this new appraisal, see § 6.06[A][1], *supra.* In *Rapid-American Corp. v. Harris*, 603 A.2d 796 (Del. 1992), the Delaware Supreme Court used the new appraisal in valuing shares of a parent corporation and included the control premium the parent corporation (a holding company which held shares) had in its subsidiaries.

an unfair price in equity. Thus, the new appraisal will usually be the remedy for minority shareholders in a freezeout so long as there has been fair dealing.[67]

Weinberger clarified several issues while leaving others unclear. Even if the ultimate burden of proof is on the defendant to show the transaction was fair, the plaintiffs have the initial burden to demonstrate some basis for invoking the fairness obligation. It eliminated the business purpose test and clarified entire fairness to include both fair dealing and price required in freezeout transactions.[68] In *Weinberger* there was no fair dealing because among other things the report prepared by fiduciaries of UOP on the highest price Signal would pay was not disclosed to the minority shareholders of UOP[69] and the rushed process. Thus, fair dealing was a fair process and not just about disclosure.

The approval of a majority of the minority of UOP was ineffective because there was a lack of complete candor when the shareholders voted since they did not know about the unfair dealing. The court did suggest that shareholder approval could shift the burden to the plaintiff.[70] The court did not clarify what happens if there was an independent negotiating committee.[71]

Further, *Weinberger* suggested that appraisal would not be appropriate for cases of "fraud, misrepresentation, self-dealing,[72] deliberate waste of corporate assets, or gross and palpable overreaching." But the decision failed to clarify when in freezeouts appraisal would be the exclusive remedy.[73] Plaintiffs prefer seeking equity as opposed to appraisal, where the minority shareholders could

---

[67] Claims of unfair dealing in the merger itself are not usually appropriate for appraisal but can be brought in a separate action in equity challenging the merger in Delaware. In the short form merger context where there is no claim of unfair dealing allowed in equity. *See* note 79, *infra.* But if there are claims of unfair dealing not related to the merger then those claims are appropriate for an appraisal proceeding.

[68] Entire fairness may also be required in an arms-length transaction. While normally such transactions are subject to the business judgment rule, if the rule is rebutted then the defendants have to prove entire fairness. *See Cede & Co. v. Technicolor, Inc.* 634 A.2d 345 (Del. 1993). For a discussion of entire fairness in duty of care cases, see § 8.03[C], *supra.*

[69] But this did not mean the controlling shareholders had to disclose their best deal so long as the directors of the subsidiary are not involved in the valuation nor confidential information from the corporation was used. *See Rosenblatt v. Getty Oil Co.*, 493 A.2d 929 (Del. 1985).

[70] For a discussion of shareholder ratification, see § 10.03[C][2](a)(ii), *infra.*

[71] For a discussion of the use of a committee of independent directors, see § 10.03[C][2](a)(i), *infra.*

[72] Since freezeouts involve self-dealing the court could not mean that freezeouts are not subject to appraisal which would have been contrary to the thrust of the opinion. The self-dealing reference could mean behavior by the control group acting in a conflict of interest other than the transaction itself or unfair dealing.

[73] Other states have followed different aspects of the Delaware approach. The new expanded appraisal has influenced other states' appraisal proceedings. In *Stringer v. Car Data Systems, Inc.*, 841 P.2d 1183 (Ore. 1992), the controlling shareholders of a closely held corporation implemented a freezeout merger. The issue was whether the minority shareholders could seek relief other than an appraisal. The court found that the minority was limited to an appraisal, even if the majority shareholder acted arbitrarily or not in good faith. The complaint made no claim for damages apart from the fair value of the shares. The court appeared to follow *Weinberger* by allowing the use of a variety of financial valuations in determining fair price and by indicating that appraisal may not be

seek to enjoin the transaction or if the merger takes place receive rescissory damages or other equitable relief. Since courts rarely rescind a merger after the fact, rescissory damages would be the norm. Rescissory damages could be greater than fair value under the new appraisal because the shareholders would be able to claim damages based upon the fact that rescission would normally give them back their shares. Thus, if you cannot get your shares then the equivalent rescissory damages would allow them a share of the benefits to the acquirer that resulted from the merger. Such elements of value from the accomplishment of the merger are usually not allowed under the new appraisal as being too speculative.[74] An action in equity brought as a class action may also encourage settlement for a higher price and potential attorneys' fees for plaintiffs' lawyers.

[2] Post *Weinberger* Cases

In a variety of different transactions[75] involving the controlling shareholders, plaintiffs argue that the controlling shareholders must prove that they acted with entire fairness, i.e., fair dealing and fair price. Fair dealing looks at the process. Included in the process are issues relating to timing, initiation, structure and negotiation of the transaction. Disclosure is also an issue requiring complete candor of all material facts.[76] Fair price looks at economic and financial factors. Entire fairness is not a bifurcated test, but the court will look at all aspects of fairness. The board has to present evidence of the "cumulative manner by which it discharged all of the fiduciary duties."[77]

[a] Fair Dealing

In *Rabkin v. Philip A. Hunt Chem Corp.*,[78] the Delaware Supreme Court restated *Weinberger*'s view of unfair dealing as requiring more than non-disclosure, including other procedural fairness issues such as timing, structure and negotiation. The defendant had purchased its shares from the control group. Contractually it agreed also to pay the minority shareholders the same consideration if it purchased those shares within a year. After the year had passed, a freezeout merger was proposed that would have paid the minority a lower price. The minority shareholders claimed unfair dealing by the controlling shareholder through its manipulation of the timing of the transaction.

---

exclusive if there is self-dealing, fraud, deliberate waste, misrepresentation or other unlawful conduct.

[74] Under Del. Gen. Corp. L. § 262(h), fair value in appraisal shall be "exclusive of any elements of value arising from the accomplishment of expectation of the merger." See *Cede & Co. v. Technicolor, Inc.*, 684 A.2d 289 (Del. 1996) (the court viewed the elimination of speculative elements of value as a result of the merger as a narrow exception), discussed in § 6.06[A][1], note 45, *supra*.

[75] In addition to freezeouts, other conflicts of interests can arise with the controlling shareholders such as contracts between the corporation and the controlling shareholder.

[76] *Kahn v. Tremont*, 694 A.2d 422 (Del. 1997). The court indicated materiality meant that there was a substantial likelihood that the omitted fact would have assumed actual significance in the deliberations of the reasonable shareholder (citing the materiality test used in federal securities law under the *Northway* case). See § 7.06[E], *supra*.

[77] *Cinerama v. Technicolor, Inc.*, 663 A.2d 1134 (Del. 1995).

[78] 498 A.2d 1099 (Del. 1985).

Defendants claimed no unfair dealing under *Weinberger* because there was full disclosure and the only remedy for the minority was an appraisal.

The alleged bad faith of the controlling shareholders in *Rabkin* in not following the contract (that is, unfair dealing) went beyond issues of mere inadequacy of price; therefore, appraisal was not the exclusive remedy.[79] Thus, if there is a lack of fair dealing and the shareholder's claim is not essentially over inadequate value, a class action in equity could be brought seeking greater damages or relief than provided for in the new appraisal.[80] Thus most freezeouts will claim a breach of fiduciary duty and unfair dealing allowing a proceeding in equity on the issue of entire fairness and thus avoiding appraisal.[81]

[i]   Negotiating Committee of Independent Directors

In trying to lessen the scrutiny placed on their decisions, the controlling shareholders may use the *Weinberger* suggestion and have a group of independent directors as a committee of the board[82] negotiate over the

---

[79] In *Glassman v. Unocal Exploration Corp.*, 777 A.2d 242 (Del. 2001), the Delaware Supreme Court held that in a short form merger appraisal was the exclusive remedy and that entire fairness is not required. Since the short form merger statute allows a 90% or more shareholder vote to effectuate a merger without the usual formalities (no prior notice, board meetings or vote), an equitable claim requiring fair dealing conflicted with the statute which was aimed at providing a simple inexpensive means to merge. If the controlling shareholder took some unfair advantage prior to the merger (e.g., taking advantage of a depressed market), that may be relevant in determining fair value in appraisal. But any claims for equitable damages like rescissory damages are not allowed in appraisal. For a discussion of short form merger, see § 6.02[C], *supra.*

[80] In *Cede & Co. v. Technicolor, Inc.*, 542 A.2d 1182 (Del. 1988), the shareholders in an appraisal proceeding discovered facts indicating fraud. The Delaware Supreme Court allowed them to bring the fraud action to set aside the merger along with an appraisal proceeding to determine the fair value of the shares. The court indicated that a fraud action makes available broader remedies than an appraisal. If the fraud action succeeded there could be rescissory damages. The shareholder did not have to elect either remedy since they are alternative remedies and were not the result of the same known facts. The cases were consolidated to avoid a double recovery. The court also indicated that the test for fairness is not bifurcated between fair dealing and fair price but must be examined as a whole. In California, however, appraisal appears to be the exclusive remedy even with unfair dealing, which can be compensated in the appraisal proceeding. *See Steinberg v. Amplica, Inc.*, 729 P.2d 683 (Cal. 1987).

[81] The Delaware Supreme Court, in *Kahn v. Lynch Communication Sys., Inc.*, 638 A.2d 1110 (Del. 1994), indicated that fairness is the usual standard in freezeout mergers thus allowing an action in equity. The issue of the exclusivity of appraisal as a remedy in fereezeouts is not uniform. Some statutes make an exception for appraisal in control transactions or if the action is unlawful or fraudulent. Some make appraisal the only remedy in all cases. *See* F. Hodge O'Neil & Robert B. Thompson, OPPRESSION OF MINORITY SHAREHOLDERS & LLC MEMBERS 5-130 (2d ed 2005).

[82] Under stock market rules, if a corporation is controlled by a 50% or more shareholder it is exempt from the requirement of a majority of independent directors on the board or on its committees (except the audit committee). The controlled corporation must disclose in its proxy materials the reasons why it opted for the exemption. *See, e.g.*, NYSE Listed Company Manual § 303A. Some controlled corporations may go beyond the market rules and, for example, have independent directors on other committees. The use of independent directors may also be an attempt by the controlling shareholder to attract investment from other shareholders. In terms of agency costs this can be viewed as a bonding cost. For a discussion of agency costs, see § 5.03[C][1], *supra.*

freezeout merger.[83] Controlling shareholders would like to limit judicial scrutiny to the business judgment rule. Under Delaware law, the use of independent directors to review transactions with controlling shareholders will shift the burden of proof but fairness is retained and the business judgment rule will not apply.[84] This shift of burden will be in equity where the fairness inquiry is litigated. The rejection of the use of the business judgment rule in this context recognizes that the presence of a controlling shareholder and its probable role in the selection of the independent directors to the board cannot assure that its decision was in fact equivalent to an arm's length bargain.[85]

An important issue is whether the directors serving on the negotiating committee are in fact independent. Under Delaware law independence requires an inquiry of whether a particular director lacks independence through either domination or control.[86] Domination can result from personal or familial ties, through force of will or when a director is beholden to the interested party.[87] But even if the directors are found to be independent, if there is a controlling shareholder, the decision of those directors can still be challenged by a plaintiff. In order to have the burden shift to the plaintiff, the independent directors must be able to act on behalf of the minority shareholders.[88]

---

[83] 457 A.2d 701, 709–710 n.7 (1983). The effect of either disinterested board approval or independent directors on judicial scrutiny of controlling shareholders actions is similar to the issues raised with the state statutes involving interested director's transactions. For a discussion of those statutes, see § 9.03[B], *supra.*

[84] This is different from Delaware's approach to interested director's transactions when there is no controlling shareholder where Delaware courts will apply the business judgment rule if the transaction is approved by independent directors. For a discussion of the Delaware approach to such transactions, see § 9.03[B][3](a), *supra.*

[85] This approach is consistent with Delaware's approach to the use of special litigation committees appointed by a majority of interested directors and the increased judicial scrutiny of their decisions as expressed in the *Zapata* case discussed at § 14.06[C], *infra.*

[86] In *Kahn v. Tremont*, 694 A.2d 422 (Del. 1997), the committee appointed to negotiate for the purchase of shares that would benefit the controlling shareholder was not independent. The three directors had previous affiliations with the controlling shareholder as did the advisors (financial and legal). Two of the three directors effectively abdicated (failed to fully participate and attend informational meetings) to the third who was closely connected with the controlling shareholder. Although the trial court found the price to be fair, the case was reversed because the trial court placed the burden on the plaintiff and should have been on the defendant given the lack of independent committee. According to the Delaware Supreme Court, the directors were required to demonstrate and to present evidence that the cumulative manner in which they discharged their duties would produce a fair transaction.

[87] *Orman v. Cullman*, 794 A.2d 5 (Del. Ch. 2002). The director must not be beholden or controlled by the interested director. *Aronson v. Lewis*, 473 A.2d 805 (Del. 1984). Delaware requires a subjective test, i.e., an actual director as opposed to reasonable director standard, in determining whether a particular director's interest was material to a transaction or lacked independence for being controlled by the interested party. *Cinerama v. Technicolor*, 663 A.2d 1156 (Del. 1995). For a discussion of independence, see § 5.02[F], *supra.*

[88] In *Levco International Fund v. Reader's Digest Ass'n, Inc.*, 803 A.2d 428 (Del. Ch. 2002), the independent directors were faced with a recapitalization plan which they had negotiated that was alleged to harm the Class A shareholders (non voting shares held by the minority which were publicly traded shares). While Class A would now receive voting rights, the overall value of their equity interest lost $100 million. The independent directors, in approving the recapitalization plan, focused on how the recapitalization would affect the corporation and not on the fairness to the Class A. The

In *Kahn v. Lynch Communication Sys., Inc.*,[89] ("Kahn 1") Alcatel owned 43.3% of the shares of Lynch Communications. The certificate of incorporation had a provision that required an 80% shareholder vote for any business combination, which meant that Alcatel had veto power. The board consisted of 11 directors of whom 5 were Alcatel's designees. When an acquisition was proposed with Telco, Alcatel opposed it and instead proposed an acquisition of a corporation connected with it. The independent directors rejected the proposal. Alcatel then proposed to purchase the remaining shares (56.7%) of Lynch for $14 per share which would eliminate the public shareholders. The committee of independent directors concluded that the price was too low and began negotiations. Alcatel finally raised its offer to $15.50 and indicated that if it was refused it would then proceed with an unfriendly tender offer at a lower price.[90] The committee approved the sale.

Although Alcatel owned less than majority control, the court concluded based upon how Alcatel had influenced decisions in the past that Alcatel was a controlling shareholder and dominated Lynch's corporate affairs. The court looked carefully at the activities of the committee to see if in fact there was an exercise of arms-length bargaining by them. Here, the committee could not sell to anyone else since Alcatel had veto power because of the supermajority vote requirement. Although the committee at three different times rejected Alcatel's offers, the threat by Alcatel to take the last offer, or face a low tender offer, was an ultimatum that ended any semblance of an arms-length bargain. The committee had no power to say no to the proposed freezeout. Thus, because of the coercion, the burden remained on the controlling shareholder to prove entire fairness.

After the case was remanded in *Kahn*, the Chancery Court found that Alcatel had met its burden to prove entire fairness even though there was some coercion in the process. The Delaware Supreme Court in *Kahn v. Lynch Communication Sys., Inc.*[91] ("*Kahn 2*") agreed and found that the previous finding that Alcatel had the burden of proof was not decisive on the issue of entire fairness. Further the focus of the coercion in *Kahn 2* was on the shareholders unlike *Kahn 1* which was on the negotiating committee. Under *Kahn 2* such coercion would have had to be material in order create liability per se. No coercion was found since all other shareholders were treated equally.[92] The court indicated that under *Weinberger* the test of entire fairness was not bifurcated but required an examination of all aspects of the transaction to see if it was entirely fair. In fair dealing, the court agreed that when looking at the other elements of fair dealing such as timing, initiation, structure and

claim of breach of fiduciary duty against the directors was sufficient to support a preliminary injunction.

[89] 638 A.2d 1110 (Del. 1994).

[90] For a discussion of the use of the tender offer to freezeout shareholders, see § 10.03[C][2][c], *infra*

[91] 669 A.2d 79 (Del. 1995).

[92] The coercion was immaterial because there were economic factors at play that produced the decision to sell and the minority were all treated equally and offered cash.

negotiation that Alcatel had met its burden.[93]

[ii]   Shareholder Ratification

In Delaware, there is no statutory requirement that a merger or other transaction with a controlling shareholder must be approved by a majority of the minority shareholders. The merger statutes generally require a majority vote[94] which means the controlling shareholder can force the merger since it has the votes and is entitled to vote as it pleases.[95] In some cases like in *Weinberger*, the controlling shareholder will optionally require that the transaction be conditioned upon the approval of a majority of minority shareholders which allows the minority to veto it. The reason for this optional requirement is to try to limit judicial scrutiny. Generally, such approval in the context of a controlling shareholder shifts the burden of proof to the plaintiff but a fairness test is retained as opposed to applying either the business judgment rule or waste test.[96] The fairness inquiry will be in the action in equity. The controlling shareholder has the burden of proving the ratification was proper and informed.[97] In *Weinberger* the failure to fully inform the shareholders about the unfair dealing meant that the vote did not shift the burden.

The reason to retain the fairness test even if the minority shareholders are necessary to authorize a transaction and there is full disclosure is the recognition that transactions with controlling shareholders need closer scrutiny. When controlling shareholders are involved in a transaction there is a concern that there could be a possibility of process manipulation in the voting. The mere presence of the controlling shareholder seeking some action it favors could influence the voting. If the majority of the minority in fact veto the transaction then the controlling shareholder remains in control and could take actions or retaliation that could harm the minority (e.g., change the dividend policy or implement an unfair freezeout.) But even when the controlling shareholders do not threaten actions against the minority shareholders, the possibility of coercion colors the process.[98] Thus, like the use of a committee of independent directors (who may be influenced by the controlling shareholders), a court may not be certain that the shareholders are accepting the transaction because it is fair. Thus, minority shareholders need protection beyond their informed vote.[99]

---

[93] In terms of fair price, the lower court found Alcatel's expert on valuation more credible then the plaintiff's expert, which was affirmed by the Delaware Supreme Court. Once the defendant proved fair price, the plaintiff would have had to show credible evidence of the merits of a greater price.

[94] *See* Del. Gen. Corp. L. § 251(c) (majority of all shareholders are required to approve a merger).

[95] For a discussion of optional shareholder ratification when voting is required, see § 9.06[B], *supra*.

[96] For a discussion of shareholder voting and the waste test, see § 9.04[C][1], *supra*.

[97] For a discussion of the duty of disclosure, see § 8.07, *supra*.

[98] See *Lacos Land Co. v. Arden Corp.*, 517 A.2d 271 (Del. Ch. 1986), discussed in note 9, *supra*.

[99] *See Kahn v. Lynch Communication Sys., Inc.*, 638 A.2d 1110 (Del. 1994). *See also In Re Wheelbrator Technologies Shareholder Litigation*, 663 A.2d 1194 (Del. Ch. 1994). discussed at § 9.06[B], *supra*.

[b] Buisness Purpose

Some courts disagree with Delaware's approach and have retained a business purpose test.[100] In *Coggins v. New England Patriots Football Club, Inc,*[101] the Massachusetts court found that a business purpose test was an additional useful test of fairness in freezeout mergers. Under this approach, the controlling shareholders must be able to show how the legitimate goals of the corporation are furthered by the transaction. Only if there is a business purpose will the court then look at fairness.

[c] The Controlling Shareholder's Tender Offer

A controlling shareholder could decide to acquire 100% ownership of the corporation by not proposing a feezeout merger. Instead it can in two steps try to accomplish the same result. First, it can make a tender offer directly to buy the shares of the minority shareholders it does not own and try to acquire enough shares to end up owning at least 90% of the corporation. With 90% ownership the second step is to effectuate a short form merger to eliminate those minority shareholders who did not tender their shares. In the first step tender offer, the board of directors has no formal role under the statutes and there is no shareholder voting. The shareholders can either tender their shares or not.[102] Generally, in a voluntary tender offer there is no right for the shareholders to receive a particular price so long as there is full disclosure and no coercion.[103] If the shareholders do not like the price they do not have to tender their shares. In the second step the short form merger statute involves no shareholder voting or process prior to the merger and thus in Delaware that merger is not subject to entire fairness standard. Thus entire fairness, which applies in freezeout mergers, does not appear to apply to the two step freezeout.[104]

The Delaware Chancery court in *In Re Pure Resources, Inc. Shareholders Litigation,*[105] was faced with a controlling shareholder attempting to use this

---

[100] *See, e.g., Alpert v. 28 Williams St. Corp.*, 63 N.Y.2d 557 (1984). In *Alpert*, the court required a limited business purpose of some "general gain upon the corporation." *Id.* at 573; *see also Leader v. Hycor Inc.*, 479 N.E.2d 173, 177 (Mass. 1985).

[101] 492 N.E.2d 1112 (Mass. 1986). The corporation had 2 classes of common stock — one voting and one nonvoting. Sullivan had acquired all the voting shares financed by personal loans. He needed to use the corporate assets to secure the loans and help pay them. In order to do so, he needed to eliminate the other shareholders to assist his goals and not the corporation, i.e., no business purpose. The freezeout merger was approved (the non-voting common had a right to vote since the merger affected them). Although the merger was found to be illegal since here was no business purpose, the court awarded damages but would not order rescission of the merger since the passage of time (ten years) had made it not feasible. Instead the rescissory damages were awarded based upon the value of the corporation ten years after the merger.

[102] For a discussion of the hostile tender offer, see Chapter 12, *infra*.

[103] *Solomon v. Pathe Communications Corp.*, 672 A.2d 35 (Del. 1996). Coercion in a tender offer usually involves a wrongful threat that forces the shareholders to tender.

[104] In *Glassman v. Unocal Exploration Corp.*, 777 A.2d 242 (Del. 2001), the Delaware Supreme Court held that in a short form merger appraisal was the exclusive remedy and that entire fairness is not required. *See* note 79, *supra*. For a discussion of short form merger, see § 6.02[C], *supra*.

[105] 808 A.2d 421 (Del. Ch. 2002).

two step process. They made a tender offer over the objections of the independent directors for what they believed was inadequate price. The court had to decide if entire fairness was required, like in other freezeout merger cases involving the controlling shareholders or, because it was initially a tender offer, should judicial scrutiny be limited to disclosure and coercion issues in the tender offer. The court was faced with two strands of Delaware law: the protection of minority shareholders in controlled mergers and freezeouts, and the right to make a tender offer directly to the shareholders[106] without board involvement.[107] The court recognized the need to treat tender offers differently but also recognized the need to protect minority shareholders as Delaware courts in freezeouts.[108] Because of the potential for coercion when a controlling shareholder makes a tender offer, the court indicated that some fiduciary duty will apply but not entire fairness. Instead, the court focused on the process surrounding the tender offer. The controlling shareholder's tender offer will be considered non-coercive only when (1) subject to a non-waivable majority of minority tender (similar to the majority of minority vote in freezeouts), (2) the second step freezeout merger that eliminates those shareholders who do not tender offers the same price offered in the tender offer[109] and (3) there was no retributive threats by the controlling shareholder. In addition, the independent directors must be allowed the freedom and time to give their opinion on the tender offer.

Thus there is a dichotomy of treatment between freezeouts by mergers with entire fairness required and a tender offer and short form merger freezeout

---

[106] In the tender offer, the controlling shareholder is on one side of the offer and the minority is on the other so arguably there is no conflict of interest unlike the freezeout context where the controlling shareholder is on both sides of the merger (acquiring the corporation and controlling it). But in the tender offer, the controlling shareholder could have access to inside information and is tendering to dispersed shareholders who need to act quickly on the tender. In a tender offer without a second step short form merger, the shareholders who do not tender do not receive the offered consideration. While in a freezeout merger the shareholder who votes no can still get the merger price.

[107] Directors are not involved in a tender offer under state statutes unlike mergers which require board approval and directors when required to act do so pursuant to their fiduciary duty. But Delaware courts allow directors a major role to play in tender offer and when they do so fiduciary duty is implicated. For a discussion of directors and defensive tactics in tender offers, see § 12.05[A], *infra*.

[108] In the tender offer, the controlling shareholder is on one side of the offer and the minority is on the other so arguably there is no conflict of interest unlike the freezeout context where the controlling shareholder is on both sides of the merger (acquiring the corporation and controlling it). But the controlling shareholder could have access to inside information and is tendering to dispersed shareholders who need to act quickly on the tender.

[109] In a tender offer without a second step short form merger, the shareholders who do not tender do not receive the offered consideration and may remain in the corporation that is thinly traded or subject to a lower priced freezeout. While in a freezeout merger the shareholder who votes against the merger can still get the merger price. The court in *In re Pure Resources, Inc. Shareholders Litigation* described this as a prisoner's dilemma, i.e., in the tender offer there are consequences in not tendering and not knowing what the other shareholders will do. Thus the court required that there must be the second step short form merger at the same price as the tender offer. If the second-step merger offers a lower price then the first-step tender offer then it is a front loaded two-tier offer which Delaware courts view as coercive. For a discussion of this tactic in tender offers, see § 12.04[A], *infra*.

that requires no coercion but fairness is not an issue. This differing approach to freezeouts has raised the issue of whether there needs to be similarity to the two approaches. Controlling shares will prefer the tender offer approach to avoid the litigation costs associated with an entire fairness inquiry in the merger context.[110] The Delaware Chancery Court, in *In re Cox Comminications, Inc. Shareholder Litigation*,[111] recommended to the Delaware Supreme Court an approach to resolve the issue of disparate treatment. The court suggested that in the merger freezeout, both the use of an independent director negotiating committee and requiring a majority minority shareholder approval together should mean that a fairness inquiry will be replaced by the business judgment rule which is similar to how the law treats arms length bargain mergers.[112] In the tender offer and subsequent freezeout in order to have similar treatment and avoid imposition of an entire fairness standard the protections of *Pure* would be required but in addition the independent committee would also have to recommend the tender offer in order to have the protection of the business judgment.[113] Whether the Delaware Supreme court will adopt this approach of the dual requirement of majority minority approval and an independent negotiating committee in both contexts removing a fairness inquiry and obviating the concerns about the presence of controlling shareholder is not clear.

[D]   Federal Law

The historical limitations of the appraisal process and other state court remedies lead minority shareholders into federal court in an attempt to fashion relief based on federal securities law claims. Because many freezeouts involve voting by shareholders of publicly traded corporations, the federal proxy rules are often involved. These rules have many requirements that underlie a policy of full disclosure. SEC Rule 14a-9 is a general catchall prohibition of the use of false and misleading statements in proxy solicitations.[114] Shareholders who claim that there are material misrepresentations and omissions in the proxy material received from the control group can try to bring a cause of action for relief.[115]

---

[110] An empirical study shows that minority shareholders receive less in tender offer freezeouts compared to merger freezeouts. *See* Guham Subramanian, *Post Siliconix Freeze-Outs: Theory and Evidence*, 36 J. LEGAL STUD. 1 (2007).

[111] 879 A.2d 604 (Del. Ch. 2005).

[112] *See* Guham Subramanian, *Fixing Freeze-outs*, 115 YALE L.J. 2 (2005) (suggested this approach). *But see* Faith Steveman, *Going Private at the Intersection of the Market and the Law*, 62 BUS. LAW. 775 (may 2007) (argues for the need to retain fairness unless there was market test or auction in the transaction).

[113] Ronald J. Gilson & Jeffrey N. Gordon, *Controlling Controlling Shareholders*, 152 U. PA. L. REV. 785 (2003) (the court adopted their proposal).

[114] For a discussion of SEC Rule 14a-9, see § 7.06[B], *supra*.

[115] Even if there is a lack of disclosure under the proxy rules if the votes of the minority shareholders are not required for the freezeout, then there is no violation because of the lack of causation under SEC Rule 14a-9. *Virginia Bankshares, Inc. v. Sandberg*, discussed at § 7.06[G], *supra*. But if as a result of the lack of disclosure the shareholders lost some remedy under state law such as an action in equity or appraisal then causation may be found allowing a federal cause of

[1] SEC Rule 13e-3

In addition to the proxy rules, Section 13(e) of the Federal Securities Exchange Act of 1934 ("Exchange Act") empowers the SEC to issue rules to avoid fraudulent, deceptive and manipulative acts whenever an issuer purchases its equity securities. Since freezeouts usually involve a stock repurchase, this legislative grant allows the SEC to regulate freezeouts. In 1977, the SEC reacted to the going private phenomena by issuing a proposed Rule pursuant to Section 13(e)(1) which would have required that the freezeout transaction itself be fair. Many commentators questioned whether the SEC had the legislative authority to issue such a rule because fairness is a fiduciary duty issue governed by state corporate law. The SEC withdrew its proposal requiring fairness,[116] and in its place issued SEC Rule 13e-3. Rule focuses on extensive disclosure in going private transactions and freezeouts including the issuer's judgment on the fairness of the freezeout and the material facts upon which that judgment is made.[117] Thus, although it is a full disclosure rule, SEC Rule 13e-3 creates securities law liability for unfair transactions if they are accompanied by a lack of disclosure.[118]

[2] SEC Rule 10b-5

SEC Rule 10b-5, issued by the SEC pursuant to its authority under Section 10(b) of the Exchange Act, has broad language that on its face prohibits fraud in the purchase or sale of any securities.[119] In a freezeout, a SEC Rule 10b-5 cause of action may arise for the minority shareholders if there is a lack of full disclosure that forces the minority shareholders to exchange in the merger (that is, sell) their shares. In *Santa Fe v. Green*,[120] minority shareholders of a Delaware corporation were frozen out in a short form merger and offered $150 cash for their shares (the physical assets were appraised at $640 per share). With a short form merger, a control group owning more than 90% of the shares could effectuate the merger without a shareholder vote or prior notice.[121] Under Delaware law, the shareholders could have sought an appraisal but at that time appraisal was usually avoided given its limitations and the new appraisal created in *Weinberger* had not yet been established.[122] Since the case was pre-*Singer*[123] it was assumed that an appraisal was the only state remedy. Minority

---

action. Since many of the freezeouts seek shareholder ratification by requiring a majority of the minority vote, that should also satisfy the causation requirement.

[116] The SEC did not concede that it did not have the power to issue a rule with a fairness requirement. *See* Act Release No. 33-6100 (Aug. 2, 1979), 515 Sec. Reg. & L. Rep. at A.3, E-1.

[117] *See generally Guidelines on Going Private*, 37 Bus. Law. 313 (1981). The focus of the rule is on transactions that result in the cessation of the reporting requirements under the Exchange Act. For a discussion of the reporting requirements, see § 7.02[B], *supra*.

[118] Thomas Lee Hazen, THE LAW OF SECURITIES REGULATION § 11.8 (4th ed. 2001).

[119] For a discussion of SEC Rule 10b-5, see § 13.02, *supra*.

[120] 430 U.S. 462 (1977).

[121] Because no shareholder voting was required in Delaware, the federal proxy rules did not come into play. For a discussion of the short form merger, see § 6.02[C], *supra*.

[122] For a discussion of appraisal and its limitations, see § 6.06, *supra*.

[123] For a discussion of *Singer*, see § 10.03[C], *supra*.

shareholders instead sought a federal remedy hoping for greater damages and relief.

The shareholders tried to claim a federal cause of action under SEC Rule 10b-5. They argued that a remedy existed under the Rule because there was fraud resulting from the gross undervaluation[124] or a breach of fiduciary duty in treating the minority unfairly by merging with no business purpose and without prior notice.[125] Because there was this alleged fraud in the sale of securities (the forced freezeout merger), they claimed a federal cause of action under SEC Rule 10b-5 which explicitly prohibits fraud.

The Supreme Court in *Sante Fe* found no fraud under the Rule since there was no lack of disclosure by the control group. There was also no prior notice requirement for short form mergers under Delaware law and thus no deception. The Court clearly limited the use of Rule 10b-5 to cases involving deceit, holding that causes of action based on breach of fiduciary duty without a disclosure claim belong in state court. The Court looked to the statutory language of Section 10(b) (as opposed to the Rule issued by the SEC pursuant to the statute) which did not use the word "fraud" but used the words "manipulative" and "deceptive." The words of the statute control how the Rule will be interpreted. Manipulation was viewed as a term of art to deal with practices that artificially affect market activity and are not disclosed which was not involved in the case. Deception involves a lack of full disclosure or misrepresentation. This use of the particular language in Section 10(b) indicated Congressional intent for the statute, and the Rule issued pursuant to that statute, to require some deception in the purchase or sale of securities in order to be covered by the law.

Part IV of the Court's opinion, which was dictum, stressed the Court's reluctance to "federalize the substantial portion of the law of corporations that deals with transactions in securities, particularly where established state policies of corporate regulation would be overridden." This suggested that broadly speaking, even if there was a breach of fiduciary duty involving a lack of disclosure, i.e., a deceit, in the purchase or sale of securities, there should be no Rule 10b-5 cause of action because state corporate law dealt with fiduciary duty issues not federal securities law.

Although Part IV of *Green* suggested that most fiduciary duty claims even with deceit should be in state court and not in federal, many lower courts have ignored the broad implications of Part IV. Those courts would allow a SEC Rule 10b-5 federal cause of action for breaches of fiduciary duty if there was also a colorable claim of lack of full disclosure and that it was material. Thus, a SEC Rule 10b-5 cause of action may arise in a freezeout not involving a short form merger[126] if the lack of disclosure had an effect on the shareholders. For example the deceit precluded the minority shareholders from exercising their

---

[124] Breaches of fiduciary duty, particularly unfair acts by the fiduciary, are viewed by some courts as a "constructive fraud."

[125] The Second Circuit had found no cause of action on the mere breach of fiduciary duty but found a deceit because the lack of prior notice meant the minority shareholders were unable to seek an injunction. *Green v. Santa Fe Industries, Inc.*, 533 F.2d 1283 (2d Cir. 1976).

[126] Currently under Delaware law in a short form merger the minority shareholders can only seek

right to seek an appraisal[127] or from seeking equitable relief in state court[128] or was material when a majority of the minority shareholders were needed to authorize the merger. Federal securities law continues to be important in regulating freezeouts, but only in the context of a deceit involving a material lack of full disclosure.

§ 10.04 SALE OF CONTROL

Generally when the control group sells its shares, they are selling their personal property, which does not automatically implicate any breach of fiduciary duty. Controlling shareholders who sell their controlling shares often receive a premium from a purchaser, that is, they receive more for their shares than the current market price.

For example, assume there is a corporation with a value of $1000 and a controlling shareholder owns 52%. If someone wishes to buy control, they need to deal with the 52% owner initially. Otherwise, the most they could purchase would be the 48% owned by the minority and the purchaser would be a minority shareholder. Arguably, the 52% interest is worth only $520, but a buyer may offer more (for example $600) in order to induce the sale by the controlling shareholder and obtain control.

In sale of control cases, an issue arises as to whether it is fair to other shareholders that the control group receive this premium.[129] Why is the purchase of control worth a premium and what does the premium ($80 in our case) represent? Are the minority shareholders harmed by the sale? The premium may represent the advantages of control, which include the ability to establish business policy and decide how the business will run,[130] as well as the ability to receive the perquisites of control, including reasonable salary and benefits from legitimate self-dealing transactions. In this case, the buyer is willing to pay the premium because she thinks that she can run the business more efficiently, or integrate it with her other operations. If the result of the acquisition of control increases the value of the corporation from $1000 to say

---

appraisal and not entire fairness in equity so notice would not have provided them with any substantive rights. *See* note 79, *supra.*

[127] To elect the appraisal remedy in a long form merger, there is generally a requirement the shareholder vote against the transaction and file a notice within a short time frame. If a shareholder does not receive full disclosure thus does not vote against the transaction, then the appraisal right may be precluded from a lack of disclosure allowing a Rule 10b-5 cause of action.

[128] *See, e.g., Goldberg v. Meridor,* 567 F.2d 209, 220–21 (2d Cir. 1977), *cert. denied,* 434 U.S. 1069 (1978) (because the action of the controlling shareholder caused the corporation to sell its shares for an unfair price was not disclosed to the minority shareholders and there was a possible injunctive remedy under state law for the minority shareholders, there was deception in connection with a purchase or sale of shares allowing a remedy under Rule 10b-5).

[129] If a corporation in which there is no control group is sold to a purchaser, the shareholders of the selling corporation who become shareholders of a new corporation with a controlling shareholder may be entitled to receive a control premium because they have become minority shareholders. For a discussion of sale of control in hostile tender offers, see § 12.05[A][5], *infra.*

[130] *Zeitlin v Hanson Holdings, Inc.,* 48 N.Y. 2d 684 (1979) (the court rejected an equal opportunity rule that the premium need to be shared with and offered to the minority shareholders which would require a tender offer as contrary to New York law).

$2000, than this would benefit all shareholders. The buyer's 52% will be worth $1040 (a gain of $440 from the purchase price of $600) while the 48% minority will be worth $960 (a gain of $480). Society also benefits when the increased value reflects more efficient use of the assets.

The premium may also enable the control group to unfairly use corporate assets for its own advantage only. Thus, the $80 premium paid may represent the value the control group is paying to extract more than $80 by misappropriation or self dealing or use of corporate assets exclusively for their own benefit. Is the premium being paid really for a corporate asset[131] and should the premium be shared with other shareholders?[132] In addition, should all shareholders be entitled to have their shares purchased at the same price?

Sale of control raises the issue of whether a rule of equal treatment of shareholders should be a goal of corporate law.[133] If one believes that control is a corporate asset or believe that the possible self-dealing by the sale of control is not always easy to identify or pursue by *ex ante* litigation, then an equal opportunity rule may be a good legal response.[134] Such a rule would assist the minority by requiring the buyer to offer to buy control ratably among all shareholders (i.e. a pro rata sharing rule) or require buyers to offer to purchase 100% of the shares at the same price (i.e., a mandatory bid rule).[135]

A pro rata sharing rule allows a purchaser to buy as many shares as they want to obtain control without being required to buy 100% but she must make that offer to all shareholders. For example, if a purchaser wants only 52% of the shares she would offer to all the shareholders the same price and buy them pro rata depending on how many shares accept the offer. In our example, assuming all the shareholders wants to sell than the controlling shareholder's could sell

---

[131] Since the control person is only able to use the control through corporate mechanisms which gives it value that other shares lack, it has been argued that the value is really a corporate asset. Adolf Berle & Gardner Means, THE MODERN CORPORATION AND PRIVATE PROPERTY 207–252 (rev. ed. 1968).

[132] In *Mendel v. Carroll*, 651 A.2d 297 (Del. Ch. 1994), a control group had proposed a freezeout transaction that would have paid the minority $25.75 per share. An outside group offered to buy all the corporation for $27.80 per share. There was no obligation of the control group to accommodate the outside offer or pay a premium to the minority since they were in control and nothing indicated that the $25.75 price was unfair. The control group was not required to sell to the outsider and share the premium with the minority. The court did not find under the circumstances that the *Revlon* duty to sell at the best price was implicated. For a discussion of *Revlon* duties, see § 12.05[A][3], *infra*.

[133] The issue is also raised whenever the corporation repurchases shares from some shareholders while excluding others. This issue has been raised in closely held corporations. *Compare Donahue v. Rodd*, 328 N.E.2d 505 (Mass. 1975) (purchase of shares from a controlling shareholder by the corporation required equal opportunity for the minority shareholder), *with Nixon v. Blackwell*, 626 A.2d 1366 (Del. 1993) (fairness does not mean equal treatment especially given the fact that the treatment of the non-employee shareholders was consistent with the founder's policy). For a discussion of equal opportunity in closely held corporations, see § 11.07[B], *infra*.

[134] *See* William Andrews, *The Stockholder's Right to Equal opportunity in the Sale of Shares*, 78 HARV. L. REV. 505 (1965).

[135] In other countries when a buyer purchases a certain percentage of a publicly traded company, she is required to make a compulsory bid and offer to buy the rest at the same price. For example, in the United Kingdom, The City Code on Takeovers Rule 9.1 requires one who acquires 30% control to bid for the remaining shares at the highest price paid within 12 months.

only 52% of her shares leaving her as a 24.96% minority shareholder. The former controlling shareholders would now be minority shareholders and would have to trust the new controlling shareholders and be willing to accept the same price as the other minority shareholders to become a minority shareholder without any financial inducement to sell her shares.[136]

A mandatory bid rule requires the purchaser to offer to buy 100% of the shares at the same price. It would mean that the controlling shareholder would not get a premium compared to what the minority shareholders were paid. It will also make acquisitions more difficult and expensive because purchasers would be required to buy the whole corporation without partial bids. In the example, it could cost over a $1000 to induce the shareholders to sell as opposed to $600 for control. Thus a mandatory bid requirement will increase the cost of the acquisition and may deter purchasers who either are unwilling or cannot afford to buy 100%.

Since many of these acquisitions that involve a sale of control are viewed as value enhancing, there is generally no requirement of a pro rata sharing[137] or a mandatory bid.[138] Neither is there a general requirement that a buyer who privately purchases control must make either a pro rata purchase or offer the same price if and when she decides to buy out the minority.

The New York Court of Appeals has summed up the general view of sale of control as follows:

> Recognizing that those who invest the capital necessary to acquire a dominant position in the ownership of a corporation have the right of controlling that corporation, it has long been settled law that absent looting of corporate assets, conversion of a corporate opportunity, fraud or other acts of bad faith, a controlling stockholder is free to sell, and a purchaser is free to buy, that controlling interest at a premium price.[139]

---

[136] *See* George Jarvis, *Equal Opportunity in the Sale of Controlling Shares: A Reply to Professor Andrews*, 32 U. CHI. L. REV. 430 (1965).

[137] There is a limited equal opportunity rule pro rata rule in a public tender offer governed by federal securities law. In the public tender offer, the offeror can decide how many shares she wants to offer to buy and then all shareholders are required to be offered an equal opportunity to tender their shares at the same price in the tender offer. If they want to tender for less than 100% then they must buy the shares tendered on a pro rata basis. *See* SEC Rule 14d-10. The law does not require a purchaser to offer to buy all the shares in the tender offer but can tender for whatever amount she decides. A purchaser is not precluded under this rule from buying controlling shares privately outside the public tender offer at one price and then make a tender offer for the remaining shares at a different price so long as the private sale was not part of the tender offer. For a discussion of the requirements of tender offers under federal securities law, see § 12.06, *infra*.

[138] In the 1980s some state statutes were enacted that have either a pro rata or mandatory bid rule that requires equal treatment of all shareholders in certain public tender offers. It was designed to limit the use of a controversial tactic used by bidders in hostile tender offers involving a front loaded two tier tender offer. The tactic has a bidder in a first step offer a higher price for control in the tender offer, and then once in control in a second step offer a lower price to freezeout the minority. For a discussion of the front loaded two tier tender offer, see § 12.04[A], *infra*. For a discussion of state statutes and tender offers, see § 12.07, *infra*.

[139] *Zeitlin v. Hanson*, 397 N.E.2d 387 (1979). The court recognized that control is not always about abuse but can have value because it allows the purchaser to influence the corporate affairs.

[A]   Looting

In *Gerdes v. Reynolds*, the majority shareholders of an investment company sold their shares for a large premium. The company resembled a mutual fund in that its assets consisted primarily of shares in publicly traded companies and cash. Those assets were liquid and easily turned into cash. The purchasers used the acquired control to loot the company of its primary liquid assets. Since the shares owned by the business were traded in the stock market, their value was easily ascertained. Based upon the value of these assets (minus the liabilities and preferred shares), the value of the common shares in the investment company was approximately $.06 a share. The purchaser paid $2 per common share for control. The court recognized that the common shares in the business could be worth more and as much as $0.75 because there may be some good will in the business and there may be value associated with control of some companies represented by the shares owned. But that value was still much lower than $2 paid for control.

Why would someone pay $2 for assets (primarily cash and liquid securities) with a maximum value of $0.75? If this was a business that did not involve investment in marketable securities, but was a business whose value depended upon the ability of the assets to generate profits, it is likely that the value of the business would be higher than the value of its underlying assets per share. A business is usually valued not on its underlying asset value but in its ability to use those assets to generate earnings.[140] But this business primarily invested in the shares of publicly traded companies whose value is set by the stock market and which can be easily replicated. The value of the investment company would generally equate with its net asset value (i.e., the share values in the market minus the liabilities of the company). If some of those shares held represented a control position in those companies there could be greater value than the market price based upon the value from the control premium. But here the only reason to pay an amount "grossly in excess of the value of the stock" and seek the immediate resignation of the directors was to steal those liquid stocks leaving other investors including creditors at risk. As a result the directors were found liable for their sale of control even though they did not know the purchasers would loot the company. Given the nature of the assets it was foreseeable that the only reason for the purchase at the premium price for control was to loot the business.[141]

A.L.I. Corp. Gov. Proj. § 5.16 allows for sale of control at a premium so long as there is fair dealing. But there is a lack of fair dealing if there is no disclosure to the other shareholders with whom the controlling shareholder dealt in connection with the transaction or it is apparent that the purchaser will violate the duty of fair dealing by obtaining a significant financial benefit from the corporation once in control. *See also Tyron v. Smith*, 229 P.2d 251 (Ore. 1951) (shareholders can freely sell their shares representing their personal property and there is usually no fiduciary duty with other shareholders in the sale unless there is fraud or control over the minority's shares or use of corporate assets). *See generally* Einer Elhauge, *The Triggering Function of Sale of Control Doctrine*, 59 U. Chi. L. Rev. 1465 (1992).

[140] For a discussion of valuation and earnings, see § 4.05[C], *supra*.

[141] In order for a seller to be liable there must be circumstances to create suspicions and put a prudent man on his guard. The controlling shareholders are not insurers but, if circumstances warrant, they may be required to investigate and, "unless such a reasonable investigation shows that

[B]   The *Perlman* Case

Perlman v. Feldmann[142] dealt with the sale of control issue and explored the idea of equal opportunity for all shareholders to share in the premium paid to the controlling shareholders (a pro rata sharing). The minority shareholders of Newport Steel brought a derivative action against Feldmann and other associates. Feldmann was the dominant shareholder and president who sold, with his associates, a 37% interest in Newport Steel Corp., constituting de facto or working control. The purchaser was Wilport, a customer for the Newport steel. Because of the Korean War, a shortage of steel existed which allowed Feldmann to develop a plan whereby purchasers paid in advance for the steel. The plan provided the business with interest free cash advances to help finance the business. Wilport paid Feldmann a premium over the market and book values of the company to buy control and be able to purchase the steel. The shareholders claimed that Feldmann had breached his duty of loyalty by selling control for the premium.

The court recognized that this was not an ordinary case of duty of loyalty because there was no fraud, misuse of confidential information, contracting with the corporation or looting. But the court recognized that the reason for the sale was to afford Wilport the advantages of being in control of a business when it needed a product that was in short supply. Given these facts, the case seemed to be about a theft of a corporate opportunity or misuse of a corporate asset, that is, Feldmann by selling control to Wilport denied Newport the ability to require Wilport to pay in advance.[143] In addition, Newport would be deprived of using their market advantage to establish any new business. Thus, the court placed the burden on the defendant, finding liability for the difference between the premium paid and the value of the stock without control.

As a derivative suit (since the theft of corporate opportunity primarily harms the corporation), the recovery would typically go to the corporation. The court recognized, however, that if Feldmann paid the control premium back to Newport, then Wilport would benefit as a 37% owner of Newport. The court decided that this was a case in which although a derivative cause of action, the recovery would go to the shareholders other than Wilport. Thus, the

---

to a reasonable man no fraud is intended or likely to result the sellers must refrain from the transfer of control." *Swinney v. Keebler Co.*, 480 F.2d 573, 578 (4th Cir. 1973). The duty of care of the seller to the other minority shareholders as opposed to the buyer is grounded in tort law. It stems from the principal that each person owes a duty to those who may foreseeably be harmed by her action and to take such reasonable steps to avoid the harm. Thus the selling shareholder is not a surety for his buyer but if circumstances would alert a reasonably prudent person to a risk that the buyer is dishonest or not truthful in a material way, there is a duty to make a reasonable inquiry and exercise due care. *Harris v. Carter*, 582 A.2d 222 (Del. Ch. 1990); *see also DeBaun v. First Western Bank and Trust*, 46 Cal. App. 3d 686 (1975) (when the seller became aware of previous actions taken by the buyer that would have alerted a reasonable person of a likelihood of looting, the seller had a duty to act reasonably and should have investigated at least from public records that would have precluded dealing with the buyer).

[142] 219 F.2d 173 (2d Cir. 1955).

[143] For a discussion of corporate opportunity, see § 9.05, *supra.*

shareholders had an equal opportunity in the premium which was allocated pro rata to all the shareholders including Feldmann.[144]

Given the strong statements in the opinion about the fiduciary obligations of controlling shareholders, the case could be viewed as establishing an equal opportunity rule and that control was a corporate asset. But the case stands for a narrower view that equal opportunity will be the rule if the seller is in effect selling a corporate asset or opportunity, or acting in a detrimental way toward the corporation or other shareholders. In some ways *Perlman* is like *Gerdes*, treating the theft of corporate opportunity or misuse of a corporate asset like the looting of a corporate asset.

[C] The California Approach

The California Supreme Court took a stricter view of control transactions in *Jones v. H.F. Ahmanson.*[145] The controlling shareholders ("the control group") of United Savings and Loan Association ("Association") decided to profit from the rise in the market value of savings and loan companies. Since Association was essentially a closely held corporation, its shares were not actively traded. One way to profit would have been for Association to do a public offering of shares result ing in its shares trading in the stock market.[146] As a result, existing shareholders would be able to cash in on the interest in the business.[147]

Instead of going public and benefitting all shareholders, the control group transferred their shares (that is, 87% of the shares of Association) to a holding company (United Financial) which would then become the parent corporation of Association. The control group now controlled United Financial (which controlled Association with its 87% ownership) and then had two different public offerings of United Financial securities. Most of the proceeds from the sales of United Financial securities went to the control group, which previously had been in control of Association. The control group retained enough shares of United Financial to also remain in control of that company through which they continued to indirectly control Associated. The plan had the effect of allowing the control group to cash in on their investment in Association through the sale of United Financial securities. The minority shareholders of Association were

---

[144] The result of the case suggests that because Wilport paid a premium for control and all the other shareholders received a pro rata payment, Wilport could then use the corporate opportunity without concern. For a discussion of derivative litigation, see Chapter 14, *infra*.

[145] 460 P.2d 464 (Cal. 1969).

[146] When a corporation goes public it can sell its own shares to more investors with the proceeds going to the corporation (a primary offering) or sell the shares of the existing shareholders with the proceeds going to them (a secondary offering). For a discussion of going public and federal securities law, see § 7.03, *supra*.

[147] Association could also go public by effecting a stock split. A stock split involves taking existing stock and creating more shares. For example if a corporation has 1000 shares outstanding and there is a 1000 to 1 stock split there will be 1,000,000 shares. A shareholder owning 10 shares would now own 10,000 shares and retain the same percentage. However, with more shares and subsequent sales, there is likely to be increased trading of those shares in a stock market. With trading, the shareholders have the ability to cash in by selling in the market.

not given the same opportunity to also transfer their shares to United Financial and share in the increased value from those sales.

Jones v. H.F. Ahmanson Diagram

Before the transaction:

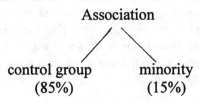

The control group transfers its Association shares to United Financial which then becomes a holding company with control of Association through its ownership of the 87% shares. The control group in exchange receives shares of United Financial (Step 1).

STEP 1

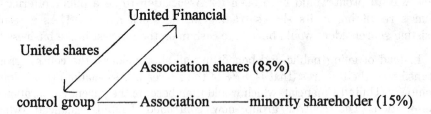

United Financial then sells its shares to the public (the control group maintains control of United Financial) and the proceeds from the sale to the public go to the control group while the minority shareholders of Association remain (Step 2).

STEP TWO

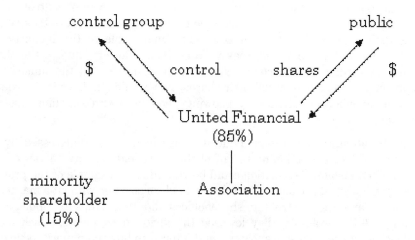

Minority shareholders of Association brought a direct suit against the controlling shareholders for breach of fiduciary duty. Defendants argued that they were merely selling their shares and still indirectly controlled Associated through United Financial. There was no breach by the defendants because the sale of their shares to United Financial and the going public where they cashed in was a legitimate transfer of their controlling shares for a premium. There was no looting or theft of a corporate opportunity. Arguably they could have been accused of taking away the opportunity of Association itself to go public by the formation of United Financial in which case the situation would have been similar to that in *Perlman.* But if liability was based on theft of a corporate opportunity, the cause of action should have been derivative in nature because the harm alleged was primarily to the corporation.

The California Supreme Court allowed plaintiffs to bring a direct suit, which suggests an individual harm.[148] The plaintiffs were not required to bring a derivative suit, claiming corporate harm.[149] That a direct suit was allowed is very significant because it meant that controlling shareholders who use control for their advantage, including its sale, have a direct fiduciary obligation to the minority shareholders, without reference to how they treat corporate assets.[150]

---

[148] Some courts have allowed a direct action even if the litigation was derivative in nature in the closely held corporation but the court never suggests that as the rationale for allowing a direct suit. For a discussion of derivative litigation in closely held corporations, see § 14.02[D], *infra.*

[149] Another possible claim for corporate damage was the fact that the controlling shareholders arranged for the pledge of Association's assets and earnings as security for United Financial's debt. But again this would usually result in a derivative suit not a direct suit as was brought here.

[150] In some derivative suits the court could order recovery directly to the shareholders. For a discussion of direct recovery, see § 14.02[E], *infra,* and *Perlman v. Feldman,* 219 F.2d 173 (2d Cir. 1955), discussed in § 10.04[B], *supra.*

This approach meant there was a higher fiduciary duty for controlling shareholders selling their shares, and differed from the traditional approach that looked at the harm to the corporation.

The court indicated that there was a "comprehensive rule of good faith and inherent fairness to the minority in any transaction where control of the corporation is material. . . ." Because the controlling shareholders took actions using their control to obtain an advantage unavailable to the minority and without any business purpose, they violated their fiduciary duty to the shareholders. According to the court, even if they had afforded the minority an opportunity to exchange or sell their shares, they would still have the burden of establishing inherent fairness by showing good faith or compelling business purpose.

The broad statements about fiduciary duty in the case, buttressed by the allowance of a direct action on behalf of the shareholders, may be viewed in a more limited fashion. Association could be viewed as an example of the problem faced by minority shareholders in a closely held corporation without a market for its shares and the controlling shareholders did take steps to oppress the minority.[151] For example, they lowered the dividend payments, which meant smaller returns for the shareholders, and offered to buy the minority shares at low prices. But *Jones* did not limit its holding to closely held corporations and appeared to be a strong statement about the fiduciary obligations of controlling shareholders.[152]

[D] Sale of Office

When a sale of control takes place, the directors usually resign and select the designated nominees of the purchaser to replace them as directors. While the purchaser could arrange for a shareholder vote, they prefer to act quickly and without that expense. These resignations raise an issue of whether an illegal sale of office has occurred.[153] Courts recognize the reality that if the purchaser has actual or de facto control, then such replacements are legitimate because a legitimate shift in control should allow them to exercise control and need not wait until the annual meeting to elect new directors. The problem occurs if the purchaser buys less than 51% and at what point does the ownership interest equate with de facto control and assure that if there is was election they would be able to replace the directors?[154] In a publicly traded corporation the percentage needed could be significantly less than 51%.

---

[151] Some states allow for direct actions for essentially derivative suits in the context of closely held corporations. *See* § 14.02[D], *infra.* Oppression of minority shareholders in closely held corporations can also mean higher fiduciary duties. *See* § 11.07[B], *supra.*

[152] *Jones* has been applied to publicly traded corporations. *See Klaus v. Hi-Shear Corp.*, 528 F.2d 255 (19th Cir. 1975). Unlike other cases, the controlling shareholders were liable without engaging in deception, harming the corporation or self dealing through control of the directors.

[153] In *Brecher v. Gregg*, 392 N.Y.S.2d 776 (1975), the president sold his 4% stock interest for a premium with a promise to resign and have the purchaser's designees selected to the presidency and two directorships. The court indicated that a sale of only 4% of the shares with a promise of control was illegal and contrary to public policy.

[154] In *Caplan v. Lionel Corp.*, 246 N.Y.S.2d 913 (1964), the New York court found that 3%

ownership did not constitute working control allowing for the replacement of the directors by the purchaser. In *Essex Universal Corp. v. Yates*, 305 F.2d 572 (2d Cir. 1962), a 28.3% seller attempted to get out of a contract for sale (the price of the shares had increased) claiming that a provision in the contract calling for replacement of the directors was illegal under New York law and thus tainted the entire contract. If in fact control was not sold, than the transfer would have been illegal as *Caplan* indicated. The court rejected the argument that there was no sale of control. Judge Lumbard found that in a publicly traded corporation a 28.3% ownership was a practical certainty of control which the seller could try to rebut. Judge Friendly concurred, but felt that if he were deciding the law as a state judge he might find sales of less than 51% with resignations to violate public policy. He found the practical uncertainty test difficult to apply and would prefer an actual election of directors decide the issue.

Chapter 11

SPECIAL PROBLEMS OF THE CLOSELY HELD CORPORATION

§ 11.01 INTRODUCTION AND OVERVIEW

[A]   Definitions of a Close Corporation

The closely held, or "close," corporation, has been referred to as the incorporated partnership. As with a partnership, the closely held corporation often, but not necessarily always, has only a handful of participants. That, however, is not the distinguishing characteristic of the closely held corporation.[1]

The hallmark of the closely held corporation is the owners' desire to control the identity of the "partners" and keep ownership "close."[2] The owners may wish to limit shareholding to family members, employees, persons who live in the vicinity of the corporation's business, and the like. Usually, ownership is kept "close" through share transfer restrictions that are often found in a "buy-sell agreement," but also found in the articles of incorporation or the by-laws.[3] The legal and practical ins and outs of these agreements are extremely important to any attorney who does corporate work.[4]

Another distinguishing characteristic of the closely held corporation is the absence of a market for shares. While the owner may not be able to sell shares because of share transfer restrictions, more likely the owner may not be able to sell simply because no share market exists. In turn, no market exists, despite the corporation's possession of valuable assets or a successful ongoing business, because in the standard corporate governance model majority rules.

---

[1] In fact, many of the statutory definitions of closely held corporation that contained numerical limitations have been amended to eliminate them. *But see* Del. Gen. Corp. L. § 342(a)(1) (30 shareholder limitation).

[2] That is not ordinarily a problem in partnership law, which provides that "[n]o person can become a member of a partnership without the consent of all the partners." Uniform Partnership Act § 18(g); Revised Uniform Partnership Act § 401(I). In contrast, unless provided otherwise, shares in a corporation are freely transferable.

[3] The Model Statutory Close Corporation Supplement, promulgated by the American Bar Association in conjunction with the Model Business Corporation Act, has a simple buy-sell agreement in the statute itself. *See id.* §§ 10–17. The agreement governs share transfers in all corporations electing to be treated as a close corporation under the statute unless the participants opt out of that part of the statute.

[4] For that reason, this Chapter contains an extensive discussion of buy-sell agreements, see § 11.04 *infra.*

The American Bar Association lists six attributes that in its opinion constitute good evidence that a close corporation is involved: (1) ownership "by a small number of persons"; (2) a high degree of overlap between the shareholders and the managers and employees; (3) a need to customize the management structure because the business is too small to support the cost of corporate formalities or because a traditional of several lawyers is inappropriate; (4) shareholders have little investment liquidity; (5) no readily observable market price exists for the ownership interests; and (6) deadlocks may arise because of the small number of shareholders.[5]

In contrast, in *Elmaleh v. Barlow*,[6] five shareholders sued the corporation and an officer-director-shareholder (Barlow) of Molecular Insight Pharmaceuticals, Inc. Molecular had slightly less than 70 shareholders. It then sold common and preferred shares to various investors, one of which was Barlow, who subscribed for 38.36% of the common and 58.50% of the preferred offerings. When the board of directors approved a repricing plan which would have increased Barlow's stake further, shareholders alleged the violation by Barlow of the fiduciary duty participants owe one to another in a closely held corporation, under the seminal Massachusetts 1975 opinion in *Donahue v. Rodd Electrotype Co.*[7] The 2005 court applied a 3 part test; "The *Donahue* Court deemed a close corporation to be typified by: (1) a small number of stockholders; (2) no ready market for the corporate stock; and (3) substantial majority stockholder participation in the management, direction, and operations of the corporation." The court found Molecular was not a close corporation, dismissing the case against Barlow.

[B] Illiquidity and Exploitation

In that standard model, a majority of shares elects all of the directors,[8] and may amend articles of incorporation, sell the assets, or merge the corporation with another entity. In a corporation with a market for its shares, shareholders who are dissatisfied with the decisions made by the majority may vote with their feet — by simply selling their shares. In the closely held corporation, however, they are not able to do so. This presents the first half of the classic closely held corporation problem, illiquidity.

The second half of the problem is that the majority, knowing of the minority's illiquidity, and feeling the power of majority rule, may attempt to exploit the minority. The majority may do so through excessive salaries for themselves and family members, generous perquisites, denial of minority voice in governance, or denial of a return through dividends. Thus, the classic close corporation problem is "illiquidity and exploitation."[9] The illiquidity and exploitation

---

[5] Committee on Corporate Laws, ABA Section of Business Law, *Managing Closely Held Corporations: A Guidebook*, 58 Bus. Law. 1077 (2003).

[6] 19 Mass. L. Rep. 684 (Super. Ct. 2005)

[7] *See* § 11.07[B], *infra.*

[8] That is under so-called straight voting, as distinguished from cumulative voting which a handful of states require and most others allow. See the discussion in § 5.05[A][1], *supra.*

[9] John A. C. Hetherington and Michael P. Dooley, *Illiquidity and Exploitation: A Proposed*

problem attracts lawyer, judicial, and legislative attention because the participants in such ventures frequently have significant amounts of human and investment capital dedicated to the enterprise. Shareholders may be employees or family members who derive significant amounts of their livelihood from the enterprise. They may be sons or daughters of the founders of the firm for whom their ownership represents their principal legacy from a deceased parent. As to investment capital, participants in a closely held corporation often have a disproportionate amount of their personal assets "tied up" in the corporation. Thus, in the illiquidity and exploitation setting, the stakes for various participants often are high in a relative, if not also in an absolute, sense.

[C] Corporate Law Responses to the Illiquidity and Exploitation Situation

The history of the law's development in the area of closely held corporations has been before the fact (*ex ante*) and after the fact (*ex post*) attempts to deal with all or certain aspects of the illiquidity and exploitation problem. *Ex ante*, before attempts at exploitation have surfaced, attorneys have anticipated potential exploitation through contractual provisions which vary from normal governance rules, such as supermajority quorum and voting requirements giving minority factions added power, to employment contracts for shareholder employees, to comprehensive shareholder agreements combining variations from the ordinary governance rules with added protections for the minority in terms of employment, distributions, and so on. Legislatures have also responded by enacting special statutory provisions applicable to closely held corporations. In general, these provisions make clear the ability of participants and their lawyers to vary from the governance and financial model the corporation law sets up for other corporations.[10]

Ex post, close corporation statutes have two effects. One result of such statutes is to render agreements more likely to withstand judicial or shareholder attack. In a bygone era, courts struck down provisions in shareholder agreements as attempts to handcuff or sterilize the board of directors, or as illegal attempts to operate a corporation as if it were a partnership.[11] Another result for close corporation statutes is to create special

---

Statutory Solution to the Remaining Close Corporation Problem, 63 Va. L. Rev. 1 (1977).

[10] An attorney representing a would-be minority participant in a closely held enterprise may take the view that, without "more," a minority interest may be worth very little no matter how valuable the assets or the business of the enterprise. Most likely, the "more" will be a contract that may guarantee employment for the minority participant, implement special governance rules, such as supermajority voting giving minority owners a measure of negative control (veto power), provide for compulsory buy-out of the minority upon the happening of certain contingencies, or something similar. These types of contractual arrangements and their enforcement may be viewed as a substitute of sorts for the ability to exit by way of the market which exists in publicly held firms.

[11] Indeed, a provision in the Delaware close corporation statute provides that no agreement that "relates to any phase of the affairs" of a Delaware close corporation "shall be invalid on the ground that it is an attempt by the parties to the agreement or by the stockholders of the corporation to treat the corporation as if it were a partnership . . . ." Del. Gen. Corp. L. § 353. In order for this provision to apply one must specially file as a close corporation in Delaware. See § 11.06, *infra.*

remedies for closely held corporation participants such as dissolution for deadlock or oppression, appointment of a provisional director, and mandatory share repurchases.

In litigation occurring after the fact of exploitation, judges have come to demonstrate solicitude for the situation in which closely held corporations and minority participants frequently find themselves. Appellate courts in a number of jurisdictions have created heightened fiduciary duties owed not merely to the corporation but by all the participants one to another, akin to partners in a partnership.[12] Furthermore, courts have given new meaning to the term oppression as that term is used in involuntary dissolution statutes. And increasingly, courts have been willing to grant remedies tailored to the problem of illiquidity and exploitation found in the closely held corporation context.[13]

§ 11.02   OBTAINING AND MAINTAINING A MEASURE OF CONTROL

[A]   Preview

In any corporation, including a closely held one, the principal objective is to obtain one or more seats on the board of directors.[14] A board seat will give a minority faction a "window" on corporate affairs, if not a measure of control. In some cases, by voting together on a consistent basis or by getting the majority to agree, a group of minority shareholders may be able to elect some directors and then maintain whatever control they possess over corporate affairs. To achieve these objectives, a number of classical devices have been used, alone or in combination. Those devices are (1) shareholder pooling agreements, (2) irrevocable proxies, (3) voting trusts, (4) class voting, and (5) cumulative voting.

The norm for shareholder voting is that the shareholder attends the shareholders' meeting, listens to the discussion, and then votes for a director or slate of directors or on resolutions proposed by management or other shareholders. Strictly speaking, proxy voting is a variation of the norm of attendance and voting. A proxy is simply a specialized agency for the voting of shares created by one who may not attend the meeting (the proxy giver) to one who will (the proxy). Under modern corporation statutes, shareholders may vote by proxy as a matter of right and not merely as a matter of grace.[15] Voting by proxy is such a common variation, however, that it is no longer thought of in those terms.

---

[12] The leading case is *Donahue v. Rodd Electrotype*, 328 N.E.2d 505 (Mass. 1975).

[13] For reference purposes, there exist two comprehensive, multi-volume treatises dealing with the subject of closely held corporations, both authored by the late Dean F. Hodge O'Neal and Professor Robert Thompson of Vanderbilt University. They are O'Neal and Thompson, CLOSE CORPORATIONS (3rd ed. 1995), and O'NEAL AND THOMPSON'S OPPRESSION OF MINORITY STOCKHOLDERS (2nd ed. 1997).

[14] For a discussion of the standard or basic model of corporate governance, see Chapter 5.

[15] *See* MBCA § 7.22. Under terminology introduced by the Model Business Corporation Act, the shareholder and principal is the proxy giver, the writing utilized (traditionally called the proxy) is the"appointment form," and the agent who will attend the meeting is the "proxy."

All of the share voting devices to be discussed are departures from the norm of attendance and voting and involve *ex ante* means to provide a minority with some board representation. A consequence of that feature is that, when they were first examined by courts, many of these devices encountered some judicial hostility that, by and large, has disappeared today. However, this hostility has affected how legislation has been written and some of the devices used by attorneys and others. Judicial hostility also resulted because many of these devices were used secretly in earlier times. In the robber baron era of the nineteenth century, secret voting agreements and voting trusts were utilized to control corporations by persons with disproportionately small share holdings.[16]

[B]   Shareholder Voting Agreements

In addition to proxy voting, a second variation from the norm is the shareholder voting agreement, also known as a shareholder pooling agreement. These agreements provide that all signing shareholders shall vote as they shall agree or, failing agreement, as a designated individual (i.e., the family lawyer, a trusted aunt) directs. Alternatively, the agreement may provide that all signatories agree to vote as a majority of the group, or "pool," decides.

This standard situation of attendance and voting may not suit the participants in a close corporation. For example, consider a 50-50 corporation, the Winchester Apple Corporation, owned by two families, A and B. Family B has five members spread throughout the United States, except for the oldest sibling, who has remained in Winchester and takes an active role in corporate affairs. The absent siblings have little interest in active participation other than getting together from time to time, even if only by telephone, to discuss Winchester Apple corporate affairs. They know, however, that it is important for them to "stick together," pursuing a common course of conduct. If one or more siblings were to splinter off, voting independently or with the other 50 percent owner, family A, family B could lose its say in corporate affairs.

A shareholder voting agreement might fit the family B siblings' needs.[17] As previously stated, a voting agreement provides that the signing shareholders agree to pursue a common course of conduct as they agree, in the election of directors, or across the entire spectrum of shareholder affairs, including amendments to the articles of incorporation and major transactions such as merger, sale of assets or dissolution.[18] In the event of failure to agree, a stated consequence follows so that the pooling agreement is more than merely an illusory contract (an agreement to agree). The stated consequence may be that, for example, in the event of a failure to agree, all signatories agree to vote as a majority of them decides. Alternatively, in the event they fail to agree, the stated consequence may be that all the signatories agree to vote as a third party directs them.

---

[16] See the discussion of vote buying and other practices in § 5.05[E], *supra*.

[17] Another solution might be class voting, discussed in § 11.02[F] *infra*.

[18] See the discussion of shareholders' roles in the traditional corporate governance model in § 5.05, *supra*.

The classic case is *Ringling Bros. Combined Shows v. Ringling.*[19] The widows of two Ringling brothers each held 315 shares of the famous circus corporation. The third shareholder, John Ringling North, owned 370 shares. The corporation had cumulative voting which assured each owner of having representation on the board.[20] By voting together, the two Ringling widows were able to control 5 seats (instead of 4 if voting individually) on a 7 person board of directors. The two widows combined their voting power using a pooling agreement. In the event of their failure to agree on who the fifth director should be, or on any other question, their pooling agreement appointed their lawyer as arbitrator. He could then determine how the shares would be voted.

At the annual meeting, however, Aubrey Ringling Haley, through her second husband, declined to follow the arbitrator's command as to the fifth director. He voted for himself and his wife, while the other widow voted as the arbitrator had directed. The result was that the fifth director did not receive enough votes to win. Pursuant to cumulative voting, John Ringling North then would be able to elect three rather than two directors.

Turmoil ensued. The other widow Ringling sued to enforce the agreement. The court found that the agreement was not an illusory agreement, since a stated consequence followed a failure to agree, namely, empowerment of the arbitrator. In fact, the court upheld the agreement in its substantive aspects. The court refused, however, to constitute the shareholder who had complied as the proxy of the recalcitrant shareholder (Ms. Haley). Thus, the court would not specifically enforce the agreement, ordering the shares voted as the arbitrator had decided. Instead, in a somewhat punitive manner, the court threw out all of the Haley votes as having been cast in violation of the agreement. The consequence was that, for the ensuing year at least, John Ringling North would control the board by a three to two margin.

The *Ringling* decision exhibits no hostility toward the substance of the pooling agreement but it does refuse to grant specific performance of the agreement according to its supposed terms. As to the substance, the court found the pooling agreement to be a "well recognized means by which a shareholder may effectively confer his voting rights upon others while retaining various other rights." As to the remedy, however, the court found that the agreement fails to spell out the consequences if one or the other signatory to the agreement refused to follow the arbitrators' decision and the court refuses to supply the missing terms, as the Vice Chancellor below had done. Nonetheless, two pieces of the fallout from the decision in *Ringling* are: (1) that many statutes now expressly provide that shareholder voting agreements shall be specifically enforceable[21] and, (2) knowledgeable attorneys are careful to spell out in detail the consequences should one or the other party breach a shareholder voting agreement. The consequences may resemble empowerment of the arbitrator

---

[19] 53 A.2d 441 (Del. 1947).

[20] For discussion of cumulative voting, see § 5.05[A][1], *supra.*

[21] *See, e.g.*, MBCA § 7.31 ("Two or more persons may provide for the manner in which they will vote their shares by signing an agreement for that purpose" and "[a] voting agreement created under this section is specifically enforceable").

and the proxy arrangement, as in *Ringling*, or a provision requiring all shares to vote, or be voted, as a majority of shares in the pool so decides. Enforceability of shareholder voting agreements is not the area of concern that it once was.[22]

[C]   Irrevocable Proxies

A third variation from the norm of attendance and voting is not merely a proxy, but an irrevocable proxy. Since a proxy arrangement is merely an agency, ordinarily it is revocable at the will of the principal. This is because the essence of agency is said to be loyalty and obedience to the principal. If the principal should have any reason to doubt the agent's loyalty, she is able to revoke the agency, no questions asked.[23] The foregoing is of course subject to the right of the agent to seek damages if the agent has a contract under which the dismissal is wrongful. But, ordinarily, the dismissed agent cannot get his or her job back.

Corporate law, however, goes further than agency law. Statutes provide that, even if not specifically revoked, a proxy arrangement is considered revoked by a later dated proxy given to another, by the shareholder's attendance at the meeting, or, in any case, by the passage of eleven months' time.[24]

Suppose, for example, that Rand Bank holds 50 percent of the shares of Winchester Apple Corporation. As security for a loan to the corporation, the bank requires both family A and family B to pledge a portion of their shares. With the shares, Rand Bank and the loan agreement also require the pledging shareholders to give the bank an irrevocable proxy to vote those shares, good for the life of the loan. The legal question, should a dispute later arise, is whether a court would uphold the irrevocable feature of this proxy (agency) relationship.

In turn, resolution of that question depends upon whether the agency is "coupled with an interest."[25] Coupled with an interest is a bit like obscenity under one famous description in that "you know it when you see it." Some authors of corporate texts do not even attempt to define the term, contenting themselves with recitation of fact patterns of a great many cases in which proxies have been held to be "coupled" or not "coupled with an interest." The typical interest involves an interest in the shares. Nonetheless, the distillation of those cases is that the irrevocability of any agency so styled, including a proxy, will be upheld when the agency is given to protect not only the interests of the

---

[22] For example, in *Ramos v. Estrada*, 8 Cal. App. 4th 1070, 10 Cal. Rptr. 3d 838 (Cal. Ct. App. 1992), the court sanctioned enforcement of an extreme provision requiring a sale of shares back to the corporation as the consequence of a failure to vote as a majority of shares agreed, as provided by the shareholder pooling agreement. The court noted that the transaction "does not constitute a forfeiture and that they violated the agreement voluntarily, aware of the consequences of their acts."

[23] In fact, the agency terminates if, without the knowledge of the principal, the agent acquires interests adverse to the principal or is disloyal. Restatement (Second) of Agency § 112.

[24] *See* MBCA § 7.22.

[25] The restatement uses another common law term for the same concept, "powers given as security." *See* Restatement (Second) of Agency § 138.

principal but in addition some independent interest of the agent, over and above the normal agent's interests such as employment, compensation, and the like.

Thus, as with Rand Bank, if a bank is willing to lend funds to a corporation but has doubts about the stability of shareholders, or wishes to be in a position to block any merger or sale of assets, the bank might request a proxy to vote all or some of the shareholders' shares during the period of the loan. That proxy would be considered coupled with an interest (especially if the shares are collateral for the loan) and its irrevocability feature upheld because the proxy was given to protect some independent interest of the proxy holder, here as lender, as well as the interests of the proxy giver. By contrast, if managers of the corporation solicit proxies that are irrevocable for five or ten years, they may not be found to be "coupled with an interest" because the proxy relationship is not necessary to protect any interest of the proxy holder independent of the agency itself or an interest in the shares themselves.

A number of cases in close corporation settings hold that a proxy given to a fellow shareholder to protect interests common among a group of shareholders is given to protect independent interests, as described above, and will be held to be coupled with an interest.[26] Thus, if Indiana Jones is to go to North Africa on a three year archeological sojourn, he could give an irrevocable proxy to his sister, and fellow shareholder, in the Kokomo Bullwhip Corp., to vote his shares, for the three year period, pursuant to a shareholder agreement. Should Indiana return early and challenge the arrangement, in all probability, he would lose. Given to a fellow shareholder, such proxy would be held coupled with an interest; its irrevocability provision would be good.

In *Haft v. Haft*,[27] the issue was whether the court should find the proxy holder's interest in maintaining his status as a corporate officer (CEO) sufficient to find the proxy coupled with an interest and therefore to uphold its irrevocability. Herbert Haft, founder of the Dart Drug chain, transferred his shares (57% of the company) to his son, Roland. In payment, Roland gave back to his father a promissory note and a lifetime irrevocable proxy to vote the shares.

Later, Roland purported to revoke the proxy. The court upheld the irrevocability and Roland lost. The court found that a proxy given to protect an ongoing contract of employment was "coupled with an interest" under the 1967 revision to Del. Gen. Corp. L. § 212(e), requiring "either an interest in the stock or *an interest in the corporation generally.*" Herbert Haft's independent interest in maintaining his position as CEO was "sufficient under our law to render specifically enforceable the express contract for an irrevocable proxy."

---

[26] *See, e.g., State ex rel. Everett Trust & Savings Bank v. Pacific Waxed Paper Co.*, 157 P.2d 707 (Wash. 1945). Modern statutes achieve the same result. *See* Del. Gen. Corp. L. § 212(e); MBCA § 7.31.

[27] 617 A.2d 413 (Del. Ch. 1995).

[D]   Voting Trusts

A more extreme departure from the norm of attendance and voting, is the voting trust. The hallmark of the voting trust is the complete separation of ownership from the other aspects of ownership. As will be seen, the shareholders participating in such a trust actually endorse their share certificates over to the trustee, who may give back to the shareholders a "certificate of beneficial interest." Voting trusts are often used to maintain control, or to insure stability in management of corporate affairs, often at the insistence of creditors or venture capitalists.

As has been seen, in a shareholder pooling agreement, the stated consequence follows only if the parties fail to agree. In the first instance, the shareholders are able to meet, discuss the issues, and decide upon a course of conduct. Thus, in a pooling agreement, there is only partial separation between voting and other aspects of ownership. The separation occurs only if the parties to the agreement cannot agree. In a voting trust agreement, the shareholders may discuss matters but the trustee has no obligation to listen to them. A complete severance of voting and ownership has occurred, with all voting rights lodged in the trustee's hands.

Cases challenge voting trusts, or arrangements contended to be equivalent to voting trusts, as "illegal voting trusts." An illegal voting trust is simply one that fails to comply with statutory requirements that the voting trust be of record at the corporation's principal offices (not secret) and be limited in duration, often ten years.[28] If the arrangement is unconventional, and is not of record or limited in duration, the issue presented is whether the device or arrangement is a voting trust. Several famous cases deal with that issue.

In *Lehrman v. Cohen*,[29] the two families owning the Giant Food supermarket chain each held a class of stock for that family: AC shares for the Cohen family and AL shares for the Lehrman family. As a tie breaker, the corporation issued a single share of a third class of shares to the attorney, Joseph Danzansky. The only right or privilege of the AD class of shares was to elect a fifth director.

After a falling out, the Lehrman family challenged the arrangement as a voting trust because it separated voting from ownership and the AD shareholder had no real equity interest. They argued that, as a voting trust, the arrangement was an illegal voting trust, that is, one that simply did not comply with the statute. The Delaware Supreme Court did not agree, for under the

---

[28] *See, e.g.*, MBCA § 7.30 (shareholders must transfer shares to trustee, trustee must deliver list of beneficial owners and trust agreement to the corporation's principal offices, and trust is "valid for not more than 10 years after its effective date"). In 1994, Delaware abolished the 10 year limitation on duration on voting trusts and other voting devices, DGCL § 218(c), while MBCA § 7.31 eliminated the duration limitation only for devices other than voting trusts. Voting trust statutes came about out of a historical suspicion of secret voting arrangements dating from the robber baron era of the nineteenth century. *Accord Oceanic Exploration Co. v. Grynberg*, 428 A.2d 1 (Del. 1981) ("'[O]ur case law makes clear that the main purpose of a voting trust statute is to avoid secret uncontrolled combinations of stockholders formed to acquire control of the corporation to the possible detriment of the non-participating shareholders.'").

[29] 222 A.2d 800 (Del. Ch. 1966).

arrangement there was no complete separation of "the voting rights of the AC or the AL stock from the other attributes of ownership." The court based that decision on its finding that, under the arrangement, the Lehrmans and the Cohens "have not divested themselves of their voting rights, although they may have diluted their voting power." If the Lehrman and Cohen directors reached an accord on a point, which they did for many years, the AD share arrangement was irrelevant and no separation of ownership from control would be present. A by-product of the case is to legitimize possible use of a third class of shares as a tie-breaker between two evenly divided factions in a corporation.

Lehrman v. Cohen, however, rested upon an earlier, and famous, Delaware case, *Abercrombie v. Davies*.[30] *Abercrombie* applied the test of earlier Delaware cases, "that one essential feature that characterizes a voting trust is the separation of the voting rights of stock from the other attributes of ownership." The court found a voting trust in an arrangement in which six owners holding 54 percent of the American Independent Oil Co. transferred stock certificates and voting power, using irrevocable proxies, to eight designated agents, agreeing that the vote of seven of the eight agents would bind the group. The shareholder agreement here, combined with the irrevocable proxies, resulted in a separation of the voting rights from the shares.

The previous sentence describes the physical arrangement, sometimes legally required, that accompanies formation of the voting trust. The participating shareholders actually endorse and deliver share certificates to the trustee who may then return to shareholders "certificates of beneficial interest." The certificate represents return to the shareholder of all rights associated with shareholding except the right to vote the shares on all or some issues which come before the shareholders.[31] The latter right, of course, remains with the trustee for the period of the trust.

Grafted onto, or impliedly incorporated into, the trust instrument — as well as in other voting devices, such as irrevocable proxies or pooling agreements — is the proper purpose doctrine. Thus, for example, a trust that is found to have fraud, illegality, or reaping a benefit to the detriment or exclusion of minority shareholders as its purpose, would violate the proper purpose doctrine even though the trustee is merely doing the participants' bidding and is not, therefore, in breach of her fiduciary duty of loyalty. A trust formed to elect directors who will disregard the environmental laws or who will permit the looting of the corporation by the majority shareholder would run also afoul of the proper purpose doctrine.[32]

---

[30] 130 A.2d 338 (Del. Ch. 1957). Under Delaware law today the use of irrevocable proxies and a shareholder's agreement would not be found to be a voting trust. Del. Gen. Corp. Law § 218(d).

[31] A trust agreement could, for example, bestow upon the trustee the power to vote in the election of directors but provide that the power to vote on merger or sale of all or substantially all of the assets remains with the participating shareholders.

[32] The late Supreme Court Justice William O. Douglas berated secret voting trusts as "vehicles for corporate kidnapping." Such a use certainly could be made of a voting trust as, for example, in the case when a working majority uses a voting trust to put directors in office who will permit looting of the corporation or allow looting to occur due to neglect. Mr. Justice Douglas, however, seemed to

Also important to remember is that a voting trust is a trust. The trustee owes fiduciary duties of care and loyalty to the participating shareholders. What exactly that might mean in context is the subject of *Wharehime v. Wharehime*,[33] John Wharehime, CEO of a successful food company, Hanover Foods (HFC), was also the trustee of a voting trust. He proposed issuance of a new class C preferred stock which would have superstock rights (35 votes per share) to HFC's 401(k) plan, which was administered by certain HFC directors Wharehime had elected. The superstock voting rights would spring into being only upon a prolonged dispute among the Wharehime siblings and would exist for 5 years after the issuance.

The complaint was that the springing voting rights would give the directors elected by John Wharehime 5 extra years control, beyond the voting trust's 10 year term, over the company, including appointment to the CEO position. John Wharehime and the directors maintained that the arrangement was necessary to give the company added stability, facilitating a major round of financing, which would redound to the voting trust beneficiaries in the long run. In contrast, the participating shareholders maintained the arrangement to be an entrenchment attempt to benefit John Wharehime who also was a trustee The Supreme Court of Pennsylvania applied a subjective standard of good faith (some would say warm heart) to one who was a voting trustee. It buttressed its findings with a provision of the voting trust agreement constituting, in its opinion, "a definition of the fiduciary obligation": "The Trustee will use his best judgment in voting the stock held be him, and assumes no responsibility for the consequence of any vote cast, or consent given by him, in good faith." "If the parties had intended to limit the trustee's authority . . . they would have included a provision . . . ," said Chief Justice Cappy.[34] The dissent pointed out that such a trust provision constitutes a defense to *duty of care* violations by a trustee. It has no applicability to situations of divided loyalties. "[The] duty of *absolute* loyalty to the beneficiaries must pervade any and all actions a trustee undertakes." The principle admits of "no leeway." "Good faith is not a defense

---

be unmindful of how the proper purpose doctrine or fiduciary duty might be invoked to curb such conduct.

Voting trusts do have legitimate purposes. As with a pooling agreement, a trust may be utilized to bind together for a time a shareholder group. If members of the group, say siblings who, as a group, control or share control of the corporation, bicker, argue and have a difficult time arriving at a consensus, as a pooling agreement may require them to attempt to do, a voting trust may be the better device to lend a measure of stability to corporate affairs. For a period of years, the trustee has the power to vote the shares as she thinks fit. After the shareholders have achieved a degree of maturity, perhaps the trust may terminate and a pooling arrangement attempted at that time.

Another use of voting trusts is in corporate reorganizations under the bankruptcy code. The plan of reorganization may require the common shareholders to put shares into a voting trust in order to insure a period of stability in corporate affairs, even after the corporation has emerged from bankruptcy.

[33] 761 A.2d 1138 (Pa. 2000), *on appeal from remand*, 777 A.2d 469 (Pa. Super. 2001), *reversed*, 860 A.2d 41 (Pa. 2004) (finding no irreparable harm which would support entry of an injunction).

[34] *Id.* at 1141.

against a claim of disloyalty." The trustee must at all times serve the beneficiaries' best interests.[35]

An old legal saying is that a trustee may not, under any circumstances, purchase at her own sale. By contrast, a corporate director may deal with the corporation on whose board she sits if she makes full disclosure and obtains disinterested decisionmakers' approval or, in any case, if she can demonstrate that the transaction's terms are fair.[36] In *Wharehime*, the court seemed to apply a director standard to one who was serving as a trustee. Nonetheless, the case points to a resurgence in the use of voting trusts. Angels, venture capitalists, and other mid stage financiers today often insist that high tech and other corporate entrepreneurs put their shares in trust for a period of years in order to facilitate stability in governance until such time as the corporation becomes able to do an initial public offering.

[E]   Class Voting

Class voting of shares is another means of implementing a power sharing arrangement in a small corporation. It may also provide for minority representation on the board by giving the minority a class of shares that allows them to elect some directors. Recall that the Winchester Apple Co. is controlled by two families. The more geographically dispersed of the two families, family B, must stay together if they are to maintain their share of control. If they begin to part ways, family A members may pursue a divide and conquer strategy, recruiting members of B family into the family A camp. If that occurs, family A may be permanently in control of the corporation.

One way to cement family B members together is through a shareholder voting agreement. Another method is amendment of the articles of incorporation to provide for class voting.[37] An amendment would provide for two classes of shares, identical in all respects except for voting rights. "A" shares, to be held by the A family, would have the right to elect two directors on a five person board. "B" shares, to be held by the B family, would also have the right to elect two directors to the board.[38]

With class voting, the divide and conquer or co-optation strategy on behalf of family A is not possible. If they co-opt one of the five family B siblings, that shareholder is of no help to them, for she only has the right to vote for B directors. She cannot help family A to obtain an additional director or to convert a B director into an A director.

Given the even number of directors elected by the two families, a possibility of director deadlock (protracted 2-2 standoff) exists. The articles could deal with

---

[35] The duties of care and loyalty and the differences between them are discussed, *inter alia*, in §§ 8.01[A] & [B] and 9.01[A], *supra*.

[36] See, e.g., § 9.03, *supra*.

[37] The Model Act language is "voting group," defined as "all shares of one or more classes or series that under the articles of incorporation or this Act are entitled to vote and be counted together collectively on a matter at a meeting of shareholders." MBCA § 1.40(26).

[38] In Model Act terms, the corporation would have voting group A and voting group B.

this risk in several ways. The provision might be that the four directors elect a fifth director, but the A and B directors could deadlock on election of the fifth director down the road. The articles could provide that, in that instance, mandatory arbitration becomes necessary. Another possible tie-breaker could be the provision for a third class of shares whose only right would be to elect a fifth director, as with the AD share in *Lehrman v. Cohen*. The single share of that third tie-breaker share class could be placed with a neutral party.

[F]   Cumulative Voting

In the election of directors, cumulative voting gives a shareholder the right to cast votes equal to the number of shares she holds times the number of director positions standing for election. She may take those votes and cumulate them on one or two of the positions open for election rather than being required to spread her votes evenly over all positions up for election.[39] It is important to note that, in the area of publicly held corporations and as a matter of mandatory state constitutional or corporate code provisions, cumulative voting is fading from the scene. However, cumulative voting schemes are very much in evidence and can be important in governance and power-sharing arrangements in smaller and closely held corporations. Generally today, however, because of the former consideration, a cumulative voting scheme must be provided for *ex ante*, in the articles of incorporation.

Assume, for example, that Winchester Apple is to undertake expansion and to do so, the corporation has to raise equity capital. The board of directors proposes to sell to two additional families or groups, shares representing a 30 percent interest in the corporation. The prospective purchasers, however, are unlikely to agree to the purchase unless they receive, among other things, some voice in corporate governance. A means to do so would be to expand the board to 7 members and to provide for cumulative voting. In that manner, the two new participants would be able to elect 2 directors to the board. Those two directors alone would not be able to control decision-making, although they would have a window on corporate affairs. And, if family A and family B disagreed and were deadlocked, the directors representing the new participants would have the important swing vote. Cumulative voting is an important tool for corporate planners working in closely held and small corporation settings.[40]

[G]   Summary

In closely held corporations, devices involving shareholder voting, such as voting agreements, irrevocable proxies, voting trusts, class or group voting provisions, and cumulative voting, all may be regarded as variations from the normal model of corporate governance. For the most part, these devices have

---

[39] See the discussion of the mechanics of cumulative voting in § 5.05[A][1], *supra*.

[40] Once cumulative voting has been installed, some thought must be given to preventing the majority from amending articles of incorporation to remove it. An express supermajority requirement for removal, or a provision that cumulative voting shall be a vested shareholder right, may be two methods by which that objective may be achieved. See the discussion of ways to undercut cumulative voting in § 5.05[A][1], note 113, *supra*.

their greatest utility in the area of closely held corporations. These arrangements, which relate to share voting and limited issues, such as election to the board or amendments to the articles, are only one variety in a large array of shareholder agreements used in the close corporation context.

§ 11.03 PROTECTING SHAREHOLDER EXPECTATIONS IN CLOSELY HELD CORPORATIONS *EX ANTE*

[A] Contract

Along with obtaining and maintaining a seat on the board of directors, the best method to protect the interests of the close corporation shareholder is a contract to deal with other issues. Hopefully, the shareholder will have negotiated for one or more contractual protections against the illiquidity and exploitation problem. Alternatively, the corporate attorney may have anticipated shareholder needs and provided for them. The contract may be as basic as a salary-tenure agreement for the shareholder as manager or employee. On the other hand, the contract may be a comprehensive shareholder agreement that contains a number of governance and other provisions, such as a salary-tenure agreement, greater than majority quorum or voting provisions for some or all transactions, limitations on the authority of the board of directors, provisions for succession in case of death or disability of the founders, and provisions for minimum annual distributions should there be inactive shareholders. The intricacies of such agreements, however, require quite a bit of background.

[B] Long-Term Shareholder Tenure and Salary Agreements

These agreements, which provide long-term job security (tenure) and salary for close corporation participants, interfere with the standard model of corporate governance by taking control over certain decisions away from the board of directors. Judicial hostility toward attempts to depart significantly from the model a corporation statute sets up, either for publicly held or for smaller corporations, continued well into the 1930s.[41] Statutes then contained a provision, carried over into modern enactments in less imperative form,[42] that the business and affairs of a corporation be managed by a board of directors. Courts interpreted those provisions of the corporation law as mandatory.[43]

---

[41] For a discussion of the standard, or basic, model of corporate governance, see Chapter 5.

[42] *See, e.g.*, MBCA § 8.01(b) ("All corporate powers shall be exercised by or under the authority of, and the business and affairs of the corporation managed under the direction of, its board of directors").

[43] Early cases included *Manson v. Curtis*, 223 N.Y. 313, 119 N.E. 559 (1918) (contract providing for a passive board for one year was "illegal," as it would have "sterilized the board of directors") and *Faulds v. Yates*, 57 Ill. 416 (1870) (contracts binding boards disenfranchise future shareholders in whole or in part and, for that reason, are void).

Mandatory adherence to corporate norms is demonstrated by the decision of the prestigious New York Court of Appeals in *McQuade v. Stoneham.*[44] McQuade was a New York City magistrate who purchased a ten percent interest in the closely held corporation that owned the New York Giants baseball club. The other ten percent minority shareholder, McGraw, was the team's on-field manager. Defendant Stoneham's share interest was 35 percent. The three gentlemen entered into an agreement in two parts. First was an agreement as shareholders to use their "best endeavors" to elect each other as directors. Second was an agreement to keep Stoneham in office as president, McGraw as vice president and McQuade as treasurer, all at specified salaries.

McQuade and Stoneham quarreled, principally over Stoneham's repeated invasion of the corporate treasury. Stoneham then caused McQuade's ouster as director and officer of the baseball club. McQuade then sued on the agreement, seeking to recover his positions. Chief Justice Roscoe Pound held that "[s]tockholders may, of course, combine to elect directors." The first part of the agreement was valid and McQuade could possibly regain his position as a director.[45] But McQuade could not regain his position and salary as treasurer because, citing "public policy," the court felt "constrained by authority to hold that a contract is illegal and void so far as it precludes the board of directors . . . from changing officers, salaries or policies or retaining individuals in office, except by consent of the contracting parties."[46]

Such a holding is fatal to many closely held corporate schemes in which a shareholder invests her money in the enterprise but expects her primary return in a capacity as officer or employee rather than as investor. The validity of a long term contract to keep a participant employed or in office is the crucial link in the transaction and the key to participation in the first place, as the New York Court of Appeals implicitly began to recognize a scant two years later in *Clark v. Dodge.*[47]

Dodge owned 75 percent of a pharmaceutical company but was inactive in management. Clark owned 25 percent, acted as general manager, and had sole possession of the formulae for the manufacture of the corporation's product. Dodge and Clark then entered into an agreement to keep Clark in office as director and general manager so long as he should be "faithful, efficient and competent." In return, Clark agreed to disclose the formulae to Dodge's son and to instruct him in the details and methods of manufacture used by the company. After a falling out, Dodge ousted Clark and Clark sued for reinstatement both as a director and corporate officer.

---

[44] 189 N.E.2d 234 (N.Y. 1934).

[45] Part 1 of the agreement was nothing more than a shareholders' voting, or pooling, agreement, discussed in § 11.02[B], *supra.*

[46] Although noting that public policy "is a dangerous guide in determining the validity of a contract," in refusing to enforce McQuade's contract the court did invoke public policy which, in this context, probably means protection of minority shareholders and of creditors. Reliance on such policy seemed curious, as no minority or creditor had been heard to complain of McQuade's arrangement and there was evidence that he was not doing a proper job.

[47] 199 N.E.2d 641 (N.Y. 1936).

The court asked itself "[a]re we committed by the *McQuade* case to the doctrine that there may be no variation, however slight or innocuous, from [the] norm [that 'the business of a corporation shall be managed by its board of directors'], where salaries or the retention of individuals in office are concerned?" The Court decided that it was not, wondering "[i]f the enforcement of a particular contract damages nobody — not even, in any perceptible degree, the public — one sees no reason for holding it illegal, even though it impinges slightly upon the broad provision of section 27." Here, where all shareholders were signatories to the agreement, there was "no damage suffered by or threatened to anybody" and "damage suffered or threatened is a logical and practical test," not public policy or the intention of the legislature. Moreover, with the requirement that Clark remain in office only so long as he continued to be "faithful, efficient and competent," any impingement on the statutory norm was slight and any harm to the creditors was remote.

Attorneys now could draft shareholder agreements binding present and future boards in the matter of shareholder employment or exclusive areas of responsibility or jurisdiction for various participants, and so on. In so doing, they had some assurance that the contract could withstand judicial scrutiny. There are limits to these agreements, however.

One limit may be where the shareholder agreement completely sterilizes the board and purports to do so over a long period of time. In *Long Park, Inc. v. Trenton-New Brunswick Theaters Co.*,[48] the New York Court of Appeals held that *Clark v. Dodge* could not bear the weight of a 19 year agreement by three shareholders to grant to one of them full authority to manage the corporation's movie theaters. The agreement contained no "out," the ability to terminate the agreement on 90 days notice by either party or that it should continue in effect only so long as the manager remained "faithful, efficient and competent."[49]

[C]   Less Than Unanimous Shareholder Agreements

The area for variation from the statutory model may also be said to be more circumscribed when there are non-contracting shareholders. In the leading case *Glazer v. Glazer*,[50] through a series of corporations, some with non-contracting minority participants, the three Glazer brothers contracted to divide amongst each other various corporate offices. The court upheld the agreement, after noting that the minority shareholders either "knew or consented" or "did not object or claim prejudice from the brothers' agreement." In so doing, the Fifth Circuit distilled the analysis of recent decisions in the field of closely held corporations:

---

[48] 297 N.Y. 174, 77 N.E.2d 633 (1948).

[49] Later in New York, the legislature permitted any restrictions as long as they complied with the statute. N.Y. Bus. Corp. Act § 620(b) provides that "a provision in the certificate of incorporation otherwise prohibited by law because it improperly restricts the board in its management of the business of the corporation" shall be valid "[i]f all the incorporators or holders of record of all outstanding shares . . . have authorized such provision" and all subsequent shareholders are given notice.

[50] 374 F.2d 490, 406 (5th Cir.), *cert. denied*, 389 U.S. 831 (1967).

> The better-reasoned decisions . . . go directly to the . . . questions: Does the company have non-contracting shareholders? If so, is the agreement unfair or fraudulent as to them? Would they be injured by its enforcement? . . . In recent years, courts have shown less reluctance in enforcing shareholder salary-tenure agreements where the number of outside shareholders was small. This is in keeping with modern corporate theory, which emphasizes the realities of management and shareholder interests in each situation.

Other courts have upheld such long term employment and salary agreements by implying one of the terms discussed above — that the contract remains valid and enforceable only so long as the shareholder employee remains loyal and competent.[51] So long as that is the case, the likelihood of damage to the corporation, or the non-contracting shareholders, from the agreement is non-existent or slight.

These issues arose once again in *Triggs v. Triggs*.[52] A father transferred 35 shares each to his three sons, and a further 36 shares to favored son and heir apparent. Heir apparent and father then agreed to vote each other in as Chairperson (father) and CEO (heir apparent). Father also gave favored son an option to purchase father's remaining 113 shares upon father's death.

Father and favored son fell out. Father instead bequeathed his 113 shares to the other two sons. Favored son then sued to enforce the option agreement. His brothers responded that the voting agreement was invalid under *Manson v. Curtis* and *Clark v. Dodge* because the agreement had not been unanimous (signed by all shareholders). Moreover, the voting agreement posed a risk of great harm to the non-signatory shareholders.

In the New York Court of Appeals, the majority opinion sidestepped the legal issue. The agreement never did "fetter the authority" of the board of directors. The corporation and its directors largely ignored the agreement. There always were 3 or 4 independent directors. The board not only reduced the chair's "guaranteed" salary; it later eliminated the position. There was no harm to the non-signatory shareholders. The court upheld the agreement and the option.

In dissent, Judge Gabrielli's far more restrictive view was that agreements that fetter the board's discretion are valid only when "the violation of the statutory mandate is minimal and, more importantly, that there is no danger of harm either to the general public or to other shareholders." He would have found that installation of corporate officers with salaries guaranteed for 10 years posed a danger of harm sufficient to strike down the agreement and the option it contained.

---

[51] *See, e.g., Puro v. Puro*, 393 N.Y.S.2d 633, 637 (A.D. 1976).

[52] 26 N.Y.2d 305, 413 N.Y.S.2d 325, 385 N.E.2d 1254 (1978).

[D]   Other Agreements Affecting Directors' Discretion

In closely held corporations, as officer-employees, shareholders may wish to guarantee themselves exclusive jurisdiction, or freedom from some forms of interference at least, in various areas of corporate affairs. One may wish exclusive control over product design, another over manufacture or sales, and yet another over the front office. All agreements of these types impinge upon the board of directors' statutory prerogative to manage the corporation's business and affairs. Often such agreements limit not only the discretion of the current board but of boards and board members far into the future.[53]

As the discussion of *McQuade v. Stoneham, Clark v. Dodge,* and other cases illustrates, much of the history of the evolution of special recognition for close corporations came from cases initially striking down, and later upholding, agreements that to some degree "sterilize" the board of directors. One case, however, illustrates the length to which courts may now go in upholding agreements that sterilize the board of directors, at least in the closely held corporate context.

In *Zion v. Kurtz,*[54] a shareholders' agreement gave the minority shareholder an absolute veto power. Without the minority shareholder's consent, the corporation "could not engage in any business or activities of any kind, directly or indirectly." It is difficult to imagine a more complete sterilization of the board of directors.

Nevertheless, the court upheld the arrangement. More instructive, however, is the length to which the court went. The New York court pointed to the Delaware statutory close corporation provisions. One such provision provides that in a close corporation a shareholders' agreement "is not invalid . . . on the ground that it so relates to the conduct of the business and affairs of the corporation as to restrict or interfere with the discretion or powers of the board of directors."[55] Another provides that "[t]he certificate of incorporation of a close corporation may provide that the business of the corporation shall be managed by the stockholders of the corporation rather than the board of directors."[56]

The only difficulty was that the corporation, Lombard-Wall Group, Inc., had never elected to be treated under the special Delaware close corporation provisions. The Delaware statute provided a close corporation had to elect in its

---

[53] In publicly held corporations the same considerations apply. In *Carmody v. Toll Brothers, Inc.,* 723 A.2d 1180 (Del. Ch. 1998), discussed in § 12.04[B][1], *infra,* the chancellor struck down a 10 year poison pill takeover defense that could only be modified or rescinded by the directors who adopted it or their direct nominees, a so-called "deadhand poison pill." The court found that the " 'deadhand provision' unlawfully restricts the powers of future boards." For the same reason (fettering future directors' discretion), in *Quickturn Design Systems v. Shapiro,* 721 A.2d 1281 (Del. 1998), the Supreme Court of Delaware struck down a "no hand" poison pill which provided that it could not be modified by any director group, new or old, for six months after a change in control of the corporation.

[54] 405 N.E.2d 681 (N.Y. 1980).

[55] Del. Gen. Corp. L. § 350.

[56] Del. Gen. Corp. L. § 351.

certificate of incorporation that is was a Delaware close corporation.[57] The New York court remedied that deficiency by citing to the provision of the shareholders' agreement requiring defendant Kurtz, as well as other signatories, to execute and deliver "further instruments and documents and take, or cause to be taken, all such other and further action as [may be] necessary, appropriate or desirable to implement and give effect to the Stockholders Agreement." In essence, the court provided that Kurtz's forced concurrence to a Delaware close corporation election was a necessary prerequisite to upholding the minority shareholder's veto power.

Not all courts are willing to bend or stretch the normal rules for closely held corporations. Surprisingly, Delaware has taken a very firm stance against relaxation of these rules. In *Nixon v. Blackwell*,[58] a closely held corporation discriminated against certain shareholders. The corporation funded an Employee Stock Ownership Plan and purchased key personnel life insurance on the lives of eight officer-employees. Those steps provided liquidity so that the class A employee shareholders could obtain cash for their shares upon death, disability or retirement. The class B shares, 30 percent of which were owned by the non-employee shareholders who were descendants of the corporation's founder, enjoyed none of those benefits, and, in turn, they sued.

The Delaware Supreme Court held that, in Delaware, there are no special judge-made rules for closely held corporations. Instead, shareholders in such settings had to obtain whatever additional protection they could through "definitive shareholder agreements."[59] The Delaware statutes are of no help either, because the Delaware statutory chapter, "Close Corporations: Special Provisions," "applies only to a corporation which is designated as a 'close corporation' in its certificate of incorporation, and which fulfills other requirements." The court refused a court-ordered remedy, such as a buy-out, or other relief from the locked-in minority shareholders against whom the corporation and its directors were practicing blatant discrimination — a classic case of illiquidity and exploitation.

[E]   Comprehensive Shareholder Agreements

Allowance for relaxed adherence to corporate norms for closely held corporations surfaced in judicial opinions upholding shareholder salary-tenure agreements in closely held corporations. Commentators urged courts to go further and uphold any reasonable contractual arrangement in a closely held corporation, even if it infringed upon corporate norms or provisions of the

---

[57] Del. Gen. Corp. L. § 342(a). *See also* Del. Gen. Corp. L. § 341(a) ("[u]nless a corporation elects to become a close corporation under this subchapter in the manner prescribed . . . it shall be subject in all respects to the provisions of chapter, except the provisions of this subchapter").

[58] 626 A.2d 1366 (1993).

[59] This holding was of no solace to plaintiffs because they had been gifted the shares, which were non-voting, and had no bargaining power. Nonetheless, Chief Justice Veasey pontificated: "[t]he tools of good corporate practice are designed to give a purchasing minority stockholder the opportunity to bargain for protection before parting with consideration." The implication is that an investor better have an attorney before purchasing a minority interest in a Delaware corporation because there will be little gap filling or other help from Delaware courts afterwards.

statute not obviously mandatory, as long as creditors and fundamental public policy remained unharmed.[60] The Supreme Court of Illinois in *Galler v. Galler*[61] did so early on and in resounding fashion. *Galler* involved a comprehensive agreement between two 47½ percent shareholders "to provide income for the support and maintenance of their immediate families." The agreement had not one, but a number of provisions that handcuffed present and future directors: (1) the shareholders purported to amend the by-laws fixing the number of directors; (2) they agreed to vote each other and their spouses in as directors; (3) gave the surviving spouse as shareholder the right to fill board vacancies in case of the death of a director; (4) provided for minimum annual dividends, given a certain level of accumulated earned surplus; (5) contained a salary continuation provision benefitting the surviving spouse of a deceased signatory; (6) in the event of a shareholder's death, required a mandatory share buy back by the corporation to fund payment of estate taxes.

The agreement infringed upon the traditional prerogatives of directors in a number of ways. The intermediate appellate court found the agreement to be "in substantial disregard of the provisions of the Corporation Act," concluding that "the public policy of this state demands voiding this entire agreement."

The Supreme Court of Illinois reversed, upholding all the various provisions of this comprehensive shareholders' agreement and delivering a perceptive statement of the reasons for differing judicial treatment of close corporations:

> At this juncture it should be emphasized that we deal here with a so-called close corporation . . . . For our purposes, a close corporation is one in which the stock is held in a few hands, or in a few families, and wherein it is not at all, or only rarely, dealt in by buying and selling. Moreover, it should be recognized that shareholder agreements similar to that in question here are often, as a practical consideration, quite necessary for the protection of those financially interested in the close corporation. While the shareholder of a public issue corporation may readily sell his shares in the open market should management fail to use, in his opinion, sound business judgment, his counterpart in the close corporation often has a large total of his entire capital invested in the business and has no ready market for his shares should he desire to sell. He feels, understandably, that he is more than a mere investor and that his voice should be heard concerning all corporate activity. Without a shareholder agreement, specifically enforceable by the courts, insuring him a modicum of control, a large minority shareholder might find himself at the mercy of an oppressive or unknowledgeable majority . . . . For these and other reasons too voluminous to enumerate here, often the only sound basis for protection is afforded by a lengthy,

---

[60] *See, e.g.*, William Cary, *How Illinois Corporations May Enjoy Partnership Advantages: Planning for the Closely Held Firm*, 48 Nw. U. L. Rev. 427 (1953); Delaney, *The Corporate Director: Can His Hands Be Tied in Advance?*, 50 Colum. L. Rev. 52 (1950); Note, *A Plea for Separate Statutory Treatment of the Close Corporation*, 33 N.Y.U. L. Rev. 700 (1958).

[61] 203 N.E.2d 577 (Ill. 1965).

detailed shareholder agreement securing the rights and obligations of all concerned.[62]

Galler remains a strong, articulate statement in favor of differing judicial treatment of close corporations, regardless of whether legislatures have acted.[63]

Galler v. Galler was not, however, a green light for ignoring the corporate statute in close corporation cases. An Illinois appellate court found it necessary to state so in *Somers v. AAA Temporary Services, Inc.*[64] At issue was an attempt by shareholders to amend by-laws to reduce the number of directors from three to two. But the Illinois statute stated that the power to amend the by-laws is "vested in the board of directors," unless the articles of incorporation changed that pattern. Nonetheless, defendants urged the court to uphold the reduction in number of directors, citing *Galler*. The appellate court, however, refused to do this, stating: "The *Galler* Court did not say that the Illinois Business Corporation Act may be disregarded in the case of a close corporation. Slight deviations from corporate norms may be permitted. However, action by the shareholders which is in direct contravention of the statute may not be permitted."

§ 11.04   RESTRICTIONS ON SHARE TRANSFERABILITY

[A]   Introduction

As has been noted,[65] an important feature of the closely held corporation is an agreement permitting participants in the corporation reasonably to control who their "partners" will be. This form of agreement is ubiquitous in the world of small corporations. The agreements may be in the articles, the by-laws, a separate agreement, or a portion of a longer comprehensive shareholder agreement.

Three basic types of restrictions are used in the context of close corporations: (1) first refusals, which prohibit a sale of shares unless the shares are first offered to the corporation, the other shareholders, or both, on the terms the third party has offered; (2) first options, which prohibit a transfer of shares unless the selling shareholder first offers the shares to the corporation, the other shareholders, or both, at a price fixed under the terms of the buy-sell or similar agreement, often in accordance with a formula contained therein; and (3) consent restraints, which prohibit a transfer of shares without the permission of the corporation's board of directors or other shareholders.

Share transfer, or buy-sell agreements, actually serve several purposes. First, the "buy-sell" agreement enables the shareholders to keep ownership "close," giving them the opportunity at least to limit ownership to themselves or

---

[62] 203 N.E.2d 577, at 583–84 (citations omitted).

[63] A little-noted factor perhaps strengthening the *Galler* holding further is that there existed a non-signatory minority shareholder, Rosenberg, who did not become involved in the litigation and for whom the court evidently concluded little potential for harm existed.

[64] 284 N.E.2d 462 (Ill. App. Ct. 1972).

[65] See the discussion of what a close corporation is in § 11.01, *supra*.

to those whose ownership fits with their business plan. Second, by definition of death, disability, or cessation of employment as triggering events, the agreements may be seen as providing a degree of liquidity to close corporation shareholders or their heirs or legatees. Third, some signatories may view the agreement as a means of keeping the existing shareholders "in," preventing them from selling, or from selling other than at very disadvantageous terms.

The latter is an illicit purpose and introduces the tension that exists in the area. Because such agreements do restrict the ability of a shareholder to alienate her shares, or dictate some or all of the terms upon which she may do so, buy-sell agreements bump up against, if not run afoul of, centuries old proscriptions forbidding restraints on alienation of property and interests therein.

[B]   Umbrella Test — Unreasonable Restraint Upon Alienation?

In *Allen v. Biltmore Tissue Corp.*,[66] the estate of a deceased shareholder-employee was obligated by contract first to offer the estate's shares back to the corporation at their original $5 issue price. The corporation chose to exercise its option but offered $20 per share. The estate's executors declined the offer, presumably because the fair market value of the shares was much higher and because 21 years had passed between the date the share transfer restriction was adopted and the date of the shareholder's death.

Judge Fuld began with enunciation of the umbrella test, that share transfer restrictions are "subject to the time-honored rule that there be no unreasonable restraint upon alienation." Reviewing cases applying that principle, he concluded that "what the law condemns is, not a *restriction* on transfer, but an effective *prohibition* against transferability itself." An effective prohibition may be set in place by a great disparity in fair value and the "various methods or formulae for fixing the option price . . . employed in practice — *e.g.*, book or appraisal value, often exclusive of good will." Nonetheless, the court upheld the buy-sell option at original issue price, concluding that "more than a mere disparity between option price and current value must be shown" in order to prove up a case of unreasonable restraint on alienation.[67]

A later New York case, *Rafe v. Hindin*,[68] found an unreasonable restraint in a so-called consent restriction. In a two shareholder corporation, a shareholder could sell only to the other shareholder or transfer to a third party only upon written permission from the other shareholder. Since there were no guarantees or promises that consent would not be unreasonably withheld, the court found that "the restriction amounts to an annihilation of property. The restriction is not only unreasonable, but it is against public policy."

---

[66] 141 N.E.2d 812 (N.Y. 1957).

[67] Valuation of corporations and other businesses is discussed in § 4.05, *supra.*

[68] 288 N.Y.S.2d 662 (App. Div.), *aff'd*, 244 N.E.2d 469 (N.Y. 1968).

In truth, "consent" buy-sell agreements have received varied treatment by the courts.[69] What courts seem to search for is a determination of whether the agreement has the intent and result of keeping shareholders in (a restraint on alienation), or merely the result of allowing fellow shareholders the opportunity to control who their "partners" will be (permissible private ordering).

A by-product of the view that transfer restrictions may amount to impermissible restraints on alienation is the corollary that such agreements are to be "strictly construed," against restriction and in favor of alienability. A second corollary flowing from the same source is the principle that triggering events, and the obligations that become incumbent upon signatories upon the happening of a triggering event, must be "clearly stated" or they will not be enforced. Thus, a "sale or disposition" triggering event was held not applicable to a share transfer after death because not "clearly expressed," even though a sale by a deceased shareholder's executor is also a "sale or disposition."[70] Another court held that a restriction upon an attempted sale applies only to sales to third parties and not to transfers to fellow shareholders.[71]

Recent decisions apply the "strict construction" as well as the "clearly stated" rule. For example, a recent Pennsylvania decision states that, "[b]ecause alienation is an inherent attribute of corporate stock, however, restrictive amendments are not favorites of the law and are strictly construed."[72] Nonetheless, the trend is to abandon at least the "strict construction" rule because such agreements are ubiquitous and their terms are a familiar and accepted part of the corporate landscape. Thus, in *Burns v. Rennebohn Drug*

---

[69] *Compare Lonyear v. Hardman*, 106 N.E. 1012 (Mass. 1914) (consent agreement not palpably unreasonable or unconscionable), *with Tracey v. Franklin*, 67 A.2d 56 (Del. Ch. 1949) (two shareholder consent arrangement found to be impermissible restraint on alienation and against public policy).

[70] *Globe Slicing Machine Co. v. Hasner*, 333 F.2d 413, 415 (2d Cir. 1954) (New York law). *See also Seven Springs Farm, Inc. v. Croker*, 801 A.2d 1212 (Pa. 2002), in which the Supreme Court of Pennsylvania decided (wrongly in this author's view) that "transfers, assigns [or] sells" language describing triggering events did not include a merger. Merger of a ski corporation into another entity did not trigger a right of first refusal the minority shareholder thought he had by virtue of a buy-sell agreement. "[M]erger is a corporate act, not a shareholder act," the court found, even though securities and tax law have long held that a merger involves the sale of securities. *Accord: Frandsen v. Jensem-Sundquist Agency, Inc.*, 802 F2. 941 (7th Cir. 1986) (Posner J.) ("The distinction between a sale of shares and a merger is such a familiar one that it is unbelievable that so experienced a businessman as Frandsen would have overlooked it"). *Cf.* SEC Rule 145 (1972) (a merger is a sale, abolishing the former "no sale" rule applicable to mergers).

[71] *Birmingham Artificial Limb Co. v. Allen*, 194 So.2d 848, 850 (Ala. 1967). Practicing attorneys have evolved long lists of triggering events, partly as a result of the strict construction and clearly stated corollaries. Thus, inter vivos transfers may be defined to include not only sales to third parties, but transfers to fellow shareholders, gifts, and transfers in a divorce. Leaving little to chance, a drafter may spell out that transfer upon death includes not only bequests, but also intestate succession. Cessation of employment with the corporation or disability may be included as triggering events. Some drafters include what has been termed the "Russian roulette" provision wherein, upon deadlock, or prolonged deadlock, as defined in the agreement, the shareholders draw straws or roll a die, or the like. The short straw has the right to force the purchase of his shares (a "put" in the language of securities options) by the other shareholder.

[72] *Rouse & Associates, Inc. v. Delp*, 658 A.2d 1383, 1384 (Pa. Super. 1995).

Stores,[73] a Wisconsin court found the "strict construction rule" supposedly applicable to corporate share transfer restrictions to be "anachronistic," in part because share transfer restrictions are so common is small corporations. Another way in which the law may be bending is that many courts analyze restrictions in contract terms, moving away from property based concepts such as restraints on alienation.

Such a case is *The Capital Group Companies, Inc. v. Armour.*[74] The question was whether restrictions in a share transfer agreement blocked distribution of rights in the shares (half the dividends or half of proceeds upon sale), rather than the shares themselves, in a California divorce case in which a Capital Group employee's shares were an asset of the marital community. Capital Group went to Delaware, seeking a declaratory judgment that the agreement was valid and blocked the partial transfer in question. The Vice Chancellor held that Del. Gen. Corp. L. § .202, which validates share transfer restrictions, still subsumes a common law reasonableness requirement ("bears some reasonably necessary relation to the best interests of the corporation"). But restrictions need not be "the least restrictive alternative" to be reasonable. He found a transfer restriction applicable to the division of dividends in a divorce to be reasonable. Such a restriction was conducive to keeping the interests of employee-shareholders aligned (not dissipated) with the interests of the company. The cases demonstrates the modern tendency to uphold share transfer restrictions rather than to scrutinize them for flaws.

[C] Other Legal Aspects of Share Transfer Restrictions

[1] Legal Capital and Funding

If the corporation purchases the shares, the purchase will be a distribution. Under older legal capital schemes, the corporation will have to have earned or capital surplus equal to or greater than the purchase price. Under modern statutory schemes, the corporation may not make the purchase if doing so would make the corporation insolvent, either in the bankruptcy or equity sense.[75]

Buy-sell agreements may provide that the corporation is to maintain life or disability insurance on the shareholders' lives. With a mandatory obligation in the event of death or disability, the corporation then has a funding source to which it can look for part or all of the necessary funds. For example, in *Concord Auto Auction, Inc. v. Rustin*,[76] the corporation had maintained a $375,000 life insurance policy on the life of a key shareholder.

---

[73] 442 N.W.2d 591, 596 (Wis. Ct. App. 1989).

[74] 2005 Del. Ch. LEXIS 38 (Mar. 15, 2005) (Lamb, VC).

[75] See the discussion of these financial aspects in § 4.04[C], *supra.*

[76] 627 F. Supp. 1526 (D. Mass. 1986).

[2]   Procedural Aspects

Procedure relating to sales of shares may be so cumbersome or difficult that a court later finds the procedure an earmark of an intention to impose a *de facto* restraint upon alienation.[77] Along those lines, in *Ling & Co. v. Trinity Sav. & Loan*,[78] the duty to notify fellow shareholders was placed upon the selling shareholder. The court noted that "[c]onceivably the number of stockholders might be so great as to make the burden too heavy upon the stockholder who wishes to sell . . . ." As with disparity in price, discussed in the next subsection, the issue is whether the procedure is intended to be, or has the effect of, exerting a chilling effect on the desire of a shareholder to sell, or otherwise transfer, her shares.

[3]   Disparity Between Buy-Out Price or Formula and Fair Price

By definition, in the close corporation arena, no established market for shares exists and, therefore, no market price exists. Consequently, if the restriction is an option rather than a right of first refusal, the agreement must state a price or a formula for arriving at a price. The most frequent avenue for attack on share transfer restrictions opens when the buy-out price or formula is significantly less than fair or probable market value. The argument is that the disparity is so great as to exert a chilling effect on any potential transfer.

Many buy-out formulae are utilized, including book value, appraised value, or periodic revision.[79] In *Helms v. Duckworth*,[80] the periodic revisions of the price never were made. Following the elder shareholder's death, the remaining shareholder admitted that he never intended to adjust the price upwards. The appellate court held that his breach of fiduciary duty "warrants cancellation of the agreement by a court of equity." Presaging later case holdings in Massachusetts and elsewhere,[81] the court also stated that "[w]e believe that the holders of closely held stock in a corporation such as shown here bear a fiduciary duty to deal fairly, honestly, and openly with their fellow stockholders and to make disclosure of all essential information." Presumably, in the context of share transfer restrictions, the shareholder must bring that duty to bear in his efforts to undertake periodic re-examinations of the price.

In another periodic revision case, however, the court upheld the agreement despite a failure to "review the price annually," as required by the agreement,

---

[77] Cumbersome procedures could include requirements that a shareholder wishing to sell first notify other shareholders who have an option for 90 days after an appraisal of the shares has been made, for appraisal by a panel of three appraisers (one chosen by the shareholder, the next by the corporation, and the third by the first two appraisers), and successive options for the other shareholders first and then for the corporation. By the time the shareholder has run through the lengthy procedure for which the agreement calls, her putative purchaser probably will have lost interest.

[78] 482 S.W.2d 841 (Tex. 1972).

[79] For these and other valuation methods, see § 4.05, *supra*.

[80] 249 F.2d 482 (D.C. Cir. 1953).

[81] See the discussion of the so-called *Donahue* principle in § 11.07[B], *infra*.

and a great disparity between the buy-out and fair values. The court abjured arguments that the price was unfair or unjust: "specific performance of an agreement to convey will not be refused merely because the price is inadequate or excessive."[82]

The trend is to uphold agreements when the challenger's argument is confined to price disparity. As one court explained, "[t]hat the price established by a stockholders' agreement may be less than the appraised or market value is unremarkable."[83] Often noting the prevalence of such agreements in the business world, courts have upheld disparities of 4 to 1 and even 1000 to 1.[84] If an extreme disparity in price is accompanied by signs of overreaching, insufficient notice, or perhaps extreme unsophistication on the part of the party against whom the agreement is sought to be enforced, then perhaps a challenge may be mounted against enforcement of the agreement. But the trend among courts today is to uphold buy-sell agreements certainly if nothing more than a disparity in price is demonstrated, and in other cases as well.

The Capital Group Companies, Inc. v. Armour[85] illustrates the latter part of this trend. The question before the court was whether an agreement's share transfer restrictions which blocked distribution of rights in shares (half the dividends, half the sales proceeds, if any — not transfer of the shares themselves) given to a spouse in California divorce proceeding. The husband had received shares as a corporate employee. The court held that Del. Gen. Corp. L. § 202, which legitimates share transfer restrictions still subsumes a common law requirement that such restrictions be reasonable ("bears some reasonably necessary relation to the best interests of the corporation"). But the court found reasonable a purpose for a share transfer restriction to limit the total number of shareholders, thereby avoiding applicability of SEC periodic reporting and other costly regulations. The court found reasonable a purpose to keep employees' interests aligned (and not dissipated) with corporate interests. Restrictions "need not be the least restrictive alternative"; they need only to be reasonable. Delaware courts have always been reluctant to invalidate share transfer restrictions. The SRA provisions were valid and enforceable and the proposed transfer of rights in the shares violates the restrictions. The court

---

[82] *Concord Auto Auction, Inc. v. Rustin*, 627 F. Supp. 1526 (D. Mass. 1986), citing *Allen v. Biltmore Tissue, supra.*

[83] *Evagelist v. Holland*, 537 N.E.2d 589, 592 (Mass. App. Ct. 1989). Another alternative is to read the agreement so as to lessen the disparity. In *Piedmont Publishing Co. v. Rogers*, 193 Cal. App. 2d 171, 14 Cal. Rptr. 133 (1961), plaintiff offered movie actress Mary Pickford $126,812.36 for her one third interest in a North Carolina television station she had helped establish. Independent estimates placed the value at $400,000. In the agreement, the buyout formula was stated as "total book value . . . (total amount of issued common stock at par plus the amount of earned and other surplus)." The court read "*total* book value" and "*other* surplus" to add "good will" to book value. In turn, the court opined, good will would include the fair market value of the television broadcasting license (carried on the books at the cost of the original FCC fee, probably only a $1000 or so), and the fair market value of the station's network affiliation agreement with NBC (probably not carried on the books at all).

[84] *Compare Jones v. Harris*, 388 P.2d 539 (Wash. 1964) ($26,000 option price upheld when current value was $92,000), *with In re Mather's Estate*, 189 A.2d 586 (Pa. 1963) (1000 to 1 disparity enforced).

[85] 2005 Del. Ch. LEXIS 38 (Mar. 15, 2005).

granted the injunction to Capital Group, a Delaware corporation.

[4]   Notice

Uniform Commercial Code § 8-204 provides in part that, "[a] restriction on transfer of a security imposed by the issuer, even if otherwise lawful, is ineffective against a person without knowledge of the restriction . . . unless the restriction is noted conspicuously on the security certificate." As to uncertificated securities, which are relatively rare in the close corporation area, the section provides that the restriction is ineffective unless the registered owner "has been notified of the restriction."

Ling and Co. v. Trinity Sav. & Loan[86] holds that a line of ordinary type on the certificate margin does not satisfy U.C.C. § 8-204 and that the restriction was, therefore, unenforceable. In order for print to be conspicuous, "something must appear on the face of the certificate to attract the attention of a reasonable person when he looks at it."

It is so important that the Official Comment notes that the section "does not deal with private agreements between stockholders containing restrictive covenants as to the sale of the security."[87] Therefore, in the case of purely intra-shareholder agreements, lack of notice on the certificate may not alone be fatal and may simply constitute evidence in support of an argument that enforcement of the agreement against a particular party is unfair or unjust.

§ 11.05   OTHER GOVERNANCE FEATURES OF THE CLOSELY HELD CORPORATION

[A]   Overview

Two other ways in which closely held corporations may vary from corporate law norms are: (1) greater than majority quorum and voting requirements for meetings, and (2) a strong tendency to act in an informal manner, that is, not to have meetings at all. Both of these aspects of the law governing close corporations have received considerable judicial attention.

[B]   Greater Than Majority Quorum and Voting Requirements

For valid action to take place at a meeting, a critical mass of shares or, in the case of directors, persons, must be present. Once that critical mass, called a quorum and usually a majority (50 percent plus 1), is present, discussion supposedly ensues. A vote is then taken. On more routine matters, traditionally, a valid vote is a majority of those shares or persons present (that is, a majority of a quorum). In the shareholder case, but absent specific authority, not in the

---

[86] 484 S.W.2d 841 (Tex. 1972).

[87] Official Comment to U.C.C. § 8-204, at note 5.

director case, presence is presence either in person or by proxy.[88] For the shareholder vote on certain fundamental changes, such as merger, sale of all or substantially all assets, amendment of articles, or dissolution of the corporation, the vote required by a particular statute may be higher, namely, a majority of all shares entitled to vote and not merely of those present in person or by proxy.[89] In a handful of jurisdictions, requirements remain that for fundamental changes, two-thirds of the shares entitled to vote must approve the proposed change.

In closely held corporations, all participants not only own shares but may have intimate connections with the enterprise, either as employees, relatives, or neighbors. Close corporation shareholders expect to be able to participate in a meaningful way in governance and control, and, if only at times, decision making. Consequently, majority rule does not suit that level of involvement. Under majority rule, resentments may be quick to build up as coalitions calcify and deny other shareholders the meaningful participation they thought they would have. Supermajority, unanimous quorum, and voting requirements are methods for solving these problems and fulfilling shareholder expectations in the more intimate closely held corporate environment. They do pose a risk, however, because supermajority requirements make it easier for participants to block decisions and thereby deadlock the corporation.

Courts have expressed hostility to planners' deviations from the norm. In *Benintendi v. Kenton Hotel*,[90] the New York Court of Appeals struck down requirements for unanimity at both shareholder and director levels. In so doing, the court espoused a rigid concessionist view of the corporation: "The State, granting to individuals the privilege of limiting their individual liabilities for business debts by forming themselves into an entity separate and distinct from the persons who own it, demands in turn that the entity take a prescribed form and conduct itself, procedurally, according to fixed rules." The court read the statute not to permit any deviation from a majority requirement.

A nearly contemporaneous Virginia decision invalidated unanimous vote requirements, also emphasizing a practical result. In *Kaplan v. Block*,[91] the court noted the ease with which a single shareholder or director might deadlock a corporation in which a unanimity requirement exists: "A recalcitrant director who is also a stockholder may embalm his corporation and hold it powerless . . . ."

---

[88] See the discussion of the basic governance model in Chapter 5.

[89] The sponsors of the MBCA have amended the Act to provide that fundamental changes (e.g., mergers, amendment of articles), now may be approved by a majority of votes present at a meeting, given a quorum of at least 50% of the votes entitled to be cast. *See Changes in the Model Business Corporation Act Fundamental Changes*, 54 Bus. Law 685 (1999). The changes have resulted in plurality (more votes for than against) rather than majority (50% plus one of the shares present) voting throughout the Model Act.

[90] 60 N.E.2d 829 (N.Y. 1945).

[91] 31 S.E.2d 893 (Va. 1944).

Legislatures balanced the competing considerations and enacted statutes permitting greater than majority quorum and vote requirements.[92] In *Adler v. Svingos*,[93] the court upheld a shareholder unanimity agreement that allowed a one third shareholder interest to block sale of the corporation's business, a restaurant. The court analogized the unanimity agreement, and the resulting blocking power, to the veto upheld in *Zion v. Kurtz*.[94] "The principles set forth in Zion are controlling here," the court concluded in upholding the unanimous voting requirement.

Thus, today, hostility to greater than majority quorum and voting requirements seems to have disappeared. In publicly held corporations supermajority voting requirements may be an integral part of a shark repellent package designed to ward off takeover players.[95] In closely held corporations, planners include such provisions to create the more intimate level of participation in governance of those corporations that shareholders and directors desire. Nonetheless, planners need to be aware that, as the Massachusetts court noted, supermajority requirements bestow upon a minority shareholder or group, a measure of negative control, or veto power, over decisions. Subject of course to fiduciary duties,[96] the minority shareholder or group may use the veto power so created to engage in strategic and opportunistic behavior, holding the corporation and the majority hostage until the minority's demands are met. Corporate planners need to give thought to such considerations before implementing greater than majority or unanimous quorum or vote requirements.

[C]   Informal Action By Shareholders and Directors

Participants in closely held corporations tend not to observe corporate formalities such as notice of meetings, formal meetings, resolutions, votes, minutes of meetings, and so on. There is a long history of corporate law coming to terms with reality, namely that directors and shareholders do not observe the formalities that statutes envision, because they feel them to be foolish "play acting," believe that it is a contrivance by their attorney to obtain additional fees, or cannot come together in the way envisioned because of other responsibilities. Today, statutes permit action by both shareholders[97] and directors[98] on an informal basis. The shareholders or directors memorialize any action taken by a written document known as a consent, which they circulate

---

[92] A modern version thereof is MBCA § 7.27 ("The articles of incorporation may provide for a greater quorum or voting requirement for shareholders . . . than is provided for by this Act"). *See also* MBCA § 8.24 (similar authorization for directors except quorum may also be lower but no lower than "one-third of the fixed or prescribed number of directors").

[93] 436 N.Y.S.2d 719 (App. Div. 1981).

[94] Discussed in § 11.03[D], *supra.*

[95] For a discussion of takeover defenses, see § 12.04, *infra.*

[96] See *Smith v. Atlantic Props., Inc.*, 422 N.E.2d 798 (Mass. 1981), discussed § 11.07[B], *infra.*

[97] *See* MBCA § 7.04(a).

[98] *See* MBCA § 8.21.

among themselves and sign. The ability of participants in closely held or any other corporation to act informally is discussed in detail in Chapter 5.[99]

§ 11.06   CLOSE CORPORATION STATUTES

Approximately fifteen jurisdictions have provisions in their corporate statutes that expressly enlarge freedom of contract for corporations that make an election to be treated as a "close corporation."[100] For the most part, the close corporation provisions are grouped into a separate chapter of the corporations code.[101]

Delaware's operative provisions first sanction sterilization of the board of directors by means of shareholder contract: "A written agreement among the stockholders of a close corporation holding a majority of the outstanding shares . . . is not invalid as between the parties to the agreement, on the ground that it so relates to the conduct of the business and affairs of the corporation as to restrict or interfere with the discretion of powers of the board of directors."[102]

Escalating, another provision provides that the corporation may dispense with a board altogether: "The certificate of incorporation of a close corporation may provide that the business of the corporation shall be managed by the stockholders . . . ."[103] A third operative provision makes clear the effect of a close corporation election:

> No written agreement among the stockholders [which] . . . relates to any phase of the affairs of such corporation, including but not limited to the management of its business or declaration and payment of dividends or other division of profits or the election of directors or officers or the employment of stockholders by the corporation or the arbitration of disputes, shall be invalid on the grounds that it is an attempt by the parties to the agreement or by the stockholders of the corporation to treat the corporation as if it were a partnership or to arrange relations among the stockholders or between the stockholders and the corporation in manner that would be appropriate only among partners.[104]

---

[99] The latitude permitted both by statutes and courts for acting informally is discussed in detail in § 5.06[B][1], *supra*.

[100] Alabama, Arizona, Delaware, Illinois, Kansas, Maryland, Pennsylvania, Rhode Island, Texas, and Wisconsin require an election to be treated as a close corporation. There is also a "Model Statutory Close Corporation Supplement" promulgated by the American Bar Association's Committee on Corporate Laws.

[101] One example is California. Its special close corporation provisions are scattered throughout the California corporations code. *See, e.g.*, California Corp. Code §§ 158(a), 705(e), 706. Other similar statutes include those of Florida, Georgia, Maine, Michigan, Minnesota, Montana, New Jersey, New York, North Carolina, Ohio, and South Carolina.

[102] Del. Gen. Corp. L. § 350.

[103] Del. Gen. Corp. L. § 351.

[104] Del. Gen. Corp. L. § 354.

Other provisions make clear the power of Delaware courts to come to the aid of close corporations in case of deadlock.[105]

Adoption of special close corporation chapters ceased around 1980. Modern corporation statutes have become so enabling that they contain all, or almost all, of the latitude planners need to draft contracts and suit the needs of participants in closely held corporations.[106] The statistics are that the number of elections to be treated under special close corporation statutes are disproportionately small.[107]

§ 11.07   PROTECTING SHAREHOLDER EXPECTATIONS IN THE CLOSE CORPORATION *EX POST*

[A]   Resetting the Problem

Many closely held corporations do not have in place special contractual arrangements of the type discussed, and even if they have contracts, they may be limited in scope. The participants may enter the business trusting that the other investors will act fairly and not think contractual protections necessary. They may not have relationships with attorneys who could help them put in place such contractual relationships and may not want to expend resources for legal advice. Without contractual protections, the participants in such corporations often find themselves face-to-face with the age-old close corporation problem of illiquidity and exploitation.

When *ex post*, those participants bring their disputes to court, courts have responded in positive ways. One principal way has been to hold that participants in a close corporation owe fiduciary duties, not only to the corporation, but to one another, akin to partners in a partnership, and that the duty owed is a heightened one. The second principal way is to articulate new tests of when shareholders have been "oppressed" by those in control of the corporation and thus, may be able to seek involuntary dissolution of the corporation. The threat of involuntary dissolution, or other intermediate remedies courts have evolved for close corporations, is often enough to procure better treatment for the minority participant, often including purchase of her shares at a fair price.

Forms exploitation may take are salaries, bonuses, perquisites, and fringe benefits for the majority shareholders with less or nothing in the way of benefits for the minority. For example, the brother who remained in the home town now runs the tool and die business the father founded, takes a generous salary as president and general manager, and enjoys an automobile, health and life insurance and other benefits at corporate expense. The other sibling, who is also a shareholder, lives in a distant state and receives little or nothing, even though her share interest is the principal legacy her parents bequeathed her. Content

---

[105] *See, e.g.*, Del. Gen. Corp. L. § 353 ("Appointment of a Provisional Director in Certain Cases").

[106] An influential piece was Dennis S. Karjala, *A Second Look at Special Close Corporation Legislation*, 58 Tex. L. Rev. 1207 (1980).

[107] *See* 1 O'Neal and Thompson, CLOSE CORPORATIONS § 1.19 (3rd ed. 1998).

to receive a salary, the brother running the corporation is loathe to cause the corporation to pay dividends.[108] The situation festers for a number of years.

The sister could bring a suit to compel payment of dividends. Those suits seldom succeed because the declaration of dividends is a central prerogative of directors. The directors' decision not to pay a dividend receives core business judgment rule protection.[109] Courts have held that a shareholder must make "bad faith" or similar showings before a court will consider ordering the declaration and payment of dividends.[110]

Another line of approach is to bring suit alleging that payment of at least a portion of the brother's salary and benefits constitutes a breach by directors of their fiduciary duty or even a gifting or waste of corporate assets.[111] The difficulty with this approach is that, even if a breach of fiduciary duty is found, fiduciary duty is owed to the corporation. The remedial consequence is that, for violation of duty, the remedy is payment back to the corporate treasury of the portion found illicit. That is not a remedy the sibling necessarily desires. She may not wish to penalize her brother, denying him financial benefits. What she really desires is similar benefits, or the financial equivalent, that her sibling enjoys: she really wishes to obtain "me too" type relief.

[B]   Heightened Fiduciary Duty in the Close Corporation Setting

In *Donahue v. Rodd Electrotype Co.*,[112] the plaintiff's deceased spouse, Joseph Donahue, had worked on the shop floor, eventually achieving a position as plant superintendent but never participating in overall management of the business. Along the way, Mr. Donahue acquired 50 shares in the corporation. Harry Rodd managed the corporation and, at the time of his approaching retirement, his sons had succeeded him in managing Rodd Electrotype. Essentially, the Rodd sons caused the repurchase by the corporation of Harry

---

[108] In some cases, the denial of a return may be part of a plan to force the minority to sell out to the majority at an unfair price. See, for example, the discussion of *Donahue v. Rodd Electrotype* in § 11.07[B], *infra*.

[109] See the discussion of the business judgment rule in § 8.03[C], *infra*.

[110] *See, e.g., Gottfried v. Gottfried*, 73 N.Y.S.2d 692 (1947) ("bad faith" and not "mere existence of adequate surplus" required before court will compel a dividend); *Schmitt v. Eagle Roller Mill Co.*, 272 N.W.2d 277, 280 (Minn. 1937) ("the declaration of a dividend rests in [directors'] sound discretion and one will not be compelled unless they act fraudulently, oppressively, unreasonably or unjustly"); *Romanik v. Lurie Home Supply Center, Inc.*, 435 N.E.2d 712 (Ill. App. Ct. 1982) (same); *Zidell v. Zidell*, 560 P.2d 1086 (Or. 1977) (not enough for family member shareholder to show that corporation could afford dividends, that he had left the corporate payroll and received nothing, and that directors had provided no documentary evidence or formal studies supporting decision not to pay dividends; complete credence given to directors' testimony about corporation's future needs for cash "possibly" to relocate a major plant and the need for renovation of a nearly obsolescent dock). *Cf. Miller Magline, Inc.*, 256 N.W.2d 761 (Mich. App. 1977) (refusal to declare dividend found breach by directors of fiduciary duty: annual dividend of $75 per share ordered for five years).

[111] As a result, not even a majority of the shares could approve or ratify the payments. See the discussion of the limits on shareholder ratification in § 9.06, *supra*.

[112] 328 N.E.2d 505 (Mass. 1975).

Rodd's shares at $800 per share.[113] Through their attorney, plaintiffs, the widow Donahue and her son, then stepped forward and asked for the same treatment for the 50 Donahue shares. The corporation denied their request for equal treatment.

The facts visibly demonstrated the familiar pattern of illiquidity and exploitation. Several times in the years preceding the Rodd buy-out at $800, per share the corporation had offered to buy the Donahue shares, but at prices ranging from $40 to $200 per share.

As the Supreme Court of Illinois had done in *Galler v. Galler*,[114] the Supreme Judicial Court of Massachusetts held forth at length about the nature of the close corporation, the predicament in which minority shareholders frequently find themselves, and the resemblance of the relationship more to partnership than corporation. Because of this "resemblance" and "the trust and confidence which are essential to this scale and manner of enterprise, and the inherent danger to minority interests in the close corporation," said the justices, "we hold that stockholders in the close corporation owe to one another substantially the same fiduciary duty in the operation of the enterprise that partners owe one to another." Ordinarily, of course, rank and file shareholders in a corporation owe no duties to the corporation or to fellow shareholders: pursuance of self-interest is the raison d'etre of such ownership.

The Massachusetts court also perceived the duty owed as a heightened one, higher than that owed in run-of-the-mill corporations:

> [W]e have defined the standard of duty owed by partners to one another as the "utmost good faith and loyalty." Stockholders in close corporations must discharge their management and stockholder responsibilities in conformity with this strict good faith standard. They may not act out of avarice, expediency or self-interest in derogation of their duty of loyalty to the other stockholders and to the corporation.

> We contrast this strict good faith standard with the somewhat less stringent standard of fiduciary duty to which directors and stockholders of all corporations must adhere.

The remedial consequence of the *Donahue* principle was that Ms. Donahue and her son now had an opportunity for "me too" relief. Since "[t]he controlling group may not, consistent with its strict duty to the minority, utilize its control of the corporation to obtain special advantages and disproportionate benefit from its share ownership," the court announced a rule of "equal opportunity in a close corporation." Upon remand, the trial court had a choice of two forms of suitable relief. The court could order the senior Rodd to pay back to the corporation what he had received, the traditional form of relief. Or, the court could order the corporation to repurchase the Donahue shares on terms and conditions as favorable as those Mr. Rodd had received.[115]

---

[113] The sale of shares by a controlling shareholder generally is discussed in § 10.05, *supra.*

[114] Discussed in § 11.03[D], *supra.*

[115] Of course, the issue arises because corporate funds were used to repurchase Mr. Rodd's

Important to note is that the *Donahue* principle is a double-edged sword. Minority shareholders in a close corporation have duties akin to partners in a partnership, just as do the majority shareholders. In *Smith v. Atlantic Properties, Inc.*,[116] by virtue of an 80 percent vote requirement, a 25 percent shareholder had a veto power, or negative control, over certain transactions. But he could not arbitrarily or unreasonably withhold his consent. His doing so was a violation of the *Donahue* principle, rendering him liable for damage to the corporation that had resulted from his exercise of the veto power based solely upon personal tax considerations.[117]

Again, too, as Illinois courts had to do with *Galler v. Galler*, the Supreme Judicial Court of Massachusetts had to temper application of the *Donahue* principle a few years after the court had formulated it. *Wilkes v. Springside Nursing Home, Inc.*[118] offers an insight into the formation and workings of a very typical close corporation. A real estate investor brought together three other individuals to acquire a building that had formerly been a hospital, converting it into a nursing home facility. Each shareholder made an identical capital contribution. Each was to be a director and an officer. Each was to receive money from the corporation in equal amounts so long as each assumed an active and ongoing responsibility for the corporation's business. Last of all, each was apportioned an area of exclusive jurisdiction, according to their talent and inclination. Thus, one was in charge of the physical plant and grounds, one was in charge of kitchen and dietary aspects, one was in charge of the medical side of the business, and one was in charge of personnel and administrative aspects of the nursing home.

Some number of years of successful operation had passed when one shareholder, Quinn, wished to purchase a portion of the unused corporate real property. Plaintiff Wilkes, however, succeeded in prevailing on the other shareholders to force Quinn to pay a higher price for the property than Quinn had anticipated. Bad blood developed. Quinn then persuaded the other two shareholders to freeze Wilkes out of active participation in the business and to cut off payments to him. They removed Wilkes from the board, removed him from his officer position, and eliminated his salary as an employee-manager.

Essentially, Wilkes won on appeal but, in passing, the Supreme Judicial Court put the brakes on untempered application of *Donahue*:

> [W]e are concerned that untempered application of the strict good faith standard enunciated in *Donahue* to cases such as the one before us will result in the imposition of limitations on legitimate action by the controlling group in a close corporation which will unduly hamper its

shares. If a control group uses its own funds to purchase another shareholder's shares, absent violation of a buy-sell agreement, a shareholder denied the opportunity to purchase those shares has no cause to complain. *See, e.g., Zidell v. Zidell, Inc.*, 560 P.2d 1091 (Or. 1977).

[116] 422 N.E.2d 798 (Mass. 1981).

[117] Because his income put him in a high marginal tax bracket, and he did not want additional income, the defendant, Dr. Wolfson, used his veto power to block payment of dividends, even after the corporation had paid three years of substantial penalties to the IRS for excess accumulated profits. Later, the IRS assessed accumulated profits taxes for four additional years.

[118] 353 N.E.2d 657 (Mass. 1976).

effectiveness in managing the corporation in the best interests of all concerned. The majority, concededly, have certain rights to what has been termed "selfish ownership" in the corporation which should be balanced against the concept of their fiduciary duty to the minority.

In other words, absent agreement to the contrary, majority still rules in close corporations. It just does not rule as absolutely as in other corporate settings.

The Massachusetts court attempts to reconcile the tension between majority rule and the *Donahue* principle by asking "whether the controlling group can demonstrate a legitimate purpose for its action. In asking this question, we acknowledge . . . that the controlling group in a close corporation must have some room to maneuver." If, however, the majority shareholders advance a credible business purpose for actions taken that also harm the minority, "we think it open to minority stockholders to demonstrate that the same legitimate objective could have been achieved through an alternative course of action less harmful to the minority's interests." In Wilkes's case, however, the majority was never able to advance a legitimate business purpose for the actions taken. As a result, the court never had to apply the second half of its analysis.[119]

Stuparich v. Harbor Furniture Mfg., Inc.[120] enunciates principles similar to *Wilkes*. A father, the company founder, had arranged for the purchase by his son of 51.56% of the voting shares in a company that made furniture (at a loss) and owned a mobile home park (very successful). After their efforts to have the company split in two were rebuffed, the two sisters (19.05% each) brought an action claiming oppression. The court noted that they had never played any part in day-to-day corporate operations. While "their efforts to participate in corporate operations or policy [may have been] frustrating and futile," their father "was privileged to sell his shares to the son at whatever price he chose." The daughters' only conceivable right was to receive dividends. The evidence showed that they "were paid significant dividends [$800,000, 1984–1998] in the period preceding the filing of the dissolution action."[121] Otherwise, the majority continued to be able to reap the selfish benefits of majority ownership.

Gearing v. Kelly[122] is a case which demonstrates how fiduciary duty, heightened or otherwise, may rise up to harm participants in a closely held corporation. In her capacity as a director, a 50 percent shareholder, Ms. Mecham, purposely avoided a meeting knowing that, if she attended, a quorum would be present and the other two directors would outvote her, appointing to a vacancy a third director who would be in their camp. The court held her estopped

---

[119] One perceptive commentator is quite critical of *Wilkes*. "Balancing [majority rule with *Donahue* duties] provides a complete shift in focus from the classic fiduciary examination of whether an action taken was in the beneficiary's best interest to a mode of analysis that centers on the fiduciary's interest. Thus, fiduciary conduct is now analyzed by examining whether the fiduciary had a motive other than to harm the beneficiary, rather than whether the fiduciary acted in the beneficiary's best interest. [T]he *Wilkes* rule . . . abandons the altruism inherent in fiduciary analysis in return for more commercially-oriented concepts of good faith and fair dealing." Lawrence Mitchell, *The Death of Fiduciary Duty in Close Corporations*, 138 U. Pa. L. Rev. 1675 (1990).

[120] 83 Cal. App. 4th 1268, 100 Cal. Rptr. 313 (2000).

[121] *Id.* at 1278.

[122] 222 N.Y.S.2d 474 (App. Div. 1961), *aff'd* 182 N.E.2d 391 (N.Y. 1962).

to complain of the third director whom her opponents appointed anyway. The court was indignant about Ms. Mecham's attempts to "paralyze" the board by staying away. The language in the decision also could provide the raw material for argument that quorum breaking and other tactics such as Ms. Mecham's constitute violation of the heightened fiduciary duty shareholders in close corporations owe to one another, akin to partners in partnership.[123]

[C] Heightened Fiduciary Duty in Other Jurisdictions

Many state judiciaries have whole-heartedly embraced the *Donahue* principle.[124] Only one or two courts have been reluctant to embrace it, or at least to embrace it fully.[125] Nonetheless, there are a number of jurisdictions, perhaps a majority, in which no opportunity has presented itself for an appellate court to embrace, reject, or modify the *Donahue* principle. The current phase of historical development, then, consists of the spreading adoption of the principles developed in *Donahue, Wilkes,* and *Smith v. Atlantic Properties,* along with examination of the further ramifications of these doctrinal developments in the law applicable to close corporations.

[D] Two Worlds Collide: The *Donahue* Principle Meets Employment at Will

One interesting problem is the potential conflict between the *Donahue* principle and fiduciary duties akin to partners and the employment-at-will doctrine, when a shareholder-employee in a close corporation has been

---

[123] It may be argued that *Gearing v. Kelly* is a terribly misguided decision. In any case in which control breaks down 50-50, and there is an even number of directors, and one director dies or resigns, *Gearing* requires the 50 percent faction who has lost a director to turn over control of the board to the other faction for an extended period, possibly forever. *Gearing* takes away the one bargaining chip the faction has, which is to stay away from meetings and negotiate how the vacancy is to be filled. On the other hand, the case reflects early judicial discontent with the possibility of long-term deadlock and the damage to a successful business it might cause.

[124] See, e.g., *Alaska Plastics, Inc. v. Coppack,* 621 P.2d 270, 276 (Alaska 1980); *Tilis v. United Parts, Inc.,* 395 So.2d 618 (Fla. Dist. Ct. App. 1981); *Cressy v. Shanon Continental Corp.,* 378 N.E.2d 941 (Ind. Ct. App. 1978); *Hagshenas v. Gaylord,* 557 N.E.2d 316, 322 (Ill. App. Ct. 1990); *Campbell v. Campbell,* 422 P.2d 932 (Kan. 1967); *Rosenthal v. Rosenthal,* 543 A.2d 348 (Me. 1988); *Blavik v. Sylvester,* 411 N.W.2d 383 (N.D. 1987); *Grato v. Grato,* 639 A.2d 390, 398–99 (N.J. Sup. Ct. App. Div. 1994); *Freeze v. Smith,* 428 S.E.2d 841, 847–48 (N.C. Ct. App. 1993); *Crosby v. Beam,* 548 N.E.2d 217, 220 (Ohio 1989). See also *Slattery v. Bower,* 924 F.2d 6, 9 (1st Cir. 1991) (Maine law).

[125] See, e.g., *Toner v. Baltimore Envelope Co.,* 498 A.2d 642 (Md. 1985) (accepting *Donahue* in principle but declining to adopt any *per se* equal opportunity rule, thus letting stand the corporate repurchase of one branch of a family's shares without ordering a similar repurchase for plaintiff Toner). See also *Kos v. Central Ohio Cellular, Inc.,* 641 N.E.2d 265, 271 (Ohio App. 1994) (*Donahue*-like fiduciary duties in closely held entities "do not mean that minority shareholders can frustrate the will of the majority by simply disagreeing over the course of corporate action"). In *Nixon v. Blackwell,* 626 A.2d 1366 (Del. 1993), the Delaware Supreme Court indicated that fairness does not require equal treatment and that judicially created rules for minority shareholders are unavailable unless the corporation elected to be covered under its close corporation statute. Last of all, in *Harrison v. NetCentric Corp.,* 744 N.E.2d 622 (Mass. 2001), despite the number and liberality of Massachusetts close corporation precedents, the Massachusetts court applied the internal affair choice of law rule, holding that Delaware, and not Massachusetts, law controlled the affairs of a Massachusetts based close corporation which had incorporated in Delaware.

dismissed. Absent a contract, an employee is an employee-at-will who may be dismissed at any time, with or without cause. According to one Ohio court, the issue is "whether the employment of a minority shareholder in a close corporation can be terminated by the majority shareholders for ostensibly legitimate, but not particularly compelling, business reasons."[126] The court answered by formally grafting a legitimate business purpose requirement onto the employment-at-will doctrine in cases in which the corporation is closely held and the dismissed employee is also a shareholder. By contrast, in *Harris v. Marden Business Systems*,[127] a Minnesota court examined the complaint and found its tenor to be employment related, rather than a *Donahue* fiduciary claim. The court held that a minority shareholder was an employee-at-will who could be dismissed without cause. Fiduciary duties, akin to a partners in a partnership, had no role to play.[128]

Similarly, in *Merola v. Exergen Corp.*,[129] plaintiff left a good employment position to become vice-president of Exergen, with the understanding that he would have the opportunity to become a major shareholder. He never acquired a substantial position although he did invest $15,000. Five years later, the controlling shareholder (Pompei) terminated plaintiff's employment, ostensibly because plaintiff criticized the public nature of the romantic relationship Pompei had with a female employee. Plaintiff sued, alleging violation of the *Donahue* principle. The Supreme Judicial Court of Massachusetts rejected the claim, pointedly noting that "[n]ot every discharge of an at-will employee of a close corporation who happens to own stock in the corporation gives rise to a successful breach of fiduciary duty claim." As with the Minnesota court in *Harris*, the Massachusetts court found the gist of his complaint to be employment related, with the share ownership incidental to his claim.[130]

Rather than suit for breach of fiduciary duty under *Donahue*, in *McCallum v. Rosen's Diversified, Inc.*,[131] a dismissed employee (in fact, the CEO of a $400 million livestock trading company), sought a court ordered buyout of his 12,000 shares by the corporation. Such buyouts have become a preferred remedy in cases in which an "oppressed" shareholder seeks to utilize the doomsday

---

[126] *Giax v. Repka*, 615 N.E.2d 644, 649 (Ohio Ct. App. 1992).

[127] 421 N.W.2d 350 (Minn. Ct. App. 1988).

[128] Similar cases in New York include *Gallagher v. Lambert*, 549 N.E.2d 136 (N.Y. 1989) (attempt by former employee to challenge as breach of fiduciary duty share buy back triggered by cessation of employment 20 days before increase in price rejected), and *Ingle v. Glamore Motor Sales*, 535 N.E.2d 1311 (N.Y. 1989) ("[a] minority shareholder in a close corporation, by that status alone, who contractually agrees to the repurchase of his shares upon termination of his employment for any reason, acquires no right from the corporation or majority shareholders against at-will discharge").

[129] 668 N.E.2d 351 (Mass. 1996).

[130] Collision of the *Donahue* principle with the employment-at-will doctrine in cases in which shareholder-employees are discharged by close corporations are arising with some frequency. *Merola v. Exergen Corp.* is at least the third opinion on the subject by Massachusetts's highest court. *See Blank v. Chelmsford Ob/Gyn, P.C.*, 649 N.E.2d 1102 (Mass. 1995) (shareholder-employee who had signed employment agreement providing for discharge without cause had no fiduciary duty claim); *King v. Driscoll*, 638 N.E.2d 488 (Mass. 1994) (shareholder-employee dismissal gave rise to breach of fiduciary duty claim against controlling shareholders).

[131] 153 F.3d 701 (8th Cir. 1998).

weapon, judicial (involuntary) dissolution of the corporation. An emerging test of what constitutes oppression is denial of the shareholder's "reasonable expectations" by those in control of the corporation.[132]

Before the litigation, the corporation had offered McCallum $600,000 for his shares. He thought their worth to be $5 million. Applying Minnesota law, the Eighth Circuit found the "reasonable expectations" language in the Minnesota statute.

> Oftentimes, a shareholder's reasonable expectations include a significant voice in management and an opportunity to work . . . . [M]cCallum's reasonable expectations were defeated [when] RDI terminated his employment as CEO and subsequently offered to purchase his RDI shares at a small premium over the value determined by an annual valuation for RDI's ESOP . . . . On his termination, McClallum was divested of his primary expectations as a minority shareholder in RDI — an active role in the management of the company and input as an employee.[133]

Denial of reasonable expectations will not work, however, for just any shareholder-employee who has been dismissed. "We simply hold that terminating the CEO — as opposed to an employee that did not have a significant role in management — and then offering to redeem his stock, which was issued partially to lure him to remain at the company, constituted conduct toward McClallum as a shareholder sufficient to invoke" the Minnesota involuntary dissolution statute and the alternative court ordered buyout remedy that statute contains.[134]

---

[132] Suits for involuntary dissolution, oppression, and buyout remedies are discussed at length in § 11.07[E]–[H], *infra*.

[133] 153 F.3d at 703–704.

[134] Opportunistic behavior (whose permutations seem to be endless) toward a former employee, who also was a shareholder of a closely held corporation, reared its ugly head in *Jordan v. Duff and Phelps, Inc.*, 815 F.2d 429 (7th Cir. 1987). On Nov. 16, Jordan told the Duff and Phelps's chairman that he was going to resign his position (but stay on until Dec. 31). Under a Stock Restriction and Purchase Agreement, cessation of his employment required Jordan to sell his stock back to the company, which he did on Dec. 30, receiving $23,255. On January 10, Duff and Phelps announced its acquisition by Security Pacific Bank that had been in the works (but still secret) for several months. Under the merger agreement, Jordan would have received a minimum of $452,000 and a maximum of $646,000. Duff and Phelps defended on grounds that even if Jordan had not resigned he was an employee at will.

They could have fired him at any time prior to announcement of the merger. Not so, said Judge Frank Easterbrook. "[A] person's status as an employee at will does not imply that the employer may discharge him for every reason." Elaborating on his observation, the judge said: "Employment creates occasions for opportunism. A firm may fire an employee the day before his pension vests, or a salesman the day before a large commission becomes payable . . . . [N]o one doubts that an *avowedly* opportunistic discharge is a breach of contract, although the employment is at will . . . ."

Moreover, Duff and Phelps, being a closely held corporation, owed Jordan in his shareholder capacity a fiduciary duty: "Close corporations buying their own stock, like knowledgeable insiders of closely held firms buying from outsiders, have a fiduciary duty to disclose material facts . . . ." Had the corporation made full disclosure, Jordan would have rescinded his pending resignation, receiving the full benefit of the later merger.

[E]   Involuntary Dissolution Statutes

More extreme than a *Donahue* type lawsuit is a petition for involuntarily dissolution by judicial decree. The involuntary dissolution petition is the doomsday weapon in the close corporation field. The beginning point for analysis of such a petition is, of course, the statute.

The Model Business Corporation law involuntary dissolution statute is representative of such statutes and is reproduced below.[135]

The statutes have existed for a number of years, but for most of their existence have been interpreted by courts to be "jurisdictional" only. That is, if a plaintiff proves that directors are deadlocked, the shareholders are unable to break the deadlock, and irreparable harm is threatened, those showings merely get the plaintiff past the courthouse door. They do not necessarily entitle him to a decree of dissolution. The same is true with showings of shareholder deadlock or that those in control of the corporation are misapplying or wasting assets, which are other grounds listed in the statutes.

The hesitancy of courts to decree dissolution despite ample showings on the grounds listed in the statute, arose from two sources. One source was an attitude termed "judicial solicitude for the lives of fictional persons"[136] and for "the sacred cow of corporate existence."[137] Courts would not grant dissolution if they thought some vague notion of the public interest would be served by continued corporate existence. If the business was making a profit, courts would find that "no irreparable damage" was threatened, refusing to decree dissolution. The latter refusal might find the participants in the closely held corporation locked in a bitter struggle, much as in a marriage gone sour, but locked together because the venture made profits.

Critics pointed out that the public interest had nothing to do with whether a mom-and-pop business venture continued or ceased its corporate existence.[138]

---

[135] MBCA § 1430 provides in pertinent part:

The [Superior Court, Circuit Court, or court of general jurisdiction no matter how named] may dissolve a corporation: . . .

(2) in a proceeding by a shareholder if it is established that:

(i)   the directors are deadlocked in the management of the corporate affairs, the shareholders are unable to break the deadlock, and irreparable injury to the corporation is threatened or being suffered or the business and affair of the corporation can no longer be conducted to the advantage of the shareholders generally, because of the deadlock;

(ii)   the directors or those in control of the corporation have acted, are acting, or will act in a manner that is illegal, oppressive, or fraudulent;

(iii)   the shareholders are deadlocked in voting power and have failed, for a period that includes at least two consecutive meeting dates, to elect successors to directors whose terms have expired; or

(iv)   the corporate assets are being misapplied or wasted.

[136] Abram Chayes, *Madam Wagner and the Close Corporation*, 73 Harv. L. Rev. 1532, 1547 (1960).

[137] *See* Carlos Israels, *The Sacred Cow of Corporate Existence — Problems of Deadlock and Dissolution*, 19 U. Chi. L. Rev. 778 (1952).

[138] Relatively recent cases, however, continue to invoke the public interest issue. *See, e.g., Henry George & Sons v. Cooper-George, Inc.*, 632 P.2d 512 (Wash. 1981) (shareholder deadlock and ensuing

One well-known judge espoused a simple standard that if "there is a want of community of interest essential to corporate operation," dissolution should be granted.[139]

[F]   Cases of Deadlock

The other source of judicial hesitancy in granting decrees of dissolution had better grounding. In cases of deadlock in which involuntary dissolution has been sought, as matter of strategic behavior, the stronger party, not the weaker one as might be assumed, may seek the remedy. The supplicant is not always an abused minority shareholder.

In re Radom & Neidorff, Inc.[140] illustrates the point. Radom & Neidorff was a highly successful music publishing business carried on by a brother (David Radom) and a brother-in-law (Henry Neidorff). The brother-in-law died, with Radom's sister succeeding to the Neidorff interest. Complete deadlock followed. The sister refused to sign checks, including her brother's salary checks. She immediately commenced a derivative suit against him, charging him with enriching himself at corporate expense. He filed a suit for dissolution on grounds of deadlock.

The court found that "despite the feuding and backbiting, there is no stalemate or impasse . . . [indeed] the corporation is not sick but flourishing." The law to be applied dictated that "[t]he prime inquiry is, always, as to the necessity for dissolution, whether judicially-imposed death 'will be beneficial to the stockholders or members and not injurious to the public." Finding that "this was not such a case," the Court of Appeals affirmed denial of the remedy of dissolution.

The outcome may leave the parties in an intolerable situation, feuding and fighting until the business does begin to deteriorate or one attempts to murder the other. The court, however, may well have been protecting the sister. The business, musical publishing, was dependent on Radom's industry contacts and his ability. He was clearly the stronger, not the weaker, party. Had dissolution occurred, Radom could have re-opened the business the following day, owning *all* of it, free of his sister, and not merely 50 percent.

Protecting the weaker party was an express objective in *Wollman v. Littman.*[141] The plaintiff, Nierenberg group, owned a corporation that supplied the fabrics to the corporation, which converted those fabrics into artificial fur fabrics it then supplied to the garment industry. The other 50 percent group, the Littmans, were in an apparent deadlock with the Nierenbergs. The court found that both groups' misery was something they might be able to endure: "the functions of the two disputing interests are distinct, one is selling and the other

---

failure to elect new directors in corporation owning an apartment house: "the trial court should consider whether dissolution will be beneficial or detrimental to all the shareholders or injurious to the public").

[139] Judge Fuld, dissenting in *In re Radom &Neidorff, Inc.*, 119 N.E. 2d 563 (N.Y. 1954).

[140] 119 N.E.2d 563 (N.Y. 1954).

[141] 316 N.Y.S.2d 526 (App. Div. 1970).

procuring, and each can pursue its own without need for collaboration." The court also saw that the petitioning shareholder, as the stronger party, would be poised to swoop down on the remains of the business should dissolution be decreed. "[Dissolution] would not only squeeze the Littmans out of the business but would require the receiver to dispose of the inventory with the Nierenbergs the only interested purchaser financially strong enough to take advantage of the situation . . . ."

In a subcategory of deadlock cases, the corporation has outlived its original purpose and now exists only for the benefit of those in control. Because of deadlock, those in control cannot be ousted. In *Kruger v. Gerth*,[142] a retail lumber business had come to exist only for the purpose of paying the 53 percent shareholder a salary and annual bonus. "Dissolution will not be compelled unless it is found that the dominant stockholders or directors have been 'looting' the corporation's assets and impairing the corporation's capital or maintaining the corporation for their own special benefit, thereby enriching themselves at the expense of the minority stockholders," the court announced. The case brings to mind the commentators' lament about "the sacred cow of corporate existence," as does *Nelkin v. H.J.R. Realty Corp.*[143]

In *Nelkin*, in 1941, three businesses formed a corporation and acquired the building that housed their businesses. Since all shareholders were also tenants at the time, they paid reduced rentals for their space. Some years later, Nelkin had ceased doing business and another H.J.R. Realty shareholder, Richter, had sold his interest in one of the tenant companies. In 1968, after 27 years of under market rentals, Nelkin and Richter, who controlled 4/9 of the shares, began a campaign to convince the other shareholders "to disregard the shareholders' agreement and pay a fair and reasonable rent." Failing in their campaign, they sought judicial dissolution of the corporation. The court refused to grant relief, finding that "the majority shareholders have not been guilty of looting or exploiting the corporation to the detriment of the minority . . . . The discounted rentals that they have been paying since 1941 were not set arbitrarily but in accordance with the shareholders' agreement."

These cases, *Kruger* and *Nelkin*, teach that, without advance planning, even a 50 percent shareholder may become locked into a corporation with no return on their investment. If those in control of the corporation do not overreach (no "looting" or oppression), the condition may persist for years and the involuntary dissolution remedy will be of little or no aid.

[G]   Oppression Grounds

The ground for dissolution most frequently alleged by minority shareholders facing illiquidity and exploitation in a closely held corporation has been oppression. Many states have expanded the grounds for dissolution to include "oppression." The statutes, however, have left it for the courts to evolve a definition of oppression. The definitions courts have evolved have not remained

---

[142] 210 N.E.2d 355 (N.Y. 1965).
[143] 255 N.E.2d 713 (N.Y. 1969).

static. The adoption and spread from jurisdiction to jurisdiction of the "denial of reasonable expectations" as a test of what constitutes oppression, has been the most important development in the closely held corporation field over the last 25 years. A related development has been the evolution by courts, or by legislatures, of a panoply of remedies — other than dissolution — to grant in cases in which oppression has been found. Both developments make a remedy for an abused minority shareholder much more likely than it was 25 years ago.

One reason for liberalization has been the realization by courts that cessation of the legal life of an entity does not necessarily entail cessation of the economic life. Earlier courts were under the misapprehension that if they decreed dissolution, a successful or flourishing business might suddenly fail. That is not true.

In their seminal piece,[144] Professors Hetherington and Dooley found that, in 27 cases in which a plaintiff obtained a decree of dissolution, in only 6 of those cases was the corporation actually liquidated. In 16 cases one party bought out the other, and in 3 others the business was sold to an outsider. Even in cases in which plaintiffs were unsuccessful, in a surprising number of cases (16 of 27), one party bought out the other or the business was sold. Later empirical studies show equally dramatic results.[145]

Good businesses do not lock their door or otherwise cease to function because of a change in their legal status. What occurs instead, is that a decree of involuntary dissolution, or the threat of one, gives to the plaintiff shareholder a lever, or tool, for use in negotiating her way out of a deadlock or dissolution situation.

An early case which demonstrated a denial of reasonable expectations is *Meiselman v. Meiselman.*[146] Michael, the older brother, and Ira, the younger brother, owned 30 and 70 percent, respectively, of a series of corporations that operated over 30 movie theaters across North Carolina. Michael complained that as CEO, his younger brother had contracted with the family corporations in a self-dealing transaction. Michael went so far as to file a lawsuit airing his complaint. Ira retaliated by firing Michael from his position, canceling his company-paid automobile, health and life insurance, and changing locks on corporate offices.

The court examined the brothers' relationship over the years. Ira had denied Michael meaningful involvement in governance of their various corporations, consistently belittling his older brother's abilities and ideas. The Court found oppression in those acts:

---

[144] John Hetherington & Michael Dooley, *Illiquidity and Exploitation: A Proposed Statutory Solution to the Remaining Close Corporation Problem,* 63 Va. L. Rev. 1 (1977).

[145] *See* Harry Haynsworth, *The Effectiveness of Involuntary Dissolution Suits as a Remedy for Close Corporation Dissension,* 35 Clev. St. L. Rev. 25 (1987) (of 37 reported cases from 1984–85 in which a decision was reached, 20 decisions ordered one party to buy out the other while 10 decisions decreed dissolution). Of course, even after a decree of dissolution is granted, the most probable outcome is that one party will purchase the other party's interest in the corporation.

[146] 307 S.E.2d 551 (N.C. 1983).

[W]e hold that a complaining shareholder's "rights or interests" in a close corporation include the "reasonable expectations" the complaining shareholder has in the corporation. These "reasonable expectations" are to be ascertained by examining the entire history of the participants' relationship. That history will include the "reasonable expectations" created at the inception of the participants' relationship; those "reasonable expectations" as altered over time; and the "reasonable expectations" which develop as the participants engage in a course of dealing . . . .

The court added, however, that "[i]n order for a plaintiff's expectations to be reasonable, the expectations must be known to, or assumed by, the other shareholders and concurred in by them."

The New York Court of Appeals soon adopted the denial of reasonable expectations test in *In re Kemp & Beatley, Inc.*[147] In a corporation with 8 shareholders, the 2 plaintiffs owned 20.33 percent of the company and had been terminated from employment after 42 years and 35 years, respectively. The termination brought with it a complete freeze out from distribution of the company's earning which the 6 other shareholders continued to enjoy. The court found that sufficient:

[Defining oppressive conduct] has been resolved by considering oppressive actions to refer to conduct that substantially defeats the "reasonable expectations" held by minority shareholders in committing their capital to the particular enterprise . . . . A shareholder who reasonably expected that ownership in the corporation would entitle him or her to a job, a share of corporate earnings, a place in corporate management, or some other form of security, would be oppressed in a very real sense when others in the corporation seek to defeat those expectations . . . .

As with the North Carolina court, the New York court added that, "objectively viewed," the expectations must have been "both reasonable under the circumstances and . . . central to the petitioner's decision to join the venture":

Majority conduct should not be deemed oppressive simply because the petitioner's subjective hopes and desires in joining the venture are not fulfilled. Disappointment alone should not necessarily be equated with oppression.

Despite *In re Kemp &Beatley*, a lower New York court denied the dissolution remedy to a shareholder who had been denied a role in governance and dividends from an incorporated family dairy business. The court found that the plaintiff, a shareholder "two generations removed from the adoption of the corporate form," could not be said to have entered the business "with the same 'reasonable expectations' as partners do."[148] The decision seems misguided. A third genera-

---

[147] 473 N.E.2d 1173 (N.Y. 1984). Another "reasonable expectations" case is *McCallum v. Rosen's Diversified*, discussed in § 11.07[D] *supra*.

[148] *Gimpel v. Bolstein*, 477 N.Y.S.2d 1014 (1984). *See generally* Douglas K. Moll, *Shareholder*

tion shareholder makes an investment, based upon expectations of what may be forthcoming for him, each day he continues his involvement in the corporation.

[H]   Remedies in Involuntary Dissolution Cases

As has been seen, courts hesitated to grant dissolution, often with the misguided belief that dissolution would mean the end for a successful business. They also viewed the choice as binary: either grant the drastic remedy of dissolution or leave the parties in their misery. In reaction to those judicial responses, the last 25 years have seen legislatures enact statutes expressly providing for forms of intermediate relief.[149] Viewing a court petitioned for dissolution as a court of equity with inherent powers, in many jurisdictions, courts themselves have evolved lists of measures that may be taken in closely held corporations in which oppression or deadlock exists.

In an early decision,[150] the Supreme Court of Oregon listed 10 forms of relief a court might grant, in addition to dissolution: (1) ordering dissolution at a future date, in the event the parties are unable to resolve their differences; (2) appointment of a receiver to continue operation of the corporation; (3) appointment of a "special fiscal agent" to report to the court on the corporation's operations; (4) retention by the court with jurisdiction over the case; (5) an accounting; (6) an injunction against specific acts of oppression such as ordering reduction in salaries or bonus payments; (7) affirmative relief such as a required dividend or reduction and distribution of capital; (8) court ordered buy-out of one party by the other; (9) affirmative relief that the minority owner be allowed to purchase additional shares; and (10) an award of damages for injury suffered as a result of oppression. In similar fashion, the Supreme Court of New Jersey listed 13 forms of relief lower courts in that state might grant.[151]

By contrast, in *White v. Perkins*,[152] the Supreme Court of Virginia found that a lower court could order dissolution or appoint a custodian, the two alternatives provided for by statute, but that Virginia courts lacked inherent power to order other forms of relief. Finding oppression, the lower court had ordered the 55 percent shareholder to keep his personal account with the company current,

---

Oppression and Reasonable Expectations: Of Change, Gift, and Inheritance in Closely Held Corporations, 86 Minn. L. Rev. 717 (2002).

[149] For example, more than half the states now expressly provide for appointment of a custodian (who displaces the board altogether), and 20 states authorize appointment of a provisional director (who sits on the board with the other directors, often to break a deadlock). *See* Robert Thompson, *The Shareholder's Cause of Action for Oppression*, 48 Bus. Law. 699, 723 (1993). In *Abreu v. Unica Indus. Sales, Inc.*, 586 N.E.2d 661 (Ill. App. 1991), the court upheld the appointment of the plaintiff's son-in-law as a provisional director, finding no "strict requirement of impartiality" in the statute authorizing judicial appointment of provisional directors. Instead, the lodestar must be the best interests of the corporation, which may necessitate the court balancing some lack of impartiality off against "the skills and abilities necessary to fulfill the position within an urgent time frame." The son-in-law was a CPA and had worked for the corporation for 17 years, rising to General Manager of Operations.

[150] *Baker v. Commercial Body Builders, Inc.*, 507 P.2d 387 (Or. 1973).

[151] *Brenner v. Berkowitz*, 634 A.2d 1019 (N.J. 1993).

[152] 189 S.E.2d 315 (Va. 1972).

ordered payment of a dividend, and ordered severance pay for the 45 percent shareholder whose employment had been terminated.

White v. Perkins, however, is not representative. In most states, based upon their inherent powers as courts of equity, courts are crafting remedies to deal with illiquidity and exploitation problems. A Texas court found that, although the Texas Business Corporation Act does not expressly provide for the remedy of a "buy out" for an aggrieved minority shareholder, . . . "[w]e conclude that Texas courts, under their general equity power, may decree a 'buy-out' in an appropriate case where less harsh remedies are inadequate to protect the rights of the parties."[153] Judicial relief in the form of a court-ordered buy-out is the trend today when oppression or deadlock has been found.

In *Muellenberg v. Bikon Corp.*,[154] the Supreme Court of New Jersey upheld a lower court order that the ⅓ minority interest buy out the majority, which, in turn, was pursuant to a 1988 amendment of the New Jersey statute authorizing that form of relief. The court found that "while a minority buy-out of the majority is an uncommon remedy, it was the appropriate one here." The minority shareholder was an engineer who, through 10 years of marketing efforts, had built up substantial United States sales of "locking assemblies" and "shaft to hub connections" based upon Muellenberg's patents.

A classical illiquidity and exploitation case in which a court ordered a $1.9 million buy-out is *Bonavita v. Corbo*.[155] The Corbo brothers and their brother-in-law, Gerald Bonavita, built up a successful seven store retail jewelry business. Even though he only ran one retail outlet, Gerald, who owned 50 percent of the shares, received the same salary as the Corbo son, Alan, who was president and chief executive officer, and who had come to own the other 50 percent. But when Gerald died, the salary ceased. Meanwhile, Alan, his spouse, and his four children, all of whom worked in the business, drew a total in salary of $400,000. When Aunt Julia, Gerald's widow, who was receiving nothing with respect to her shares, requested a dividend be paid out of accumulated profits, her request was refused.

The corporation had been extraordinarily successful. It had retained earnings of $5 million, stockholders' equity of $4.6 million, and the so-called AAA account containing $1,390,000 in cash upon which, because of the corporation's subchapter S status, personal income taxes had already been paid. There would have been no tax impact for the Corbo family in receiving the dividend.

The court did not find the case to be one of deadlock, as in the cases in which the party in control takes advantage of the stalemate to use the corporation to provide themselves with financial benefits, such as *Kruger v. Gerth* and *Nelkin v. H.J.R. Realty*:

---

[153] *Davis v. Sheerin*, 754 S.W.2d 375 (Tex. Ct. App. 1988) (finding oppression principally in fabrication by majority shareholder of a "gift" by a 45 percent holder of his shares to the majority holder).

[154] 669 A.2d 1382 (N.J. 1996).

[155] 692 A.2d 119 (N.J. 1996).

> Although plaintiff claims there is a corporate "deadlock," . . . it is not clear what constitutes the alleged deadlock of which plaintiff complains.

> [T]his is not a case where a corporation is unable to act. It can act. And it did act. It acted by denying plaintiff's demands [for a dividend or a buy-out of her stock]. And it is the result of that action — not an inability to act — which is the basis for the plaintiff's claim . . . .

Julia's nephew, Alan, gave numerous business reasons for hoarding cash in the corporation, including the seasonal nature of the jewelry business which necessitated building up large inventories quickly, and the need for substantial renovation of two of the stores. Nonetheless, the court found, "[w]hat Julia Bonavita has, and what she will continue to have so long as Alan Corbo is able to make the kind of decisions he has been making, is a block of stock which has absolutely no value." In essence, the court found that managing a corporation so as to render a shareholder's shares worthless, constitutes oppression. "[T]here is no question that defendants' conduct has destroyed any reasonable expectation that plaintiff may have respecting her stock interest," the court concluded.

Although a compulsory buy-out was to be ordered sparingly, the court found that no other remedy would work: "there is no rational basis on which this corporation can continue to exist and operate with half its shares owned by the Corbo interests and half by the Bonavita interests. There must be a divorce."

In *Pedro v. Pedro*,[156] the court used reasonable expectations not as a definition of oppression but as a measure of damages in fashioning a remedy for oppression. Plaintiff, one of 3 brothers who each owned 1/3 of a successful leather goods company, complained of significant discrepancy in the books (upwards of $270,000 was missing). Investigations by accountants backed him up. Rather than follow up their brother's complaints, his brothers terminated his employment. They lied to employees, telling them that he had a nervous breakdown. The court awarded him substantial damages for: (1) what he could have expected for his stock under the Stock Restriction Agreement (buyout rather than dissolution); (2) damages to him (versus the corporation) for breaches of fiduciary duty (which his brothers owed directly to him under the *Donahue* principle); (3) damages for what the court found to have been a reasonable expectation of lifetime employment (at least to age 72); and (4) substantial attorney's fees on common law grounds that his brothers had "acted arbitrarily, vexatiously or otherwise not in good faith."

[I] Valuation Issues in Court Ordered Buyouts

When the court orders this remedy, as an alternative to ordering a dissolution, the court may be called upon to review the fairness of the price offered by one party to the other, or the share price determined by a special master or appraiser. Two questions that arise are whether the court should apply, or approve application of, a "minority discount" and, further, a "lack of marketability discount." A minority discount is a "second stage adjustment for

---

[156] 489 N.W.2d 798 (Minn. App. 1992).

valuing minority shares . . . because the minority shareholder lacks corporate decision-making power." *Charland v. Country View Golf Club, Inc.*[157] describes a lack of marketability discount as a further reduction in the value of shares because no ready market exists in which the shares could be sold or resold.

In *Charland*, the plaintiff owned a 15 percent interest in a golf course. He sued for involuntary dissolution of the corporation. The corporation's response was to make a statutory election to purchase the plaintiff's shares. During the pendency of the action, the corporation sold the golf course for $2 million, so total value was not at issue. What was at issue was whether plaintiff would receive $300,000 (15% $2 million), or some lesser sum.

The court declined to apply any discounts, following other decisions which have reasoned that "had the plaintiffs proved their case and had the corporation been dissolved, each shareholder would have been entitled to the same amount per share. There would be no consideration given to whether the shares were controlling or noncontrolling."[158] So, too, with a lack of marketability discount: had the minority shareholder obtained dissolution, each party would obtain their pro rata share of the proceeds of a liquidation. When a buyout takes place instead, the minority shareholder should not have a discount applied to his pro rata share, or the equivalent, representing lack of a market for those shares.[159]

The Supreme Court of Iowa has urged caution in applying minority or lack of marketability discounts to shares in closely held corporations. The prospect of obtaining the minority's shares, and doing so at a discount from "fair" value, may create inordinate incentives for the majority to squeeze out the minority by one means or another.[160]

[J]   Conclusion

Ex post, a minority, or even a 50 percent, shareholder in a closely held corporation, who feels that she has received rough treatment at the hands of those who are in control of the corporation, has a number of choices. She may sue for breach of fiduciary duty, requiring the defendants to pay back to the corporation benefits they have received. She may also invoke the *Donahue* principle and the "equal opportunity" rule of that case, alleging that she is entitled to benefits parallel to those the controlling faction is receiving. She may sue alleging oppression, seeking involuntary dissolution of the corporation if the statute authorizes it. She also may establish oppression under the liberalized test that "denial of reasonable expectations" (for example, dividends, salary, meaningful participation in governance) in a closely held corporation constitutes oppression. In her suit for involuntary dissolution, she may also seek forms of alternative relief, ranging from appointment of a provisional director or of a

---

[157] 588 A.2d 609 (R.I. 1991).

[158] Citing *Brown v. Allied Corrugated Box Co.*, 91 Cal. App. 3d 477 (1979), and *Blake v. Blake Agency, Inc.*, 486 N.Y.S.2d 341 (App. Div. 1985).

[159] *But see McCauley v. Tom McCauley & Son, Inc.*, 724 P.2d 232 (N.M. 1986) (trial court has discretion to apply a discount); *Blake v. Blake Agency, supra* note 146 (no minority discount but lack of marketability discount applied).

[160] *See Security State Bank, Hartley, Iowa v. Ziegeldorf*, 554 N.W.2d 884 (Ia. 1996).

custodian to a court ordered buy-out of her interest. What is most interesting of all may be that these substantive and remedial principles applicable to close corporations are the product of the last quarter century.

Chapter 12

HOSTILE TENDER OFFERS

§ 12.01 INTRODUCTION

If A Corporation wants to acquire control of B Corporation, there are several methods it can use to accomplish the transfer of corporate control. A Corporation can purchase the shares of B Corporation, the assets of B Corporation, or effectuate a merger with B Corporation.[1] Whichever method is chosen, however, the transaction will more easily occur if the Board of Directors of B Corporation (the "target") is in favor of the transfer. If it is not, the acquisition of control is called "hostile," and the mechanisms available for obtaining control are substantially reduced. The hostile tender offer raises significant legal and policy issues.[2]

If A Corporation (the "bidder") wants to attempt a takeover of B Corporation without the approval of its management in a hostile acquisition, there are only two means available.[3] The first is a proxy fight in which the bidder solicits the target's shareholders to vote for its slate of directors.[4] If successful, the new board of directors can facilitate a friendly acquisition of B Corporation by approving the acquisition or removing any defensive tactics that block the bidder. The second is the tender offer where the bidder can make an offer directly to the target's shareholders to buy their shares, thereby giving control of the target to the bidder.[5] Technically, a tender offer does not involve the board of directors of the target. Because of target defensive tactics (some of which operate after a bidder has acquired a fixed percentage of shares), bidders usually must convince the target directors to remove the tactic or use a proxy fight to remove directors prior to the tender offer.[6]

---

[1] For a discussion of acquisition techniques, see Chapter 6, *supra*.

[2] *See* § 12.03, *infra. See generally* Arthur R. Pinto, *Corporate Takeovers Through the Public Markets in the United States*, 42 Am. J. Comp. Law 339 (Supp. 1994).

[3] State law requires that the target's board of directors approve a merger or a sale of assets but not a tender offer, which is between the bidder and the shareholders.

[4] For a discussion of the proxy fight, see § 5.05[C], *supra*.

[5] While the bidder can make some purchases of the shares in the stock market or privately, there are reasons why there needs to be a tender offer. *See* note 34, *infra*.

[6] The directors of the target that oppose the bidder will usually implement defensive tactics to thwart the hostile offer which raises fiduciary duty issues. *See* §§ 12.04[B], 12.05, *infra*. For a discussion of proxy fights to facilitate an acquisition, see § 5.05[C][2], *supra*.

§ 12.02 THE RISE AND FALL OF HOSTILE TENDER OFFERS

Beginning in the late 1970s through the 1980s, the tender offer became an effective means of gaining control of corporations in which the management was hostile to the acquisition and, thus, became a major phenomenon, increasing in number and size.[7] Because shareholders were often offered a substantial premium in cash over the current market price for control, they were induced to tender their shares to the bidder.[8] A significant explanation for the development of hostile tender offers is that they are a response to the separation of ownership from control and serve to monitor corporate managers by providing a mechanism for their removal if they operate the company inefficiently or in their own interests. Thus, they are an important component of the market for corporate control.[9] This explanation, however, is controversial and cannot alone explain the tender offer phenomenon.

There is no one satisfactory explanation for this increase in tender offers during this period, but there are several factors that may help to explain it. Hyperinflation in the 1970s meant that many companies' hard assets were more valuable than the goods they produced, and it became economical to buy corporations for their existing assets as opposed to investing in new assets. Inflation also leads to lower stock market prices.[10] Many mature businesses were no longer growing but were still generating cash, which in some cases the managers failed to use in a way that would maximize shareholder value.[11] A number of targets were conglomerates (that is, corporations that owned a diverse number of businesses) that failed to produce gains for their sharehold-

---

[7] *See* Edward R. Bruning, *The Economic Implications of the Changing Merger Process*, *in* HOSTILE TAKEOVERS, ISSUES IN PUBLIC AND CORPORATE POLICY 47 (David L. McKee ed. 1989). However, hostile takeovers have always represented a small percentage of all takeover activity. For example, in 1986 there were 40 such takeovers out of 3,300. It was the threat of a hostile takeover and the fact that large corporations can be a target that created the controversy. *See generally* Michael C. Jensen, *Takeovers: Their Causes and Consequences*, J. ECON. PERSP. (Winter 1988).

[8] The stock markets also facilitate acquisitions by allowing shares to be sold in the markets to other investors after a tender offer is announced. These purchasers provide a higher price to those shareholders wanting to sell prior to the completion of the tender offer. For example, if the market price of the target is $10 and a bidder announces an offer of $15, purchasers are willing to buy the shares with the possibility of a successful tender. The purchases push the share price higher to, for example, $14. These purchasers are called arbitragers who hope to profit from the spread between the market price and the ultimate tender offer price. Their role in takeovers is controversial. While they supply liquidity to the market by allowing shareholders the ability to quickly sell at a higher price then before the bid, they also have a short-term interest in making the most profit from a successful takeover and will inevitably support the bidder.

[9] For a discussion of the separation of ownership from control, see § 5.02[E][1], *supra.* For a discussion of the market for corporate control, see § 12.03[A], *infra.*

[10] *See* Peter F. Drucker, *Corporate Takeovers — What Is To Be Done?*, PUB. INTEREST (Winter 1986).

[11] *Id.* at 7–8. For example, the conglomerate movement of the 1960s, which some described as empire building by managers, produced large companies in unrelated fields which generally failed to meet expectations. This meant that there were companies selling in the stock market at prices lower than their realizable asset values if broken up. Samuel N. Levin, *Raiding the Establishment: New Perspectives on Takeover Law*, 26 U. RICH. L. REV. 507 (1992); *see also* Randall Morck et al., *Do Managerial Motives Drive Bad Acquisitions?*, 45 J. FIN. 31 (1990).

ers.[12] The markets were becoming more institutionalized and these institutions were more receptive than individual shareholders to tender offers because they had a legal duty to maximize the return on their investments.[13] Attitudes toward debt changed as the United States became a more debtor-oriented society. The availability of credit and the growth of the high-yield (or what is popularly called the "junk") bond market made money available as loans for high-risk investments including hostile acquisitions. The development of this market meant that bidders could borrow to finance the tender offer, making even very large corporations vulnerable to a tender offer, which raised the stakes both economically and politically.[14] Attitudes toward tender offers changed; investment banking firms, law firms, banks and even corporate executives who had once viewed the business of tender offers as unseemly could no longer resist the high fees or the success of many early takeovers.[15] Political changes, which included the deregulation philosophy of the government in the 1980s, fostered the belief in markets (including the market for corporate control) over government regulation.[16]

Following the 1980s, there are fewer hostile tender offers,[17] but their threat remains. The decline in the prevalence of tender offers in the 1990s was related to many factors including an economic recession, the collapse of the junk bond market and the highly publicized prosecutions of some of its most important participants, and an overall tightening of credit. In addition, public attitudes changed. For example, several spectacular bankruptcies occurred which were

---

[12] The idea behind a conglomerate is that if a corporation has excellent management those skills can be applied to different kinds of businesses. Critics suggest that investors can diversify their investments themselves by buying different shares and do not benefit from the diversification of a conglomerate. Many of the conglomerates established in the 1960s failed to perform in the stock market making them targets for hostile tender offers aimed at breaking up the businesses.

[13] Martin Lipton, *Corporate Governance in the Age of Finance Corporation*, 136 U. PA. L. REV. 1, 7–9 (1987). *But see* John Pound, *The Effects of Institutional Investors on Takeover Activity: A Qualitative Analysis*, Investor Responsibility Center (November 1985) (a study from 1981–84 indicating that the level of institutional ownership had no effect on premiums or success of takeovers). For a discussion of the increasing role of institutions in corporate governance, see § 5.02[E][2], *supra*.

[14] *See generally* Connie Bruck, THE PREDATORS BALL: THE INSIDE STORY OF DREXEL BURNHAM AND THE RISE OF THE JUNK BOND RAIDERS (1989) (an excellent and readable account of Michael Millkin and the junk bond phenomenon). The increased use of debt to purchase companies involves leveraging. For a discussion of leveraging, see § 4.03, *supra*.

[15] John Brooks, THE TAKEOVER GAME 251–55 (1987). There may even have been a sociological reason since many of the bidders and their advisors were corporate outsiders challenging the establishment. *See* Levin, note 11, *supra*.

[16] Takeovers were viewed in a positive way by the Reagan administration. *See* Council of Economic Advisors, 1985 Economic Report of the President 192–94 (1985) (advocated the law and economics view that tender offers were good for the economy). Deregulation in certain industries, such as financial services, oil and gas, transportation and broadcasting also made more corporations vulnerable. *See* Jensen, note 7 at 24, *supra*. Antitrust enforcement also became less significant. *See* Andrei Shleifer & Robert W. Vishney, *The Takeover Wave of the 1980s*, 249 SCIENCE 745, 747–48 (Aug. 17, 1990).

[17] In 1988, the value of hostile takeovers were $127.1 billion while in 1992 that figure fell to $1.8 billion. Petruno, *Get Ready for a New Breed of Hostile Takeover*, LOS ANGELES TIMES, Feb. 10, 1993, at D3.

traceable to the use of large amounts of corporate debt for a takeover (or defense against one). The loss of many jobs in some major restructurings associated with takeovers affected the public mood. Legal reaction to tender offers quickly evolved into judicial deference to defensive tactics and legislative enactments of pro-management tender offer statutes, which will be discussed below.

The decline in hostile tender offers is not necessarily permanent or irreversible. Various acquisition techniques have risen and fallen in popularity over time as market conditions have changed and the legal, regulatory and political climates have shifted. When direct tender offers became more difficult, there was a resurgence of proxy fights to try to replace the hostile directors with new directors willing to negotiate a friendly transaction and remove defensive tactics. The decline in tender offers had also changed approaches to corporate governance, increasing the role played by institutional investors and independent directors in monitoring management.[18]

§ 12.03 POLICY ISSUES

Hostile tender offers have generated a considerable amount of legal, political and economic debate. The policy debate raised questions not only of whether tender offers were beneficial to the companies involved or the economy as a whole, but also of what motivated a bidder to pay a premium over the market price for shares of the target, whether those premiums represented gains and, if they did, the source of those gains.

[A] Proponents

Some who defended hostile tender offers as beneficial are of the view that takeovers represented a market solution to the problems of corporate mismanagement. Their thesis is that market-based competitive solutions were ultimately the most efficient for the economy and, therefore, the market for corporate control should be encouraged and facilitated while any encumbrances should be removed. This "market for corporate control" theory is built upon the efficient market hypothesis, which assumes that by using all publicly available information the trading markets were informationally efficient in pricing shares at levels that best represent the values of their respective corporations.[19] Accordingly, any failure by incumbent management to maximize the value of a corporation would be reflected in the price of its shares when trading in an efficient market. Such management failures would attract a bidder to offer a premium to shareholders for a controlling interest in the corporation, in the belief that the bidder could operate the corporation more efficiently and achieve benefits that would exceed the premium paid. For example, a bidder might find a target whose shares were trading at $10 a share and realize that by reorganizing the corporation and running it more efficiently the value of the corporation on a per share basis could be $20. The bidder would be willing to pay a premium over the market price of $10, such as $15, because of the

---

[18] For a discussion of the activism of institutional investors, see § 5.02[E][2], *supra*.

[19] For a discussion of the efficient market hypothesis, see § 5.02[D], *supra*.

perceived ultimate value of $20. Thus, the bidder would provide a premium over the market price to shareholders which was beneficial to them (i.e., $5), replace inefficient management and shift corporate assets to a more efficient use in the hopes that the tender offer would produce a higher valued corporation (i.e., $20 and a $5 gain). This possibility of a tender offer served as an incentive for managers to run the corporation efficiently, because if they did not they could face a hostile offer which would replace them.[20] Thus, tender offers were but one of several market mechanisms to make sure companies were run efficiently and in the interests of their shareholders.[21]

[B] Opponents

Some opponents of hostile tender offers argue that they are harmful to shareholders because the future value of the target would be higher than the bidder's offer and, thus, shareholder gains are usurped by the bidder. Furthermore, the dynamics of some tender offers make it more likely than not that shareholders feel they must tender into an offer or risk being left as a very small minority in a controlled subsidiary corporation, susceptible to being bought out later on unfavorable terms.[22] Opponents also believe that tender offers are harmful to other corporate constituencies besides shareholders, such as employees, creditors and the communities in which target corporations have facilities. Hostile takeovers are seen as hurting the economy as a whole by merely reshuffling assets and not producing any real economic gains. There is, moreover, the concern that in reality tender offers are not aimed at inefficient companies, but, rather, bidders are seeking well-run corporations.[23]

Hostile tender offers also divert target management's attention from long-run performance and, instead, force them to place too much emphasis on short-term profit-making to keep the company's share price high enough to ward off a hostile offer.[24] Some critics also contended that the increased use of debt in financing hostile tender offers caused severe economic problems[25] and decreased the overall competitiveness of United States companies in world markets.

Critics of hostile tender offers have attacked the efficient market hypothesis, which underlies the market for corporate control theory, arguing that the stock markets were not truly efficient. By attacking the hypothesis, they hoped to

---

[20] *See generally* Easterbrook & Fischel, *Proper Role of Target's Management in Responding to a Tender Offer*, 94 HARV. L. REV. 1161, 1173–74 (1981).

[21] See discussion of market mechanisms in § 5.03[C][2], *supra*. Proxy fights are also part of the market for corporate control. *See* § 5.05[C], *supra*.

[22] See discussion of bidder tactics at § 12.04[A], *infra*.

[23] *See generally* Martin Lipton, *Corporate Governance in the Age of Finance Corporatism*, 136 U. PA. L. REV. 1 (1987).

[24] *Id.*

[25] *Compare* Kenneth M. Davidson, *Where Do Merger Profits Go?*, J. BUS. STRAT. 47 (May/June 1987) (leveraging not only risks bankruptcy but limits investment in new capital goods, and money paid in takeovers has not resulted in increased investment), *with* Michael C. Jensen, *The Agency of Free Cash Flow, Corporate Finance and Takeovers*, 76 AM. ECON. REV. 323 (1986) (increased debt is beneficial in limiting management's ability to hoard free cash flow and limit dividends).

prove that all the claimed gains resulting from tender offers were illusory (that is, the premium over the market reflected undervaluation by the stock market and not mismanagement).[26] Some question the underlying studies that supported the theory pointing out anomalies in the stock markets, since a truly efficient market should not be "beaten" in any consistent way.[27] Others argue that, although the trading markets may be efficient in the daily pricing of small percentages of shares or even single shares, such pricing did not reflect the value of the enterprise as a going concern.[28]

In the end, the great variety of businesses involved in tender offers and the different effects of hostile takeovers make it difficult to determine whether such offers have created overall welfare gains.[29] It is generally conceded that tender offers have produced significant gains to target shareholders by paying them large premiums over the market price of their shares prior to the tender offers. In many cases, however, the bidders' shares have not gained from the acquisitions and may even have lost value. For example, prior to the tender offer, the market price of the bidder was $20 and the market price of the target was $10. If the tender offer was $15 for the target, then after the tender offer was successful, the bidder (assuming equivalent size companies for the hypothetical) should have a value greater than $35 ($20 $\mp$ $15). Many studies reveal that the bidder is not often valued at a price greater than $35 (sometimes even less), which indicate no gain for the bidder but a gain for the target's shareholders, who received the $5 premium (i.e., from $10 to $15). However, the fact that before the tender offer the two companies were valued at $30 and now the combined are worth more than that amount shows an overall net gain from the tender offer. This is because the overall amount of gain paid to target shareholders is much greater than any possible losses incurred by the bidder suggests that some direct gains have resulted from the tender offers.[30]

---

[26] For a discussion of the efficient market, see § 5.02[D], *supra.*

[27] *See, e.g.,* Gordon & Kornhauser, *Efficient Markets, Costly Information, and Securities Research,* 60 N.Y.U. L. Rev. 761 (1985); William Wang, *Some Arguments that the Stock Market Is Not Efficient,* 19 Calif. L. Rev. 341 (1986). Some economic literature not only question the accuracy of the underlying tests for market efficiency but suggest that "noises" (which are influences unrelated to rational expectations about assets) may play a greater role in market pricing. *See* Donald C. Langevoort, *Theories, Assumptions, and Securities Regulation: Market Efficiency Revisited,* 140 U. Pa. L. Rev. 851 (1992). *See also* Andrei Shleifer & Laurence H. Summers, *The Noise Trader Approach to Finance,* J. Econ. Perspectives 19 (Spring 1990); Lynn Stout, *Are Takeover Premiums Really Premiums? Market Price, Fair Value, and Corporate Law,* 99 Yale L.J. 1235 (1990).

[28] *See* Louis Lowenstein, *Pruning Deadwood in Hostile Takeovers: A Proposal for Legislation,* 83 Colum. L. Rev. 249, 274–76 (1983).

[29] In 1983, in response to developments in the tender offer area, including the large size of such offers, the Securities and Exchange Commission (SEC) set up an Advisory Committee. While there were some specific recommendations, the Committee concluded that there was insufficient basis to conclude whether takeovers were either beneficial or detrimental to the economy, to the market or to shareholders. SEC Advisory Comm. on Tender Offers, *Report of Recommendations* 7–9 (1983) There are numerous studies and arguments that have tried to deal with this question. *See, e.g.,* Corporate Takeovers: Causes and Consequences (Alan J. Auerbach ed. 1988); Knights, Raiders, and Targets (John C. Coffee, Jr. et al. eds. 1988).

[30] Bernard S. Black, *Bidder Overpayment in Takeovers,* 41 Stan. L. Rev. 597, 598 (1989) (suggesting premiums to target shareholders of 50%). One study suggested average returns of 30% and conceded that bidder shareholders have had wealth effects of zero and in some cases negative.

There have been many studies and attempts to explain the source of these overall net gains to target shareholders (i.e. where did the $5 increase in value in our example come from).[31] One explanation was that takeovers resulted in value maximizing efficiencies. The efficiencies could be from synergy gains, or the reduction of agency costs, as a result of the tender offer. Sources of synergies from the combined businesses included increased operating efficiency of the new corporation, or financial synergy, from the ability of the combined businesses to raise capital at lower costs. Reduction of agency costs suggested that replacement of inefficient management and the redirection of excess cash to the shareholders produced the gains. There were also expropriation explanations for the gains. This view suggested that, in effect, the combination of the corporations resulted in transfers from the U.S. Treasury to target shareholders by leveraging the purchase. This resulted from the use of tax advantages realized from financing the acquisition with debt which allows a tax deduction for interest. Other transfers could have come from restructuring the business with similar shifts of wealth from creditors, employees and consumers to the shareholders. Some have suggested that, in fact, there was no real gain to target shareholders because an inefficient market was pricing the shares and the tender offer was only setting the right price for the shares.[32]

§ 12.04 TACTICS

During the 1980s one federal court observed that:

> Contests for corporate control have become ever more frequent phenomena on the American business scene. Waged with the intensity of military campaigns and the weaponry of seemingly bottomless bankrolls, these battles determine the destinies of large and small corporations alike. Elaborate strategies and ingenious tactics have been developed both to facilitate takeover attempts and to defend against them. Skirmishes are fought in company boardrooms, in shareholders' meetings, and, with increasing regularity, in the courts.[33]

Its explanation for this was that the wealth effects of the bidder may not be observed because they are disguised in other information or as a small part of the bidder's wealth. Another explanation was that competition in the offer meant excess returns to the target. The study rejected the argument that poor investment by the bidder was the source of the lack of gains. *See* Gregg A. Jarrell & Annette B. Paulsen, *The Returns to Acquiring Firms in Tender Offers: Evidence from Three Decades*, 18 Fin. Mgmt. 12 (1989).

[31] *See* Roberta Romano, *A Guide to Takeovers: Theory, Evidence and Regulation*, 9 Yale J. Reg. 119 (1992); Reiner Kraakman, *Taking Discounts Seriously: The Implications of "Discounted" Share Prices as an Acquisition Motive*, 88 Colum. L. Rev. 891 (1988) (discusses why premiums are paid).

[32] *Id.* Other explanations for takeovers that did not increase overall value after the tender offer were the result of motivations by bidders for diversification and self-aggrandizement, non-beneficial use of excess cash flow by bidders and hubris resulting in overbidding for the target. Professor Romano argued that there was substantial support for the synergy gains explanation for the increased value from tender offers and less support for the other explanations. She also concluded that the "overwhelming balance of research viewed takeovers favorably and the more restrictive the approach to takeovers, the more ill-conceived the regulation." *Id.* at 177.

[33] *Norlin Corp. v. Rooney Pace, Inc.*, 744 F.2d 255, 258 (2d Cir. 1984).

As discussed below, there are a variety of offensive tactics used by bidders and a variety of defensive tactics used by targets.

[A]   Bidder Tactics

A bidder does not generally acquire a target by purchasing a controlling amount of shares in the public securities markets, but, instead, a bidder uses a tender offer to all shareholders to gain control.[34] Bidders in a tender offer are subject to the disclosure and timing requirements imposed by federal securities law.[35] Bidders are not generally required to tender for all the shares of a corporation, but most bidders at least seek enough shares to gain control (usually at least 51%) to avoid being a minority shareholder owning a large percentage of shares without the benefits of control. Under federal securities law, all the target shareholders are entitled to an equal opportunity to tender their shares in the tender offer, but the bidder is not required to unconditionally accept the tendered shares and may set conditions for its eventual acceptance of them, such as receipt of a certain number of shares. If more shares are tendered than the bidder wants, the shares tendered are purchased from the tendering shareholders on a pro rata basis.[36] A bidder can offer different kinds of consideration, cash is often used because it is easier to value than securities and does not require registration under the Securities Act of 1933.[37]

Bidders often want the benefits of 100% control of the target. Owning all the shares means no minority shareholders and allows the bidder to use the assets freely including borrowing against them to help pay for the acquisition. Since there will always be some holdouts who do not tender their shares, the bidder will notify the target shareholders in the tender offer that it will need to acquire those shares not tendered in a second-step freeze out merger after the first step tender offer is complete. In that merger, the remaining shareholders usually

---

[34] There are several explanations why a bidder does not use open-market purchases to gain control but a tender offer. Under federal securities law a bidder must disclose ownership within 10 days of acquiring 5% of a corporation's shares. *See* § 12.06[B] *infra*. This disclosure signals the market of a possible tender offer and the market price will reflect that information. While a bidder can still try to buy control in the stock market, it may not be able to purchase control quickly and may be left with a large noncontrolling minority interest. Shareholders who learn of the purchases may now hold out waiting for a higher price. The conditional tender offer overcomes this problem of shareholders who will not sell to open-market purchasers in the hopes of extracting a higher price, because in a tender offer all shareholders are offered the same price and opportunity to tender. If the tender offer succeeds, the bidder has control. If it fails, the bidder will have a minority position the size of which depends on how many shares it purchased prior to the tender offer. Another explanation for the use of the tender offer is that it serves as a signaling device. A bidder cannot really gain control through market purchases, because there may be insufficient shareholders in the market willing to sell, but the tender offer informs the target shareholders of the increased value of the target which then may induce them to sell in the tender offer. Market purchases may also take time to acquire control which could allow another bidder to come in to compete. Once a tender offer is made, a bidder is restricted to purchasing the shares through the offer and may not purchase them in the market. Lloyd R. Cohen, *Why Tender Offers? The Efficient Market Hypothesis, the Supply of Stock, and Signaling*, 19 J. LEGAL STUD. 113 (1990).

[35] For a discussion of the Williams Act, see § 12.06, *infra*.

[36] *Id.*

[37] For a discussion of the Securities Act of 1933, see § 7.03, *supra*.

receive cash for their shares and the bidder then owns 100% of the target.[38] The bidder wants to structure the tender offer to be sure that enough shares are tendered to give it control.

One of the most controversial bidder tactics that had been used to attract as many sellers as possible in the first step tender offer is called the front-loaded two-tier tender offer. If for example, a target's shares are selling for $20 in the market and the bidder is willing to pay $25 per share for all the shares, the bidder could offer a cash premium in the tender offer of, $30 for only 51% of the shares, to gain control. At the same time, it will announce that after the tender offer is accepted, it will use its control to merge the target and buy out the minority shareholders at a lower price, such as $20 in cash or securities. This tactic generated controversy because it was considered coercive since shareholders that did not tender initially would only receive the lower price. Since shareholders did not know how the other shareholders planned to respond to the tender, they had to tender for fear of losing the premium on at least 51% of their shares.[39]

The bidder's use of debt to finance the purchase has also raised issues. Once the target is acquired, the increased debt may result in restructuring of the corporation with sales of assets to help pay off some of the debt. This "bust up" takeover may adversely affect the target and its employees. The increased leveraging which adds more debt to the business burdens existing creditors with greater risks and may also hurt the economy because more debt increases the possibility of default and bankruptcy. However, the shareholders who receive cash for their shares and no longer have any interest in the target are arguably unaffected.

There have also been cases in which a bidder has bought target shares and threatened a hostile tender offer. This threat has often been enough to force target directors, as a defensive tactic, to have the target purchase those shares at a premium over the market. As a result, the bidder agreed to avoid the takeover. This tactic is called greenmail and raises issues of whether the directors are benefitting the corporation or themselves by precluding the tender offer.[40] It is interesting to note that Congress rarely enacted legislation dealing with tender offers in the 1980s, but did impose an excise tax on greenmail payments.[41]

---

[38] For a discussion of freezeouts, see § 10.03, *supra*.

[39] *See* Lucien Bebchuk, *Towards Undistorted Choice and Equal Treatment in Corporate Takeovers*, 98 HARV. L. REV. 1693 (1985). This tactic led some states to pass fair price statutes which require a bidder, after acquiring a certain percentage of the shares, to offer to buy the remaining shares at the same price. *See* § 12.07, *infra*. The use of poison pills by targets has effectively eliminated this bidder tactic because the pill can be viewed as a reasonable response to the coercive effect of the tactic. *See* § 12.04[B][1] *infra*.

[40] Greenmail arguably can instigate an auction for the target by a different bidder where shareholders would benefit. Jonathan Macey & Fred McChesney, *A Theoretical Analysis of Corporate Greenmail*, 95 YALE L.J. 13 (1985). *But see* Jeffrey Gordon & Lewis Kornhauser, *Takeover Defense Tactics: A Comment on Two Models*, 95 YALE L.J 295 (1986) (finding benefit of greenmail payments to be very limited).

[41] I.R.C. § 5881. Congress also used the tax code to deal with an unpopular defensive mechanism

[B]   Target Tactics

The lexicons of defensive tactics are legion. Many are implemented prior to any actual bid. Some tactics try to delay a bidder from taking immediate control. Delays raise the costs of a bid, create uncertainty and may have the effect of precluding it. Other tactics are aimed at precluding the bidder from using certain offensive tactics such as front-loaded two-tier offers or at limiting the bidder's ability to finance the transaction through borrowing (that is, leveraging).

Some tactics require amendments to the corporate articles and, thus, involve a shareholder vote.[42] For example, by staggering the terms of directors so that some (such as one-third) of the directors are elected each year, immediate control of the board is prevented until the bidder can elect a majority.[43] Other articles amendments try to make it more difficult for the bidder to acquire shares that are not tendered or to finance the bid. For example, an amendment can require a super-majority or disinterested shareholder vote before a successful bidder can sell assets to finance the bid or implement a freezeout merger to eliminate the minority shareholders who did not tender. Articles provisions may also establish a fair price for all shares in a tender offer or compulsory redemption of shares not tendered at a fair price even if the bidder does not want to acquire those shares.[44] There can also be a recapitalization of the corporation through amending the articles to create two classes of shares from an existing single class. This tactic can be the ultimate defense, because one class of shares held by the public can have limited voting rights and another supervoting class of shares holds the significant voting power. If the latter shares are owned by the managers, a hostile tender offer is virtually impossible.[45]

Target directors can also implement defensive tactics prior to or during a bid without a shareholder vote.[46] Target managements have restructured the target

---

called golden parachutes, which involved granting favorable employment contracts to target managers who left if a tender offer was successful. While arguably beneficial to shareholders because the golden parachutes protected managers if they lost their jobs and thus eliminated a conflict of interest when there was a hostile tender offer. The parachutes were limited in deductibility and subject to an excise tax. I.R.C. §§ 280G, 4999.

[42] Targets have used a variety of "shark repellant" amendments to its bylaws and articles to make a takeover more difficult, although they rarely prevent a takeover itself. Such amendments must be permitted by the state's statute and enacted by either the directors or shareholders as provided in the enabling statute. *See generally* Hochman & Folger, *Deflecting Takeovers, Charter and Bylaw Techniques*, 34 Bus. Law. 537 (1979). When shareholders vote in favor of defensive tactics, they are less likely to be illegal.

[43] See, e.g., Model Bus. Corp. Act Ann. § 8.06 (4th ed. 2008), which requires a shareholder vote to amend the articles to provide for as little as 1/3 of the directors to be elected each year.

[44] *See generally* Ronald J. Gilson, *The Case Against Shark Repellant Amendments: Structural Limitations in the Enabling Concept*, 34 Stan. L. Rev. 775 (1982). These tactics may not in fact deter an offer, although the requirement of redemption of all shares makes an offer more expensive and may have a more significant impact on a bidder's decision to tender.

[45] For a discussion of the one share and one vote controversy, see note 145 at § 5.05[A], *supra.* See also the discussion of the *Williams* case at § 5.05[D], the text at note 193, *supra.*

[46] Defensive tactics are generally subject to review by courts under principles of fiduciary duty.

to make it less appealing to a bidder by selling off or granting an option to sell significant assets (called the "crown jewel defense") or by splitting the corporation into different component corporations to increase its overall value. There can also be a self-tender, where the target purchases shares from its shareholders which may raise the value of the target, solidify the ownership interest of the managers or be coupled with restructuring or recapitalization that makes the target less attractive.[47] A target trying to thwart an unwanted bid may also seek another bidder to serve as a "white knight" and come to the target's rescue. The target can sell a block of shares to a friendly "white squire" who will side with managers and usually sign a "stand still agreement" limiting future purchases of target shares and agreeing to support the managers. With a friendly block of shares agreeing not to accept a hostile bid, a tender offer becomes more difficult. Targets have also established employee share ownership plans which are often intended to increase productivity but can place a significant number of shares in the hands of employees who may favor managers over bidders. A target may make a tender offer more costly if successful by implementing expensive policies that may result from the change of control. For example, a plan to pay employees increased benefits or provide its customers with increased protection such as refunds if there is a takeover that adversely affects them. Targets have also increased their debt which limits a bidder's ability to finance the tender offer with debt through leveraging the target. After gaining control, the bidder may need the target's assets to support that debt. The managers may also take over ownership of the corporation by going private through a management buyout to preclude a hostile takeover. The going private often involves the use of debt, and they are often called leveraged buyouts.[48]

[1]   Poison Pills

While corporate lawyers and investment bankers have created a large number of different defensive tactics, the "shareholder rights plan" or "poison pill" defense remains the most significant, because of its ability to thwart an unfriendly takeover and give control to the target directors.[49] The plans have a variety of provisions, but in general at some initial triggering event (usually the announcement or threat of a tender) the target issues to its shareholders "Rights." (i.e., options). The Rights are not immediately effective and can be redeemed by the target board but after a subsequent triggering event (such as the purchase of a certain percentage of the target's shares), the Rights become non-redeemable and effective. These Rights at that point allow the shareholders to obtain securities (equity or debt) at a substantial discount. These discounted securities can be from the bidder (called a "flip over" plan) or from the target

---

See discussion at § 12.05, *infra.* Courts are particularly concerned with acts by directors whose purpose is to thwart shareholder voting. *See* § 12.05[A][7], *infra.*

[47] Self-tenders are also subject to the Williams Act. *See* discussion at note 130, *infra.* For an example of a self-tender used as a defensive tactic in the *Revlon* case, see note 80, *infra.* Another example is the self tender used in *Unocal* discussed at § 12.05[A][2], *supra.*

[48] For a discussion of management buyouts and freezeouts, see § 10.03, *supra.*

[49] Over 1700 companies have adopted such plans. Dennis J. Block et al., THE BUSINESS JUDGMENT RULE 1085 (5th ed. 1998). Pressure by institutional shareholders have convinced a number of companies to either drop their poison pills or subject them to a shareholder vote.

(called a "flip in" plan).[50] The issuance of these securities pursuant to these Rights have the effect of making the hostile tender offer more expensive for the bidder by either adversely affecting r the target (a flip over plan) or the bidder itself (flip in plan).

The poison pill in the case of *Moran v. Household International, Inc.*,[51] was an example of a flip over plan. Under the plan there were two triggering events as described:

> Triggering Event 1. Bidder announces a tender offer for 30% or more of the target's shares. Target issues Rights (i.e., options) to buy preferred shares of the Target (seems to look like a financing technique but in fact this is not the purpose of the Rights). The target directors have the right to redeem those Rights for nominal consideration (i.e., $0.50 each).

> Triggering Event 2. Bidder purchases 20% or more of the Target's shares. If Event 1 has not occurred then the Target issues Rights (i.e., options) to buy preferred shares of the Target. Under Event 2, the Target directors now have no right to redeem those Rights. The Rights now give the Target's shareholders the option to buy $200 worth of the Bidder's shares for $100.[52]

Under triggering Event 2, the fact that the Target's shareholders can buy the Bidder's shares at a discount hurts the Bidder's current shareholders by diluting the value of their shares with the discounted shares (i.e., buying them at a 50% discount). It is the ability of the Target shareholders to harm the Bidder that makes this a "flip over" poison pill (i.e., the Rights affect the Bidder adversely). This only becomes binding under Event 2 because under Event 1 the board can always redeem the Rights and thus preclude use of the pill. The only way the Target's shareholders can have the option to buy the Bidder's shares under the plan is if the Bidder decides at some point after acquiring control of the Target through a tender offer to do a second step freezeout merger in order to own 100% of the Target. After the merger the Bidder is now bound by the contract rights of the Target including this option to buy its shares at a discount (the acquiring corporation in a merger assumes the liabilities and contracts of the acquired corporation). The bidder could try to tender for 100% of the shares and the Rights together but in any tender offer there are always holdouts since not all shareholders respond to the tender. Because Bidders cannot expect to get 100% of the shares in a tender offer they need to do a second step freezeout merger to

---

[50] The "flip in" plans are more prevalent, because a "flip over" plan requires a merger with the bidder to create the binding obligation. For an example of a "flip in" plan, see note 79, *infra.*

[51] 500 A.2d 1346 (Del. 1985).

[52] The purchase of 20% or more of the Target in Event 2 is more threatening to the Target than the announcement of the tender offer for 30% or more in Event 1. That is why the board cannot redeem the Rights in Event 2. In Event 1, the issuance of the Rights with the power to redeem gives the Target directors the ability to negotiate for its redemption with the Bidder who has not yet purchased the 20%. If the Bidder buys more than 20% without a redemption by the board (i.e., Event 2) the pill will be effective.

acquire the remaining shares if they want to own 100% of the Target.[53] In most cases the bidder wants 100% ownership. If the bidder borrowed to make the tender offer then the bidder needs to transfer that debt to the target. Owning 100% allows the bidder to use the Target's assets to support this debt help finance the bid and have complete control of the business without minority shareholders. The "flip over" pill is in ineffective if the Bidder decides not to acquire 100% through the merger and is willing to have remaining minority shareholders.

In *Moran*, the poison pill plan was upheld, although the plaintiffs claimed that the directors had no power to adopt it. First, the plaintiffs argued that there was no statutory authority to issue the Rights in this context. The court found such authority because the Delaware statute permitted issuance of rights and preferred shares even though they are traditionally used for financing and not for a defensive tactic in takeovers. There was no statutory limitation to their use in this context. Second, plaintiffs contended that the plan usurped the share-holders' right to receive a tender offer. The court found that the poison pill did not preclude a tender offer. A bidder could still buy less than 100% of the corporation and so long as there was no subsequent merger the pill option would not apply. A bidder could also buy 19.9% (the trigger for non redemption was 20%) and lead a proxy fight to fill the board with directors in favor of the tender offer who would then redeem the pill.[54] Third, the plaintiffs argued that the plan

---

[53] The second step merger will involve a controlling shareholder in a freezeout transaction which raises fiduciary issues. *See* § 10.03, *supra*. The merger is often structured as a triangular merger. *See* § 6.02[A], *supra*.

[54] Some plans tried to restrict newly elected directors from redeeming the poison pills. This attempts to change the directors through a proxy fight to redeem the pill and implement a friendly acquisition would not work. These so called "dead hand" provisions only give directors that remain on the board ("continuing directors") as opposed to newly elected directors the right to redeem. If valid, such a poison pill can make a corporation takeover-proof. In *Ivancare Corp. v. Healthdyne Technologies, Inc.*, 968 F. Supp. 1578 (N.D. Ga. 1997), such a provision was upheld under Georgia law. Georgia had enacted a broad anti-takeover statute that explicitly validated poison pills. See discussion of state statutes at § 12.07, *infra*. Other courts have expressed concern over the attempt by directors to preclude actions taken by new directors. In *Carmody v. Toll Brothers, Inc.*, 723 A.2d 1180 (Del. Ch. 1998), the Delaware Chancery court allowed a cause of action challenging the "dead hand" provision as violating Delaware law. The court looked to Del. Gen. Corp. L. § 141(d) which required directors who have distinctive rights or greater voting rights to be provided for in the certificate. The "dead hand" provision could have also violated § 141(a) which provides that the directors including newly elected ones have the power to manage unless otherwise provided for in the certificate. The "dead hand" provision could be viewed as improperly taking power away from the future board by the existing board. In addition the plan improperly interfered with shareholder voting under *Blausius* and because it precludes a proxy fight and violates *Unocal* and *Unitrin*. For a discussion of these cases, see § 12.05[A] *infra*. *See also Bank of New York Co. v. Irving Bank Corp.*, 528 N.Y.S.2d 482 (1988), *aff'd* 533 N.Y.S.2d 411 (1988) (invalidating a poison pill "dead hand" provision as violating New York law that required an amendment to the articles to restrict the powers of the board). Corporations reacted to the invalidity of the "dead hand" by putting a time frame, such as after 6 months, on the ability of the new board to redeem the poison pill and this has been described as a "no hand" or "delayed redemption" pill. Unlike the dead hand pill, the plan did not discriminate between new and old directors and had a limited life. It did not preclude a friendly deal, although the delay of 6 months may prove costly to the bidder. In *Mentor Graphics Corp. v. Quickturn Design Systems, Inc.*, 721 A.2d 1281 (Del. 1998), the Delaware Supreme Court found a "no hand" pill with a 6 month delay violated Delaware law because it impermissibly limited the board's statutory power to manage under Del. Gen. Corp. L. § 141(a). Any limitation on such power should

fundamentally restricted shareholders' right to conduct a proxy contest. The broad language of the plan could suggest that soliciting proxies was a triggering event. The court found, however, that the poison pill did not restrict a proxy fight since seeking shareholders' votes was not a triggering event under the plan.[55]

There has been much litigation over poison pills and other defensive tactics and whether they were properly implemented under state law. While most state statutes allow flexibility in directors' actions, their activities cannot violate mandatory statutory rules or provisions of the corporation's bylaws or articles of incorporation.[56] Even if there is compliance with the letter of the law, the implementation and the actual use of defensive tactics such as poison pills involve questions of fiduciary duty.[57]

The poison pills and other defensive tactics remain controversial.[58] Some view defensive tactics as preventing a successful takeover and benefitting the

---

be set forth in the certificate. In addition, directors have a fiduciary duty, and contracts or provisions which limit the fiduciary duty of future boards are usually invalid. Under this reasoning, the "dead hand" and "no hand" pills violate Delaware law.

[55] The court also analyzed the defensive tactic under the *Unocal* modified business judgment rule. *See* § 12.05[A][2], *infra*. The court found no violation. There was a majority of outside directors which were informed and not grossly negligent in the decision making process. The directors did not act to entrench themselves and were concerned about the threat posed by potential bidder tactics such as coercive front-loaded two-tier offers and bust up tender offers. Thus, the poison pill plan was found, under the *Unocal* test, to be a reasonable response to the threat posed. The poison pill did not preclude a takeover. Since there was no hostile tender offer when the plan was adopted, the court indicated it would look again at the plan when it was actually in use during a tender offer.

[56] *See Bank of New York Co. v. Irving Bank Corp.*, note 54, *supra.* Courts have also decided whether the pill violates the substance of state law. *See, e.g., Asarco v. MRH Holmes A Court*, 611 F. Supp. 468 (D.N.J. 1985) (applying New Jersey law, a poison pill improperly discriminated between shareholders). *See Mentor Graphics*, note 54, *supra.*

[57] In *Moran*, note 51, *supra*, the court indicated that it will look at both the implementation of a defensive tactic and its use in the context of an actual tender offer to see if there is a breach of fiduciary duty. Pre-planned tactics are often easier to justify and may only be subject to the business judgment rule. The Delaware court indicated that pre-planning "might reduce the risk that, under the pressures of a takeover bid, management will fail to exercise reasonable judgment."

[58] Early studies of the effects of poison pills have shown different results. *Compare Georgeson & Co*, Poison Pill Impact Study II (Oct. 31, 1988) (shares with pills outperformed shares without), *with* A Study on the Economics of Poison Pills (1985– 1986 Transfer Binder) FED. SEC. L. REP. (CCH) ¶ 83,971 (Mar. 5, 1986) (target shares declined upon adoption of a pill). *See generally* John Coates, *Takeover Defenses in the Shadow of the Pill: Critique of the Scientific Evidence*, 79 TEX. L. REV. 271 (2000) (two decades of research on poison pills and other takeover defenses does not support the belief-common among legal academics-that defenses reduce firm value). Some shareholders, particularly institutional shareholders, do not like poison pills and have used the proxy system to try to limit poison pills. They have sponsored precatory shareholder proposals to recommend that poison pills either be cancelled or subject to a shareholder vote. In some cases they have tried to amend the by laws to require a shareholder vote for a pill. *See Int'l Bhd of Teamsters Gen. Fund v. Fleming Cos.*, 975 P.2d 907 (Okla. 1999) (the court found under Oklahoma law that shareholders could require a vote). Such proposals raise an issue of allocation of power between shareholders and directors. Although *Fleming* suggested that Delaware law would be similar it remains unclear if shareholder could require a vote on poison pills given the power the board has in implementing them. *See Mentor Graphics Corp. v. Quickturn Design Systems, Inc., supra* note 54, *supra* (the Delaware Supreme Court found attempts to limit future board's actions on poison pills as violating Delaware law because it impermissibly limited the board's statutory power to manage under Del. Gen. Corp. L. § 141(a). The holding may suggest that poison pills are a board issue that shareholders cannot directly vote

incumbent management.[59] Poison pills are usually implemented by directors without a shareholder vote. But, they also can be viewed as necessary to protect the corporation and its shareholders from offensive tactics of the bidder that arguably hurt the corporation or its shareholders.[60] A poison pill plan also may result in a higher price for the shareholders. For example, the directors' power to redeem a poison pill prior to a bidder purchasing a certain percentage of shares may encourage the bidder to negotiate with the directors and possibly increase the bidder's offer to avoid the pill's impact. But when a poison pill is in place and the target directors refuse to redeem it, the bidder will usually buy sufficient shares under the percentage that triggers the non redemption of the pill and then does a proxy fight to hopefully convince the target shareholders to elect new directors nominated by the bidder. If elected the new directors will then reeem the pill and facilitate a friendly acquisition.[61]

§ 12.05 STATE LAW

When a target's management and directors institute actions to defend the corporation from the hostile takeover, they are usually faced with a charge of breach of fiduciary duty to the corporation and its shareholders under state law. Fiduciary duty is generally divided between the duty of care, and, when there is a conflict of interest or lack of good faith, the duty of loyalty. With the duty of care, directors are liable only for neglecting their duties, not for misjudgments and, thus, any judicial inquiry focuses on the decision-making process, not the decision with the burden of proof on the plaintiff. The decisions are generally protected by the business judgment rule, which presumes that directors have acted in good faith and in the corporation's best interest. Duty of loyalty generally applies when the directors are in a conflict of interest. The important distinction between the two duties is that in a duty of loyalty analysis involving a conflict of interest and not good faith, the directors usually have the burden of proof as to the fairness of their decision and, thus, the courts scrutinize the process and the substance of the decision with a greater possibility of liability.[62]

Those who favor hostile tender offers have argued that the target's defensive tactics place directors in a conflict of interest, because they are concerned with keeping their positions, and, thus, the duty of loyalty should apply and not the

---

on). For a discussion of allocation of power, see § 5.05[C][3], *infra.*

[59] *See* Patrick J. Thompson, *Note, Shareholder Rights Plans: Shields or Gravels*, 42 VAND. L. REV. 173 (1989).

[60] In fact, some controversial bidder tactics, such as the front-loaded two-tier offer, have been abandoned, and one reason is that courts allowed target directors to use defensive tactics, such as the poison pill, to avoid them. *See, e.g., Moran*, note 51, *supra* (the court viewed the possibility of coercive front-loaded two-tier tender offers and bust-up tender offers as reasons to allow the implementation of the poison pill plan).

[61] For a discussion of proxy fights to facilitate acquisitions, see § 5.05[C][2], *supra.*

[62] For a discussion of fiduciary duty, see § 8.01, *supra.* There is also a duty of disclosure within fiduciary duty. In *Lynch v. Vickers Energy Corp.*, 383 A.2d 278 (Del. 1978), the court held that in making a tender offer to minority shareholders there was an obligation of "complete candor" on the part of the controlling shareholder.

business judgment rule.[63] Those who oppose hostile takeovers view the implementation of defensive tactics as similar to other business decisions protected by the business judgment rule.[64] In fact, in most cases, the use of defensive tactics have resulted in the application of an enhanced standard of review involving a modified business judgment rule or proportionality test under the Delaware case of *Unocal Corp. v. Mesa Petroleum Co.*[65]

[A]   Delaware Approach

[1]   The *Cheff* Case

In response to the debate over both offensive and defensive tactics, the courts have tried over time to establish a rule that reflects the conflicting arguments and interests involved. At first, the Delaware courts adopted a strong business judgment view of takeovers. In *Cheff v. Mathes*,[66] a Delaware court was faced with a greenmail case, in which the target directors had voted to purchase the shares of a potential bidder for a premium over the market price so that the bidder would not make a hostile tender offer. The potential bidder was purchasing the target's shares on the market and seeking a seat on the board while criticizing management of the target. The target's purchase of shares from the bidder was challenged in a derivative suit alleging it was a perpetuation of control by the target directors.

The court's decision recognized the directors' need to defend proper business practices but also recognized the potential conflict of interest that arises when directors are acting solely or primarily to perpetuate their control. There was, however, a recognition that, at least for the outside directors, this potential conflict of interest differed from the traditional duty of loyalty case that involved a direct pecuniary interest. Thus, the court did not apply either the traditional business judgment rule or duty of loyalty standard. Instead the court shifted the burden to the defendant directors to show whether there were reasonable grounds to believe a danger to corporate policy or effectiveness existed. The potential bidder in this case has a poor reputation and caused unrest at the corporation. Their burden was satisfied by a showing of good faith and reasonable investigation. This intermediate standard between duty of care and of loyalty focused more on the motive of target directors and permitted the

---

[63] Some commentators argue for director passivity when faced with a hostile tender offer, allowing any offer above the market price to be given to the shareholders. Defensive tactics raise the costs for bidders and will deter not only the specific tender offer but tender offers in general. Any actions which limit the advantages of tender offers and the market for corporate control should be restricted. Frank Easterbrook & Daniel Fischel, note 20, *supra*. Others argue that directors should be allowed to facilitate an auction for the target and even use defensive tactics to seek the highest bid for the shareholders. *See generally* Lucien A. Bebchuk, *The Case for Facilitating Competing Tender Offers*, 95 Harv. L. Rev. 1028 (1982); Ronald Gilson, *A Structural Approach to Corporations: The Case Against Defensive Tactics in Tender Offers*, 33 Stan. L. Rev. 819 (1981).

[64] *See* Martin Lipton, *Takeover Bids in the Target's Boardroom*, 35 Bus. Law. 101 (1979).

[65] 493 A.2d 946 (Del. 1985). For a discussion of the test, see § 12.05[A][2], *infra*.

[66] 199 A.2d 548 (Del. Ch. 1964).

purchase of the shares because of the threat the potential bidder posed to corporate policy.

[2]   The *Unocal* Test

Even though the *Cheff* view modified the business judgment rule by shifting the burden of proof, it was still difficult to successfully challenge directors' defensive tactics. Some courts reviewed the justifications of the directors (which were not too difficult to create) and then required a showing by the plaintiff that impermissible motives predominated the directors' decision.[67] That was a difficult test for plaintiffs. But in the 1980s tender offers became more significant in size and number with bidders offering large premiums to shareholders (often in cash) and directors using corporate assets to thwart bids. The Delaware courts could not ignore the potential shareholder gains in a tender offer and possible self-dealing by managers to prevent the offer. But there was still a recognition that directors had a responsibility to the corporation and possibly to other constituencies.

In *Unocal Corp. v. Mesa Petroleum Co.*,[68] the bidder Mesa Petroleum owned 13% of Unocal and commenced a front loaded two-tier takeover for the target. The first tier, or step, was acquiring approximately 37% at $54 cash and then indicated that with its 51% stake it would implement the second step. The second step was a freezeout merger to acquire the remaining approximately 49% for securities with a face value of $54 but which would in fact trade at a lower price because the securities were highly subordinated to other debt and risky (called "junk bonds"). The target board, which consisted of a majority of outside directors, saw the tender offer as being at an inadequate price and that the front loaded two-tier tender offer was coercive to the shareholders. The target responded with a self-tender for $72 cash to purchase the 49% of the Unocal shares not included in Mesa's first tier offer.[69] The target's self tender excluded Mesa[70] and was funded with new Unocal debt which had restrictive covenants. This use of substantial debt made Unocal highly leveraged which had the effect of restricting Mesa's ability to eventually finance its tender offer with more debt. Bidders would often borrow to make the tender offer and then when in control use the target's assets to support that debt.

Mesa challenged the self tender as beyond the power of the board and even if within its power it was a breach of fiduciary duty. Mesa argued for a standard fairness because of the exclusion while Unocal argued that it acted in good faith

---

[67]   *E.g., Johnson v. Trueblood*, 629 F.2d 287, 292–93 (3d Cir. 1980).

[68]   493 A.2d 946 (Del. 1985).

[69]   Initially the self tender was conditioned on Mesa actually acquiring the 37% in its tender but that was dropped because of concern that most Unocal shareholders would tender in the self tender and Mesea would not be able to purchase sufficient shares to meet the condition. Thus the self tender was made irrespective of Mesa's tender offer.

[70]   The directors were advised that they need a corporate purpose to exclude Mesa. The exclusion was felt necessary because if Mesa was included it would mean that fewer Unocal shareholders would be included in the self tender. This would defeat the goal of compensating the shareholders who would be eliminated in the freezeout merger. In addition, Mesa would receive payments in the self tender that could be used to finance their unfair tender offer.

and with due care to protect the company and shareholders. The Delaware Supreme Court recognized that when the directors implement a defensive tactic there arises "the omnipresent specter that a board may be acting primarily in its own interests, rather than those of the corporation or its shareholders . . . ." The court reiterated the *Cheff* rule but with an additional focus:

> If a defensive measure is to come within the ambit of the business judgment rule, it must be reasonable to the threat posed. This entails an analysis by the directors of the nature of the takeover bid and its effect on the corporate enterprise. Examples of such concerns may include: inadequacy of the price offered, nature and timing of the offer, questions of illegality, the impact on "constituencies" other than shareholders (i.e., creditors, employees, and perhaps even the community generally), the risk of nonconsumption, and the quality of securities being offered in the exchange.[71]

Thus, in enacting a defensive tactic the board must prove (1) that it had reasonable grounds for believing that a danger to corporate policy and effectiveness existed (the threat), and (2) that the defensive tactic was reasonable to the threat posed (the response).[72] In addition, according to the court, the presence of a majority of independent directors unaffiliated with the target materially enhances the directors' proof.[73] This test differs from the normal application of the business judgment rule by placing the initial burden on the directors and allowing some scrutiny of not just the process but also the substance of the decision.[74] The first step focuses on the threat and directors acting in good faith after reasonable investigation. The second step allows the court to balance the defensive tactic with the threat (that is, whether the response was proportionate to the threat). Thus, the Delaware courts have chosen a test that does not implicate a fairness review but uses a heightened scrutiny that is a modified business judgment or proportionality test.

The *Unocal* court rejected the idea of fairness or that directors should be passive or that the decisions of directors in this context are similar to other

---

[71] *Id.* at 955.

[72] Threats often involve an inadequate offer but can also involve an opportunity loss, structural coercion or substantive coercion. *See* note 108, *infra.* A.L.I. Corp. Gov. Proj. § 6.02 allows the directors to take any action that has a foreseeable effect of blocking a tender offer if the action is a reasonable response to the offer. The board may take into account factors relevant to the best interests of the corporation and shareholders including the offer's legality and whether it would threaten the corporation's essential economic prospects. Other constituencies can be considered if it would not significantly disfavor long-term shareholder interests. But unlike Delaware, the burden of proof is on the plaintiff to show that the board's response was unreasonable.

[73] *Unocal*, 493 A.2d at 955.

[74] Some states have enacted statutes which reject this test for the traditional business judgment rule. For example, Indiana Code § 23-1-35-1 (1989). Courts have also used the traditional duty of care analysis to review defensive tactics. In *Hanson Trust PLC v. ML SCM Acquisition, Inc.*, 781 F.2d 264 (2d Cir. 1986), the court used New York law to find that the target directors breached their duty of care when they quickly and without a valuation granted a crown jewel lockup to a white knight which also included participation by the target's management in the takeover. The court placed the initial burden on the plaintiff but found a failure to exercise due care which was heightened under the circumstances of the lockup.

business decisions that are protected by the business judgment rule. As a result, the _Unocal_ test gives directors significant latitude while allowing some closer judicial scrutiny of the tactics.[75] The court approved the self tender defensive tactic and, thus, allowed discrimination among shareholders in the self tender which excluded the bidder.[76] The decision was based on threats of Mesa's inadequate front loaded two tier offer, considered coercive, and the threat that Mesa may be looking for greenmail and to be bought out by Unocal for a premium to go away.

[3]   The _Revlon_ Test

The _Unocal_ decision lead to litigation on the two-part test in the context of specific offers and tactics.[77] In _Revlon, Inc. v. MacAndrews & Forbes Holding, Inc.,_[78] the court was faced with the application of the _Unocal_ test. Initially, the bidder tried to negotiate a friendly acquisition but was rebuffed claiming an inadequately priced offer. Revlon used several defensive tactics to avoid the takeover, including a poison pill[79] and a self tender.[80] The tactics had the positive effect of raising the tender offer bid to a higher cash price that could no

---

[75] Delaware could not really allow directors of targets who selected it as their state of incorporation to be unprotected from the threat of a takeover since they could try to reincorporate in another state which has stronger protection for target directors. Complete deference to the directors would anger shareholders especially institutional investors. In addition, Delaware probably understood that giving complete control to incumbent management could hurt shareholders which might have pressured Congress to federalize corporate law, thereby eliminating Delaware's franchise.

[76] This self-tender defense, which excludes the bidder, is no longer permitted under SEC Rules which requires an equal opportunity to all shareholders in the tender offer. _See_ note 140, _infra._

[77] Commentators have suggested that "decisions applying the _Unocal_ rule do not successfully teach us how to measure the dimensions or import of either the requisite threat or the appropriate response so as to be able to tell whether the latter is reasonable in relation to, or proportionate to, the former." Victor Brudney & William Bratton, CORPORATE FINANCE 1092 (4th ed. 1993).

[78] 506 A.2d 173 (Del. 1985).

[79] Revlon used a poison pill that was a Notes Purchase Rights Plan. (i.e., "flip in" poison pill). Under the plan, all Revlon shareholders would receive a dividend of one Note Purchase Rights ("Rights") for each share held by them. The Rights entitled the holder to exchange his or her Revlon shares for a $65 Revlon note paying 12% interest with a one year maturity ("Note"). The Rights became effective only after a Bidder acquired 20% or more of Revlon's shares. Prior to the 20% purchase, the board of Revlon could redeem the Rights for $0.10 each. The fact that Revlon's shareholders can convert their shares for the Note of $65 (a price viewed as much higher then anyone would have paid for the shares) would make Revlon less attractive to a Bidder. It meant that Revlon would take on more debt with the issuance of the Notes and that within a year it would have to pay on the Notes the high price of $65 cash which meant that a substantial amount of cash would have to be raised. Because the effect of the Notes made Revlon (the Target) less attractive to a Bidder it is called a "flip in" poison pill. While Revlon involved the use of Notes other "flip in" pills could involve preferred stock of the target that would have a claim against the Target. Some poison pills allow the Target shareholders to affect the Bidder adversely makes those plans a "flip over" poison pill. See discussion of those pills in § 12.04[B][1], _supra._

[80] In the self tender, Revlon offered to buy 10 million common shares from its shareholders for notes and preferred shares valued at $57.50 in exchange for those common shares which was a higher price than the bidder's offer at that time. The notes received by the shareholders had covenants which restricted Revlon's ability to incur debt or sell assets thus limiting the bidder's flexibility of using the target's assets if successful in its tender offer (the directors could waive the covenants).

longer be viewed as unfair.[81] The target found Forstmann Little, a white knight, who was willing to offer a competing bid for the target in return for (1) a "no shop provision" by the target (Revlon would not look for another bidder), (2) a $25 million cancellation fee if the bid failed, and (3) a crown jewel lockup (the white knight was given the right to buy a valuable division of the target at a discount price if it should fail in its offer). The effect of these transactions was to lockup in favor of the white knight and effectively end the bidding. The first bidder would not want the business without the crown jewel.

The bidder challenged the actions of Revlon's board as a breach of fiduciary duty. The *Revlon* court indicated that lockups which encourage bids are permissible, while those that end bids are not. Here the court concluded that Revlon's directors had breached their fiduciary duty. In finding a competing bid, Revlon had been effectively put up for sale by the directors and the breakup of the company had become a reality. The court enjoined the lockup and required an enhanced scrutiny under *Unocal* and held that when a target is up for sale the directors cannot play favorites. The target directors' duty under *Revlon* changes from preservation of the target to maximization of value to the shareholders; that is, they are auctioneers.[82]

While *Unocal* suggested that directors can be concerned with other corporate constituencies during a takeover, *Revlon* indicated that such concerns are permissible only if there are rationally related benefits accruing to shareholders. But, once there is an auction for the business and the object is no longer to protect the corporate enterprise, such interests are inappropriate and the corporation should be sold to the highest bidder.

[4]   The *Time* Case

Unocal and particularly *Revlon* together suggest that the Delaware courts were taking a more active role in scrutinizing defensive tactics with a greater emphasis on shareholder concerns. But, at the time, it was unclear when the

---

[81] The poison pill and self tender forced the bidder to increase its bid to a point where it was close to the $57.50 value Revlon had used in the self tender and thus no longer unfair. As a result, these tactics met the *Unocal* test (i.e., they were a reasonable response to the initial inadequate offer by the bidder). Once Forstmann Little entered the bidding the directors had to redeem the poison pill and waive the covenants in the notes (*see* note 80, *supra.*) because it could also harm Forstmann. As a result the value of the notes decreased (the protection against future lending was gone which meant that there could be more debt issued, i.e., more leveraging, which would increase the risk to the note holders) and the note holders were threatening litigation. One of the reasons the managers sought Forstmann was Forstmann's promise to assist the note holders by maintaining its value. As a result of favoring Forstmann, the directors breached their duty of loyalty because this protection of the note holders (i.e., creditors) not the shareholders when the target was up for sale was found to be motivated by their fear of personal liability.

[82] For a discussion of judicial scrutiny of lockups, see § 12.05[A][9], *infra*. The *Revlon* test can be triggered by a sale and breakup of the corporation in the form of an auction, management buyout or some type of restructuring. When the corporation is up for sale the directors' responsibilities are significantly altered, although their duties remain unchanged under *Unocal*. If the directors favored one bidder, then the court determines if the shareholders' interests were enhanced and if so, whether the response was proportionate to the threat posed. If both tests are met, then the business judgment rule will apply. *See Mills Acquisition Co. v. Macmillan, Inc.*, 559 A.2d 1261 (Del. 1989).

obligations of *Revlon* within *Unocal* to auction the company would apply.[83] The Delaware Supreme Court decision in *Paramount Communications, Inc. v. Time, Inc.*[84] put to rest any idea of the courts actively substituting its judgment for those of outside directors on most takeover issues.[85] In that case, the Time directors were able to defend the company from a cash offer from Paramount that ended up at $200 a share when Time's shares had been trading at $126 prior to the offer. Time had originally negotiated a friendly merger with Warner Brothers to pursue a strategic plan of expansion before Paramount made its bid. Time directors feared that the company's shareholders would now vote to reject the merger because of Paramount's substantial cash offer.[86] So Time changed the transaction from the original merger between Warner and Time and instead Time made a friendly cash tender offer for 51% of the shares of Warner. With Time using cash and making a tender offer, there would be no vote by Time's shareholders. The remaining 49% of Warner would be acquired later for cash and securities.

Paramount argued that there was now a *Revlon* duty to auction Time since it was effectively put up for sale by the original merger agreement. It further argued that the requirements of *Unocal* were not met because there were no reasonable grounds to believe Paramount's offer posed a threat and the response of Time was intended to entrench the management and, thus, was unreasonable. The court rejected the use of *Revlon* in this context. The court did not find that the negotiations with Warner meant a dissolution or breakup of Time was inevitable. Here, Time's response of a friendly cash tender offer to Warner was defensive and did not put Time up for sale. Time was allowed to pursue its long-term strategy of combining with Warner Brothers.[87]

---

[83] Another issue was: if the bidder did not use any controversial tactics but offered a fairly priced all-cash deal, could the target resist the bid by the "just saying no" defense under *Unocal* (a play on Nancy Reagan's drug policy)? Some case law suggested that all-cash and all-share bids were not sufficient threats to justify the use of a poison pill defense to preclude the offer. *See City Capital Associates Ltd. Partnership v. Interco Inc.*, 551 A.2d 787 (Del. Ch. 1988). Based on the broad discretion given to the directors in *Time* to pursue long-term corporate strategy, however, the courts may allow the defense in the *Time* situation which involved an all cash and all shareholder bid by Paramount. *See generally* Jeff Gordon, *"Just Say Never?" Poison Pills, Deadhand Pills, and Shareholder-Adopted By-laws: An Essay for Warren Buffett*, 19 Cardozo L. Rev. (1997).

[84] 571 A.2d 1140 (Del. 1989).

[85] *Time* and *Unitrin* (discussed at § 12.05[A][4] and [6], *infra*) together give target directors a lot of discretion.

[86] It is interesting to note that the shareholders were going to vote on the merger with Warner because a vote was required under New York Stock Exchange rules since the transaction involved a significant issuance of Time shares that would dilute the interests of the Time shareholders. Under Delaware law, however, Time shareholders had no right to vote, because Warner was merging into a wholly-owned subsidiary of Time, not Time itself (that is, a triangular merger). For a discussion of triangular mergers, see § 6.02[A], *supra*.

[87] The court indicated that *Revlon* duties arise when a corporation initiates active bidding by seeking to sell itself or reorganizes itself in a way that involves a breakup. The duty also arises when, in response to a bid, a long-term strategy is abandoned and the corporation seeks an alternative involving a breakup. The court did not address whether *Revlon* was implicated if there was a change of control for some other reason. See discussion of the *QVC* case at § 12.05[A][5], *infra* (sale of control implicates *Revlon*).

Using the *Unocal* test, the court looked at the first part (the threat) and determined that inadequate value or coercive tactics were not the only threat a target faces. Paramount's offer was all cash at a substantial premium and was not a coercive front-loaded two-tier offer. Paramount argued that inadequate value or coercion were the only threats under *Unocal* and its offer was fair and should be allowed to go forward. The court disagreed and indicated there were other threats to justify Time's defensive tender offer for Warner. One threat was Time's concern that its shareholders would tender to Paramount without an understanding of the proposed plan with Warner. In addition, Paramount's offer had conditions which created uncertainty and skewed a comparative analysis between the tender offer and Time's plan. Paramount's offer arguably was designed to upset the initial vote for the merger with Warner and confuse shareholders.

Under the second part of the test (the response), the reasonableness of the defense depended on the threat. Thus, Time's directors were permitted to respond to protect the company's pre-existing plan, but not in an overly broad manner. The court, however, decided to defer to the directors on the "selection of a time frame for achievement of corporate goals."[88] This decision gave a great deal of deference to independent directors in both identifying a threat and in determining what was best for the corporation in its response. The focus was not on shareholder choice but on the directors' view of the future of the target under an existing business plan. The court indicated that deciding which was a better deal for the shareholders in this case was up to the directors.

Thus, under *Time*, there appeared to be no general obligation to sell a corporation simply because there happened to be a substantial premium in cash offered to shareholders in a tender offer (even at a fair price) when such a sale would upset a business plan. *Time* appears to be distinguishable from *Revlon* because there was no planned breakup of Time.

[5]　The *QVC* Case

The *Time* decision seemed to give directors wide discretion and limit the *Revlon* enhanced duty and obligation to seek the best price. The Delaware Supreme Court's opinion in *Paramount Communications Inc. v. QVC Network, Inc.*,[89] however, suggested that the *Time* decision favoring directors of the target was not so broad. Paramount agreed to be acquired by Viacom in a friendly acquisition involving cash and shares of Viacom worth $69.14 and a "No-Shop Provision" which limited Paramount's ability to accept another bid.[90] In addition, if (1) Paramount terminated its agreement with Viacom because of a competing offer, (2) Paramount's stockholders did not approve the transaction

---

[88] The court was unwilling to enter the debate between the short-term value of Paramount's bid with the alleged long-term value of Time's strategy. The court stated that "the question of 'long-term' versus 'short-term' values is largely irrelevant because directors, generally, are obliged to charter a course for a corporation which is in its best interests without regard to a fixed investment horizon." *Id.* at 1150.

[89] 637 A.2d 34 (Del. 1994).

[90] The court found that such provisions cannot define or limit the directors' fiduciary duty under Delaware law. The issue is also dealt with in the *Omnicare* case discussed at § 12.05[A][9], *infra.*

with Viacom, or (3) Paramount's directors recommended a competing transaction, Viacom would receive a $100 million termination fee and the option ("stock option") to buy 24 million Paramount shares (19.9% of Paramount) at $69.14.[91] Although the shareholders of Paramount would own shares in the new merged company, the controlling shareholder of Viacom, Sumner Redstone, would own 70% of the new company.

QVC offered to acquire Paramount at a higher price than Viacom had offered. The directors of Paramount viewed the Viacom offer as fitting into Paramount's long-term business strategy and a means to increase shareholder value. As a result, and with some irony, Paramount, which was defeated in *Time*, relied on the *Time* decision on the basis that, like Time's acquisition of Warner, it had a strategic merger and there was no planned breakup of the business. The Paramount directors did not seriously consider the QVC bid even though at one point it was $1.3 billion higher than Viacom's bid. The directors refused to withdraw any of their defensive tactics, including the termination fee, stock option to Viacom and the company's poison pill.

QVC sued to enjoin Viacom's offer and Paramount's use of defensive tactics and to seek invalidation of the termination fee and stock option.[92] The court decided that *Time* did not apply and that the *Revlon* duty was triggered by the proposed merger with Viacom. The court found that the change of control that would result from Viacom's proposed acquisition of Paramount justified the application of *Revlon*, and was not limited to circumstances when the breakup of the corporation was inevitable. The court found it significant that in *Time* there was no change of control since Time and Warner were both public companies with widely dispersed shareholders and no controlling shareholders. The Time shareholders retained an equity interest in the new company (Time Warner) which had no controlling shareholders. Conversely, in *QVC* there was a change of control.[93] Paramount had no controlling shareholders, but Viacom did have one. After Viacom's purchase, Paramount's public shareholders would be

---

[91] The effect of these provisions was to compensate Viacom for the expenses it incurred in making its offer in the event that Paramount went with a competing bidder or Paramount's shareholders did not approve the Viacom transaction. The provisions also made it more expensive for the other bidder because of the cost of the termination fee and the need to buy the shares Viacom could purchase under the stock option (that is, an additional 19.9%). *See* note 92, *infra.*

[92] The stock option was worth approximately $500 million to Viacom if QVC's offer was accepted. QVC would have had to pay $90 for each additional share that Viacom could have purchased under the stock option for $69.14 making QVC's offer more expensive. The Delaware Supreme Court affirmed the trial court's injunction against Paramount using defensive tactics that favored Viacom and the trial court's invalidation of the stock option. While the termination fee of $100 million was found to be reasonable by the lower court to cover Viacom's expenses, the Supreme Court did not reverse that holding because it was not raised on appeal. But, the court did discuss all the defensive measures taken as a whole as being problematic, suggesting that such a fee might be unreasonable in light of all the defensive tactics.

[93] According to the court, sale or change of control takes place when a majority of voting shares are acquired by a single person or entity or a cohesive group acting together which results in a significant diminution in voting power to those who become minority shareholders. As a result, the court will now be required to determine if in fact there is an acquiring group in control to see if the merger will subject the public shareholders to future loss of a premium. The court will also have to determine if ownership of less than 51% can be de facto control as it often is in the case when shares are widely dispersed among the public.

minority shareholders in a company controlled by Viacom's controlling shareholder (Sumner Redstone). According to the *QVC* court, when there was a change of control and the target shareholders became minority shareholders then their voting rights became a formality. It was this loss of voting power which was part of the compensation paid when a corporation is sold. Furthermore, the controlling shareholder could at some point decide to deny the minority shareholders the long-term benefits of the merger by cashing them out in a subsequent freeze out merger.[94] This loss of control by the sale of Paramount to Viacom required compensation to Paramount's shareholders (the public shareholders were entitled to a control premium), and, thus, Paramount's directors were subject to the enhanced scrutiny of *Revlon*. Thus, in a change of control context, directors must focus on the objective to secure a transaction offering the best price reasonably available for the shareholders. While there is no single method required for seeking the best value, an auction is one possibility.

In *QVC* there was an enhanced duty under *Unocal* which required judicial determination on the process of the board's decisions and a determination on the reasonableness of the board's actions (that is, whether they were within a range of reasonableness). Here, the board was required to seek the best price because there was a proposed diminution of shareholder voting power; the control premium belonging to the public shareholders was being sold; and the court was concerned with actions impairing voting rights. This enhanced scrutiny looked at the adequacy of the process, including the information used, and examined the reasonableness of the actions themselves under the circumstances. The burden was on the directors to prove they were adequately informed and acted reasonably. The court indicated that judges should recognize the complexity of the determination as to best price and the directors are usually best equipped to make that decision. Thus, the court should not second guess the decision, so long as on balance it is within the range of reasonableness, looking for a reasonable decision not a perfect one.

Under this standard, the Paramount directors had an obligation to be diligent and obedient in examining both bidders, to act in good faith, to obtain and act on all information reasonably available on the issue of best value, and to negotiate actively and in good faith with both Viacom and QVC. The directors had decided to enter a strategic merger with Viacom, which involved a change of control, and approved certain defensive tactics to facilitate the transaction. The court decided that this activity and the subsequent disparate treatment of a competing bidder were the result of an unreasonable process and a breach of fiduciary duty.[95]

---

[94] For a discussion of freeze out mergers, see § 10.03, *supra*.

[95] The result of the decision created a bidding auction between QVC and Viacom. Viacom ultimately succeeded in acquiring Paramount and not only raised its bid to around $10 billion from around $8 billion, but provided the Paramount shareholders with some protection for a set period from a decline in the value of the Viacom securities they received. Thus, if the Viacom securities received by Paramount shareholders did not maintain their value as projected, more securities would have to be issued. That protection could have required Viacom to issue an additional $700 million of its securities to the former shareholders of Paramount.

The *QVC* decision was a strong statement about shareholder choice, but there was also strong support for directors having a major role in tender offers. *QVC* indicated that whenever there is a change of control either in a tender offer or a merger, an enhanced scrutiny will apply. This test should also apply in an arms-length bargain merger, where there is no control group acquiring the corporation, if the shareholders are losing their equity position by receiving cash and nonvoting securities. This does not mean that directors are required to seek another bidder or hold an auction if there is such a sale. But, the directors must be able to justify the value negotiated and, if there is a competing bid, treat all parties fairly.[96]

[6]   The *Unitrin* Case

In *Unitrin, Inc. v. American General Corp.*,[97] the Delaware Supreme Court reversed the lower court's injunction of the target Unitrin's repurchase or self tender of its own shares to thwart American General's hostile takeover. The Unitrin directors, who owned 23% of the shares, did not sell their shares to Unitrin in the self tender. Thus, the self tender had the effect of reducing the number of shares outstanding and increasing the percentage of Unitrin shares owned by the directors who did not sell to 28%. Their increased ownership allowed them to block a merger with someone owning more than 15% of the shares because of a super-majority shareholder vote requirement of 75% in the certificate for such mergers.[98]

The Delaware Supreme Court agreed with the lower court that the *Unocal* test should apply since the self tender decision was a defensive measure. Both courts agreed that under the first prong of the test (the threat), the board had

---

[96] In *Barakn v Amsted Industries, Inc.* 567 A2d 1279 (Del. Sup. 1989), the Delaware Supreme Court indicated that *Revlon* does not require every change of control requires a heated bidding contest but only that directors act with "scrupulous concern for fairness to shareholders." Thus if there are alternative bids then the directors cannot favor one over the other. If there is only one bid the directors may decide to canvass the market if there are no reliable grounds to judge the bid's adequacy. But if there is reliable evidence to evaluate the fairness of an offer, they need not do a market test.

In *Ryan v. Lyondell Chem. Co.*, 970 A.2d 235 (Del. 2009), the Delaware Supreme Court held that *Revlon* duties to get the best price do not arise simply because the company is in "play." The duty to seek the best price occurs when the company, in response to an offer or acting on its own initiative, embarks on a transaction resulting in a change of control. The fact the directors of the target decided to "wait and see" does not implicate *Revlon* and could not be viewed as a lack of good faith (there was no duty of care liability possible because of a § 102(b)(7) provision in the articles). *Revlon* duties arise when there are negotiations but there are no set of requirements that must be satisfied and the Lyondell directors' failure to take any specific steps during the sale process could not have demonstrated a conscious disregard of their duties, i.e., lack of good faith. Only if the directors had knowingly and completely failed to undertake their duties would they have breached their duty of loyalty. Since the Lyondell directors were disinterested and independent, "the inquiry should have been whether those directors utterly failed to attempt to obtain the best sale price." *Id.* at 244.

[97] 651 A.2d 1361 (Del. 1995).

[98] This shark repellent provision precluded a merger with anyone owning more than 15% of the shares unless approved by a majority of the incumbent directors or by a 75% shareholder vote. The effect here was that once a bidder owned 15% the directors could block the merger even if they were replaced because they would still own 28% of the shares after the repurchase and the bidder could not get the requisite 75% required voter.

met its burden of reasonable investigation and good faith in determining the threat or threats (i.e., inadequate price and antitrust concerns). The inadequate price was viewed as substantive coercion, i.e., the target shareholders might accept an inadequate offer because of ignorance or mistaken belief of the target's long term value.

The two courts differed on the second prong (the response) concerning the proportionality of the defense. The Delaware Supreme Court recognized that defensive tactics that affect shareholder voting require careful scrutiny under *Unocal.*[99] Here, the increased share ownership by the directors arguably affected shareholder voting in two ways. First, there was a poison pill which was nonredeemable when someone acquired 15% of the shares. Second, in order to eventually own 100% of the corporation, the bidder (if it owned 15% or more) would need a merger that required a super majority vote under the articles (i.e., a 75% shareholder vote). The self tender defense left the target directors with 28% of the shares. Thus, in order to avoid both the pill and the supermajority merger vote, the bidder could buy 14.9% and then would try to replace the board through a proxy fight, redeem the pill and effectuate a friendly merger by the usual shareholder majority vote. Although the increased share ownership of the directors made a proxy fight and a merger more difficult, the court found that neither a proxy contest nor a merger could be vetoed by the directors and both remained viable alternatives so long as the bidder initially purchased less than 15%.

The lower court found the repurchase defensive tactic under the *Unocal* test[100] to be disproportionate, because it was "unnecessary." The Delaware Supreme Court found an "unnecessary" analysis was incorrect under Delaware law — the lower court should not have substituted its decision for the board's decision. The Court indicated that there was a higher likelihood that defensive tactics would lack proportionality under the *Unocal* test when the tactics were found to be draconian by either being preclusive of a tender offer or coercive to the target shareholders. But if the defensive tactic was not draconian, then under *Unocal's* proportionality test, the enhanced scrutiny shifted to the range of reasonableness. That would result in judicial restraint and greater deference to the directors' decisions.

In *Unitrin*, the defensive tactic was a limited nondiscriminatory self-tender which was not draconian (i.e., a tender offer was not precluded and the self-tender was not coercive). If a proxy fight or a merger was possible, even if difficult, it is, not precluded. If not draconian, the lower court was instructed to determine the reasonableness of the defensive tactic by considering whether the board's actions if done in a nontakeover context would have been routine. The court was to consider how the tactic compared to the threat (for example, a mild threat required a mild response), and whether the board properly recognized that all shareholders are not alike. In *Unitrin*, the self tender provided liquidity

---

[99] The court looked to two Delaware Supreme Court cases, *Blausius Industries, Inc. v. Atlas* and *Stroud v. Grace*. For a discussion of both cases, see § 5.05[D], *supra.* For a discussion of shareholder voting and tender offers, see § 12.05[A][7], *infra.*

[100] For a discussion of the *Unocal* test, see § 12.05[A][2], *supra.*

to some shareholders who wanted to tender. If the response was proportionate, then the business judgment rule would apply.

[7]　Shareholder Voting and Tender Offers

Often in battles for corporate control, target directors can take actions that adversely affect shareholder voting. In tender offers because of certain defensive tactics like poison pills bidders will have to undertake a proxy fight to get control of the board to remove the defensive tactic in order to facilitate a friendly acquisition.[101] Thus defensive tactics may sometimes adversely affect the voting rights of shareholders in the proxy fight or otherwise. While the *Unocal* and *Unitrin* tests usually apply when the target directors initiate defensive tactics in a tender offer, some of those tactics could adversely affect the voting rights of shareholders. As discussed previously, the Delaware courts also protect shareholder democracy when voting rights are implicated. Under *Blausius Industries v. Atlas Corp.*,[102] the Delaware Chancery Court required a strict duty of loyalty and compelling justification for actions taken for the primary purpose of impairing shareholder voting.

It remained unclear how the *Unocal* test which focuses on reasonableness and proportionality would interplay with the stricter test of compelling justification articulated by *Blausius*.[103] The Delaware Supreme Court in *MM Companies, Inc. v. Liquid Audio, Inc.*,[104] clarified the use of the two tests.

---

[101] For a discussion of proxy fights to facilitate acquisitions, see § 5.05[C][2], *supra.*

[102] 564 A.2d 652 (Del. Ch. 1988). *Blausius* involved a proxy fight for control of the corporation where directors took steps to thwart shareholder voting. For a discussion of *Blausius* and shareholder democracy and voting, see § 5.05[D], *supra.*

[103] In *Hilton Hotels Corp. v ITT Corp.*, 978 F.Supp. 1342 (D. Nev. 1997), the target ITT was subject to a hostile takeover by Hilton. ITT believed that the offer was inadequate and delayed calling the annual meeting. The court found no problem with the delay because under Nevada law the corporation had 18 months to call the meeting. ITT also implemented defensive tactics. The tactics involved restructuring ITT into 3 different corporations one of which would have 93% of the current assets and 87% of the current revenues of ITT. In setting up that corporation, it would have in place numerous antitakeover defenses (which the target did not have), such as a poison pill; staggered board and a super majority provision requiring and 80% shareholder vote to remove the directors without cause or remove the staggered board or remove the 80% super majority provision. The shares of the new corporation with the defensive provisions would be distributed to ITT's shareholders as a dividend and would then be publicly traded. The Nevada court looked to Delaware law for guidance in determining Nevada law and used the *Unocal, Blausius* and *Unitrin* tests. According to the court when the issue relates to power over corporate assets, the *Unocal* test would usually apply but if the issue is one of power between the board and shareholders then *Blausius* could apply. If *Blausius* was implicated it would apply as part of *Unocal's* requirement of proportionality. Here the staggered board was viewed as preclusive because current ITT shareholders were unable to exercise their current right to determine who was on the board. There was also an entrenchment effect because the existing directors were to be put on the new staggered board with longer terms and more difficult to be removed. In addition because of the adverse effect on shareholder voting by not allowing theshareholders to vote for or oust the directors at the upcoming annual meeting there was no compelling purpose for it under *Blausius*.

[104] 813 A.2d 1118 (2003). In *MM Companies*, the bidder sought to buy the target but was opposed by the target's directors. They even tried to cancel a scheduled annual meeting of the shareholders but were ordered by the court to hold it. The target had a staggered board of 5 directors which meant that there were three classes of directors with the three year terms that would delay a bidder from

Under *MM Companies*, the *Blausius* standard of enhanced judicial review will apply within the *Unocal* test when the defensive action's primary purpose is to interfere or impede with the shareholder franchise in contested elections of directors.[105] In that case, the first step is to use the *Blausius* standard of compelling justification. According to *MM Companies* the *Blausius* standard of compelling justification must be met as a condition precedent to judicial consideration of whether the defensive tactic was proportionate or reasonable to the threat under *Unocal*. Only after the tactic passes that scrutiny does the court use *Unocal* and *Unitrin* to determine if the defensive tactic was draconian, i.e., coercive or preclusive and result in close scrutiny. If not then under *Unitrin* the reasonableness of the response is reviewed with greater deference to the independent directors on the board.

[8] Summary

When shareholders challenge the defensive actions of target directors the enhanced standard of review of *Unocal* generally applies[106] which looks at the threat to the corporation and response to it. The strengths of the *Unocal* test are that it applies when the directors' conduct is defensive and allows the courts significant discretion in dealing with the variety of takeover scenarios. Its weaknesses are its lack of clarity and its inclination to defer too much to the directors. When the test applies, the court looks at the threat and the response. The initial burden is on the directors, and the courts look first at the reasonableness test that focuses on the good faith determination of the threat to the target. The use of a majority of independent directors enhances the proof. The threat is often based on the belief that the bidder has offered insufficient value, but other threats are possible.[107] It could involve the hostile bid depriving

---

electing a majority of directors at one annual meeting. When the bidder sought to elect two directors at the annual meeting (they were successful) and amend the bylaws to increase the number of directors by 4 (they were unsuccessful), the incumbent directors used their power prior to the election to amend the by laws to increase the number of directors by 2 (from 5 to 7) and then select directors to fill the 2 vacancies. The target directors were concerned that if some of the incumbent directors resigned then the bidder's directors if elected could gain control or possibly deadlock the board or their presence would create tension within the board. The actions by the board increasing the board to 7 would not have precluded the bidder from taking control. If the bidder was successful in adding the 4 new directors it proposed in addition to the 2 it did elect it, the bidder would have elected 6 of the 11 (original 5 plus 2 added by the directors plus 4 if the bidder had prevailed). Thus directors expansion of the board with 2 directors did not preclude the possibility of gaining control by the bidder. This was unlike *Blausius* where the directors did try to preclude insurgents from taking control of the board. Even though the bidder only won 2 directors the board increase from 5 to 7 intiated by the directors would have diminished the bidder's influence on the board and undermine shareholder voting. Thus this action had a primary purpose of interfering with the shareholder vote in electing directors. See discussion of *Blausius* at § 5.05[D], *supra*.

[105] *Blausius* could apply even if the defensive tactic does not actually prevent the election of directors or there is no outright challenge to control.

[106] If the directors are acting out of a conflict of interest like in Revlon then the duty of loyalty would apply. *See* note 81, *supra*.

[107] In *Ivanhoe Partners v. Newmont Mun. Corp.*, 535 A.2d 1334 (Del. 1987), the Delaware Supreme Court indicated that "the board may under appropriate circumstances consider the inadequacy of the bid, the nature and timing of the offer, questions of illegality, the impact on constituencies other than shareholders, the risk of nonconsummation, and the basic shareholders'

target shareholders of a superior alternative (an opportunity loss), treating non-tendering shareholders differently and distorting shareholder choice (structural coercion like *Unocal*) or the shareholders may tender to an undervalued tender offer because shareholders disbelieve management's view (substantive coercion like *Unitrin*).[108] The court then looks at the proportionality of the target's response to the threat. Under *Unitrin*,[109] if the defensive tactic is viewed as draconian (that is, either preclusive of tender offers or coercive to shareholders), it will be closely scrutinized and will likely fail. If the response is less than draconian, then the judicial scrutiny looks at the range of reasonableness (that is, whether the tactic was proper and proportionate to the threat). In that case, there will be judicial restraint and the court will not usually substitute its judgment for that of the directors.

If the corporation seeks to sell itself by initiating active bidding, abandons a long-term strategy and seeks alternatives that include the breakup of the business (*Revlon*), or attempts to effect a change of control (*QVC*), then the *Revlon* duty of getting the best available price for the shareholders will apply. Without a change of control or breakup, there appears to be no general obligation to sell the corporation, even if a premium that reflects a fair price is offered by a bidder. This is especially true when the tender offer upsets a business plan.[110]

Actions by directors that are unilateral and whose primary purpose is to interfere or impede the effective exercise of the shareholders' franchise in a contested election are also carefully scrutinized by the courts. Under *MM Compnaies* when the defensive action's primary purpose is to interfere or impede shareholder voting, the *Blausius* compelling justification test applies and must be a condition precedent before scrutinizing the directors' response.[111] If shareholders are involved in the approval of the defensive tactics, that will also influence the level of scrutiny.[112]

The overall effect of Delaware's judicial deference to most defensive tactics makes a direct hostile tender offer by a bidder unlikely. Instead a bidder will either negotiate to remove the defensive tactics or announce a hostile offer but also initiate a proxy fight to elect new directors who will remove the defensive tactics. When the tactics are removed then there can be a friendly acquisition.[113] Many of the defensive tactics can be removed by the directors but only prior to the bidder purchasing a specific amount of shares (found in the poison pill or

interests at stake, including the past actions of the bidder and its affiliates in other takeover contests." *Id.* at 1341–42.

[108] Ronald J. Gilson & Reinier Kraakman, *Delaware's Intermediate Standard for Defensive Tactics: Is There Substance to Proportionality Review?*, 44 Bus. Law. 247, 267 (1989).

[109] *Unitrin, Inc. v. American General Corp.*, 651 A.2d 1361 (Del. 1995).

[110] *Paramount Communications, Inc. v. Time, Inc.*, 571 A.2d 1140 (Del. 1989).

[111] For a discussion of shareholder voting and tender offers, see § 12.05[A][7], *supra.* For a discussion of shareholder democracy, see § 5.05[D], *supra.*

[112] For a discussion of shareholder ratification, see § 9.06, *supra.*

[113] A bidder could make a tender offer conditional or a successful proxy fight to change to board and redeem any defenses. For a discussion of a proxy fight to facilitate an acquisition, see § 5.05[C][2], *supra.*

possibly in a state statute).[114] Thus, the bidder will usually purchase as many shares as it can without reaching the limit prescribed that precludes the new board from removing the defensive tactic. Institutional shareholders often play an important role in supporting the bid or trying to change the defensive tactics.[115]

[9]   Judicial Scrutiny of Deal Protection

In the context of friendly acquisitions, an acquirer may only be willing to make an offer to buy a corporation if it can be assured of success. The fear is that through their efforts and interest in the corporation, someone else may come in to compete and acquire the corporation. The corporation to be acquired may also want to induce the acquirer to make an offer. In order to minimize this result, parties will contract "lock up" provisions that will try to assure the deal. In some cases the acquirer may seek to lock up the deal by restricting the ability of the corporation to accept another offer by a "no shop" provision or a limitation on providing information to the other bidder. They may also seek compensation for making their bid through a termination fee or an option to buy shares[116] or other corporate assets[117] that will come into play if there is another bidder. Under *Revlon*, if there is a sale or change of control or the breakup of the company is inevitable or the target initiates active bidding, then such lockups are inoperative and the directors are obligated to sell at the highest price.[118] But many merger transactions do not implicate *Revlon*; should the courts use the business judgment rule or the enhanced scrutiny of *Unocal* to deal protection devices in that context?

In *Omnicare, Inc. v. NCS Healthcare, Inc.*,[119] NCS was the subject of competing bids by Omnicare and Genesis Health Ventures, Inc. ("Genesis").

---

[114] Poison pills have a triggering amount which that when met makes the tender offer difficult. For a discussion of poison pills, see § 12.04[B][1], *supra*. Some state statutes designed to make a hostile bid more difficult also have a triggering amount. For example, Delaware's business combination statute becomes effective with a 15% or more purchase of shares. *See* note 150, *infra*.

[115] For example, institutions have initiated shareholder proposals (which tend to be advisory) or amendments to the bylaws (which tend to be mandatory) that limit the defensive tactics of directors. *See* note 58, *supra*. For a discussion of proxy fights to change policy, see § 5.05[C][3], *supra*.

[116] The tactic is effective because the compensation may be expensive enough to thwart another bidder. In *QVC* Viacom negotiated a $100 million termination fee and an option to buy 24 million Paramount shares (19.9% of Paramount). As a result of QVC's higher competing bid this option was worth approximately $500 million to Viacom if QVC's offer was accepted. The Delaware Supreme Court applied *Revlon* and affirmed the lower court's injunction on the option and did not address the issue of the termination fee that was found to be reasonable by the lower court. For a discussion of *QVC*, see § 12.05[A][5], *supra*.

[117] In *Revlon* the court invalidated an asset lock up given to the white knight that allowed it to purchase divisions of Revlon at a discount if it failed to acquire the corporation. According to the court a lock-up is not *per se* illegal under Delaware law and can entice other bidders to enter a contest for control of the corporation, creating an auction for the company and maximizing shareholder profit. However lockups which end an active auction and foreclose further bidding operate to the shareholders' detriment. *Revlon, Inc. v. MacAndrews & Forbes Holdings*, 506 A.2d 173, 184 (Del. Sup 1985).

[118] For a discussion of *Revlon*, see § 12.05[A][3], *supra*.

[119] 818 A2d 914 (Del 2003).

NCS had two classes of shares with Class A having 10 votes and Class B one vote per share. NCS had been going through difficult times and was in default on its debt obligations. Its stock was trading in a range from $.09 to $.50. Over almost a two year period NCS was unable to find an appropriate solution to its problems until Omnicare offered to acquire NCS in an asset purchase in bankruptcy. The amount offered would not have been enough to provide any recovery to NCS's shareholders and was felt to be inadequate. Genesis was also interested in NCS. NCS board appointed an independent committee of directors to negotiate a possible sale of the corporation.[120] Genesis was concerned that its negotiations with NCS would be a "stalking horse" for another acquirer. They planned to provide for some recovery for the shareholders. But they demanded an exclusivity agreement with NCS before negotiating and it was granted. The protective devices provided that the directors were bound to submit any Genesis merger to a shareholder vote.[121] Genesis also required that the majority shareholders, Outcalt and Shaw (their control was in owning the super majority Class A shares and not a majority of the equity), enter a shareholder agreement where they obligated themselves to vote in favor of the Genesis offer which meant that the required majority shareholder vote in a merger was secured.[122] Because of these protections a higher bid from another bidder was impossible unless the directors had a fiduciary out provision allowing them to act.

Omnicare discovered that NCS was in negotiations and was concerned that it could be sold to a competitor like Genesis. Omnicare made its proposal that also included payments to shareholders but, because of the exclusivity provision with Genesis, the committee did not respond. The committee felt a response would violate the exclusivity agreement which could drive Genesis away. But the offer from Omnicare was used to extract a higher bid from Genesis. Genesis demanded an immediate acceptance or it would walk away. The committee met and unanimously agreed to the Genesis proposal followed by the approval of the entire board. They weighed the certainty of the Genesis offer and the fear that they could walk away possibly leaving them with no deal.

Omnicare sought to enjoin the merger and announced a tender offer for the shares of NCS. Genesis allowed NCS to enter into discussions with Omnicare and eventually a new deal was struck with Omnicare by the board committee. But Genesis maintained that under its merger agreement the NCS was binding that it must be submitted for a shareholder vote even if it was not approved by the board and an inferior deal. Since Genesis already had the majority vote through the shareholder agreement with the controlling shareholders, they would succeed.

---

[120] The independent board committee had no employees or major shareholders of NCS. Because of the precarious financial condition and close to insolvency it was believed that the fiduciary duty of the board included the corporation as a whole and not just to shareholders. Insolvency usually means that the shareholders are wiped out and no longer the owners. For a discussion of fiduciary duty in the zone of insolvency, see § 5.02[A], *supra*.

[121] Under the Delaware statute a merger can be submitted for a shareholder vote even if the approval of the board of directors is withdrawn later. Del. Gen. Corp. L. § 251(c).

[122] The shareholder agreement granted an irrevocable proxy to Genesis to vote the shares which made the contract enforceable. For a discussion of the use of irrevocable proxies in shareholder agreements often used in closely held corporations, see § 11.02[C], *supra*.

The Delaware Supreme Court in analyzing the legal issues needed to determine what standard of judicial scrutiny should apply. The court discussed how the usual standard for an arms-length bargain transaction is the business judgment rule but recognized that in some case greater scrutiny may be required before the rule applies. For example, the *Unocal* modified business judgment or proportionality standard applies to defensive tactics in a hostile takeovers. Further there are *Revlon* duties that come into play when there is a change of control, the target initiates an active bidding contest or the breakup of the company is inevitable. The court analyzed the deal protection devices in the Genesis merger under a *Unocal* standard of review with enhanced scrutiny and not under *Revlon*.[123] That scrutiny looks at the process including the information used and reasonableness of the circumstances with the burden on the directors. Applying the two step *Unocal* test the court first looked at the threat which was that Genesis offer would have been lost without any comparable firm offer and then was the response reasonable to the threat. Under *Unitrin* there is closer scrutiny when the response is draconian as either coercive or preclusive. Here the court found the response was both coercive and preclusive because the shareholders had to accept the Genesis merger as a fait accompli because of the deal protection devices.[124] Even though the board removed its recommendation of the merger and recommended against the merger, it was of no avail because of the requirement that there be a shareholder vote on the Genesis merger and the shareholder agreement giving them the required majority vote.

The court also found the deal protection provisions unenforceable as being invalid because the provisions operated to prevent the board from exercising its fiduciary duty to minority shareholders when a better deal was presented by Omnicare. Thus NCS board had no authority to "lock up" with Genesis. The directors are obligated to negotiate for a fiduciary out clauses in the merger agreement so they can accept a better offer. According to the court, the board is empowered to give a bidder reasonable structural and economic defenses and incentives and fair compensation if the acquirer loses out to another bidder. But they must be economic and reasonable and they cannot limit the directors' fiduciary duty. There is no authority for an absolute lockup without a fiduciary out clause. Thus fiduciary out clause are now the norm for merger agreements even though the create uncertainty for an acquirer succeeding.

This case produced a rare dissent of two judges in the Delaware Supreme Court who would have under the facts of this case deferred to the board that was independent and acted in good faith and in an informed manner. The actions by the board and controlling shareholders were in the context of insolvency and creditor pressures and should not have been subject to judicial ex post review

---

[123] The lower court determined that *Revlon* would not apply because there was no change of control and NCS had not initiated a bidding contest.

[124] It would be coercive if it forces shareholders into an alternative. It would be preclusive if it deprives shareholders of the right to the tender offer or precludes the bidder from seeking control through a proxy contest. The dissent did not think that the fact that the majority shareholder was bound to vote for the Genesis merger was coercive to the minority shareholders nor was the kind of preclusion that raises concerns under *Unitrin* which focused on the board's unilateral actions that did involve shareholders.

The dissent sees value in lockups. The lock up allows for some certainty which has value. The acquirer may pay a higher price if they are assured of the deal and the target benefits from the certainty of the transaction. If the acquirer does not bid then the opportunity may be lost and may result in a negative perception of the target. The dissent disliked the bright line test of the majority requiring a fiduciary out clause.[125] Their view is the *Unocal* should not apply but the business judgment rule and that this case should have limited application.[126]

§ 12.06   FEDERAL SECURITIES LAW — THE WILLIAMS ACT

Generally, corporate law is an issue of state law,[127] but there are clear areas in which federal interests in interstate commerce and, more particularly, the functioning of the public markets for securities have resulted in legislative and regulatory developments at the federal level that do regulate corporate behavior.[128] A prime example can be seen in the area of tender offers.

[A]   History

Hostile tender offers for shares of public corporations involve extensive use of interstate facilities and are accomplished through the purchase of publicly traded securities. During the 1960s, tender offers were often announced after the stock markets closed on a Friday, with the period open for tenders to close early the next week, sometimes even on Monday. These so-called "Saturday night specials" were felt by Congress to frustrate the federal interest in informed investment decision-making by forcing shareholders to make up their minds about tendering their shares very quickly, and without information adequate to evaluate the offer or the bidder. Other techniques by which control was acquired were also deemed inappropriate to our capital market structure. For example, no requirements existed that ownership of shares be disclosed before an accumulation of an amount equal to a controlling block was assembled. Congress also felt that this kind of "secret" transfer of control did not comport with the model of full and fair disclosure contemplated by the securities laws. In addition, state corporate law which deals with the relationship between shareholders and directors of the target was either ineffective or inapplicable to the relationship between a target and a hostile bidder. "Saturday night specials"

---

[125] *See* Sean J. Griffith, *The Costs and Benefits of Precommitment: An Appraisal of* Omnicare v. NCS Healthcare, 29 J. Corp. L. 569 (2004) (argues against a bright line test and the hostility to precommitment strategies will harm shareholder welfare).

[126] In *Orman v. Cullman*, 2004 Del. Ch. LEXIS 150 (Oct. 20, 2004), the court found that the controlling shareholders agreement to vote against any competing merger for 18 months was not illegal because the contract was entered into by shareholders and not the directors. In addition the minority shareholders had the power to reject the proposed deal. The fact that such a rejection would mean no future deal for 18 months might influence the shareholder vote but did not make the lockup illegal.

[127] There are some limited federal incorporations laws. *See* § 1.09, note 54, *supra*. The Supreme Court has said the relationship between corporations and their shareholders is a matter traditionally relegated to state law. For a discussion of the *Sante Fe* case, see § 10.03[D][2], *supra*.

[128] For a discussion of federalism, see § 5.02[H], *supra*.

and secret accumulations of control, to the extent Congress found them to be abusive practices, were beyond the scope of state law.

In 1968, Congress responded to these perceived problems by enacting the Williams Act, which amended Sections 13 and 14 of the 1934 Exchange Act.[129] Much of the legislation, like federal securities regulations in general, focuses on disclosure. However, the Williams Act and the rules promulgated thereunder contain a variety of both procedural and substantive rules that govern the conduct of tender offers, by either a bidder or self tender by the target.[130]

[B]　Disclosure Rules

The disclosure scheme starts with Section 13(d), which requires any person who acquires more than 5% of a class of equity securities of a public corporation to file a disclosure statement with the SEC within 10 days of the purchase.[131] The statement includes the identity of the purchaser, the number of shares owned, when purchased, how paid for, and the intentions of the purchaser with regard to the company. This information must be updated when there are changes in the information disclosed. This disclosure provides the target, its shareholders, the market and the SEC with notice of a possible takeover attempt. These disclosures are intended to prevent "secret" accumulations of control.

Once a tender offer commences other statutory provisions come into play.[132] For example, § 14(d)[133] requires the bidder to file materials used in connection with the offer with the SEC and requires a disclosure statement similar to, but more extensive than, required by § 13(d) which must be distributed to the shareholders of the target.[134] Target management is required to make a recommendation to the shareholders regarding the tender offer[135] and is also

---

[129] Williams Act, Pub. L. No. 90-439, 82 Stat. 454 (1968) (codified as amended at 15 U.S.C. §§ 78m(d)-(e), 78n(d)-(f) (1982)). *See generally* Marc I. Steinberg, Understanding Securities Law § 13.04 (3rd ed. 2001).

[130] A company may make an offer to purchase its own shares from its existing shareholders. This kind of transaction, called a "self-tender," might occur for a variety of reasons, for example, to effect a partial recapitalization of the company unrelated to the market for corporate control. Self-tenders may also occur, however, as defensive measures in anticipation of or in response to a hostile bid, or as an alternative to one. *See, e.g.,* note 80, *supra.* Such transactions have been governed since 1979 by Rule 13e-4. Rule 13e-4 sets up a scheme for issuers which parallels in most respects that established by § 14(d) and the rules thereunder for third party tender offers.

[131] 15 U.S.C § 78m(d) (1982). A copy of the form must be sent to the company whose shares are the subject of the filing, and to the principal exchange on which the security trades.

[132] The term "tender offer" is not defined by the statute or in the regulations. Courts have attempted to define the term by reference to the factors that Congress cited in setting forth the dangers to the federal interest which gave rise to the Williams Act. *Wellman v. Dickinson,* 475 F. Supp. 783 (S.D.N.Y. 1979) (uses an eight factor test). The absence of a definition in the statute allows for application of the law to novel situations that Congress intended to regulate.

[133] 15 U.S.C. § 78n(d) (1982).

[134] Schedule 14D-1.

[135] Rule 14e-2.

required to prepare, file and send a disclosure document[136] in connection with its recommendation.

[C]   Other Rules

Generally speaking, once a tender offer is commenced,[137] it must remain open for the receipt of share tenders for at least twenty business days, which may be extended by the bidder and will be automatically extended in the event the bidder changes its terms.[138] Shareholders who tender their shares have the right to withdraw their shares at any time while the tender offer remains open.[139] This right of withdrawal enables target shareholders to tender into a competing bid during the time the offer remains open. If a bidder seeks to purchase less than all of the outstanding shares of the target it does not own, and if more shares are tendered into the offer than the bidder wishes to purchase, it must purchase its shares from each of the tendering shareholders on a pro rata basis and at the same price.[140] In addition, tender offers subject to the Williams Act must be open to all the holders of the class of securities sought.[141]

[D]   Section 14(e)

Section 14(e) is an anti-fraud provision that prohibits material misstatements and omissions and manipulation and fraudulent practices "in connection with any tender offer."[142] Section 14(e) was often a major focus of hostile tender offer litigation, given its broad language and the usual claim that the parties have failed to fully disclose all material facts.[143]

---

[136] Schedule 14d-9.

[137] The date of "commencement" of a tender offer is important in defining the parties' obligations under the Williams Act, and is defined in Rule 14d-2.

[138] Rule 14e-1. Any increases in the consideration prior to the expiration of the offer must be offered to be paid to those who have previously tendered. § 14(d)(7).

[139] § 14(d)(5). After 60 days the bidder must return the shares tendered that have not been paid for to prevent the bidder from tying up the shares.

[140] § 14(d)(6); Rule 14d-8. This is a limited equal opportunity rule. For a discussion of equal opportunity in sale of control cases, see § 10.04[B], *supra*.

[141] Rule 14d-10. The rule (known as the "all holders rule") requires that the consideration paid must be the highest paid to the class during the tender offer. The rule was added by the SEC in direct response to the holding of the Delaware Supreme Court in *Unocal* which upheld under state corporate law the validity of a tender offer that excluded the bidder. See § 12.05[A][2], *supra*.

[142] 15 U.S.C. § 78n(e) (1982). Many of the Williams Act rules apply only to tender offers of corporations that are publicly traded and subject to § 12(g) of the 1934 Act (companies listed on a national exchange or with 500 shareholders and $10 million in assets). Section 14(e) is not so limited. Section 14(e) empowers the SEC to issue rules. One such rule is SEC Rule 14e-3, which deals with insider trading and tender offers. For a discussion, see § 13.04[C], *supra*.

[143] Private litigants are not given an express remedy under § 14(e), but most courts imply a cause of action for at least equitable relief. In *Piper v. Chris-Craft Indus. Inc.*, 430 U.S. 1 (1973), the Supreme Court denied an action for damages for a defeated bidder but did not preclude equitable relief for the bidder or an implied private cause of action for damages for target shareholders. *Id.* at 42, 47–48. The Court emphasized that the Williams Act was enacted for the protection of target shareholders, which would not have been furthered by an action for damages by the bidder. *Id.* at 35.

As discussed above, management of targets have devised a broad range of defensive tactics in response to hostile tender offers. Litigation was brought under § 14(e), claiming that its prohibition of manipulative, deceptive and fraudulent acts or practices should work to prohibit the use of some of these tactics or provide a cause of action for shareholders for damages when a tender offer was withdrawn or changed as a result of the target's defensive actions. Bidders and target shareholders have argued that defensive tactics artificially affected the market for the target's shares and constituted manipulative conduct under § 14(e). They have also argued that actions depriving shareholders of an opportunity to tender were fraudulent under § 14(e).

In *Schreiber v. Burlington Northern, Inc.*,[144] the Supreme Court found that based on its language, § 14(e) was not intended by Congress to require more than full disclosure. Thus, activities that are challenged as fundamentally issues of substantive fairness or breaches of fiduciary duty are not governed by the Williams Act but by state law.[145] Thus, litigants may argue under the Williams Act that there was a lack of disclosure concerning the defensive tactic.[146] Substantive unfairness is not a disclosure defect and therefore is not cognizable under § 14(e).

§ 12.07 STATE TAKEOVER STATUTES

[A] Introduction

State legislatures reacted to the rise of hostile tender offers by enacting statutes that generally have the effect of restricting such offers. The first generation of statutes was designed to directly thwart the tender offer and could apply to corporations incorporated in another state. The second generation statutes, enacted after *Edgar v. MITE Corp.*,[147] limit their application to corporations incorporated in the state and with a significant presence, and provide a regulatory format similar to other corporate rules. These statutes evolved and took a variety of forms in different states.[148] In some cases the statute permits the corporation to either opt in or opt out of its coverage. There are disclosure statutes that are similar to the Williams Act but

---

For a discussion of implied causes of action under federal securities law, see § 7.06[C], *supra.*

[144] 472 U.S. 1 (1985).

[145] The Court's reasoning in *Schreiber* is similar to that used in *Santa Fe v. Green* in limiting the scope of actions under Rule 10b-5. See discussion at § 10.03[D][2], *infra.*

[146] There are certain disclosure obligations under the Williams Act that may affect defensive tactics. For example, under SEC Rule 14d-9, targets seeking protection from a tender offer by finding another bidder, may be required to disclose those negotiations.

[147] 457 U.S. 624 (1982) (the Supreme Court found a first generation statute unconstitutional). For a discussion of *Edgar*, see § 12.07[C][1], *infra.*

[148] *See generally* Arthur Pinto, *The Constitution and the Market for Corporate Control: State Takeover Statutes After CTS Corp.,* 29 WILL. & MARY L. REV. 699 (1988). There is also a fourth generation statute that applies to corporations not incorporated in the state (called foreign corporations), but with some other substantial nexus, such as the location of the headquarters. Whether these statutes violate the Commerce Clause is unclear as a result of the rational of the *CTS* case. *See id.* at 754-778.

require additional information by a bidder. There are constituency statutes that allow or require the directors to consider interests other than shareholders, such as employees and creditors when responding to a tender offer or to take a long term view for the corporation.[149] Some statutes expressly permit the adoption of poison pills as a defensive tactic or explicitly adopt the business judgment rule for defensive tactics. Fair price statutes require an offer of a fair price to all shareholders and preclude front-loaded two-tier offers. Cash-out statutes allow the shareholders to demand that a bidder after purchasing a certain percentage of shares buy the remaining shares at the highest price paid, which discouraged partial bids for the corporation.

The third generation statutes do not directly try to regulate the tender offer but allow the bidder to tender for as many shares as it likes but severely restrict the use of those shares unless the target board approves the offer. For example, a voting rights statute requires a disinterested shareholder vote to give voting rights to a bidder who bought a substantial number of shares without board approval (the board may also force a redemption of the shares by the corporation). The additional time required for the shareholder vote and the possibility of purchasing shares without voting rights made hostile bids more difficult.

There is also a business combination statute that requires board approval of purchases of shares over a certain percentage otherwise the bidder may be precluded from a subsequent business combination with the target for many years[150] The bidder is free to make a tender offer but after acquiring shares over the percentage, failure to get board approval limits the bidder's options. For example, the bidder could not effectuate a business combination (such as a freezeout merger) to acquire the shares that were not tendered in order to own 100% of the target. Even if the tender offer seeks 100% of the shares, there will always be some shareholders who do not tender. Complete ownership may be necessary to facilitate borrowing (that is, leveraging) to finance the bid.[151] Under these statutes the bidder has to wait years before being able to do a business combination.[152]

---

[149] The constituency statutes allow the directors to consider interests other than shareholders when faced with a takeover. This also rekindles the debate over corporate responsibility and the purpose of a corporation. See discussion at § 5.02[A], *supra.*

[150] Delaware's response was important because so many large corporations are incorporated there. It enacted Del. Gen. Corp. Law § 203 which is a version of the business combination statute and applies to corporations incorporated in Delaware. The law requires a bidder (1) after acquiring 15% of a target's voting shares, to either have received board approval for the purchase or for future business combinations with the bidder; or (2) to purchase at least 85% of the target's shares (excluding shares owned by inside directors and certain employees shares option plans) in the same transaction in which the bidder exceeded 15%; or (3) to receive board approval for the business combination along with the vote of 2/3 of the disinterested shareholders. Failure to meet these requirements restricts the bidder from effectuating a business combination with the target for up to three years.

[151] Poison pills can also limit the bidder's ability to acquire 100% of the target. See the discussion of "flip over" poison pills at § 12.04[B][1], *supra.*

[152] Under New York's business combination statute it would take 5 years. N.Y.B.C.L. § 912.

[B]   Policy Issues

These statutes raise several issues, some of which parallel the debate over hostile tender offers. State legislatures usually acted in response to the disruptive effects tender offers have on local investors and local industry, including the relocation of assets and jobs to other states. In many cases a statute was explicitly passed in the context of a tender offer for a local publicly traded company.[153] Much of the legislation is inconsistent with the view that the market for corporate control is beneficial. Indeed, many of the statutes were designed as additional defensive weapons for management's use in fighting hostile tender offers. While the laws may not preclude offers, they increase the costs of tender offers, which may limit their number and thus reduce the benefits of the market for corporate control.[154] However, some of these statutes arguably enhance shareholder interests.[155] Since many of the statutes permit the directors to opt out of their provisions, they may force a bidder to negotiate with the directors to avoid the statute's effect. This may allow the directors to extract a higher price from the bidder or create time to find another bidder to offer a higher price. The statutes may also be used to restrict harmful tactics employed by bidders.[156]

These statutes have raised the question of the role of the federal government in corporate governance. Although there were calls for Congress to enact federal legislation to supersede some or all of these state statutes, Congress declined to do so. The strong tradition of state corporate law and the fact that many state and federal politicians felt that tender offers were not beneficial, meant that these statutes remained.

As a result of the pro-management bias of many of these statutes, the tactics of tender offers changed around them. These statutes, combined with the use of poison pills, force bidders to purchase shares of the target below the threshold that precludes a board from action on the defensive tactic, then start a proxy fight initially to replace the directors or to pressure the directors to change their view of the offer. If the directors change their view of the tender offer or the proxy fight is successful, the board could respond positively to the takeover and opt out of the statute or redeem the poison pill.[157]

---

[153] *See* Roberta Romano, *The Political Economy of Takeover Statutes*, 73 Va. L. Rev. 111 (1987).

[154] *See, e.g.*, Jonathan Macey, *State Anti-Takeover Legislation and the National Economy*, 1988 Wisc. L. Rev. 467.

[155] There is a debate over whether these statutes are harmful to target shareholders. Roberta A. Romano, *supra* note 153, at 182–86 (concluding no significant effect on the value of target firms in certain states enacting statutes). *But see* Jo Watson Hackle & Rosa Anna Testani, *Note: Second Generation State Takeover Statutes and Shareholder Wealth*, 97 Yale L.J. 1193 (1988) (finding some statutes decrease a target's value).

[156] For example, statutes requiring a fair price for all the target shares eliminate the coercive front-loaded two-tier offer because the bidder may no longer offer a higher premium to buy control and then pay a lower price for the remaining shares in a second-step merger. *See also* Richard Booth, *The Promise of State Takeover Statutes*, 86 Mich. L. Rev. 1635(1988).

[157] For example, under Delaware's business combination statute, purchases of 15% or more of the target's shares restricts the bidder unless there was board approval prior to the purchase. *See* note 150, *supra.* A bidder could purchase 14.9% of the target's shares and then start a proxy fight to

The enactments of these takeover statutes created somewhat of a dilemma for the law and economics view of corporate law. That view believes that markets should be the primary protection for shareholders. One such market is the one for corporate charters, which was viewed as protecting shareholders because the states compete in that market, offering regulation that protects shareholders in order to attract the incorporations.[158] Under that thesis, state takeover statutes must be beneficial otherwise states would see corporations reincorporating to avoid their harmful effects. Yet these statutes clearly were intended to limit the market for corporate control, which law and economics scholars believe is also important to shareholder protection.[159]

[C]   Constitutionality

These statutes also raise two issues of a federal constitutional dimension. One is whether Congress in enacting the Williams Act exercised its exclusive power to regulate tender offers and thus preempted these statutes under the Constitution's supremacy clause.[160] Since Congress did not explicitly preempt state law, the issue becomes whether compliance with both federal and state law is impossible or the state law is an obstacle to the purpose of the federal law. The second issue is whether these statutes violate the Constitution's commerce clause by unreasonably burdening interstate commerce.[161]

[1]   The *Edgar* Case

The Supreme Court faced these questions in two cases and the opinions reflect the underlying policy debate on tender offers. In *Edgar v. Mite Corp.*,[162] a majority of the Court found a first generation Illinois statute violated the commerce clause. The statute gave power to a state official to enjoin a nationwide tender for being unfair or for lacking full disclosure. The statute was found to impose an excessive burden upon interstate commerce when compared to the State's interests. The burden was the statute's interference with nationwide tender offers, which adversely affected shareholders throughout the country and the economy overall. The Court's analysis accepted the benefits espoused by those favoring the market for corporate control, and viewed the statute's interference with that market as impermissible.[163] Illinois argued it

---

replace the board with directors who will approve the subsequent purchase. For a discussion of proxy fights to facilitate an acquisition, see § 5.05[C][2], *supra.*

[158] For a discussion of the market for corporate charters, see § 1.09, *supra.*

[159] *See generally* Arthur R. Pinto, *Takeover Statutes: The Dormant Commerce Clause and State Corporate Law,* 41 MIAMI L. REV. 473, 492–96 (1987).

[160] U.S. Const. art. VI, cl. 2.

[161] U.S. Const. art. I, § 8.

[162] 457 U.S. 624 (1982).

[163] The Court noted that the Illinois statute's frustration of hostile tender offers took away substantial benefits from shareholders who lost an opportunity to tender their shares at a premium; a reallocation of economic resources to their higher valued use which improves efficiency and competition was impeded; and an incentive for management to run the corporation well and keep the shares price high was diminished. 457 U.S. at 643. This approach reflects the law and economic view of the benefits of hostile tender offers. *See* § 12.03[A], *supra.*

had an interest in protecting investors, but the Court found that Illinois had no legitimate interest in protecting the nonresident shareholders affected by the statute. The State also argued it had an interest in regulating the internal affairs of corporations incorporated in Illinois.[164] The Court indicated that while a state has an interest in the internal affairs of companies incorporated there, a tender offer involved transfers of shares by or among shareholders, was not a matter of the internal affairs of the target. In addition the statute could apply to corporations not incorporated in Illinois but which had a significant presence in the state (e.g., location of its principal executive offices and 10% of its capital in Illinois). However, a majority did not find the statute preempted by the Williams Act.[165]

[2]　The *CTS* Case

Five years later, in *CTS Corp. v. Dynamics Corp. of America*[166] the Court upheld an Indiana statute that differed from the Illinois statute, but had the practical effect of limiting a bidder's ability to conduct a hostile tender offer. The statute only applied to corporations incorporated in Indiana and did not involve direct regulation of the tender offer. Instead the statute was a third generation statute directed at what happens after the shares are acquired by a bidder. The statute dealt with voting rights, a matter within the internal affairs of a company and traditionally regulated by the incorporating state. The Indiana statute provided that if anyone bought more than a certain percentage of shares, constituting "control shares," they would need to get shareholder approval from the other disinterested shareholders in order to have voting rights in those shares.[167] The rationale for the law was to allow the shareholders to act collectively, by voting to ensure a fair tender offer and possibly to avoid coercive bids.

Thus, the statute did not legally prohibit a tender offer as the Illinois statute in *Edgar* did. Yet, it effectively limited acquisitions because, without voting rights, control is divorced from the acquisition of even a majority of the shares. If the shareholders voted to permit the acquisition and allow voting rights, shareholder approval could take up to 50 days creating delays, uncertainty and raising costs for a bidder.

The Court upheld the statute. It rejected the preemption argument because the tender offer could take place within the time requirements of the Williams Act. The statute did not favor either side in the tender offer, but instead protected shareholders, which was the basic purpose of the Williams Act. The statute was also found not to unreasonably burden interstate commerce because although the law could hinder tender offers, voting rights were a traditional

---

[164] For a discussion of the internal affairs doctrine, see § 1.09, *supra*.

[165] A plurality opinion argued that the delays caused by the Illinois statute favored target management and was preempted because Congress had intended neutrality in tender offers and the statute violated that purpose. *Id.* at 630–40.

[166] 481 U.S. 69 (1987).

[167] Ind. Code § 23-1-42-1 to -11 (Supp. 1986). *See, e.g., id.* § 23-1-42-1. The statute requires a shareholder vote to vest voting rights at three thresholds of ownership: 20%, 33 1/3%, and 50%. *Id.*

state corporate law concern. So long as both residents and nonresidents had equal access to shares, the Court would not interfere with state regulation of a corporation's internal affairs since that could also affect other corporate governance regulation.[168]

The *CTS* decision means that most state tender offer statutes that do not directly regulate the tender offer and which apply to targets incorporated in the state will be constitutional.[169] It is interesting to note that *Edgar* was decided in 1982 when tender offers were accelerating and deregulation was in vogue. *CTS* was decided in 1987 when the general attitude towards hostile tender offers and their effects was becoming more negative. Contemporaneously, there were notorious insider trading scandals involving individuals who misused tender offer information. The attitude of the opinions in the two Supreme Court cases reflects the evolution of the broader debate over hostile tender offers. In *Edgar*, the Court accepted the market for corporate control rationale, while in *CTS* the Court says that the Constitution "does not require the States to subscribe to any particular economic theory."[170]

After the *CTS* case, the most significant judicial view of state takeover statutes has been the Seventh Circuit decision in *Amanda Acquisition Corp. v. Universal Foods Corp.*[171] The court upheld a Wisconsin business combination statute against attack on both preemption and commerce clause grounds. The business combination statute limited a bidder, who had not received the target directors' approval, from merging with the target or using the target's assets for three years. This delay substantially affected a bidder who planned to use the target assets to fund the offer and to restructure the target. While the court clearly did not like the statute because of its limitations on hostile tender offers, the statute did not adversely affect the process of the actual tender offer that the Williams Act was intended to protect. The court engaged in no balancing under the commerce clause because the incorporating state had the power under the internal affairs doctrine to regulate mergers.[172] Thus, statutes that affect tender offers but do not directly interfere with the tender offer itself, and that limit their application to corporations incorporated in their state, should be constitutional.

---

[168] As the Court indicated: "It thus is an accepted part of the business landscape in this country for states to create corporations, to prescribe their powers, and to define the rights that are acquired by purchasing shares. A state has an interest in promoting stable relationships among parties involved in the corporations it charters, as well as ensuring that investors in such corporations have an effective voice in corporate affairs." 481 U.S. at 91.

[169] The *CTS* decision raises interesting questions about the extent to which a state, other than the incorporating state, can regulate corporations which have a major presence in the state. The decision seems to suggest that the commerce clause may limit regulatory power to only the incorporating state, which would invalidate many state corporate law provisions regulating foreign corporations incorporated in another state. *See* Pinto, *supra* note 148, at 754–78.

[170] 481 U.S. at 92.

[171] 877 F.2d 496 (7th Cir.), *cert. denied*, 493 U.S. 955 (1989).

[172] The court suggested that the statute's constitutionality did not depend on whether the law benefitted investors. The court believed that the market for corporate charters, where states compete for incorporation, would eventually provide a remedy. See the discussion in § 1.09, *supra.*

Chapter 13

SEC RULE 10b-5 DISCLOSURE AND INSIDER TRADING

§ 13.01 SEC RULE 10b-5 DISCLOSURE AND INSIDER TRADING

The SEC promulgated Rule 10b-5 in 1943, pursuant to authority granted by Section 10(b) of the Securities Exchange Act of 1934 ("1934 Act").[1] Since that time, Rule 10b-5 has been the general antifraud rule applicable to "the purchase or sale of any security." The rule prohibits material omissions or misleading statements, whether oral or written.[2] The latter may be in a formal prospectus or merger agreement, or in a handwritten sales pitch.

The rule is a true catchall. Even though an issuer or broker-dealer has complied with an SEC or self-regulatory organization form calling for item-and-answer disclosure,[3] Rule 10b-5 nonetheless applies and requires disclosure of any remaining material information. The Supreme Court has also held that securities law remedies, and in particular Rule 10b-5, are cumulative rather than alternative. Thus, a plaintiff alleging an omission or misleading statement in a formal prospectus filed with the SEC may pursue both the implied remedy under Rule 10b-5 and any applicable express remedy as well, such as that under Securities Exchange Act Section 11.[4] Rule 10b-5's jurisdictional means are very

---

[1] Securities Exchange Act of 1934 § 10(b) provides:

> It shall be unlawful for any person, directly or indirectly . . . [t]o use or employ, in connection with the purchase or sale of any security registered on a national securities exchange or any security not so registered, any manipulative or deceptive device or contrivance in contravention of such rules and regulations as the Commission may prescribe as necessary or appropriate in the public interest or for the protection of investors.

[2] SEC Rule 10b-5 provides;

> It shall be unlawful for any person, directly or indirectly, by the use of any means or instrumentality of interstate commerce, or of the mails, or any facility of any national securities exchange,
>
> (a) to employ any device, scheme, or artifice to defraud,
>
> (b) to make any untrue statement of a material fact or to omit to state a material fact necessary in order to make the statements made, in light of the circumstances under which they were made, not misleading, or
>
> (c) to engage in any act, practice, or course of business which operates or would operate as a fraud or deceit upon any person,
>
> in connection with the purchase or sale of any security.

[3] Examples include registration statements filed with the SEC when new securities are sold, or annual 10-K or quarterly 10-Q reports publicly held corporations file with the SEC. For discussion of requirements to file such documents, see § 7.02, *supra*.

[4] *Herman & MacLean v. Huddleston*, 459 U.S. 375 (1983). For discussion of the 1933 Act, see § 7.01, *supra*.

broad, prohibiting material misstatements or omissions "by the use of any means or instrumentality of interstate commerce, or of the mails, or of any facility of any national securities exchange." No requirement exists that the transaction itself be in interstate commerce. Use of the mails, telephone, or cyber-facilities in accomplishing the transaction will satisfy the jurisdictional means.[5] Because the rule prohibits conduct in connection with the purchase or sale of *"any"* security, the rule does not limit its scope to securities of publicly held corporations. The upshot of those two observations is that a misrepresentation in a wholly intrastate transaction, in the securities of a small or closely held corporation, may be actionable in federal court under SEC Rule 10b-5.[6]

Some observers refer to Rule 10b-5 as the "insider trading rule" although it covers a wide range of fraudulent activity beyond insider trading. Roughly speaking, insider trading involves use of nonpublic information by any person "having a relationship [director, officer, attorney] giving access, directly or indirectly, to information intended to be available only for a corporate purpose and not for the personal benefit of anyone."[7] By use of the information to trade or to tip others who trade, such person makes a gain, or in the case of trading on negative news, foregoes a loss by remaining silent when there is a duty to speak. Rule 10b-5 and its opaque provisions are the foundation stones for the entire insider trading edifice, at least under federal law.[8] This Chapter deals with insider trading and its prohibition at length.

Insider trading cases are a subset of a set of Rule 10b-5 cases, namely, cases of silence, rather than misstatement, by a person in a fiduciary or similar relationship. That set is a smallish part of the universe of potential Rule 10b-5 cases, which includes affirmative misstatements, half-truths, or omissions by any person (and not merely fiduciaries) in oral statements, informal writings, formal writings, and legal documents, including merger documents, prospectuses, other SEC filings, and so on.

The Rule's reach is illustrated by *The Wharf (Holdings) Ltd. v. United International Holdings, Inc.*[9] which holds that the Rule can quite easily extend to cases of promissory fraud. Wharf enlisted plaintiff United's assistance in applying for the cable television franchise in Hong Kong. To obtain assistance (United even sent employees to work in Hong Kong), and a standby commitment for a future capital infusion, Wharf granted United an option on 10 percent of the

---

[5] A wholly intrastate telephone call will suffice. *Myzel v. Fields*, 386 F.2d 718 (8th Cir. 1967), *cert. denied*, 390 U.S. 951 (1968). Use of any jurisdictional means in the transaction will do: the omission or misstatement need not necessarily be transmitted by such means. *See, e.g., United States v. Kunzman*, 54 F.3d 1522, 1527 (10th Cir. 1995).

[6] Such a suit will also have to be brought in federal court, as the Securities Exchange Act of 1934 ("1934 Act") provides for exclusive federal subject matter jurisdiction. 1934 Act § 27. Oddly enough, under the more convoluted Securities Act of 1933, state courts have concurrent jurisdiction with federal courts. Securities Act § 22.

[7] *In re Cady, Roberts & Co.*, 40 S.E.C. 907 (1961).

[8] The majority view is that state law prohibits insider trading, under an expanded form of the so-called special facts doctrine or under fiduciary duty generally. State law prohibition of insider trading is discussed in § 13.05, *infra*.

[9] 532 U.S. 588 (2001).

stock in the new venture, an oral (but detailed) promise United was able to show Wharf had no intention of ever fulfilling. Mr. Justice Breyer held that United's suit was more than a mere breach of contract action for a failure to deliver securities. It was securities fraud, governed by Rule 10b-5, because "United's claim . . . is not that Wharf failed to carry out a promise to sell it securities. It's claim is that Wharf sold it a security (the option) while secretly intending from the very beginning not to honor the option." United recovered $67 million in compensatory and $58.5 million in punitive damages.

This Chapter's first objective is to describe the concepts needed to navigate that large Rule 10b-5 universe. Chapter 7 contains an introduction to antifraud rules generally and discusses some of the same concepts, sometimes with a different focus. Rule 10b-5 has its own jurisprudence, such as in the areas of standing (the "purchaser-seller rule"), reliance (transaction causation) and reliance substitutes (fraud on the market theory), loss causation, and the "in connection with" requirement.[10]

This Chapter's second objective is to navigate the smaller Rule 10b-5 insider trading universe.

The insider trading exposition requires introduction of a third grouping of antifraud rule jurisprudential concepts. These include the nature of the insider trading prohibition, the definition of an insider, the tipper-tippee relationship, the misappropriation theory of insider trading, insider trading penalties (including criminal enforcement), and state law evolution of the prohibition against insider trading. The insider trading discussion must also ask whether insider trading should be prohibited at all. A respectable school of law professors and economists maintains that insider trading should be permitted, if not encouraged. To some extent, events have swept that school aside, as insider trading became "the" crime of the 1990s and the twenty-first century, and countries around the world have enacted prohibitions against insider trading, many basing their legislation on the U.S. common law model. The debate remains an interesting one.

§ 13.02   DISCLOSURE CONCEPTS AND ELEMENTS OF A CAUSE OF ACTION UNDER RULE 10b-5

[A]   Implication of Private Rights of Action

In 1946, a federal district court accepted the existence of an implied right of action under Rule 10b-5.[11] On several subsequent occasions, the Supreme Court ruled on issues in Rule 10b-5 cases without comment on the existence of a right by investors to sue for damages or for injunctive relief.[12]

---

[10] Many of these requirements stem from the requirements of a cause of action for deceit or fraud under common law. Under SEC Rule 10b-5, and other general securities law antifraud rules, federal courts have had to decide which of these common law requirements should be imported into federal securities law, either wholly or in relaxed form as requirements for plaintiffs.

[11] *Kardon v. National Gypsum Co.*, 69 F. Supp. 512 (E.D. Pa. 1946).

[12] *See, e.g., Affiliated Ute Citizens v. United States*, 406 U.S. 125 (1972); *Superintendent of Ins.*

A fair guess is that, if the issue were to arise for the first time today, the Supreme Court would hold that no private right of action exists, leaving enforcement of the rule to the SEC alone. However, in the 1979 case of *Touche Ross & Co. v. Redington*,[13] the Court noted its acquiescence "in the 25 year-old acceptance by the lower federal courts of an implied action under § 10(b)." In *Basic v. Levinson*,[14] the court re-affirmed that conclusion: "Judicial interpretation and application, legislative acquiescence, and the passage of time have removed any doubt that a private cause of action exists for a violation of § 10(b) and Rule 10b-5." Today the existence of a private right to sue under the rule is seldom questioned.[15]

[B]   Standing to Sue

Who would be harmed by a belated report of a spectacular mining discovery by a company which had earlier denied the find?[16] In *SEC v. Texas Gulf Sulphur Co.*, the information would have served investors well. Knowing that the price of TGS shares had risen from 30 to 58 1/4 in 32 days, all of the world could say they were harmed by the delayed release of the news of the mining discovery. Had potential investors known, they would have purchased TGS shares. The potential for fictitious claims, though, is obvious.

Standing requirements are used to limit the universe of potential claimants to those who probably have cognizable injury and among whom the chance for fabricated claims is less. The Rule 10b-5 standing rule would cut off even the limited class of plaintiffs who already owned TGS shares and who, because of the delayed release of the news, forwent additional TGS share purchases and profits. That is so, because the class of whose claims the antifraud rule will take cognizance is limited to those who have actually purchased or sold the security at issue. Early in the history of Rule 10b-5, Judge Augustus Hand crafted the "purchaser-seller," or so-called *Birnbaum*, rule to define the class of persons who probably had injury cognizable under the rule and among whom the chance of fictitious claims would be small.[17] Thus, although all potential investors could say they were harmed by the misleading and delayed report of the facts, none of them actually bought or sold securities. In *Texas Gulf Sulphur*, the class which could potentially recover was defined as consisting of those who *sold* on the basis of an earlier, misleading press release. That is the only class of persons, of all the classes of persons with potential harm, which could meet the standing rule.[18]

---

of the State of New York v. Bankers Life & Cas., 404 U.S. 6 (1971).

[13] 422 U.S. 560 (1977).

[14] 485 U.S. 224 (1988).

[15] For further discussion on implication of private rights under the federal securities laws, see § 7.06[C], *supra.*

[16] *See SEC v. Texas Gulf Sulphur Co.*, 401 F.2d 833 (2d Cir. 1968), *cert. denied*, 394 U.S. 976 (1969).

[17] *Birnbaum v. Newport Steel Co.*, 193 F.2d 461 (2d Cir. 1952). Judge Hand found the standing requirement subsumed in Section 10(b)'s language that the misleading statement or omission occur "in connection with the purchase or sale of any security."

[18] The defendant does not have to have been a purchaser or seller to be held liable under Rule

Persons who have been harmed may be cut off by the standing rule. For example, imagine an investor who owns shares of a thinly traded over-the-counter stock. She telephones her registered representative (usually called her broker) for a progress report. He tells her to "hold." Several day later, she notices that the trading volume is up and the price is down. Still later, negative news about the corporation is forthcoming. Still later yet, she learns that the broker had been tipping more favored clients to sell or had himself been liquidating a position. She has significant losses. She is the very type of person Rule 10b-5 is designed to protect. Nonetheless, she cannot invoke the rule: she neither purchased nor sold-she held-and she therefore has no standing.

Blue Chip Stamps v. Manor Drug Stores[19] is just such a case. Blue Chip had settled an antitrust action by means of a consent decree. The decree required Blue Chip to offer, on advantageous terms, shares in a reorganized Blue Chip to retailers who had used the stamp service in the past. Not wanting to share what apparently was a good deal, the "New Blue Chip" company painted a pessimistic picture for the offerees by disclosing high redemption rates for the trading stamps, which would severely depress profits.

Rule 10b-5 prohibits the very type of activity New Blue Chip had undertaken, but the plaintiff retailers had not purchased the securities. The fraudulent acts had caused them *not* to purchase. Under traditional Rule 10b-5 analysis, they had neither purchased nor sold and therefore lacked standing. Compelled by the equities, the Ninth Circuit carved out an exception to the purchaser-seller requirement. If plaintiffs were members of an identifiable group who had a contractual or other right to purchase or sell, and who had been victimized by fraud, they could sue under Rule 10b-5 despite the lack of a purchase or sale.

On appeal, the Supreme Court reaffirmed the purchaser-seller standing rule, noting that "litigation under Rule 10b-5 presents a danger of vexatiousness different in degree and kind from that which accompanies litigation in general." The purchaser-seller rule reduces the danger of vexatiousness simply by preventing "widely expanded class[es] of plaintiffs."

Limiting the class of plaintiffs is useful because "in the field of securities laws governing disclosure of information even a complaint which by objective standards has very little chance of success at trial has a [disproportionate] settlement value . . . ." Justice Rehnquist noted that "[t]he second ground for fear of vexatious litigation is based on the concern that, given the generalized contours of liability, the abolition of the *Birnbaum* rule would throw open to the trier of fact many rather hazy issues of historical fact the proof of which depended almost entirely on oral testimony." In other words, abolition of the purchaser-seller requirement would open courts to claims of "I would have purchased had I known" (or "I would have sold had I known").

In the absence of the *Birnbaum* doctrine, bystanders to the securities marketing process could await developments on the sidelines without risk,

---

10b-5. This aspect of the rule has been criticized because a corporation which issues a misleading press release but does not profit may be held liable to purchasing or selling investors for millions of dollars.

[19] 421 U.S. 723 (1975).

claiming that inaccuracies in disclosure caused nonselling in a falling market and that unduly pessimistic predictions by the issuer followed by a rising market caused them to allow retrospectively golden opportunities to pass.[20]

Blue Chip Stamps firmly established the purchaser-seller standing rule. After *Blue Chip Stamps*, a few questions remain, such as whether a plaintiff who has not purchased or sold may seek injunctive relief against misstatements or omissions affecting the market.[21] For purposes of the basics of actions under Rule 10b-5, however, the purchaser-seller standing rule is one of the fundamentals.[22]

[C]   Materiality

To run afoul of the disclosure rules, the fact misstated or omitted must be one to which the reasonable investor would attach importance in the making of her decision.[23] The omitted or misstated fact, if known, must be such that it would have assumed actual significance in the deliberations of the reasonable shareholder. A fact is a material fact if there exists a substantial likelihood that a reasonable shareholder would consider it important in deciding whether to purchase or sell a security.

In *Folger Adam Co. v. PMI Industries, Inc.*,[24] the Court of Appeals reversed a trial court instruction which "repeatedly stated that a material fact is one that would alter the total mix of available information." The court found that the jury instruction "never mentioned, much less highlighted, the critical distinction between facts that are important enough to assume actual significance in a reasonable investor's deliberations, and facts that are so important that they would change an investor's decision whether to consummate the transaction." To be material, a fact need not be "outcome-determinative" or one which would have caused a reasonable investor "to alter its views as to the desirability of proceeding with the purchase." Material facts are those which would have a propensity to affect the reasonable investor's thought process.

Courts have also faced a related issue: at what point in time do merger or other takeover talks between corporations become material requiring disclosure?[25] Corporations engaged in such talks generally have incentives to keep talks confidential as long as possible, for a number of reasons: disclosure could set off a bidding war, increasing the acquisition price; disclosure could put

---

[20] 421 U.S. at 747.

[21] *Compare Advanced Resources Int'l v. Tri-Star Petroleum Co.*, 4 F.3d 327 (4th Cir. 1993) (must be a purchaser or seller), *with Kahan v. Rosenstiel*, 424 F.2d 161 (3d Cir. 1970) (plaintiff in suit for injunctive relief need not be a purchaser or seller).

[22] Because mergers and other acquisitions involve shares being converted into something else, the conversion is considered a sale for Rule 10b-5 standing purposes.

[23] See *TSC Industries v. Northway, Inc.*, 426 U.S. 438 (1976), and the discussion of materiality generally in § 7.06[E], *supra.*

[24] 938 F.2d 1529 (2d Cir. 1991).

[25] *See, e.g.*, Douglas M. Branson, *SEC Nonacquiescence in Judicial Decisionmaking: Target Company Disclosure of Acquisition Negotiations*, 46 MD. L. REV. 1001 (1987).

the target corporation "in play" if the negotiations fail; and premature disclosure could "mislead investors and foster false optimism."[26]

The Supreme Court reviewed the issue in *Basic, Inc. v. Levinson.*[27] For thirteen years, Combustion Engineering, Inc. had been interested in acquiring Basic, Inc. In 1976, the Federal Trade Commission changed its position regarding relevant markets for antitrust law purposes, making Combustion's objective more realistic. Beginning in September, 1976, Combustion made inquiries of Basic. During 1977 and 1978, Basic issued three statements denying that it was engaged in merger negotiations.[28] In December, 1978, Basic reversed course, announcing that Combustion would acquire Basic for $46 per share.

Basic shareholders brought actions on behalf of those who sold Basic stock during the two-month period in which the inaccurate statements attributable to Basic had been circulating, thereby causing class members to forego the premium price Combustion would pay in the merger. The District Court granted summary judgment to Basic, Inc., on grounds that any misstatements by it were immaterial.

At the time, the Third Circuit had adopted the position that "because merger negotiations are inherently tentative, disclosure of their existence itself could mislead investors." Thus the court adopted "an agreement-in-principle . . . price and structure rule" as to materiality.[29] Would-be merger partners would not have to disclose until they had signed a letter of intent or similar document, setting out the price (dollars or shares of the acquiring company) and the form of the proposed transaction (merger, share exchange, cash tender offer and so on).

In the *Basic* case, the Sixth Circuit took a different position, holding that if the corporate defendant made a statement denying the existence of merger discussions, and that statement was untrue, that denial is automatically material because it is untrue. The Sixth Circuit expressly rejected the Third Circuit approach.[30] In turn, the Supreme Court rejected the Sixth Circuit approach, noting that "it is not enough that a statement is false or incomplete, if the misrepresented fact is otherwise insignificant."

The Supreme Court refused to adopt a test of materiality based on price and structure on the grounds that the fundamental premise of the securities laws is disclosure and not secrecy. Moreover, "investors are [not] nitwits, unable to

---

[26] *Basic, Inc. v. Levinson*, 485 U.S. 224 (1988).

[27] 485 U.S. 224 (1988).

[28] One Basic, Inc., press release stated that "management is unaware of any present or pending company development that would result in the abnormally heavy trading activity . . . in company shares." Similar statements were also found in a newspaper article. It is important to note that such statements may literally be true. Merger negotiations do not cause share prices to rise. Trading on rumors of such negotiations does. If a company is reasonably certain that negotiations have been kept confidential, and there are no leaks and thus no credible rumors, then management truly is unaware of any development causing the share price to rise.

[29] *Greenfield v. Heublein, Inc.*, 742 F.2d 751 (3d Cir. 1984).

[30] *See Levinson v. Basic, Inc.*, 786 F.2d 741, 749 (6th Cir. 1986).

appreciate-even when told-that mergers are risky propositions until the closing.' ' Instead, the Court left the matter of materiality of merger negotiations "to be determined on the particular facts of each case."

Generally, materiality "will depend at any given time upon a balancing of both the indicated probability that the event will occur and the anticipated magnitude of the event in light of the totality of the company activity."[31] Again, generally, but not always, a merger will be an event of great magnitude in the totality of a company's activity. The probability of that event occurring is, however, altogether a different matter:

> Generally, in order to assess the probability that the event [of merger] will occur, a factfinder will need to look at the highest corporate levels. Without attempting to catalog all such possible factors, we note by way of example that board resolutions, instructions to investment bankers, and actual negotiations between principals or their intermediaries may serve as indicia of interest . . . . No particular event or factor short of closing the transaction need be either necessary or sufficient by itself to render merger negotiations material.

Although proving itself very useful on another point,[32] at least to plaintiffs, *Basic, Inc. v. Levinson* did little to aid American corporations in the very real quandary they face in deciding whether or not to disclose merger negotiations.[33]

[D]   State of Mind

State of mind is a measure of the degree of fault ("scienter").[34] Courts typically recognize five "levels" of fault, or five culpable states of mind: strict liability, negligence, recklessness, knowing conduct, and intentional conduct. Intent is to be distinguished from motive. "[M]otive is the desire or inducement which incites or stimulates a person to do an act," while intent "is the purpose or resolve to do the act" itself.[35]

Although motive obviously underlies intent, and may well be "illegitimate" in most insider trading cases, it is not an element of an offense under Rule 10b-5 and its proof is therefore not essential. Conversely, proof of a legitimate motive does not mitigate against a finding of a culpable state of mind. A corporation whose motive behind a dissembling press release is the quite legitimate desire to acquire additional leases in the vicinity of a major mineral discovery still was

---

[31] *Levinson v. Basic, Inc.*, 485 U.S. at 238 (quoting *SEC v. Texas Gulf Sulphur Co.*, 401 F.2d. at 849).

[32] By adopting the "fraud on the market" reliance substitute a number of circuits had adopted, see § 13.02[G], *infra.*

[33] The Court did suggest that a corporation in possession of material information regarding a merger could choose to remain quiet, answering inquiries with "no comment."

[34] See also the discussion of the requisite state of mind under the proxy area antifraud rule in § 7.06[F], *supra.*

[35] W. LaFave & A. Scott, HANDBOOK ON CRIMINAL LAW 208 (1972).

potentially liable under Rule 10b-5.[36] The corporation issued the misleading press release knowingly.[37]

In the early 1970s, several circuit courts of appeal had come to hold that, based upon a lack of reasonable care, a defendant could be held liable for damages under Rule 10b-5.[38] Some commentators lamented that state of the law and opposed any liability based upon negligence. A person or corporation might be held liable for great sums, based merely upon a slip of the pen.

In *Ernst & Ernst v. Hochfelder*,[39] the Supreme Court set out to remedy the situation. Leston Nay, owner of a small Chicago securities firm, solicited investments in fictitious "escrow accounts" based upon a high rate of interest. Nay began the scheme in 1942, using newly invested funds to pay interest on older accounts and diverting funds to his personal use. In order to maintain itself, the scheme had to recruit additional new investors each year. In 1966, the market became saturated. Collapse was near. In that year, Nay took his life and disclosed the Ponzi scheme in a suicide note.[40]

Since Nay's estate was judgment-proof, Nay's victims sued Ernst & Ernst, the auditors of Nay's firm. Plaintiffs contended that had Ernst & Ernst personnel audited properly, they would have discovered Nay's "mail rule," which dictated that only Nay, and not his employees, could open mail addressed to Leston Nay. Uncovering the mail rule, plaintiffs theorized, Ernst & Ernst auditors would have dug deeper, exposing the Ponzi scheme years before Nay's suicide note.

The case set the stage nicely for the Supreme Court. No one could say that Ernst & Ernst's conduct amounted to anything more than a mere lack of

---

[36] *See SEC v. Texas Gulf Sulphur Co.*, 401 F.2d 833 (2d Cir. 1968).

[37] Advocates of a statutory definition of insider trading often include proof of a motive to trade based upon public information as an element of the definition. Alternatively, they have urged that good motive, or alternative motive (medical emergency, need to pay children's law school tuition bills) should be a defense to a charge of insider trading. *See generally* Symposium, *Defining "Insider Trading,"* 39 ALA. L. REV. 337 (1988); Note, *Toward a Definition of Insider Trading*, 41 STAN. L. REV. 377 (1989). Such, however, has not been the state of the law. Motive, while relevant, has been neither an element of a plaintiff's or prosecutor's 10b-5 case nor has it been a defense. At least two recent decisions have, however, held that defendants accused of insider trading may avoid liability if they demonstrate that they did not base their trades on, or "use," the insider information they possessed. *See United States v. Smith*, 155 F.3d 1051 (9th Cir. 1998); *United States v. Adler*, 137 F.3d 1325 (11th Cir. 1998). *Cf. United States v. Teicher*, 987 F.2d 112, 120 (2d Cir. 1993) (mere possession of inside information while trading satisfies the test for liability). In the "use" rather than mere "possession" debate, the SEC has by rule codified its traditional position. *See* SEC Rule 10b5-1 (trading while "aware of the material nonpublic information when the person makes the purchase or sale" is trading "on the basis of material non-public inside information" for purposes of the rule, except in cases of advance written plans for purchases or sales).

[38] *See, e.g., Royal Air Properties v. Smith*, 312 F.2d 210 (9th Cir. 1962); *Ellis v. Carter*, 291 F.2d 270 (9th Cir. 1961).

[39] 425 U.S. 185 (1976).

[40] A Ponzi scheme is a form of fraud in which the promoter promises and pays high rates of interest or other return, however denominated — for a time. The returns paid are primarily from the capital committed by new investors. All such schemes collapse eventually, when the promoter becomes unable to recruit a sufficient number of new investors. *See* D. Dunn, PONZI — THE BOSTON SWINDLER (1975) (biography of Carlo Ponzi (1882-1949)).

reasonable care. The Court's opinion began by asking "whether an action may lie under . . . Rule 10b-5, in the absence of an allegation of intent to deceive, manipulate, or defraud." The opinion answers merely, though, the question of whether negligence will suffice.

The *Hochfelder* Court began its analysis by observing that Section 10(b) makes unlawful the use or employment of "any manipulative or deceptive device or contrivance" in violation of such rules as the SEC may promulgate under the section. The Court then noted:

> The words "manipulative or deceptive," when used in conjunction with "device or contrivance," strongly suggest that § 10(b) was intended to proscribe knowing or intentional misconduct . . . . [T]he use of the words "manipulative," "device," and "contrivance" . . . make quite unmistakable a congressional intent to proscribe a type of conduct quite different from negligence. Use of the word "manipulative" is especially significant. It is and was virtually a term of art when used in connection with securities markets. It connotes intentional conduct designed to deceive or defraud investors by controlling or artificially affecting the price of securities.[41]

The Court also addressed the SEC's argument that subsections (2) and (3) of Rule 10b-(5) encompass negligent behavior. Indeed, on its face, clause (2) seems to provide for strict liability. The Court held that the scope of an SEC rule could not exceed the scope of the statutory authority pursuant to which the SEC had promulgated the rule. Having interpreted Section 10(b)'s statutory language as limited to prevention of knowing, intentional, or possibly reckless conduct, the Court could not extend the scope of the statute to validate a rule issued by the SEC pursuant to Section 10(b) that would hold a defendant liable for negligent conduct.[42]

Post-*Hochfelder*, two important questions remained. The first question was whether the SEC could obtain an injunction against acts that merely were negligent, even if a private party could not. The Supreme Court applied the same standard of scienter for the SEC in *Aaron v. SEC*.[43] Because the Supreme Court in *Hochfelder* had emphasized the language of Section 10(b), the result in *Aaron* was consistent with *Hochfelder*.

The second, and the more interesting, question was whether an allegation of recklessness (as opposed to knowing or intentional conduct) could ground a recovery of damages under Rule 10b-5. In a famous *Hochfelder* footnote, the

---

[41] 425 U.S. at 197–99.

[42] The point is important in states' securities laws, most of which contain an antifraud rule modeled after Rule 10b-5 but as a matter of legislative adoption rather than mere rule. Many state courts have thus held that negligence will ground a claim for damages under their securities laws. *See Kittilson v. Ford*, 608 P.2d 264 (Wash. 1980) ("[I]n contrast to the federal scheme, the language of Rule 10b-5 is not derivative but is the statute in Washington"); *State v. Larson*, 865 P.2d 1355 (Utah 1993) (same). *See also* Douglas M. Branson, *Collateral Participant Liability Under State Securities Laws*, 19 PEPP. L. REV. 1027, 1046 (1992).

[43] 446 U.S. 680 (1980).

Court had left that question unanswered.[44] Subsequently, all of the federal courts of appeal decided that proof of recklessness, at least of the high conscious disregard sort, would ground a damage recovery.[45] Many circuits follow the so-called *Sundstrand* description of what sort of conduct satisfies the conscious disregard standard of recklessness:

> Reckless conduct may be defined as a highly unreasonable omission, involving not merely simple, or even inexcusable negligence, but an extreme departure from the standards of ordinary care, and which presents a danger of misleading buyers and sellers that is either known to the defendant or is so obvious that the actor must have been aware of it.[46]

Pleading and proving the requisite state of mind, or what defense interests refer to as "scienter," is the heart of any disclosure or fraud case under Rule 10b-5.

[E] Pleading State of Mind

With the Private Securities Litigation Reform Act (PSLRA) of 1995,[47] pleading state of mind has taken on independent significance. The PSLRA requires that a plaintiff alleging a securities fraud claim, such as one under Rule 10b-5, must "state with particularity facts giving rise to a strong inference that the defendant acted with the requisite state of mind." The act also requires that "if an allegation regarding [a] statement or omission is made on information and belief, the complaint shall state with particularity all facts on which that belief is formed." Last of all, blending with those two PSLRA requirements is the pre-existing requirement of Federal Rule of Civil Procedure 9(b) that in a complaint alleging fraud "the circumstances constituting fraud shall be stated with particularity," in contrast to the notice pleading that is standard under modern rules of civil procedure. Pleading fraud with particularity is similar to an exercise in Journalism 101: as with a good news story, the complaint must state the what (the omission or statement), when, where, who (the speaker) and how (the statement was misleading).

In securities fraud actions today, the first battle is fought, and the entire war is often won or lost, at the pleading stage. Post-PSLRA, the federal courts have differed in their opinions as to what the ground rules should be for that battle.

---

[44] See 425 U.S. 193–94, n.12: "In certain areas of the law recklessness is considered to be a form of intentional conduct for purposes of imposing liability for some act. We need not address here the question whether, in some circumstances, reckless behavior is sufficient for civil liability under § 10(b) and Rule 10b-5."

[45] *See Hollinger v. Titan Capital Corp.*, 914 F.2d 1564, 1568 & n.6 (9th Cir. 1990) (citing cases from 11 circuits), *cert. denied*, 499 U.S. 976 (1991).

[46] *Sundstrand Corp. v. Sun Chemical Corp.*, 553 F.2d 1033, 1044 (7th Cir.), *cert. denied*, 434 U.S. 875 (1977).

[47] For a discussion of the act generally, see § 14.09[B], *infra.*

In *Novak v. Kaskas*,[48] plaintiff class representatives complained that Ann Taylor, Inc., owners of an upscale women's clothing store chain, had overstated profits by understating inventory writeoffs for out-of-date fashions and other inventory. Instead, the company pursued a "Box and Hold" practice which did not require an immediate writeoff and reduction in profits. Over a short period of time, "Box and Hold" inventory had increased form 10 to 34 % of Ann Taylor's total inventory.

The *Novak* court reviewed the split among the federal circuits about what the PSLA requires. There exist at least four interrelated, and unresolved, issues:

(1) Does the PSLRA raise the pleading standard, and not merely incorporate the pre-PRSLA Second Circuit "strong inference" standard?

(2) Does the PSLRA require plaintiffs to prove a greater degree of scienter than previously had been the case?

(3) Is pleading motive and opportunity insufficient to meet the pleading standard?

(4) Must the plaintiff name confidential sources (e.g., whistle blowers within the company) in order to plead fraud "with particularity" (the who of what, when, where, who and how)?

Most particularly, in *In re Silicon Graphics Inc. Sec. Litig.*,[49] the Ninth Circuit had answered all of those questions with a resounding (and pro defendant) "Yes."

By and large, Judge Walker of the Second Circuit came out the other way. Congress adopted the pre PSLRA "strong inference" standard because Congress used the exact words the Second Circuit had used in its pre-PSLRA decisions. Given that level of clarity, no need existed to resort to legislative history, which does contain some "conflicting expressions."

Skipping to question (3), pleading motive and opportunity could satisfy the standard. Plaintiffs may allege the requisite scienter by pleading "concrete benefits that could be realized by one of more of the false statements . . . . Opportunity would entail the means and likely prospect of achieving concrete benefits." Thus, a plaintiff could allege, for example, that the speakers were masking the real (negative) situation while they were divesting themselves of shares based upon inside information. Pleading generalized goals as motives, such as the desire to maintain a high credit rating, or to maintain a high stock price, to prolong one's stay in corporate office, will not do.

What will suffice to satisfy the pleading standard for scienter are allegations that "defendants (1) benefitted in a concrete and personal way . . . ; (2) engaged in deliberately illegal behavior; (3) knew facts or had access to information suggesting that their public statements were not accurate; or (4) failed to check information they had a duty to monitor."

---

[48] 216 F.3d 300 (2d Cir. 2000).

[49] 188 F.3d 970 (9th Cir. 1999).

Judge Walker found that post-PSLRA recklessness, defined as "an extreme departure from the standards of ordinary care," or "an egregious refusal to see the obvious, or to investigate the doubtful," still to be sufficient. The *Silicon Graphics* court has held that the PSLRA raised the level of scienter required, from "recklessness" as it was known pre-PSLRA, to "conscious recklessness." Last of all, in the Second Circuit "plaintiffs who rely on confidential sources are not always required to name those sources, even when they make allegations on information and belief concerning false and misleading statements . . . [p]rovided they are described . . . with sufficient particularity to support the probability that a person in the position occupied by the source would posses the information alleged." By contrast, in the Ninth Circuit the complaint must "name names" of formerly confidential sources. To the extent that plaintiffs' securities lawyers rely, or rely heavily, on sources within companies to reveal wrongdoing, *Silicon Graphics* strikes a telling blow.

In *Novak*, the Second Circuit re-instated plaintiffs' complaint, which the district court had dismissed. The court found that Ann Taylor corporate officers knew they had serious inventory problems; deliberately refused to mark down inventory so as artificially to inflate profits; knowingly sanctioned procedures that violated the company's established mark down policy; and "made repeated statements to the investment community either offering false reassurances that inventory was under control or giving false explanations for its growth."

[F]   Reliance (Transaction Causation)

In a common law fraud case, a plaintiff must plead and prove that he heard or saw the offending misstatement and that it played a significant part in a decision to purchase, invest, tender, or the like. In cases of omission, the plaintiff's task becomes more difficult. Proof that one relied on the absence of information or upon silence is difficult, if not impossible.

In the securities area, courts have recognized the difficulty of proof of reliance in omission cases. They have recognized that "we can't say **A** acted, bought, or sold in reliance on what **B** didn't tell him. What we can say in the latter case is that a *reasonable investor* who knew the omitted fact *probably* would not have bought or sold."

Given proof of materiality, at least in silence cases, we presume reliance: if a reasonable investor would have considered it important if the fact had been disclosed, we will presume the particular plaintiff would have considered it important.

In *Affiliated Ute Citizens of Utah v. United States*,[50] two bank employees failed to disclose the higher price for which shares were selling in the market made by the bank. They did not make this disclosure because they were actively engaged in buying up the shares of former Ute tribe members who used the bank as custodian for their stock. The Tenth Circuit denied a recovery because the plaintiffs had not proven reliance on any misstatements. The Supreme Court reversed:

---

[50] 406 U.S. 128 (1972).

Under the circumstances of this case, involving primarily a failure to disclose, positive proof of reliance is not a prerequisite to recovery. All that is necessary is that the facts withheld be material in the sense that a reasonable investor might [would] have considered them important in the making of this decision.[51]

Given materiality, the presumption of reliance makes particular sense in a case of face-to-face dealing.[52] The plaintiff may be assumed to have thought, "if it was important [material] he would have told me." After *Affiliated Ute*, courts nonetheless extended the presumption of reliance to cases of silence involving share transactions taking place over anonymous markets such as stock exchanges.[53] More recently, however, this issue has become less important with the development of a reliance substitute called the "fraud on the market" theory, discussed in the following subsection. In cases of alleged misstatement, however, the requirement that a Rule 10b-5 plaintiff prove reliance may persist.[54]

The reliance issue also arises in cases of misrepresentation. A presumption of reliance or a reliance substitute versus positive proof of reliance as an issue looms large because much disclosure litigation is class action litigation. If proof of individual reliance is required, and the investor class is of any size, the individual issues may overwhelm the common issues. Due to a perceived lack of commonality, or of manageability, the court may not certify the class under Federal Rule of Civil Procedure 23.[55]

In cases in which the plaintiff is alleging reliance on a misrepresentation, it is not necessary for the plaintiff actually to have seen the press release, quarterly report, or other document containing the alleged misstatement. In such cases proof of indirect reliance is sufficient. For example, if the plaintiff had relied on a broker or other adviser, who had relied upon a newspaper report about the issuer corporation, which in turn had been influenced by the misleading annual report, proof of those facts establishes reliance. If the plaintiff can link her conduct (buying shares) to the defendant's fraud by showing that "the fraud was a 'substantial' or 'significant contributing cause,' the plaintiff has shown sufficient reliance to support her 10b-5 claims."[56]

---

[51] 406 U.S. at 153–54.

[52] In *Affiliated Ute*, as well as many other face-to-face transactions, a duty to disclose arises because of the fiduciary relationship between the defendant (e.g., the bank in *Affiliated Ute*) and the purchaser or seller of securities.

[53] See *Shapiro v. Merrill Lynch, Pierce, Fenner & Smith*, 495 F.2d 228 (2d Cir. 1974); see also *Peil v. Speiser*, 806 F.2d 1154 (3d Cir. 1986).

[54] See *Wilson v. Telecommunications Corp.*, 648 F.2d 88 (2d Cir. 1981); *Vervaecke v. Chiles, Heider & Co.*, 578 F.2d 713 (8th Cir. 1978).

[55] With a smaller class of up to even several hundred, the court may conduct mini-trials, with groups of ten to twelve plaintiffs giving evidence on the reliance issue in each mini-trial session. The class is therefore manageable and may be certified.

[56] *Panzirer v. Wolf*, 663 F.2d 365 (2d Cir. 1981), *vacated as moot*, 459 U.S. 1027 (1982) (plaintiff purchased on basis of Wall Street Journal story in turn influenced by misleading annual report).

The plaintiff's reliance must be reasonable. Plaintiffs cannot make out a case by pointing to representations of outlandish or preposterous facts. The reasonableness of a plaintiff's reliance is to be judged with the following factors in mind:

> (1) the sophistication and expertise of the plaintiff in financial and securities matters; (2) the existence of long-standing business or personal relationships; (3) access to the relevant information; (4) the existence of a fiduciary relationship; (5) concealment of the fraud; (6) the opportunity to detect the fraud; (7) whether the plaintiff initiated the stock transaction or sought to expedite the transaction; and (8) the generality or specificity of the misrepresentations.[57]

In disclosure documents involving startup operations or projections of future performance, cautionary language will often in essence say "do not rely on this," or "do not place great reliance on this." Courts have held that in cases in which the cautionary language is risk-specific, rather than generalized boilerplate, the language "bespeaks caution." An investor who later claims that the projections caused him to purchase may prove reliance, but will not be able to prove that the reliance was reasonable, given the cautionary language.[58]

The PSLRA has now introduced a statutory safe harbor for forward looking statements (projections of revenues or profits, statements of corporate plans or objectives, statements of future economic performance generally, and the like) that are accompanied by "meaningful cautionary statements identifying important factors that could cause actual results to differ materially from those in the forward-looking statement."[59] Courts are directed to entertain motions to dismiss based upon the safe harbor and the presence of cautionary language, no matter how great the disparity between the projection or other forward looking statement and the reality which unfolds. The PSLRA safe harbor for forward looking statements is the reason why you will see cautionary language in every corporate press release, earnings report, proxy statement, annual report, and so on.

There are several important exclusions. For example, the safe harbor is only available to SEC reporting companies. It also does not apply to disclosure documents in connection with tender offers, initial public offerings, or penny stock (less than $5 per share) offerings.

[G]　The Fraud on the Market Theory Reliance Substitute

The fraud on the market theory is a reliance substitute that may be utilized in cases involving publicly traded securities. Often, investors may not be able to prove even indirect reliance. Alternatively, differing proofs as to reliance among

---

[57] *Zobrist v. Coal-X, Inc.*, 708 F.2d 1511, 1516 (10th Cir. 1983).

[58] *See generally* Donald C. Langevoort, *Disclosures That "Bespeak Caution,"* 49 Bus. Law. 481 (1994).

[59] Securities Exchange Act of 1934 § 21(E).

investors may defeat class certification. Some investors may have relied upon the offending statement directly, and some indirectly, while others did not rely at all.

All investors, however, do rely on the integrity of prices in the securities markets, namely, that those prices accurately reflect all available information about the issuer corporation. Moreover, developed securities markets are efficient. They reflect almost instantaneously all public information about companies.[60] If, however, the corporation has issued disclosures that are false or misleading, or which contain material omissions, then market prices will not accurately reflect the state of affairs within the issuer corporation. Investors' reliance on the integrity of the market in purchasing or selling will have been misplaced. This is the fraud on the market theory which may be used as a substitute for reliance. Several circuit courts have recognized this theory.[61]

The Supreme Court gave the fraud on the market theory national currency with its decision in *Basic, Inc. v. Levinson*.[62] The Court began by noting that "modern securities markets, literally involving millions of shares changing hands daily, differ from face-to-face transactions contemplated by early fraud cases." The lower court had accepted the presumption created by the fraud on the market theory, and the Supreme Court agreed that it was correct: "Requiring a plaintiff to show a speculative state of facts, *i.e.*, how he would have acted if omitted material information had been disclosed or if the misrepresentation had not been made, would place an unnecessarily unrealistic burden on the Rule 10b-5 plaintiff who has traded on an impersonal market." The Court went on to accept the theory:

> The presumption [of reliance on the market] is also supported by common sense and probability . . . . It has been noted that "it is hard to imagine that there ever is a buyer or seller who does not rely on market integrity. Who would knowingly roll the dice in a crooked crap game?" Indeed, nearly every court that has considered the proposition has concluded that where materially misleading statements have been disseminated into an impersonal, well-developed market for securities, the reliance of individual plaintiffs on the integrity of the market price may be presumed.[63]

Successful invocation of the fraud on the market theory establishes a presumption, and only a presumption, of reliance. As with other presumptions, this one may be rebutted:

> Any showing that severs the link between the alleged misrepresentation and either the price received (or paid) by the plaintiff, or his decision to trade at a fair market price, will be sufficient to rebut the

---

[60] See the discussion of the Efficient Capital Market Hypothesis (ECMH) in § 5.02[C], *supra*.

[61] *See, e.g., Peil v. Speiser*, 806 F.2d 1154, 1160–61 (3d Cir. 1986) ("The misstatements may affect the price of the stock, and thus defraud investors who rely on the price as an indication of the stock's value, By artificially inflating the price of the stock, the misrepresentations defraud purchasers who rely on the price as an indication of the stock's value.").

[62] 485 U.S. 224 (1988). Also discussed in connection with materiality of merger negotiations in § 13.02[C], *supra*.

[63] 485 U.S. at 246–47 (citation omitted).

presumption of reliance. For example, if [defendant Basic, Inc.] could show that the "market makers" were privy to the truth about the merger discussions here with Combustion, and thus that the market price would not have been affected by their misrepresentations, the causal connection would be broken: the basis for finding that the fraud had been transmitted through the marketplace would be gone. Similarly, if, despite [defendant Basic]'s allegedly fraudulent attempt to manipulate market price, news of the merger discussions credibly entered the market and dissipated the effects of the misstatements, those who traded Basic shares after the corrective statements would have no direct or indirect connection with the fraud.[64]

Defendants labor mightily to defeat application of the fraud on the market theory for two reasons. One reason is that the theory's application establishes what otherwise would be a difficult element of a plaintiff's case. A second reason is that the theory applies uniformly to all members of a class, paving the way to class certification. Besides contending that the link between the alleged misrepresentation and the plaintiff's action was severed, defendants argue that the market had the correct information or attempt to raise doubt about the efficiency of the market in which the securities traded.

Freeman v. Laventhol & Horwath[65] identifies five factors for determining market efficiency: "(1) a large weekly trading volume; 2) the existence of a significant number of reports by securities analysts; (3) the existence of market makers and arbitragers in the security; (4) the eligibility of a company to file an S-3 Registration Statement [for widely held public companies with a proven track record]; and (5) a history of immediate movement of the stock price caused by unexpected events or financial releases." Under the *Freeman* factors, a court could refuse to apply the fraud on the market theory even to less actively traded portions of the New York Stock Exchange or NASDAQ lists.

The fraud on the market theory is a valuable tool for plaintiffs and for securities law class action attorneys.

[H]   Loss Causation

In a Rule 10b-5 case, the plaintiff must establish not only a causal link between the defendant's alleged wrongdoing and the plaintiff's conduct (transaction causation), but also a causal link between the defendant's acts and the plaintiff's loss or damages (loss causation). If the plaintiff alleges that the defendant issuer published profit projections which did not come to fruition, and that the projections caused the plaintiff to purchase shares, but the fall in share price followed the filing of a major antitrust suit against the corporation, reliance (transaction causation) may be present but loss causation would not be. The antitrust suit is a superseding cause that intervened to cause the plaintiff's damage.

---

[64] *Id.* at 248–49 (footnotes omitted).

[65] 915 F.2d 193, 199 (6th Cir. 1990).

Judge Posner explained the concept in *Bastian v. Petren Resources, Inc.*,[66] involving an oil and gas investment that had gone bad:

> [Plaintiffs] suggest no reason *why* the investment was wiped out. They have alleged the cause of their entering into the transaction in which they lost money but not the cause of the transaction turning out to be a losing one. It happens that 1981 was a peak year for oil prices and that those prices declined steadily in the succeeding years. When this happened the profitability of drilling for oil plummeted . . . . Suppose that because of the unexpected drop in oil prices after 1981, all or the vast majority of the oil and gas limited partnerships formed in 1981 became worthless. Then it would be highly unlikely that the plaintiffs' loss was due to the defendants' fraud.

The causation that the plaintiff must prove is straight causation, as in the cause-in-fact phase of a torts case. Thus, the plaintiff must prove that "but for the defendant's acts (misstatement, omission), the decrease in market price (and loss) would not have occurred." Alternatively, the plaintiff must prove that the misstatements or omissions were a "substantial factor" in producing the loss the plaintiff has suffered. The Private Securities Litigation Reform Act (PSLRA) codifies this requirement, providing that "the plaintiff shall have the burden of proving that the act or omission of the defendant alleged to have violated the Act caused the loss for which the plaintiff seeks to recover damages."[67] The PSLRA loss causation requirement, and its interpretation by the Supreme Court in *Dura Pharmaceuticals, Inc. v. Brouda*,[68] are further developed in the discussion of the PSLRA itself.

[I]   The "In Connection With" Requirement

A backstop requirement to the causation requirements is the requirement that the defendant's wrongful acts must have occurred "in connection with" the purchase or sale of a security as stated in Section 10b. The "in connection with" requirement is a means of testing whether the connection between securities, or even securities markets generally, and the fraud alleged, is too attenuated.[69] One application is to the temporal sequencing of events. If the plaintiff purchased shares at $30, a false press release regarding the state of pivotal contract negotiations caused the share to rise to $40, and then correcting information saw the share price fall to $25, the defendants' wrongdoing did not

---

[66] 892 F.2d 680 (7th Cir.), *cert. denied*, 496 U.S. 906 (1990). See also *In re Carter-Wallace Securities Litigation*, 150 F.3d 153 (2d Cir. 1998), holding that, contrary to the lower court's finding, complex technical advertisements for a new drug, which appeared in medical journals, could have been actionable as "in connection wit the purchase of sale of securities." All plaintiffs need show is that the advertisements had been utilized by market professionals, such as analysts, in evaluating the stock of the company that had manufactured the drug.

[67] Securities Exchange Act of 1934 § 21D(b)(4). *See generally* Thomas Lee Hazen, Securities Regulation § 12.11, at 622 (4th ed. 2002).

[68] 544 U.S. 336 (2005) (discussed in § 14.09[C][2], *infra*).

[69] *See, e.g.*, *Ketchum v. Green*, 557 F.2d 1022, 1029 (3d Cir.), *cert. denied*, 434 U.S. 940 (1977) ("[B]oth the 'connection' and 'causation' principles speak to the degree of proximity required between a misrepresentation and a securities transaction").

occur "in connection with" the plaintiff's purchase. Similarly, if the plaintiffs' securities purchase or sale occurred months after the conduct alleged, one line of defense would be that the purchase or sale had not taken place "in connection with" the alleged wrongdoing.[70]

The in connection requirement reached the Supreme Court in *SEC v. Zandford*.[71] Distinguish two cases. In case one, a broker sells securities in a customer's account. Later, in an independent act, the broker misappropriates the cash in the account. The securities laws do not apply to the misappropriation. In case two, the broker (Zandford) misappropriates cash pursuant to a plan or pattern initiated with liquidation of the securities, followed by misappropriation of the funds. In the latter, "the scheme to defraud and the sale of securities coincide." Such a relationship between the acts is sufficient to satisfy SEC Rule 10b-5's requirement that alleged fraud must occur "in connection with the purchase or sale of a security. Rule 10b-5 does not limit itself to misrepresentations or omissions relating to the value of securities.

[J]   Privity

A common law fraud claim could not lie in the absence of direct dealings between the plaintiff and the defendant.[72] In the securities markets, the vast majority of transactions take place through intermediaries: there are no direct dealings. Investors purchase and sell through the medium of anonymous stock exchanges or over-the-counter markets.

In *Goodwin v. Agassiz*,[73] the president and general manager of a mining company purchased the plaintiff's shares through the Boston Stock Exchange. They did so while in possession of undisclosed information about a new mining theory that might benefit the company greatly. Insofar as the plaintiff rested his claim on common law deceit or misrepresentation, it would not lie: "The stock of the cliff Mining Company was bought and sold on the stock exchange. The identity of buyers and sellers of the stock . . . was not known to the parties and could not have been ascertained." In other words, no privity could be established.

Rule 10b-5 has no privity requirement. Elimination of such a requirement is one area in which it may be unequivocally stated that Rule 10b-5 lowers significantly a plaintiff's burden from what it would have been at common law.

[K]   Secondary Liability for Disclosure Violations

Secondary violators become liable because someone else, the primary violator, has violated the securities laws, including disclosure rules such as Rule 10b-5. Plaintiffs often pursue such secondary violators because the primary

---

[70] *See generally* Barbara Black, *The Second Circuit's Approach to the "In Connection With" Requirement of Rule 10b-5*, 53 Brook. L. Rev. 539 (1987); Edward Fletcher, *The "In Connection With" Requirement of Rule 10b-5*, 16 Pepp. L. Rev. 913 (1989).

[71] 535 U.S. 813 (2002) (Stevens, J.).

[72] *See Ultramares Corp. v. Touche, Niven & Co.*, 174 N.E. 441 (N.Y. 1931) (Cardozo, C.J.).

[73] 186 N.E. 659 (Mass. 1933).

violator, often the issuer of the securities, has become judgment-proof, or nearly so. For 25 years or more, plaintiffs joined as defendants corporate directors and officers, accountants, business consultants, attorneys, bankers, celebrity spokespersons, and similar "collateral participants" in securities transactions, in the Rule 10b-5 area alleging that those persons had "aided and abetted" the primary violators' violation.[74] The plaintiff had only to prove that the secondary defendant had rendered "substantial assistance" to the primary defendant when, in the exercise of the slightest care, they should have known that the primary violator was engaged in wrongdoing. That wrongdoing could have been in the form of misleading statements or material omissions in a press release, prospectus, private placement memorandum, or other document.

In *Central Bank of Denver v. First Interstate Bank of Denver*,[75] the Supreme Court put an abrupt end to "aiding and abetting," and probably other implied secondary liability theories under Rule 10b-5 as well. The Court simply found that no statutory basis existed for such liability. In the Private Securities Litigation Reform Act of 1995,[76] Congress did resurrect "aiding and abetting" liability but only in actions by the SEC.

Plaintiffs still pursue secondary defendants in securities cases, on the basis of express secondary liability provisions in the securities laws,[77] or on the basis that in reality collateral participants are primary violators as well.[78] Suffice it to say that after *Central Bank*, and the demise of "aiding and abetting" liability, establishing the liability of collateral participants in securities transactions should be a bit more difficult under Rule 10b-5, except perhaps in an earth shaking case.

The late 2001 bankruptcy of Enron Corp., the seventh largest corporation in the U.S. by market capitalization, and *Fortune* magazine's most innovative company for three consecutive years, was such a case. To preserve its debt rating, Enron had implemented an "asset lite" business plan whereby, when it could not sell assets in arm's length transactions, it moved assets, including liabilities relating to those assets, into approximately 900 special purpose entities (SPEs) (partnerships, LLCs, corporations, and so on). Ultimately, Enron had "out placed" 57 percent of its assets and a much greater percent of its liabilities. These transfers were done in open disregard of the accounting rules governing such transfers. For example, they were not "true sales" because Enron financed, and its personnel controlled, the supposedly independent SPEs.

---

[74] *See generally* Douglas M. Branson, *Collateral Participant Liability Under the Securities Laws-Charting the Proper Course*, 65 OR. L. REV. 327 (1986).

[75] 511 U.S. 164 (1994).

[76] See the discussion in § 14.09[B], *infra*.

[77] The controlling persons provisions are examples. *See* 1933 Act § 15 ("Liability of Controlling Persons"); 1934 Act § 20 ("Liability of Controlling Persons and Persons Who Aid and Abet Violations").

[78] *See, e.g.*, Douglas M. Branson, *Chasing the Rogue Professional After the Private Securities Litigation Reform Act of 1995*, 50 SMU L. REV. 91 (1996).

In *In re Enron Corporation Securities, Derivative & ERISA Litigation*,[79] Judge Melinda Harmon wrote a 163 page opinion resolving the collateral participants' motion to dismiss the plaintiffs' complaint for failure, *inter alia*, to meet the PSLRA state of mind pleading standards.[80] The collateral participants included the banks, the law firm (Vinson & Elkins) and the accounting firm (the now defunct Arthur Anderson) who, over and over, aided Enron in setting up its elaborate scheme of off-the-books entities. The court held that the collateral participants were liable as primary violators because they had not remained silent. Instead, for example, "Vinson & Elkins . . . choose not once, but frequently, to make statements to the public about Enron's business and financial situation. [V&E] was not merely a drafter, but essentially a co-author of the documents it created for public consumption."

The repetition of illicit transactions provided circumstantial evidence sufficient that "the scienter pleading requirement is satisfied [at least in part] by allegations of a regular pattern of related and repeated conduct involving the creation of unlawful, Enron-controlled SPEs, sale of unwanted Enron assets to these entities in clearly non-arm's length transactions . . . in order to shift debt off Enron's balance sheet and sham profits onto its books." Moreover, the motive of greed was accepted by Judge Harmon as sufficient under a "motive and opportunity" strong inference of scienter test. The concrete benefits were, for example, that V&E derived 7 percent of its revenue from Enron. Arthur Anderson partners decided to keep Enron as a client, despite warnings that it was risky to do so, because they foresaw the Enron account expanding from $57 to over $100 million in yearly billings.

Judge Harmon kept most of the collateral participants in the case. They had "failed to monitor matters they had professional duties to monitor," "knew facts or had access to information suggesting that their public statements were not accurate," and "benefitted in a concrete and personal way" from their lapses.[81] In fact, one of the mysteries of Enron is why so many collateral participants, as gatekeepers and monitors of Enron's performance, including attorneys, accountants, and bankers, did not perform as professional standards would require.[82]

The Supreme Court, however, revisited secondary liability under Rule 10b-5 in *Stoneridge Investment Partners, LLC v. Scientific-Atlanta, Inc.*,[83] reaffirming its *Central Bank* holding of no aiding and abetting liability. The case involved the liability of "secondary actors" in "scheme liability." Charter, a cable television operator, needed additional revenues to meet Wall Street projections. Charter arranged to pay an additional $20 per set-top box Scientific-Atlanta and

---

[79] 235 F. Supp. 2d 549 (S.D. Tex. 2002).

[80] Discussed in § 13.02[E], *supra*.

[81] See *Novak v. Kaskas* and note 47, *supra*.

[82] *See, e.g.*, Douglas M. Branson, *Enron — When All Systems Fail: Creative Destruction or Roadmap to Corporate Governance Reform?*, 48 Vill. L. Rev. 989 (2003); John C. Coffee, Jr., *Understanding Enron: It's About the Gatekeepers, Stupid*, 57 Bus. Law. 1403 (2002); Roger C. Crampton, *Enron and the Corporate Lawyer: A Primer on Legal and Ethical Issues*, 58 Bus. Law. 143 (2002).

[83] 552 U.S. 148 (2008).

Motorola supplied for ultimate use by cable customers. The two defendant suppliers also agreed to "round trip" the money, immediately using it to purchase advertising from Charter. Charter amortized the outflow (the boxes' cost) over several years while it booked the inflow (advertising fees) entirely as revenue in the instant accounting period. The scheme added $17 million to Charter's quarterly revenue.

The issue was whether participants in the scheme (Scientific and Motorola), who had neither spoken to investors nor had a duty to speak, could nonetheless be liable under Rule 10b-5. Scientific and Motorola were collateral participants in a securities transaction ("secondary actors," in Justice Kennedy's words), or participants in a scheme (in the plaintiff's words). *Central Bank* eliminated secondary liability for collateral participants. They become liable, if they are liable at all, as primary actors, that us, because they themselves made statements to investors or actively participated in a statement made by others ("group speech"). The Court buttressed its reaffirmation of these principles with several arguments.

In its 1995 enactment of the PSLRA, Congress re-authorized aiding and abetting liability "only in actions by the SEC but not by private parties," despite being urged by the SEC and others to enact a wider re-authorization. The PSLRA amendment, limited as it was, supported the conclusion that no other secondary liability exists. Moreover, supply contracts, and their fictitious nature *vel non*, lie within "the realm of ordinary business operations . . . governed, for the most part, by state law."

The Court couched its ultimate conclusion in reliance terms. Because there had been no statements or actionable silences, investors in Charter did not rely on anything spoken by defendants. Rue 10b-5 requires reliance and there was nothing upon which investors could have relied. The district court properly dismissed securities law claims against Scientific-Atlanta and Motorola.

§ 13.03   THE PROHIBITION OF INSIDER TRADING: IS IT GOOD OR BAD?

In 1966, Dean Henry Manne published a book entitled "Insider Trading and the Stock Market." In that small volume, Dean Manne set forth a number of arguments as to why insider trading, the use by senior corporate managers and directors of nonpublic investment information, should be made legal, subject to regulation (or not) by individual corporations.[84] At the time, Dean Manne, then a young law teacher, was vilified in the law reviews and elsewhere.[85]

Henry Manne went on to become one of the founders of the jurisprudential school known as the law and economics movement. Throughout the 1980s, the L & E school dominated corporate law teaching and scholarship. Many of its

---

[84] Henry Manne, INSIDER TRADING AND THE STOCK MARKET 111-58 (1966).

[85] *See, e.g.*, Roy Schotland, *Unsafe at Any Price: A Reply to Manne "Insider Trading in the Stock Market,"* 53 VA. L. REV. 1425 (1967). *Cf.* Henry Manne, *Insider Trading and the Law Professors*, 23 VAND. L. REV. 547 (1970).

adherents shared Dean Manne's view about insider trading.[86]

The arguments in favor of insider trading are many, not all of which can be reviewed here. Some of those arguments include the following. First, profits made by insiders through their trading constitute rewards for their entrepreneurial efforts ("Entrepreneur Rationale") A second, and closely related, argument holds that insider trading profits constitute the very type of performance-based compensation that aligns corporate officials' interests with those of shareholder owners ("The Ideal Performance-Based Compensation"). If the insiders manage well, the corporation's share price increases and everyone, owners and agents alike, benefits, because the law permits the insiders to take share positions based upon favorable news not yet made public. Third, insider trading helps move stock prices quickly in the correct direction and magnitude, reflective of events occurring within the particular company, thereby contributing to stock market efficiency, which is beneficial to investors ("Enhancement of Accurate Securities Pricing"). Fourth, insider trading harms no one because if the inside information needed to be secret, those who sell when insiders are buying or those who buy when insiders are selling would have bought or sold anyway ("No One is Harmed").

A rebuttal of each of these four arguments follows:

Entrepreneurs. Senior managers and directors of publicly held corporations are for the most part not entrepreneurs. They are stewards, charged with preserving and enlarging the wealth of enterprise often founded years before by the true entrepreneurs. Moreover, they are among the most highly compensated individuals in our society. Permitting them to trade on nonpublic information would rend the socio-economic fabric and truly constitute an example of the rich getting richer.

The Ideal Performance-Based Compensation.[87] Insiders who possess negative news may sell before other investors receive the news and react. The scenario of badly performing managers being able to preserve their compensation, or at least suffer losses much smaller than rank and file shareholders suffer, gives pause. Law and economics scholars reply that the law could prohibit insiders from short selling or undertaking other types of transactions that would permit insiders to benefit from possession of negative information. In that manner, draftspersons could devise a regulatory scheme that would allow insiders to trade only on news of positive events.

Professor Easterbrook has suggested that even insider trading on positive news may induce managers to select overly risky projects for the corporation, because increased volatility in stock prices gives managers greater opportunities for insider trading profits.[88] In the longer run, individual corporations and the

---

[86] *See, e.g.,* Jonathan Macey, *From Fairness to Contract: The New Direction of the Rules Against Insider Trading,* 13 HOFSTRA L. REV. 9 (1984).

[87] The leading exposition of this view is Dennis Carlton & Daniel R. Fischel, *The Regulation of Insider Trading,* 35 STAN. L. REV. 857 (1983).

[88] Frank Easterbrook, *Insider Trading, Secret Agents, Evidentiary Privileges, and the Produc-*

economy would suffer.

Enhancement of Accurate Securities Pricing. Consider a researcher at a drug company who has a promising discovery. If she is permitted to trade on insider information, she may delay for a day before she makes disclosure of her discovery to the director of research. She uses that day to arrange funding for her share purchases and takes a position in the stock.

The researcher then makes the disclosure to the research director. For similar reasons, the research director may also delay for two days before disclosing to the relevant corporate vice-president. For similar reasons, the vice-president delays, and then the COO delays, and then the CEO delays, all while they load up on the stock. The delays that would tend to result from such hierarchical disclosure would effectively make markets less informationally efficient, not more.

No One is Harmed. On a macro-economic basis, commerce and industry would be harmed. Would-be investors would believe that the cards are stacked against them if insider trading were to be permitted. If they withdraw from investing in any significant numbers, markets are weakened, making it more difficult for corporations to raise capital in the primary markets.[89]

Argument over the merits of the insider trading prohibition continues. Two observations may be made. One is that investors know that all investors in the stock market are not on an equal footing, in terms of their abilities and the investment information available to them, just as athletes on a playing field differ in size and ability. However, trading on information intended to be available only for a corporate purpose, not possessed by other players in the market, is beyond the rules of the sport, so to speak, or so the vast majority of investors feel. In terms of the sports metaphor, the insider trade is the flagrant foul, or the tackle out of bounds. That sentiment about insider trading rings true around the world, as most industrialized nations of the world have enacted into law prohibitions against the practice.

The other observation is that prohibition of insider trading, including criminal prosecution for violations, is here to stay. In 1980, the administration of President Ronald Reagan began deregulation of vast areas in which government had regulated for decades, including the securities area. But one area of securities regulation the Reagan administration chose not to deregulate and, indeed, consciously chose to regulate with renewed and additional vigor, is the insider trading area. The 1980s and 1990s witnessed criminal prosecutions and lengthy prison sentences for insiders who traded on non-public information.[90] That renewed emphasis on insider trading enforcement has continued into the new century.

---

tion of Information, 1981 Sup. Ct. Rev. 309, 322 (1981).

[89] Professors Steinberg and Wang have demonstrated that investors are harmed by insider trading on a micro-economic basis as well. *See* Marc Steinberg & William K. S. Wang, INSIDER TRADING, Ch. 3, "The Harm to Individual Investors from a Specific Insider Trade" (1996).

[90] Congress also took significant actions to increase the penalties for insider trading, such as the Insider Trading Sanctions Act (ITSA). For a discussion of ITSA, see § 13.04[I], *infra.*

Examination of the competition in the marketplace of ideas regarding the merits (or lack thereof) in prohibiting insider trading is interesting. What is clear is that competition has ended, at least for the time being. Those who favor a strong prohibition on insider trading are in the ascendancy, now and for the foreseeable future.

§ 13.04 THE LAW OF INSIDER TRADING

[A] Common Law Background

The common law approach to insider trading was based upon an action in fraud. While insider trading may involve a misrepresentation or half-truth, most insider trading involves a lack of disclosure (that is, silence). Bringing an insider trading common law fraud action has several problems. If there was a misrepresentation or half-truth, a common law cause of action required privity, which meant that a fraud action could not reach trading in impersonal markets.[91] But even in face-to-face transactions, if one party bought or sold with inside information, there could be no cause of action for silence unless the law imposed a duty to speak. A fiduciary relationship could impose a duty to speak on the defendant, but many courts, when faced with a corporate insider having purchased shares directly from a shareholder, found no liability. Their reasoning was that, although the insider had been a fiduciary, she owed her duty to the corporation and not to the shareholders when purchasing shares. If the corporation sued the insider, the courts responded that the trading had not harmed the corporation — it had no damages. The shareholder had suffered the harm.[92] Fiduciary duty proved inept at policing trading by insiders.

There were exceptions. In *Strong v. Repide*,[93] a corporate director had purchased plaintiffs' shares in the Philippine Sugar Estates Development Company. Defendant was in charge of negotiations to sell the corporation's principal assets, land in the Philippines, to the United States at a large profit. The corporation then intended to liquidate, distributing the sales proceeds. The sale of a principal asset, coupled with the intent to liquidate, were "special facts" justifying an exception to the rule that permitted a trading fiduciary to remain silent.[94] What constituted "special facts" was never defined but seemed to require some episodic event in the life of a corporation, such as a liquidation, a forthcoming merger or takeover bid, and so on, coupled with active involvement by the insider in the event or transaction.[95]

---

[91] See the further discussion of insider trading under modern state law in § 13.05[D], [E], *infra.*

[92] Two cases that illustrate this approach are *Percival v. Wright*, 1 Ch. 421 (1902), a turn-of-the-century English case, and *Goodwin v. Agassiz*, 186 N.E. 659 (Mass. 1933).

[93] 213 U.S. 419 (1909).

[94] In *Strong*, the defendant director also used a dummy purchaser to disguise his identity as the true purchaser. Offers to purchase by the director himself would have raised inevitable questions. A good many courts also developed a secret purchaser exception to the normal nondisclosure rule. *See, e.g., Mansfield Hardwood Lumber Co. v. Johnson*, 263 F.2d 748, *explained*, 268 F.2d 317 (5th Cir. 1959) (Louisiana law).

[95] Expansion of the definition of "special facts" has been a principal method whereby, in the

Some courts refrained from legal formalism, condemning all insider trading. They based their conclusions on fiduciary duty. This was often called the "Kansas Rule," named after Kansas courts' uniform condemnation of insider trading through finding a fiduciary duty running also from the insider to the shareholder.[96] Even under this broadened view, however, purchasers of shares from an insider may not have had a remedy because they were not shareholders at the time of the purchase and thus no fiduciary relationship could have existed at the relevant point in time.

In most jurisdictions, however, the historical gap between fraud law and fiduciary duty persisted. The federal judiciary and Rule 10b-5 stepped into that gap, passing state judiciaries by and developing the modern law of insider trading.[97]

[B]   The Nature of the Insider Trading Prohibition

Questions to be answered include what is the nature of the prohibition on insider trading, how long does it last, and who is subject to the prohibition? Further areas for discussion include the civil and criminal sanctions for insider trading and the approach modern state courts take to the practice. This subsection deals with only the first of those questions.

The prohibition visited upon the insider is "disclose or abstain."[98] Because the prerogative to disclose usually is the corporation's, and not the insider's, the effective prohibition becomes to "abstain" from trading, or from tipping others to trade. In smaller corporations, of course, the insider may be an effective alter ego of the corporation and may be able to disclose. It will also be easy to do if the transaction takes place in the face-to-face setting. The insider merely discloses the nonpublic information to the person with whom he is trading.

In anonymous markets, including even a local over-the-counter market, although conceivably the insider may be able to disclose, it may not be easy to do so. It is not sufficient for the insider to post a notice on a telephone pole, because the prohibition visited upon the insider lasts until the information is not only disclosed, but has been effectively disseminated to the market. The insider who has the prerogative to disclose nonetheless may be unable to persuade the local newspaper editor to publish the insider's press release or other notice. In that case, the insider's duty to abstain may persist for some time.

Much of the foregoing is a teaching of *SEC v. Texas Gulf Sulphur Co.*[99] One TGS director, Coates, waited until the corporation issued a press release regarding a major mineral discovery in Northern Ontario, Canada. That press release corrected an earlier press release that had been literally true but

---

modern era, state courts have come to enforce a broad insider trading prohibition as well. See the discussion in § 13.05[D], [E], *infra.*

[96] *See Hotchkiss v. Fisher,* 16 P.2d 531 (Kan. 1932).

[97] For a discussion of how some state courts have subsequently fashioned a remedy, see § 13.05[E], *infra.*

[98] *See In re Cady, Roberts & Co.,* 40 S.E.C. 907 (1961).

[99] 401 F.2d 833 (2d Cir. 1968) (en banc), *cert. denied,* 394 U.S. 976 (1969).

misleading, stating that TGS had been exploring in the area for years and that to date most of the activity had "revealed either barren pyrite or graphite without value." TGS issued the correcting release in a ten to fifteen minute announcement, commencing at 10:00 am. At 10:20 am, Coates telephoned his son-in-law stockbroker, placing an order for 2000 TGS shares for a trust Coates controlled. If disclosure alone lifted the prohibition, Coates would have been free to trade and to tip his son-in-law. But disclosure alone does not free the insider of the prohibition:

> The reading of a news release, which prompted Coates into action, is merely the first step in the process of dissemination required . . . . [A]t the minimum Coates should have waited until the news media could reasonably have been expected to appear over the media of widest circulation, the Dow Jones broad tape, rather than hastening to insure an advantage to himself and his broker son-in-law . . . .

Had Coates waited ten to fifteen minutes to trade he nonetheless would have participated in much, if not all, of the price increase in TGS shares from $31 to 58 1/4 six weeks later. His lack of patience (or his greed) cost him dearly.

[C]   Who is an Insider?

A traditional insider is a person who, because of a fiduciary or similar relation, is afforded access to nonpublic investment information from her corporation. The paradigmatic insider is the senior corporate official or director in a corporation, although professionals such as attorneys, accountants, and investment or commercial bankers may also become insiders, or temporary insiders, when they learn of nonpublic information during the course of performing services for the corporation.

For many years, *In re Cady, Roberts & Co.*[100] was a starting point in the analysis of an insider trading case. *Cady Roberts* extended the disclose-or-abstain obligation beyond classical insiders. The "obligation [to disclose or abstain] rests on . . . the existence of a relationship giving access, directly or indirectly, to information intended to be available only for a corporate purpose and not for the personal benefit of anyone . . . ." Because of *Cady Roberts*, the concept of who was subject to the disclose-or-abstain obligation who is an insider-seemingly became flexible and open-ended. Courts began bestowing insider status on anyone who had "access" to nonpublic information.

Re-application of *Cady* principles had to await the Supreme Court decision in *Chiarella v. United States*, 17 years later.[101] In the intervening years, the federal courts had defined who is an insider by use only of an access test. Anyone, classical insider or not, who had access to material nonpublic investment information, became an insider.[102]

---

[100] 40 S.E.C. 907 (1961).

[101] 445 U.S. 222 (1980).

[102] In *Chiarella*, 588 F.2d 1358, 1365 (2d Cir. 1978), the Second Circuit attempted to set some limits to the "access" approach to the definition of an insider. Judge Kaufman molded a "regular receipt" test to determine who besides the classical insider may be subject to the disclose-or-abstain

Vincent Chiarella was an employee in a financial printing house. He had access to offering documents on behalf of tender offerors. Tender offers are made at substantial premiums above existing market prices.[103] Mr. Chiarella would calculate who the target corporation was to be. He would then purchase shares in the still-sleeping market. Once the tender offer was announced, the target company shares would rise in price. Mr. Chiarella would sell his shares at a substantial profit.

The SEC referred Mr. Chiarella's case to the Department of Justice for criminal prosecution.[104] He was prosecuted and convicted for willful violations of Section 10(b) and Rule 10b-5.

In *Chiarella*, Mr. Justice Powell began analysis of the Second Circuit's opinion and of who is an insider by a careful re-reading of *Cady Roberts*. Instead of placing the emphasis on "access," as lower federal courts had been doing, Justice Powell shifted back to the full wording: "the existence of a *relationship* giving access to nonpublic information." He found that "the duty to disclose arises when one party has information 'that the other [party] is entitled to know because of a fiduciary or similar relation of trust and confidence between them.'" The requirement of a fiduciary relationship relates to the common law notion that without it there is no duty to disclose. Throughout the opinion, he emphasized that the duty owed, if it is owed at all, is owed to the other party to the transaction (that is, the purchaser or sellers of the shares). The opinion thus built to a conclusion that rejected the notion that Rule 10b-5 imposed a duty to the market place as a whole:

> We cannot affirm petitioner's conviction without recognizing a general duty between all participants in market transactions to forgo actions based on material, non-public information. Formulation of such a broad duty, which departs radically from the established doctrine that a duty arises from a specific relationship between two parties . . . should not be undertaken absent some explicit evidence of congressional intent.[105]

The Court thus repudiated the policy basis underlying broad insider trading prohibitions:

> The Court of Appeals . . . failed to identify a relationship between petitioner and the sellers that could give rise to a duty. Its decision thus rested solely upon its belief that the federal securities laws have

---

rule: "Anyone, corporate insider or not, who regularly receives material nonpublic information may not use that information to trade without incurring an affirmative duty to disclose. And if he cannot disclose, he must abstain from buying or selling." Judge Kaufman intended that the "regular receipt" test govern the "cogs" and "auxiliaries" of the securities industry-persons who by virtue of strategic positions have regular access to material nonpublic information, such as a financial printer like Chiarella.

[103] See the discussion of tender offers in Chapter 12, *supra*.

[104] Earlier, the SEC had sought an injunction against Mr. Chiarella. As a condition of letting Chiarella off with a relatively painless consent decree, the SEC required Chiarella to disgorge the $30,011.39 profit he had made. At the time, such a civil proceeding was a form frequently taken by SEC enforcement.

[105] 445 U.S. at 233. For a discussion of the misappropriation theory that can create misappropriation liability, see § 13.04[E] and [F], *supra*.

"created a system providing equal access to information necessary for reasoned and intelligent investment decisions." . . . The use by anyone of material information not generally available is fraudulent, this theory suggests, because such information gives certain buyers or sellers an unfair advantage over less informed buyers and sellers.[106]

The Court labeled such reasoning "defective" because "not every instance of financial unfairness constitutes fraudulent activity." The ingredient needed to make silence fraudulent is a "duty to disclose," absent in Chiarella's case because Chiarella owed no duty to the sellers of the shares he purchased. The attempts of the SEC and the lower courts to use Rule 10b-5 to create a duty to the marketplace as a whole and to put investors in parity as to access to information had failed. Almost as an afterthought, Mr. Chiarella went free.

If the window washer in a downtown office building peers through the window and reads papers on the desk of a CEO, and invests in the shares of the corporation because of important news about the corporation he discovered in peering through the window, he has access. His access, however, does not arise from a "fiduciary or similar relationship of trust and confidence" to those persons who sell shares while he is buying. He is not liable if he trades on the information.

The attorney or independent accountant who performs services on the corporation's behalf stands on a different footing. He has access, and he has a "fiduciary or similar relationship."[107] The relationship Chiarella had, however, was with the bidder company, and *Chiarella* requires a fiduciary or similar relationship with the other parties to the transaction, that is, the shareholder of the target corporation who sold the shares. The professional may be in a similar posture: although he has access and a fiduciary responsibility to a bidder, he would not be liable under *Chiarella* principles.[108]

After *Chiarella*, the SEC exercised its authority under Securities Exchange Act Section 14(e) to define and prescribe "fraudulent, deceptive or manipulative" acts or practices in the tender offer area. SEC Rule 14e-3 fills the gaps *Chiarella* creates in the law when someone has information from either the bidder or the target of a tender offer and trades on that information. Rule 14e-3 prohibits any "person who is in possession of material information relating to [a] tender offer" to trade on that information without any reference to a duty.[109] The Second Circuit held en banc by a 10-1 vote that the SEC had power to promulgate the rule.

---

[106] 445 U.S. 231–32 (citation omitted).

[107] *See Dirks v. SEC*, 463 U.S. 646, n.14 (1983): Under certain circumstances, such as where corporate information is revealed legitimately to an underwriter, accountant, lawyer, or consultant working for the corporation, these outsiders may become fiduciaries of the shareholders. The basis for recognizing this fiduciary duty is not simply that such persons acquired nonpublic corporate information, but rather that they have entered into a special confidential relationship in the conduct of the business of the enterprise and are given access to information solely for corporate purposes.

[108] *See Moss v. Morgan Stanley, Inc.*, 719 F.2d 5 (2d Cir. 1983) (under *Chiarella*, investment bank employee who represented bidders not liable to seller of target corporation shares).

[109] For discussion of the SEC power to issue the rule, see the discussion of *United States v. O'Hagan* in § 13.03[F], *infra*. For a discussion of Section 14(e) and tender offers, see Chapter 12, *supra*.

[D]   Tipper-Tippee Liability

An insider who passes information to another person knowing that the other person will trade is a tipper. Whether she trades or not, a tipper has the same liability as an insider who actually trades. The recipient of the information is a tippee, and also has insider trading liability, but only if she trades. If the tippee in turn tips another individual, she also becomes a tipper. Her recipient is a sub-tippee, or remote tippee. One can envision a chain of remoter and remoter tipper-tippees, although at some point an argument may be made that the information is no longer nonpublic information.

The definitive tippee liability case is *Dirks v. SEC*.[110] Raymond Dirks was an insurance industry analyst at a New York brokerage firm. Equity Funding Corp. was a high flying Wall Street darling whose business involved selling clients life insurance and mutual fund shares. Distributions on the shares would pay the premiums on the life insurance (equity funding). Dirks received a tip from a disgruntled former Equity Funding officer (Secrist) that its assets were vastly overstated. Dirks flew to Los Angeles where Equity Funding was located. Lower level Equity Funding employees corroborated some of the fraudulent practices Dirks suspected.[111] After two weeks, Dirks returned to New York, where he advised his firm's clients to sell off their positions in Equity Funding shares. In an administrative proceeding, the SEC proceeded against Dirks's license but, recognizing the role he had played in exposing a massive fraud, the Commission only censured him. The Commission found that he had "aided and abetted" his firm's clients' Rule 10b-5 violations. Dirks appealed.

The Supreme Court found the tippee's obligation to be derivative of the tipper insider's obligation ("there must be a breach of the insider's fiduciary duty before the tippee inherits the duty to disclose or abstain"). The Court thus expanded upon *Chiarella v. United States* and its requirement of a fiduciary relationship but in the context of tipper-tippee liability. Not any tipper-tippee access to an inside source will be sufficient to ground liability:

> The SEC's [access] theory of tippee liability . . . appears rooted in the idea that the antifraud provisions require equal information among all traders. This conflicts with the principle set forth in *Chiarella* that only some persons, under some circumstances, will be barred from trading while in possession of material nonpublic information.

The Court analyzed the important market efficiency and other economic interests that were at stake:

> Imposing a duty to disclose or abstain solely because a person knowingly receives material nonpublic information . . . could have an inhibiting influence on the role of market analysts . . . necessary to the preservation of a healthy market. It is commonplace for analysts to 'ferret out and analyze information,' . . . and this is often done by

---

[110] 463 U.S. 646 (1983).

[111] Dirks also contacted the *Wall Street Journal's* Los Angeles bureau chief. Dirks urged him to write a story about Equity Funding but he refused to do so. He felt that such a massive fraud could not have gone undetected and that any story would be libelous.

meeting with and questioning corporate officers and others who are insiders . . . . It is the nature of this type of information . . . that such information cannot be made simultaneously available to all of the corporation's shareholders or the public generally.[112]

The Court then devised a more limited test of tippee liability. It first became "necessary to determine whether the insider's 'tip' constituted a breach of the insider's fiduciary duty." That, in turn, depends upon "[w]hether the insider personally will benefit, directly or indirectly from his disclosure. Absent some personal gain, there has been no breach of duty to stockholders."[113]

Dirk's tipper, Secrist, received no benefit and therefore violated no fiduciary duty. He, and other Equity Funding employees, were "motivated by a desire to expose . . . fraud," not a desire to commit one. Secrist's additional motive was not to procure a benefit but to seek revenge for his dismissal.

The benefit test of when the tipping fiduciary violates her duty is a broad one, not limited to financial and other tangible benefits. If a corporate CEO tips senior managers of other corporations during their weekly golf outing, she could be found to have received a benefit, either in the form of enhanced reputation or in the form of actual or expected reciprocal exchanges of information. Alternatively, she could be viewed as having made a gift to her golf partners.[114]

In *SEC v. Switzer*,[115] no direct or indirect benefit to the source of the information was found. The insider source thus breached no fiduciary duty and no derivative liability on the part of the alleged tippee could be found. The tippee in that case was Barry Switzer, then football coach at the University of Oklahoma. Allegedly, Switzer was sitting in the bleachers at a track meet behind George Platt, CEO of TIC Corp. and a director of its Phoenix Resources Co. subsidiary. Switzer began eavesdropping on a conversation between Mr. and Ms. Platt. He overheard that an announcement of a "possible liquidation" of Phoenix might be made that week. That weekend Switzer and his cronies, with whom he had invested in the past, organized a scheme to make substantial purchases of Phoenix shares. Later, a liquidation involving payment of a large premium was announced. Switzer and his syndicate profited handsomely.

The court merely applied *Dirks*. Platt, the insider, received no benefit and thus did not breach a fiduciary duty. Because the tippee's duty is derivative of the tipper's, the tippee cannot be held liable if the tipper breached no duty. Switzer escaped liability. Eavesdroppers and others who accidentally overhear may not

---

[112] 463 U.S. 657–59.

[113] *Id.* at 662. In a strong dissent, Justice Blackmun found no support for the requirement of personal gain in order to breach a fiduciary duty. Commentators have agreed. *See, e.g.*, Donald Langevoort, *The Insider Trading Sanctions Act of 1984 and Its Effect on Existing Law*, 37 VAND. L. REV. 1273, 1292 (1984). Lower courts have had little trouble finding the requisite benefit to the tipper, finding an "enhanced personal relationship" (possibly amorous) with a female tippee or "an enhanced professional relationship" with a tippee to suffice.

[114] *See Dirks*, 463 U.S. at 664 (The element of fiduciary duty and exploitation of nonpublic information also exist when an insider makes a gift to a trading relative or friend. The tip and trade resemble trading by the insider himself followed by a gift of the profits to the recipient.").

[115] 590 F. Supp. 756 (W.D. Okla. 1984).

be held liable as tippees, which seems a partial roadmap to evasion of the twin prohibitions on tipping and trading on nonpublic information so received.[116]

[E]   The Misappropriation Theory

United States v. Chiarella left open the possibility that many nontraditional insiders would be able to profit unfairly from their positions. While SEC Rule 14e-3 required no duty and could be used against individuals trading on information about tender offers, other "outsiders" who wrongfully received non-tender offer information that could affect share prices had no duty to shareholders on the opposite side of share trades. Often these "outsiders" have stolen or misappropriated market information from one source in order to purchase shares of other corporations in which they owe no fiduciary or similar duty to anyone. Arguably, under *Chiarella*, no duty to those with whom one trades means no Rule10b-5 insider trading liability.

To remedy this situation courts developed the misappropriation theory. The misappropriation theory "holds that a person commits fraud 'in connection with' a securities transaction, and thereby violates § 10(b) and Rule 10b-5, when she misappropriates confidential information for securities trading purposes, in breach of a duty owed to the source of the information,"[117] rather than in breach of a duty to the investor on the opposite side of the trade, as in the "classical" case of insider trading. The misappropriation theory is not a catchall. Instead, it is the last on a list of four ways to define insiders or their equivalents upon whom the "disclose or abstain" prohibition is visited. Those four ways are:

1. A classical insider or equivalent who by virtue of a [fiduciary or similar] relationship has access to nonpublic information and has a duty to disclose arising from a relationship of trust and confidence between parties to a securities transaction (for example, the corporate director in *Matter of Cady, Roberts & Co.*).

2. A temporary insider, or quasi-insider: an attorney, accountant, banker, consultant or other person who temporarily becomes a fiduciary of the corporation.[118]

3. A tipper or a tippee who meets the receipt of a benefit and tipper breach of fiduciary duty test for tipper-tippee liability (*Dirks*).

4. Someone who steals (or converts) the information in violation of a duty owed to the owner of the information (a misappropriator), or their tippee ("fraud on the source").

---

[116] Had coach Switzer overheard information about a forthcoming tender offer, he would have violated Rule 14e-3 by trading because, under that rule, mere possession of such information is sufficient.

[117] *United States v. O'Hagan*, 521 U.S. 642, 117 S. Ct. 2199 (1997).

[118] The Court in *Dirks v. SEC*, 463 U.S. at 655, n.14, observed that "where corporate information is revealed legitimately to an underwriter, accountant, lawyer, or consultant working for the corporation, those outsiders may become fiduciaries of the shareholders" and have a responsibility to abstain or disclose accordingly.

The misappropriation theory traces its roots to Mr. Chief Justice Burger's dissent in *Chiarella v. United States*.[119] Justice Burger was incensed that Vincent Chiarella would go free. He found that "the evidence shows beyond all doubt that Chiarella, working literally in the shadows of warnings in the print shop, misappropriated-stole to put it bluntly-valuable nonpublic information entrusted to him in the utmost confidence. He then exploited his ill-gotten informational advantage by purchasing securities." Chief Justice Burger posited an alternative theory of liability, based upon violation of a duty to the owner or rightful possessor of the information: "I would read § 10(b) and Rule 10b-5 to encompass and . . . to mean that a person who has misappropriated nonpublic information has an absolute duty to disclose that information or to refrain from trading."

Chief Justice Burger included, four (and possibly five, including Justice Stevens) justices subscribed to the theory, as a theory, but the majority felt that "we need not decide whether this theory has merit for it was not submitted to the jury." Thus was planted the seed that grew into the misappropriation theory of insider trading liability.

A question under the misappropriation theory is whether a "mere thief" will do, or whether by their theft the thief must breach "a fiduciary duty to the lawful possessor of non-public information." The court in *SEC v. Cherif*[120] posed that question. First National Bank of Chicago had employed Cherif from 1979 until late 1987. After his dismissal, Cherif kept his magnetic identification card. On weekends, with the card, Cherif gained access to the bank's offices and its Specialized Finance Department, which provided financing for takeovers, leveraged buyouts and other "deals." Cherif rifled former co-workers desks, obtaining names of target companies and investing in them. His profits for seven months totalled $247,000.

Running through the checklist, Cherif was not a classical insider; the bank had dismissed him. Nor was he a tippee; no one gave him the information. Instead, he was a trespasser and a thief. The only theory left with which to pinion liability on Cherif was misappropriation. But Cherif contended that he was only a thief, that the misappropriation theory required that the theft be in violation of a fiduciary duty, and that his fiduciary duty ceased when the bank dismissed him. His conduct "may have amounted to theft, but it did not constitute fraud," he argued.

The Seventh Circuit reviewed the cases from other Courts of Appeals, adopting the misappropriation theory. The Court then quoted Restatement (Second) Agency § 395, which posits a continuing duty by a former agent "not to use or communicate information confidentially given him by the principal or acquired by him during the course . . . of the agency." Cherif breached that fiduciary duty by misuse of his key card, his knowledge of the internal procedures of the bank, and other confidential information acquired during his employment. "His trades were 'in connection with' a fraudulent scheme to gain access to material, non-public information" in violation of Rule 10b-5. "Cherif

---

[119] 445 U.S. 222 at 239 (1980).

[120] 933 F.2d 403 (7th Cir. 1991), *cert. denied*, 502 U.S. 1071 (1992).

betrayed a trust in a way that a mere thief does not." Misappropriation thus requires a theft in violation of a fiduciary or similar duty to the source of the information.

SEC v. Materia[121] involved facts nearly identical to *Chiarella.* Materia was a financial printer who purchased shares in target corporations, just like Chiarella. His conviction on the basis of misappropriation was upheld. *United States v. Libera*[122] involved a printer who provided two traders with advance copies of *Business Week* magazine. The traders reaped profits by investing in shares of companies that received favorable mention in the magazine's "Inside Wall Street" column. The case held that a tippee may be liable either on a tip from a classical insider (*Dirks*) or on a tip from a misappropriator (the printer here). "The tipper's knowledge that he or she was breaching a duty to the owner of confidential information suffices to establish the tipper's expectation that the breach will lead to some kind of misuse of the information."

In *SEC v. Musella,*[123] the trial court applied the misappropriation tipper-tippee doctrine to an office manager at the prestigious New York law firm of Sullivan & Cromwell. The office manager tipped to two different groups of traders the names of target corporations for whom Sullivan & Cromwell clients were going to make bids.

In *United States v. Bryan,*[124] however, the Fourth Circuit rejected the theory. Bryan was the director of the West Virginia state lottery. He purchased shares in corporations about to receive state lottery contracts. He was convicted of insider trading, based upon his misappropriation of information.

The Fourth Circuit reversed, finding that under the misappropriation theory the act (theft of information) does not occur "in connection with" the deception and the purchase or sale of securities:

> The misappropriation of information from an individual who is in no way connected to . . . securities is simply not the kind of conduct with which the securities laws . . . are concerned. In essence the misappropriation theory disregards the specific [Section 10(b)] requirement of deception, in favor of a requirement of a mere fiduciary duty breach, and then artificially divides into two discrete requirements-a fiduciary breach and a purchase of sale of securities the single indivisible requirement of deception upon the purchaser or seller of securities . . . .[125]

---

[121] 745 F.2d 197 (2d Cir. 1984), *cert. denied,* 471 U.S. 1053 (1985).

[122] 989 F.2d 596 (2d Cir. 1993).

[123] 578 F. Supp. 425 (S.D.N.Y. 1984).

[124] 58 F.3d 933 (4th Cir. 1995).

[125] 58 F.3d at 949.

[F]   The Misappropriation Theory in the Supreme Court

Post-*Chiarella*, the misappropriation theory made two trips to the Supreme Court. Only on the second trip did the Court reach the merits of the theory. The first trip, however, was interesting indeed.

Foster Winans was one of several *Wall Street Journal* reporters who researched and wrote "Heard on the Street" columns for the *Journal*. "Heard on the Street" is the most widely read investment advice column in the United States. A pessimistic or negative report, or an enthusiastically positive one, in "Heard on the Street" may move a corporation's stock price up or down several points.

Winans and his colleagues would write columns, which the *Journal* would then keep in reserve for publication at a later date. When Winans learned from the publication schedule that one of his columns was coming out of reserve, he tipped two stockbrokers through an intermediary (Carpenter). The brokers moved quickly into stocks and then quickly out again when the particular "Heard" column had the expected effect on market prices. Winans had received a forty-page manual from the *Journal* which had seven pages devoted to conflicts of interest for journalists. He also knew that company policy deemed all news material gathered on the job to be company property.

The scheme was uncovered, to the acute embarrassment of the *Wall Street Journal*. The United States Attorney prosecuted Winans and his confederates under the misappropriation theory. They were convicted. On appeal,[126] they argued that other Second Circuit misappropriation cases, such as *Materia*, were inapposite because in those cases the information was misappropriated by employees who owed a duty of confidentiality not only to their employers, but also to their employers' clients, which sought to buy shares of the corporations whose shares the insiders traded. In other words, appellants argued that the misappropriation theory may be applied only where the information is misappropriated by corporate insiders or so-called quasi-insiders.[127] Winans, the journalist, owed no duty to anyone other than the *Journal*, which he breached by tipping as to the content and publication schedule for future "Heard" columns.

That breach of duty was sufficient, the Second Circuit held. But what if the *Journal* itself chose to trade on information to appear in future "Heard" columns? The Court noted, without deciding, that the *Journal* could make those trades, while at the same time continuing to forbid Winans from trading or tipping and, in that case, Winans could still be prosecuted if he violated the *Journal*'s rule and misappropriated.[128]

---

[126] *United States v. Carpenter*, 791 F.2d 1024, *aff'd*, 484 U.S. 19 (1987).

[127] 791 F.2d at 1028.

[128] 791 F.2d at 1033 (footnote omitted):

Appellants argue that it is anomalous to hold an employee liable for acts that his employer could lawfully commit. Admittedly, the employers in [previous cases] were investment banks that would barred by the federal securities laws from trading or tipping in securities of their clients, while in the present case the *Wall Street Journal* . . . might perhaps

And what if the *Journal* permitted some or all of its reporters to trade, as an added "perk" of the job? There then would be no breach of fiduciary or other relationship of trust and confidence, no misappropriation, and no violation of Rule 10b-5.[129]

The Supreme Court granted a writ of *certiorari*. The case was argued. The Court did not reach a decision, Mr. Justice White noting that "[t]he Court is evenly divided with respect to the convictions under the securities laws and for that reason affirms the judgment below on those counts."[130]

Ten years later the misappropriation theory of insider trading made its way back before the Court in *United States v. O'Hagan*.[131] The Court affirmed a conviction under the theory.

James O'Hagan was a partner in a large Minneapolis law firm that the English company, Metropolitan PLC (Grand Met), retained in preparation for a possible tender offer for shares of Pillsbury Co., headquartered in Minneapolis. O'Hagan did no legal work for Grand Met but he found out about the potential takeover. He proceeded to purchase call options (that is, a right to buy shares at a fixed price for a time period) on 250,000 shares of Pillsbury and purchased long another 5000 shares, at $39 per share. Subsequently, O'Hagan's law firm withdrew from representing Grand Met. A month later, when Grand Met announced its bid, Pillsbury's share price rose to $60. O'Hagan made a $4.3 million profit.

O'Hagan was disbarred by the Supreme Court of Minnesota. He was convicted in state court, then sentenced to 30 months imprisonment. The SEC obtained a 57-count indictment, a trial was had, and O'Hagan was convicted and sentenced to a 41-month term of imprisonment.

The Court of Appeals for the Eighth Circuit reversed. Applying the reasoning of *United States v. Bryan*, quoted above, the court rejected the misappropriation theory as a basis for Section 10(b) liability. Noting the split among circuits, the Supreme Court granted *certiorari*.

The Supreme Court upheld the misappropriation theory. It rejected the notion that the fiduciary or other duty of trust and confidence must run in the same direction as the offending purchase or sale, as it does in the classical insider trading case. "The misappropriation theory comports with § 10(b)'s language, which requires deception 'in connection with the purchase or sale of any security,' not deception of an identifiable purchaser or seller." Hence, the deception may run one direction, toward the trader or tipper's employer or

---

lawfully disregard its own confidentiality policy by trading in the stock of companies to be discussed in forthcoming articles. Another criticism of that approach is that criminal behavior then results from the terms of a particular employment contract.

[129] Initially, the SEC had argued that Winans and Carpenter owed a duty to the readers of the *Journal* but dropped that contention when First Amendment issues were raised.

[130] 484 U.S. 19 (1987). The justices did unanimously affirm the convictions of Winans and his confederates on federal wire and mail fraud counts.

[131] 521 U.S. 642 (1997).

client, and the trade run another. The Court thus expressly rejected the criticism of the misappropriation theory by the Fourth Circuit in *United States v. Bryan.*

In terms of technical Rule 10b-5 law, the Court had to demonstrate how the "misappropriator's deceptive use of information [can] be 'in connection with the purchase or sale of [a] security.'" "This element is satisfied," the Court noted, "because the fiduciary's fraud is consummated, not when the fiduciary gains the confidential information but when, without disclosure to his principal, he uses the information to purchase or sell securities." As a corollary, "[s]hould the misappropriator put such information to other use," rather than trading in securities, "the statute's prohibition would not be implicated."

The Court did point to a means whereby O'Hagan may have been able to do what he desired to do. He could brazenly have told his law firm, as his employer and as agent for Grand Met, that he had knowledge of the possible bid and that he planned to use the information to trade. "Because the deception essential to the misappropriation theory involves feigning fidelity to the source of information, if the fiduciary discloses to the source that he plans to trade on the nonpublic information, there is no 'deceptive device' and thus no § 10(b) violation, although the fiduciary-turned-trader may remain liable under state law for breach of the duty of loyalty."[132]

The last matter with which the Court had to deal was to avoid *Chiarella's* reasoning. The Court in *Chiarella* emphasized that Section 10(b) liability "is premised upon a duty to disclose arising from a relationship of trust and confidence between parties to a transaction."[133] How could the Court square a doctrine premised upon violation of a relationship of trust and confidence running the other way, to the possessor of the nonpublic information, with that statement from *United States v. Chiarella*?

The *O'Hagan* Court found that those statements "rejected the notion that § 10(b) stretches so far as to impose a 'general duty between all participants in market transactions to forgo actions based on material, nonpublic information,' and we confine them to that context." In other words, the narrow statement in *Chiarella* was a matter of emphasis, utilized to create a stark contrast with some general duty to everyone in the marketplace. Moreover, *Chiarella* is "an opinion carefully leaving for future resolution the validity of the misappropriation theory, and therefore cannot be read to foreclose that theory."

The result in *O'Hagan* delighted the SEC, which, over the years, had had more than its share of defeats in the Supreme Court. *O'Hagan* does not answer all questions that may arise under the misappropriation theory of insider trading, nor smooth over the theory's logical inconsistencies.[134] *O'Hagan* does,

---

[132] That, of course, would be a civil rather than criminal matter. And as the discussion of *United States v. Carpenter* intimates, the employer or client could conceivably grant the trader or tipper permission to trade or tip, in which case even a duty of loyalty case might fall by the wayside.

[133] 445 U.S. 222, at 230.

[134] With Rule 10b-2, the SEC has attempted to answer some of those questions, providing a non-exclusive list of relationships of trust and confidence that will convert a mere thief into a

though, firm up the list of four ways in which, as a matter of federal law, the disclose-or abstain prohibition may be visited upon someone.

[G]   Tippees of Misapporiators

To the categories of persons upon whom the "disclose or abstain" prohibition may be visited (classical insider, temporary insider, tipper-tippee, and misappropriator) must be added a fifth category, the tippee of a misappropriator. An illustrative case is *United States v. Falcone*.[135] Each edition of *Business Week* magazine contains a widely read investment advice column, "Inside Wall Street." Favorable mention of a company and its stock in the column often has an effect on the stock's market price. McGraw-Hill, *Business Week's* publisher, used Curtis Circulation Co. as its nationwide distributor. In turn, Hudson News Agency, which runs kiosks and stores in airports and other venues across the U.S., received a substantial number of copies each week from Curtis, with strict instructions not to release them until after 5:00 PM on Thursdays. Each Thursday morning, Greg Salvage, a Hudson employee, would fax an advance copy of the "Inside Wall Street" column to Smath, a stock broker who was Salvage's next door neighbor. Smath tipped Falcone, who profited from advance receipt of this nonpublic market information.

Falcone thus represents not only the case of a misappropriator (Salvage, who not only knew of his employer's confidentiality policy but was in charge of enforcing it) who stole information in violation of a fiduciary or similar duty owed to the owner of the information, but also of a tippee-tipper (Smath), and a remote tippee (Falcone). According to the Second Circuit, the required elements for tippee liability in the misappropriation context are "(i) a breach by the tipper of a duty owed to the owner of the nonpublic information; and (ii) the tippee's knowledge that the tipper had breached the duty."[136]

Falcone made a feeble protestation as to the latter but the prosecutors had testimony to the contrary. "Smath testified that defendant [Falcone] paid him $200 for each column, substantially in excess of the magazine's sales price." Based upon that circumstantial evidence, the jury was justified in finding that Falcone had knowledge that the original tipper had breached the duty owed to the owner of the information.

---

misappropriator. The list includes persons who have agreed to maintain information in confidence, persons to whom information is communicated who have a history, pattern or practice of sharing confidences with the possessor of the information, and persons who receive information from a spouse, parent, child or sibling.

[135] 257 F.3d 226 (2d Cir. 2001).

[136] Quoting an almost identical case involving theft of *Business Week's* "Inside Wall Street" column, *U.S. v. Libera*, 989 F.2d 596 (2d Cir. 1993). Still another very similar case was *U.S. v. Carpenter*, discussed in § 13.04[F], *supra* (misappropriation of the publication schedule for "Heard on the Street" column of the *Wall Street Journal*).

[H]   Remedies and Enforcement

Persons who trade "contemporaneously" with trading by an insider, tippee, or misappropriator may sue for damages. In 1988 Congress adopted the Insider Trading and Securities Fraud Enforcement Act (ITSFEA), which added a new Section 20A ("Liability to Contemporaneous Traders for Insider Trading") to the Securities Exchange Act of 1934. The section statutorily recognizes what the courts first recognized in 1946, in *Kardon v. National Gypsum Co.*,[137] a right of a purchaser or seller to sue the person who sold or bought while in possession of inside information. The legislative history of Section 20A seems to indicate that the section codifies a private right of action against both classical insiders and misappropriators.[138]

Those who were contemporaneous traders, that is, those whose trades occurred "not more than a few days apart from the defendant's," may sue.[139]

The amount of damage, as opposed to the existence of a right to sue, is another issue. In the early days of Rule 10b-5, it was thought possible that all contemporaneous traders could recover from the insiders who trade.[140] In such a case, the amount of liability would far outstrip the profit made or the loss avoided by the insider. The first court to put its foot down and vigorously disagree with such a proposition was the Court of Appeals for the Sixth Circuit in *Fridrich v. Bradford.*[141] Bradford received a tip about an insurance company merger. He purchased 1225 shares of Old Line Insurance stock, selling the shares after the merger was announced. He made a $13,000 profit. The district court held him liable to a class of persons who sold when Bradford was buying. The court awarded those plaintiffs $361,186.75 and Bradford's liability to all contemporaneous sellers was estimated at $800,000.

The Sixth Circuit treated the problem as one of causation. "Defendants' trading did not alter plaintiffs' expectations when they sold their stock, and in no way influenced plaintiffs' trading decision." The court stated that there must be a "causal link" between defendant's trading on insider information and plaintiffs' damage.

Of course, there is causation. Had Bradford complied with the obligation placed upon him by his tippee status, he would have disclosed and waited for dissemination of the information, before trading. Had that occurred, presumably plaintiffs would not have sold their shares. The Sixth Circuit was correct,

---

[137] 69 F. Supp. 512 (E.D. Pa. 1946).

[138] *See SEC v. Clark*, 915 F.2d 439 (9th Cir. 1990) ("The House Committee reporting on the bill acknowledged that the misappropriation theory had split the Supreme Court in *Carpenter*, yet nonetheless endorsed the theory as consistent with the broad objectives of § 10(b) and Rule 10b-5."). Another view is that Congress did not endorse the theory but let the courts decide, which the Supreme did in *United States v. O'Hagan.*

[139] *See Neubronner v. Milkin*, 6 F.3d 666 (9th Cir. 1993). *See also* William Wang, *The "Contemporaneous" Traders Who Can Sue an Insider Trader*, 38 Hastings L. J. 1175 (1987).

[140] It was even possible to claim damages for trades taking place in the entire period in which the information had not been disclosed, which could be a period of months.

[141] 542 F.2d 307 (6th Cir. 1976), *cert. denied*, 429 U.S. 1053 (1977).

though, in identifying that there existed a problem concerning the scale between the degree of an insider or tippee's fault and the amount of potential damages.

In *Elkind v. Liggett & Myers*,[142] the court noted again the problem of "Draconian, exorbitant damages, out of all proportion to the wrong committed, lining the pockets of all interim investors and their counsel." The court considered and rejected the so-called out-of-pocket measure of damages applied to a corporate issuer of securities who makes a misleading statement. Under that measure, if investors purchase one million shares at $50 which, but for the puffing misrepresentation by the corporation, would only have sold for $40, the corporation is liable for $10 million.

The case of trading or tipping is different. "Except in rare face-to-face transactions . . . uninformed traders on an impersonal market are not induced by representations on the part of a tippee to buy or sell," as they are when a corporate issuer makes a glowing, and false, representation. "Usually they ['victims of insider trading'] are wholly unacquainted with and uninfluenced by the tippee's misconduct."

Liggett & Myers had tipped certain persons to a forthcoming low earnings report. The tippee then sold 1800 shares on the open market, avoiding a price decline from $55 to $46 per share. The investors sued the tipper, which is permitted, even if the tipper has not traded. The Court reviewed other measures of damage, adopting instead of "out-of-pocket" the "disgorgement" measure. The insider trader, tipper, or tippee's liability is capped at the amount of the profit made or the loss avoided ($9.35 per share in the case at bar). Those who sue the insider or tippee recover pro rata if the sum of their claims exceeds the profit made or the loss avoided. In the case of a loss avoided, the loss is calculated using the share price at the time the information is disclosed ($55 here) and at the time at which the court concludes the information has been effectively disseminated ($46, two days after disclosure).

In Section 20A of the Securities Exchange Act, Congress adopted the "disgorgement" measure of damages for the statutory cause of action.[143] Before Section 20A's enactment, many lower federal courts had adopted the disgorgement measure. The question that arises is whether the disgorgement measure of damage results in under-deterrence of insider trading and creates a moral hazard for those who regularly come in contact with inside information. The one-time trader may think that if all she has to do is give up any profit if she is caught, the proposition is "heads I win, tails I break even." The potential repeat player thinks that, if she trades ten times, makes $100,000 each time, and gets caught twice, she disgorges $200,000 and retains $800,000.

The risk of criminal enforcement, or of having to defend an SEC civil action for injunctive relief, increases the cost for an insider and hence the amount of

---

[142] 635 F.2d 156 (2d Cir. 1980).

[143] *See* Securities Exchange Act § 20A(b)(1) & (2) ("The total amount of damages imposed- . . . shall not exceed the profit gained or loss avoided in the transaction" but "[t]he total amount of damages . . . shall be diminished by the amounts, if any, that such person maybe required to disgorge [in an SEC proceeding] or [in a proceeding for civil penalties]").

deterrence but not significantly so. The SEC and the Justice Department have limited prosecutorial resources to devote to insider trading enforcement.

With the "disgorgement" measure of damages and the problem of under-deterrence in mind, Congress adopted the Insider Trading Sanctions Act of 1984. The Act added a new Section 21A ("Civil Penalties for Insider Trading") to the Securities Exchange Act of 1934. The SEC is authorized to bring an action against insider traders for a civil penalty which "shall not exceed three times the profit gained or loss avoided as a result of such unlawful purchase, sale or communication [tip]." The penalty may be in addition to disgorgement of the profit or the loss avoided, which the SEC may procure or private litigants recover in a suit for damages.[144]

In 1988, Congress extended the civil penalty provision to controlling persons (brokerage firms, banks, investment advisers, law firms) of persons who trade or tip. To obtain the penalty, however, the SEC must show that the controlling person "knew or recklessly disregarded the fact that such controlled person was likely to engage in the act or acts constituting the violation." Alternatively, the SEC may show that the controlling person "knowingly or recklessly failed to establish, maintain or enforce any [required] policy or procedure." The 1988 amendments impose an obligation upon broker-dealers to develop and maintain adequate internal controls and supervision systems to prevent securities law violations by their employees.[145]

The insider trading area is conceptually difficult but must be understood. SEC civil and criminal enforcement is much more frequent than it was 25 years ago. The Supreme Court's decision in *O'Hagan* affirms use of a tool (the misappropriation theory) that the SEC has been using for some time. Congress, too, has climbed on the insider trading enforcement bandwagon, with statutory recognition of civil liability, severe civil penalty provisions, and extension of those provisions to controlling persons.

[I] SEC Regulation FD

An issuer or a person acting it is behalf may impart material information to a research analyst, an institutional investor, an investment advisor, or holder of a significant quantity of the issuer's securities. Were the recipient of the information to trade, or tip others to do so, the insider trading and tipping prohibitions, with civil and criminal penalties, would apply. But to deal with the selective, or differential, disclosure problem in instances in which insider trading is not implicated, the SEC needed additional tools.

Through a new regulation promulgated in 2000, Regulation FD (for Fair Disclosure) (SEC Rules 100–103), the SEC has once again attempted to level the playing field, to insure a parity of information for all investors, at least for non public information being disclosed by corporate sources.[146]

---

[144] Thus, insiders may have to pay four times the profit made or the loss avoided by their insider trading.

[145] Securities Exchange Act § 15(f).

[146] Regulation FD is violated when an SEC reporting company, or any person acting on its behalf,

The SEC attempted to charge a violation of Regulation FD but was rebuffed in *SEC v. Seibel Systems, Inc.*.[147] The district court granted a defense Rule12(b)(6) motion to dismiss the SEC's civil complaint, on grounds that officers of Seibel had not violated Regulation FD. The CFO had made positive statements about Seibel's future prospects ("the order pipeline was growing," "activity levels were good or better than" previous quarters). He did so at 2 private conferences. Simultaneously, the Seibel CEO made public statements that the company's results looked to be flat, or even slightly negative. The SEC charged the CFO with selective disclosure and a violation of regulation FD.

"Regulation FD deals exclusively with the disclosure of material information. The regulation does not prohibit persons speaking on behalf of an issuer from providing more positive or negative interpretations, or their optimistic or pessimistic subjective general impressions, based upon or drawn from the material information available to the public," the judge observed in a common sense way. Persons who speak need neither use "identical words" nor impart the exact same substance, as the SEC staff seemed to assert. The court found that the information the CFO had alleged leaked was neither material nor non public. The case represents a slap on the wrist for the SEC in its efforts to "level the playing field."

State court judges read the newspapers. They have witnessed these events unfold, through the takeover boom of the 1980s and into the current century. When presented with issues regarding the treatment of insider trading under state law, they have not stood still. The modern evolution of the insider trading prohibition in the state courts must then be is the subject to which this chapter turns.

§ 13.05   THE INSIDER TRADING PROHIBITION UNDER STATE LAW

[A]   Common Law

Trading on insider information was not necessarily conduct of which common law courts approved.[148] Rather, strait-jacketed by legal formalism, turn of the century judges were unable to reach the practice utilizing the legal tools at their proposal.

---

makes selective disclosures to a broker dealer, an investment adviser, an investment manager, or to a holder of the company's stock. when it is reasonably forseeable that the person may buy or sell the corporation's securities. The selective disclosure itself violates the rule "when the person making the disclosure either knows, or is reckless in not knowing, that the information he or she is communicating is both material and nonpublic." In cases of non intentional disclosure, the issuer must "promptly" make public disclosure. Promptly "means as soon as reasonably practicable (but in no event after the later of 24 hours or the commencement of the next day's trading on the New York Stock Exchange"). In cases of intentional violations, senior officials at an issuer must take immediate corrective action. Certain violations of Regulation FD would also constitute tipping for civil and criminal liability purposes.

[147] 384 F. Supp. 2d 694 (S.D.N.Y. 2005).

[148] *Compare* Frank Easterbrook & Daniel Fischel, THE ECONOMIC STRUCTURE OF CORPORATE LAW 264 (1991) (majority rule at common law permitted insiders to trade), *with* Douglas M. Branson,

For example, when shareholders sued traditional insiders (officers or directors), alleging that the insider's trade breached a fiduciary duty, courts were quick to note that the duty, if any, was owed to the corporation and not to any particular shareholder. Courts dismissed plaintiffs' breach of fiduciary duty claims because the gist of the complaint was that the shareholder who sold to or bought from the insider, and not the corporation, had been harmed.[149]

Other common law plaintiffs pursued fraud claims against trading insiders. That is, they alleged that the director or officer who engaged in affirmative misrepresentations or who answered inquiries with half-truths was liable in tort to her purchaser or seller, just as any other citizen would be in a commercial transaction.[150] However, in many cases, the plaintiff could complain only of a director's silence, not of affirmative misrepresentation or misleading half truth. At common law, silence was actionable only if a duty to speak existed. A duty to speak existed only if a fiduciary or similar duty was owed. As has been seen, the formalistic view, however, was that a corporate fiduciary owed a duty to the corporation and not to the shareholder.

As greater numbers of shares were traded over the medium of a stock exchange, a plaintiff also could no longer allege that she had been in privity with the defendant. Common law fraud required privity of dealing between the parties.[151] Other insider trading claims failed on this basis.

[B]   Common Law Exceptions: The Kansas Rule

A few courts condemned all insider trading. A prohibition of silence by a fiduciary when in possession of material nonpublic investment information was called the "Kansas rule" because the courts of that state marked out a position which uniformly condemned insider trading.[152] They held that insiders owed a

---

Choosing the Appropriate Default Rule-Insider Trading Under State Law, 45 Ala. L. Rev. 753 (1994) ("There exist no fewer than five state law foundations upon which judges could base (and have based) findings of civil or criminal liability for insider trading").

[149]   This was in part the rationale of *Goodwin v. Agassiz*, 186 N.E. 659, 660 (Mass. 1933), turning back a challenge to share purchases by two corporate officers who possessed information about a valuable new mining methodology or theory the corporation possessed. Earlier, English courts had reached the same conclusion. *See Percival v. Wright*, 2 Ch. 421 (1902).

[150]   One common scenario involves a shareholder who, before selling to the insider, asks whether there are any plans afoot to merge or sell the corporation. The insider answers "no," knowing full well that a plan does exist to sell the assets of the corporation and liquidate it. The common law of fraud often would give a remedy in such cases of half truth. Indeed, one of the early rule 10b-5 cases was similar. *See Kardon v. National Gypsum Co.*, 69 F. Supp. 512 (E.D. Pa. 1946) (half truth or false reply to question of whether any negotiations were then pending for sale of the company).

[151]   *See Goodwin v. Agassiz*, 186 N.E. at 661 (as a tort claim, plaintiff's case failed as transactions took place on the Boston Stock Exchange and, hence, the required privity was lacking).

[152]   The leading case is *Hotchkiss v. Fisher*, 16 P.2d 531, 534 (Kan. 1932) (in dealing with a shareholder a corporate director was under a duty to act fairly toward her and "to communicate . . . all material facts in connection with the transaction"). *See also Blakesley v. Johnson*, 608 P.2d 908 (Kan. 1980) (same); *Newton v. Hornblower*, 582 P.2d 1146 (Kan. 1978) ("strict fiduciary relationship" owed to shareholders in share dealing matters); *Sampson v. Hunt*, 564 P.2d 489 (Kan. 1997) ("very strict fiduciary duty"). California and Georgia had similar precedents. *See Taylor v. Wright*, 159 P.2d 980 (Cal. Ct. App. 1945); *Oliver v. Oliver*, 45 S.E. 232 (Ga. 1903).

446 SEC RULE 10b-5 DISCLOSURE AND INSIDER TRADING CH. 13

"strict" or "very strict" fiduciary duty to disclose to shareholders with whom those insiders dealt.[153]

[C]   Common Law Exceptions: Special Facts Doctrine

In *Strong v. Repide*,[154] a corporate director had purchased plaintiff's shares in the Philippine Sugar Estates Development Company. Defendant was in charge of negotiations to sell the corporation's principal assets, land in the Philippines, to the United States government at a large profit. The corporation then intended to liquidate, distributing the profits. The sale of a principal asset, coupled with an intent to liquidate, were "special facts" justifying an exception to the normal rule that may have permitted a trading defendant to remain silent. Plaintiff Strong could recover from the purchasing fiduciary.

While in *Strong v. Repide* the Court held "there are cases where, by reason of the special facts, such duty [to disclose] exists," the Court gave no comprehensive definition of the types of facts that constitute "special facts." Usually, the special facts involved the director's or officer's knowledge of the probability or the certainty of an episodic event in the corporation's life (such as a forthcoming merger, takeover bid, or liquidation as in *Strong. v. Repide*). Other forms of material nonpublic information such as a drastically higher (or lower) earnings reports, a forthcoming favorable contract or new product, or the departure or arrival of key personnel were not sufficient to invoke the doctrine. The exact line of what separated material facts and special facts was never, however, defined.

[D]   Modern Expansion of the Special Facts Doctrine

In *Bailey v. Vaughn*,[155] the court reviewed a great number of state appellate court opinions in the insider trading area. The court found that the special facts doctrine states the majority state law rule.[156] Moreover, the court concluded that a special fact is any fact "that bears upon the potential increase [or decrease] in value of the shares."

The expanded special facts doctrine seems to represent the majority view among state courts today.[157] Special facts include any material facts which the insider knows a reasonable investor or shareholder would want to know in making the decision to buy or sell.

---

[153] Even the Kansas rule did not protect the investor who bought shares from the insider because there was not existing duty running from the insider to the new investor in the corporation.

[154] 213 U.S. 419 (1909).

[155] 359 S.E.2d 599 (W. Va. 1987).

[156] "[W]e are drawn to the conclusion that a director who solicits a shareholder to purchase his stock and fails to disclose information not known to the shareholder . . . shall be liable to the shareholder . . . ." 359 S.E.2d at 603.

[157] See, e.g., *Van Schaack Holdings v. Van Schaack*, 867 P.2d 896 (Colo. 1994), in which the court adopted a broadened special facts doctrine to hold liable insiders who purchased plaintiff's shares while in possession of information that the new Denver, Colorado airport would in part be built on land owned by the corporation. The court swept aside any limited definition of special facts, adopting a standard that special facts include all material facts.

[E]   Finding Harm to the Corporation from the Insider's Trading

Another state law approach to insider trading is based on the principle that insider trading damages the corporation as well as the trading shareholder and, thus, violates fiduciary duties owed by the insider to the corporation. Although several of the cases are well-known, the theory has had mixed acceptance and cannot be stated to have the currency of the expanded special facts doctrine.

In *Diamond v. Oreamuno*,[158] the New York Court of Appeals found that insider trading does harm the corporation and violates duties the insider owes to it:

> Although the corporation may have little concern with the day-today transactions in its shares, it has a great interest in maintaining a reputation of integrity, an image of probity, for its management and in insuring the public acceptance and marketability of its stock. When officers and directors abuse their position in order to gain personal profits, the effect may be to cast a cloud on the corporation's name, injure stockholder relations and undermine public regard for the corporation's securities.[159]

Diamond permits a derivative suit for insider trading, which allows for a corporate recovery.[160] *Diamond*, however, has not found widespread acceptance and several courts have expressly rejected its reasoning. In *Schein v. Chasen*,[161] the Supreme Court of Florida emphasized that under Florida decisions "actual damage to the corporation must be alleged." The court strongly intimated that the corporate president's act of tipping two stock brokers to a forthcoming lower earning's report had not harmed the corporation. Only the shareholders who had purchased at a higher price while tippees were selling had suffered cognizable harm. Similarly, applying Indiana law, in *Freeman v. Decio*,[162] the Seventh Circuit refused to follow *Diamond*, finding any harm to the corporation from insider trading to be non-existent or *de minimis*.

By contrast, the A.L.I. Project states that "Section 5.04 rejects [*Freeman v. Decio*] . . . and in so doing follows the result reached . . . in *Diamond v. Oreamuno*."[163] A federal district court decision found that New Jersey law would

---

[158]   248 N.E.2d 910 (N.Y. 1969).

[159]   248 N.E.2d at 912. The New York court relied upon an older Delaware decision, *Brophy v. Cities Service Co.*, 70 A.2d 5 (Del. Ch. 1949), which came to a similar conclusion that trading by insiders also harms the corporation.

[160]   A difficulty with a derivative action and a recovery by the corporation is that, in a federal Rule 10b-5 action, the insider might also be held liable to the persons who sold or purchased when the insider traded. In addition, a derivative suit would not help those who sold shares since they no longer own corporate shares and get no benefit from a corporate recovery.

[161]   313 So. 2d 739 (Fla. 1975).

[162]   589 F.2d 186 (7th Cir. 1978).

[163]   A.L.I. Corp. Gov. Proj. § 5.04, comment (d)(2)(a) at 270 ("Use by a Director or Senior Executive of Corporate Property, Material Non-Public Corporate Information, or Corporate Position").

follow *Diamond* and find state law liability for insider trading. The court expressly refused to follow *Freeman v. Decio* and take "such limited view of potential harm to the corporation."[164]

§ 13.06 REGULATION OF INSIDER TRADING UNDER SECTION 16 OF THE SECURITIES EXCHANGE ACT OF 1934

[A] Statutory Provisions

Section 16 is the original explicit insider trading provision, dating from 1934. Section 16(b) presumes that any officer, director or holder of 10% or more of an SEC reporting company[165] who purchases and sells or sells and purchases within a 6 month period is presumed to have traded on inside information. Such person is therefore made liable to the corporation for the profit and subject to a derivative suit. The provision is commonly referred to as "the short swing profits provision." Section 16(a) is a reporting provision.

Immediately after a corporation achieves reporting status, or after the director, officer or 10% holder (insider) achieves status as director, officer or 10% holder, the insider must file a report with the SEC indicating all equity securities of the issuing corporation of which they are the beneficial owner. Under the original legislation, in the first 10 days of any month following a month in which a change in their beneficial ownership has occurred, these insiders must file a report with the SEC. Under the post-Enron Sarbanes Oxley legislation, effective in 2003, the reporting requirement is in near real time, "before the end of second business day following the day on which the subject transaction has been executed."[166] The § 16 insider must now file reports electronically. The SEC must post such "statements on a publicly accessible Internet site not later than the end of the business day following [the] filing," as must the issuer on its corporate website (if the issuer maintains a corporate website).[167]

Certain schools of investment research follow very closely the filing of Section 16(a) reports on the theory that investment success may be achieved by doing what the insiders have been doing. Various publishers sell market letters that do nothing else but report Section 16(a) filings. With near real time reporting under Sarbanes-Oxley, the timely and widespread availability of information in insider trading reports has been enhanced still further.

---

[164] *In re Orfa Securities Litigation*, 654 F. Supp. 1449, 1457 (D.N.J. 1987).

[165] Those include corporations with a class of shares listed on a national stock exchange (12(b) corporations) and those corporations traded OTC with a class of equity securities held by 750 or more persons and $10 million or more in assets (12(g) corporations). See the discussion in § 7.02[A], *supra*.

[166] Securities Exchange Act of 1934 § 16 (a)(2)(C).

[167] *Id.*, § 16(a)(4)(B), (C).

Section 16(c) contains a prohibition on insiders selling short the equity securities of their corporation.[168] Since that is so, the reference in Section 16(b) to liability for "sale and purchase" must have a reference to other than short selling. The reference is intended to govern the situation in which insiders sell shares they own, presumably because of adverse information, replacing those securities in their portfolio with securities purchased at a lower price after the information has been disseminated through the markets.

[B]   Parties Plaintiff and Calculation of Damages

Section 16(b) liability is often referred to as "draconian" or "in terrorem," in part because it is strict liability but also because of the manner in which damages are calculated. "The only rule," the Second Circuit noted in an early case,[169] "whereby all possible profits can surely be recovered is that of the lowest price in, highest price out within six months."[170]

Assume that an insider enters into the following transactions:

(1)	7/01/98	Buys 100 shares at $115
(2)	5/15/99	Sells 100 shares at $93
(3)	5/18/99	Buys 100 shares at $90
(4)	5/21/99	Buys 100 shares at $95
(5)	5/23/99	Sells 100 shares at $97
(6)	5/26/99	Buys 100 shares at $105
(7)	5/29/99	Sells 100 shares at $108
(8)	8/10/99	Sells 100 shares at $115

An accountant or stock broker examining these transactions would probably conclude that the insider made a profit of $300 on transactions (2) and (3), $200 on (4) and (5), $300 on (6) and (7), and $0 on (1) and (8), closing the account with a total profit of $800.

Using the "lowest price in, highest price out" rule, however, the following tabulation is made:

Purchases (lowest first)			Sales (highest first)			Profit
100	@	$90	100	@	$115	$2500
100	@	$95	100	@	$108	$1300

---

[168] A short seller borrows securities from a broker-dealer, promptly selling them in the market. The short seller believes that either the market as a whole, or the market for a particular stock, is going to fall. He profits by re-purchasing shares in the market at the lower price, replacing the securities he borrowed and sold with the securities purchased at the lower price. Section 16(c) makes unlawful the sale by any officer, director or 10% holder "if the person selling the security or his principal . . . does not own the security."

[169] *Smolowe v. Delendo*, 136 F.2d 231, 239 (2d Cir.), *cert. denied*, 320 U.S. 751 (1943). *Gratz v. Claughton*, 187 F.2d 46 (2d Cir.), *cert. denied*, 341 U.S. 920 (1951), is another early case reaching the same conclusion.

[170] This is referred to as the "lowest purchase price, highest sale price" rule. *Whittaker v. Whittaker Corp.*, 639 F.2d 516, 530 (9th Cir. 1981).

Thus, according to this method of computation, there is a total Section 16(b) profit of $3,800. Under this theory, all transactions which yield losses are ignored.[171] The wording of Section 16(b) allows the court to match all sales and purchases even if the sale precedes the purchase. If, however, the recovery inures to the benefit of the corporation, seemingly few cases will be brought. What is in it for a shareholder? While the corporation as a whole receives the profits, it is the shareholder's attorney who is entitled to attorney fees in an amount which appellate courts have directed should be more than adequate because it is a form of statutory derivative suit.[172]

That attorney may seek a plaintiff from a wide variety of eligible candidates. The only textual reference in the section requires that the plaintiff must be the "owner of [a] security . . . of the issuer" at the time suit is "instituted." Thus there exists no requirement for ownership at the time of the wrong complained of, in contrast to the contemporaneous ownership requirement in derivative suits.[173] The plaintiff can own "any equity security" of the issuer: a warrant to purchase stock, as well as ownership of stock itself, will do.

In *Gollust v. Mendell*,[174] the Supreme Court reviewed these aspects of Section 16 in deciding whether the section required continuous ownership, similar to that required in derivative litigation. A Section 16 plaintiff brought a suit against beneficial holders of Viacom International. During the pendency of the suit, International was merged into a subsidiary of Viacom, Inc. By analogy to derivative action cases, defendants claimed that plaintiff had lost standing to maintain the suit.

The Court disagreed, finding that Section 16 confers standing of "signal breadth." A requirement that a Section 16 plaintiff have some "financial stake in the outcome" of the suit does enter the picture, but it is the result of Article III of the Constitution's case or controversy limitation of federal court jurisdiction, which requires a person maintaining a suit to have a stake in the outcome. The text of Section 16(b) itself does not require continuous ownership. Thus plaintiff's new shares in a Viacom subsidiary that had absorbed International sufficed to satisfy the Article III requirement.

[C]   Who is an Officer for Section 16 Purposes?

"Officer" includes presidents, chief executive officers, chief operating officers, vice-presidents in charge of a principal business unit or division, principal financial officers, principal accounting officers, and other persons who perform significant policy making functions for the registrant. In 1991, through adoption

---

[171] The hypothetical is based upon Robert W. Hamilton & Jonathan R. Macey, *Cases and Materials on Corporations* at 1086–87 (8th ed. 2003).

[172] *Smolowe, supra*, 136 F.2d at 241. For a discussion of attorney fee awards in derivative suits, see § 14.08[B], *supra.*

[173] In fact, Section 16(b) requirements for plaintiffs are very lax compared with those applicable to derivative action plaintiffs. For a discussion of the latter, see § 14.03, *infra.*

[174] 501 U.S. 115 (1991).

of extensive regulations, the SEC did make clear that Section 16 does not apply to officers who have a title such as vice-president but no significant policy making function.[175]

[D]   Insider Status at Only One End of a Swing

Section 16(b) provides that "[t]his subsection shall not be construed to cover any transaction where such [a 10%] beneficial owner was not such both at the time of the purchase or sale, or the sale and purchase, of the security involved." A question arises as to whether the purchase that lifts an owner to 10% status counts for Section 16(b) purposes. Can that purchase be matched with a subsequent sale within six months? For example, is shareholder X, who owns 9%, purchases 2%, and sells the entire 11% holding less than 6 months later, liable to the corporation?

In *Foremost-McKesson, Inc. v. Provident Securities Co.*,[176] the Supreme Court held that a 10%, or more holder was not liable unless he qualified as such before he made the purchase in question. Thus, the purchase that first lifts a beneficial owner above 10% cannot be matched with a subsequent sale for Section 16(b) liability purposes. Under *Foremost-McKesson*, then, shareholder X would not be liable because he was not a 10% holder on the "front end of the swing." If, in the example, after purchasing the 11%, shareholder X purchased 4% and then sold the entire 15%, X would be liable for the profit on the 4%, if within the six month period.

Through its regulations, the SEC has made clear that transactions completed before a person became an officer or director are not subject to Section 16.[177] On the opposite end of a transaction, however, the rule is different. In *Feder v. Martin Marietta Corp.*,[178] the court held that an officer or director who purchased while an officer but later resigned and then sold within 6 months, is liable to the corporation under Section 16(b).

[E]   Takeover Players and Section 16(b)

Defeated bidders often have on hand more than 10% of the equity securities of a target corporation. Because they usually have borrowed a significant portion of the purchase price, often at high interest rates, they may be under significant pressure to sell. They may also wish to sell before the share price declines in response to the defeat or abandonment of the tender offer. Usually, however, when contemplating such a sale, takeover players face the prospect of significant Section 16 short swing profit liabilities. The Supreme Court has helped solve at least part of their problem.

---

[175] *See* SEC Rule 16a-1(f). In its 1991 rulemaking, the SEC also attempted to clarify a number of other points, such as Section 16's application to derivative securities such as puts, call, options, and so on.

[176] 423 U.S. 232 (1976).

[177] SEC Rule 16a-2(a).

[178] 406 F.2d 260 (2d Cir. 1969), *cert. denied*, 396 U.S. 1036 (1970).

In *Reliance Electric Co. v. Emerson Electric Co.*,[179] the Court approved of a "two step" transaction. The case involved a defeated takeover player who held 13.2% of the target. The player first sold 3.6%, reducing its holding to 9.6%. Subsequently, it sold the 9.6%, all within six months. The Court held that while Section 16(b) applied to the first transaction, and profit from it would have to disgorged, Section 16(b) did not apply to the second transaction.

One year later, the Court approved of the "pragmatic approach" to Section 16(b). If a director, officer or 10% holder enters into an "unorthodox" transaction (that is, nontraditional sale such as a merger, corporate reorganization, or stock reclassification) that could not possibly have involved the evil at which the section aims (utilization of inside information), the transaction will not be within the reach of Section 16(b).

In *Kern County Land Co. v. Occidental Petroleum*,[180] Occidental purchased a foothold position in Kern County Land Co. of more than 10%. Kern County defeated Occidental's takeover attempt by a defensive merger with Tenneco. In the merger, Occidental received Tenneco shares for its Kern County shares within 6 months of the original purchase. An issue arose as to whether the receipt of the Tenneco shares in the merger was a sale of Kern County shares for Section 16(b) purposes.[181] The Court held that the purchase of Kern County shares and the forced exchange of them in the Tenneco-Kern County merger did not trigger Section 16(b) because no possibility existed that Occidental had inside information relating to Kern County Land, which had been overtly hostile to Occidental. The merger was not a simple purchase or sale but an unorthodox transaction. Thus, although Section 16(b) supposedly portends strict liability, the courts will be "pragmatic," examining the potential for abuse when the courts face unorthodox transactions such as the forced sale in the merger context.

---

[179] 404 U.S. 418 (1972).

[180] 411 U.S. 582 (1973).

[181] Another issue was whether the granting of an option by Occidental to Tenneco to buy back the Tenneco shares was covered by Section 16(b). The option was granted less than six months after Occidental had received the original Kern shares. Was the granting of the option a sale under Section 16)(b), rather than the actual transfer of the shares? The Court held that the grant of the option by Occidental was not a sale by it under Section 16. If Occidental had an option to sell the shares to Tenneco, as opposed to Tenneco having the option to buy the shares, the result could have been different.

Chapter 14

CORPORATE LITIGATION

§ 14.01 INTRODUCTION

Corporate litigation breaks down into two broad categories, direct and derivative. If one or more shareholders sue the corporation alleging that the corporation has denied them a contract right associated with shareholding (rights to dividends or disclosure, for example), the action is direct. The shareholder may maintain the action in his or her own name. If the shareholder alleges a special and distinct injury over and above a diminution in the value of shares, the action is also direct. In a direct action, damages recovered are paid to the shareholders.[1]

By contrast, if shareholders sue to vindicate the violation of a duty owed to the corporation, either fiduciary duties owed by corporate directors or officers, or obligations of a third party pursuant to a contract with the corporation, the action is derivative. Any recovery goes to the corporate treasury. A central tenet of corporate law has long been that the board of directors manages the business and affairs of a corporation.[2] Those affairs include litigation by the corporation or by shareholders in the corporate name, or rights of the corporation to commence litigation.

In the mid-nineteenth century, American courts of equity developed a device whereby a shareholder could, under certain circumstances, step into the corporation's shoes, in order to vindicate wrongdoing to the corporation when the directors would not do so. The device is known as the derivative action, because the shareholder "derives" whatever rights she has from the corporation. Derivative actions are useful in cases in which the alleged wrongdoers are members of the group bestowed with the power to manage, that is, some of the directors or officers themselves. In some cases, through sympathy or friendship, the remaining directors may choose not to pursue wrongdoing directors.[3]

---

[1] In 2004, in *Tooley v. Donaldson, Lufkin & Jenrette, Inc.*, 845 A.2d 1031 (2004), discussed in § 14.02[F], *infra*, the Supreme Court of Delaware threw out the "special injury" test, substituting a different inquiry to determine whether a shareholder action is direct or derivative.

[2] For a discussion of the role of the board, see § 5.06, *supra*. *See also* MBCA § 8.01(b) ("All corporate powers shall be exercised by or under the authority of, and the business and affairs of the corporation managed under the direction of, its board of directors"); Del. Gen. Corp. L. § 141(a) ("The business and affairs of every corporation organized under this chapter shall be managed by or under the direction of a board of directors").

[3] In other cases, the wrongdoer is a third party who has breached a contract with the corporation or, vis-a-vis the corporation, the wrongdoer is a tortfeasor.

The device flourished in the United States but, then, the "strike suit" era developed. Justice Hugo Black described a strike suit as a suit "by people who might be interested in getting quick dollars by making charges without regard to their truth or falsity so as to coerce corporate managers to settle worthless claims in order to get rid of them."[4] Two attributes of a strike suit are likely to be a plaintiff with a small shareholding, and an attorney seeking a quick fee.

In a publicly held corporation, an owner of one share out of twenty million may bring a derivative action. If the alleged wrongdoing is egregious enough, or publicized enough, the corporation may face a multiplicity of suits brought by a number of persons with small or medium size shareholdings.[5]

On the attorney side of the strike suit phenomenon, counsel, who by conferring a benefit on a corporation, may recover a fee from the corporate treasury through settlement or judgment. If the named plaintiff alone was required to pay the fee, few suits would be brought and, in those in which some measure of success has been achieved, the remaining shareholders would be unjustly enriched.[6] The solution is that all those benefitted, namely the corporation and the other shareholders, pay the fee of the "private attorney general" whose actions benefitted them.

To counteract the danger of a multiplicity of worthless "strike suits," state legislatures put in place a number of procedural hurdles which a shareholder-plaintiff in a derivative action must cross. These include requirements that plaintiffs: (1) post security for the defendant's costs; (2) be "record" owners of shares; (3) verify the truth of their pleadings, rather than plead based upon "information and belief"; (4) adequately represent shareholder interests;[7] (5) own shares contemporaneously with the wrongdoing of which they complain; (6) maintain shareholding continuously during the pendency of the proceeding; and (7) exhaust intra-corporate remedies by demand on the board of directors to take action, possibly followed also by demand on their fellow shareholders.

More recently, with the takeover boom and widespread media coverage of corporate affairs, the last twenty years have seen another strike suit era. Within days of the announcement of lower earnings reports, adoption of takeover

---

[4] *Surowitz v. Hilton Hotels Corp.*, 383 U.S. 363, 371 (1966).

[5] The requirement that a shareholder must proceed by means of a derivative action tends to reduce, but not eliminate, a multiplicity of suits. "[A]ny other rule would admit of as many suits against the wrongdoer as there were stockholders in the corporation." *Wells v. Dane*, 63 A. 324, 325 (Me. 1905).

[6] In economic analysis, the other shareholders would seek a "free ride" on the efforts of the plaintiff and her lawyer. They will lend no financial support to the prosecution of the suit but will share in any benefit if the suit is successful. Incentives for attorneys are also thought necessary to solve collective action problems among shareholders. Because of free rider and other problems, it is costly (if not impossible) for shareholders to unite in order to remedy wrongdoing. Attorneys step forward to fill that void. For a discussion of the collective action problem of shareholders in publicly traded corporations, see Chapter 5, *supra*.

[7] In *Cohen v. Beneficial Industrial Loan Corp.*, 337 U.S. 541, 549 (1949), the Supreme Court stressed that a derivative action plaintiff assumes "a position, not technically as a trustee perhaps, but one of a fiduciary character. He sues, not for himself, but as a representative of a class comprising all those who are similarly situated . . . . He is a self-chosen representative and a volunteer champion."

defenses perceived as anti-shareholder, or announcement of SEC or other governmental investigations, derivative and class action attorneys file a variety of lawsuits against publicly held corporations. After the suits are filed, plaintiffs' counsel compete to be named lead counsel with power to control the lawsuit, its settlement, and, more importantly, apportionment of the attorneys' fees received from the corporate treasury.

These abuses have lead to reform efforts. The reform proposals of the American Law Institute,[8] and the American Bar Association's Committee on Corporate Laws, in its Model Business Corporation Act, are the principal reform efforts discussed in this chapter. Both proposals make frequent comparisons with the Delaware case law.[9]

Reforms of the first and second strike suit eras have made derivative litigation very difficult and have re-kindled interest in direct actions. The emphasis on direct actions, and the avoidance of derivative ones, has fueled a reprise of the class action lawsuit. Recently, shareholder litigation has taken the form of direct corporate and securities law claims. For instance, many plaintiffs now institute actions in which they allege that the corporation failed fully to disclose, or disclosed in a misleading way, events occurring within the corporation. Also, such litigation is often driven by the prospect of large fees for class counsel.[10] Recent regulation of securities class actions, including Congress's enactment of the Private Securitieis Litigation Reform Act (PSLRA) of 1995 and the Securities Litigation Uniform Standards Act (SLUSA) of 1998, is the penultimate subject in this chapter.

---

[8] *See* A.L.I. Corp. Gov. Proj. §§ 7.01-7.25.

[9] One criticism of these reform efforts is that they make a complex topic more complex and do so driven by events in the world of *Fortune 500* corporations. Meanwhile, in the remainder of the United States, conditions may be the opposite of what the "reformers" posit them to be: plaintiff-shareholders have genuine stakes in the outcome of litigation, no corporate plaintiffs' bar exists, and the independence of corporate directors is not so assured. Yet, the reforms purport to govern derivative litigation in all its forms. *See generally* Douglas M. Branson, *The American Law Institute Principles of Corporate Governance and Structure and the Derivative Action: A View from the Other Side*, 43 WASH. & LEE L. REV. 399 (1986) (litigation from the view point of a practitioner in Portland, Oregon or Portland, Maine).

[10] A leading proponent of reform highlights attorney control, the absence of monitoring by the client shareholder, and the quest for large fees as the principal evils of corporate litigation. *See, e.g.,* John C. Coffee, Jr., *The Unfaithful Champion: The Plaintiff as Monitor in Shareholder Litigation*, 48 LAW & CONTEMP. PROBS. 5 (Summer 1985); Coffee, *Rescuing the Private Attorney General: Why the Model of the Lawyer as Bounty Hunter is Not Working*, 42 MD. L. REV. 215 (1983). Professor Coffee's views are important, as he served as the author (reporter) of the A.L.I. Corp. Gov. Proj. derivative action provisions.

§ 14.02 THE NATURE OF THE DERIVATIVE SUIT: DIRECT VERSUS DERIVATIVE, PRO RATA RECOVERY, AND OTHER PRELIMINARY ISSUES

[A] The Nature of the Derivative Suit

A derivative action is an action brought by shareholders on behalf of the corporation. The derivative action is initiated to remedy an alleged wrong to the corporation perpetrated either by those in control of the corporation, such as officers, directors or controlling shareholders, a third party, such as a supplier who has breached a contract with the corporation, or both. In the case of a supplier who has allegedly breached a contract with the corporation, the plaintiff may allege a cause of action against the third party supplier, and may also plead in the alternative against the directors. Plaintiff can allege mismanagement (duty of care) by the board, in that board members were indifferent or inattentive to the breach by the third party of an important contract. Alternatively, plaintiff could allege self-dealing (duty of loyalty): that for some *quid pro quo*, the directors favored the interests of the supplier as a friend, associate, family member, or the like, over the best interests of the corporation.[11]

The action is "founded on a right of action existing in the corporation itself, and in which the corporation itself is the appropriate plaintiff,"[12] but which, for some reason (for example, inattention, mismanagement, conflict of interest) the corporation did not assert. A derivative action allows a shareholder "to step into the corporation's shoes and to seek the restitution he could not demand on his own."[13]

Courts and commentators have perceived of the derivative suit as being two suits in one:

> A bill filed by stockholders in their derivative right . . . has two phases — one is the equivalent of a suit to compel the corporation to sue, and the other is the suit by the corporation, asserted by the stockholders in its behalf, against those liable to it. The former belongs to the complaining stockholders; the latter to the corporation. The complaining stockholders are allowed in derivative bills to bring forward those two causes of action in one suit.[14]

Of these suits, a later Delaware court stated that "[t]he stockholder's individual right to bring the action does not ripen, however, until he has made a demand on the corporation which has been met with a refusal by the corporation to assert its causes of action . . . ." Later in its opinion, the court stated:

---

[11] Fiduciary duties are discussed generally in Chapters 8 and 9.

[12] *Daily Income Fund, Inc. v. Fox*, 464 U.S. 523, 528 (1984).

[13] *Cohen v. Beneficial Indus. Loan Corp., supra*, 337 U.S. at 548.

[14] *Cantor v. Sachs*, 162 A. 73, 76 (Del. Ch. 1932). *Accord Brown v. Tenney*, 532 N.E.2d 230, 231 (Ill. 1988) ("The derivative action really consists of two causes of action: one against the directors for failing to sue; the second based upon the right belonging to the corporation).

The stockholder's right to litigate is secondary to the corporate right only for so long as the corporation has not decided to refuse to bring suit. Once the corporation refuses, or impliedly refuses, to assert an apparently valid claim, involving breach of fiduciary duty by the directors, the stockholder is vested with a primary and independent right to redress the wrong by bringing a derivative suit.[15]

[B]   Direct Versus Derivative — Special or Distinct Injury Rule

Assume a corporation that has allegedly paid a dividend in the form of financial benefits for some, but not all, common shareholders. The aggrieved shareholders (those who did not share in the financial benefit) may certainly bring a derivative action, alleging that the directors carelessly violated an obvious precept of corporate law — that all shares of the same class be treated equally (duty of care claim). Alternatively, aggrieved shareholders could allege that, in making the discriminatory payments, directors served the interests of friends and family members who received the benefit rather than the best interests of the corporation (duty of loyalty claim).

Yet, because of all the procedural and other requirements surrounding the derivative action,[16] such as the need to post bond or to make a demand on the directors, plaintiffs tend to view derivative actions as something to be avoided. An important threshold issue is whether an action, based on a claim such as the payment of a dividend to some of a class of shareholders,[17] may be maintained as a direct action: "A direct action can be brought either when there is a special duty, such as a contractual duty, between the wrongdoer and the shareholder, or when the shareholder suffers injury separate and distinct from that suffered by other shareholders."

In *Sax v. World Wide Press, Inc.*,[18] the court found that plaintiff stated only derivative claims in an action in which he alleged that defendants conspired to deplete corporate assets, and thereby depressed the value of stock, and that defendants allegedly diverted assets to their own use. Each of Sax's allegations spoke of "an injury suffered by all of World Wide's shareholders and not by Sax alone."[19]

---

[15] *Maldonado v. Flynn*, 413 A.2d 1251, 1262–63 (Del. Ch. 1980), *modified sub nom.*, *Zapata Corp. v. Maldonado*, 430 A.2d 779 (Del. 1981).

[16] These requirements are discussed in §§ 14.03–14.04, *infra.*

[17] Based upon *Hanson v. Kake Tribal Corporation*, 939 P.2d 1320, 1327–28 (Alaska 1997) (allegation that the corporation has paid a dividend, or somehow benefited some shares of a class to the exclusion of other shares of the same class, alleges special or distinct injury and is direct).

[18] 809 F.2d 610 (9th Cir. 1987). The Ninth Circuit found the question of direct versus derivative as one of state law. However, the court stated that "[o]nce state law characterizes the action as either direct or derivative, the applicable procedural rules are determined by federal law."

[19] The Delaware Supreme Court emphasizes that "[t]he distinction between derivative and individual actions rests upon the party being *directly* injured by the alleged wrongdoing . . . he must be injured *directly* or *independently* of the corporation." *Kramer v. Western Pac. Indus.*, 546 A.2d 348, 351 (Del. 1988).

If the allegation is that mismanagement or self dealing has resulted in a decline in the value of one's shares, the action is always derivative. There are several telltale signs. First, the duties owed and violated (duties of care and loyalty) run from the corporate officials to the corporation and not to anyone within it, such as a shareholder. Second, the harm resulting is to the corporation directly, and only indirectly to the shareholder, through decline in the value of shares. Third, the recovery, if any, will go directly to the corporation, to make it whole, and not to any individual shareholder's pocket.

Thus, in *In re Paxson Communication Corp. Shareholders' Litigation*,[20] the plaintiff alleged that a shareholder (Lowell Paxson), owning 75% of the voting shares, had manipulated the business for his own personal benefit. He had caused the corporation, which owned 63 television stations, to abjure a $20 per share takeover bid from Fox News in favor of a "white squire" transaction with NBC. For an investment of $415 million, NBC received warrants (options to purchase), convertible preferred securities, and options on some of Paxson's shares sufficient to give NBC 49% control if NBC desired. Plaintiffs brought the action as a direct action, citing older cases holding that an action complaining of unwarranted dilution was direct.

Cutting it finer than had the precedents, the Chancellor held that dilution claims are direct "where a significant shareholder's interest is increased at the sole expense of the minority [stockholders]." By contrast, when the diluting share issuances benefitted a third party, such as NBC, the action was derivative. The shareholders would have no "special injury," that is, all the shareholders, Paxson included, would suffer dilution, even though, beneath the surface, the very "end and aim" of the transaction was to keep Lowell Paxson in control, at the expense of the minority shareholders, who had to forgo an attractive offer from Fox News. The case was dismissed for failure to make a demand on the board of directors, a requirement of derivative but not of direct litigation.

Two observations may be made. One is that flexibility which once existed and which a creative plaintiff may have been able to exploit to her benefit, may be more circumscribed. For example, in *Eisenberg v. Flying Tiger Line, Inc.*,[21] plaintiff objected to the reorganization of the airline corporation into a holding company, that is, a parent corporation which would hold shares of the airline corporation, which then would be a subsidiary. Defendant claimed that any injury occasioned by formation of the holding company was to the airline corporation. To avoid posting a bond, plaintiff Eisenberg argued that his action was direct: the holding company formation and his ownership of shares now in the holding company deprived him of a vote that would directly affect airline operations ("the reorganization deprived him and other minority stockholders of any voice in the affairs of their previously existing operating company"). So viewed, the injury was direct and not derivative: no bond or other security for costs could be required.[22]

---

[20] 2001 Del. Ch. LEXIS 95 (2001).

[21] 451 F.2d 267 (2d Cir. 1971).

[22] Similar creativity was exhibited in *Reifsnyder v. Pittsburgh Outdoor Advertising Co.*, 173 A.2d 319 (Pa. 1961). Plaintiff complained that a controlling shareholder had used corporate funds to

The other point is that trial courts have discretion. In cases in which either a direct or derivative action may lie, the trial court may permit the plaintiff to proceed as she wishes.[23]

If both direct and derivative claims will lie, the choice is the plaintiff's. The ALI Project therefore provides: "[i]f a transaction gives rise to both direct and derivative claims, a holder may commence and maintain direct and derivative claims simultaneously . . . ."[24] Thus, in a case posited earlier, in which directors caused a corporation to pay discriminatory dividends, the denied shareholders could proceed directly, seeking damages to put them in parity with those who had received the dividend. They could also proceed derivatively, alleging that in causing the corporation to pay a discriminatory dividend, directors had violated their duties of care and loyalty. The claim might be that the directors are liable to the corporation for the corporation's costs in defending the direct suit by the shareholders. Being derivative, the claim would produce a recovery for the corporation. Plaintiff-shareholders would be able to proceed on their direct claims, their derivative ones, or both.

[C]   Direct Versus Derivative — Denial of Contract Rights Associated With Shareholding

Even if a shareholder is not able to establish separate and distinct injury, she may be able to proceed in a direct action if she can establish denial by the corporation or directors of some right belonging to the shareholders. The Delaware Chancellor has stated that:

> To set out an individual action, the plaintiff must allege either "an injury which is separate and distinct from that suffered by other shareholders" . . . or a wrong involving a contractual right of a share-holder, such as the right to vote, or to assert majority control, which exists independently of any right of the corporation.[25]

As the Chancellor points out, the shareholder's relationship with her corporation is primarily contractual.[26]

---

repurchase property from the shareholder which was, seemingly, a harm to the corporation. Plaintiff was able to avoid derivative characterization by arguing that the repurchase diluted plaintiff's voting power, emphasizing direct injury to minority shareholders.

[23] "Courts generally have wide discretion in interpreting whether a complaint states a derivative or a primary claim." *Hanson v. Kake Tribal Corporation*, 939 P.2d 1320, 1327 (Alaska 1997), *quoting* 12B FLETCHER'S CYCLOPEDIA OF THE LAW OF PRIVATE CORPORATIONS § 5911 (rev. ed. 1993).

[24] A.L.I. Corp. Gov. Proj. § 7.01(c); *see also Lipton v. News Int'l, Inc.*, 514 A.2d 1075, 1079–80 (Del. 1986) (even though corporate shareholder filed direct and derivative claims, it proceeded only with the individual action: settlement amounting to payment of greenmail was not subject to judicial review as settlement of a derivative action).

[25] *Moran v. Household Int'l, Inc.*, 490 A.2d 1059, 1069, *aff'd*, 500 A.2d 1346 (Del. 1985) (citations omitted) (shareholder action challenging adoption of poison pill takeover defense is derivative); *see also Elster v. American Airlines*, 100 A.2d 219, 223 (Del. Ch. 1953) ("a wrong affecting any particular right which he is asserting — such as his preemptive right as a stockholder").

[26] *See Trustees of Dartmouth College v. Woodward*, 17 U.S. (4 Wheat) 518 (1819). For further discussion of the contractual view of the corporation, see § 5.03[C], *supra*.

The shareholder's contract begins with the articles of incorporation. Actions to enforce its provisions are direct (for example, "actions to enjoin an ultra vires act").[27] But the shareholder's contract is much broader, containing many implied terms as well. Those terms have their genesis in statutes and in the common law of corporations. A manner of pleading a direct claim is to state it in just those words: that the defendants are breaching a contract, denying plaintiff a right commonly associated with shareholding.[28]

The ALI Project catalogues a long list of contractual rights:

(1)   actions to enforce a right to vote, to protect preemptive rights, to prevent the improper dilution of voting rights, or to enjoin the improper voting of shares;

(2)   actions to compel dividends or to protect accrued dividend arrearages;

(3)   actions challenging the use of corporate machinery or the issuance of stock for a wrongful purpose (such as an attempt to perpetuate management in control . . .);

(4)   actions to enjoin ultra vires or unauthorized acts;

(5)   actions to prevent oppression of, or fraud against, minority shareholders;

(6)   actions to compel dissolution, appoint a receiver, or obtain similar equitable relief;

(7)   actions challenging the improper expulsion of shareholders through mergers, redemptions or other means;

(8)   actions to inspect corporate books and records;

(9)   actions to require the holding of a shareholders' meeting or the sending of notice thereof; and

(10)   actions to hold controlling shareholders liable for acts undertaken in their individual capacities that depress the value of the minority's shares.[29]

Although one may be able to disagree about one or another item on the ALI list, the enumerated items deal with rights associated with shareholding.

---

[27] The ultra vires doctrine is discussed in § 1.09, *supra.*

[28] An action to enforce any "side agreement" would be direct as well, even if the agreement creates duties viewed primarily as running to the corporation. *See Hikita v. Nichiro Gyogyo Kaisha, Ltd.,* 713 P.2d 1197 (Alaska 1997) (in side agreement, defendant shareholder agreed to provide capital and technical expertise to the corporation).

[29] A.L.I. Corp. Gov. Proj. § 7.01, Comment c.

[D]   Direct Versus Derivative — Closely Held Corporation Exception

A growing number of jurisdictions permit actions that should be derivative claims to be prosecuted in a direct action, if the corporation is closely held. The reasons are varied. With its procedural complexity, a derivative action is overkill in the close corporation. A widely accepted view of the close corporation perceives the participants as owing not just duties to the corporation but to each other, akin to partners in a partnership.[30] Shareholders are able to proceed directly against shareholder-directors for violation of those duties.[31] Last of all, the risk of a multiplicity of actions is much less in a corporation with three or four shareholders.

"[A]n increasing number of courts are abandoning the distinction between a derivative and a direct action because the only interested parties are the two sets of shareholders" lined up on either side of the dispute.[32] Multiplicity of suits is an issue that is minimized, but not eliminated, in the closely held corporation.[33]

The right to trial by jury in direct actions may form the basis of an attempt to characterize the action as direct rather than derivative. Since derivative suits are equitable in nature, there may be no jury trials. In *Schumacher v. Schumacher*,[34] a majority shareholder's brother and spouse sued the majority shareholder, his "partner" in a Goodyear tire retail store. The trial court held that the claims contained in the complaint constituted allegations of a breach of fiduciary duty, triable to the court and not to a jury.[35] The North Dakota Supreme Court held that the action could be direct, triable to a jury. In doing so, the court applied the ALI Project's "closely held corporation exception" to the derivative action norm.[36]

Objectors to the overwhelming trend include one well respected corporate law scholar, Judge Frank Easterbrook of the Seventh Circuit, who believes that corporation means corporation, with all its baggage, including the derivative suit:

> Ohio, like a few other states, has expanded the "special injury" doctrine into a general exception for closely held corporations. The American Law Institute recommends that other states do the same. The

---

[30] This practice is often referred to as the *Donahue* principle, after *Donahue v. Rodd Electrotype Co.*, 328 N.E.2d 505 (Mass. 1975), and discussed in Chapter 11.

[31] *See, e.g., Crosby v. Beam*, 548 N.E.2d 217, 221 (Ohio 1989) (because of "heightened" duties directly owed, "suit by a minority shareholder against the offending majority or controlling shareholder may proceed as a direct action").

[32] *Richards v. Bryan*, 879 P.2d 638 (Kan. Ct. App. 1994).

[33] *See generally* Douglas M. Branson, CORPORATE GOVERNANCE § 11.08, at 612 (1993) (suggesting that a court might avoid the problem by requiring the action to be brought as a class action on behalf of all objecting shareholders).

[34] 469 N.W.2d 793 (N.D. 1991).

[35] The right to trial by jury in derivative actions is discussed in § 14.08[A], *infra.*

[36] A.L.I. Corp. Gov. Proj. § 7.01(d).

premise of this exception may be questioned. Corporations are *not* partnerships. Whether to incorporate entails a choice of many formalities. Commercial rules should be predictable; this objective is best served by treating corporations as they are . . . . So it is understandable that not all states have joined the parade.[37]

Judge Easterbrook found that Delaware would require closely held corporation participants to proceed derivatively.[38]

Most arguments against the close corporation exception center around the rights of third parties. Because a direct action produces a direct recovery, rather than putting funds back into the corporate treasury, creditors may legitimately complain. The derivative action protects them; the direct action does not.

The American Law Institute has fine-tuned its closely held exception to take into account the problems of creditors whose rights may intervene and the potential of a multiplicity of suits:

> In the case of a closely held corporation, the court in its discretion may treat an action raising derivative claims as a direct action . . . and order an individual recovery, if it finds that to do so will not (i) unfairly expose the corporation or defendants to a multiplicity of actions, (ii) materially prejudice the interests of creditors of the corporation, or (iii) interfere with a fair distribution of the recovery among all interested persons.[39]

Despite Judge Easterbrook's view of the parade, the dominant trend today is for state courts to join the parade, recognizing an exception for closely held corporations, whether they rely upon the ALI Principles or not.[40]

[E]   Pro Rata (Individual) Recovery in Derivative Actions

The norm in an action based upon violation of a fiduciary or other duty owed to the corporation, is that the recovery goes to the corporate treasury. In close corporations, a growing number of courts permit plaintiff-shareholders to proceed directly, resulting in direct payment of damages. Plaintiff-shareholders recover damages in proportion to the shares they hold (pro rata).

In other cases involving closely held and other corporations, courts continue to style the action as derivative but permit any recovery to go directly to

---

[37] *Bagdon v. Bridgestone/Firestone, Inc.*, 916 F.2d 379 (7th Cir. 1990), *cert. denied*, 500 U.S. 710 (1991) (citations omitted).

[38] Citing *Abelow v. Symonds*, 156 A.2d 416 (Del. Ch. 1959), and *Taormina v. Taormina*, 78 A.2d 473 (Del. Ch. 1951).

[39] A.L.I. Corp. Gov. Proj. § 7.01(d).

[40] Recent adoptions include *Barth v. Barth*, 659 N.E. 559, 560 (Ind. 1995) (minority shareholder in Barth Electric, Inc., complained that president and majority shareholder had paid excessive salaries to himself and his family; used corporate employees to perform services at his and his son's homes; dramatically lowered dividends; and appropriated corporate funds for personal investments; remanded for trial court application of A.L.I. Corp. Gov. Proj. § 7.01). *See also Richards v. Bryan, supra* (Kan. Ct. App. 1994); *Derouen v. Murray*, 604 So. 2d 1086, 1091 (Miss. 1992). *See generally* Branson, *supra* note 32, at 613, n.89.

shareholders. The theory of these "pro rata recovery" cases is that, if the wrongdoers own a substantial amount of shares, and if the damages are paid to the corporate treasury, the recovery flows in part to the wrongdoers.[41] Although not facially limited to close corporations, in practice, individual recoveries are found in closely held corporations.

To illustrate, suppose that shareholders Chico and Harpo, owning 20% each, complain that the majority 60% shareholder, Rufus T. Firefly, has used corporate funds and facilities to benefit himself to the extent of $500,000. In a pro rata recovery, rather than ordering Firefly to pay $500,000 to the corporate treasury, the court enters a $200,000 judgment (40% of $500,000) directly in favor of Chico and Harpo.

Professor Melvin Eisenberg questions the premise judges adopt in ordering pro rata recoveries, namely, that pro rata recovery should be decreed to prevent the wrongdoers from sharing in the recovery.[42] He points out that more deterrence against future defalcations is procured by having Rufus T. Firefly pay all $500,000 back to the corporation. By only having to pay Chico and Harpo $200,000, Firefly is "let off the hook." Firefly will gladly take the pro rata option every time.[43]

One court firmly opposed to pro rata recovery is the New York Court of Appeals. In *Glenn v. Hoteltron Systems, Inc.*,[44] defendant Jacob Schachter had diverted a corporate opportunity of Ketek Electric Corporation to Hoteltron from which Hoteltron had earned $362,243. Despite the presence of only two shareholders, each owning 50% (Schacter and plaintiff Herbert Kulik), the court would not countenance a pro rata recovery:

> [Plaintiff's] injury was real, but it was derivative, not direct. Thus, the Appellate Division properly ruled that those profits should be returned to Ketek Corp.
>
> [Plaintiff] argues that this result is inequitable because [the wrong-doing director, Schachter] will ultimately share in the proceeds of the

---

[41] See, e.g., the reasoning in *Lynch v. Patterson*, 701 P.2d 1126, 1130 (Wyo. 1985):

[C]ourts sometimes permit pro-rata recovery by individual shareholders to prevent an award from reverting to the wrongdoers who remain in control of the corporation . . . .

. . . Corporate recovery would simply return the funds to control of the wrongdoers.

Direct recovery assures that [plaintiff] Patterson will reap some benefit from his lawsuit. We refuse to order payment into the corporate treasury in this case and risk necessitating a subsequent suit by Patterson to compel the directors to declare a dividend or apply the funds to legitimate corporate purposes.

Lynch was adopted by the Supreme Court of Arkansas in *Hall v. Staha*, 858 S.W.2d 672, 678 (Ark. 1993) (minority shareholders permitted direct recovery of excessive salaries approved by controlling shareholders for themselves).

[42] See Melvin Eisenberg, CARY AND EISENBERG ON CORPORATIONS 948 (8th ed. 2000).

[43] *Accord* Edward Grenier, Jr., *Pro Rata Recovery by Shareholders on Corporate Causes of Action as a Means of Achieving Corporate Justice*, 19 WASH. & LEE L. REV. 165 (1962) ("[W]hen the defendants are directors guilty of flagrant and willful breaches of fiduciary duty toward the corporation, full payment of the corporate damages should be exacted . . . . In less serious situations only pro rata recovery may be justifiable . . . .").

[44] 547 N.E.2d 71 (N.Y. 1989).

damage award. But that prospect exists in any successful derivative action in which the wrongdoer is a shareholder of the injured corporation . . . .

It is true that this anomaly is magnified in cases involving closely held corporations because the errant fiduciary is likely to own a large share of the corporation . . . . We conclude, however, that this consideration does not require a different damage rule for close corporations.

While awarding damages directly to the innocent shareholder may seem equitable . . . other interests, particularly those of the corporation's creditors, should not be overlooked. The fruits of a diverted corporate opportunity are properly a corporate asset. Awarding that asset directly to a shareholder could impair the rights of creditors whose claims may be superior to that of the innocent shareholder.[45]

Courts that do permit pro rata recovery do so in several sets of circumstances: in the closely held corporation situation; when the corporation is in liquidation and, presumably, provision has been made for creditors;[46] and when former shareholders later discover wrongdoing that has been concealed.

Of course, the last example, the discovery of wrongdoing by former shareholders after they have disposed of their shares, could not result in a derivative suit due to the requirement that a plaintiff-shareholder must maintain continuous ownership from filing through final adjudication of the action.[47]

In *Watson v. Button*,[48] a former 50% owner sued the general manager, the other half-owner, to recover for embezzlements occurring prior to plaintiff's sale of his shares. Ordinarily, a suit to remedy embezzlement would be derivative, with the recovery going to the corporation. The *Watson* court noted that plaintiff "cannot bring a derivative action since he is no longer a stockholder" but decided to follow "courts in other states [that] have held that a former stockholder, who parted with his shares without knowledge of a prior wrongful misappropriation of corporate assets by the directors, may recover from the directors the amount by which the misappropriation has reduced the value of his prior shareholdings."[49]

---

[45] Delaware also does not permit a direct recovery. In *Keenan v. Eshleman*, 2 A.2d 904 (Del. 1938), the court held that directors' excessive salaries and ratification by a larger number of shareholders "constituted fraud on the corporation." Nonetheless, the court refused to order a direct award to the complaining minority shareholders, holding such to be "contrary to the settled general rule."

[46] *See Sale v. Amber*, 6 A.2d 519 (Pa. 1939).

[47] See the discussion in § 14.03[C], *infra*.

[48] 235 F.2d 235 (9th Cir. 1956).

[49] *Accord Kirk v. First Nat'l Bank*, 439 F. Supp. 1141 (M.D. Ga. 1977). Delaware also may allow a direct recovery by a former shareholder confronted with these circumstances. See the dictum in *Keenan v. Eshleman, supra* note 44 ("If the case were one where the corporation had ceased to operate, its controlling stockholder had converted all of its assets and it was denuded of all its property, it might be that the minority stockholders would be entitled to a decree against the culpable officer for payment to them of their equitable share of the assets which the defendant had in his possession.").

In appropriate circumstances, courts may consider alternative recovery vehicles such as a pro rata recovery for a direct action, or a derivative action with the usual limitations such as verification, security for expenses, and demand, but with a pro rata recovery at the end.[50]

[F]   The *Tooley* Test in Delaware

Credit Suisse acquired 71% of Donaldson Lufkin & Jenrette (DLJ) from AXA Financial agreeing to pay therefor with a combination of stock and cash. Credit Suisse agreed to acquire the minority shares solely with cash. The minority holders complained of a 22 day postponement in closing the cash merger, resulting to them a loss of the time value (22 days' worth) of the money to be received. Seemingly, the minority shareholders suffered a "special injury," because they were to be paid all in cash while majority shareholder AXA would receive stock and cash.[51]

The Court of Chancery found against the plaintiff shareholders: they had failed to allege "special injury"; their action was therefore derivative rather than direct; and, since they had given up their shares in the subsequent merger, the plaintiffs lacked the continuous ownership which the contemporaneous ownership rule (see *infra*) requires in derivative actions.

The Supreme Court did Chancery one better: it threw out the special injury rule altogether, finding it "not helpful." Instead, the "issue must turn *solely* on the following questions: (1) who suffered the alleged harm (the corporation or the suing stockholders); and (2) who would receive the benefit of any recovery (the corporation or the stockholders, individually)?"[52]

On the basis of its new rule, and contrary to Chancery, the court found the action not to be derivative. But "it does not necessarily follow that the complaint states a direct cause of action. [I]t states no claim at all." The complaint based itself upon rights that the plaintiffs alleged were being violated but did not yet have. "The claim will not be ripe until the terms of the merger are fulfilled." It seems as though the plaintiffs might better have proceeded on breach of contract and of the covenant of good faith and fair dealing rather than breaches of fiduciary duty, as they did.

The new test has met with approval, at least in Delaware. In a subsequent case, *Gatz v. Ponsoldt*,[53] Chancellor Chandler noted:

> The Supreme Court's *Tooley* decision simplified the analysis required to distinguish between direct and derivative actions, discarding the old "special injury" test. The analysis now focuses on the following questions: "Who suffered the alleged harm-the corporation or the suing

---

[50] *See generally* Douglas M. Branson, CORPORATE GOVERNANCE § 11.08 (1993); Richard A. Booth, *Derivative Suits and Pro Rata Recovery*, 61 GEO. WASH. L. REV. 1274 (1993).

[51] 845 A.2d 1031 (Del. 2004).

[52] *Id.* at 1033.

[53] 2004 Del. Ch. LEXIS 203 (Nov. 5, 2004).

stockholder individual-and would receive the benefit of the recovery or other remedy?"[54]

It is too soon to tell whether other jurisdictions will find the new Delaware test helpful, or merely "old wine in new bottles."

§ 14.03   QUALIFICATIONS OF A PROPER PLAINTIFF-SHAREHOLDER

[A]   Record Ownership

The vast majority of shares in publicly traded corporations are held in nominee, or "street" (Wall Street) name, rather than in shareholders' names, or "record" ownership.[55] From a shareholder-investor standpoint, the reason for the use of the nominee is convenience in buying and selling. Persons who are record owners usually have a share certificate. To retrieve the certificate from a safety deposit box and deliver it to a broker's office is inconvenient, requiring far more effort than a mere telephone call, as is possible when shares are in street name.[56]

Statutes in many jurisdictions have eliminated requirements that derivative action plaintiffs be record owners.[57] Delaware arrives at the same result through case law.[58] There are pockets of resistance, though. Whether because of resistance by corporations, or mere failure to modernize corporate law, a few jurisdictions still require that the plaintiff in a derivative suit be a record owner of shares.[59]

---

[54] *Id.* at *25.

[55] For a discussion of ownership, see § 5.05, note 222, *supra.*

[56] In an early time, fewer (probably around 50 percent) of shares were held in nominee or street name. Reformers therefore pushed through state legislatures provisions that derivative action plaintiffs had to own shares in their own name, that is, be record owners. It is unclear whether the reformers' intent was to eliminate half the shareholders as potential plaintiffs, or because those "reformers" had a genuine belief that street name shareholders were far more transient, and therefore less likely to have a recognizable interest in corporate governance.

[57] *See* MBCA § 7.40(2) ("'Shareholder' includes a beneficial owner whose shares are held in a voting trust or held by a nominee on the beneficial owner's behalf"). A.L.I. Corp. Gov. Proj. §§ 1.22 (definition of holder) and 7.02 (standing to commence a derivative action) are similar, as are statutes in California and New York. *See* Cal. Corp. Code § 800(b)(1); N.Y.B.C.L. § 626(a).

[58] The leading case is *Rosenthal v. Burry Biscuit Corp.,* 60 A.2d 106 (Del. Ch. 1948). *See also Jones v. Taylor,* 348 A.2d 188 (Del. Ch. 1975); *Harff v. Kerkorian,* 324 A.2d 215 (Del. Ch. 1974).

[59] *See, e.g.,* Col. Rev. Stat. § 7-4-121; Iowa Code Ann. § 496A.43; Mass. Gen. L. Ch. 156B, § 46.

[B]   Contemporaneous Ownership

[1]   Introduction

Another requirement is that the plaintiff own shares at the time the wrong about which she complains occurred,[60] and that she maintain ownership continuously throughout pendency of the pleadings. An interruption or termination of shareholder status automatically ousts plaintiff on lack of standing grounds.

Exceptions include continuing wrongs and double derivative actions.[61] A provision in the ALI Project would also grant standing to a non-contemporaneous owner if the alleged wrongdoing had remained undisclosed at the time of acquisition of the shares. A plaintiff may also evade the contemporaneous ownership requirement by proceeding in a direct rather than derivative action. Last, if a plaintiff acquired shares by operation of the law, such as by bequest, intestate succession, or by order of court in a marital dissolution, the action may be maintained despite lack of contemporaneous ownership.

[2]   Basis for the Rule

Many trace its origins to Judge, later Dean, Roscoe Pound in *Home Fire Ins. Co. v. Barber.*[62] Judge Pound hypothesized that "the right of the stockholder to sue exists because of special injury to him for which he otherwise has no redress. [Thus] one who held no stock at the time of the mismanagement ought not to be allowed to sue, unless the mismanagement or its effects continue and are injurious to him . . . ." The reasoning behind the requirement is that the law should not permit one to buy into a lawsuit through purchase of shares in a corporation in which possible wrongdoing has occurred.

A modern exposition of the rule was made by the United States Supreme Court in *Bangor Punta Operations, Inc. v. Bangor & Aroostook Railroad Co.*[63] In 1969, Amoskeag Co. purchased from Bangor Punta Corporation a railroad, Bangor and Aroostook Railroad (BAR), for $5 million. In 1971, Amoskeag caused BAR to sue its former owner for $7 million, allegedly on account of wrongdoing in the days when Bangor Punta owned BAR. Relying upon *Home Fire Ins. v. Barber*, Mr. Justice Powell denied BAR a recovery based upon two fundamental principles of derivative action law.

---

[60] The rule is most frequently stated in the rules of civil procedure. *See, e.g.*, Fed. R. Civ. P. 23.1:

> In a derivative action brought by one or more shareholders or members to enforce a right of a corporation or of an unincorporated association, the corporation or association having failed to enforce a right which may properly be asserted by it, the complaint shall be verified and shall allege (1) that the plaintiff was a shareholder or member at the time of the transaction of which the plaintiff complains or that the plaintiff's shares or membership thereafter devolved on the plaintiff by operation of law . . . .

[61] Discussed in § 14.03[B][4], [5], *infra*.

[62] 93 N.W. 1024 (Neb. 1903). However, the rule is mentioned earlier. *See, e.g., Hawes v. Oakland*, 104 U.S. 450 (1892).

[63] 417 U.S. 703 (1974).

First, plaintiff had to have been a shareholder at the time of the wrong of which plaintiff complains. Amoskeag purchased its share interest subsequent to Bangor Punta's alleged mismanagement; it was not a contemporaneous owner.

Second, "a shareholder may not complain of acts of corporate mismanagement if he acquired shares from those who participated or acquiesced in the allegedly wrongful transaction."[64] This latter principle, the "tainted share rule," exists independently of the contemporaneous ownership rule.[65]

The court noted further the basis for the rule. Presumably, the current shareholder paid a price that reflected the harm done by the earlier wrongdoers' acts. Any recovery, direct or indirect, by the subsequent shareholder would represent a windfall. For example, in *Bangor Punta*, Amoskeag paid $5 million to Bangor Punta for a 98.3% of BAR. Amoskeag then turned around to seek $7 million in damages from the seller. Mr. Justice Powell noted that:

> The equitable principles of *Home Fire* preclude Amoskeag from reaping a windfall by enhancing the value of its bargain to the extent of the entire purchase price plus an additional $2,000,000. Amoskeag would in effect have acquired a railroad worth $12,000,000 for only $5,000,000. Neither the federal antitrust or securities laws nor the applicable state laws contemplate recovery by Amoskeag in these circumstances.

Even if the purchasing shareholder knows nothing of the wrongdoing during an earlier time period, permitting recovery to the non-contemporaneous holder may represent a windfall. The reason, reflected in the widely accepted efficient market hypothesis, is that securities markets incorporate in the price of shares all currently available information about the corporation issuing the shares, assuming that the information has been in some way made public.[66]

[3] Possible Exception: Undisclosed Wrongdoing

At least twice in his *Bangor Punta* opinion, Mr. Justice Powell noted that "Amoskeag did not contend . . . that the purchase transaction was tainted by fraud or deceit."[67] The implication of Justice Powell's observation is that, if the wrongdoing remained concealed at the time of the purchase, the purchase price would not reflect the harm caused by the wrongdoing. The reasoning in cases such as *Home Fire Ins.* and *Bangor Punta* does not apply.

The drafters of the 1975 revision of California's corporations code picked up upon Justice Powell's dictum. Under California's statute, the judge may dispense with the requirement of contemporaneous ownership if "the plaintiff acquired the shares before there was disclosure to the public or to the plaintiff

---

[64] *Bangor Punta*, 417 U.S. 703 (1974).

[65] This is discussed further in § 14.03[D], note 78, *infra*.

[66] The United States Supreme Court accorded judicial recognition to the efficient market hypothesis in *Basic Inc. v. Levinson*, 485 U.S. 224 (1988) (accepting as a matter of federal securities law the so-called fraud on the market reliance substitute), discussed in § 13.02[G], *supra*.

[67] 417 U.S. at 711. *See also id.* at 716 ("No fraud or deceit of any kind is alleged to have been involved in the transaction").

of the wrongdoing."[68] The ALI Project provides that "[a] holder of an equity security has standing to commence and maintain a derivative action if the holder . . . acquired the equity security . . . before the material facts relating to the alleged wrong were either publicly disclosed or were known by, or specifically communicated to, the holder."[69]

By contrast, in its codification of derivative action principles, the American Bar Association rejected the approach of the ALI, California, and several other jurisdictions. The ABA's Model Business Corporation Act retains a hard and fast contemporaneous ownership requirement as "simple, clear and easy to apply."[70]

[4] Exception: Continuing Wrong

A principle that may enable a subsequent purchasing shareholder to avoid the contemporaneous ownership requirement is to find that the wrong committed is a continuous one, extending into the period of the named plaintiff's share ownership. Often, a cause of action may accrue during a previous owner's ownership. The current owner may seek to recover damages on the theory that the wrongdoing has continued into the new period of ownership. Application of the theory seems highly fact specific, with similar cases coming out differently depending upon the court involved.[71] Some courts hold that payments under a contract entered into by the corporation before plaintiff's purchase of shares constitute a continuing wrong while others do not.[72]

[5] Exception: Double Derivative Actions

An owner of shares in a parent corporation or holding company, may sue to remedy wrongdoing in a subsidiary. This action is called a double derivative action. A complete exposition on the subject of double derivative actions is contained in *Brown v. Tenney*.[73]

Brown and Tenney were the two shareholders of a corporation engaged in commodities trading. Anticipating future diversification, Brown and Tenney

---

[68] Cal. Corp. Code § 800(b)(1)(ii).

[69] A.L.I. Corp. Gov. Proj. § 7.02(a)(1). In *Rifkin v. Steele Platt*, 824 P.2d 32 (Col. App. 1991), on *Bangor Punta* type facts, the court held that subsequent buyers of shares could retain a corporate recovery for wrongdoing that had occurred prior to their share purchase if, on remand, the trial court "finds that the purchase price did not reflect the wrongdoings."

[70] MBCA § 7.41 and Official Comment, 45 Bus. Law. 1241, 1243 (1990).

[71] Delaware, for example, has conflicting caselaw on the continuing wrong theory. *See, e.g., Nickson v. Filtrol Corp.*, 262 A.2d 267 (Del. Ch. 1970) (retention of bonds previously purchased did not constitute a continuing wrong; court extremely skeptical of continuing wrong theory). *But see Maclary v. Pleasant Hills, Inc.*, 109 A.2d 830 (Del. Ch. 1950) (plaintiff who purchased after directors wrongfully resolved to issue shares but before shares actually issued, permitted to proceed on continuing wrong theory).

[72] *Compare Palmer v. Morris*, 316 F.2d 649 (5th Cir. 1963) (continuing payments constitute a continuing wrong; later purchasing shareholder had standing), *with Goldie v. Yaker*, 432 P.2d 841 (N.M. 1967) (payments on land contract assumed as payment for allegedly watered shares did not constitute a continuing wrong).

[73] 532 N.W.2d 230 (Ill. 1988).

formed a holding company, which then held the shares of their operating company.[74] Later, Brown sued Tenney. Tenney successfully moved to dismiss on the ground that Brown was not a contemporaneous shareholder in the subsidiary in which the wrongdoing had occurred. The Supreme Court of Illinois reversed, calling the double derivative action "a longstanding doctrine of equity jurisprudence." The court found the double derivative action to have "nearly universal acceptance." Combined with rigid application of the contemporaneous ownership rule, Justice Moran found that:

> The additional layer in the corporate structure [represented by a parent corporation or holding company] would prevent the righting of many wrongs and would insulate the wrongdoer from judicial intervention.

> To prevent this from occurring . . . courts have fashioned a remedy from the single derivative cloth — the double derivative suit . . . . The right to bring the derivative action falls to the shareholder when the holding company fails to protect its property and assets.

The same principles might allow a shareholder in a grandparent (parent of the parent) corporation to complain of wrongdoing in a subsidiary. This would result in a "triple" derivative action. In some corporate group structures, even a quadruple derivative action is conceivable.

[C] Continuous Owner

Sales of shares, gifts of shares, or merger of the issuing corporation,[75] even if contrived to end the plaintiff's lawsuit, are events that extinguish the named plaintiff's right to maintain a shareholder suit. Ownership must be maintained though trial and appeal, if any.

In *Merritt v. Colonial Foods, Inc.*,[76] the court upheld dismissal of a suit in which a merger had no purpose other than elimination of the plaintiff's standing. The court reasoned that other remedies exist. "If a proposed merger is sought to be used for the cover-up of wrongful acts of mismanagement, a court of equity in an action making a direct attack on the merger can and will protect the innocent shareholder victim."[77] The court found that when standing to maintain a derivative suit has been eliminated on grounds of lack of continuous ownership, the complaining parties may bring a direct action for fraud.[78]

---

[74] As they diversified, Brown and Tenney formed a new subsidiary for each new business with the shares to be held by the holding company. Brown and Tenney themselves would own shares in only the holding company. Such a corporate structure is very common in the banking industry in which banks have subsidiaries in banking, credit card issuance, investment management, and so on.

[75] Mergers and other acquisition forms are discussed in Chapter 6.

[76] 505 A.2d 757 (Del. Ch. 1986).

[77] *Id.* at 762, quoting *Bokat v. Getty Oil Co.*, 262 A.2d 246 (Del. 1970).

[78] *See, e.g., Cede & Co. v. Technicolor, Inc.*, 542 A.2d 1182 (Del. 1988) ("[n]o one would assert that a former owner, suing for the loss of property through deception or fraud, has lost standing to right the wrong that arguably caused the owner to relinquish ownership . . . ").

Another exception to the continuous ownership requirement is found "where the merger is in reality a reorganization which does not affect plaintiff's ownership of the business enterprise."[79] In other words, if, by virtue of the merger, nothing changes with the exception of the substitution of one share certificate for another in a substantially equivalent enterprise, the merger does not eliminate plaintiff's standing. A merger or share exchange to form a holding company is a good example.

An example of a share exchange is when a shareholder of an operating company, such as an airline, becomes a shareholder of an airline holding company by exchange of one share for another. In one such case,[80] the Delaware Chancery Court permitted the ex-airline shareholder to continue prosecution of his pre-merger derivative suit. "The structure of the old and new companies is virtually identical," the court remarked, finding that "the instant action is really [or had become by way of the merger] a double derivative suit." Conversely, if what plaintiff receives in the merger represents "property interests distinctly different" (for example, cash, shares in a larger new entity) from that which was held previously, the former shareholder no longer has standing to maintain a derivative action.

One case goes beyond these parameters. In *Blasband v. Rales*,[81] plaintiff owned shares of Easco Hand Tools, Inc. Plaintiff filed suit complaining that Easco directors had invested in junk bonds as a favor to a broker-dealer associate rather than as a matter of sound business judgment. Prior to filing the suit, the directors caused Easco to be merged into the larger Danaher Corp. The District Court denied standing because the shareholder no longer owned Easco shares. The Third Circuit reversed. Although Blasband no longer owned shares in the subsidiary, he did now own shares in the parent corporation. His suit was analogous to a double derivative action and could continue.

[D] Clean Hands Requirement

The derivative suit is a creature of equity. Most often, the underlying claims of breaches of fiduciary duty are equitable as well. Thus, courts require plaintiff to have cleans hands.[82] If the plaintiff has any complicity in the wrongdoing, either as shareholder, officer, director or in some other capacity, she is not an adequate representative of the shareholder class.[83]

---

[79] *Lewis v. Anderson*, 477 A.2d 1040, 1046 (Del. 1984).

[80] *Schreiber v. Carney*, 447 A.2d 17 (Del. Ch. 1982).

[81] 971 F.2d 1034 (3d Cir. 1992).

[82] *Rosenthal v. Burry Biscuit Corp.*, 60 A.2d 106, 111–13 (Del. Ch. 1948).

[83] Under the tainted shareholder rule, even the purest shareholder may be disqualified if she has taken her shares from a wrongdoer or one who has assisted in the alleged wrongdoing. A leading case is *Courtland Manor, Inc. v. Leeds*, 347 A.2d 144 (Del. Ch. 1975). The corporation operated a nursing home, while a limited partnership owned the facility. The plaintiff complained that, as shareholders and directors, the limited partners had caused the corporation to enter into a lease that was disadvantageous to the corporation and highly favorable to the partnership. Before commencing the action, the plaintiff purchased the shares of some control group members who had negotiated or agreed to the lease transaction. Chancellor Brown noted the clean hands rule: "[o]ur courts have recognized the basic principle that one who acquires his stock from a shareholder who participated

[E]   Adequate Representation Requirement

The "adequate representation requirement" in derivative suits has two components: one, that the plaintiff-shareholder be an adequate representative of the shareholders in general and, second, that counsel be able adequately to prosecute the case.

The rationale behind the rule is the same as the rationale behind the adequate representation requirement in class actions:

> In order to give a judgment rendered in a derivative action res judicata effect, we impose a requirement of fair and adequate representation on the named plaintiffs. This specter of res judicata, by which a decision is binding on all the shareholders, makes the named plaintiff in a shareholder derivative suit similar to a representative in a class action.[84]

The preclusive effect and the accompanying judicial economy are achieved only if the plaintiff-shareholder and counsel are found to be adequate representatives of the class.[85]

Shareholders who have some complicity in the wrongdoing alleged, and thus have unclean hands, are not adequate representatives of the shareholder class. Even a shareholder with no complicity may be an inadequate representative if that shareholder has a side agenda that will interfere with prosecution of the shareholder lawsuit.[86] Shareholders who are aggrieved ex-employees, competi-

---

in or acquiesced in a corporate wrong lacks the capacity himself to complain of it."

"A shareholder may not complain of acts of corporate mismanagement if he acquired his shares from those who participated or acquiesced in the wrongful transaction." The reason is that, presumably, the price the would-be plaintiff paid for the shares reflects the harm done by the prior wrongdoing. A suit, and a recovery therein, would be a windfall. By contrast, if the price does not reflect the wrongdoing, the proper suit by the holder of the tainted shares is against her seller for fraud.

Another leading tainted share case is *Ettridge v. TSI Group, Inc.*, 548 A.2d 813 (Md. 1988) (citations omitted):

The second principle, precluding suit by those who acquired their shares from one who participated or acquiesced in the allegedly wrongful transactions, is grounded not only in the same considerations [as the contemporaneous ownership rule and its concern with windfalls] but also in the equitable doctrine of unclean hands — "he that hath committed inequity shall not have equity." A purchaser of stock generally acquires the rights that his transferor had.

[84] *Palmer v. United States Sav. Bank of Am.*, 553 A.2d 781, 785 (N.H. 1989) (citations omitted).

[85] *Hansberry v. Lee*, 311 U.S. 32 (1940) (due process dictates that judgment in a class suit is res judicata only if named or representative parties were adequate representatives of the class).

[86] When assessing adequacy of representation, Delaware applies a less exacting standard:

A plaintiff . . . will not be disqualified simply because he may have interests which go beyond the interests of the class . . . . Likewise, purely hypothetical, potential, or remote conflicts of interest will not disqualify a derivative plaintiff.

A defendant has the burden of proof in a motion to disqualify a derivative plaintiff and must show that a *serious* conflict exists and that the plaintiff cannot be expected to act in the interests of the others because doing so would harm his other interests.

Emerald Partners v. Berlin, 564 A.2d 670, 674 (Del. Ch. 1983) (emphasis added) (citations omitted).

tors, or shareholders in a competing corporation may not be adequate representatives.[87]

Another ground for objection is that physical infirmities or age make it unlikely that the representative party will pursue the claim vigorously. Courts generally do not give much credence to such defense arguments.[88] Delaware Chancellor William Chandler faced motions to disqualify two plaintiffs in *In re Fuqua Industries, Inc., Shareholders Litigation.*[89] One held 12,008 Fuqua shares but had failing memory and other faculties. The other (Freberg) held 25 shares, "his knowledge of the case was at best elliptical," and he had "general ignorance of six or seven other lawsuits in which he was" the named plaintiff. The defense castigated him as "a puppet for fee-hungry lawyers." The chancellor turned back the motion to disqualify on grounds that "Freberg does in fact understand the basic nature of the derivative claims, even if barely so."

Hunger for fees also does not disqualify. "[T]hat lawyers pursue their own economic interest in bringing derivative litigation cannot be held grounds to disqualify a derivative plaintiff. To do so is to impeach a cornerstone of sound corporate governance. Our legal system has privatized in part the enforcement mechanism for policing fiduciaries by allowing private attorneys to bring suits on behalf of nominal shareholder plaintiffs."

Secondly, though, for adequate representation to exist, "the plaintiff's attorney must be qualified, experienced and generally able to conduct the proposed litigation."[90] Occasionally, a court examines a derivative action attorney's qualifications, finding them wanting.[91] More frequently, the issue that arises is not mere technical competency but conflict of interest.

Most typically, the conflict lies in the attorney's attempt to act both as plaintiff and as attorney in the action. More than a handful of jurisdictions have adopted a *per se* rule of inadequate representation and plaintiff disqualification in these cases.[92]

---

[87] Ex-employees: see *Recchion v. Kirby*, 637 F. Supp. 1309 (W.D. Pa. 1986); *Roberts v. Alabama Power Co.*, 404 So. 2d 629 (Ala. 1981). *See also Steinberg v. Steinberg*, 434 N.Y.S.2d 877 (App. Div. 1980) (derivative action by estranged spouse of CEO of public company found "deliberately instituted to obtain leverage in the matrimonial proceeding" — representation inadequate). Competitors: see *Rose v. Tidelands Capital Corp.*, 438 F. Supp. 684 (N.D. Ala. 1977); *DuPont v. Wyley*, 61 F.R.D. 615 (D. Del. 1973).

[88] *See, e.g., Fradkin v. Ernst*, 98 F.R.D. 478 (N.D. Ohio 1983) (plaintiff was a stroke victim who had difficulty communicating; court held plaintiff was an adequate representative); *Koenig v. Benson*, 117 F.R.D. 330 (E.D.N.Y. 1987) (language deficiency not a barrier).

[89] 752 A.2d 126 (Del. Ch. 1999).

[90] *Wetzel v. Liberty Mutual Ins. Co.*, 508 F.2d 239 (3d Cir. 1975).

[91] *See, e.g., Rogosin v. Steadman*, 71 F.R.D. 514 (S.D.N.Y. 1976) (counsel had no independent memory of the case).

[92] *See, e.g., Zylstra v. Safeway Stores, Inc.*, 578 F.2d 102 (5th Cir. 1978); *Kramer v. Scientific Control Corp.*, 534 F.2d 1085 (3d Cir. 1976); *Turoff v. May Co.*, 531 F.2d 1357 (6th Cir. 1976); *Hedges Enter. Inc. v. Continental Group*, 81 F.RD. 461 (E.D. Pa. 1979); *Camp v. Chase*, 476 A.2d 1087 (Conn. 1983).

Delaware does not follow a *per se* rule of attorney disqualification. In *Emerald Partners v. Berlin*,[93] the court disqualified an attorney who, with her spouse, controlled a partnership holding 2.2% of the publicly held corporation involved in the case. The court focused on the potential for real, and not merely hypothetical, violations of the Rules of Professional Conduct, as enacted in Delaware and a number of other jurisdictions. One consideration is the likelihood that the attorney may be a witness in the case.[94] A real conflict may also arise when the attorney looks to a fund created by the lawsuit for her fee, setting up a conflict between the roles of claimant and attorney.

Thus, a derivative action plaintiff and the attorney have a long checklist that they must go through before typing a name in the caption of the complaint. Once they have placed the name in the caption of the complaints they intend to file, attention must then turn to statutory and other derivative actions "reforms" enacted in the first strike suit era.

[F]   Selection of Lead Counsel

When suspected wrongdoing has occurred in a publicly held corporation, typically plaintiffs' attorneys file multiple lawsuits. Often, pursuant to defense motions, the court will consolidate the lawsuits. Part of that process is that one plaintiff will become lead plaintiff and one law firm will become lead counsel, with power to parcel out work and control conduct of the litigation. The traditional method for choosing lead counsel has been negotiation and agreement among the attorneys.

Recently, Delaware Chancellor Chandler noted, "[m]embers of the Court of Chancery have been asked, with increasing frequency, to become involved in the sometimes internecine struggles within the plaintiffs' bar over the power to control, direct and (one suspects) ultimately settle shareholder lawsuits."[95] The Chancellor first made clear that an allegedly once important factor, the first to file in a race to the courthouse, "has neither empirical nor logical support." Instead, he formulated a three part test for occasions when (reluctantly) judges must resolve the issue of appointment of lead counsel. The court should consider the "quality of the pleading," "give weight to the shareholder plaintiff that has the greatest economic stake in the outcome" [but not "mechanically applied"], and "accord some weight to whether a particular litigant has prosecuted its lawsuit with greater energy, enthusiasm, or vigor" than other litigants.

---

[93] 564 A.2d 670 (Del. Ch. 1989).

[94] *See, e.g., In re Conduct of Kinsey*, 660 P.2d 660 (Or. 1983) (attorney who stipulated to his non-appearance as a witness so that his law firm could continue to defend the derivative action sanctioned and reprimanded by state supreme court).

[95] *TCW Technology Ltd. Partnership v. Intermedia Communications, Inc.*, 2000 Del. Ch. LEXIS 147 (2000), subsequently consolidated as *In re Digex Shareholders Litigation*.

§ 14.04 REFORMS OF THE EARLIER STRIKE SUIT ERA

[A] Overview

In the 1930s, state legislatures enacted "reforms" that made it more difficult for shareholders to bring derivative suits, including statutory requirements for record ownership and for contemporaneous ownership. Two other reforms enacted during that time were the verification requirement and the need to post security for expenses.

[B] Verification Requirement

A strike suit era reform that survives today is the requirement that a derivative action plaintiff "verify" the complaint.[96] Verification requires that a plaintiff read the allegations and attests that, in good faith and based upon personal knowledge, she believes them to be true. A verified complaint must be signed by the plaintiff. In contrast, most modern pleading is stated to be based on "information and belief." In most non-derivative actions, the attorney signs the pleading on the client's behalf.

Because the verification requirement is relatively rare in most forms of litigation, verification could represent a potential time bomb for the derivative action plaintiff and the attorney. Often, especially with publicly held corporations, the plaintiff races to the courthouse. The attorney will have based the lawsuit upon information gleaned from a newspaper article or similar report. The nominal plaintiff will verify the complaint despite a lack of personal knowledge and upon what later is found to be a flimsy investigation. Defense lawyers may discover all of this through deposition of the plaintiff-shareholder. The defense then may move to disqualify plaintiff, her attorney, or both, on the grounds of inadequate or false verification.

In *Surowitz v. Hilton Hotels Corp.*,[97] Mr. Justice Black diffused the time bomb. He discussed the issue of verification by an older immigrant lady (Ms. Surowitz) with "a very limited English vocabulary" who had invested $2,000 in Hilton shares. The plaintiff had signed a detailed complaint as requested by her attorney son-in-law (with the appropriate name Irving Brilliant). The trial court held her verification to be a false affidavit and therefore a nullity. The complaint was dismissed as having failed to meet the verification requirement.

Justice Black took an instrumentalist view. Verification had been adopted to "discourage 'strike suits' by people who might be interested in getting quick dollars by making charges without regard to their truth so as to coerce corporate managers to settle worthless claims . . . ." The instant action was not "a strike suit or anything akin to it . . . . Mrs. Surowitz was not interested in anything but her own investment." Her verification, "not on the basis of her own knowledge and understanding, but in the faith that her son-in-law had

---

[96] *See, e.g.,* Fed. R. Civ. P. 23.1 ("In a derivative action brought by one or more shareholders . . . the complaint shall be verified . . . .").

[97] 383 U.S. 363 (1966).

correctly advised her," was sufficient. Under the law established by the *Surowitz* case, the verifying plaintiff need only demonstrate that someone in whom she has confidence has investigated the allegations and believes them to be true. *Surowitz* is a landmark case that has diffused the verification requirement as a viable weapon for derivative action defendants.[98]

[C]　Security for Expenses Requirements

Another requirement is that a shareholder-plaintiff, or at least a party plaintiff with a small stake in the corporation,[99] undertake to pay defendants' costs should the plaintiff lose or abandon the litigation.[100] Such an undertaking normally consists of a promise to pay (a bond) that may be required to be collateralized in whole or in part. Undertakings may be collateralized by placing cash or negotiable securities in the registry of the court. The exact arrangements vary.

Providing such security is a daunting proposition for a plaintiff with a small stake. Told by his lawyer of a need not only to sign the complaint but also to put up $5,000 or $7,500, and a promise to pay even more, many potential plaintiffs simply evaporate.

State legislatures in a half dozen of the two dozen or so jurisdictions having security for costs statutes have eliminated them, in part because they deny citizens access to the courts.[101] In states which still retain a security for costs statute, defense lawyers can be expected to seek the posting of bonds and security thereon in extremely large amounts to discourage plaintiffs from pursuing their lawsuits.[102]

The available evidence is that, perhaps hesitant to close the doors to any class of litigant, courts resist defense entreaties, ordering security for expenses in amounts that are reasonable, if not downright small.[103] Several courts, too, have noted that defendants misconstrue such rules when they attempt to find the

---

[98] There are, however, limits. *See, e.g., Roussel v. Tidelands Capital Corp.*, 438 F. Supp. 684 (N.D. Ala. 1977) (plaintiff who admitted to verifying complaint without even having read it was inadequate representative).

[99] Statutes based upon earlier versions of the Model Act dispensed with the requirement if plaintiff owned either 5% of the company or shares valued at more than $25,000. *See, e.g.*, Ariz. Gen. Corp. L. § 49(C)(1976).

[100] New York adopted the first such statute in 1944. *See* N.Y.B.C.L. § 627.

[101] The Revised Model Act substitutes a provision making clear courts' power after the fact to "order the plaintiff to pay any defendant's reasonable expenses (including counsel's fees) incurred in defending a proceeding if it finds that the proceeding was commenced or maintained without reasonable cause or for an improper purpose." MBCA § 7.46(2). A.L.I. Corp. Gov. Proj. § 7.04 adopts the same approach. Delaware, too, has never had a security for expenses requirement for derivative action plaintiffs.

[102] The United States Supreme Court refused to find security for expenses statutes to be unconstitutional. *Cohen v. Beneficial Industrial Loan Corp.*, 337 U.S. 541 (1949) (finding also that such statutes are a matter of state substantive law which, under *Erie*, federal courts must apply in derivative actions brought in federal court based upon diversity of citizenship).

[103] *See, e.g., Malott v. Randall*, 523 P.2d 439 (Wash. Ct. App. 1974) ($100,000 requested but only $10,000 ordered); *Gaudosi v. Mellon*, 269 F.2d 873 (2d Cir. 1959) ($3000). Another tactic courts have

English attorney fee rule (prevailing party receives fees from losing party) incorporated in the statute. Because the security for costs statutes do not incorporate a "loser pays all" rule as to fees, the bond and/or other security need not be so large as to cover all anticipated attorney fees. In ordering a bond of only $3000, a New Jersey court noted that:

> The statute does not in terms direct the allowance of costs and counsel fees, but merely provides for security out of which . . . fees might thereafter be allowed in the court's discretion. [The statute] cannot reasonably be construed as in itself assuring a defendant corporation that it will be reimbursed for costs and counsel fees. The statute merely made more potent the sanction that was available to the Chancellor — charging counsel fees against a bad faith suitor — by making the availability of such money a prerequisite to maintenance of suit.[104]

Nonetheless, plaintiffs seek to avoid security for expenses statutes where they continue to exist. One manner is to avoid derivative allegations, pleading direct claims. A second and related strategy is to plead federal securities rather than state corporate law claims to which courts have at times held security for costs statutes are not applicable.[105] A third is to find joint plaintiffs or intervenors to help qualify for a statutory exemption (for example, a party holding more than $25,000 in shares).[106]

Security for costs statutes are another of the strike suit reforms that may gradually lose significance. However, corporate litigators practicing today must remain aware of the requirements and fashion strategy accordingly.

§ 14.05   THE DEMAND RULE

[A]   Overview

The lynch pin of the modern strike suit reforms is the demand requirement. Rules of civil procedure commonly provide that "[t]he complaint shall also allege with particularity the efforts, if any, made by the plaintiffs to obtain the action the plaintiff desires from the directors or comparable authority."[107]

Demand is not merely a pleading requirement. Substantive state corporation laws require that plaintiffs make such a demand.[108] The United States Supreme Court has held that the demand requirement is a device whereby state

---

used is stay the effectiveness of the order to post security so that the plaintiff can find intervenors who will help defray the expense.

[104] *De Bow v. Lakewood Hotel and Land Assoc.*, 145 A.2d 493, 497 (N.J. Super. Ct. App. Div. 1958).

[105] *McClure v. Borne Chemical Co.*, 292 F.2d 824 (3d Cir.), *cert. denied*, 368 U.S. 939 (1961); *Fielding v. Allen*, 181 F.2d 163 (2d Cir.), *cert. denied*, 340 U.S. 817 (1950).

[106] *See, e.g., Baker v. MacFadden Publications*, 300 N.Y. 325, 90 N.E.2d 876 (1950).

[107] Fed. R. Civ. P. 23.1.

[108] Thus, the law of the state of incorporation, rather than the forum state's law, will govern demand.

corporate law has made an important substantive allocation of power among shareholders, directors, and the corporation.[109]

Demand is the means whereby the board of directors, which is charged with managing the corporations business and affairs, has an opportunity to manage litigation in the corporation's name or on its behalf. Demand also presents an opportunity for intra-corporate dispute resolution. By receiving and acting upon a demand, the board may save the corporation great expense. Demand may also filter out abusive strike suits.

[B]   Demand Refused

A shareholder generally makes demand by letter to the board of directors, a senior manager, such as the CEO, or to the corporation's counsel. In the letter, the shareholder sets out the grievance. No format or specific level of certainty or content is required. The demand should eventually end up in the hands of the board of directors.[110]

The demand requirement has three common law branches: demand "refused," demand "accepted," or demand "excused." In a demand refused case, the board "rejects" the demand after due deliberation, preceded by investigation of the facts. Demand may be refused either because the board has concluded that the law has not been violated, or because pursuing the corporations rights would not be in the corporation's best interests. The corporation then notifies the shareholder-plaintiff or opposing counsel that the demand has been rejected.

Sometimes the affair may end there. Other times, the shareholder files a lawsuit. In such a lawsuit, the corporation would likely move to dismiss or move for summary judgment in its favor on the grounds that the board has considered and refused the demand, that the law charges boards and not courts with management of the corporation's business and affairs, and that the business judgment rule shields from judicial scrutiny the board's decision that the proposed litigation should not ensue.

The demand refused scenario is thus not favorable to plaintiffs, presenting as it does two uphill battles for plaintiffs: first, at the intra-corporate stage, and then after an action is filed in court. The demand refused scenario is made even more unpalatable by the Delaware decision in *Speigel v. Buntrock*,[111] in which the Supreme Court of Delaware held that "[b]y making a demand, a stockholder

---

[109] *Kamen v. Kemper Fin. Serv., Inc.*, 500 U.S. 90 (1991) ("The Court of Appeals thus erred by fashioning a uniform federal common law rule abolishing the futility exception in derivative actions"), *reversing, Kamen v. Kemper Fin. Serv., Inc.*, 908 F.2d 1338 (7th Cir. 1990) (Easterbrook, J.).

[110] In the case of repetitive or duplicative demands, the American Law Institute provides that the demand must still reach the board of directors but allows the board to utilize a summary procedure in dealing with such a demand. *See* A.L.I. Corp. Gov. Proj. § 7.09 and Comment (e). Corporate counsel advocate that a senior corporate official, such as the general counsel, deal with a shareholder demand in such circumstances.

[111] 571 A.2d 767 (Del. 1990).

tacitly acknowledges the absence of facts to support a finding of futility," that is, concedes the ability of the board to deal impartially with the demand.[112]

The difficulty is that *Speigel* creates a disincentive to explore alternative dispute resolution. A plaintiff who conducts preliminary discussion with the corporation or its counsel may have made a demand, thereby conceding the ability of the board, and given up any realistic alternative to court proceedings later on if the intra-corporate approach fails to yield fruit.[113]

[C]   Demand Accepted

In the demand accepted scenario, the board of directors notifies the shareholder that the board intends to take action on the demand. The corporation may hire special counsel or conduct an investigation. After investigating plaintiff's claims, the corporation may either go ahead with the action or settle. Settlement may occur with or without the filing of an action against the alleged wrongdoers.

Settlement may pose problems. The shareholder may fear that, via the board of directors, the corporation will accept demand and then administer a slap on the wrist or enter into a sweetheart settlement with the alleged wrongdoers. The settlement and the feckless prosecution scenarios give pause to plaintiffs.[114] Once the board accepts demand, the shareholder no longer has any rights in the litigation: the shareholder's name is dropped from the complaint in the realignment of parties, she will not be entitled to participate in discovery or settlement discussions, and she will not even be entitled to be copied on pleadings and other court papers.[115] She will have no window on the litigation at all.

Another feature of the demand accepted landscape is the nature of settlement. Federal Rule of Civil Procedure 23.1 provides that "a derivative action shall not be dismissed or compromised without the approval of the court, and notice of the proposed dismissal or compromise shall be given to

---

[112] The court rejected the argument that, in making credible insider trading allegations against directors of Waste Management, Inc., and demand thereon, plaintiff Speigel preserved his right to argue that demand was excused. *But see Scattered Corp. v. Chicago Stock Exchange*, 701 A.2d 70 (Del. 1997) (nothing in *Speigel* prevents a court from closely examining claims that, in actual operation, a special litigation committee or board which refused a demand lacked disinterestedness).

[113] An attorney may advise an aggrieved shareholder to either make demand, knowing that demand refused will be the effective end of the dispute, or avoid the corporation altogether. The shareholder thus should abjure the kind of pre-suit, pre-filing negotiation or discussion that may occur in any other form of litigation, and which ethical and collegial attorneys feel is their duty to undertake.

[114] *See, e.g., Powell v. Western Ill. Elec. Co-op.*, 536 N.E.2d 231 (Ill. App. Ct. 1989).

[115] *Powell, supra.* Indirectly, courts give added credence to intra-corporate resolutions if the corporation allows the plaintiff-shareholder to continue involvement in the litigation. *See, e.g., Joy v. North*, 692 F.2d 880, 892 (2d Cir.) (a special litigation committee ("SLC") might permit plaintiff's counsel to be present at depositions and to cross-examine witnesses), *cert. denied*, 460 U.S. 1051 (1983). *Cf. Peller v. Southern Co.*, 911 F.2d 1532, 1538 (11th Cir. 1990) (lack of good faith when SLC refused even to release to plaintiff summaries of witness interviews). *See generally* Douglas M. Branson, CORPORATE GOVERNANCE § 11.35, at 701–02 (1993).

shareholders or members in such manner as the court directs." Two types of settlement are possible: a possible settlement with the alleged wrongdoer — a director or directors or senior executive — on the underlying claim, and a settlement with the shareholder-plaintiff in the derivative action itself.

In *Wolf v. Barkes*,[116] the Second Circuit held that Rule 23.1 does not require judicial approval of the settlement the corporation reaches with the "true" defendants. That feature of the landscape enlarges the potential field of play for a sweetheart settlement.[117]

Frequently, corporations do proffer the settlement for court approval in order to gain protection against suit over the same facts by other shareholders.[118] The corporation then has res judicata as a shield in subsequent litigation. However, the prevailing law follows *Wolf v. Barkes*. Thus, the corporation may accept demand, commence an action, and then quickly settle. The complaining shareholder is entitled to neither notice of the settlement nor a window of opportunity to examine or to challenge the settlement.[119]

[D]   Demand Excused

[1]   Introduction

Because "demand refused" and "demand accepted" conjure up unpalatable scenarios, experienced shareholder rights attorneys turn first to the "demand excused" branch of the common law of demand. Alleging that the law "excuses" demand, the attorney proceeds directly to court, filing a summons and complaint and causing the corporation and the individual defendants to be served with process.

The common law excuses demand in several sets of circumstances: when the corporation is threatened with irreparable harm; when it is a closely held corporation;[120] when the corporation has taken an extraordinarily long period of time and still has not responded; when demand has been made and the corporation takes no position on the issue; and when demand is excused as "futile."

---

[116] 348 F.2d 994 (2d Cir.), *cert. denied*, 382 U.S. 941 (1965).

[117] The rationale in *Wolf* is that, by virtue of its res judicata effect, settlement of the derivative component will bind all other shareholders. Judicial examination of the adequacy of representation is necessary. By contrast, settlement of the underlying dispute binds only the parties thereto: the corporation and the wrongdoers. Any other shareholder remains free to sue. The corporation then would plead the earlier settlement as an affirmative defense. The court entertaining the second suit could review the settlement as to fairness, adequacy or representation, and so on, at that time.

[118] See the authorities cited in Douglas M. Branson, CORPORATE GOVERNANCE § 11.36, at 706 (1993).

[119] The A.L.I. Project does provide for court approval of settlements but makes clear that the complaining shareholder need not necessarily be involved. A.L.I. Corp. Gov. Proj. § 715(a) ("[T]he board or a properly delegated committee, without the agreement of the plaintiff, may *with the approval of the court* enter into a settlement with, or grant a release to, a director, a senior executive, or a person in control of the corporation, or an associate of such person, with respect to any claim raised on behalf of the corporation in the action.") (emphasis added).

[120] See the discussion of close corporations and derivative litigation in § 14.02[D], *supra*.

[2]   The Futility Exception

[a]   Introduction

The law will not command an act which, if done, would be futile. Requiring a shareholder to make demand upon a board of directors who will not give that demand a fair hearing would be to require a futile act. A board of directors may be unable to give a demand a fair hearing because a critical mass of the directors who would act,[121] are likely to be motivated by an illicit objective in their treatment of the shareholder demand, if it were made. An illicit objective could be revenge, spite, jealousy, or some other base motive. Usually, plaintiff's counsel alleges that the board is disabled because either a critical mass of the directors have a material interest in the subject matter of the underlying claim or suit (subsection (b)), or they are dominated or controlled by a fellow director or shareholder who does have such a conflict of interest (subsection (c)).

[b]   Legal Tests for Demand Futility

The best font of general principles regarding demand futility is the 1984 Delaware Supreme Court opinion in *Aronson v. Lewis.*[122] In *Aronson*, the directors had approved a generous ten year salary, bonus, and consulting arrangement for a controlling shareholder, aged 75, to whom the directors were likely beholden for their positions. Justice Moore went out of his way to state that a 47% shareholder in a publicly traded corporation is not necessarily in control, which seems preposterous.

The guiding principle is that "where officers and directors are under an influence which sterilizes their discretion, they cannot be considered proper persons to conduct litigation on behalf of the corporation."[123] In applying that principle, a trial court must ask itself:

> [W]hether, under the particularized facts alleged, a reasonable doubt is created that: (1) the directors are disinterested and independent [or] (2) the challenged transaction was otherwise the product of a valid exercise of business judgment. Hence, the Court of Chancery must make two inquiries, one into the independence and disinterestedness of the directors and the other into the substantive nature of the challenged transaction and the board's approval thereof.[124]

The quoted language has been interpreted to mean that demand will be excused when plaintiff has created a reasonable doubt that, had the board acted, the

---

[121] The Supreme Court of Delaware has held that it is an issue of fact of how much participation by one, two or more disabled directors is sufficient to taint the "collective independence" of a collegial body such as the board of directors. *See Cede & Co. v. Technicolor, Inc.*, 634 A.2d 345, 364 (Del. 1993). Decisions in an earlier era held, or strongly hinted, that participation by even one director with a disabling conflict tainted the board's decision. *See, e.g., Bowman v. Gun*, 193 A. 271, 274 (Pa. 1937); *Teft v. Schaefer*, 239 P.2d 837, 838 (Wash. 1925). That is not, of course, the current view.

[122] 473 A.2d 805 (Del. 1984).

[123] *Mayer v. Adams*, 141 A.2d 458, 461 (Del. 1958).

[124] *Aronson, supra.*

directors would have been entitled to the business judgment rule's protections, (a) either with regard to the decision on the shareholder demand, or (b) at the prior time at which the directors approved the challenged transaction.[125]

From a plaintiff's point of view, *Aronson* seems to formulate a fairly liberal standard. From that point on, however, *Aronson* dismisses as insufficient a number of contentions. Nomination and election of all the directors by the alleged wrongdoers is insufficient to establish "domination and control." The threat of personal liability alone is insufficient to establish disinterestedness. Further, approval of a seemingly questionable series of transactions was held insufficient to establish "reasonable doubt."

Aronson v. Lewis thus establishes a fairly liberal test for demand futility but overall sends a message that demand is to be excused only sparingly, at best.[126]

New York seems to have retained flexibility better than Delaware. In *Marx v. Akers*,[127] an IBM shareholder challenged the IBM board's action in raising the annual retainers of 15 of 18 outside directors from $20,000 to $55,000 plus 100 IBM shares, and for voting for unreasonably high compensation for IBM executives, including the 3 executives who sat on the board. The board had acted at a time when IBM was in great financial difficulty. As to the first allegation, demand was excused because a majority of the directors were interested in the decision. New York case law leaves it open for a trial court to find that demand is excused because "(1) a majority of the directors are interested in the transaction, or (2) the directors failed to inform themselves to a degree reasonably necessary about the transaction, or (3) the directors failed to exercise their business judgment in approving the transaction."[128]

The victory for plaintiff was short-lived. The court went on to find that the underlying factual claim, that the increase from $20,000 to $55,000 amounted to wrongdoing, failed to state a cause of action. The plaintiff would have to allege

---

[125] The court's subsequent opinions in *Grobow v. Perot*, 539 A.2d 180 (Del. 1988), and in *Levine v. Smith*, 591 A.2d 194 (Del. 1991), made clear that the test is disjunctive.

[126] Judge Frank Easterbrook was critical of the *Aronson* formulation in *Starrels v. First Nat'l Bank of Chicago*, 870 F.2d 1168, 1175 (7th Cir. 1989):

> If "reasonable doubt" in the *Aronson* formula means the same thing as "reasonable doubt" in criminal law, then demand is excused whenever there is a 10% chance that the original transaction is not protected by the business judgment rule. Why should demand be excused on such a slight showing? Surely not because courts want shareholders to file suit whenever there is an 11% likelihood that the business judgment rule will not protect a transaction.

Marx v. Akers, 666 N.E.2d 1034, 1938 (N.Y. 1996) notes the *Starrels* criticism of the reasonable doubt test and also notes that the test may be "overly subjective, thereby permitting a wide variance in the application of Delaware law to similar facts."

[127] 666 N.E.2d 1034 (N.Y. 1996). For a discussion of *Marx* and compensation, see § 9.04[A], note 79, *supra*.

[128] 666 N.E.2d at 1039, 1041. Elaborating on the need of the board to be diligent, the court stated:

> Demand is excused because of futility when a complaint alleges with particularity that the board of directors did not fully inform themselves about the challenged transaction to the extent reasonably appropriate under the circumstances . . . . The "long standing rule" is that a director "does not exempt himself from liability by failing to do more than passively rubber-stamp the decisions of the active managers."

waste of corporate assets, which he could not do on the facts of the case. As to the allegation regarding increased compensation for the full time executives, demand was required and the allegation properly dismissed. A majority of directors which approved that compensation were not interested in that transaction: "[a] board is not interested 'in voting compensation for one of its members as an executive or in some other nondirectorial capacity, such as a consultant to the corporation.' "

[c]   Disabling Conflicts of Interest

Material interests that disable include financial or pecuniary interests or familial associations. For example, assume a 5 person partnership sold real estate to the corporation which was later found to be seismically unstable and unsuited for the corporation's purposes. A shareholder brings a derivative action alleging duty of loyalty violations, challenging the directors' failure to rescind the transaction, and claiming damages from those directors who were on both sides of the transaction. The shareholder alleges that three of nine directors benefitted as partners in the selling partnership. The shareholder might also allege that two other partners were family members of two other directors, lacking independence. The shareholder would allege that demand is excused as futile because not only a critical mass, but a majority of the directors (five of the nine) have either conflicts of interest that disable them, or lack independence, and as a group are likely to prevent the board from giving any demand fair treatment.[129]

Vexed questions include what types of interests might disable. Merely being named as defendants in the lawsuit does not disable directors so named. Receipt of directors' fees or long board service do not automatically disable. In the above illustration, plaintiffs' attorneys may name all nine directors, alleging that in originally approving the transaction, and later by failing to cause the corporation to bring suit once the facts had become known, the remaining four directors are not disinterested.[130] Thus, the plaintiff actually alleges that the remaining four directors violated their fiduciary duty of loyalty by serving the best interests of fellow directors rather than those of the corporation. This type of make weight allegation never suffices.[131]

---

[129] A few jurisdictions hold that if a majority of the directors are interested, and/or lack independence, the board is disabled and unable to deal with the demand. *Miller v. Register & Tribune Syndicate, Inc.*, 336 N.W.2d 709 (Iowa 1983), is the leading case. Under Delaware law, seemingly there is an issue of fact as to whether such a board would be altogether disabled but, in *In re Limited, Inc., Shareholders Litigation*, 2002 Del. Ch. LEXIS 28 (2002), the court held demand excused after finding that, on the surface, 6 of 12 directors lacked independence from the Chairman and CEO Wexner.

[130] *But see Marx v. Akers*, 666 N.E.2d 1034 (N.Y. 1996) (similar to Delaware, demand could be excused in a case in which a majority of directors has "self interest in the transaction at issue" or "a loss of independence because a director with no direct interest is 'controlled' by a self-interested director"). Alternatively, "[d]emand is excused because of futility when a complaint alleges that the board of directors did not fully inform themselves about the challenged transaction to the extent reasonably appropriate under the circumstances."

[131] *See, e.g.*, A.L.I. Corp. Gov. Proj. § 1.23(c)(2) ("the fact a director is named as a defendant does not make the director interested . . . if the complaint against the director is based only on the fact

[d] Lack of Independence

Even though directors may have had no pecuniary interest in the transaction under attack, plaintiffs may allege that directors are beholden to a controlling shareholder, a family member, the CEO, or some other person who does have an interest in approval of the transaction or refusal of a demand. These directors are sometimes said to have been dominated. In more polite terms, the allegation and finding will be that they lack independence.

A question is whether significant social or professional relationships, such as many years' membership in the same exclusive golf club as a fellow director who is a party to the challenged transaction, may disqualify a director. Delaware[132] and the Model Business Corporation Act[133] arguably say "no" to that question, emphasizing direct pecuniary interests and rejecting purely social ties. Through its general definition of "interested," the ALI Project disables only those who are parties to the transaction itself, or have a "material pecuniary interest," either directly or through "an associate of the director or officer, or a person with whom the director . . . has a business, financial or familial relationship . . . ."[134]

A recent spate of cases has dealt with cases on the spectrum between financial contacts, on the one hand, and purely social contacts, on the other, between the challenged director and the person plaintiffs claim dominate or controls her. In *In re Walt Disney Company Derivative Litigation*,[135] shareholders challenged the $140 million severance payment, under a "no fault termination," to Michael Ovitz after Ovitz had seriously underperformed in one year as President of Disney. Ovitz was a long time friend and associate of Disney CEO Michael Eisner. Plaintiffs filed suit without making demand, alleging that a majority of Disney directors were beholden to Eisner and thus lacked independence. Demand, they alleged, was excused.

---

that the director approved of or acquiesced in the transaction or conduct that is the subject of the action"); *Lewis v. Graves*, 702 F.2d 245 (2d Cir. 1983) ("that a corporation's directors have previously approved transactions subsequently challenged in a derivative suit does not inevitably lead to the conclusion that those directors . . . will refuse to take up the suit"); *Aronson v. Lewis*, 473 A.2d 805 (Del. 1984) ("the mere threat of personal liability for approving a questioned transaction, standing alone, is insufficient to challenge either the independence or disinterestedness of directors").

[132] *See, e.g., Pogostin v. Rice*, 480 A.2d 619, 624 (Del. 1984) ("Directorial interest exists whenever divided loyalties are present, or a director either has received, or is entitled to receive, a personal financial benefit from the challenged transaction which is not shared by the other shareholders").

[133] The Model Business Corporation Act "conflicting interest" provisions limit such an interest to an "interest a director of the corporation has respecting the transaction . . . if the director knows that he or a related party [(*e.g.*, brother-in-law, son, daughter)] is a party to the transaction or has *a beneficial financial interest* . . . ." MBCA § 8.60(1)(I).

[134] A.L.I. Corp. Gov. Proj. § 1.23(a)(3). Another question is whether a corporation may nonetheless respond to a demand by scripting around a critical mass or majority of directors who are interested in the underlying transaction. One court has said unequivocally that the board of directors is disabled if a majority of directors is colorably implicated in the challenged conduct or transaction. The court held that, in those circumstances, the board simply has no power to respond in any way to a demand as by appointing a litigation committee. *Miller v. Register & Tribune Syndicate, Inc.*, 336 N.W.2d 709 (Iowa 1983).

[135] 731 A.2d 342 (Del. Ch. 1998).

The court found that, indeed, certain directors did seem to lack independence: Eisner's personal attorney and his personal architect, both board members, constituted that group. Yet three directors who were Disney executives reporting to Eisner were not by that alone "disqualified." Nor was the principal of the elementary school Eisner's children had attended disqualified. Last of, the President of Georgetown University, which Eisner's son had attended and to which he had given a $1 million gift, was not disqualified.

The Supreme Court of Delaware reversed, finding that under certain circumstances the plaintiffs might be able to plead a case that would withstand a motion to dismiss.[136]

On remand, the plaintiffs shifted gears.[137] Rather than alleging that they had raised a "reasonable doubt" that a majority of directors who would pass on the demand lacked independence, plaintiffs switched to the other prong of *Aronson v. Lewis, infra*, alleging that the directors who passed on the original contract and no fault termination had not been entitled to protection of the business judgment rule because they had not made "*any* business judgment." The board had permitted, and then rubber stamped, Eisner's negotiation of the employment contract with his friend Ovitz. Similarly, the board had conducted the no fault termination "with a similar Ostrich like approach."

Post-Enron Delaware decisions seem to find lack of independence with greater ease. In *In re Limited, Inc., Shareholder Litigation*,[138] the Chancellor found that executives who reported to the CEO whose family benefitted by the transaction and who both received $1.8 million in annual compensation, lacked independence. The court emphasized that the test of independence is a subjective one: "whether that particular director [and not a mythical reasonable one] is either beholden to the controlling shareholder or so under his influence that their discretion is sterilized" but found independence lacking nonetheless. So, too, was a Brown University administrator found to lack independence because he received a $150,000 annual consulting fee from The Limited. On a subjective basis, the court seemed to assume that such an amount of money would loom large for a university staff person.

Most interesting was the court's treatment of Limited director G. Gordon Gee, former president of Ohio State University (subsequently, president of Brown University and then Chancellor of Vanderbilt University). At Ohio State, Gee had successfully raised $25 million from CEO Wexner for a performing arts center. Citing the precedent of Georgetown's president in the Disney case, defendants pressed the court for a finding that Gee should be treated as independent as well. Without much explanation, the court found the other way, holding demand excused in the plaintiffs' duty of loyalty case because half (6 of 12) Limited's directors lacked independence.

---

[136] *Sub nom., Brehm v. Eisner*, 746 A.2d 244, 258 (Del. 1999).

[137] 825 A.2d 275 (Del. Ch. 2003).

[138] 2002 Del. Ch. LEXIS 28 (2002).

Similarly, in a recent case, a Delaware court found that director members of a special litigation committee (SLC) lacked independence sufficient for them to review allegations against Oracle Inc.'s CEO Larry Ellison and other executives for insider trading and breach of fiduciary duty. The challenged directors both taught at Stanford University (one is an esteemed law professor). Ellison and Oracle had many ties to Stanford, including sizeable monetary contributions to the university. The court found that the SLC had failed to carry its burden to establish its independence, albeit in the SLC rather than the demand excused context (the test of independence would be the same in both contexts).[139]

[3] Threat of Irreparable Harm

Both the ALI Project[140] and the Model Business Corporation Act[141] excuse demand in cases in which the corporation is threatened with irreparable harm. Little case law exists but the proposition is not controversial.[142]

[4] Closely Held Corporations

As has been seen,[143] a trend has developed for courts to dispense with the requirement that corporate claims be raised derivatively in the case of closely held corporations. Subsumed in such holdings is the excuse of any requirement that the complaining shareholder first make a demand on the board of directors.

[5] Delay

"Courts require a plaintiff to exhibit some patience. However, plaintiff's patience need not be infinite."[144] Courts' decisions vary widely on the issue of reasonableness of delay. One court refused to excuse demand after even an eight month delay in responding in a "complex case."[145] Another court excused demand when twenty seven days had passed, and the issues raised by the demand were straightforward.[146] A few decisions held that two months is insufficient delay to excuse demand while other decisions have held that a three month delay did free plaintiff to proceed to the courthouse.[147] The Model Business Corporation Act permits a plaintiff to file if 90 days have passed since

---

[139] *In re Oracle Corp. Derivative Litigation*, 824 A.2d 917 (Del. Ch. 2003).

[140] A.L.I. Corp. Gov. Proj. § 7.03(b) ("only if the plaintiff makes a specific showing that irreparable injury to the corporation would otherwise result, and in such instances demand should be made promptly after commencement of the action").

[141] MBCA § 7.42.

[142] *See, e.g.*, A.L.I. Corp. Gov. Proj. § 7.03, Reporter's Note 4 at 66 ("No cases were found that explicitly posed [the irreparable injury] issue").

[143] See the discussion in § 14.02[D], *supra.*

[144] Branson, CORPORATE GOVERNANCE § 11.28 at 678 (surveying cases).

[145] *Mozes v. Welch*, 638 F. Supp. 215 (D. Conn. 1986).

[146] *Rubin v. Posner*, 701 F. Supp. 1041 (D. Del. 1988).

[147] *Compare Recchion v. Kirby*, 637 F. Supp. 1309 (W.D. Pa. 1986) (two months' delay did not justify filing by plaintiff) and *Allison v. General Motors Corp.*, 604 F. Supp. 1106 (D. Del. 1985) (same), *with Lewis v. Sporck*, 646 F. Supp. 574 (N.D. Cal. 1986) (three months held ample time for a board to respond).

demand was made and no response has been forthcoming.[148]

[6]   Neutrality

The Supreme Court of Delaware has held that a corporation may not remain neutral and has held that a corporation's "position of neutrality must be viewed as tacit approval" of the shareholder going forward with her suit.[149] If the corporation does not speak to the demand, and pointedly refuses to do so, or does so noncommittally, the shareholder's suit may go forward.

[E]   Demand On Shareholders

The theory is that a complaining shareholder should also make a demand on the shareholders if the acts of which she complains could be ratified by a majority of the shares.[150] Conceivably, a shareholders group or the directors could convene a shareholders' meeting to do precisely that. However, if a shareholder alleges ultra vires or illegal acts by directors, or a gift or waste of corporate assets, demand on the shareholders would be excused. Shareholders are not able to ratify those acts unless they do so unanimously. Demand on shareholders would also be excused when the alleged wrongdoers hold a majority of the shares.[151]

The leading case is *Mayer v. Adams*,[152] in which the Supreme Court of Delaware agreed with the principles that it is not necessary to make a demand on shareholders if the suit is based upon a wrong which is not capable of being ratified. The minority view, exemplified by the Massachusetts case of *Alberti v. Green*,[153] holds that demand must be made on the shareholders in every case and that if shareholders in good faith vote to dismiss the action, the vote is binding on the corporation and the courts.[154] Other courts have rejected the distinction between ratifiable and non-ratifiable acts.[155]

---

[148] MBCA § 7.42(2).

[149] *Kaplan v. Peat, Marwick, Mitchell & Co.*, 540 A.2d 726 (Del. 1988).

[150] *Wolgin v. Simon*, 722 F.2d 389 (8th Cir. 1984) (allegations that directors were self-dealing in fending off hostile takeover did not excuse demand under Missouri law); *Zimmerman v. Bell*, 585 F. Supp. 512 (D. Md. 1984) (same — Maryland law).

[151] *Heilbrunn v. Hanover Equities Corp.*, 259 F. Supp. 936 (S.D.N.Y.). The same result may be obtained when the alleged wrongdoers hold a controlling, but less than majority, interest. *Gotesman v. General Motors Corp.*, 268 F.2d 194 (2d Cir. 1959). For a discussion of shareholder ratification, see Chapter 9, *supra*.

[152] 141 A.2d 458 (Del. 1958). Since fiduciary duty claims can be viewed as constructive fraud and fraud cannot be ratified, shareholder demand is excused.

[153] 372 N.E.2d 534 (Mass. App. Ct. 1978).

[154] *See also S. Solomont & Sons Trust, Inc. v. New England Theatres Operating Co.*, 93 N.E. 2d 241 (Mass. 1950).

[155] See *Bell v. Arnold*, 487 P.2d 545 (Col. 1971), where demand on 26,000 shareholders was not excused:

> [The non-ratifiable nature of the wrongs] is not an acceptable reason or a valid excuse for not making a demand on shareholders here. The purpose of making a demand on the shareholders is to inform them of the alleged nonratifiable wrongs; to seek their participation in available courses of action, such as, the removal of the involved directors

Statutes in New York and California deliberately omit any reference to demand on shareholders.[156] The Model Act is rather coy about the question. It requires "demand . . . upon the corporation."[157] Its predecessor referred to "demand upon the board of directors."[158] The commentary states that the change was made because some corporate decisions to sue or not to sue "would fall within the authority of an officer of the corporation."[159] An argument may be made that the MBCA intends to eliminate a requirement that demand be made upon shareholders. The ALI Project contains a straightforward statement that "[d]emand on shareholders should not be required."[160] The latter is undoubtedly the correct modern view. In corporations of any size, the focus of demand and other matters relating to derivative litigation should be on the board of directors and not on the shareholders.

§ 14.06 TERMINATION OF LITIGATION: THE ADVENT OF THE SPECIAL LITIGATION COMMITTEE DEVICE

[A] Background

The mechanism by which corporations have come to find their voice for speaking out about whether or not a derivative action should continue is the Special Litigation Committee (SLC). To form an SLC, the board of directors delegates to a committee of two or three directors all the board's power with respect to the litigation. Often, the board amends the bylaw dealing with board size, adds two or three new director positions, and appoints to those positions persons who had no conceivable connection with the alleged wrongdoing. These "expansion" directors then staff the SLC. In a case in which a demand has been made, the board creates the SLC after an initial determination that the plaintiff's claims are colorable. In a case in which demand is alleged to be excused on futility grounds, the board creates the SLC soon after the plaintiff files suit to try to have the SLC deal with the merits of the litigation.

In the 1960s and 1970s, United States corporations and their representatives made a number of illegal foreign payments (bribes and kickbacks) in order to procure business abroad. In the 1970s, the Committee to Reelect the President (CREP) solicited a number of illegal corporate campaign contributions for Richard M. Nixon's 1972 campaign. United States law criminalizes corporate contributions to partisan political efforts.

---

and the election of new directors who will seek the redress required in the circumstances . . . .

[156] Cal. Corp. Code § 800(b); N.Y.B.C.L. § 626. *See also Syracuse Television, Inc. v. Channel 9 Syracuse, Inc.*, 273 N.Y.S.2d 16 (App. Div. 1966) (requirement was eliminated in 1963 because "it was considered too onerous").

[157] MBCA § 7.42(1).

[158] MBCA § 7.40(b) (withdrawn).

[159] MBCA § 7.42, Official Comment 2; 2 MBCA Annotated 7-336 (3rd ed. 1985 & Supp. 2003).

[160] A.L.I. Corp. Gov. Proj. § 7.03(c).

In the 1970s, the Securities and Exchange Commission had on its hands several hundred such cases in which the aforesaid practices had occurred, but had not been disclosed by the corporations involved. To deal with its crowded docket, the SEC instituted a voluntary compliance program. Those corporations which thoroughly investigated their own affairs, developed procedures for dealing with possible illegal payments, and then voluntarily disclosed the payments received only a slap on the wrist from the SEC. That being so, quite rapidly, corporations developed the use of committees of outside directors, assisted by independent legal counsel, to investigate and then deal with illegal payment problems.[161]

It was only a matter of time before the same techniques came to be used by corporations faced with derivative litigation. An early case is *Gall v. Exxon Corp.*,[162] in which officials of Exxon's Italian subsidiary had made $59 million in contributions to political interests in Italy. After shareholder Gall filed suit alleging demand futility, Exxon amended its bylaws to provide for a "Special Committee on Litigation," staffed with three newly or recently appointed directors. In turn, the retired Chief Justice of the New Jersey Supreme Court served the committee as counsel. After four months and over 100 interviews with witnesses, the committee issued an 82 page report, which concluded that "it would be contrary to the best interests of Exxon and its shareholders for Exxon, or anyone on its behalf, to institute or maintain a legal action against any present or former Exxon director or officer."[163] Citing a number of older precedents, the court found that:

> Since it is the interests of the corporation which are at stake, it is the responsibility of the directors of the corporation to determine, in the first instance, whether an action should be brought on the corporation's behalf. It follows that the decision of corporate directors whether or not to assert a cause of action rests within the sound business judgment of the management.[164]

Neither would the court look into the merits of the litigation committee's recommendation that the litigation not go forward:

> It is clear that absent allegations of fraud, collusion, self-interest, dishonesty or other misconduct of a breach of trust nature, and absent allegations that the business judgment exercised was grossly unsound, the court should not at the instigation of a single shareholder interfere with the judgment of the corporate officers.[165]

The court dismissed Ms. Gall's action.

---

[161] The development is described in Arthur Matthews, *Internal Corporate Investigations*, 45 OHIO ST. L. J. 655 (1984). An internal corporate investigation of illegal payments is described in *Upjohn Co. v. United States*, 449 U.S. 383 (1981) (parameters of attorney-client privilege when corporate employees communicate with corporate counsel).

[162] 418 F. Supp. 508 (S.D.N.Y. 1976).

[163] *Id.* at 514 (footnote omitted).

[164] *Id.* at 515.

[165] *Id.* at 516.

[B]   Application of the Business Judgment Rule

Higher profile cases followed in 1979. Within weeks, the United States Supreme Court and the New York Court of Appeals gave imprimaturs to use of the special litigation committee device and the modern history of derivative litigation truly began.

In *Burks v. Lasker*,[166] a case involving an investment company,[167] the United States Supreme Court drew attention to directors' possible state law powers to dismiss derivative litigation. Relying on a handful of older state law decisions,[168] the Court found that the Investment Company Act of 1940 imposed no federal law obstacle to dismissal if the investment company's state of incorporation facilitated it.

A few weeks later, in *Auerbach v. Bennett*,[169] the New York Court of Appeals held that "[t]he substantive aspects of a decision to terminate a shareholder's derivative suit . . . are beyond judicial inquiry," if the decision has been made by a committee of disinterested directors, based upon a reasonable investigation. In other words, the New York court bestowed a high degree of business judgment rule protection to shield the board recommendation to dismiss from judicial review as to the merits of the decision itself, if the board has satisfied its burden of proof that the process leading to the decision met business judgment rule standards.[170] The New York court did make clear that the directors on the SLC have the burden of proving their disinterestedness and the diligence of their investigation.

With the takeover boom in the 1980s, a flood of derivative litigation ensued. In those cases, if the plaintiff-shareholder proceeded directly to court alleging a right to do so on grounds that demand was excused as futile, the corporate response became well scripted. Counsel would recommend that the directors amend the corporate bylaws to expand the number of directors. The board would then appoint to those two or three[171] newly created positions, persons

---

[166] 441 U.S. 471 (1979).

[167] The popular name for an open-end investment company of the type involved in *Burks* is a mutual fund. The Investment Company Act of 1940 regulates investment company affairs on an extensive basis. 15 U.S.C. §§ 80a-1B80a-64. In the first instance, however, investment companies are corporations chartered under and governed by the laws of a particular state, namely, the state in which the fund promoters chose to incorporate.

[168] *MeKee v. Rogers*, 156 A. 191 (Del. Ch. 1931); *Rice v. Wheeling Dollar Savings & Trust Co.*, 130 N.E.2d 442 (Ohio Common Pleas 1954); *Goodwin v. Castlton*, 144 P.2d 725 (Wash. 1944) (shareholder approval of a settlement rather than director recommendation of dismissal).

[169] 393 N.E.2d 994 (N.Y. 1979).

[170] Under the traditional business judgment rule, these matters (directors' disinterest, some diligence in informing themselves, and so on) are presumed with the burden of proof on lack of process usually on the plaintiff, although as a practical matter, a trial lawyer defending directors would offer proof on such issues.

[171] Or perhaps one. In *Lewis v. Fuqua*, 502 A.2d 962, 967 (Del. Ch. 1985), however, the court did note that "[i]f a single member committee is to be used, the member should, like Caesar's wife, be above reproach." The court thus refused to follow the recommendation of a one person SLC that litigation not be pursued against Fuqua Industries' senior management because the one person, Terry Sanford, former governor of North Carolina and former North Carolina senator, had been

who have no possible connection to the alleged wrongdoing and whose integrity and independence were unquestioned (local Episcopal bishop, and the like). The board would then constitute the two or three new directors as the SLC. The SLC would hire special counsel, usually a law firm that had not for some time represented, or never represented, the corporation in any matter. Special counsel would then appear in court asking the court for a lengthy continuance while the SLC investigated the wrongdoing alleged.[172]

Thereafter, the committee, assisted by counsel,[173] undertakes a lengthy and voluminous investigation. Counsel thoroughly researches the law governing the conduct alleged to be wrongful. After due investigation and deliberation, the SLC compiles a final report in which it generally recommends that the court dismiss the action as "not in the best interests of the corporation." That report is then appended to a motion, generally for summary judgment, and filed with the court.

Under the *Auerbach* approach, the court then examines the SLC's proof as to the disinterestedness of the participating directors and the diligence they have exercised. Finding a decision, a degree of diligence in making it, disinterestedness on the committee members' parts, and a rational basis for the decision made, the court must then dismiss the action. The court may not linger, delving into the pluses and minuses of the decision itself.

[C] Delaware and the *Zapata* Second Step

In the late 1970s and early 1980s, a number of decisions upheld *Auerbach* procedures, dismissing derivative suits without any review of the SLC decision itself. Many of those decisions involved Delaware corporations but were educated *Erie* guesses made by federal courts as to what Delaware would do, that is, follow an *Auerbach*-like approach.

To the surprise of many onlookers, when a case finally reached the Supreme Court of Delaware, that court did not follow the *Auerbach* business judgment rule approach. In *Zapata Corp. v. Maldonado*,[174] Zapata's 10 directors had caused the re-issue of stock options to themselves at a new, lower exercise price following a decrease in the market price to a point below the old exercise price. In reviewing the corporation's response to Maldonado's shareholder suit, the Delaware court left room for what has become known as the "*Zapata* second step." Despite a review of SLC compliance with the business judgment rule,

---

tainted by a $10 million dollar gift by Fuqua Industries to Duke's Business School when he was president of Duke University.

[172] *See, e.g.*, A.L.I. Corp. Gov. Proj. § 7.06 ("[T]he court should stay discovery and all further proceedings by the plaintiff in a derivative action and upon such conditions as the court deems appropriate pending the court's determination of any motion made by the corporation {to dismiss base upon action by the board of directors").

[173] If the investigation is found to have been by counsel with little or no meaningful participation by the directors, the court may reject the "committee" recommendations as not having been made by the SLC. *See, e.g., Peller v. Southern Co.*, 911 F.2d 1532 (11th Cir. 1990) (committee recommendation rejected despite retention of former Attorney General Griffin Bell and large Georgia law firm in part because of lack of directorial involvement).

[174] 430 A.2d 779 (Del. 1981).

based upon the SLC's proof on those issues, a Delaware court may, in its discretion, proceed to a review of the merits of the SLC's recommendation.

That outcome results from the observation that dismissal of a derivative suit against corporate officials is not merely another case of business judgment such as whether to market a new product or modernize a plant. "[I]t seems to us that there is sufficient risk in the realities of a situation like [this] one . . . to justify caution beyond adherence to the theory of business judgment." The court noted that "we must not be unmindful that directors are passing judgment on fellow directors in the same corporation and fellow directors, in this instance, who designated them to serve both as directors and committee members. The question naturally arises whether a 'there but for the grace of God go I' empathy might not play a role."[175]

Thus was born the *Zapata* second step. After a review of the SLC's good faith, independence, and diligence (adequacy of investigation), based upon the proof offered by the directors (step one):

> The Court should determine, applying its own independent business judgment, whether the [SLC] motion should be granted. (This step shares some of the same spirit and philosophy of the statement made by the Vice-Chancellor: 'Under our system of law, courts and not litigants should decide the merits of litigation') . . . . The second step is intended to thwart instances where corporate actions meet the criteria of step one, but the result does not appear to satisfy its spirit, or where corporate actions would simply prematurely terminate a stockholder grievance deserving of further consideration in the corporation's interest.

[D]   Structural Bias and Other Criticisms

No matter which of the early approaches (*Auerbach* or *Zapata*) is under consideration, shareholder activists and attorneys had a number of criticisms of the procedure. A pervasive criticism arises from the "there but for the grace of God go I" syndrome hypothesized by the *Zapata* court. By and large, directors tend to come from the same socio-economic group. They tend to have common backgrounds and interests. They have a natural, and somewhat strong, tendency to empathize with one another.[176] SLC members receive a subliminal message as to how, barring unforeseen circumstances, the matter is to be resolved. Once appointed, SLC members' board service does not terminate upon completion of the committee's work. In every instance or, arguably to some critics, every instance in which the "right outcome" has been reached, SLC members will continue as directors, receiving annual retainers and meeting fees,

---

[175] *Id.* at 787–89.

[176] A leading piece by a law professor and a psychologist is James Cox & Harry L. Munsinger, *Bias in the Boardroom: Psychological Foundations and Legal Implications of Corporate Cohesion*, 48 LAW & CONTEMP. PROB. 83 (Summer 1985).

and enjoying the prestige of a directorship, long after the SLC has concluded its work.[177]

" 'Structural bias' may be defined as inherent prejudice against any derivative action resulting from the composition and character of the board of directors" and of special litigation committees.[178] No court has accepted the structural bias argument directly, and two noted commentators have termed it "pop psychology" and a "silly but harmless academic argument."[179] By contrast, several courts have expressed their belief that structural bias does exist.[180] The Supreme Court of Iowa noted that much of the concern over use of SLCs "has been focused on the 'structural bias' approach, which suggests that it is unrealistic to assume that members of independent committees are free from personal, financial or moral influences which flow from the directors who appoint them."[181]

Courts have not relied directly on the concept because when their suspicions have been aroused, courts have been able to pinpoint a source of actual bias or conflict on the directors' part. Thus, what may have begun as a structural bias case is resolved in actual bias terms.[182]

The search for actual bias is be an extensive one. "[T]he Court of Chancery must exercise careful oversight of the bona fides and [the SLC's] process." "[T]he SLC has the burden of establishing its own independence by a yardstick that must be 'like Caesar's wife'-above reproach. Moreover, . . . the SLC analysis contemplates not only a shift in the burden of persuasion but also the availability of discovery into various issues, including independence."[183] In *Beam*, the Delaware Supreme Court noted that only through discovery had

---

[177] One partial answer to structural bias allegations is to staff an SLC with "disinterested persons," who will have no expectation of board service after their work is done. *See, e.g.,* Joel Seligman, *The Disinterested Person: An Alternative Approach to Shareholder Derivative Litigation,* 55 Law & Contemp. Prob. 357 (1992). The idea has not been widely adopted, although Michigan and North Carolina have statutes authorizing court appointment of disinterested persons. *See* Mich. Bus. Corp. Act § 450.1495(1); N.C. Bus. Corp. Act § 55-7-40(c).

[178] Marc Steinberg, *The Use of Special Litigation Committees to Terminate Shareholder Derivative Suits,* 35 U. Miami L. Rev. 1, 24 (1980).

[179] Michael P. Dooley & E. Norman Veasey, *The Role of the Board in Derivative Litigation: Delaware Law and the Current ALI Proposals Compared,* 44 Bus. L. 503, 534 (1990). An actual bias case with elements of structural bias is *In re Oracle Corp. Derivative Litigation,* 824 A.2d 917 (Del. Ch. 2003), discussed in § 14.05[D](2)(c), in which the court refused to afford business judgment rule protection to an SLC recommendation when the two committee members were Stanford University professors and both the corporation and the defendant CEO had made, or had promised to make, significant contributions to Stanford).

[180] *See, e.g., Hassan v. Clevetrust Realty Inv.,* 729 F.2d 372, 376–77 (6th Cir. 1982) ("The problems of peer pressure and group loyalty exist *a fortiori* where the members of a special litigation committee are . . . carefully selected by the majority of directors").

[181] *Miller v. Register and Tribune Syndicate, Inc.,* 336 N.W.2d 709, 716 (Iowa 1983).

[182] See the cases collected in Douglas M. Branson, Corporate Governance § 11.30, at 686–86 (1993).

[183] *Beam ex rel. Martha Stewart Living Omnimedia, Inc. v. Stewart,* 845 A.2d 1040, 1055 (Del. 2004).

plaintiffs found ties to Stanford University both by the director members of Oracle, Inc., SLC, and the corporation, which was a principal contributor to Stanford.[184]

The structural bias argument is nonetheless important, for two reasons. One is that, in the future, a court may well reject an SLC recommendation to dismiss based upon structural bias grounds. Two is that suspicion of widespread structural bias in SLC's operations may be an ingredient in a judicial choice of a *Zapata*-like intermediate approach over a strict *Auerbach* business judgment rule approach. Indeed, at least two courts already have so stated.[185]

Another criticism of the SLC device is that the committee's recommendation need only be that continuation of the litigation is not "in the best interests of the corporation," even though the wrongdoers have violated the law or run roughshod over their common law fiduciary duties. In most instances, SLC members and counsel will be able to script cases to come out on balance for discontinuation of litigation, based upon factors likely to be present in almost every case. Thus factors such as the drain on executive time, adverse impact on employee morale and customer relationships, increased stress levels, and adverse public relations generally can always be cited, and will tip the balance in all but the most egregious cases of wrongdoing.

The answer to the criticism is that, in an early and persuasive opinion, *Joy v. North*,[186] Judge Winter of the Second Circuit marked out a high road that leaves some room for use of makeweight factors. Judge Winter set out two makeweight factors a committee and a court could take into account if, but only if, the potential recovery for the corporation in the suit was small in relation to shareholders' equity. They are "the impact of distraction of key personnel by continued litigation" and "potential lost profits that may result from the publicity at trial." If recovery in the litigation is likely to be large, however, impact of distraction and potential lost profits from adverse publicity are irrelevant:

> Judicial scrutiny of special litigation committee recommendations should thus be limited to a comparison of the direct costs imposed upon the corporation by the litigation with the potential benefits. We are mindful that other less direct costs may be incurred, such as negative impact upon morale and upon the corporate image. Nevertheless-, . . . such factors, with the two exceptions noted, should [never] be taken into account. Quite apart from the elusiveness of attempting to predict such effects, they are quite likely to be related to the degree of corporate wrongdoing, a spectacular fraud being generally more news- worthy and damaging to morale than a mistake in judgment . . . .

---

[184] The *Oracle* case is discussed, *inter alia*, in § 14.05[C][2][d] Lack of Independence, *supra*.

[185] See the discussion of *Alford v. Shaw*, 358 S.E.2d 323 (N.C. 1987), and *Houle v. Low*, 556 N.E.2d 51 (Mass. 1990), *infra*.

[186] 692 F.2d 880 (2d Cir. 1982), *cert. denied*, 460 U.S. 1051 (1983). As a diversity case, the court was applying Delaware law.

The ALI Project is more cryptic. In dismissing an action, the court must find that "the board or committee was adequately informed under the circumstances and reasonably determined that dismissal was in the best interests of the corporation, *based upon grounds that the court deems to warrant reliance.*"[187]

A third criticism of the SLC approach, even under the *Joy v. North* limitation, is that not every determination should be a strict cost-benefit analysis. In certain cases, a corporate expenditure of $10 to recover $5 may be a worthwhile expenditure because other values are served. One value is deterrence of venal and opportunistic conduct by corporate officials. Another is elimination of the moral hazard problem created by a situation in which a director may be tempted to self-deal to the extent of $5 because he knows that the cost of detecting and prosecuting his defalcation exceeds that amount.

A fourth, and telling criticism, is that no SLC has ever recommended that derivative litigation continue against sitting directors, as opposed to former directors or senior executive officers.[188] As the North Carolina Court of Appeals observed after reviewing the nearly fifty early cases, "[n]ot one committee, in all these instances, has decided to proceed with the suit."[189]

As with a flesh and blood person, a fictional being such as a corporation should be able to choose not to enforce its legal rights. A neighbor may choose not to sue a neighbor who cuts across her backyard, even though all the elements of trespass are present. Corporations should be able to make such choices. The question arises, however, "How does the corporation find its voice in order to make that choice, especially when some element of the closest thing a corporation has to an alter ego, its board of directors, is implicated in the underlying allegation of wrongdoing?" The question then becomes not the legitimacy of the SLC device — which is so well-established in corporate jurisprudence as to be beyond challenge. The real question is how to allow the corporation to have its voice, but with fine tuning which offsets the likelihood or possibility of actual or structural bias with some additional procedural safeguards such as the possibility of a *Zapata* second step or that egregious cases at least will see the full light of day through means of trial or other hearing. Those "fine tuning questions," along with the choice among *Auerbach, Zapata,* or something in between, have been the issues that have confronted courts in subsequent cases.

---

[187] A.L.I. Corp. Gov. Proj. § 7.10(a)(2).

[188] *Cf. In re Continental Illinois Sec. Litigation,* 732 F.2d 1302, 1314 (7th Cir. 1984) (SLC recommendation that suits over wrongdoing in energy loan loss cases continue against *former* bank officers). A study of more recent SLC cases finds that committees decide to settle cases or pursue them again one or more of the defendants 40% of the time. *See* Minor Myers, *The Decisions of Corporate Special Litigation Committees: An Empirical Investigation,* 84 IND. L.J. ___ (forthcoming 2009).

[189] *Alford v. Shaw,* 324 S.E.2d 878 (N.C. Ct. App. 1985), *rev'd,* 349 S.E.2d 41 (N.C. 1986), *earlier opinion withdrawn,* 358 S.E.2d 323 (N.C. 1987).

[E]   Recent Cases

Generally speaking, courts that have rendered authoritative opinions in the matter, that is, state supreme and appellate courts construing state corporation law (rather than federal courts making educated *Erie* guesses) have utilized *Zapata* as a starting point. By contrast, approximately a dozen legislatures have enacted statutory pathways that enact a version of the near strict business judgment rule approach authoritatively adopted in *Auerbach v. Bennett.* Most have done so by adoption of the Model Business Corporation Act's derivative action proposals promulgated in 1990 by the American Bar Association's Committee on Corporate Laws.[190] Meanwhile, Delaware has retreated from the bold overture first made in *Zapata v. Maldonado.* Delaware has done so by sharpening the distinction between "demand refused" and "demand excused" cases, judicially providing that a Delaware court may not review on the merits an SLC recommendation in a demand refused case. The basis for the distinction, other than to cut back *Zapata's* reach, is difficult to understand.[191]

Assume for example, a ten person board, with four directors interested in the transaction challenged in the derivative suit, and six directors who are disinterested and independent. Since a majority is disinterested, if the shareholder makes demand, he tacitly concedes the independence of the board to respond to that demand. If the disinterested directors vote 4-2 to reject the demand, any judicial review is limited to good faith and the reasonableness of the investigation.

By contrast, if the board has six interested directors and four disinterested, demand is excused and a *Zapata* second step review may be made. If the board responds by appointment of a three director SLC, which votes 3-0 that the litigation is not in the corporation's best interests, the Delaware court may, in its discretion, review that decision. The Delaware court may also examine how disinterested and independent the SLC members are. It seems as though more of a need for judicial review may exist in the first case rather than in the second. Yet Delaware law provides the opposite.

---

[190] *See* Committee on Corporate Laws, *Changes in the Model Business Corporation Act — Amendments Pertaining to Derivative Actions*, 45 BUS. LAW. 1241 (1990) (proposing Subchapter D to Chapter 7, Shareholders).

[191] The latter development is an outgrowth of *Levine v. Smith*, 591 A.2d 194 (Del. 1991). Levine was another General Motors shareholder who sued over the $900 million hushmail payment to GM director H. Ross Perot. Roger Smith was the CEO and Chairman of GM during the period when its fortunes were lagging. Unlike another group of suits in which shareholders alleged that demand was excused as futile, plaintiff Morton Levine made demand, which was promptly refused. Levine then filed suit. GM moved for a protective order against the interrogatories and requests for production which sought to examine the merits of the Perot share repurchase. The Chancery Court granted the order; the Supreme Court affirmed, stating that in a demand "excused" case:

> [T]he act of establishing a special litigation committee constitutes an implicit conces-
> sion by a board that its members are interested in the transaction and that its decisions are
> not entitled to the protection of the business judgment rule . . . . [A] board of directors
> concedes demand futility when it is both interested and establishes a special litigation
> committee to resolve the derivative plaintiff's suit. Therefore, demand is excused and
> discovery is allowed. There is not a basis for such presumption to be extended to a demand
> refused case.

Id. (citations omitted).

At any rate, all of this is very confusing.[192] The only safe thing that can be stated is that in, a demand refused case in a Delaware court, the only issues for the court to consider are lack of diligence in investigation and lack of good faith (base motive dominates). By contrast, in a demand excused case, the issues also include the board's disinterestedness, or lack thereof, and the merits of the board's decision itself (*Zapata* second step).

The North Carolina Supreme Court refused to follow the Delaware distinction, adopting a "broadened" *Zapata* approach in *Alford v. Shaw.*[193] The court found "no justification for [a] limitation" of the "two step judicial inquiry to cases in which demand upon the corporation was futile and therefore excused." Thus, in "*all* derivative suits," including demand refused cases, and "even where the directors are not charged with fraud or self-dealing:"

> [T]hat a special litigation committee . . . recommends that the action should not proceed, while carrying weight, is not binding upon the trial court; rather, the court must make a fair assessment of the report of the special committee, along with all the other facts and circumstances in the case, in order to determine whether the defendants will be able to show that the transaction complained of was just and reasonable to the corporation.

In *Alford v. Shaw,* the court withdrew an earlier opinion that had endorsed the use of *Auerbach v. Bennett* in North Carolina.[194]

In its later decision, the Supreme Court of North Carolina surveyed:

> [T]he recent trend among courts which have been faced with the choice of applying an *Auerbach*-type rule of judicial deference or a *Zapata*-type rule of judicial scrutiny has been to require judicial scrutiny on the merits of the special litigation committee's report . . . . We interpret the trend away from *Auerbach* among other jurisdictions as an indication of growing concern about the deficiencies inherent in a rule giving great deference to the decisions of a corporate committee whose institutional symbiosis with the corporation necessarily affects its ability to render a decision that fairly considers the interest of plaintiffs . . . . Such concerns are legitimate and, upon further reflection, we find that they must be resolved not by slavish adherence to the business

---

[192] The *Levine* court returned to the issue again at a later point:

> The focus of a complaint alleging wrongful refusal of demand is different from the focus of a complaint alleging demand futility. The legal issues are different; therefore, the legal standards applied to the complaints are necessarily different. A shareholder, by making a demand upon a board before filing suit "tacitly concedes the independence of a majority of the board to respond. Therefore, when a board refuses a demand, the only issues to be examined are the good faith and reasonableness of the investigation." When a shareholder files a derivative suit asserting a claim of demand futility . . . the basis for such a claim is that the board is (1) interested and not independent; and (2) that the transaction attacked is not protected by the business judgment rule.

Id. at 209 (citations omitted).

[193] 358 S.E.2d 323 (N.C. 1987), *withdrawing the court's earlier opinion,* 349 S.E.2d 41 (1986).

[194] *See* 349 S.E.2d 41 (N.C. 1986).

judgment rule . . . .[195]

In Massachusetts, the Supreme Judicial Court reached a similar result but seemingly makes the *Zapata* second step mandatory, in part because of "the danger of 'structural bias' recognized by so many courts and commentators."[196]

In *Houle v. Low*, the court held that:

> The balancing of . . . various concerns *requires* reviewing judges to go beyond establishing the committee's independence, good faith and the adequacy of its investigation.

> The judge *must determine*, on the basis of the evidence presented, whether the committee reached a reasonable and principled decision . . . . In conducting its review, the court should look to factors such as those identified by the ALI, which include the likelihood of a judgment in the plaintiff's favor, the expected recovery as compared to the out-of-pocket costs, whether the corporation itself took corrective action, whether the balance of corporate interests warrants dismissal, and whether dismissal would allow any defendant who has control of the corporation to retain any significant improper benefit. See ALI Principles of Corporate Governance § 7.08.[197]

The permutations multiply. In *PSE & G Shareholder Litigation*,[198] the New Jersey Supreme Court declined to follow either the MBCA, Delaware or New York (*Auerbach*) approaches. The court faced actions alleging that directors of an electric utility with nuclear power plants had recklessly overseen the plants' operation. The Nuclear Regulatory Commission had assessed over $2 million in fines against the company. The court did follow *Alford v. Shaw* in holding that the same standard of review would govern both "demand excused" and "demand refused" cases. That standard of review would be a "modified business judgment rule," the elements of which are that (1) the directors acting were independent and disinterested; (2) acted in good faith and with due care in their investigation; and (3) the board's decision was reasonable." The latter finding ("was the decision to terminate reasonable?") would necessitate some inquiry into the merits and seems *Zapata*-like. The New Jersey rule would also permit plaintiff shareholders to undertake limited discovery.

Lastly, intermediate appellate courts in several states have confronted the issue: some have not followed *Auerbach*,[199] while others have.[200] In *In re UnitedHealth Group Incorporated Shareholders Derivative Litigation*,[201] a

---

[195] 358 S.E.2d at 325–26 (citations omitted).

[196] *Houle v. Low*, 556 N.E.2d 51 (Mass. 1990).

[197] *Id.* at 59 (emphasis added).

[198] 801 A.2d 295 (N.J. 2002).

[199] *See, e.g., Millsap v. American Family Corp.*, 430 S.E.2d 385 (Ga. Ct. App. 1993); *Lewis v. Boyd*, 838 S.W.2d 215 (Tenn. Ct. App. 1992). *Cf. Atkins v. Hibernia Corp.*, 182 F.3d 320 (5th Cir. 1999) (*Erie* guess that Louisiana courts would follow *Auerbach*).

[200] *See, e.g., Desigoudar v. Meyercord*, 108 Cal. App. 4th 173, 133 Cal. Rptr. 2d 408 (2003).

[201] 754 N.W.2d 544 (Minn. 2008) (on certified question from federal district court).

stock options backdating case, the Supreme Court of Minnesota adopted the *Auerbach* approach in its entirety.

To complete discussion of the topic, it is necessary to consider the current proposals for legislative reform, namely the ALI Project and Model Business Corporation Act proposals. The judicial decisions draw heavily upon these proposals. Indeed, a Pennsylvania Supreme Court decision adopts the ALI proposals in their entirety, going so far as to attach the text of the ALI black letter as an appendix to its opinion.[202] The ALI schematic, which is intended to be different, and hopefully better than, the Delaware approach, makes demand universal (never excused on futility grounds) but does not provide for any stated consequence should demand not be made or refused, as in Delaware. Instead, under ALI Corporate Gov. Proj. § 7.10, the court's power to review the merits of an SLC recommendation hinges upon whether the complaint colorably alleges duty of loyalty rather than duty of care claims. In the latter case, the court should end its inquiry after an examination of business judgment rule factors. In the former case, the court may inquire into the merits of the SLC's recommendations.

§ 14.07   PROPOSED REFORMS OF THE MODERN STRIKE SUIT ERA

[A]   The ALI Proposals Briefly Considered

The ALI Project reporters came up with the idea that has become the centerpiece of modern reforms: universal demand. To implement universal demand, the legislature enacts a statute that eliminates the demand "excused" branch, or the futility sub-branch thereof.[203] Every shareholder-plaintiff must make a pre-suit demand which then must be accepted or refused on the corporation's part.

In controversial eleventh hour deliberations, the ALI reporters compromised their position.[204] The compromise calibrates the standard of judicial review, and hence, judicial deference to a board or board committee (SLC) decision, based upon the claim raised by the plaintiff's allegations. Thus, if the underlying claim raises the issue of duty of care; compensation approved by disinterested directors (ALI § 5.02); certain approved uses of corporate property or

---

[202] *See Cuker v. Mikalauskas*, 692 A.2d 1042, 1049 (Pa. 1997) ("We specifically adopt §§ 7.02–7.10 and 7.13 of the *ALI Principles*.").

[203] *Kamen v. Kemper Fin. Serv., Inc.*, 500 U.S. 90 (1991), discussed *supra*, would seem to cut against a court doing so on its own motion; even a state court might be reluctant as the demand doctrine is well-established "embedded" common law.

[204] The original ALI proposals adopted a universal demand requirement, but to some extent trivialized it. Those proposals allowed the equivalent of a *Zapata* second step in demand refused cases. The judge could look into the merits of the board's or a committee's decision that demand be refused. House counsel of large corporations and groups such as the Business Roundtable reacted strongly to those proposals, predicting an era of "corporate governance by litigation." The result was the compromise provision between duty of care and duty of loyalty cases, as described in the described in the previous section text.

information (ALI § 5.04); diversion of a fully disclosed corporate opportunity; or competition with the corporation that has been approved by disinterested directors (ALI §§ 5.05, 5.06), the standard of judicial review follows the business judgment rule.[205] The court looks to the process leading to demand refusal: were the decision-makers disinterested, did they inform themselves adequately, and did they have some rational (not necessarily reasonable) basis for the decision made?[206]

In other cases, such as conflict of interest transactions other than those enumerated, or cases in which a director received a "significant improper benefit," the standard of judicial review ratchets upward. In addition to examining whether the board or committee refusing demand "was adequately informed under the circumstances," the court may inquire into whether the board "reasonably [not merely rationally] determined that dismissal was in the best interests of the corporation, based upon grounds that the court deems to warrant reliance." The latter is, of course, similar to the *Zapata* second step.

[B]   The American Bar Association (Model Business Corporation Act) Proposals

The ALI drafters may have opened a Pandora's box when they introduced the universal demand concept. That is because the American Bar Association Committee on Corporate Laws took universal demand and turned it around. Instead of trivializing demand somewhat, the ABA drafters made demand all important. Demand is required in all cases and, in all cases in which directors refuse demand, judicial review is limited to business judgment rule factors:

> A derivative proceeding shall be dismissed by the court on motion by the corporation if one of the groups specified in subsections (b) [disinterested directors, disinterested committee of directors] or (f) [panel of one or more independent persons appointed by the court] has determined in good faith after conducting a reasonable inquiry upon which its conclusions are based that the maintenance of the derivative proceeding is not in the best interests of the corporation.[207]

The ABA proposal probably does no harm in the arena of larger publicly held corporations in which "independent" directors are truly independent and tend to be persons of stature who will not permit their integrity and reputation to be comprised in any way.[208] But the Model Business Corporation Act is the corporate law of most of the noncommercial jurisdictions in which smaller corporations predominate and director independence is a matter of shades of

---

[205] A.L.I. Corp. Gov. Proj. § 7.10(a)(1).

[206] See, e.g., the A.L.I. codification of the business judgment rule, A.L.I. Corp. Gov. Proj. § 4.01(c), discussed in § 8.03[C], *supra.*

[207] MBCA § 7.44(a). Section 7.44(f) authorizes the court to appoint a panel of one or more independent persons to act as if the panel were an SLC. Such a panel might be sought in the instance in which a majority of directors is interested in the transaction.

[208] See the discussion of institutions' and others' role as relational investors in § 5.02[E], *supra.*

gray rather than black and white.[209] Given the latter fact, the ABA proposals probably should have left in place the relief valve of judicial review, at least in some cases, as with the *Zapata* second step or the ALI proposals.

In *Einhorn v. Culea*,[210] the Supreme Court of Wisconsin noted the absence of judicial review as support for added vigilance by trial courts. The Wisconsin Legislature had adopted the MBCA derivative action subchapter, with universal demand and no judicial review of the merits of an SLC determination. Therefore, "[j]udicial review to determine whether the members of the committee are independent and whether the committee's procedure complies with the statute is of utmost importance, because the court is bound by the substantive decision of a properly constituted and acting committee."

Ms. Justice Abrahamson emphasized that "[g]iven the finality of the ultimate decision of the committee to dismiss the claim, judicial oversight is necessary to insure that the special litigation committee is independent . . . ." She directed trial courts to examine at least seven factors:

(1)   A committee member's status as a defendant and potential liability.

(2)   A committee member's participation in or approval of the alleged wrongdoing.

(3)   A committee member's past pr present business or economic dealings with an individual defendant.

(4)   A committee member's past or present personal, family, or social relations with individual defendants.

(5)   A committee member's past or present economic relations with the corporation.

(6)   The number of members on a special litigation committee.

(7)   The roles of corporate counsel and independent counsel.

"It is vital for a [trial] court to review whether each member of a special litigation committee is independent. The special litigation committee is, after all, 'the only instance in American Jurisprudence where a defendant can free itself from a suit merely by appointing a committee to review the allegations of a complaint.' "[211]

[C]   Summary

Courts have adumbrated at least five different positions. Most pro-defendant is the business judgment rule application of *Auerbach,* also reflected in the Model Act provisions adopted in roughly a dozen states, but which also (unlike New York) eliminates the demand futility branch altogether. Less pro-defendant, but still pro-defendant, is the ALI position, adopted in its entirety by the Supreme Court of Pennsylvania. Moving into the pro-shareholder portion of

---

[209]   *See, e.g.*, Douglas M. Branson, *Recent Changes to the Model Business Corporation Act: Death Knells for Main Street Corporation Law*, 72 NEB. L. REV. 258 (1993).

[210]   612 N.W.2d 78 (Wis. 2000).

[211]   612 N.W.2d 78, 90, quoting *Lewis v. Fuqua*, 502 A.2d 962, 967 (Del. Ch. 1985).

the spectrum, one encounters the *Zapata v. Maldonado* theory in which the court may, in its discretion, review the merits of an SLC recommendation. Delaware would be even more pro-shareholder, at least on the relative scale of things, if Delaware courts also could undertake the *Zapata* second step in reviewing demand refused as well as demand futility cases. Unfortunately, Delaware limits *Zapata* to demand excused cases while the North Carolina Supreme Court in *Alford v. Shaw* applies *Zapata* to all demand cases. Last of all, similar to North Carolina, and most pro-shareholder of all is Massachusetts, which, some contrary language in the *Houle v. Low* opinion notwithstanding, judicially requires the trial judge to undertake a version of the *Zapata* second step in every case.

§ 14.08   RIGHT TO TRIAL BY JURY, ATTORNEYS' FEES, AND MISCELLANEOUS ISSUES

[A]   Right to Trial By Jury

Fiduciary duties have their genesis in trust law, at the heart of the Chancery Court's jurisdiction. The derivative action itself was the creation of the equity courts. Hence, for many decades the prevailing view was that derivative actions belong exclusively to the equity courts: there was no right to trial by jury.

The landscape was altered, at lease under federal law, by the decisions of the United States Supreme Court in *Beacon Theatres, Inc. v. Westover*[212] and *Dairy Queen v. Wood*,[213] which interpreted the Seventh Amendment of the United States Constitution as requiring that all claims in law and all issues of fact common to both legal and equitable claims first be tried to a jury. Then and only then could a judge, sitting as chancellor, decide the factual issues unique to equitable claims and apply the law to facts found by the jury and judge, respectively.

In *Ross v. Berhard*,[214] the Court extended *Beacon Theatres* and *Dairy Queen* to derivative actions. The Court held that "[t]he Seventh Amendment question [of right to jury trial in derivative actions] depends on the nature of the issue(s) to be tried rather than the character of the overall action."

Thus, questions pertaining to plaintiff's right to maintain the action are questions for the chancellor. Questions such as "was demand made or excused?," "was there adequate representation?," and so on, are for the court. The issues in the case on the merits must then be taken up issue by issue. Assume that the corporation has failed to sue a major supplier who has breached a contract. The plaintiff might assert three claims: breach of contract, breach by directors of their duty of care in not remedying the breach, and, in the alternative, breach by the directors of their duty of loyalty, perhaps because some of the directors have familial or financial relationships with the supplier. Issue by issue, the plaintiff

---

[212] 359 U.S. 500 (1959).

[213] 369 U.S. 469 (1962).

[214] 396 U.S. 531 (1970).

would try the contract claim to a jury. Plaintiff would try the breach of fiduciary duty claims to the judge. In rendering his decision, the judge would have to take as his raw material the jury's findings on any issue of fact also germane to the equitable claims.[215]

The Seventh Amendment, however, does not apply to the states. As a result, *Beacon Theaters, Dairy Queen,* and *Ross v. Berhard* will not apply to state courts, although some state judiciaries choose to follow the federal practice.[216]

[B]   Attorneys' Fees in Derivative Actions

[1]   Entitlement: Common Fund Versus Common Benefit Cases

The shareholder attorney in a derivative action looks to the corporate treasury for payment of her fee, based upon one of two rationales. In a case in which the action produces a monetary fund, the rationale for award of the fee is that the other beneficiaries of the recovery, in this case, other shareholders, would be unjustly enriched if the named plaintiff had to bear all legal costs or if the attorney received nothing. The "common fund" theory, establishing a right to fees from the fund itself, and in this case, indirectly from the corporation, has long been recognized.[217]

The second rationale is a variant of the first. Even though the attorney's actions have produced no fund, counsel will nonetheless be entitled to a fee if she has produced a "common benefit," a case outcome that directly or indirectly will benefit shareholders other than the named plaintiff. Examples might include an injunction resulting in improved disclosure to fellow shareholders before they vote on a transaction, the negation of an election, production of extensive amendments to corporate bylaws, adoption of a code of conduct or of a policy statement governing senior executives and other employees, and so on.

In *Mills v. Electric Auto-Lite Co.*,[218] the plaintiffs established the misleading nature of disclosure in a corporate merger. The proxy statement failed to disclose that a number of the target corporation (Auto-Lite) directors recommending a "yes" vote of the merger were nominees put on the board by

---

[215] *See De Pinto v. Provident Security Life Ins. Co.*, 323 F.2d 826 (9th Cir. 1963) (issue by issue approach utilized in derivative action).

[216] One state alternative to the federal issue by issue approach is to take a hard look at the plaintiff's case overall. The judge then characterizes it as "primarily legal" or "primarily equitable." In the latter case, the parties will try the derivative action to the judge sitting as chancellor *See, e.g., Hyatt Bros., Inc. Ex rel. Hyatt v. Hyatt*, 769 P.2d 329 (Wyo. 1989) (shareholder derivative action held primarily legal; case remanded for jury trial of six count complaint, even though equitable remedies such as an accounting and specific performance sought).

[217] Seminal cases include *Trustees v. Greenough*, 26 L. Ed 1157, 15 Otto 527 (1882) (to deny a fee out of the common fund "would not only be unjust to [plaintiff and her lawyer] but . . . would give to the other parties entitled to participate in the benefits of the fund an unfair advantage"), and *Sprague v. Ticonic Nat'l Bank*, 307 U.S. 161 (1939) (plaintiff and her lawyer entitled to fee when they have established a right to a fund from which others eventually will benefit).

[218] 396 U.S. 375 (1970). For a discussion of *Mills* as a securities case, see § 7.06[C] and [G], *supra.*

the acquiring corporation by virtue of its pre-existing 50% share interest. The "yes" votes of the other shareholders were important because the prevailing law required a two-thirds vote to approve the merger. A common type of relief in such a case might be corrective disclosure followed by re-solicitation of the shareholders, and not damages or creation of a common fund (although in *Mills*, no such action was sought but only damages were sought, and the Court remanded for a determination of the appropriate relief). In any form, the relief could include attorney's fees: "[t]hat this suit has not yet produced, and may never produce, a monetary recovery does not preclude an award based upon [the common benefit] rationale." When the litigation has "conferred a substantial benefit on members of an ascertainable class,"[219] plaintiff and her attorney are entitled to fees and costs under the "common benefit" common law exception to the American rule against fee shifting.

In a later case, *Alyeska Pipeline Service Co. v. Wilderness-Society*,[220] the Court tightened considerably the ability of federal courts, in the absence of express statutory authorization, to shift fees from a losing defendant to a plaintiff who had achieved some measure of success. Significantly, the Court left undisturbed the common fund and common benefit exceptions to the rule against fee shifting.

A last question in regard to entitlement is the question of causation. A truculent defendant might say of bylaw amendments or an increase in a takeover bid price, "we were going to do it anyway — the plaintiff's suit actually played little or no part" in producing the benefit or creating the fund. Indeed, the corporate defendant may have refused to deal with the plaintiff-shareholder altogether.

Delaware, whose courts entertain numerous requests for judicial approval of fee awards or the attorney fee component in class and derivative action settlements, employs a presumption of "causation by sequence." First, the key is a benefit: a settlement or judgment is not a prerequisite to a fee award.[221] Second, the plaintiff's suit must have had some merit, in the sense that it could have survived a hypothetical motion to dismiss. Third, the corrective action (for example, improved disclosure, increase in takeover price) must have occurred prior to settlement or abandonment of the suit.[222] Fourth, there must be a plausible causal relationship between the lawsuit and the corrective actions. In the latter inquiry, chronology weighs heavily. "Once it is determined that action benefiting the corporation chronologically followed the filing of a meritorious suit, the burden is upon the corporation to demonstrate 'that the lawsuit did not in any way cause their action.' " Moreover, appellate review of the determination of causation is under an "abuse of discretion" standard highly deferential to trial court determinations.[223]

---

[219] 375 U.S. at 393–94.

[220] 421 U.S. 240 (1975).

[221] *Chrysler Corp. v. Dann*, 223 A.2d 384, 387 (Del. Ch. 1966).

[222] *Allied Artists Pictures Corp. v. Baron*, 413 A.2d 876 (Del. 1980).

[223] *Tandycrafts, Inc. v. Initio Partners*, 562 A.2d 1162, 1165 (Del. 1989) (plaintiff obtained temporary injunction and improved proxy statement disclosure that arguably resulted in defeat of

[2]　The Cosmetic (Collusive) Settlement Problem

Since a route to a fee award may be "corporate therapeutics," as well as production of a common fund, a plaintiff's attorney may trade a slap on the wrist (non-monetary settlement) in return for a tacit agreement to a generous attorney fee in the derivative or class action settlement proffered to the court for approval. Everyone seems to win: the attorney obtains a good fee, the defendant corporation has to pay far less, and the court conserves valuable judicial resources that would otherwise have been expended in continuation of the lawsuit. The potential losers are the shareholders who might have benefitted more by a strong push for a monetary settlement or judgment. In theory, the court approval requirement exists to prevent collusion. However, in practice, courts may be too busy to give the settlement anything but a cursory review.

The cosmetic settlement problem is often alleged to be graced further by unseemly collusion. The plaintiff's attorney and corporate counsel reach a tentative early agreement regarding settlement. A silent component of that agreement will be a long delay, during which, by virtue of extensive discovery, voluminous legal research, and protracted discussion and negotiation of details, the plaintiff's attorney amasses billable hours. Counsel amasses those hours to justify the fee to the court.

For those and other reasons, the late Judge Henry Friendly admonished the reporters of the ALI Project that resolution of the cosmetic settlement be given a high priority in their work.[224] Perhaps as a result, the ALI Project directs courts evaluating proposed derivative action settlements to "place special weight on the net benefit, including pecuniary and non-pecuniary elements, to the corporation."[225]

Another safeguard against collusive settlements is the caution that ordinarily, but not always, the class or derivative plaintiff's attorney's fee should only be negotiated after all other elements of the settlement are in place.[226] The settlement on the merits should not be held hostage pending a negotiated fee or other self serving arrangement for the plaintiff's attorney.

---

proposed amendments to articles of incorporation, the court holding that "[t]he definition of a corporate benefit . . . is elastic" and that "[c]hanges in corporate policy or, as here, a heightened level of corporate disclosure, if attributable to the filing of a meritorious suit, may justify an award of counsel fees").

[224] *See also Saylor v. Lindsey*, 456 F.2d 896, 899–900 (2d Cir. 1972) (Friendly, J.); *Allegheny Corp. v. Kirby*, 333 F.2d 327, 347 (2d Cir. 1964) (Friendly, J., dissenting).

[225] A.L.I. Corp. Gov. Proj. § 7.14(b).

[226] A.L.I. Corp. Gov. Proj. § 7.14, Comment, at 213. Several federal courts went so far as to prohibit simultaneous negotiation of class action settlements and attorney fee award. The Supreme Court refused to endorse blanket prohibition of simultaneous negotiation. *See Evans v. Jeff D.*, 475 U.S. 717, 732 (1986).

[3]   Computation of Fee Amounts: Lodestar Versus Percentage of Recovery Methods

The lodestar is a fee computation method based upon hours expended by the plaintiff's attorney. It prevailed through the 1970s and 1980s. The 1990s and new century have seen a return to computing attorney fee awards based upon a percentage (15 to 30%) of the common fund or of the value of the benefit conferred upon the corporation.

The 1973 Federal Judicial Manual for Complex Litigation states that "the reasonableness of the fee arrived at should not rest primarily on the selection of a percentage of the recovery." Fee awards proceedings should instead look to "the time and labor required and the effect of the allowance on the public interest and the reputation of the courts."[227] This, in turn, lead to widespread application of the hour-based fee determination known as the lodestar method.

The number of billable hours expended (for example, 1500 hours) multiplied by the attorney's normal billable rate ($200 per hour), adjusted for the location in which the litigation has been prosecuted (for example, New York rates would not be applied in Boise or Birmingham), produces a product known as the lodestar ($300,000). The judge then applies to the lodestar a multiplier, usually in the range from 1.2 to 1.9. Multipliers less than 1.0 are rare.[228] The lodestar multiplied by the multiplier yields the fee (1.5 $300,000 = $450,000). In this way, judges can assess whether the fee agreed upon by the parties is within the acceptable range.[229]

The latest trend has been a turn away from the lodestar back to the percentage of recovery system as the preferred method of fee computation.[230]

---

[227] FEDERAL JUDICIAL MANUAL FOR COMPLEX LITIGATION § 1.47.

[228] Rather than delivering the direct slap in the face a multiplier of 1.0 would represent, judges dissatisfied with an attorney's work frequently discount the billable hours instead. *But see In re Washington Public Power Supply Sys. Lit.*, 19 F.3d 1291, 1299 (9th Cir. 1994) (given the large size of the fee, multiplier of only 1.0 upheld; the court refused to apply a larger "risk multiplier," on grounds that "law firms showed no reluctance to take the case and that firms' high hourly rates already reflected some of the risk in the case").

[229] Two early lodestar method cases are *Lindy Bros. Builders, Inc. v. American Radiator & Standard Sanitary Corp.*, 487 F.2d 161 (3d Cir. 1973), and *Detroit v. Grinnell Corp.*, 495 F.2d 448 (2d Cir. 1974). Selection of the appropriate multiplier depends upon the presence or absence of a number of enhancement factors: the intricacy, novelty, and complexity of the issues; particular obstacles to be overcome, such as statute of limitations arguments or multiple defense motions for summary judgment; the difficulty encountered in unearthing the facts; the reputation, skill, and resources of defense counsel; the wholly or partly contingent nature of the representation and, accordingly, the risk of nonpayment for the attorney; the amount of business the attorney may have had to forego successfully to prosecute the action; the time the litigation had been pending and the stage it had reached, such as discovery completed, class certification, eve of trial, and so on. *But see In re Boesky Sec. Lit.*, 888 F. Supp. 551, 569–70 (S.D.N.Y. 1995) (four factor formula utilized: the contingent nature of the expected compensation; the consequent risk of non-payment; the quality of the representation; and the results achieved).

[230] Federal judges have excoriated the lodestar method and the wasted effort judicial review often entails. *See, e.g., In re Activism Sec. Lit.*, 723 F. Supp. 1373, 1375 (N.D. Cal. 1989) ("Is this process necessary? Under a cost-benefit analysis, the answer would be a resounding 'no.' "); *In re Oracle Sec. Lit.*, 131 F.R.D. 688 (N.D. Cal. 1989) ("the lodestar method . . . is thoroughly

Critics of lodestar methodologies focus upon the extensive expenditure of attorney and judicial time in preparing and reviewing fee applications. The lodestar method also creates strong incentives for attorneys to "run the clock" throughout the pendency of the lawsuit, delaying any settlement or judicial review until still additional hours have been billed. By enhancing the multiplier based upon factors such as "difficulty of the case," and "novelty and complexity of the issues," the lodestar method also compensates attorneys for "betting on long shots." Some experts question whether attorney fee awards and the methods of computing them ought to encourage the more meritorious cases (the "sure" and "near sure things") rather than the "long shots" to be brought to court.[231]

The A.L.I. Project envisions a percentage of recovery method as a cap on fees that otherwise would be awarded under an hourly based method such as the lodestar. The ALI black letter provides that: "[a] successful plaintiff in a derivative action should be entitled to recover a reasonable attorney's fee award and other reasonable litigation expenses . . . but in no event should the attorney's fee award exceed a reasonable proportion of the value of the relief (including non-pecuniary relief) obtained by the plaintiff . . . ."[232]

[4] Objectors and Intervenors

Class and derivative litigation against publicly held corporations draws the attention of many onlookers. One set of those onlookers include "objectors," who appear at the court hearing at which the parties seek approval of the settlement. Objectors may object to the terms of the settlement, the amount of the fee award to plaintiffs' counsel, or to the award of any fee at all. Their motives may be mixed but one prevalent motive is base. On threat of derailing the settlement, the objector's counsel seeks to obtain a portion of the fee that otherwise would go entirely to plaintiff shareholders' attorneys.

A procedural question is whether the objector must formally move to intervene in the litigation or may just appear. One consequence may be, that failing intervention, the objector will have no standing to appeal an adverse ruling. The Seventh Circuit has adopted a "no intervention, no standing rule."[233] In contrast, the Second Circuit has held that an objecting shareholder has a sufficient interest to have standing to appeal a ruling adverse to her interests.[234]

Kaplan v. Reed involved a so called parasitic lawsuit, one which seeks to "piggy back" itself on to an early suit, governmental investigation, or other

---

discredited by experience"); *In re Union Carbide Sec. Lit.*, 724 F. Supp. 160, 170 (S.D.N.Y. 1989) ("[A percentage method] is consistent with the new learning . . . which we believe will proceed from West to East and take us back to straight contingent fee awards bereft of largely judgmental and time-wasting computations and multipliers"). *But see In re Boesky Sec. Lit.*, 888 F. Supp. 551, 561and 565 (S.D.N.Y. 1995) (lodestar mandatory under existing Second Circuit precedent).

[231] *See, e.g.*, John Leubsdorf, *The Contingency Factor in Attorney Fee Awards*, 90 YALE L. J. 73 (1981).

[232] A.L.I. Corp. Gov. Proj. § 7.17.

[233] *Felzen v. Andreas*, 134 F.3d 873 (7th Cir. 1998).

[234] *See, e.g., Kaplan v. Reed*, 192 F.3d 60 (2d Cir. 1999).

proceeding. Two years earlier Texaco had settled a civil rights suit brought by African American Texaco employees. The settlement included increased forward pay, a $115 million lump sum payment, and formation of a Texaco Task Force on Equality and Fairness. Kaplan then brought a shareholder's derivative action against Texaco's directors for duty of care violations. Texaco settled that suit by promising to indicate in its annual report that copies of the Task Force reports could be obtained and to include a short "Statement of Equality and Tolerance" in contracts with outside vendors. The settlement also provided for attorney's fees up to $1.4 million, $1 million of which the trial court awarded.

Texaco shareholder Rand, who was also an attorney, appeared at the hearing, objecting to, *inter alia*, the fee award. On appeal, the Second Circuit took the extraordinary step of reversing altogether, remanding with instructions to the trial court to award no fee whatsoever. The court did recognize that fees may be awarded when a derivative action results in a "substantial non-monetary benefit to the corporation." The benefit, however, must be "something more than technical in its consequence and . . . one that accomplishes a result which corrects or prevents an abuse which would be prejudicial to the rights or interests of the corporation." The Texaco proceeding was not such a case.

"Even by the most liberal definition of 'substantial benefit,' the settlement in the case before us does not meet the test." The Task Force reports had been available to shareholders for the asking all along. There was no evidence that a clause in vendor contracts was needed. The settlement did not seek "to prevent a sequence of misconduct from reoccurring," nor did it seek to remedy past securities law violations persons within a company.

Kaplan v. Reed marks a tightening up of standards for when pure corporate therapeutics benefits will merit any sort of attorney's fee.

[5] The *WorldCom* Case

Although technically brought under the federal securities laws rather than state corporate law, *WorldCom*[235] is instructive because, among other things, it was the largest piece of shareholder litigation ever filed. WorldCom had issued $17 billion in bonds, of which $15.3 billion were outstanding at the time of settlement. In approving the settlement, Judge Denise Cote found that it was of "historic proportions": $6.5 billion, allocated at a rate of $426.66 per $1,000 to 834,000 of 4 million class members who had filed claims. In reviewing a proposed class or derivative action settlement, a court must "carefully scrutinize the settlement to insure its fairness, adequacy, and reasonableness, and that it was not the product of collusion":

[A] district court must consider the following [nine] factors;

(1) the complexity, expense, and likely duration of the litigation, (2) the reaction of the class to the settlement, (3) the stage of the proceeding and the amount of discovery completed, (4) the risks of establishing liability, (5) the risks of establishing damages. (6) the risks of maintaining the class action through the trial, (7) the ability of the defendants to

---

[235] 388 F. Supp. 2d 319 (S.D.N.Y. 2005). (Cote, J.).

withstand a greater judgment, (8) the range of reasonableness of the
settlement fund in light of the best possible recovery, [and] (9) the range
of reasonableness of the settlement fund to a possible recovery in light
of all the attendant risks of litigation.[236]

Judge Cote found the settlement the product of strenuous negotiations, keying
on the unusual fact that only 7 of 834,000 claimant had filed objections with the
court.

A second stage of settlement hearings is approval of the attorneys' fees
provided for in the settlement. Judge Cote approved plaintiffs' law firms' (2
firms) fees calculated on the percentage of recovery method at 5.5% of the
settlement, or $194,600,000. She used the lodestar method of fee calculation only
as a cross-check, noting "the fees sought were the equivalent to a lodestar
multiple of 4.0," an unusually high amount. She applied a 6 factor test, known as
the *Goldberger* factors:

> (1) the time and labor expended by counsel; (2) the magnitude and
> complexities of the litigation; (3) the risk of the litigation; (4) the quality
> of the representation; (5) the requested fee in relationship to the
> settlement; and (6) public policy considerations.[237]

A powerful institutional investor lead plaintiff, the New York State Common
Retirement Fund, had $300 million at stake. As lead plaintiff, NYSCPF had
negotiated a 5.5% fee. "A district court is not required to adhere to a retainer
agreement [previously negotiated] . . . . Nonetheless, when class counsel in a
securities lawsuit have negotiated an arm's length fee agreement with a
sophisticated lead plaintiff possessing a large stake in the litigation . . . the court
should give the terms of the fee agreement great weight."[238]

[C]   Statute of Limitations or Laches?

Often in smaller corporations, a plaintiff delays taking action when she
suspects mismanagement. She may do so due to a "wait-and-see" attitude, the
difficulty of obtaining reliable information, or active concealment by the
wrongdoers. If she does delay, she may find that any litigation she proposes may
run up against a time bar. The question is what that time bar will be.

Defendants may contend that breach of a fiduciary duty is a tort, to be
governed by a two or three year statute of limitations or an even shorter "tort
reform" one or two year statute. The modern view is that the relationship
between a shareholder and her corporation is contractual, with both the
corporations law and the common law of fiduciary duty supplying terms implied
in that contract. Thus, if a statute of limitations applies to our delaying
shareholder's claims, the proper statute is the one applicable to contract actions,
usually six years.[239]

---

[236] *Id.* at 337.

[237] *Id.* at 355.

[238] *Id.* at 356.

[239] *See Hanson v. Kake Tribal Corp.*, 939 P.2d 1320, 1325 (Alaska 1997) ("The relationship

There may be even more latitude than that in breach of the duty of loyalty cases. Because a suit for a breach of fiduciary duty is not a mere tort or contract claim, but "a serious breach of trust," the Delaware Chancellor long ago held that the applicable time bar may not be a statute of limitations at all but laches (that is, the passage of a great deal of time accompanied by a material change of position on the defendant's part).[240] Laches would require an additional passage of time than would any statute of limitations. In addition, the defendant pleading this affirmative defense would have to demonstrate some change in position that would make it inequitable now to bring him to account.[241]

[D]   Who Pays?

Professors Bernard Black, Brian Cheffins, and Michael Klausner conducted extensive empirical research on the settlement of corporate litigation. Essentially, they found that, in shareholder class or derivative litigation, directors seldom, if ever, had to contribute to any settlement fund from their own pockets. Any contribution on directors' behalf was made by the insurance carrier who had written the "D & O" liability insurance purchased by the corporation.[242] The professors, however, may have spoken too soon.

Shortly after the professors reached their conclusions, in early 2005, settlements in both the Enron and WorldCom lawsuits contained as an integral part payment by directors from their own assets (principal residences and retirements excluded). Directors paid $24 million in WorldCom and $13 million in Enron, which amounted to 20% of their net assets. The lead institutional plaintiffs insisted upon such personal payments, initially insisting on payments of 30% of personal assets. Thus, Bert Roberts, the Board Chair at WorldCom, paid in $3.5 million, and the dean of Georgetown University Law School, who was a WorldCom director as well, had to contribute a substantial amount. These payments caused considerable anguish among directors who, while persons of means, for the most part were not super wealthy.

It remains to be seen whether in future cases lead plaintiffs take a page from NYSCRF, NYCERS and CALPERS play books, insisting on personal contributions by corporate directors, at least in the settlement of headline grabbing cases.

---

between a corporation and its shareholders is primarily contractual," *citing Trustees of Dartmouth College v. Woodward*, 4 Wheat 518 (1819) (Marshall, J.) (six year contracts statute governs shareholder class claims for discrimination in matter of dividends). *But see Demoulas v. Demoulas Super Mkts., Inc.*, 677 N.E.2d 159, 172 (Mass. 1997) (claim for breach of fiduciary duty sounds in tort; three year statute of limitations governs).

[240] *Bovay v. H.M. Byllesly & Co.*, 38 A.2d 808, 819–20 (Del. Ch. 1944).

[241] The doctrine has had a mixed history in the Delaware courts. One case limits its reach to "particularly egregious conduct," "extraordinary cases which involve, at a minimum, allegations of self-dealing, [where] the benefit of the statute [of limitations] will be denied to those corporate officers and directors who profited personally from their misconduct." *Halpern v. Barran*, 313 A.2d 139, 142 (Del. Ch. 1973) (citations omitted).

[242] Black, Cheffins & Klausner, *Outside Directors Liability*, 58 Stan. L. Rev. 1055 (2006).

§ 14.09   THE REPRISE OF THE SHAREHOLDER CLASS ACTION

[A]   The Death of the Derivative Action and the Rise of the "Stock Drop" Class Action

In the 1980s, with a special litigation committee, a corporation could sidetrack all but the most egregious breach of fiduciary duty claims. Derivative litigation had come to have a number of potential outcomes most of which, from a plaintiff's perspective, were "bad." Quite naturally, plaintiffs' attorneys turned to pursuit of direct rather than derivative claims.

Direct claims might arise under state law, as in the Delaware duty of candor-disclosure cases,[243] or more frequently, under federal securities laws. The bull market of the 1990s brought to the market an unprecedented number of initial public offerings (IPOs) of securities, many by high tech corporations engaged in biotech and computer software and hardware. Each disappointing quarterly earnings report, product failure, or other corporate pratfall brought forth multiple class action lawsuits. A significant drop in the share price of newly public companies often means multiple class actions were filed.

In these "stock drop" lawsuits, plaintiffs' attorneys often filed skeletal complaints, attributing the drop in share price to a particular cause.[244] Plaintiff law firms maintained stables of professional plaintiffs who owned small, 5 or 10 share lots in several hundred corporations.[245]

The consequence of class action filings was allegedly that new public firms nearly always settled, often for substantial amounts, regardless of the lack of merit in the plaintiffs' claims.[246] Newly public companies viewed securities class litigation as a form of blackmail. A lobbying effort over several years finally resulted in Congress enacting the "Private Securities Litigation Reform Act of 1995 (PSLRA)."[247]

---

[243] *See, e.g.,* Douglas M. Branson, Corporate Governance § 10.07 (1993) ("Emergence of a New Duty — The Duty of Candor-Disclosure"); Lawrence Hamermesh, *Calling Off the Lynch Mob: The Corporate Directors' Fiduciary Duty of Disclosure,* 49 Vand. L. Rev. 1087 (1996).

[244] Races to the courthouse took place because being first to file had some bearing on who, among various class action attorneys, would be named lead counsel when and if the various actions were consolidated. Designation as lead counsel carried with it certain emoluments, such as a larger share of the fee and the right to parcel out the workload among the various plaintiffs' firms participating in the law suit.

[245] The paradigm is Harry Lewis, a non practicing attorney who owns shares in over 800 corporations, and who was the named plaintiffs in over 50 reported Delaware opinions and another 50 or so federal court opinions in the ten year period 1975–85 alone. Harry Lewis's activities are described in Douglas M. Branson, *The American Law Institute Principles of Corporate Governance and the Derivative Action: A View From the Other Side,* 43 Wash. & Lee L. Rev. 399, 418 and n.108 (1986).

[246] The most touted piece of evidence was a controversial study by a Stanford University law professor, Jane C. Alexander, *Do the Merits Matter? A Study of Settlements in Securities Class Actions,* 43 Stan. L. Rev. 497 (1991). *Cf.* Joel Seligman, *The Merits Do Matter. . .,* 108 Harv. L. Rev. 438 (1994).

[247] Pub. L. No. 104-67, 109 Stat. 737 (codified in scattered sections of the Securities Act of 1933

[B]   The Private Securities Litigation Reform Act (PSLRA) of 1995

By and large, the Private Securities Litigation Reform Act constitutes a new "add on" code of civil procedure for securities class actions.[248]

A few of its salient features are:

- **Ineligible Plaintiffs:** A plaintiff may be a "lead plaintiff, or an officer director or fiduciary of a lead plaintiff, in no more than 5 securities class actions . . . during any 3-year period." This provision is intended to narrow considerably the potential scope of professional plaintiffs' involvement.

- **Prohibition of Plaintiff Compensation:** The Act prohibits payment of "incentive payments" for those professional plaintiffs who remain eligible to act.

- **Certification By Plaintiffs:** The attorney must file a certification averring that "the plaintiff has reviewed the complaint and authorized its filing;" pledge that plaintiff did not purchase the security at the direction of counsel or "in order to participate in any private action" arising under the securities laws; promise that the plaintiff will appear for his deposition and testify at trial; identify other actions in which she has served or sought to serve as class representative in the previous three years; and more. The named plaintiff must swear to this certificate.

- **Publication and Upset Provision — Statutory Requirement for the Quest for the Most Appropriate Plaintiff (MAP):** Within twenty days of filing, plaintiff's attorney must publish a notice of the pendency of the action "in a widely circulated national business-oriented publication." Within the ensuing 90 days, if any person or entity with a larger shareholding comes forward, the court must presume that that person or entity is the MAP.[249] If the MAP moves to be substituted for the named class representative, the court must oblige.

- **Heightened Pleading Standards:** The Federal Rules of Civil Procedure mandate only notice pleading. The rules do require that a plaintiff plead fraud "with particularity."[250] An exception to the exception, however, is that "[i]ntent, knowledge, and other condition of

---

and the Securities Exchange Act of 1934, 15 U.S.C. §§ 77z-1, 78j-1, 78u-4, -5).

[248] *See, e.g.,* Douglas M. Branson, *Running the Gauntlet: A Description of the Arduous, and Now Often Fatal, Journey for Plaintiffs in Federal Securities Law Actions,* 65 U. CINN. L. REV. 3 (1996); Branson, *Chasing the Rogue Professional After the Private Securities Litigation Reform Act of 1995,* 50 SMU L. REV. 91 (1996).

[249] A likely effect is that the few professional plaintiffs who do survive will be upset by MAPs holding a mere 100 or 200 shares. Knowing also that you may soon lose control of the action provides a disincentive for attorneys to file in the first place. Last of all, the MAP provision was designed by a law professor who thought that institutional investors would come forward to take over securities class litigation and manage that litigation in a responsible manner.

[250] Fed. R. Civ. P. 9(b).

mind of a person may be averred generally." The PSLRA negates the effect of Federal Rule 9, installing heightened pleading standards for pleading state of mind, or "scienter." For each defendant, and for each disclosure or nondisclosure sued upon, plaintiffs must "state with particularity facts giving rise to a strong inference that the defendant acted with the requisite state of mind." This is a high threshold for plaintiffs to cross.

- **Stay on Discovery:** A plaintiff will have to meet the heightened standard without the benefit of discovery. If a securities class action defendant files a motion to dismiss, the court is required to stay all discovery until that motion has been resolved. Every defense lawyer files an immediate motion to dismiss on grounds that the complaint fails to meet the pleading standard. The stay on discovery kicks in and the plaintiff's ability to obtain information to meet the pleading standard is reduced accordingly.

- **Mandatory Rule 11 Review of Plaintiff's Pleadings:** In contrast to Federal Rule of Civil Procedure 11, which has been amended to make sanctions optional (court "may" rather than "shall" impose sanctions), and which has a 30 day cooling off period during which an attorney may withdraw the offending pleading, the PSLRA resurrects the old mandatory rule 11. Moreover, the PSLRA requires judges to conduct a Rule 11 review, including "in the record specific findings regarding compliance by each party and each attorney" with Rule 11.

- **Fee Shifting Provision:** If the court, in its mandatory Rule 11 review, finds that the plaintiffs have violated Rule 11 in the allegations of the complaint, the presumptive sanction is not merely the other side's cost in responding to the offending allegation. Instead, the sanction becomes all of the attorney's fees "incurred in the action" by the other side. Since many defense efforts will be mounted by large law firms in which lawyers tend to have high billing rates and the staffing of defense efforts tends to be generous, the potential sanction could be large.

Overall, the Private Securities Litigation Reform Act of 1995 has the effect of making it much more difficult to bring a class action based upon federal securities laws.

[C]   Particularized Issues Under the PSLRA

[1]   Pleading

Under the PSLRA, plaintiffs must "state with particularity facts giving rise to a strong inference that the defendant acted with the required state of mind."[251] Lower courts have struggled over what such a standard requires. In *Tellabs, Inc. v. Makor Issues & Rights, Ltd.*,[252] in attempting to provide some guidance, Justice Ginsburg struck a middle course. She held that lower courts

---

[251] Codified as, *inter alia*, Securities Exchange Act § 21(b)(2).

[252] 551 U.S. 308 (2007).

must engage in comparative evaluation of plausible explanations of the conduct of which plaintiffs complain, that is, that corporate officers acted out of a neutral or benevolent motive rather than with an intent to defraud. "To qualify as 'strong' [under the PSLRA] . . . an inference of scienter must be more than merely plausible or reasonable-it must be cogent and at least as compelling as any opposing inference of nonfraudulent intent."[253] "Cogent" and "compelling" seems to be the key words under the PSLRA pleading standard.

[2]　Loss Causation

The PSLRA requires that securities fraud complaints"specify" each statement alleged to have been misleading and to whom it is attributable. Moreover, the statute imposes on plaintiffs "the burden of proving that the defendant's misrepresentations caused the loss for which the plaintiff seeks to recover."[254] In *Dura Pharmaceuticals, Inc. v. Broudo*,[255] Michael Broudo purchased shares in Dura Pharmaceuticals at $39 per share. Dura's hopes rested on FDA approval of a spray device for asthma suffers. Dura had to announce that its earnings would be lower than expected due to slow drug sales. Eight months after that Dura then had to announce that had not received the FDA approval it has earlier ballyhooed for the spray device. The share price fell to $21.

Dura bought a class action alleging that due to the misrepresentations, Dura's stock price had been inflated. He had purchased in reliance on the integrity of the market (fraud on the market reliance substitute).[256] Justice Breyer rejected the Ninth Circuit's acceptance of the theory that "plaintiffs establish loss causation if they have shown that the price *on the date of purchase* was inflated because of the misrepresentation."

"Normally, in such cases as this (*i.e.*, fraud-on-the-market cases), an inflated purchase price will not itself constitute or proximately cause the relevant economic loss," began Justice Breyer:

> [T]he logical link between the inflated share purchase price and any later economic loss in not invariably strong . . . . [I]f the purchaser sells later after the truth makes its way into the marketplace, an initially inflated purchase price *might* mean a later economic loss. But that is far from inevitably so. [T]he lower price might reflect, not the earlier misrepresentation but changed economic expectations, changed investor expectations, new industry-specific facts, conditions, or other events . . . . Other things being equal, the longer the time between the purchase and the sale, the more likely that this is so, *i.e.*, the more likely that other factors caused the loss.
>
> [T]he most logic alone permits us to say is that the higher purchase price will *sometimes* play a role in bringing about a future loss. [O]ne

[253] *Id.* at ___.
[254] Securities Exchange Act § 21D(b)(2)–(4).
[255] 544 U.S. 336 (2005).
[256] Discussed in § 13.02[G], *supra.*

might say that the inflated purchase price suggests that the misrepresentation "touches upon" a late economic loss. To "touch upon" a loss is not to *cause* a loss, and it is the latter that the law requires.[257]

The Court rejected Brouda's claim, leaving the plaintiffs' bar in a tizzy as well. The case requires plaintiffs and their lawyers to exclude intervening or so-called confounding events and their possible effect on price, as best they can do so, a difficult task. The shorter the passage of time between purchase at a price alleged to be inflated and the closing of the class period, however, the less cogent or compelling the exclusion of such alternative explanations need be. Proof of loss causation represents yet another higher barrier to recovery imposed by the PSLRA on plaintiffs.[258]

[3]   Selection of the Most Appropriate Plaintiff

The district court presumes that the would-be plaintiff (often an institutional investor) with the most at stake (the largest losses) is the most appropriate plaintiff. If that prospective plaintiff would be an adequate representative of the class (no material conflicts of interest or side agendas, represented by competent counsel) and represents claims typical of the class as a whole (again no side agendas, or non-shareholder axes [e.g., disgruntled former employee] to grind), the court should appoint that investor as lead plaintiff. But what happens if the presumptive plaintiff fails to pass muster under adequacy and typicality tests? What does the court do then?

Can the court reach out in the first instance to a would-be plaintiff who has less at stake but negotiated a better fee deal with the counsel it wishes to have represent the class? *In re Cavanaugh*[259] deals with these questions in a principled way. In a case involving shareholders of Copper Mountain Networks, Inc., the district court chose as plaintiff a shareholder whose losses were only $59,000 but who had negotiated a beneficial fee agreement (up to 15% of any recovery, with an overall cap of $8 million). In doing so, the court bypassed the Cavanagh group, whose losses were 55 time greater ($3,327,000) but which had negotiated a fee arrangement topping out at 30%, as the recovery increased, albeit with Milberg Weiss, one of the top shareholder plaintiff firms.

The PSLRA directs courts to designate as plaintiff the contender "most capable of adequately representing the interest of class members." But the Act defines capable "narrowly." "The 'most capable' plaintiff . . . is the one who has the greatest financial stake in the outcome of the case, so long as he meets the requirements of Rule 23" (adequacy and typicality). The court is to be satisfied with a certain level of adequacy and of typicality, not that the investor under consideration is the best or most typical putative representative of the group. If a district court finds a prospective plaintiff lacking, the court is not then free to roam. It must then entertain the application of the investor with the next largest financial stake, and so on, down the line. Judge Kozinski lays out a

---

[257] 544 U.S. at 342–43.

[258] *See generally* Jill Fisch, *Cause for Concern: Causation and Federal Securities Fraud*, __ Iowa L. Rev. __ (forthcoming 2009).

[259] 396 F.3d 726 (9th Cir. 2002).

3 step procedure which the PSLRA requires lower courts to follow in selecting the most appropriate from a group of would-be plaintiffs. The district thus erred in not having designated the Cavanaugh group as lead plaintiff.

[D] The Securities Litigation Uniform Standards Act (SLUSA) of 1998[260]

Following the 1995 enactment of the PSLRA, shareholder attorneys turned to state courts. They filed suits alleging violations of state securities acts ("Blue Sky Laws") and common law claims, sometimes intending to pursue state claims to a judgment or settlement. Other attorneys filed parallel federal and state class actions. They used the state action only as vehicle to obtain the discovery that could now not be had in federal court because of the PSLRA.

SLUSA puts an end to many of these practices. SLUSA regulates "covered class actions," basically defined as any suit (class, or a group action naming more than 50 shareholder plaintiffs) that purports to represent more than 50 shareholders. Further it regulates those suits only as to "covered securities," securities trading on the NYSE, AMEX or NASDAQ or "a security of the same issuer that is equal in seniority" or is senior to the covered security.

In covered actions involving covered securities, SLUSA bestows on defendants the right to remove the state court action to a federal court, where the PSLRA will apply.

Generally, the battle, if there is one, is then fought over plaintiffs' motions to remand to state court. Grounds for such argument may include the following:

- The claim relates to debt securities issued in a private placement or "seeks to enforce a contractual agreement between an issuer and an indenture trustee," both statutory exceptions.

- More generally, as in the forgoing, the claim relates to a breach of contract or other claim rather than the misleading disclosure or material omission claims which are SUSLA's province. In *MDCM Holdings, Inc. v. Credit Suisse First Boston Corporation,*[261] plaintiff issuer of securities brought an action on behalf of itself and other hot IPO market issuers whose IPOs had been underwritten by Credit Suisse. In return for allocations of hot issues shares, Credit Suisse required the favored customers to share their subsequent profits with Credit Suisse. Credit Suisse, of course, had already been compensated by issuers through the "spread," typically 7 percent of the gross offering proceeds. The court found that "MDCM alleges that Credit Suisse signed numerous contracts in which it promised to do one thing but did another . . . . The contract claims do not involve allegations of misrepresentation or omissions by Credit Suisse." The court remanded the case to state court.[262]

---

[260] Codified as Securities Act of 1933 § 16(b) and Securities Exchange Act of 1934 § 28(f).

[261] 216 F. Supp. 2d 251 (S.D.N.Y. 2002).

[262] *See also Green v. Ameritrade, Inc.,* 120 F. Supp. 3d 795 (D. Neb. 2000) (after removal, plaintiff

- Disclosure claims which confine themselves exclusively to allegations of violations of the Securities Act of 1933 are not removable.[263] In that Act, Congress gave state courts an express grant of concurrent jurisdiction. SLUSA does not overrule that, although undoubtedly this is a loophole engendered by oversight on the drafters' part.

- The "Delaware Carveout," Part I: actions brought exclusively as derivative actions are not removable even if they contain lack of disclosure or misleading disclosure claims.

- The "Delaware Carveout," Part II: even group or class (direct rather than derivative) claims involving disclosure may not be removed if they invoke that sub branch of state law fiduciary duty requiring full and fair disclosure. This is the Delaware creation known as the "duty of candor." In the main, the duty of candor requires directors and senior executives to make full and fair disclosure when, in one form or another, they seek shareholder approval, of mergers, tender offers, share buybacks, and the like

In *Gibson v. PS Group Holdings, Inc.*,[264] defendant contended that an action brought under the Delaware Carveout, but in a California court, was removable. "Defendants reason that because PS Group is incorporated in Delaware and Plaintiff filed suit in California, this action does not come within the Delaware carve-out." The federal court disagreed: "[n]othing in the language [of SUSLA] suggest that Congress intended to restrict the venue of preserved class actions to the issuer's state of incorporation." The court remanded the case to the California state court.

SLUSA reached the Supreme Court in *Merrill Lynch, Pierce, Fenner & Smith v. Dabit*.[265] As a Merrill Lynch stockbroker, Dabit brought a carefully crafted class action, contending that because of undue and unlawful influences the investment banking side of ML had caused ML research analysts to make recommendations in which the analysts did not believe, or which were unjustified by their research, and upon which retail brokers like Dabit had relied.[266] To escape removal under SLUSA, Dabit alleged that he and members of the class continued to hold shares based upon the false research recommendations, giving rise to state law breach of contract and fiduciary duty claims against ML. Thus their state law claims did not invoke SLUSA, which

---

amended compliant, deleting fraud, misrepresentation and state securities claims and leaving only breach of contract claims: court ordered remand back to Nebraska state court).

[263] *See, e.g., In re Waste Management, Inc., Sec. Litigation*, 194 F. Supp. 2d 590 (S.D. Tex. 2002) (applying Securities Act of 1933 § 22, which provides that "The district courts of the United States . . . shall have jurisdiction of offenses and violations of this title . . . concurrent with State and Territorial courts" and expressly providing that no claims under the act are removable to federal court).

[264] 2000 U.S. Dist. LEXIS 3158 (2000).

[265] 547 U.S. 1503 (2006).

[266] The case was further fallout from the 2003 prosecution by New York Attorney General Elliott Spitzer of 10 major financial firms, alleging rampant investment banking research department conflicts of interest. The 10 firms settled that case, *inter alia*, by promises to provide unbiased, independent securities research and payment of $1.4 billion.

covers claims made over "a misrepresentation or omission . . . in connection with the purchase or sale of a covered security."

Justice Stevens, writing for a unanimous court, held that "purchase or sale of a security" in SLUSA was not so limited as it is in SEC Rule 10b-5 jurisprudence.[267] Any fraud or misrepresentation allegation that "coincides with" or "touches upon" the purchase or sale of a security is removable to federal court under SLUSA, The power to remove is not just limited to actual purchases or sales.

Dabit involved removal. Three months later, in *Kircher v. Putnam Funds Trust*,[268] another SLUSA case, the Court held that district court orders to remand cases earlier removed by defendants to federal court were not appealable. Thus, defendant would have to be prepared to go to trial in state court, able to raise objections only in later appeal on the merits.

§ 14.10 LAWYERING PROBLEMS IN CORPORATE LITIGATION

[A] Attorney-Client Privilege

The attorney-client privilege is one of the oldest privileges for confidential communication known to the common law. An attorney may not reveal disclosures made to him in confidence for the purposes of procuring legal advice. Because the privilege belongs to the client rather than to the attorney, only the client may waive it. The purpose of the privilege is to encourage full and frank communication between attorneys and their clients with a view to promoting the broad public interest in the observance of law. The privilege recognizes that sound legal advice or advocacy serves the public interest, and depends upon the attorney being fully informed.

In the usual case, the client relates the facts to the attorney, who may ask questions, and then render legal advice back to the client. That, too, is the model courts had in mind when they evolved a "control group" test for when the statements of corporate agents would be shielded by the corporation's privilege. If senior management personnel, who could be said to possess an identity analogous to the corporation as a whole, related facts to the corporation's attorney for purposes of obtaining legal advice, those senior managers could invoke attorney-client privilege in any suit against the corporation on those discussions.

Upjohn Co. v. United States[269] changed the manner in which we think of the attorney-client privilege in the corporate context. Upjohn executives learned that one of its foreign subsidiaries had paid overseas bribes to government officials in order to procure business. Upjohn's in-house counsel consulted with the Chairperson of the board and with Upjohn's outside attorneys. He then

---

[267] The 10b-5 purchaser-seller rule is discussed in § 13.02[B] *supra*.

[268] 547 U.S. 633 (2006).

[269] 449 U.S. 383 (1981).

undertook an investigation to ascertain the exact depth of the problems. He sent a questionnaire to "all Foreign and area managers" worldwide, emphasizing that Upjohn needed full information concerning any such payments. Following analysis of the responses, Upjohn voluntarily submitted a report to the Securities and Exchange Commission.

The Internal Revenue Service immediately issued a summons to Upjohn for the questionnaires in order to determine if any bribes paid had improperly been deducted as an ordinary and necessary business expense. The Sixth Circuit rejected Upjohn's invocation of privilege "to the extent that the communications were made by officers and agents not responsible for directing Upjohn's response to legal advice." Only the higher-ups in the "control group" could invoke the privilege.

The Supreme Court rejected the control group test as defining the ambit of the privilege. An organization of any size does not fit the one-on-one mind's eye model of attorney-client communication and privilege. In an organization, middle level and lower level managers may furnish the factual material to the attorney, who then renders legal advice to the senior or upper level managers:

> In the corporate context . . . it will frequently be employees beyond the control group . . . who will possess the information needed by the corporation's lawyers. Middle level — and indeed lower level — employees can, by actions within the scope of their employment, embroil the corporation in serious legal difficulties . . . .
>
> . . . The attorney's advice will also frequently be more significant to noncontrol group members than to those [higher-ups] who officially sanction the advice, and the control group test makes it more difficult to convey full and frank legal advice to the [middle and lower level] employees who will put into effect the client corporation's policy.

Upjohn vastly increases the field of play for the attorney-client privilege in the corporate setting.[270]

---

[270] Although *Upjohn* creates no road map for application of its principles, commentators have done so:
- the communication must be one that would not have been made but for contemplation of legal services;
- the communication's content must relate to the legal services being rendered;
- the information-giver must be an employee, agent or independent contractor of the corporation;
- the communication must be made in confidence; and
- the privilege may be asserted either by the corporation or by the information-giver.

John Sexton, *A Post Upjohn Consideration of the Corporate Attorney-Client Privilege*, 57 N.Y.U. L. Rev. 443 (1982). The privilege protects the communication, not the underlying facts. In *Upjohn*, the IRS could have asked the employees about the payments but not what they told the attorney.

[B]   Attorney-Client Privilege in Derivative Litigation

The field of play for the attorney-client privilege may narrow again if the privilege is invoked in a derivative suit in which the corporation or control group members are defendants. The Fifth Circuit in *Garner v. Wolfingbarger*[271] created a judicial exception to the attorney-client privilege when the litigation is between the corporation and its shareholders, on the ground that in rendering advice to the corporation, an attorney is in some sense also acting on behalf of the shareholders. In other words, the corporation, in part, asserts the privilege against itself, or a near alter ego. The court found the privilege to be neither as absolute and inflexible as the corporation contended nor as "totally unavailable" as the shareholders contended. Instead, the court held that the "availability of the privilege [is] subject to the right of stockholders to show cause why it should not be invoked in the particular instance." The court listed the following "indicia that may contribute to a [judicial] decision of the presence or absence of good cause:"

> [T]he number of shareholders and the percentage of stock they represent; the bona fides of the shareholders; the nature of the shareholders' claim and whether it is obviously colorable; the apparent necessity or desirability of the shareholders having the informa-tion . . . ; whether, if the shareholders' claim is of wrongful action by the corporation, it is of action criminal, or illegal but not criminal, or of doubtful legality; whether the communication related to past or to prospective actions; whether the communication is of advice concerning the litigation itself; the extent to which the communication is identified versus the extent to which the shareholders are blindly fishing; the risk of revelation of trade secrets or other [proprietary] information . . . .

The Ninth Circuit has held that the potential exception to the privilege as outlined by *Garner* is limited to derivative actions in which the corporation, although a nominal defendant, is the true party-plaintiff.[272] By contrast, the Fifth Circuit has held that the *Garner* factors' presence may lead to a judicial decision of good cause not to uphold the privilege in a shareholder class action.[273] Many of the *Garner* factors could be present in closely held and smaller corporation litigation, leading to a decision not to uphold the attorney-client privilege when it is asserted against shareholder litigants.

[C]   The Corporation as Client

Many attorneys who do little corporate work appear as if they represent the board of directors, or the chief executive officers, or the majority shareholder, rather than the corporation as a whole. The Model Rules of Professional Conduct (Model Rules) make clear that "[a] lawyer employed by or retained by an organization represents the organization acting through its duly authorized

---

[271] 430 F.2d 1093 (5th Cir. 1970).

[272] *Weil v. Investment/Indicators, Research & Mgmt.*, 647 F.2d 18 (9th Cir. 1981).

[273] *Ward v. Succession of Freeman*, 84 F.2d 780 (5th Cir. 1988), *cert. denied*, 490 U.S. 1065 (1989).

constituents." Thus, the attorney must be on guard not to over identify with or unduly favor directors, the CEO, or majority shareholders.

If a shareholder sues the corporation and some or all of its directors, the corporation's attorney may defend all of them, at least until such time as the interests of the corporation and of those in control begin to diverge. At that point, when a conflict of interest arises on the attorney's part, she must resign from representing one or the other, or possibly both.[274] The attorney also may have to resign if it appears that she may be a witness. That is often true when a transactional lawyer or her law firm also undertakes the defense of the corporation or its officials.[275] The defending firm will have to step aside when it becomes apparent that one of its members will have to testify. Of course, in many forms of routine litigation, an attorney is called upon to defend both the corporation and the individuals without a conflict ever arising.

A controversial proposal to the Model Rules calls for an attorney to engage in whistle blowing, at least on an intra-corporate basis. The obligation is triggered if the attorney "knows that an officer, employee or other person associated with the organization is engaged in action, intends to act or refuses to act in a matter related to the representation that is a violation of a legal obligation to the organization, or a violation of law which reasonably might be imputed to the organization, and is likely to result in substantial injury to the organization."[276] The lawyer might ask the relevant corporate actor to reconsider the matter, or "advis[e] that a separate legal opinion on the matter be sought for presentation to appropriate authority in the organization." If those alternatives do not solve the problem, the attorney must then consider "referring the matter to higher authority in the organization, including, if warranted by the seriousness of the matter, referral to the highest authority that can act," which in the corporate setting will be the board of directors. If the highest authority does not act, then the attorney should resign.

The ABA proposal on whistle blowing was controversial and never approved by the ABA although some states have chosen to adopt the provision. The Securities and Exchange Commission has long maintained that attorneys who practice before it must engage in the same sort of "internal whistle blowing" when they know of wrongdoing that implicates the securities laws.[277] The ethical obligations of corporate lawyers and the various problems that may arise when the client is an organization such as a corporation, are beyond the scope of a work such as this. Nonetheless, discussion of the decisions in *Upjohn v. United*

---

[274] Model Rule of Professional Conduct 1.7. Anticipating future conflict, some attorneys never undertake dual representation initially.

[275] *See In re Conduct of Kinsey*, 660 P.2d 660 (Or. 1983) (severe censure of a transactional attorney who stipulated not to testify so that his law firm could continue to defend a derivative suit over a transaction he had engineered).

[276] Proposed Model Rule of Professional Conduct 1.13(b).

[277] *See In the Matter of Carter and Johnson*, SEC Exchange Act Release No. 17597 (Feb. 28, 1981). At an earlier time, the SEC maintained that upon exhaustion of internal remedies, securities attorneys were under an obligation to "blow the whistle" to the SEC. *See SEC v. National Student Marketing Corp.*, 457 F. Supp. 682 (D.D.C. 1978). With *Matter of Carter and Johnson*, the SEC abandoned that position.

States, Garner v. Wolfingbarger, and the ABA Model Rule pertaining to the "Organization as Client" furnishes a good introduction to the topic.

[D] Sarbanes Oxley Act (SOA) § 307: The Conflict Between "Reporting Up" and the Prohibition on Disclosure of Client Confidences

In the aftermath of the Enron and WorldCom corporate debacles, many observers asked "Where were the lawyers?" Among others, the SEC declined to deal with the question, although the Commission was prodded by Professor Richard Painter, of the University of Illinois College of Law, who has long labored at the intersection of corporate-securities law and attorneys' professional responsibility. Senator John Edwards of North Carolina then introduced Professor Painter's proposed addition to what became SOA as a floor amendment. The section governs all attorneys (outside and inside house counsel) who represent publicly held corporations. When those attorneys encounter "evidence of material violation of securities law or breach of fiduciary duty or similar violation by the company or an agent thereof," the attorney's "reporting up" duties are triggered. The attorney's first report is to be to the Chief Executive Officer (CEO) or the Chief Legal Officer (CLO). Failing "appropriate action" by those individuals, or their subordinates, the attorney has a "further duty to report [the evidence of wrongdoing] to the audit committee, independent directors or the full board of directors."

Despite opposition by almost everyone, including the American Bar Association, major law firms, and their corporate clients, the final legislation included the "reporting up" provision as § 307. The provision contains many vagaries ("similar violation"? "appropriate action"?) but through extensive rule making the SEC has taken steps to clarify the vagaries.

While matters have smoothed themselves out at the federal level, SOA § 307 encountered rough sailing with some state bar associations, who advised their members that, in some instances, actions taken under the section would constitute a breach of the client confidentiality rules. American Bar Association (ABA) Model Rule of Professional Conduct MRPC 1.6 provides only that "a lawyer may reveal information relating to the representation of a client to the extent a lawyer reasonable believes necessary . . . to prevent reasonably certain death or substantial bodily harm." Previous efforts to amend the rule to excuse attorney breaches of their duties of confidentiality in cases of serious fraud had failed.[278]

The collision was averted in August, 2003, when the ABA House of Delegates approved changes to MRPC 1.13 ("Organization As A Client") to make clear that reporting up of the type mandated by Sarbanes Oxley does not violate the rules.

---

[278] *See generally* Susan P. Koniak, *When the Hurlyburly's Done: The Bar's Struggle with the SEC,* 103 COLUM. L. REV. 1236 (2003).

§ 14.11   INDEMNIFICATION AND INSURANCE

[A]   Overview

Before agreeing to serve as a director, especially on the board of a publicly held corporation, an individual will want to know what protections she will have if she is named as a defendant in a class action, derivative suit, or governmental proceeding involving the corporation's affairs. Protection includes payment for, or provision of, legal services to the director. Protection also includes full or partial payment of any settlement or judgment in proceedings against the directors.

Indemnification is an agreement to make a person whole in light of possible or anticipated losses and expenses. A plaintiffs' attorney will also want to know if indemnification provisions exist in a corporation, since the directors of a corporate defendant themselves may not have sufficient assets to pay any settlement or judgment. Corporations often purchase "D & O" insurance (director and officer insurance) to indemnify directors or to provide a fund for the payment of plaintiffs if an action results in settlement or judgment. Plaintiff's counsel will want to know if insurance exists and what exceptions the insurance policy makes in its coverage.

Under common law, employees have rights to indemnification for expenses and losses incurred as a result of carrying out their employment responsibilities.[279] Corporate directors, however, are not employees. Rather they are members of a collegial group in which their power resides.[280] For that reason, an influential New York case held that, after successfully defending themselves in a derivative action, directors were not entitled to indemnification as employees, or to any indemnification at all.[281]

Thus was born the need for indemnification statutes and their historic emphasis on directors rather than employees, officers, or other agents. The policies behind adoption of such acts are several. In the absence of indemnification, capable persons would refuse to serve as corporate directors. Indemnification also ensures that directors continue to take appropriate risks. Without provision for indemnification, directors would be overly cautious. Most of all, directors should be encouraged to defend themselves against groundless claims. On the other hand, if indemnification is over-inclusive, it protects wrongdoers.

[B]   Indemnification Statutes

Today, claims against corporate directors include a broad range of allegations: CERCLA (Comprehensive Environmental Response and Cleanup Liability Act) and other environmental claims, civil rights claims, tortious

---

[279] The idea came from agency law. *See* Restatement (Second) of Agency §§ 438–40 (1958).

[280] See the discussion of the board of directors in § 5.06, *supra.*

[281] *New York Dock Co. v. McCollum*, 16 N.Y.S.2d 844 (1939). *See also Greisse v. Lang*, 175 N.E. 222 (Ohio 1931) (same).

interference with contractual rights claims, illegal foreign and other payment allegations, and ERISA (Employment Retirement Income Security Act) claims, as well as allegations of breach of the fiduciary duties of care and of loyalty. Directors generally have no protection against such claims unless they or an attorney has taken affirmative steps. The reason is that corporate indemnification statutes are permissive or enabling — they are not self-implementing.

The exception is that regardless of the lack of implementation, "a corporation *shall* indemnify a director who was wholly successful, on the merits or otherwise, in the defense of any proceeding to which he was a party because he is or was a director of the corporation."[282] The New York statute provides for mandatory indemnification for "[a]ny person who has been successful, on the merits or otherwise, in the defense of a civil or criminal action."[283]

All other indemnification is permissive unless made mandatory by a provision in the articles of incorporation or bylaws, or by a contract. Two questions that arise are: (1) under what standard will the director's past conduct be evaluated, and (2) who will apply that standard to the facts? Under the MBCA, the director must show that he acted "in a manner he reasonably believed to be in the best interests of the corporation."[284] A director still may be denied indemnification if he is found to have received "a financial benefit to which he was not entitled."[285]

The director who seeks indemnification may make those showings in any of several forums. He may seek approval from a majority of a quorum of disinterested directors, from "independent" or "special" legal counsel, or from a majority of the shareholders.[286] Those entities must make two decisions: whether the director met the standard of conduct (the eligibility decision) and whether the corporation should utilize its resources to indemnify him (the authorization decision). In addition, the director may go to court to have those decisions made. Although a court proceeding may entail additional cost or delay, there is a benefit, even if the standard of conduct has not been met. Unlike other decision-makers, a court may nonetheless grant indemnification if it determines, "in view of all the relevant circumstances, that it is fair and reasonable" to do so.[287]

---

[282] MBCA § 8.52 (emphasis added).

[283] N.Y.B.C.L. § 723(a).

[284] MBCA § 8.51(a)(1)(ii)(A). *Cf.* Del. Gen. Corp. L. § 145(a) ("in a manner he reasonably believed to be in or *not opposed to* the best interests of the corporation") (emphasis added). The standard is different in criminal matters. *See* MBCA § 8.51(a)(1)(iii) ("in the case of any criminal proceeding, he had no reasonable cause to believe that his conduct was unlawful").

[285] MBCA § 8.51(d)(2).

[286] MBCA § 8.55. If the pathway of board authorization is chosen, "no language in [Del. G. Corp. L.] § 145 impose a presuit demand requirement" before a director sues to enforce her rights to indemnity. *Stifel Financial Corp. v. Cochrane*, 809 A.2d 555 (Del. 2002).

[287] MBCA § 8.54(a)(3).

The range of coverage (what types of proceeding are covered) arose in *Reinhard & Kreinberg v. Dow Chemical Co.*[288] In a case that rocked the corporate world, Dow dismissed directors Reinhard and Kreinberg for allegedly surreptitiously attempting to sell the company. Dow then sued the former directors in federal court in Michigan. The directors answered with $100 and $75 million counterclaims respectively.

The directors then sued in Delaware on grounds that Dow was not advancing them their legal expenses, as it was permitted (Del Gen Corp. L § 145) had obligated itself to do in connection with directors' defense of claims. Chancellor Chandler analyzed the issue in term of "what does defense mean?" Relying on an earlier Delaware precedent,[289] the Chancellor held that "defense" includes counterclaims, but only ones that under the applicable rules of civil procedure are compulsory, an issue to be decided by the Michigan court.

The analysis seems correct. If a plaintiff had not sued a director, the director may well have let lie fallow the claims they must now assert or forever lose.

[C]   Advance of Fees and Other Expenses

A director who is sued or a target in a proceeding does not wish to wait for indemnification decisions and eventual reimbursement. He wishes funds to hire counsel, pay for expert witnesses, and for other expenses of litigation as he goes along. Indemnification statutes provide for the "advance of funds to pay for or reimburse the reasonable expenses incurred by a director."[290] To receive an advance, a director must provide the corporation with a written affirmation of his good faith belief that his conduct meets the relevant standard of conduct for indemnification, along with an undertaking to repay any funds advanced if he is not entitled to mandatory indemnification or it is ultimately determined that his conduct does not meet the relevant standard. Importantly, the undertaking need not be secured and "may be accepted without reference to [the director's] financial ability to make repayment."

Sarbanes Oxley § 402 makes it unlawful for a public company "to extend or maintain credit, [or] to arrange for the extension of credit, in the form of a personal loan to, or for, any director or officer." *Tafeen v. Homestore, Inc.*[291] held that the prohibition does not apply to prevent the advancement of expenses to a former senior executive, who otherwise would be entitled to such advances under Homestore's bylaws. *Envirokare Tech, Inc. v. Pappas*[292] deals with the SOX prohibition's effect on advancements to current officers and directors. Judge Louis Kaplan held the prohibition applicable only to "personal loans." He held further that advancements of expenses to an officer or director sued by reason of being a corporate official were not personal loans. The issue (the

---

[288] 2008 Del. Ch. LEXIS 39 (Mar. 28, 2008) (letter opinion of Chandler, J.). (letter opinion of Chandler, J.)

[289] *Citadel Holding Corp. V. Roven*, 603 A.2d 818 (Del. 1992).

[290] MBCA § 8.52(a).

[291] 2004 Del. Ch. LEXIS 38 (Mar. 22, 2004) (Chandler, J.).

[292] Unreported decision (S.D.N.Y., Mar. 16, 2006).

interaction of the SOX prohibition and agreements to advance litigation expenses) is likely to rise again in future cases.

[D]   Fees on Fees

One recurring issue is whether a director who has to sue to enforce her rights to indemnification may recover from the corporation not only the fees and expenses in dealing with the underlying matter but also the fees and expenses in the second action ("fees on fees"). In *Stifel Financial Corp. v. Cochrane*,[293] the Supreme Court of Delaware resolved the matter once and for all, in favor of indemnification of such expenses. The Court noted that the "language of [Del. Gen. Corp. L.] § 145(a), permitting indemnification to a party 'in any action' can be read literally to encompass the indemnification action itself." The prospect of being able to obtain of fees on fees will "encourage capable men [and women] to serve as corporate directors." On the other side of the coin, the prospect of such fees "prevents a corporation from using its deep pockets to wear down a former director, with a valid claim to indemnification, through expensive litigation."

In New York, the statutory language is different, so the New York Court of Appeals came down the opposite way, disallowing a corporate CFO (Siegel) his claim for fees on fees.[294] The court denied fees on two grounds. One, the New York statute permits indemnity for "reasonable expenses, *including attorney's fees actually and necessarily incurred as a result of such action or proceeding.*"[295] "It stretches language beyond the outer limits of meaning," said the court, "to claim that fees on fees were necessarily incurred" in the action for which indemnification is allowed.[296] Two, other statutes (MBCA, Indiana, California) expressly authorize fees on fees. In its statutory revisions, New York did not include a similar provision, one presumably of which the New York draftspersons were aware.

[E]   Implementation By Contract

Many corporations make mandatory in the articles of incorporation or bylaws what statutes permit them to do, including provisions for advances. From a director's standpoint, matters may turn sour, board composition may change, sometimes radically changing the corporate climate. In such cases, a bylaw or article may be revoked or substantially amended. For that reason, many knowledgeable directors or their attorneys insist upon a contract making mandatory (and irrevocable) provisions for indemnification, advances for expenses, and maintenance of insurance coverage. They do not rely solely upon provisions in bylaws or articles of incorporation.

---

[293] 809 A.2d 555 (Del. 2002).

[294] *Baker v. Health Management Systems, Inc.*, 98 N.Y.2d 80, 745 N.Y.S.2d 741, 772 N.E.2d 1099 (2002).

[295] 98 N.Y.2d at 84 (emphasis in the original).

[296] *Id.* at 85.

[F]   Non-exclusive Versus Exclusive Statutes, Public Policy Limits, and Consistency Limitations

A last question is whether such a contract or bylaw may provide for indemnification broader than the statutory provisions. May a corporation indemnify based upon a standard of conduct lower than the statutory standard, or provide advances without any undertaking by the director to repay? In part, the answer depends upon whether the statute is "exclusive" or "non-exclusive." The MBCA indemnification provisions are exclusive, providing that "[a] corporation may provide indemnification or advance expenses to a director or officer only as permitted by this subchapter."[297] By contrast, the Delaware and New York statutes are "non-exclusive."[298] Commentators believe that any wide variation from statutory standards (indemnifying directors for reckless or intentional misconduct, for example) would be void as against public policy and courts, including Delaware courts, would so hold.[299] Although it is "non-exclusive," the New York statute does articulate limits probably similar to those other courts would flesh out as a matter of public policy. The statute forbids indemnification of a director if an adjudication has found that "acts [were] committed in bad faith or were the result of actual or deliberate dishonesty."[300]

[G]   Overriding Requirement of Good Faith (Statutory)

Although courts seem strongly to favor indemnification, a requirement of good faith on the part of a director seeking indemnification is "statutory and cannot be waived." Nonetheless, *Owens Corning v. National Union Fire Ins. Co.*[301] shows that courts can be creative when it comes to the existence and evidence of good faith. Owens Corning (OC) paid $9,975,000 in settlement of a stock drop lawsuit. It also paid indemnification to OC directors who had paid into the settlement. OC then sought reimbursement from its D & O insurance carrier, which refused on the grounds that OC had not proffered evidence of directors' good faith. The Sixth Circuit did not follow the Ninth Circuit, which held that payment of amounts in settlement consisted of "success on the merits

---

[297] MBCA § 8.59.

[298] *See, e.g.,* Del. Gen. Corp. L. § 145(f) ("[t]he indemnification and advancement of expenses provided . . . shall not be deemed exclusive of any other rights to which those seeking indemnification . . . may be entitled under any bylaw, agreement, vote of stockholders or disinterested directors, or otherwise."); *see also* N.Y.B.C.L. § 7.21 ("Non-Exclusivity of Statutory Provisions").

[299] *See, e.g.,* Douglas M. Branson, CORPORATE GOVERNANCE § 12.14 (1993) ("Public Policy and Other Limitations on Indemnification"). The Securities and Exchange Commission has long taken the position that provisions for indemnification of corporate officers, directors, and underwriters for liabilities for violations of various provisions of the securities laws are void as against public policy, and the courts have agreed. *Globus v. Law Research Serv., Inc.*, 418 F.2d 1276 (2d Cir. 1969), *cert. denied*, 397 U.S. 913 (1970), is the leading case. *See also* SEC Regulation S-K, Items 702, 510, 512.

[300] N.Y.B.C.L. § 721. The section was applied to deny indemnification of a director in *Biondi v. Beekman Hill House Apt. Corp.*, 94 N.Y.2d 659 (2000) (no indemnification of punitive damages assessed against a director for intentional race-based discriminatory actions).

[301] 257 F.3d 484 (6th Cir. 2001).

or otherwise," entitling directors to mandatory indemnification at least as long as the directors did not admit liability.[302]

The Sixth Circuit would not accept that indemnification was mandatory. Instead, it skinned the cat in another way. The court would entertain a presumption of good faith on directors' part. OC and other typical corporate bylaws would be broad enough to entertain such a presumption. Then (presumably) it would be up to the defendant insurance company to produce evidence rebutting the presumption. Barring such rebuttal, National Union would have to reimburse OC for sums it had paid to directors.

[H]   Insurance

Directors' and Officers' ("D & O") liability insurance serves two functions: as a funding source, providing resources for defense of directors and for payment of settlements or judgments, and as a potential gap filler, filling in gaps in the indemnification statute and in the articles, bylaws or contracts implementing the statute.

Even in jurisdictions which provide that the indemnification statute is exclusive, the statutes make clear that insurance coverage may be broader than the statute. The MBCA provides that "[a] corporation may purchase and maintain insurance on behalf of an individual who is an officer or director of the corporation . . . whether or not the corporation would have power to indemnify or advance expenses to him against the same liability under this chapter."[303] Insurance, if it may be obtained, is not bounded by the exclusivity provision of the indemnification statute.

With one exception, the issue is largely an academic one. Generally speaking, if a corporation obtains D & O insurance, the coverage will be narrower rather than broader than the statute and coverage has become narrower over the years. D & O coverage will have large deductibles or co-payment requirements. There are numerous exclusions, such as for director actions taken in response to a takeover bid, in connection with securities offerings, for reckless conduct, for environmental matters, for intentional torts, and more. At times, coverage has become unavailable for even middle size publicly held corporations, or prohibitively expensive for them. That was true, for example, in 1986–87 when a general crisis in liability insurance occurred world-wide and when, in a high profile case, the Supreme Court of Delaware held directors of Trans-Union Corp. potentially liable for over $20 million for duty of care violations.[304]

The exception was that older indemnification statutes prohibited corporate payment of settlements or judgments in "actions by or on behalf of the corporation," namely, derivative suits. The policy reason was that if directors were liable to the corporation, and the corporation could turn right around to indemnify them, the whole process would be circular and the deterrent effect for directors would be nil. In states in which such limitations were placed on

---

[302] *Safeway Stores, Inc. v. National Union Fire Ins.*, 64 F.3d 1282, 1290 (9th Cir. 1995).

[303] MBCA § 8.57.

[304] *Smith v. Van Gorkom*, 488 A.2d 858 (Del. 1985), discussed in § 8.04, *supra*.

indemnification, it was nonetheless permissible to purchase insurance which would pay settlements or judgments in derivative suits. That was, and still may be, the principal area in which insurance coverage is broader than is the right to indemnify.

Rights to indemnification are of little importance if the corporation has no funds with which to pay advances or settlements of judgments. In middle size and larger publicly held corporations, the funding source often is D&O insurance. In smaller publicly held corporations, a risk of suit may exist, but insurance will be unavailable. In those corporations, directors and their attorneys often give thought to alternative funding sources such as a security interest in an asset given to a director by the corporation. The parties may agree by contract that the corporation will maintain a restricted fund for advances of defense costs.[305]

Insurance carriers could be a force for improved corporate governance but they are not, according to Professors Thomas Barker and Sean Griffin.[306] D & O insurance carriers attempt to price policies in terms of risk but otherwise play no role in assessing or attempting to improve the quality of governance in the corporations which they insure.

[I]   Summary

Holding a director of a corporation above the fray that litigation represents, financially at least, requires a platform with at least three, and perhaps four, legs. The first leg is the existence of an indemnification statute in the jurisdiction and an article, bylaw, or contract implementing and possibly making mandatory the indemnification permitted. The second leg is a funding source (possibly D & O insurance). The third leg is an exculpatory provision in the articles of incorporation capping or eliminating director liability for duty of care violations. The fourth leg is a contract in favor of the individual director, making obligatory many of the corporate obligations (to indemnify, advance, insure, and so on), so that in case of article or bylaw amendments, a change in control, or a falling out, the individual director remains protected.[307]

---

[305] *See generally* J. Phil Carlton & M.Guy Brooks, III, *Corporate and Officer Indemnification: Alternative Methods for Funding*, 24 WAKE FOREST L. REV. 53 (1989).

[306] *The Missing Monitor in Corporate Governance: The Directors' and Officers' Liability Insurance Carrier*, 95 GEO. L. J. 1795 (2007).

[307] These provisions, first authorized in 1986 by Del. Gen. Corp. L. § 102(b)(7), are discussed in § 8.05, *supra*.

TABLE OF CASES

[References are to pages.]

[References are to pages.]

[References are to pages.]

E

F

G

[References are to pages.]

[References are to pages.]

[References are to pages.]

[References are to pages.]

[References are to pages.]

T

[References are to pages.]

TABLE OF STATUTES

[References are to pages and footnotes.]

[References are to pages and footnotes.]

[References are to pages and footnotes.]

[References are to pages and footnotes.]

[References are to pages and footnotes.]

[References are to pages and footnotes.]

INDEX

[References are to pages.]

A

ACQUISITIONS (See MERGERS AND ACQUISITIONS)

ALI TEST
Generally . . . 269

ANTIFRAUD
Generally . . . 200
Causation . . . 210
Omission of misleading statement, materiality of
. . . 207
Private rights of action; implication . . . 203
Remedies . . . 214
SEC Rule 14a-9 . . . 201
Standing to sue . . . 206
State of mind requirement . . . 208

ASSETS
Intangible . . . 81
Sale of . . . 148

ATTORNEY-CLIENT PRIVILEGE
Generally . . . 518
Derivative litigation . . . 520

ATTORNEYS AND LITIGATION (See LITIGATION)

ATTORNEYS' FEES
Common fund versus common benefit cases; entitlement . . . 503
Computation of fee amounts . . . 506
Cosmetic settlement problem . . . 505
Entitlement . . . 503
Intervenors . . . 507
Objectors . . . 507
WorldCom case . . . 508

B

BOARDS OF DIRECTORS
Change of directors; proxy voting by shareholders
. . . 118
Conflict of interest; multiple boards . . . 271
Meetings
Generally . . . 132
Actions without . . . 132
Structure . . . 131

BOOK VALUE
Cost based accounting . . . 80
Depreciation . . . 81
Intangible assets . . . 81

BUSINESS JUDGMENT RULE
Generally . . . 223

BUYOUTS
Closely held corporation; disparity between buy-out
price and fair price . . . 337
Court-ordered; valuation issues . . . 358

BYLAWS, CORPORATE
Amendment of . . . 197

C

CALIFORNIA
Control of shareholders; sale of control . . . 307
Interested director transactions . . . 251

CAPITALIZATION, INADEQUATE (See INADEQUATE CAPITALIZATION)

CAPITAL STRUCTURE
Generally . . . 73

CASH FLOW
Valuation . . . 83

CAUSATION
Antifraud . . . 210
Duty of care . . . 225
Insider trading
Loss causation . . . 419
Transaction causation . . . 415
Loss causation; Private Securities Litigation Reform
Act of 1995 . . . 514

CERTIFICATIONS
Generally . . . 163

CLASS ACTIONS, SHAREHOLDER
Derivative actions, decline of . . . 511
Private Securities Litigation Reform Act of 1995
Generally . . . 512
Loss causation . . . 514
Plaintiff, selection of most appropriate
. . . 515
Pleading . . . 513
Securities Litigation Uniform Standards Act of 1998
. . . 516
"Stock drop" class actions . . . 511

CLOSELY HELD CORPORATIONS
Definitions . . . 313
Direct versus derivative suits . . . 461
Ex ante protection of shareholder expectations
Comprehensive shareholder agreements
. . . 331
Contract . . . 326
Directors' discretion, agreements affecting
. . . 330
Less than unanimous shareholder agreements
. . . 328
Long-term shareholder tenure and salary agreements . . . 326
Ex post protection of shareholder expectations
Generally . . . 359

[References are to pages.]

[References are to pages.]

[References are to pages.]

[References are to pages.]

[References are to pages.]

I

[References are to pages.]

[References are to pages.]

[References are to pages.]

[References are to pages.]

[References are to pages.]